# REDEEMING JUDGMENT

# Redeeming
# Judgment

DALE PATRICK

☙PICKWICK *Publications* · Eugene, Oregon

REDEEMING JUDGMENT

Copyright © 2012 Dale Patrick. All rights reserved. Except for brief quotations in critical publications or reviews, no part of this book may be reproduced in any manner without prior written permission from the publisher. Write: Permissions, Wipf and Stock Publishers, 199 W. 8th Ave., Suite 3, Eugene, OR 97401.

Cascade Books
A Division of Wipf and Stock Publishers
199 W. 8th Ave., Suite 3
Eugene, OR 97401

www.wipfandstock.com

ISBN 13: 978-1-60899-910-1

*Cataloging-in-Publication data:*

Patrick, Dale
    Redeeming judgment / Dale Patrick.

    xii + 664 p.; 23 cm. Includes bibliographical references and index.

    ISBN 13: 978-1-60899-910-1

    1. Judgment—Biblical teaching. 2. Bible. O.T.—Criticism, interpretation, etc. 3. Bible. N.T.—Criticism, interpretation, etc. I. Title.

BS680 J8 P37 2012

Manufactured in the U.S.A.

Biblical quotations from the New Revised Standard Version of the Bible, copyright © 1989 by the Division of Christian Education of the National Council of the Churches of Christ in the USA and used by permission.

Biblical quotations from the Revised Standard Version of the Bible, copyright © 1946, 1952, 1971 by the Division of Christian Education of the National Council of the Churches of Christ in the USA and used by permission.

# Contents

*Preface · vii*
*Abbreviations · xi*

**PART ONE**

1. Introduction · 3
2. Sin and Judgment in the Genesis of History (Genesis 1–11) · 18
3. Genesis of the People of Israel (Genesis 12–50; Exodus 1–15) · 41
4. Covenant and Law (Exodus; Leviticus) · 54
5. Individuals within the Covenant (Proverbs; Psalms) · 72
6. Judgments in the Wilderness (Exodus 32; Numbers 10–25; Deuteronomy) · 102
7. Possessing the Land (Joshua, Judges) · 121
8. The Judgment of Kings (1–2 Samuel; 1–2 Kings) · 137
9. Four Eighth Century Prophets of Judgment (Amos, Hosea, Isaiah, Micah) · 159
10. Refining Fire (Amos, Hosea, Isaiah, Micah) · 195
11. Prophecy for a New Generation (Jeremiah, Ezekiel) · 213
12. Communal Lamentation and the Prophets' Answer (Psalms, Lamentations; Hosea, Jeremiah) · 255
13. Restoring Judgment to Theology · 289

**PART TWO**

14. Resuming the Argument · 313
15. The Book of Isaiah I (Isaiah 1–39) · 331
16. The Book of Isaiah II (Isaiah 40–55) · 362
17. Prophetic Tradition and Penitential Piety (Isaiah 56–66) · 401
18. A Debate over Piety (Psalms, Job) · 425
19. Final Judgment on the Horizon · 453

20. Divine Judgment in the Synoptic Gospels
    (Matthew, Mark, Luke) · 467
21. The Suffering Servant and Son of Man
    (Matthew, Mark, Luke) · 510
22. Judgment and Redemption in the Fourth Gospel (John) · 530
23. The Lion of Judah and the Lamb of God (Revelation) · 544
24. The Wrath of God and Justification by Faith (Romans 1–11) · 562
25. Final Judgment and Redemption · 589

*Bibliography* · 613
*Scripture Index* · 621

# Preface

THIS BOOK AROSE FROM the author's sense of urgency. The Protestant church that I know and love has grown silent about the judgment of God. It is ashamed of this aspect of biblical faith. It seems that my church is bent upon living up to H. Richard Niebuhr's caricature of liberal Protestantism: "A God without wrath brought men without sin into a kingdom without judgment through the ministrations of a Christ without a cross."[1]

The book is meant to remedy this silence. Since the Bible still has putative authority in the Protestant churches, I will demonstrate the pervasiveness of the judgment of God in both Old and New Testaments. Not only do we find the act of judgment in every era, I hope to show that judgment is a necessary stage in God's saving work. Moreover, the illuminating power of the concept is confirmed by common human experience.

The word *redeem* was added to this book's title to indicate that I am proposing to reclaim this theological teaching. It is also intended to characterize judgment as an essential component of redemption. Judgment, in particular, initiates a transformation of character from bondage to sin to a penitent, reformed person and community.

I have identified my audience as liberal Protestant Christians. We used to call ourselves mainline, but the erosion of membership in these churches renders that adjective a misnomer. They include churches that accompanied immigrants to this country, like the Lutheran, Presbyterian, Reformed, and Episcopal; and those which grew up on the frontier, like the Baptist, Methodist, and Disciples of Christ. These churches tend to be liberal in doctrine and accomodationist in practice. With respect to Scripture, these denominations have accepted the critical methods of interpretation, methods that cover authorship, history, and cultural influence. Oftentimes the congregations have only

---

1. H. R. Niebuhr, *The Kingdom of God in America*, 193.

*Preface*

a vague impression of critical teaching, but most ministers have embedded it in their preaching.

There is a tendency in these same churches to accommodate to the moral ethos of modern culture, particularly the more liberal wing of modernity. One will not, for example, hear quotations of Scripture to enforce the subordination of women to their husbands; the broader culture has rendered anything but equality among the sexes unacceptable. The same is becoming the case regarding homosexuals. The texts that offend our sensibilities will not be read in church or cited in debate. Historical church teaching will be dismissed with even less qualms.

This does not mean that all biblical texts are treated in such a cavalier fashion. Very few biblical texts actually affront the liberal churchperson, and some are received with enthusiasm. What develops is a list of favorites, and it is from these that liberal preachers build up a biblical message; these texts are a "canon within the canon." Texts that are out of favor are not allowed into the mix, and others are made to conform to the inner core.

Note the reasoning of W. J. Dalton: "God is primarily a God who loves, a God who saves. Hence any eschatological statement set in the context of future judgment must take into account the inadequacy of this context and must allow for this inadequacy if conclusions unworthy of God are to be avoided."[2]

Judgment has been "ruled out" of theological consideration a priori. It is this sort of reasoning that I am opposing. I will argue that that biblical God is a loving and saving God who redeems individuals and communities from and through judgment and atonement.

While I have singled out the liberal Protestant church as the audience, I suspect that evangelical Protestant churches retreat from the message of divine judgment, or render it so innocuous that it may just as well be dispensed with. Likewise, the Roman Catholic Church has become ashamed of the message of divine judgment. The *deus ira* has dropped out of the Requiem Mass. The German Roman Catholic New Testament scholar, Marius Reiser, wrote *Jesus and Judgment* to counter the subversion of judgment in the churches. Note his characterization: "In preaching and catechesis within the churches today, the general consensus is that Jesus' message was *good news* (*Frohbotschaft*), not grim news (*Drohbotschaft*), as the handy formula would have it."[3] Reiser

---

2. Dalton, *Aspects of New Testament Eschatology*, 7.
3. Reiser, *Jesus and Judgment*, 1.

*Preface*

demonstrates, moreover, that the scholarly discussion is not much better; no one wants to hear Jesus threaten "gnashing teeth."

Although I am writing this book in opposition to the trend in both Protestant and Roman Catholic churches to avoid the subject of divine judgment, I will not be quoting preachers or scholars and refuting them. Rather, I am simply going to set forth texts that depict or reflect upon divine judgment. Even a reader who believes that wrath should be expunged from the divine attributes should be able to follow and concur with this exposition.

The church eviscerates its kerygma when it ignores divine judgment. Why do I think I am qualified to perform the task of rehabilitating it? Because I have been studying and writing on biblical law since my dissertation on law and covenant. I have also been a theologian attuned to narrative theology and the prophetic depiction of God's judgment. I have also been a student of lament and the book of Job. I have, thus, published on at least two-thirds of the texts I expound in this book. To my amazement, they have fitted smoothly into a comprehensive exposition of divine judgment. Indeed, the tight fit of all these texts confirms the propositions I am proposing.

The writing of this book began in 2003–2004. During those years my wife, Mary, and I spent an academic year teaching in a small Protestant seminary in Lesotho, a small mountain republic surrounded by South Africa. We lived in a town of about ten thousand inhabitants. There was no nightlife, giving me the time to write to my heart's content. At first I experimented with article-length exegetical pieces; as time went on, I began to link them together. By the end of our nine months in Morija, Lesotho, I had written about two-thirds of a book on divine judgment in the Old Testament.

When I returned to Drake University, I found an offer to compose a number of entries for the *New Interpreter's Dictionary of the Bible*. I set aside this manuscript to research and write dictionary entries. When I had finished the sixteen assigned to me, three years had passed and the book on divine judgment was a vague memory. To revive the project, I asked for a year's leave without pay to evaluate what I had written and finish it. We located in Tübingen, Germany, to remove ourselves from our routines and obligations and experience the stimulation of that intellectual center. I was so unsatisfied with the first draft that I essentially started over and spent the 2007–2008 academic year composing it. I returned to Drake with chapters covering all the Old Testament and the Synoptic Gospels of the New. I wrote the remaining chapters on the New Testament, and conclusion and introduction, during

*Preface*

the 2008–2009 academic year. I also used that year to teach courses using my manuscript.

As I began to submit the manuscript to potential publishers, I realized that the argument actually falls into two parts. After several rejections, I decided to offer publishers a choice between one volume and two. I think two volumes make for a cleaner argument. However, the second volume is so dependent upon the first that it may be the better part of wisdom to keep them together.

I have a number of people who have helped me bring the book to its present form. The editors at Cascade Books deserve thanks for supporting a project which is more important for what it says than for its commercial promise. I would single out K. C. Hanson for his cordiality and adaptability.

Drake University allowed me to take a leave of absence when I needed time to rewrite and complete the manuscript. Scott Caulley, director of the Institute for Research into Early Christianity, hosted my wife, Mary, and me during our year in Tübingen. He read portions of my chapters on the New Testament. The University of Tübingen was also generous and congenial for study.

Drake University students were willing to participate in several courses that used chapters from the manuscript as textbook. A number of these students were religion majors who have since gone on to seminary and ministerial careers. I have also used chapters of the manuscript in courses in Old Testament at the United Theological College in Harare, Zimbabwe, where I have been teaching in retirement.

My wife, Mary, has read every chapter of this work, some several times.

# Abbreviations

| | |
|---|---|
| ABD | *The Anchor Bible Dictionary*. 6 vols. Edited by David Noel Freedman. New York: Doubleday, 1992 |
| JBL | *Journal of Biblical Literature* |
| JSOTSup | Journal for the Study of the Old Testament Supplements |
| NIDB | *The New Interpreter's Dictionary of the Bible*. 5 vols. Edited by Katherine Doob Sakenfeld. Nashville: Abingdon, 2006–2009 |
| OBT | Overtures to Biblical Theology |
| TLOT | *A Theological Lexicon of the Old Testament*. 3 vols. Edited by Ernst Jenni and Claus Westermann. Translated by Mark E. Biddle. Peabody, MA: Hendrickson, 1992 |

# PART ONE

# 1

# Introduction

## Defining the Scope of the Investigation

ALTHOUGH THE FOCUS OF the investigation of divine judgment will not be the terms—Hebrew, Greek, or English—that denote the phenomenon, a definition of words like *judgment*, *judge*, *crime*, and *vengeance* provide a comfortable entrée. This should furnish the identifying marks of the sort of narrative or histrionic utterance that deserves our attention.

One can define *judgment* as the deliberative procedure dedicated to determining guilt and innocence with respect to social norms. Normally, the judgment, or trial, will result in the imposition of punishment or at least restrictions on the future activity of one or both parties. It may also reward one party. The persons doing the judging must have authority to deliberate and impose sanctions. This authoritative status of the "judges" may be determined by the political constitution of the society, or at least by the parties to the legal dispute. Not only the parties but the society at large must obey the ruling of the judicial body. Finally, the purposes of the judicial proceeding may be to reconcile disputing parties, avenge a wrong, curtail adverse action, but also to reform or rehabilitate an offending party.[1]

The expression "divine judgment" is straightforward. Whenever the judicial deliberation, decision, and/or imposition of a sentence is performed by God—by YHWH in the Hebrew Bible—we are speaking of divine judgment. We have numerous narratives of such events and laments and oracles that dra-

---

1. We often call our prisons *penitentiaries* or *reformatories* as an indication of what the society hopes punishment ("doing time") will accomplish.

matize them. In Genesis, for example, the Lord holds a trial of the first couple and the snake after the eating of the forbidden fruit; Cain also is subject to God's interrogation and sentencing after he kills his brother. As the narratives go on, divine intervention in human affairs becomes less direct, often mediated by human judges or the concatenation of events.

Readers might object: How can a transcendent being engage in judicial actions? Aren't we talking about humans ascribing their own actions to the deity? Let's simply sidestep such metaphysical questions in this book. The biblical narrative ascribes divine "intervention" to God, and we need not speculate about *how* he can do so to affirm *that* he did. Narrators, prophets, psalmists, and wise men were authorized to recount or dramatize such interventions and Israel was duty-bound to believe and obey. Israelites did have avenues for expressing doubts, but these were encompassed by a theological tradition that recognized divine interventions.

There is no doubt but that the Lord God of Israel is a judge, indeed the Judge of all the world. Abraham addresses him as such in Gen 18:25. According to the narrative in Gen 18:16–22, the Lord has heard the "outcry" of humans against Sodom and Gomorrah (v. 21), and he has "sent" two supernatural beings to test them. This test is their trial; if they show hospitality to the visitors, they will "clear" their name. Then the Lord turns to Abraham and tells him what he is about to do. Abraham intercedes for the cities—rather like a "friend of the court." Abraham advances the principle that the Lord should not destroy the cities if it means bringing death to the righteous among the wicked. He concludes his argument: "Shall not the Judge of all the earth do right?" The Hebrew word translated "judge" is *shophaṭ*.

The Bible not only calls the Lord a judge in judicial decisions; he is also called one when he witnesses oaths and decides conflicts between combatants (e.g., Gen 31:53; Judg 11:27). He is addressed as a judge in several psalms (e.g., Pss 50:6; 82:8); he is asked to judge in individual laments, e.g., Ps 9:5; and he is projected as eschatological judge in Pss 96:13 and 98:9. Indeed, according to *A Theological Lexicon of the Old Testament*, there are more than forty passages with the Lord as the subject of the verb *shaphaṭ*, and nineteen as subject of *dîn*, the other common verb for judging.[2] A third word, *rîbh*, also has the Lord as the subject in more than twenty passages; this word denotes disputes of various kinds, including judicial disputes.[3]

---

2. Liedke, "*dîn*," 336; Liedke, "*špṭ* 3:1397

3. Liedke, "*rîb*," 1232–36.

*Introduction*

While the ascription of judgment to God denotes an actual transaction in the course of human events, it probably should be classified as metaphorical. In theological theory, God does not need to deliberate: he knows all the facts and has an immediate grasp of the principles and concepts by which actions are classified and evaluated. Why, then, do narratives have divine deliberation? We have, for example, interrogation in Genesis 3 and 4, and testing in Genesis 18. At the very least, such trial proceedings have the rhetorical purpose of exposing sin for the sinner and the reader. It may well be that one should affirm that God's accommodation to human beings requires a renunciation of the kind of knowledge Ps 139 ascribes to him; however, that question belongs to metaphysical speculation and need not be addressed here.

The judicial activity of God is often associated with anger or wrath. According to Deena Grant, "the wrath of God is triggered by human disregard for God's authority."[4] God's wrath is not only a state of mind, it is itself an "instrument of destruction."[5] "The most frequent cause of divine wrath at Israel is the worship of idols and foreign methods of worship."[6] "Social injustice . . . is another frequent cause of God's wrath at Israel."[7] Frequently, the Lord's wrath against foreign nations is simply an expression of his protection of his people (e.g., Exod 14:28; 15:7, 19; Ps 2:5). The prophets, on the other hand, hold foreign nations to international standards of comportment (see Amos 1–2).

The most insightful justification of divine wrath is found in Abraham Heschel's *The Prophets*, where he argues that God is passionately engaged in the world, and his wrath is thwarted love.[8] One can only be angry with someone when one cares about the person. When one turns away from true good to pursue chimerical advantage, one who cares deeply invariably struggles with disappointment and anger. How much more the Lord!

Now let us turn to the biblical Hebrew words designating violations of other humans and offenses against the order established by YHWH. The word *crime* is only rarely used in English translations (only four times in the NRSV); it seems to imply a rather modern idea of the "state" as the "maker" of law. The conceptual framework of biblical law differs from ours primarily in its theological foundation. Israel's law has the explicit authority of God behind it. As Creator, God has the authority to impose behavioral norms on creatures,

---

4. Grant, "Wrath," 933.
5. Ibid.
6. Ibid.
7. Ibid., 934.
8. Heschel, *The Prophets*, 2:279–98.

## Redeeming Judgment

and as Israel's covenant partner YHWH has the community's explicit affirmation of authority to command. The law is given by God to remedy the violence and exploitation rampant in the human community. YHWH establishes the system of judges to exercise judgment for him, and he supplements this with divine sanctions.

Hebrew has an abundance of words denoting offenses against the order established by YHWH and against fellow members of society. The most common general terms are formed on the roots $ḥṭ$', $ʿwn$, $pshʿ$, $rʿʿ$ and $rshʿ$.[9]

The meaning of the verb based on $ḥṭ$' is "to miss," but this nonmoral meaning is eclipsed by its theological use, *to sin*. The verb and noun appear in accusations and confessions of sin (e.g., Exod 32:31; 1 Sam 7:6; 15:24; 2 Sam 24:10; Hos 4:7; Zeph 1:17), covering legal, social and cultic wrongdoing. Some expressions so link sin with punishment that we can speak of sin entailing its own punishment, e.g., the person "must die in his $ḥṭ$'" (e.g., Num 27:3; Deut 24:16).

The Hebrew verb *ʿawah* and noun *ʿawon* have the basic meaning of "to pervert" and "perversity." The noun is usually used figuratively with the sense of "guilt" or "iniquity" (what makes one guilty). Since the thought world of the Hebrew Bible links act and consequences, the noun *ʿawon* can mean the punishment (e.g., Gen 19:15; Jer 51:6) as well as the deed (e.g., Isa 30:13; Ezek 18:19). Just as in the case of $ḥṭ$', punishment can be passed on to later generations (e.g., Lev 26:39–40; Isa 14:21; 53:11).

The Hebrew words based upon *pashaʿ* are frequently translated by "transgress" and "transgression." This term was famously used in Amos's cycle of judgments against the nations (Amos 1:3, 6, 9, 11, 13; 2:1, 4, 6).

The various words based upon the root $rʿʿ$ bear the meaning of *bad*, frequently with the moral connotation of *evil*. The expression, "do evil in YHWH's eyes," occurs frequently (e.g., Num 32:13; Deut 4:25; 17:2; Judg 2:11; 10:6; 1 Sam 15:19; 1 Kgs 11:6; 14:22).

The noun *rashaʿ* can mean "impious" and "wicked." The noun refers first to a person who threatens (e.g., Prov 12:6; Jer 5:26) or takes the life of an innocent person (e.g., 2 Sam 4:11). Besides murder and violence, it can mean *rebellion* (e.g., Num 16:26), oppression of the poor (e.g., Ezek 18:5), and unfair commerce (e.g., Mic 6:10–11).

---

9. For the analysis of the Hebrew words cited, see the Patrick, "Crimes and Punishments," 790–91.

*Introduction*

Numerous other Hebrew words could be added to our list, but most are more specialized. The above examples should afford a general impression of the words available for denoting the acts subject to divine judgment.

There are many expressions for the imposition of the sentence. Of course, *punish* would be the most common. The English word translates the Hebrew *pqd* (e.g., Exod 32:34). The Lord is often said to "visit iniquity on the head," or something to that effect (e.g., Exod 20:5; 34:7). Also this same Hebrew word can mean "to bring evil" on someone (e.g., 2 Sam 17:14). This belongs to the world of thought in which a evil deed actually boomerangs; it comes back to haunt the doer. On the other hand, the Lord is said to "avenge" (*naqam*) a person or community for their wrongdoing. Vengeance is equivalent to "retribution" or "retaliation" when God is the actor.[10]

Since I have attached the adjective *redeeming* to the word *judgment* in the title of the book, we should also identify the terms that are translated by "redeem." The words *ga'al* and *padhah* mean "to buy back," and expand to "to ransom," "to rescue," and "to liberate." One can buy back land, houses, or crops that were dedicated to the temple; the price is the market value plus a fifth (Lev 27:15, 19, 31). A member of a family can buy land belonging to a relative to avoid the land becoming the possession of a person from outside the family (Lev 25:25–31; Jer 32:6–12). Moreover, a person should buy a relative who has been sold into slavery and set him free (Lev 25:35–54). One may also be set free by serving for seven years (according to Exod 21:2–6; Deut 15:12–18) or the years to the Year of Jubilee (Leviticus 25).[11]

A quite different meaning is given to *go'el* when a family member is murdered; a close family male relative may be called to pursue the killer and avenge the killing. In English, the *go'el* is called "avenger," though it is the same Hebrew word that is translated "redeem." The word *padhah* can be used of a substitute sacrifice; humans and donkeys cannot be sacrificed to fulfill the command to sacrifice the firstborn (Num 18:15–16); sacrificeable animals were substituted (Exod 13:13, 34:20; cp. Num 18:16). First Samuel 14:45 has the army "redeem" Jonathan after he had inadvertently violated a vow.

God "redeems" Israel or individuals (2 Sam 4:9; Lam 3:58; Pss 69:18; 72:14). The exodus is frequently described as a redeeming act of God (e.g., Deut 24:18). YHWH refuses to redeem his people according to Hos 7:13, 13:14. Other prophets promise redemption from exile (Isa 35:9–10; Mic 4:10). Isaiah 40–55 uses both *g'l* and *pdh* frequently to proclaim redemption (Isa

---

10. See Patrick, "Avenge," 356; and Patrick, "Avenger of the Blood," 357.
11. See Patrick, "Redeem, Redeemer," 753–54.

43:1; 44:22–23; 48:10; 52:9; 50:2; 51:10) and to identify YHWH (Isa 43:14; 44:14, etc.).

Only Ps 130:7–8 states that the Lord will redeem "Israel from her iniquities." This is startling because it would seem to be the theological language most common to Christian history. The closest thing to this usage is Isa 59:20; 60:16; and 63:16, all of which use "redeemer" for YHWH in contexts where Israel's sinfulness is on the author's mind. It is these few texts that justify the Christian use of "redemption."

While the strain of piety that is deeply conscious of sin and that places hope in God's power to redeem humans from it links Old and New Testaments, the title "redeemer" is not used in the New Testament. The term *redemption* is used three times in Luke (1:68; 2:38; 24:21), but none of the other gospels uses it.

Only Paul and his disciples make potent use of the word *redemption*. Romans 3:23–25a anchors it in a climatic theological assertion: "Since all have sinned and fall short of the glory of God, they are now justified by his grace as a gift, through the redemption that is in Christ Jesus, whom God put forward as a sacrifice of atonement by his blood, effective through faith." *Redemption* here must mean God's reclaiming of humans, who have sold themselves to sin (Rom 1:18—3:20) and would be destroyed in judgment. Redemption is a transaction between God, the Son and believers. Removal of guilt is involved, but also a liberation of humans from their propensity to sin.

My use of the word *redeeming* in the title of the book corresponds to Ps 130 and the letters of Paul. It is the action of God of reclaiming humans, transforming humans from "slaves to sin" to obedient creatures. The word *salvation*, on the other hand, is used simply of divine interventions to deliver humans, individuals and communities, from dire straits either of their own or others' making.[12]

## The Argument of This Study

I am working to restore the subject of divine judgment to its rightful place as a pillar of Christian theology. Of course, one cannot expect biblical theology to accomplish this task by itself. We can demonstrate that judgment pervades the scriptural narrative and teaching. One should not attempt to expound any other subject without reference to it.

---

12. For all this discussion of *redeem*, see ibid.

There are some corollaries to my thesis about the pervasiveness of judgment. One should eschew contrasting Old and New Testaments regarding the "wrathful character of God." The difference between the Testaments has only to do with the acute eschatological consciousness of the New Testament.

There is no "progress" in history toward the release of humans from the power of sin. The Lord is motivated to destroy the human species, and all living creatures with us, because he had to acknowledge "that the wickedness of humanity was great in the earth, and that every imagination of the thoughts of (their) hearts was only evil continually" (Gen 6:5). After the flood, he vows not to ever again impose collective punishment on the human race because "the imagination of [the human] heart is evil from youth" (8:21). Note that the same reason justifies a different strategy. That is characteristic of human history: God brings particular evils to an end and devises new strategies for dealing with our evil purposes. An eschatological horizon is, thus, essential to the hope of redemption. As long as history continues, it will be "fallen;" humans will be in bondage to sin. Thus, we hope in a last judgment in which the violence, injustice and godlessness that plague the human story come to an end and those whose hearts are open to grace may flourish. The Final Judgment is the climax of the judgments and new beginnings of history. None of these resolved the contradiction driving human history.

Another thesis we shall argue is that particular historical judgments must be based upon what the society knows of the will of God. All humans, we shall discover, are under a "common" law, the covenant of Noah, and can be judged according to the norms of common decency and humanity, as we say. Anyone who violates these norms should "know better." The chosen people, on the other hand, not only are duty-bound to this common human law, but to the law given to Israel as a part of the covenant. In other words, Israel is held to a higher standard. Christians are held to the same higher standard—Mosaic law as interpreted by Jesus in passages like the Sermon on the Mount.

A parallel thesis has to do with individual and communal judgment and redemption. Individual and communal judgment must be distinguished but not separated. Nations and other collectives have a common ethos and capacity to act in the world. Individuals may simply play the role of pawns in such action. As such, they may suffer, or succeed, along with the larger "organism." Yet individuals must take responsibility for what they think, feel, and do. They are what the collective made of them and must answer for who they are and what they have done. Individuals have the capacity to stand apart from their communities and formulate their own identity and course of action. Hence, they (we) must submit to personal judgment and repent of our actions, whether collectively induced or not.

The big issue for readers probably would be whether collectives have any part in the kingdom of God. Many might think that collectives are reduced to the traces they left on individuals. In other words, nations, classes, even religious communities, die with history while the individual is raised from the dead. There are, nevertheless, hints of the restoration of nations in the kingdom of God (e.g., Rev 21:24), and Paul looks forward to the reconciliation of Jews and Gentiles as the climatic event (Rom 11:28–36). Thus, we should not exclude a collective dimension to the Kingdom of God.

Finally, we will be arguing that divine judgment is not an end in itself; it serves the purpose of restoring and redeeming humans. The Lord does not wipe out the human race in the days of Noah. He starts over again with a new regimen, viz., a legal and judicial system. Judgment meted out according to the established order and the establishment of a new order does not just happen in primeval history, it recurs throughout the biblical story. Judgment may suppress a given form of evil or a particular perpetrator, but it is designed to protect and restore humans. Full redemption of humanity begins to appear on the horizon of the prophecies of national judgment, and takes center stage in prophecies of restoration and the Gospels. As Ezekiel says, "Have I any pleasure in the death of the wicked, says the Lord God, and not rather that he should turn from his way and live?" (18:23).

Along the way, we hope to make exegetical observations that will enrich the readers' understanding of judgment and redemption. Our theses are embedded in textual exposition and stand or fall according to whether they make the text the best text it can be.[13]

## The Order of the Chapters

An explanation of the organization of the argument is in order. As one would expect from a study in biblical theology, we will be expounding texts that depict or reflect on God's judgment. The first step is often to show that a text does indeed depict or reflect on divine judgment. Then we can think through what it "teaches" about the subject and how that fits with the teaching of other texts and Scripture as a whole.

---

13. On the principle of interpreting a text as the best text it can be, see Patrick and Scult, *Rhetoric and Biblical Interpretation*.

*Introduction*

Organization is important. The sequence of textual expositions sets forth the steps in a logical argument. We are attracted to Gerhard von Rad's and his student Rolf Rendtorff's thesis that narrative sequence represents the mode of Old Testament thinking.[14] The kind of logic provided by narrative sequence can be called dramatic logic. By that I mean the necessary (or natural) order of a series of incidents and interchanges. What we shall find in following the biblical narrative from judgment to judgment is a continuing expansion, redefinition, refinement, and nuancing of the concept of divine judgment. Events will have the force of precedent for later times, and the inconclusiveness of events will project the need of further judgment.

Narrative sequence is the backbone of chapters 2 through 11. The accounts of Genesis 1–11 portray the human condition; divine judgment is recurring and cumulative; the resolution is the dissolution of the unified human community. The human subjects of the story change to the ancestors of Israel in Genesis 12–50. These ancestors are called to be a "friend of the court" in conflicts between the divine judge and humanity. The ancestors become victims of oppression during their sojourn in Egypt, and the Lord's effort to free them requires the judgment of their oppressor. In the wilderness, the people are bound to the Lord in a covenant and law, and they immediately violate the divine law and are subjected to judgment. In the years that follow, the people are condemned to live forty years in the wilderness for not trusting the Lord's power to conquer the inhabitants of the promised land. The people are also judged for rebelling against their leaders. Despite all these judgments, Moses in his last address portrays the era as one of learning to live according to the will of the Lord; the judgments were only disciplining.

The conquest narrative of Joshua and Judges brings up new issues. Why are the inhabitants of Canaan losing their land and under God's decree of extinction? There are some intimations of divine judgment, but not enough to justify calling the conquest an event of judgment. What Israel is to learn is that it must avoid imitating the religion and morality of the predecessors or will face judgment. Once the people are settled, there grows a desire for a king to unite the people in their struggles against neighboring peoples, and chaos in their own ranks. The Lord permits the prophet Samuel to inaugurate the monarchy, though he quickly has to condemn the first king, Saul.

Samuel is the first of a series of prophets to intervene to choose a king or condemn a king for violating the Lord's law. David is chosen and his dynasty promised rule in perpetuity by Nathan; yet David himself is condemned by

---

14. See von Rad, *Old Testament Theology*; and Rendtorff, *The Canonical Hebrew Bible*.

*Redeeming Judgment*

this prophet for adultery and murder. Ahijah chooses Jeroboam as ruler of the northern kingdom of Israel to divide Solomon's kingdom; this occurs at the ascension of Rehoboam over the tribe of Judah in the south. Jeroboam himself is judged for various measures he took to establish his kingdom. Elijah forces a crisis in Israel over exclusive loyalty to YHWH and condemns Ahab for judicial murder and property theft. Ahab's son, Ahaziah, comes in for Elijah's condemnation for seeking healing from a Philistine god.

After Elijah, the subject of judgment passes from kings to the nation as a whole. Elijah is privately told of national judgment by the Arameans, but it is the eighth-century prophets of judgment who are called to publicly proclaim the judgment of both Israel and Judah. We have come full circle, so to speak. The human race was judged collectively in the worldwide flood and later in the dispersion of the human race during the construction of the tower of Babel. Israel, which was chosen to reverse the sin and judgment driving human history, comes in for its own collective judgment with the eighth-century prophets and their successors.

A close reading of the table of contents will reveal some chapters that are not part of the narrative sequence. In particular, chapter 5, which expounds passages focusing on individuals, isn't a part of the national-narrative sequence. The book of Proverbs contains sayings that purport to describe the fate of those who violate provisions of the law and the moral ethos of the society. The individual laments of the Psalms provide prayers for individuals in crisis situations—types of situations that could occur at any time in Israel's history. We located these within the covenant because the community exists, according to the biblical understanding, within a covenant with YHWH.

The covenant itself is not simply subsumed under the national-narrative sequence of the Pentateuch. To be sure, the covenant is struck at Sinai/Horeb, during the wilderness period. However, the covenant is a "constitution" for the people, which will exist from this time forth and develop as the conditions of national life change. We have legal corpora from various eras—all purported to be given at Mount Sinai. Is there any justification for this telescoping of history? Well, the law antedates the imposing of laws at any given time; each promulgation must conform to the law already in force and will be applied as a rule of the timeless law.

Readers should be alert to the anachronistic application of particular laws, e.g., the restriction of legitimate sacrifice to one temple (Deuteronomy 12). This provision of law was unknown until Josiah adopted the law book found in the temple (2 Kings 23). The author who composed 1–2 Kings condemned the violations of the provision from the time of Jeroboam (1 Kings 12).

I located these chapters on timeless subjects where I did because they applied to Israel and its members "from that time forth." Of course, readers cannot build up any causal sequence between particulars; such sequences would be subject to possible anachronisms.

We should note the use of communal laments in reference to the exile. It is possible that these lament were originally composed for earlier times, but readers of Scripture in its final form would naturally apply the communal laments to the nation's greatest crisis. These psalms are preserved in order for us to cry out about the destruction of the nation in the exile. The prophetic oracles of salvation answer all such outcries.

## The Second Part

The first part follows the depiction and proclamation of divine judgment through the classical prophets of judgment in the eighth through the sixth centuries BCE. The prophets did announce salvation in response to the judgment of exile. However, the idea that judgment actually facilitated redemption was only hinted at. It is the book of Isaiah that joins judgment and redemption together in one action. The prophet of the exile, the author of Isaiah 40–55, announces the dawning of salvation following judgment. Thus, the book has an action that begins in judgment and ends in salvation. Moreover, the book has to take another step when the return from exile falls short of the saving event announced from the Babylonian exile. Now the delay of salvation becomes judgment and divides the community between those who have inwardly appropriated the judgment of exile and those who have not. The division will be revealed in a "final" judgment.

According to my reading, the New Testament is a proleptic fulfillment of the message of the book of Isaiah. Part 2 of this book, titled "Transforming Judgment," begins with the Isaianic message and ends with the New Testament. It is imperative that interpreters of the New Testament appreciate the continuity of the Christian message with that of the book of Isaiah. This means recognizing the continuation of the message of divine judgment in an eschatological key. The Christian message is not of an escape from judgment, but of a transformation of judgment from constraint and retribution to purification, compunction and reconciliation.

*Redeeming Judgment*

The return to Isaiah in chapters 15, 16, and 17 could be formulated as an extension of the narrative-sequence principle (from the first part of this book to the evolution of the book of Isaiah). However, I believe that we should read the book of Isaiah as one message, justified by one prophetic commission, delivered by multiple prophets over several centuries of time. While this commission only mentions judgment, Isaiah of Jerusalem thought that judgment served a purgative purpose; indeed, there are some intimations of a redemptive purpose. A prophet of the Babylonian exile attached the announcement of the end of judgment to Isaiah's message; this prophet looked forward to a full-scale redemption followed by an eternal salvation. The disciples of this prophet returned to Jerusalem in the expectation of an "eschatological" transformation of existence, and had to adapt that message to the discouraging situation that emerged in Jerusalem. They found the need for judgment language, but applied it to one portion of the community while their own "sect" could look forward to the hopes enunciated by the Babylonian prophet.

The two chapters that follow the three on the book of Isaiah (that is, chapters 18 and 19) are "emanations" (so to speak) from the composite Isaiah text. The prophetic community of Isaiah 56–66 developed a piety that incorporated judgment. We are calling it "penitential piety." It appears in some famous penitential psalms and promises to penetrate the entire religious community. One can read the "debate" between Job and his friends over how to pray as a clash between classical individual lamentation and penitential prayer. The Lord does side with Job, who insists on arguing with God, but translators and interpreters have understood Job to have concluded with a penitential thanksgiving.

A number of psalms praise the Lord for his judgments, and a few of these look forward to a final judgment. This hope of a final judgment echoes passages of "eschatological praise" in Isaiah 40–55. The idea of praising God for his judgments provides an occasion to review the representation of judgment in the Old Testament texts examined in the book.

While the placement of the New Testament chapters fits the narrative-sequence principle, that does not capture the inner arrangement of the four chapters. The New Testament offers itself as an account of the fulfillment of the promises of the Old. It would be more precise to say that the New Testament brings the eschatological horizon of the Old into the present. "The kingdom of God is at hand" (Mark 1:15). Everything that happens in the New Testament emanates from this proclamation.

The five chapters devoted to the New Testament (chapters 20–24) are not chronological or sequential; rather, we begin with the proclamation of eschatological judgment, then turn our attention to the message about the person Jesus and his destiny. The proclaimer becomes the proclaimed and is expected back as the judge at the Last Judgment. Here we see the New Testament dialectic of weakness and power. The Gospel and Apocalypse of John reflect on the relationship of weakness and power in the person and work of Jesus. The last chapter on the New Testament is devoted to Romans 1–11, which presents a comprehensive argument concerning judgment and redemption; it provides a fitting wrap-up.

## Selection of Texts

Readers should notice that the book does not expound every Old and New Testament book. How did we select the passages to include? First, the text had to say something about divine judgment. Second, what they said had to contribute to the sequence or to the recurring life of the religious community. Third, the biblical texts should be well known among readers of the Bible, or deserving of being known. Fourth, I did take up texts that were congenial to my thesis that judgment is or can be redeeming.

I did not think 1–2 Chronicles enriched our understanding of monarchical era; Samuel and Kings were sufficient. The postexilic era is covered best, I think, by Third Isaiah, so Ezra-Nehemiah and the postexilic prophets were left out. Ecclesiastes might be included as a dissonant voice, one that denied divine judgment, historical or eschatological; the best reading of this nonconforming book is as a "countertestimony" to the comprehensive theological scheme of the Old Testament. One might well find insight into the appropriation of divine judgment in the book of Ruth, but the explanation would take us away from the primary line of argument.

The overall rationale for selection as well as ordering has been to make the Old and New Testaments the best texts they can be. Meaning arises, I maintain, within a transaction between text, interpreter, and interpretive community. Readers of this book will have to judge whether my exposition facilitates a rewarding reading of the Bible's judgment texts.

## The Final Form as the Text of Record

Expounding the full text that has been passed down to us in the scriptural canon provides, I am convinced, the "best text" reading of a biblical text. This is the reading strategy I have sought to adhere to throughout the book.

Let me explain what is meant by "final form." The received text in a critical edition is such a "final form." It is a public document that is largely immune to the machinations of interpreters. All exegetical arguments should appeal to a common, public text.

That does not get to the heart of the contention, though. The final form of many, probably most, Old Testament texts is a composite of sources; that is, the text was edited together from separate writings and was expanded, contracted, and modified by "editors." A final-form reading gives no cognizance to the separate sources; a critical final-form reading will incorporate the evidence used to distinguish sources while harmonizing discrepancies and balancing viewpoints.

Ronald Dworkin has compared the procedures of precedent in the common law to a compositional process in which one novelist wrote, say, a chapter, a second extended the story, and so did a third, and so forth.[15] If we allowed the later authors to rearrange and expand earlier chapters, we have an approximation of what occurred in the Hebrew Bible. Interpreters, in our view, should read the book carefully enough to identify separate authors/sources, but should construe them as contributions to one, self-consistent whole.

Readers should realize that this has not been the agenda of critical scholarship over the last two centuries. Rather, we have focused on the sources and dating, and searched for regularities in speech form and traditions. All this has served the reconstruction of Israel's history and cultural evolution. One simply cannot construct a "reliable" history of Israel without breaking down the text.

In my view, the religious communities that look to biblical texts for the Word of God should ignore or at least subordinate reconstructing ancient historical events and disentangling sources. The search for the message of the text to its original audience has tended to make it irrelevant to our own. I would advise preachers and theologians to attend to the events of biblical history as represented in the text, and to draw messages from our texts for contemporary readers. This does not mean artificial relevance, but a message that belongs to and addresses whatever era and situation the text is read in.

I am not a supporter of allegorical interpretation of texts, but I sympathize with the desire to apply the words of the reading to the concerns of the congregation. I would hope that a perspicacious biblical theology would accomplish what allegory seeks to do, but with defensible connections between text and interpretation.

---

15. Dworkin, *A Matter of Principle*.

*Introduction*

Reading the final form requires imagination and ingenuity. We have to appreciate the value of each voice in the text and yet exercise the sort of intelligence that draws the text together in a best-text reading. This may well surpass anything actually said in the text or within the original horizon of the communication.

While I have adopted the canonical reading of the text inaugurated by Brevard S. Childs and advanced brilliantly by Christopher Seitz and Rolf Rendtorff, I do want to retain as much critical insight into the origins of the text as possible. I will try to facilitate a convergence between exposition of the final form of the text and the historical-critical reconstruction of the origins of that text.

# 2

# Sin and Judgment in the Genesis of History
(Genesis 1–11)

THE FIRST ELEVEN CHAPTERS of Genesis are frequently called the *Urgeschichte* among scholars. The title is borrowed from German, where it means simply the earliest stage of human history. Narratives in Genesis 1–11 tell stories of beginnings; the concern is to explain how things came to be what they are, and what they have been from time immemorial. Since the narratives apply to all humans, seeking to mirror universal character traits, they have been of special interest to Christian theologians.

Inasmuch as this book is about divine judgment, the first thing to do is to locate divine judgment in these chapters. There is no judgment, as I am using the term, in creation. It is only after humans begin to live their story that judgment is brought to bear on them. The first act that humans do on their own is to eat the forbidden fruit, which results in divine judgment pronounced on the participants (Genesis 3). After expulsion from the garden, the original couple has two sons, and one son kills the other. This calls for divine judgment (Genesis 4). There are several divine judgments reported in Genesis 6. After the sons of God and human women mate and have children, all humans are sentenced to a shorter lifespan (Gen 6:1–3). Of much greater significance is the LORD's decision to put an end to the human race because everyone is in bondage to sin (6:5–12). Noah and his family, however, are plucked from the fire, so to speak, along with breeding stock for animal species. When the flood is over, humans are promised that it will never happen again, and law is imposed upon humans and even animals (8:20—9:17). The series of judgments on humanity comes to an end with the shattering of the unity of the people (11:1–9).

The interpretation of Genesis 3 is the most contested of these events of judgment. It has anchored the Christian doctrine of original sin. According to the theological expositors, humans "fell" from a state of righteousness (*justia originalis*) into a state of sin and guilt. The man and woman could not have violated the divine prohibition by mistake, or out of necessity; they must have freely, deliberately followed their desire when it had been aroused by the tempter. When the original couple transgressed and incurred God's wrath, all their offspring—the whole human race—were under the power of sin and therefore guilty in the eyes of God.

This reading of the chapter has been challenged by many prominent contemporary exegetes. In the critical era, scholars often broke down the text and traced parts to different groups with different agendas. No thesis built on such critical analysis is relevant to our interpretation, however, since we are committed to interpreting the extant text—the text with canonical status for the synagogue and church. Only those challenges to the orthodox Christian interpretation of Genesis 3 based on this canonical text have any standing in this book. There are several scholars who challenge the interpretation of the extant text as teaching original sin.[1]

I shall argue that the doctrine of original sin cannot be anchored in Genesis 3 alone, but if we base a case on chapters 3, 4, and 6, we have a good chance of supporting the main contentions of the doctrine. Thus, it is my contention that we do best to read these stories as building on one another.

## The Fall from Innocence

Should the story told in Genesis be titled a "fall"? That could be disputed. We can be cautious and describe the course of action as a fall from innocence. There is little reason to doubt that the human couple was in a state of innocence at the start, but lost their innocence by eating the forbidden fruit. The doctrinal question is whether the couple acted deliberately, seeking to be like God by knowing good and evil, and whether they came into bondage to sin as a result of their action. Also, was this state passed on to later generations as an inheritance? In this section we will offer an interpretation of the chapter that will consider what parts of the doctrine of sin the passage will bear.

---

1. Among these are Barr, *The Garden of Eden*; we will consult his works in the course of this exposition.

*Redeeming Judgment*

*Questions to Be Answered in Our Reading*

Before I embark on this interpretation, let me share a sequence of questions that I will be answering. I drew up the questions for my Old Testament students to discuss in groups; they proved successful in leading the students to cogent interpretations. The reader may want to answer the questions before reading the next section.

1. Does the tree of knowledge contain knowledge in its fruit, or is it the violation of the prohibition that will produce knowledge of good and evil?
2. What is the "knowledge of good and evil"?
3. What is wrong with knowing "good and evil"?
4. Does the couple know what "death" is?
5. Who is the serpent?
6. Why does the serpent want to provoke rebellion against the Lord God?
7. What is the strategy of the serpent's question?
8. In what spirit does the woman answer it?
9. Does the serpent say anything that is untrue?
10. To what desire does the serpent pitch his address?
11. Does the woman understand the serpent's appeal?
12. Is the woman vulnerable to sinful desire before she eats?
13. What is the motive for the man's eating of the forbidden fruit?
14. What is the first effect of the eating of the forbidden fruit?
15. Had the couple had sexual intercourse before eating the fruit?
16. What is the second effect of eating the forbidden fruit?
17. What is the status of shame and fear of God after this event?
18. What is the third effect of eating of the forbidden fruit?
19. Does the couple feel guilty for their act?
20. To what does the Lord God sentence the serpent?
21. To what does the Lord God sentence the woman?
22. To what does the Lord God sentence the man?
23. Were the man and woman mortal or immortal before this sentencing?
24. What is the significance of the man's naming the woman?

25. Why does the Lord God provide the couple with skins for clothes?
26. Why are Adam and Eve banished from the Garden of Eden?

## *The Prohibition*

The story told in Genesis 3 actually begins in 2:16–17. When the man has been placed in the garden, the Lord God tells him: "You may eat freely of every tree of the garden; but of the tree of the knowledge of good and evil you shall not eat, for in the day that you eat of it you shall die." This prohibition leaves gaps to fill in. First, was the power to know good and evil in the fruit or in the breaking of the commandment? If it is in the latter, the Lord God could simply have chosen a tree at random.[2]

Nothing in the text will answer this question, but we are well advised to locate the power to know good and evil in the breaking of the prohibition. First, placing the discovery after breaking the prohibition is less mythological. Second, tying the receipt of knowledge to the breaking of the prohibition makes a logical connection between the act and the result. In breaking the prohibition, the couple would assert freedom to decide their own future; it would not be left in the hands of God. This would fit well with the idea that the knowledge of good and evil is equal to moral accountability.[3] When the couple lives in a state of innocence, they simply follow their instincts supplemented by anything that God tells them. By eating what is forbidden, they have taken on responsibility for their own actions.

I am convinced that this narrative can best be read if we construe the innocent couple to be like children. Indeed, the author tells a story that we, the audience, can confirm as truthful from our own experience. As young children, we are in a state of innocence, and then we cross a threshold into a state of accountability—the age of discretion, we call it. This is what happens in the "fall." Moreover, we become conscious of our nakedness and attempt to blame others when we do something wrong.

Why would the Creator try to keep humans from "exercising their free will?" If humans have this capacity, why aren't we encouraged to use it? The

---

2. The popular tradition that it was an apple would fit the idea that the power was not in the fruit but in the violation of the commandment.

3. We know from Gen 3:22 that they gain the knowledge of good and evil in the course of the action. So the knowledge of good and evil cannot mean "everything," because they do not gain that sort of knowledge, and of course humans still do not possess it. Isaiah 7:16 uses the expression "the child knows how to refuse the evil and choose the good" for the age of discretion.

## Redeeming Judgment

Lord God knows that humans have this capacity, because to test the couple's willingness to obey, he prohibits an action. So why does the Lord God test us rather than encourage our use of free will? One thing we know: Once humans gain the knowledge of good and evil, they/we begin to mistreat each other, and human community will go downhill from there. All one has to do is think of the genocides of the twentieth century to question whether free will is good. If humans could have "willingly" remained innocent, perhaps the story would have gone better. But that was not to be. Most theologians would say that God knew that humans would fall—indeed, we know this of each other. Other possibilities were in fact empty.

It is doubtful that the innocent couple understands the existential threat of death. They may well have observed the death of fellow creatures, but this would not arouse the fear of extinction in their minds. The death of fellow creatures would simply be an event in the world around them. The warning given by the Lord God would not have been threatening enough to thwart their pursuit of whatever they desired.

### Temptation and Disobedience

The story in Genesis 3 occurs without the Lord God being present. However, that God's absence can be understood theologically, it certainly can be understood psychologically. The decision to heed the words of the serpent must be theirs alone. If the Lord God had been present, the couple would be inclined to turn to him. Or the Lord God might have intervened to thwart the action.

The story begins by introducing a new character, the snake or serpent. He is said to be one of the creatures—clever but not necessarily evil. Of course, the attribution of power of speech to this creature arouses our suspicion. Moreover, we are shocked by what the serpent says: he is stirring up rebellion against God. When the concept of the devil or Satan enters Jewish tradition, the serpent is taken to be the incarnation of this rebellious angel. I think, though, that we can suspend consideration of the serpent's identity. What the serpent does is to divulge to the innocent woman the knowledge the audience has of what is at stake in the action. The serpent represents "fallen knowledge." Moreover, the serpent seeks recruits; frequently those who have lost their innocence have an insatiable desire to explode the innocence of others.

The serpent begins by asking a question that he knows is untrue. He wants the woman to correct him. The woman not only does so, but she repeats the prohibition: "God said, 'You shall not eat of the fruit of the tree that is in the middle of the garden, nor shall you touch it, or you shall die" (3:3). She has reformulated the command, adding the prohibition against touching it. This exhibits a certain anxiety on her part; she is, as it were, putting a fence around the law. Just touching the fruit will be too strong a temptation.

The woman has unconsciously become a defender of God. This too exhibits a certain anxiety. But she is still innocent; she has no idea that God might be withholding something that would be of benefit to her. The serpent tries to arouse this suspicion. First, he denies that death will come from eating the fruit. That threat, he seems to be saying, is just to frighten you away from seizing a power that is yours to have by eating. The benefit of eating is that you will now be God's equal in knowledge—you too will know what is good and evil, and therefore gain independence.

The serpent has not overtly lied, though the New Testament calls the devil the 'father of lies' (John 8:44). The LORD God does not execute the couple, as the prohibition warned. Moreover, the couple does gain the knowledge of good and evil. Now they can get by without God telling them.

Interpreters have usually assumed that the woman understands what the serpent has told her, and deliberately disobeys the prohibition out of pride or some other deadly motive.[4] This interpretation would, unfortunately, have her lose her innocence before she eats the fruit. For her to be innocent until she eats the fruit, she would have had not to understand the serpent. This is in fact the import of v. 6: "So when the woman saw that the tree was good for food, and that it was a delight to the eyes, and that the tree was to be desired to make one wise . . ." This is a paraphrase of what the serpent says, but it lacks all traces of sin.[5] The woman has no suspicion of the LORD God, and she "translates" being equal to God by knowing good and evil into being wise. It is good to be wise, and need not be a challenge to God.

One might still say that the woman does not trust in the God who issued the prohibition. If she had, she would have obeyed him without fail. I would counter that the woman trusts the serpent too much. Being innocent, she has no capacity to envisage one who seeks to deceive or misuse her.[6] So she believes the serpent who is speaking to her as though the serpent carries a new message from those who know. In other words, the woman had no capacity to differentiate trustworthy and untrustworthy persons.

---

4. Biddle, *Missing the Mark*.

5. Exposing another character's differing perspective by paraphrase is a common literary method in the Hebrew Bible: see Sternberg, *The Poetics of Biblical Narrative*, 365–440.

6. We have to teach children to watch out for strangers.

*Redeeming Judgment*

The best way to interpret the man's eating the fruit at the woman's suggestion is that they understood themselves to share everything. As far as the woman was concerned, she had discovered a boon, and the man had no reason to doubt her.

## *The Effects and the Trial*

The woman and man have broken the commandment, and it begins to have effects on them psychologically. They have lost their innocence, and are becoming accountable. The first effect was consciousness of nakedness. We can call this a sense of shame. Why do humans experience the sense of shame about being seen naked? I think that it is because humans become self-conscious, and our bodies become an object of our consciousness. We feel that our self is exposed in our naked bodies. We want to hide our bodies most of the time so the self is not exposed to the searching eyes of others. It is instructive how often stripping people naked is used to torture them, or at least to break down their egos.

The couple may well have sexual intercourse before they fall from innocence. The text does not report such an event, but it does allude to the normalcy of sexual intercourse in marriage (2:24). Sexual intercourse is not sinful. It becomes "shameful" once the couple is fallen.

When it is time for the Lord God to walk in the garden, the couple begins to fear a meeting, so they hide. The second effect of eating the fruit is fear of God. Up until now, there is no indication from the text that they experienced such feelings in God's presence. God is still a "father figure," not the powerful, majestic, mysterious being that he will become for later humans. Why do they fear God? They may be anxious about what he will say and do in response to what they have done. This may be the beginnings of guilt; but it is expressed as a sense of shame: "I was afraid because I was naked" (v. 10).

When the Lord God calls out, "Where are you?" the couple cannot remain in hiding. The Lord God's voice still carries too much authority. The man immediately explains why they hid, and the Lord God holds a trial on the spot. The man says that he hid because he was naked. The Lord God knows immediately that they have broken the prohibition: "Have you eaten from the tree of which I commanded you not to eat?" (v. 11). The man begins the "blame game." He blames the woman, and God for giving her to him. The woman blames the serpent. This blaming of one another does expose the event; it is itself evidence that humans are beginning to experience guilt, and they are trying to salve their consciences by pinning the blame on others. Of course, all three characters are guilty, and in a perfect world all would accept blame.

How can the man and woman be held accountable for the action they did, when they did not do it in malice? The woman decides to eat because she thinks that the fruit will be good for humans, both physically and spiritually. Moreover, she hears the serpent as a benefactor. She does not respond to the suspicion and resentment that the serpent seeks to arouse in her. Why do the woman and man feel guilty and ashamed afterward, and why do readers blame them? I guess the answer would have to be that we must own up to what we have done even when we do not appreciate the full consequences of what we are doing.

The trial ends with sentencing. The serpent is sentenced to crawling and having to fight for its life against humans (3:14–15). This sentence seems to be less than the trouble the creature has caused. Christians have allegorized the sentence as the struggle between the Son of Man (Jesus) and the devil, with the cross in particular being the moment when the Son of Man's "heel" is struck, and when the Son of Man strikes the serpent's "head. This equating the serpent with the devil gives the serpent's punishment something proportionate to the action, but it stretches the text too far.

The man and the woman are sentenced to the conditions of "adult" life. Women suffer during childbirth and are under the domination of men in most societies. Men have to struggle to eke out a living from the soil, and to it they return when they die. This picture of the conditions of life belongs to traditional societies, but we too suffer, are defeated, succumb to despair and die.

### The Issue of Immortality

This subsection has the word *issue* in the title because a longtime mentor and friend of mine, James Barr, argued that Genesis 3 can best be classified as an account of the loss of immortality, not of the loss of innocence and of the consequent bondage to sin.[7] I do not agree with that thesis, but it should alert us to the significance of the subject. The expulsion from the garden is clearly keeps the human race from eating of the tree of life and gaining immortality.

Let's go back to the last verse of the divine sentence on the man:

> By the sweat of your face you shall eat bread
> until you return to the ground, for out of it you were taken;

---

7. Barr, *The Garden of Eden*, 1–20.

> you are dust and to dust you shall return. (3:19)

Reference to returning to dust closes the circle, so to speak, which started with the creation of the man from dust (2:7). Mortality is not punishment; the hard labor on the soil is. Mortality is the natural condition of human beings.

The narrative then ties up other loose ends (3:20–21). We might ask whether the story of the expulsion from the garden (3:22–24) continues the action or inaugurates a new one. The expulsion is motivated by the couple's obtaining the knowledge of good and evil (v. 22), which means that it is best understood as a continuation. The Lord God is worried by the expansion of human power because it will invariably challenge divine prerogatives. Mortality now takes on a new meaning: it is the barrier or threshold between humans and God.

The expulsion is required because the tree of life is in the garden. Eating of the fruit of that tree will communicate the power to live forever. Whether eating it just once will communicate that power, or whether continual partaking is necessary, the couple must be removed from it to avoid their usurpation of a divine prerogative.

The tree of life is the irreducible mythical feature of our story. Many cultures have such myths. Humans are not only plagued by the thought of death; they seem to feel that it could be otherwise. In this sense, the story of the fall from innocence does hint at the "loss" of immortality. If the couple had not eaten of the fruit of the tree of knowledge, they would have been permitted to eat of the tree of life.

*Reflections on Genre*

Before we take up the next judgment, we should reflect further on the kind of narrative we have in Genesis 3. The narrative refers to an event to which the author and audience had no access. We could call it myth or fiction, but it does seek to depict an event in the past of the human race. The event can be inferred from the conditions of the present. To know what happened, the storyteller can incorporate the experiences of humans throughout history. In this case, the author knew that he and his audience, and all other humans, had lost their innocence. An event had to occur to bring this about. That event is in fact repeated in the life of every adult human. We all have a childhood when we were not accountable—we were innocent, we did not know good from evil—and then we pass into a condition of responsibility, or to the age of discretion. The story told in Genesis 3 is so effective because we have personal memories of it.

This account of Genesis 3 should show that it is inappropriate to ascribe our condition to an event in the ancient past. We pass from innocence to adulthood ourselves, and this is the reason things are as they are. The story of the "original" fall is a mirror for us, to help us understand the significance of our past and present.

In my review of the story I identified traces of anxiety at various turns. I was alerted to this phenomenon by Søren Kierkegaard, whose analysis of the human psyche's moods has filled in the gaps in the story of the fall.[8] The woman and man were anxious because they were conscious of multiple possibilities, both good and bad. As a synthesis of finitude and infinitude, nature and spirit, we experience tension that can inaugurate an action to resolve it. The "fall" is the inauguration of such an action. Thus, it is not a natural process, though it seems to come naturally to every human. The "fall" involves spirit, and it is a "leap." We do not become guilty by a natural process.

The loss of innocence is irreversible. Once a person has been plunged into the responsibilities of adulthood and becomes vulnerable to sinful impulses, there is no going back. The attempt to do so will result in a false innocence. Once one becomes conscious of one's nakedness, the attempt to recover naïve innocence is futile. The nudist lifestyle is not innocent—it is quite deliberate and self-conscious.

The Bible does not counsel a return to a state of innocence. Once humans begin to experience shame, it becomes a value. Now humans *should* experience shame in certain circumstances, and being "shameless" is unworthy of a human. Fearing God is the same: the fear of God is now appropriate, and commended as the foundation of wisdom; having no fear of God is tantamount to atheism.

## Cain's Murder of Abel

The narrative of Genesis 3–4 shows us that the first couple's fall from innocence had repercussions for the history that followed. In other words, the fall of Adam and Eve entailed the fall of the human race. This does not sound logical; it sounds mythological. I have some explaining to do.

The story of the first homicide begins with the sacrifices from the two sons of Adam and Eve. Abel's sacrifice received divine approval, but Cain's did not. This is an arbitrary preference shown by God. There is no evidence that Abel is morally or spiritually superior to Cain, nor is he more earnest in his

---

8. Kierkegaard, *The Concept of Anxiety*.

offering. This is a test of Cain. Can he accept rejection and disappointment, and the shame of rejection when his brother is accepted?[9]

Cain fails the test. He is disappointed, and directs his anger against God to the person favored by God. We can term his condition envy. The LORD warns him that "sin is lurking at the door; its desire is for you, but you must master it" (Gen 4:7). I would say that it is more than "at the door," it is actually coursing through his veins. Cain is not acting from a state of innocence: he is already fallen, and he is susceptible to envy. He must exercise his will to resist this sinister power. The LORD is addressing him as a responsible human.

Cain is not able to master the power of envy. We must assume, for the sake of the moral life, that he was capable of mastering the impulse to sin. But in concrete terms, he is not able to. He is, as we say, in bondage to sin. So we are left with a paradox: humans must be able to master sinful impulses, yet in fact they are often "bound"—in bondage.

### Debate over the Root Sin

When we read the story of Cain, his motives are fairly transparent. We can say that he was overwhelmed by envy. I take the term from the tradition of the seven deadly sins. These are the coinage of early Christian monks. Whether there are only seven—pride, envy, greed, anger, lust, gluttony, and sloth—or not is irrelevant. The virtue of the scheme is that a plurality and variety are acknowledged; it fits the diversity of persons and situations.

Many theologians want to go farther. Reinhold Niebuhr, for example, identified pride as the root of all sin; he broke it down into pride of power, intellect, and righteousness.[10] He did acknowledge something of a counterweight—concupiscence. It is the "sin of weakness," as pride is assertive. In the decades since Niebuhr, a number of theologians have pointed out that for some people, not acting, not asserting oneself, is the fault.[11] If we are discussing Genesis 3, pride at least has the virtue of fitting with what the serpent says to entice the woman. However, she does not understand him. If she acts in innocence,[12] we are mistaken to seek a root sin. We should look for sinful motives only after actors have lost their innocence.

---

9. I would compare it to the arbitrariness of talent and intelligence.
10. Reinhold Niebuhr, *The Nature and Destiny of Man*, 1:186–207.
11. Biddle, *Missing the Mark*, 16–22 and elsewhere.
12. Barr, *The Garden of Eden*, 13–14, notes this as well.

So what do all sinful actions have in common? It would seem to be anything that is in tension with the will of God and the good of the community, both human and creaturely. The deadly sins are powers that take over a person and cause harm to the self and others.

## The Trial

There is no legal community yet, so the LORD must intervene to rectify the situation after Cain has murdered his brother. The LORD "hears" Abel's blood cry out. This is an odd idea, reflective of the ancient idea that the earth itself is defiled by human crimes, particularly murder. In this case, it can be taken fairly literally. The blood of the victim has entered the soil, sending a message to the Creator.

The LORD asks Cain what I would call an accusing question: "Where is your brother Abel?" (Gen 4:9). Cain's answer, denying that he knows, and disavowing any responsibility for his brother, provokes the LORD's assertion: Your brother has been murdered; you are cursed for what you did. Given that Cain's is the first crime, the first murder, there are no fixed procedures or penalties. At a later time, Cain would have been executed (Gen 9:6). Not in this first trial: the defilement of the ground dictates Cain's punishment. He is banished from it, and it will no longer yield for him. So he becomes a wanderer.

At this point, Cain is relocated into a world with other people, and he fears for his life. Nonresidents were vulnerable because no law protected outsiders. So the LORD implements the "first law": He puts a mark on Cain's forehead to indicate that Cain is under divine protection. Not that the LORD would intervene to save him, but he would exact vengeance if Cain were harmed.

## The Transmission of Sin

How did the fall from innocence of Adam and Eve get passed on to their descendents? That question arises from the fact that the first murder comes in the wake, so to speak, of the fall from innocence. In the world following the fall from innocence, humans are not only responsible and accountable, but they are susceptible to the power of sin—envy, pride, and the like.

The Augustinian tradition proposed an idea of biological transmission. This doesn't make much sense according to modern biological science, and probably always was an implausible line of thought. When Cain and Abel were born, they were innocent and had to "recapitulate" their parents' loss of innocence. This story is not told. In fact, it will not be told again in the Bible. The recapitulation of the fall from innocence seems to happen to every human, so there is no need to recount it over and over. This does not mean that the original fall caused the subsequent ones; rather, the original fall reveals what is inevitable for every human.

How, then, does the original fall condition later events? The parents probably shaped their sons' character, and thereby passed on the stamp of their parents' fall. Nevertheless, Cain's susceptibility to envy and his murder of his brother were his own doing. His parents did not produce such effects. So, we can say that the original fall shaped the world that the sons entered, but the sons' actions were "transactions" with their world for which they bear responsibility.

We have to confront one more dimension of this intergenerational transaction. There are collective sins that are a part of the world passed on from one generation to another, and these shape each generation without their active appropriation. I am thinking of sins like racism, consumerism, and nationalism; these antedate the individual and usually condition consciousness as a person develops an ethic and lifestyle. Nevertheless, the recipient of such conditioning is responsible for what he or she does and thinks of doing.

## Judgment by Flood

James Barr observed that Christian theologians searching for a textual anchor for the doctrine of original sin would do well to look to the flood story:

> [The] idea of a sudden and catastrophic fall into sin and radical alienation from God, which has been characteristic of much of Christian tradition and which was supposed to have its textual location in Adam and Eve and the Garden of Eden, actually has a much better textual basis in Genesis 6 . . . It is here, and not in the story of the Garden of Eden, that we hear that the earth was filled with violence (Genesis 6:11). It is here, and nowhere else in the Bible, that we find a statement coming close to the idea of "total depravity": "The LORD saw that the wickedness of man was great in the earth, and that the whole formation of the thoughts of his heart was only evil at all times" (Genesis 6:5). It was then, and appropriately, that God, disgusted with this state of affairs, regretted that he had made humanity at all and decided to wipe out the whole lot of them.[13]

---

13. Barr, *The Garden of Eden*, 75–76.

Rather than follow Barr's thesis in its entirety, I propose to see the judgment of the world at the time of Noah as the climax of the story of sin and judgment beginning in Genesis 2–3.

The account of the mating of the "sons of God"—probably divine beings—and human women (6:1–4) doesn't really make an adequate account of the evil that arouses God's wrath. The story, which has a shockingly polytheistic character, tells of the invasion of the human sphere by lustful beings from the divine world. The LORD seems to be angry with these sons of God, but there is no mention of their judgment. In an effort to limit the power of their offspring, the LORD shortens the lifetime of all human beings. The last verse (v. 4) explains why the story was told: to account for the origin of a heroic race known in legend.

This story would hardly explain why the LORD found the *human* species to be so evil. Rather, the story of the fall from innocence and expulsion from the garden, of the first murder, of Lamech's compound revenge, and the genealogies filling in the years between the beginning and the time of the flood provide the explanation for the LORD's judgment. In Gen 6:5—9:17, we have an account of judgment of inconceivable magnitude, wiping out human and animal life from the earth. It needs a tale of offenses equal in breadth and depth.

God's deliberation in 6:5–12 constitutes the trial. The LORD's recognition of the extent and depth of human sinfulness (6:5) sums up the teaching derived from the doctrine of original sin. Humans are in the grip of evil impulses throughout their lives—from their youth up according to the parallel text in 8:21. We might say, in the light of Genesis 3, that when humans pass from innocence to accountability, they are not only susceptible to deadly sins, they/we are invariably in their grip.

So the LORD is sorry that he had made humans; we are a failed experiment. It is time to put a stop to this tragedy. But then the LORD decides to save Noah. Noah "found favor" in God's sight; a bit later he is said to be "a righteous man, blameless in his generation" (v. 9). Nevertheless, he is still a human, subject to evil impulses like everyone else. When the LORD decides to save him, he changes his mind about bringing the story of evil and violence to an end. He has chosen to sustain creation despite its evil. This is the closest thing to theodicy in the Old Testament: God accepts evil among creatures as the cost for preserving human life at all.

It is illuminating to compare the story of Noah and the flood to the very similar accounts preserved in the *Atra Hasis* and the end of the *Gilgamesh*

## Redeeming Judgment

*Epic*.[14] According to these, one deity decides to destroy the human race, another to save it by telling a Noah-type figure to build a ship. Biblical monotheism cannot take this route: it has to explain how the LORD could both decide to destroy the human race and the animals, and to save seed for a new beginning. The storytellers could have had Noah exemplify a superior moral human or have God reform human nature, so that evil would not be so prevalent in the postflood world. Neither option was tried, however; rather, after the flood, the LORD repeats his observation about the depravity of the human race: "I will never again curse the ground because of humankind, for the imagination of the human heart is evil from youth" (8:21). What will change is how God deals with wayward humans.

Later readers of the story were uneasy about the drowning of the masses of humans without giving them a chance to change. A midrash sprang up about how Noah "preached" to his contemporaries, warning them of the coming flood and encouraging them to repent. This is what Israel expected before God judged them. Of course, the story still had to end with all but the family of Noah dead, but at least they had been given a chance.

### The Covenant between God and Noah

Once the flood subsides and the inhabitants of the ark are allowed to exit, Noah builds an altar and sacrifices one of every clean animal and bird (8:20). The LORD is pleased with the offerings and promises to himself never to repeat this sort of intervention in nature. From now on, the seasonal pattern will go on without radical disruption. Why? Because the LORD acknowledges, as quoted above, that humans are bent on sinning, and he must put up with them if he is going to sustain a world populated with creatures who bear his image. There seems to be little prospect for making humans better. So let life go on.

God does intervene to make a covenant with Noah that has principles and procedures for limiting the damage of the violent, corrupt human heart. The covenant begins with a blessing: humans, as well as animals, are going to have to repopulate the earth. Now, however, humans are permitted to eat animal meat as long as the blood of these animals has been drained (9:2–4). It is assumed that some animals will eat others as well, but they are prohibited from killing and eating humans (v. 5). The animals' fear of humans should protect humans from such attacks (most of the time).

---

14. Available in Heidel, *The Gilgamesh Epic and Old Testament Parallels*.

Humans are forbidden to kill other humans (vv. 5–6). This is the beginning of *law* governing human affairs. Humans bear the image of God, and therefore are of infinite value. Anyone who does kill a human should be executed, because the only "repayment" a killer can make for "taking" a life, as we say, is his or her own life. This is meant to be a law for all humanity. The theology of the Bible classifies the prohibition of killing humans, and the *lex talionis* for violators, as a universal law. Later readers added other common prohibitions and values to the covenant with Noah—that is, with the whole human race.

To conclude the covenant with Noah, God communicates his pledge to himself to Noah to maintain the seasonal patterns. Not only do humans have his word, they have the heavenly sign of the rainbow.

## Sin and Law

Off and on theologians have defined sin as breaking the commandment of God. The justification for doing so is the story of the original fall from innocence. The Lord tests the couple's willingness to obey. Tradition has held that the woman deliberately breaks it when she is persuaded by the serpent to do so. Our own reading of the story, however, denies that she acts with deliberate malice. She eats the forbidden fruit believing that it will be a benefit. It would be wrong to blame the fall on a deliberate act of disobedience. The couple is responsible for their action, but they have little idea of its consequence.

In any case, law does not come into play until the covenant with Noah. Here we have law covering homicide. It is known by most humans; as Paul puts it, it is a law "written on their hearts" (Rom 2:14–15). Now that humans are governed by this law, the violation of the commandment is sinful. As the law develops, a vast array of subjects comes under its sway. As long as the law represents the best interests of the community, it is possible to say that the violation of any of its provisions is sinful. However, no law is exhaustive enough to cover all the actions and motives that are sinful. Some wrongs are impossible to enforce; some are even too complicated to be brought under a rule. Harsh words and social snubs are usually wrongful, but law does not cover such contingencies.

Thus, law is what can be enforced by humans or, in the Bible, by God. However, it is not breaking a rule that makes an action sinful; it is chiefly actions under the grip of one of the deadly sins. One may break a law in pursuit of one's desire, but that is not why one has sinned.

*Redeeming Judgment*

One further observation should be noted. Most law governs the actions of individuals and groups within the legal community. Collective offenses are not covered. When the classical prophets indict the people, the offenses often reach beyond the law because the whole people are condemned. Amos's indictment of the luxury and decadence of wealthy and powerful Israelites is not the violation of any biblical law; it is, rather, a spirit of living out of step with the will of YHWH and the good of society.

## The Adaptability of God

One who has been paying close attention to the Genesis narrative will notice that the Lord seems to learn from experience and adapt to the changes humans have wrought. We find that already in Genesis 2, where the Lord is curious about what the man will name animals (2:19–20).

Of greater moment, the Lord must discover that the man needs a woman (2:18, 20). In Genesis 3, the Lord God must hold an inquiry to learn what happened. Since the couple experienced shame at their nakedness and fear the Lord once they had eaten the forbidden fruit, shame and fear become normative for human behavior. Though the Lord intends for humans to remain innocent, he adapts to their new powers and seeks to rectify situations disturbed by sin. He has to punish Cain for his murder. Then he becomes aware that humans are invariably evil and violent, and decides to destroy all life. But then he thinks better of it, and calls Noah to save a remnant for a new beginning. At the end of the flood, he devises a new order and pledges not to destroy it. God has, as it were, learned to deal with sinful humanity.

Adaptability is at variance with the doctrine of God in practically all sophisticated theologies. If God is perfect, doesn't God know the future completely; doesn't God have everything planned out; isn't God changeless, indeed timeless? One can say either that our authors were naïve and we know better, or that they knew better but depicted God graphically for the sake of their audience. I would urge readers to give full credit to the authors; they were sophisticated and perceptive. Try the idea that God accommodates himself to the capacity and character of those he is relating to. He walks around the garden when the couple is in a state of innocence but ceases to after they are expelled from the garden. Perhaps this capacity to accommodate has something to do with the Christian doctrine of the incarnation.

## The Tower of Babel

The bridge between the covenant of God with Noah and the beginning of the tower of Babel is a story of a family incident (the story of Ham seeing his father, Noah's, nakedness) that results in shame and curse. Things haven't changed since before the flood. This is followed by the genealogy of the three sons of Noah, often called the table of nations. Since the genealogy precedes the tower of Babel account, we can infer that the LORD God intends to divide the human family into a plurality of peoples before he puts down a rebellion by scattering the conspirators. The plurality of human communities living throughout the physical world is a part of the good creation, though sin exacerbates the divisions.

*Tower Construction*

The story of the construction of a tower reaching heaven is the last of the series of accounts of sin and judgment. It is a story of collective sin: humans have learned how they can amass power by joining forces. Their motive is to "make a name for ourselves" and to avoid being "scattered abroad upon the face of the earth" (Gen 11:4). The latter motive may be a response to God's decision to spread humans out around the world. Why would the tower thwart this diaspora? Perhaps a collective project will keep them united—or so they think. It is also possible that the attainment of heaven might challenge divine sovereignty. The LORD thinks along this line: "they are one people, and they have all one language; and this is only the beginning of what they will do; nothing that they propose to do will now be impossible for them" (11:6).

This judgment resembles the LORD God's thinking about the couple seizing fruit from the tree of life (3:22). His response was expulsion from the garden so that death would limit human power, keeping humans subordinate to God. Now humans have gotten around the barrier of death because the collectivity could live on indefinitely. So now God devises a scheme to undercut the power of "collective man," to divide and balance power against power.

It is noteworthy also that the sin of pride, which Reinhold Niebuhr named as the root of human sin,[15] is the driving force of this collective sin. Pride accompanies great power. The empires that the prophets pronounce judgment on typically come in for accusations of pride and related sins like avarice and

---

15. Reinhold Niebuhr, *The Nature and Destiny of Man*, 1:186–207, also 138, 139; 2:306.

violence (e.g., Isa 10:5–19; Ezek 28:1–10).[16] Unfortunately, Christian piety is seldom alert to collective sin and evil, allowing believers to participate in it as obedient citizens. It is our intent in this study to accord collective evil at least as much attention as individual sin and evil.

The judgment of the LORD is not so much punishment as suppression of a challenge to divine power. This again resembles the expulsion of the original couple from the garden. In the case of Babel, God does not hold a trial; he responds like a sovereign to a rebellion. His response, moreover, is not punishment but a measure to thwart the objectives of the rebellion. Here he undoes the power of this collective to act together. The story, of course, tells of the origin of the plurality of human languages. However, it invites an imaginative extension: there developed conflicts between the builders, conflicts involving egos and cliques, for instance. These would have been experienced as "a problem of communication," as we often say. The workers begin to abandon the project—they may even become skeptical of its viability and desirability. Some, undoubtedly, left expecting to build their own tower.

So the construction of a city and tower fails to ensure the unity of the human family, and in fact propels the centrifugal forces already operating. Now there will be no one human history either. When humans are scattered around the world, there will only be histories. The Genesis narrative narrows to one such story—to the story of the ancestors of Israel. It will be of universal significance because this people will be singled out by the LORD of history. The dispersion of the peoples of the world is the background to the story of Abraham and his descendants.

*The Issue of Progress*

The story told in Genesis 1–11 can be read as a story of progress. Each story and even some annotations of genealogical names recount how human civilization and culture are enhanced. The original couple actually advances human development by breaking out of innocence. Innocence, after all, is really an animal existence. Many thinkers have spoken of "the fortunate fall" because humans gained their freedom.

While Cain's murder of his brother is hardly a "fortunate" event, we see the beginnings of criminal law—at least the law of vengeance. Moreover, Cain is forced away from the land, thus facilitating city culture. The genealogies

---

16. One can't quite separate our story from the city of Babylon, capital of the empire that exiled Judah.

have annotations that record the "invention" of city building, herding, musical instruments. and practical metal tools (Genesis 4). Humans are increasing their mastery of the world and the adornment of their living space with the arts.

One might even say that the LORD's adaptation to human beings entails progress. We can call it the "progress of religion." God's response to the flood is the most dramatic: He introduces law as a part of his covenant with all humans through Noah. He also forswears the annihilation of humanity, no matter how evil. These are measures that he adopts to avoid causing such a catastrophe again. When the LORD plans to wipe out Sodom and Gomorrah, Abraham persuades him to respect the rights of the innocent and to accord their protection greater weight than punishing the guilty (see Gen 18:16–33).

One would be a fool, however, to read the stories of sin and judgment optimistically. "Progress" does not make humans better or life less tragic. The loss of innocence may have a good side, but it also makes humans susceptible to the power of sin. Moreover, humans are now fully conscious of suffering, death, and the impossibility of escape. When humans are dispersed about the earth, they will fight with each other for land and love. The human story changes; there are points of progress but also new dangers and causes of despair. With "progress" in technology comes power, and power can be used for evil as well as good.[17] As for the LORD, his adaptation to changing human conditions ends up balancing power, leaving an uneasy and dangerous balance. In Genesis 12, the LORD takes a new tack entirely, but it does not eliminate the need to balance power.

## Retrospect and Prospect

The purpose of this section is to review what we have found out about divine judgment in Genesis 3–11, and to look forward to the filling out of these leads in the chapters to come.

The trial of the human couple for eating the forbidden fruit is the denouement of the action involving the loss of innocence. The trial concerns what happened to bring about the disobedience of the prohibition. The man blames the woman, the woman the serpent. Both feel guilt and try to unload it on someone else. The sentence follows a certain simple logic: the serpent is sentenced to the life of snakes, the woman and man to a life as adults—a

---

17. A recurring theme in Reinhold Niebuhr's thought; see, e.g., *Faith and History*, 1–13, 218.

consciousness of guilt and suffering and death. This is pretty much what losing innocence entails. The conditions described are certainly conditions the audience knows.

If there is a moral problem with the story, it is that the fall from innocence is itself innocent: it is not a deliberate act of disobedience. How can the couple be treated as guilty? Guilt usually derives from actions that one knows to be wrong. The couple has been told not to eat the fruit, but the serpent seems to be offering good advice. The woman cannot understand his appeals to sin—suspicion of God, desire to be equal to God. If she could have understood, she would have already lost her innocence before she disobeys the Lord God's prohibition.

So it is only after they have eaten the fruit that the man and woman become conscious of having done something wrong. Why does the Lord God judge them to be guilty? Because humans have to accept responsibility for actions whose evil or negative consequences are unknown to the actors. This happens not only because of naïve innocence, but again and again in the course of life.

The expulsion from the garden is added to the penalties stipulated in the trial. Here the Lord is suppressing a possible challenge to his sovereignty.

The story of Cain's murder of Abel—the first crime—shows that once humans are thrust into a world entailing responsibility and accountability, they are susceptible to the power of sin. In Cain's case, this is the power of envy. He is angry at the Lord's arbitrary favor toward one and rejection of the other, so he assaults the human that had been God's preference.

The trial begins with a seemingly naïve question: where is your brother? Cain not only denies knowing the answer, but he disavows the responsibility to know. The Lord exposes the cover-up and sentences Cain to alienation from the land. This penalty corresponds to the negative effect Cain's deed has on the land, viz., the land's contamination. When Cain objects to the severity of the judgment, the Lord puts a sign of protection on his forehead, thereby introducing the institution of vengeance.

The judgment of the human race in Gen 6:5–12 is unusual in several respects. There has been no act for which the condemned is to be judged: rather, it is the "moral condition" of the human race that is condemned. And based on that determination, the Lord declares his intent to wipe out the whole species. This has been, as it were, a failed experiment. Then, however, he changes his mind and institutes a plan to save one righteous man, his family and breeding stock for repopulating the postflood world. This is a decisive turn: total destruction is renounced, and law is introduced to make murder the worst offense committed between humans.[18] The upshot is that God restricts collective punishment in favor of a discriminate system.

The final event of the series is the collective challenge to the LORD. The human race has figured out that they can access greater power by working together. By building a tower to heaven, they expect to attain equality with the LORD and his host. The LORD thwarts their attempt by turning the conspirators against each other. Now humans will have to live in groups alongside other groups, and in competition with them for the means of life. There will be no more collective history, and the biblical story turns to one of the many.

*Original Sin Once More*

James Barr not only rejects reading Genesis 3 as the fall of humans from innocence into sin; he maintains that the textual basis for a doctrine of universal bondage to sin is exceedingly narrow.[19] I disagree: we can maintain a healthy continuity with the traditional interpretation.

First, I think that we arrive at a best-text reading of the first eleven chapters of Genesis by taking the accounts of judgment cumulatively and sequentially. As I have already said, Genesis 3 tells of the loss of innocence, the "fall" into the age of responsibility and accountability. All humans pass through an identical fall (or loss); it seems to be inevitable for humans to claim moral independence. This state of responsibility renders humans susceptible to deadly sins. Even those who resist sinful impulses successfully are compromised in their exchanges with others. Hence, the LORD can say "that every inclination of the thoughts of their hearts is only evil continually" (Gen 6:5). Even after the judgment by flood humans are vulnerable, both individually and collectively.

Second, these stories of judgment are strategically placed at the beginning of the canonical narrative. Biblical readers are expected to read the rest of the Bible in the light of these accounts. Indeed, given the fact that the whole human race is involved, how could a reader avoid drawing conclusions about the nature and destiny of all humanity?

Third, this set of judgments foreshadows the judgments that we read about in every period of the following history. The patriarchs and matriarchs of the chosen people are not subject to divine judgment, though their lives

---

18. Other realms of law are not mentioned here, but later Jewish thinkers added all those laws of which all humans have some version.

19. Barr, *The Garden of Eden*, 6–8; also 75, 91–93.

are governed by providence (according to passages like Gen 15:18–21; 35:3; 45:4–13). Abraham, however, intercedes for Sodom and Gomorrah when he is told the Lord's plan to judge the city (Gen 18:16–33). In the story of the exodus, Pharaoh and people of Egypt come under divine judgment when they refuse to comply with the Israelite petition. We see in this story how power becomes enslaved to maintaining power. The Israelites "fall" when they build a golden calf while Moses is away receiving revelation for the people. They are subject to a series of judgments in the wilderness, which seem to foreshadow the later disasters of the chosen people. The nation lives on a trajectory toward the exiles of Israel and Judah from the time they occupy the promised land until the people are removed from it. Each of these judgments involves sin. Amos has a memorable epigram worthy of Israel's history as a whole: "You only have I known of all the families of the earth; therefore I will punish you for all your iniquities" (Amos 3:2).

# 3

## Genesis of the People of Israel

(Genesis 12–50; Exodus 1–15)

BEGINNING IN CHAPTER 12, the Genesis narrative abruptly changes its focus from the universal to the particular, from sin and judgment to the comings and goings of a family, from the vast horizon of the international world to the minutia of daily life. No longer do we have etiologies of the human condition; now it is the small beginnings of the chosen people.

The stories of the patriarchs and matriarchs of Israel differ from what follows as well as from what precedes. The people is no more than a family, and its leader is the father, whereas in the narrative that follows (the exodus from Egypt), the people has grown to a "multitude," a collection of families and a mixed, heterogeneous mass led by one of their number called by God to perform the task of nation building. The Israel of neither narrative is subject to divine judgment. In Genesis, judgment comes upon cities famous for their wickedness; it is the oppressors of the Hebrews who experience the wrath of God in the exodus. The ancestors might be said to be a "third party" in both of these accounts of judgment.

If the narratives of the patriarchs and matriarchs differ so markedly from the exodus story, why have they been combined in this one chapter? Both stories precede the revelation of the law to Israel, so the chosen people share law and moral values with the majority populations where they live. Both accounts locate the chosen people in societies under the rule of others. Both tell of divine judgment of the peoples among whom the chosen people live. In both stories God reveals himself to the people in order to fit them for their vocation.

## The Ancestors

A survey of the Genesis narrative provides a general picture of the norms and values of the characters (and of the audience). There is no account of murder, though there are violent deaths and capture in Genesis 14 and 34. The prospect of being killed does arise elsewhere. Abram (later called Abraham) worries that he will be killed in Egypt (Gen 12:11–12), so he has his wife Sarai (later called Sarah) pretend that she is his sister. She is taken into the pharaoh's house, a kidnapping that threatens to lead the pharaoh to violate the marriage. God intervenes, and the pharaoh exhibits respect for the sanctity of marriage (12:19). Indeed, the narrative demonstrates that Abraham does not need to fear for his life, and that his dissembling actually causes trouble.[1] The pharaoh rightly upbraids Abraham for lying and expels him from the kingdom (12:18–20).

Other evidence shows that marriage is respected by all the characters in the stories. According to Genesis 34, the prince of the city of Shechem, who goes by the name Shechem, either rapes or seduces Jacob's daughter Dinah. Then he asks for her hand in marriage, and Jacob and his sons agree, on the condition that Shechem and the rest of the men of the city will submit to circumcision.[2] Clearly the Shechemites honored marriage.

Unfortunately, during the period of recovery, Simeon and Levi, and perhaps others, slaughter the Shechemites. Thus, they violate the covenant between the Shechemites and Jacob's s family, and execute vengeance for the dishonor that has come upon the family. Jacob condemns his sons because of the bad name their act will give Jacob's family among the inhabitants of the land (34:30). The immorality of the act, amounting to murder, is not acknowledged in the narrative. Perhaps the curse Jacob utters against Simeon and Levi in 49:5–7 amounts to divine judgment.[3]

The moral principle of truth telling comes up frequently in these stories. Jacob deceives his blind father Isaac, with the help of Rebecca, into believing that he is blessing Esau, its rightful recipient (27:5–45). Jacob, in turn, is deceived by Laban into marrying Leah (the eldest daughter) when he thinks he was marrying the younger and more beautiful Rachel (29:15–30). There is a contest between Jacob and Laban to deceive the other most effectively. One might call this poetic justice.

---

1. In the parallel account in Gen 20:11–12, Abraham defends the truthfulness of his statement, but that doesn't justify its half-truth; it was purposely misleading, and he was exposed.

2. The agreement actually entailed group intermarriage, not just the one couple.

3. In history, Simeon declined and Levi ceased to be a territorial tribe.

Theft is an issue in several accounts besides material directly about Jacob. Rachel, Jacob's favorite wife, steals her father's *teraphim*—household gods—when Jacob seeks to return to his homeland with his family and herds. When Laban, with a posse, overtakes the fleeing family, Rachel has to hide the stolen goods by a clever ruse (31:19, 33–35). Later in Genesis, Jacob and Rachel's son Joseph, now a ruler and grain provider in Egypt, plants his "diviner's cup" in his brother Benjamin's sack of grain so that all Joseph's brothers can be arrested and charged with theft (Gen 44:1–17). Joseph tests his brothers to determine whether they have repented of what they had done to him in selling him into slavery.

Indeed, selling Joseph into slavery is the worst crime committed within the family. In Israelite law, selling a free person into slavery is a death-worthy crime (Exod 21:16). One might expect a judgment—human or divine—to resolve the Joseph story, but Joseph, who has risen to prominence with God's aid, engineers a reconciliation that saves Jacob's family from starvation as well as from the enmity of blood vengeance. Joseph offers a theological reason for adopting such a conciliatory policy (Gen 50:15–21; also 45:4–15).

Reuben's sexual liaison with Jacob's concubine Bilhah also ranks high on a list of deeds deserving judgment (see Gen 35:22). There is no narrative account of it, but it is the subject of a curse in Gen 49:3–4.

Readers may be surprised by how closely the moral perceptions and values in the ancestral narrative match their own. This fact confirms that the moral order in Genesis is a common human order. We can call it natural law, if that term is not taken in its technical philosophical sense of a comprehensive rational scheme built into the order of the human world. In any case, the narrator and characters in our story have a vision of right and wrong, value and worthlessness, honor and despicability, that is recognizable to us. The scheme is conditioned by the particular historical conditions. The narrative, for example, assumes the institution of slavery and the subordination of women. It takes little historical imagination, though, to recognize common human values in this historical guise.

It is quite noteworthy that there are no religious crimes or conflicts in the ancestral corpus. The uncanny thing about this narrative is that YHWH alone—or Elohim in those sources that withhold the divine name until the exodus—is active in the lives of the patriarchs and matriarchs, and also in the lives of their neighbors. It is YHWH who afflicts the pharaoh to warn him of Sarah's marital status (12:17), and Elohim who gives king Abimelech of Gerar the same warning (20:6). When covenants are made over wells and borders, it is the one God who witnesses (20:25–34; 26:26–33; 31:43–54). Given that this God is the only divine persona in the narrative, offenses and conflicts due to polytheism are outside its horizon.

Yet one would expect the ancestors of the Israelites to be "tempted" by the gods of Canaan, since this becomes a major issue later in the Pentateuch (viz., Exod 23:23–33; 34:12–16; Lev 20:22–26; Deut 7:1–16; 12:29–31). It is quite puzzling that the problem is unknown in Genesis. Rachel's theft of Laban's *teraphim* is the subject of humor but not censure (31:33–35). We do hear of a rite of burying images, called "foreign gods," in Shechem before the family goes on pilgrimage to Bethel (32:2–4). The account assumes the prohibition against recognizing other gods and worshiping idols, but the issue doesn't arise in any of the ancestral stories.

## The Promise to the Patriarchs

The story of Abraham is included in the sacred history because this person and his family have been chosen by YHWH, the Creator and Sovereign of the world, to be a mediator of God himself in the world. Indeed, the future Israel is the only nation so chosen. This role is bestowed on Abraham's family by the promise made to Abraham in Gen 12:1–3.

> Go from your country, and your kindred and your father's house
> to the land that I will show you.
> I will make of you a great nation,
> I will bless you, and make your name great,
> so that you will be a blessing.
> I will bless those who bless you
> And the one who curses you I will curse;
> And in you all the families of the earth will be blessed.

This communication is a command backed up with promises.[4] It inaugurates the relationship between YHWH and the first patriarch, and through him between YHWH and all the generations that trace their ancestry to him through Sarah. The command to emigrate is followed up in Gen 12:7 with the promise to give Abraham's descendants the land of Canaan. This promise is not fulfilled for hundreds of years; until the generation of Joshua, Abraham and his descendants had to live as guests of foreign countries. The whole Pentateuch reaches forward, so to speak, to the fulfillment of this promise.

---

4. Despite the frequency of the word *brk*, the divine word is not a blessing but a promise.

The promise to make Abraham's descendants a great nation is a promise of progeny and honor. The barrenness of Sarah leaves the couple in suspense, provoking problematic efforts to "aid" the fulfillment; Abraham and Sarah finally have a son when Abraham is one hundred years old and Sarah is ninety. This son, Isaac, is the link to the mass of descendants to follow. Later God commands Abraham to sacrifice this son, and all prospects of a future, but Isaac is spared when Abraham proves obedient (Gen 22:11–19). The promise to Abraham is renewed with explicit reference to descendants (22:16–18), and delivered to Isaac (26:2–5) and Jacob (28:13–15).

The promise to bless the nations that treat the patriarch or his descendants well and to exact retribution from anyone who harms them is a promise of protection. The Lord's intervention to keep the pharaoh from violating Sarah in Egypt (12:17) would constitute the first application of this promise.

The call ends with a promise that Abraham either would be recalled in blessings or would mediate a blessing to *all* nations. The Hebrew is ambiguous, so either construal is possible. The promise that Abraham and his descendents will be mediator of blessing is more powerful, and is congruent with the role Abraham plays in the judgment of Sodom and Gomorrah.[5]

## Intercession for Sodom and Gomorrah

Now we can consider the one dramatic case of divine judgment in the ancestral narrative. When YHWH approaches Abraham to divulge his plan to judge the cities, the only accusation mentioned is, "The outcry against Sodom and Gomorrah is great and their sin is very grave" (18:20). What that sin is, is unspecified. That isn't enough to condemn them; indeed, there is a need for an investigation, a "test" if you will. Even if one's doctrine of God would hold that to be unnecessary (because God is omniscient), it is needed for humans—to dispel doubt as to culpability, to teach the reader what is right and wrong.

So two angelic wayfarers travel to Sodom: the response of the men of the city to the presence of strangers in their midst determines their fate, demonstrating their depraved character. The strangers are given safe harbor with Lot, but then the house is attacked. Tradition has it that the sin of Sodom is sodomy. Yes, the men of the city desire the bodies of the two male strangers. Lot offers to placate his neighbors with his daughters—on the assumption that homosexual rape is more offensive than heterosexual rape. The men/angels do not let the daughters come to harm. The real crime of the Sodomites is not

---

5. See Patrick, "Election, Old Testament," 434–41; also Kaminsky, *Yet I Loved Jacob*.

their homosexuality but their inhospitality to strangers and their uncontrolled sexual desire. The men of Sodom would have been just as guilty of sin in God's eyes if they raped Lot's daughters (cp. Judg 19:16–30).

This test, by the way, has God acting *incognito*. The people of Sodom do not know that they are attacking the deity—or angels, if that's your take. They might have behaved themselves if they had known. It is their treatment of their fellow human beings that is being tested, though. The test *is* their trial before God, the Judge of all the earth.

When YHWH is deliberating whether he will divulge the judgment of the cities to Abraham, he formulates the purpose of election: "I have known him, that he may urge his children and his household after him to keep the way of YHWH[6] by doing righteousness and justice" (Gen 18:19). How will this benefit the Gentiles? Perhaps as a model of righteousness and witness to a higher law. When YHWH reveals his plan, though, the role expands to include intercession for the "nations of the earth" (18:18). Abraham has been invited to participate in YHWH's deliberation, a friend of the court, as it were. His particular role in this deliberation is to stand up for the humans who would suffer the Lord's wrath. It is as if the Judge of all the earth needs the voice of the subjects, a voice to balance justice with mercy.[7] Unfortunately, not even a minimum of righteous could be found, so Lot and his family have to be brought out before the destruction.

## The Exodus

The exodus is not only the deliverance of the Hebrew slaves from bondage; it is a judgment on Egypt for enslaving them and not releasing them when YHWH commands the pharaoh to do so. The commission of Moses highlights the deliverance of the slaves, and initially pharaoh is a secondary concern. When he refuses a rather minor request, the Lord begins to demonstrate his power and chastise the pharaoh for refusing. As the plagues grow in severity, we realize that the pharaoh is being tested, and will be subjected to judgment if he does not relent. The act of liberating the Hebrews, thus, becomes a severe judgment on the pharaoh and his people. It is so called in the prediction of the exodus in Gen 15:14: "I will bring judgment on the nation that they serve . . ."

---

6. Where the NRSV and RSV use Lord, we insert YHWH.

7. Actually, Abraham appeals for justice for the righteous, not mercy. If his appeal is answered, it will result in mercy toward the guilty.

The first chapter of Exodus is a bridge back to Genesis; it sets the scene for the power struggle to follow. First we are told that the family of Genesis has become a people, indeed, a minority that is becoming so big that it makes the host population uncomfortable (vv. 7, 9). Then we are told that a new ruler arose over Egypt, one who had no ties to Joseph or any of the Israelites. This could be read as a new dynasty that felt no obligation for a population favored by the previous dynasty. The ruler decides to isolate and demonize the foreigners, probably with the tacit approval of the native population. Fear of the increasing size of the minority becomes a rationale for enslaving them. They are made slaves of the state, who were assigned to the construction of two cities: Pithom and Raamses (v. 11). When enslavement did not slow down their increase, the pharaoh made a secret attempt to stop it by killing male babies at birth. This proves unsuccessful, so the foreigners grow in number as they continued to serve as state slaves.

The account of the enslavement of the descendants of Israel is what I have called elsewhere a "forensic narration."[8] That is, it describes the pharaoh's actions as evil and deserving of divine judgment. The pharaoh, in a word, is guilty of crimes against humanity. The Israelites are innocent; their only crime is fecundity. There is no suggestion in the narrative that their enslavement is punishment for some sin on their part. Later they will be censured for lack of faith (Exod 14:10–14), but that has nothing to do with being enslaved.

Though the account in chapter 1 could lead to a divine intervention to judge the pharaoh and Egypt, it does not. Rather, the commission of Moses at the burning bush highlights the deliverance of the Israelites. Once the Lord has identified himself (3:1–6), he announces in a classic oracle of salvation that he knows the suffering of his people and will remove them from their situation (3:7–8). Moses will be his human agent (3:9–10). Only in v. 10 does God mention the negotiations with the pharaoh, and the actual assignment is not described until v. 18, which is expanded on in vv. 19–22. Moses is much more worried about his credibility with his own people than he is about the pharaoh (see 3:13; 14:1, 10).

The Lord does tell Moses, "the king of Egypt will not let you go unless compelled . . . So I will stretch out my hand and smite Egypt with all my wonders" (3:19–20). This will be a power conflict between YHWH and the pharaoh, not a judgment imposed on a wrongdoer. At least that is how the interaction begins, and it only evolves into judgment when the pharaoh refuses to yield.

---

8. Patrick and Scult, *Rhetoric and Biblical Interpretation*, 57–81.

*Redeeming Judgment*

Moses has little difficulty gaining acceptance from his people (4:17–31), though it will not last. It was the pharaoh who spoke a resounding no to a modest request (5:1–9). One of the big puzzles of Moses's initial encounter with the pharaoh is why he asks not for the people's freedom but for permission to celebrate a feast in the wilderness (5:1, 3). This will be the explicit request throughout the struggle. Is this a ruse, or did Moses start out trying to alleviate the slaves' harsh conditions? The pharaoh takes Moses's request at face value (5:4), though he may have had suspicions. In any case, the Egyptian ruler seems to have thought that giving in to such an innocent, innocuous request would encourage the slaves to ask for more, until they did demand their freedom (5:2).

The pharaoh's harsh response demoralizes the Israelites, and Moses himself; it comes close to having the pharaoh's intended effect. The Lord has to reverse the mood (5:22—6:1), now without the wholehearted support of the people (5:15–21; 6:9–13). Moses and Aaron have to negotiate with the pharaoh through the use of signs (7:1–13), and the first plagues are little more than signs themselves (7:14ff.); they only constitute nuisances for the Egyptians. The Egyptian "magicians" are able to duplicate these and so undercut the demonstration of YHWH's power (Exod 7:22; 8:7; but note 8:18; 9:11).

A striking feature of this narrative is that the Egyptians have no deities. The magicians can match Moses and Aaron for a while, but the narrative does not speak of their power deriving from deities, or their invoking them. This is an amazingly different view of Egyptian culture from the one in its own literature. The Exodus narrator misrepresents Egyptian culture to make a theological point, viz., that YHWH's power and majesty not only exceed that of the gods of Egypt; he is the only power and majesty. The one exception, Exod 12:12, says that YHWH exercised "judgment" on the gods of Egypt. This judgment was an exposure of their impotence, demonstrated by their complete absence from the conflict.

How about the pharaoh himself? Now and then interpreters have identified the Egyptian ruler as the divine being against whom YHWH fights.[9] We know that Egyptian religion accorded the pharaoh the status of a god; perhaps the Israelite narrators are exposing the hollowness of this claim. However, the pharaoh was not a divine being in isolation from other gods; he "incarnated"

---

9. E.g., Labuschagne, *The Incomparability of Yahweh*, 75, says "that we are justified in saying that the bringing out of Israel is represented as a contest between Yahweh and the god-king of Egypt."

various gods according to his function and stage in life.[10] The biblical narrative ignores all such mythology and does not really portray the pharaoh as anything more than a tyrant. To be able to resist YHWH, he must be empowered by YHWH (so Exod 4:21; 9:12; 10:1, etc.). The Egyptian ruler seems actually to be enslaved to his own willfulness, and cannot abide by the counsel of prudence (10:7–11).

Though the pharaoh is merely a human being, the Lord clearly has it in mind to "get glory for myself over Pharaoh and all his host" (14:17). This is a matter of honor, of exhibiting superior power and rectitude. We might even say, to show this human ruler who is boss, who can stand tall. The aim of the Lord's action is not only to deliver Israel but to receive recognition for his status in the order of things. In the midst of the plagues, YHWH sets forth the reason he is sending a series of blows rather than simply destroying the Egyptian people: "This time I will send all my plagues upon you yourself . . . that you may know that there is none like me in all the earth. For by now I could have stretched out my hand and struck you and your people with pestilence, and you would have been cut off from the earth; but this is why I have let you live, to show you my power, and to make my name resound throughout all the earth" (Exod 9:14–16).

Of course it is understood that the God of the Hebrews (5:3) has every right to punish the Egyptians until they release the slaves; the deliverance of the one people entails coercion of the other. But YHWH uses the occasion to manifest his power, his reality, to the entire world of humans. He is actually pulling his punches so that Egypt will survive to proclaim the story of his blows.

By the time we have reached the last plague, the divine blows have become judgment of the Egyptian ruler's oppressive behavior. Actually, the announcement of the final plague sounds much like the rest:

> Thus says the LORD: About midnight I will go out through Egypt; and every first-born in the land of Egypt shall die, from the first-born of Pharaoh who sits on his throne, to the firstborn of the female slave who is behind the handmill; and all the first-born of the livestock. And there will be a loud cry throughout the land of Egypt, such as there has never been, or will ever be again . . . And all these officials of yours shall come down to me, and bow down to me, saying, "Leave us, you and all the people who follow you." And after that I will leave. (Exod 11:4–8)

---

10. Frankfort, *Kingship and the Gods*, 15–212.

## Redeeming Judgment

What makes the deed announced here an act of judgment is its finality. Every household will lose a member, and the laments will be truly heartrending. Nothing is said of the action for which it is a punishment, and it would probably be more correct to call it judgment for the Egyptians' not complying with the divine ultimatum when they had due warning. The previous plagues are like the warnings recited in Amos 4:6–12, and this last one is like Amos's warning, "Prepare to meet you God, O Israel" (v. 12).

This plague will break the resistance of the pharaoh and his servants. Indeed, the natives will give gifts to the slaves to redress the wrongs they have suffered (3:21–22; 12:33–36). While the pharaoh does not admit the wrongs he has done to the Hebrew slaves, he does send them away with the request to pray for him (12:31–32).

One might also classify the drowning of the pharaoh and his troops in the Sea of Reeds as a judgment, but this time no words are exchanged between YHWH's spokesman and the Egyptian ruler, no words to interpret the event. In truth, this drowning is a "punishment" the pharaoh brings upon himself; that is, his ego is so bent on winning that he cannot concede defeat (see 14:5). His undoing is well known in the ancient biblical Wisdom tradition. The Song of the Sea ascribes the insatiable desire to win to the Egyptians in somewhat different wording:

> The enemy said, "I will pursue, I will overtake,
> I will divide the spoil, my desire shall have its fill in them.
> I will draw my sword, my hand will destroy them." (15:9)

So the event of deliverance is not only a promise of empowerment to the poor and oppressed; it is a shattering of the power of the oppressor. YHWH asserts his destructive power at the same time that He demonstrates his justice.[1]

The Song of the Sea begins with a praise of YHWH for his saving deed (15:1), and a confession of trust combined with praise (15:2). The first strophe ends with a characterization of YHWH as a warrior. There is nothing about judgment in it, and much of the description of the overthrow of the pharaoh's army focuses on the demonstration of power and glory (e.g., vv. 6, 11).

Beginning in Exod 15:13, the Song leaves behind the overthrow of the Egyptian army to follow the fate of the Hebrew tribes on their journey to their promised home—the Lord's "abode" (v. 13). Four peoples are mentioned: Philistines, Edomites, Moabites, and Canaanites. They are not defeated in battle; they are paralyzed by fear so that they do not prevent the Israelites from passing by and settling in YHWH's "sanctuary."

One might say that the fear-inspiring presence of YHWH makes it possible to avoid the need for violent conquest and any acts of judgment against these peoples. This is not, of course, the way the conquest is depicted in the books of Joshua and Judges. At least we can say that the Song of the Sea does not conclude with a focus on YHWH's powers as a warrior but with an emphasis on his uncanny presence among his people. YHWH the warrior of 15:1–3 has become the God who will reign by spiritual force at the end.

The Exodus narrative does tell the story of a violent engagement between the liberated slaves and a desert tribe known as Amalekites (Exod 17:8–16). YHWH comes to the rescue by empowering the Israelites to fight under Joshua; the "staff" held by Moses is the source or conduit of divine power. God acts as Israel's protector and as judge of the violent, unprovoked alien tribe. Indeed, YHWH decrees, in his role as judge, that the Amalekites must be exterminated because of their assault on the vulnerable ex-slaves.

## Summary Reflection

Abraham and his progeny by Sarah were called by the Lord, Creator of heaven and earth, to be his representative on earth. Other nations will fare well or poorly according to how they treat this family (and later, nation). This people has been chosen to be an agent of blessing to the families/nations; one of their tasks is to plead for justice and mercy, as perceived from the creaturely point of view.

There is no account in the life of the family over four generations that can be said to be a divine judgment. Again and again, conflicts break out that could have resulted in such judgment, but do not. Sarah's expulsion of her slave Hagar (Gen 21:10–14) would have been murder except for God's intervention. The thefts committed by Jacob, which provoke Esau to look for an opportunity to even the score, are defused by Jacob's sojourn with Laban. When Jacob returns later, the brothers are reconciled, at least sufficiently to get along together. Simeon and Levi incur Jacob's censure for their murder of the men of Shechem, but only in his final "blessings" are they placed under divine judgment. The selling of Joseph into slavery was serious crime, but it is transformed into a boon for the family and an occasion for reconciliation. The rubric of the Joseph story—"'Even though you intended to do harm to me, God intended it for good'" "you meant it for evil, but God meant it for good" (Gen 50:20)—can actually be said to characterize the family's conflicts over four generations.

## Redeeming Judgment

The most serious event of judgment to take place in the era of the ancestors was the destruction of Sodom and Gomorrah. The Lord had the evidence of cries of distress to raise suspicion about these cities in the vicinity of the Dead Sea. He intends to test the evidence by sending two representatives to the city to see how they are treated. He consults with Abraham as well, as something of a friend of the court. Abraham seeks to persuade the divine Judge to adopt the principle that the inadvertent punishment of the innocent along with the guilty would be unjust. God adopts this principle, though even such a protective measure doesn't suffice to save these cities.

God, whose name is YHWH, has called and covenanted with Abraham and his descendants for the purpose of remedying the condition of the human race. Humans have proven to be inveterately sinful and must be dispersed to prevent a collective assault on heaven. This results in what might be called an "armed truce," a steady state that allows humans to continue but not to fulfill their true destiny. The call of Abraham inaugurates a plan to recover humans. How this is going to be accomplished is not yet clear, but a seed has been planted that will grow into the redemption of the world once an eschatological horizon becomes manifest to the people of God. At this stage it is only a call to loyalty and service. YHWH protects his newly chosen family from the consequences of their own sin as well as their neighbor's hostility. The family is to learn the will of God and to intercede for humans. In the case of Sodom and Gomorrah, Abraham counsels YHWH to protect the innocent and righteous even if it means allowing evil to flourish.

The chosen family becomes a people under common leadership in Exodus. They are born as victims of Egyptian oppression. Moses is appointed a leader, a deliverer, by YHWH. Freeing the slaves is going to require divine intervention on their side, an intervention that becomes a power struggle between the oppressive human tyrant and the divine patron of the slaves.

Moses is told to confront the pharaoh with a request for a holiday, a sacrificial feast outside Egypt. This is not a judgment pronounced on the pharaoh and his country. Only as the request is rejected and a series of plagues does not soften the pharaoh's will that the last plague and the drowning of the army have the force of judgment. Even then, the narrative focuses more on the glory YHWH gains by his spectacular deliverance of his people than on the judgment of the oppressors.

YHWH's role as patron and protector of his people continues beyond the exodus. The Song of the Sea looks forward to YHWH's fear-inspiring presence in the promised land and his empowerment of the escaped slaves to defend themselves against an attack by a desert tribe known as Amalek. Whenever YHWH gives victory to his people against their foes, it is an implied judgment on the latter. However, YHWH's saving activity for his people is the foundation.

The next phase of YHWH's activity will be the construction of an internal structure of authority and law to empower the people to govern themselves and consolidate their gains.

# 4

# Covenant and Law

(Exodus 18–40, Leviticus)

THE PEOPLE OF ISRAEL are not yet a political body when they leave Egypt. Indeed, it would be more proper to call them Hebrews or a band of escaped slaves. According to Exodus 1, the core of the group belonged to one extended family. That would have formed the basic structure, but such nascent tribal structures are notoriously fickle and unstable. Moreover, the text reports that along with the family there was a "mixed crowd" (Exod 12:38), making the band even less homogenous. This multitude did harken to Moses, but it should not surprise the reader that there are those who grumble whenever difficulties arise (Exod 15:24; 16:2–3; 17:2–3).

Among his other duties, Moses is called upon to adjudicate disputes between members of this band of Hebrews. His father-in-law advises him to delegate responsibility for this job (Exod 18:14–23). Judges should be appointed over various divisions of the people to hear all but the most difficult cases; the latter should come to Moses, the "appellate judge," so to speak, who will in turn consult the Lord. The text does not mention a written law, so one may surmise that the people are judged by an unwritten one. Such an "unwritten law" would have been a shared ethos to which all members of the community can be held accountable.

This type of legal system could have continued indefinitely; to a large extent, it did. However, in the very next chapter of Exodus, after Moses receives delegating advice, the people arrive at Mount Sinai and begin preparing to meet YHWH, at which time they will enter into a covenant with him. As a part of this covenant, YHWH imposes written law. What does the covenant and written law do for the people? Well, the fact that the "society" has become more complex and includes disparate elements may require a more formal law. Moreover, the authority structure of this nascent community is undefined. If the band of slaves is going to be established as a permanent society, it needs the covenant and law enacted in Exodus 19–24.

## Covenant

It has been common for scholars to compare the covenant between YHWH and Israel to the Hittite treaties between a suzerain and a vassal—in contemporary terms, an imperial power and a client state. This comparison has been popular since the middle of the twentieth century, when a number of Hittite treaty texts were found.[1] The protocol of the treaties is similar to the covenant texts in Exodus, Deuteronomy, and elsewhere in the Bible. If one adds the fact that the Hebrew term *berith* was used of treaties in Scripture, one has an initially plausible case. However, the word *berith* is used for a range of formal pledges of loyalty and obedience, and the covenant between YHWH and Israel could fit a number of them. I myself would compare this covenant to the one between David and the northern tribes (2 Sam 5:3); here the relationship is between a king—a sovereign—and his subjects.[2]

Exodus 19 actually provides an important formal declaration of what is established in the act of covenant making. The divine declaration begins with a commission to Moses to convey the message to the people of Israel (v. 3b); the commission is repeated at the conclusion (6b). The Lord initiates his proposal by reviewing what he has just done for the addressees:

> You have seen what I did to the Egyptians
> and how I bore you on eagles' wings
> and brought you to myself. (19:4)

This is a presentation of YHWH's credentials, as it were, to be Israel's God. The next sentence offers the people an opportunity to formally decide and declare their willingness to serve the speaker:

> Now therefore if you will obey my voice
> and keep my covenant,
> you shall be my treasured possession out of all peoples,
> for all the earth is mine. (19:5)

---

1. Mendenhall, "Covenant," 714–23.
2. My position is well covered in Patrick, *Old Testament Law*, 223–35.

*Redeeming Judgment*

If they are willing to obey YHWH as expressed in his law, YHWH—the Lord of all—will set the addressees apart; they will become his sphere of sovereignty, as the following lines indicate:

> You shall be for me a priestly kingdom
> and a holy nation. (19:6a)

When the people answer in the affirmative (19:7–8), the theocratic constitution goes into effect. First, YHWH makes an appearance before the whole mass of people (19:16–20 [21–25]). As a part of this theophany he declares the Ten Commandments in the people's hearing (20:1–17).³ Then Moses is chosen to mediate all the other words YHWH has for the people (20:18–20). Moses ascends the mountain and receives a corpus of law, beginning in 20:23 and ending in 23:19.⁴ This corpus has been titled the Book of the Covenant because it is so called in 24:7. When Moses returns from the mountain, he performs two ratification rituals. He recites the laws he has received, and when the people have reaffirmed their decision to obey YHWH he writes the words in a book, constructs altars, and offers sacrifices; he concludes the ceremony by throwing blood on the altar and the people (24:3–8). Then Moses, priests, and elders ascend the mountain to eat a sacred meal in the presence of God (24:9–12).

## Law

Law plays a central part in the action: the ceremony formally recognizes YHWH's authority to impose law on the people; then YHWH exercises that authority.

Aside from its liturgical role, the function of the written law is uncertain. We have little evidence from outside the legal corpora that written codes were actually applied in courts,⁵ yet the laws read like a practical body of legal teaching.⁶ To deduce what the Book of the Covenant was used for, we also have to

---

3. Whether the Israelites actually understood what they were hearing, or whether it took Moses to decipher it for them is ambiguous. In 20:18–20, the people respond in such a way that one could surmise that they only heard inarticulate sounds. Deut 5:22–27 says they heard the Ten Commandments, but even that chapter is ambiguous.

4. Exod 23:20–33 is not law but a prophecy of what will happen after they leave the mountain.

5. See Patrick, *Old Testament Law*, 189–203.

6. One can discern evidence in the Book of the Covenant of amendments; e.g., Exod 21:22, which states two different rules for assessment of payment. Undoubtedly the second

take into account the fact that it has moral preachments and cultic rules; these would not be used in a court setting. The code is, in my opinion, heuristic—to be read publicly, taught to judges and common people alike. It is not exhaustive of judicial or moral teaching, so we must regard it as paradigmatic. Unwritten law remained, thus, a staple for judicial decisions. The Ten Commandments highlighted the salient moral rules of action in a comprehensive fashion and the Book of the Covenant provides paradigmatic applications.

What does divine proclamation of the law do to its provisions? Many of the provisions of both the Ten Commandments and the Book of the Covenant were in circulation elsewhere; Israel did not need YHWH to make them aware that stealing is wrong, or that burning a neighbor's field by accident entails reparations to its owner. Nevertheless, YHWH's saying it changes the status of such laws essentially: they become sins against YHWH, acts of disobedience of his stated will. This gives the law additional motive force. It also institutes a different hermeneutic: once the law is framed as divine commandment, the interpreter is obliged to understand and apply it within a theological scheme.

A theory of language sheds additional light on the theological import of the covenant and law. I am referring to the proposal of J. L. Austin that speaking *does* something as well as says something. Many of the utterances humans make are not descriptive, or not only descriptive, but perform some task. Naming is one: when someone with authority bestows a name on someone or something, the name is official; the act of speaking (or writing) has the force of bringing about a new state of affairs.

Promises, agreements, and commandments have a performative character. The covenant depicted in Exodus 19–24 has all three types of performative discourse mentioned. When the covenant is ratified in chapter 24, YHWH is bound to be Israel's patron and ruler (as stated in the offer in 19:5–6), and Israel has bound itself to submit to YHWH's rule and depend upon his saving deeds (cp. Exod 24:10–11). This state of affairs originates in the ceremony. The will of YHWH has been articulated as law (or commandment), and Israel specifically accepts this law as binding upon itself (Exod 24:3, 7; cp. v. 8).

We need to nuance this characterization of Israel's obligation to the law. The laws actually govern the acts of individuals (and families, villages, and the like) within Israel, and the penalties enunciated in the law fall upon violators. Thus, when Israel accepts the divine law, it is binding its members to the stipulations and itself, as a collective entity, to their enforcement. Israel may be subject to the judgment of God for failure to perform its assignment

---

replaced the first. There may be, on the other hand, some utopian rulings.

effectively and justly, but in the Book of the Covenant this is at most implied. Perhaps only the officials acting on behalf of the community were explicitly accountable.

The covenant together with its law concerns Israel alone. Other nations are not bound to its provisions. To be sure, the subjects covered in the legal corpora of the Pentateuch are about the same as those covered in ancient Near Eastern codes; indeed, they are common to most legal traditions. In the Pentateuch, these legal subjects and teachings that all human societies share are included in the covenant with Noah (Genesis 8; 9:1–10). Only the killing of humans and animals is explicitly covered in Gen 9:4–6, but we can see from the narratives of the ancestors that theft was treated as a crime, marriage was honored, and contracts and promises were binding and enforceable. The law of the Israelite covenant covers the same subjects, but explicitly articulates them as duties owed YHWH, and provides a theological rationale for their application and performance. That is to say, in the commandments YHWH engages the community, and each member, in a personal relationship of obligation and accountability; in the judgments and institutional rules, the community's application and accountability is paramount.

## What Is Revealed

The Ten Commandments condenses biblical legal teaching to an epitome. The first table (Exod 20:3–11) enunciates the unique theological regimen of biblical religion, while the second (20:12–17) embraces common human social norms. Together the major breaches of Israelite community are placed under divine proscription.

The initial statement, "I am the Lord your God, who brought you out of the land of Egypt, out of the house of bondage," is not a commandment. The question is, what is it? Scholars have variously titled it a "historical prolog" and "self-introduction." "Historical prolog" does fit the description well enough: it recalls the beneficence of the speaker toward the addressee, enhancing the speaker's worthiness and the addressee's gratitude. The title "self-introduction" also fits because the asseveration has the force of identifying the speaker both by name and by this demonstration of power and goodness; this will become the paradigm for the Lord's activity in Israel's life. Finally, it effectively draws both speaker and addressee into the scope of the discourse.

The commandment against recognizing any deity but YHWH stands at the head of the Ten Commandments (Exod 20:23; Deut 5:7) and reappears in practically all pentateuchal corpora (Exod 20:23; 22:20; 23:13; 34:14; Deut 13; 17:2–3; cp. Lev 19:4, 26:1; Deut 27:15). This is the heart of the law revealed by YHWH. No other religious tradition has this provision, and all monotheistic religions derive from it.[7]

It should be noted that the first commandment is not an assertion of fact or even statement of faith to the effect that there exists one and only one God. Rather, it is a prohibition against recognizing any deity but YHWH, the God of Israel. The audience envisaged is prone to honoring other gods, and the prohibition means to shut the door on such practices. Recognizing YHWH is not an opinion or conviction, not a surmise from evidence and logic, nor a response to experience or emotions or tradition: it is a duty—a covenant obligation owed by this people, singly and collectively.

Closely related to the first commandment is the prohibition of making and worshipping images (Exod 20:4; 34:7; Deut 5:8; also Exod 20:23; Lev 19:4; 26:1; Deut 27:15); they are so close that many church traditions subsume the prohibition of images under the prohibition against worshipping other gods. Probably the ancient Israelites themselves could not imagine the worship of another god without an image; practically all ancient Near Eastern gods had images or totems. Yahwism was considered suspect of atheism for not having images of the deity.[8] Nor did the Israelites take to imageless worship naturally. The religious authorities had to suppress the urge to make images of YHWH (cp., e.g., Judg 8:24–28; 17:3–5; 18:30–31). The infamous "golden calves" erected by Jeroboam in his state sanctuaries were either images of YHWH or pedestals for him (1 Kgs 12:25–30). The ark, though not a pictorial image, had the qualities of an idol (see 1 Samuel 4–6). Postexilic Judaism tended toward an inanimate iconography, but it did not follow the prescription to the tee (i.e., no likeness of anything above, on, or under the earth).

As time went on, there was a tendency for idol polemic to identify the gods of the nations with their images, and to ridicule the image as a dead god. Such satire probably functioned to reinforce the proscription of the worship of other gods by Jews.[9]

---

7. A few Greek philosophers, but they do not represent full-scale religions.

8. This occurred later, when the Jews encountered the Greeks and Romans; what ancient Near Eastern peoples thought is not documented.

9. This idol polemic is the ancestor of Feuerbach's argument (in *The Essence of Christianity*) that religion is the "projection" of human qualities and needs. There were Greek philosophers who argued in the same vein.

The Book of the Covenant lays down the foundations of the judicial and moral law of the Bible. Its proximity to the Ten Commandments gives it the opportunity to apply the vision of the epitome of the law. Its image of Israelite society is simple. There is no king; a "leader" (*nagid*) is mentioned once (22:28). Priests are not mentioned but there are numerous sanctuaries in the countryside, consisting only of primitive altars. No judicial system "above" the town court is envisaged. YHWH exercises authority through the law and the lay judges/elders of each local community. The patriarchs of each family take responsibility for ensuring that their families comply with the law as well.

The code begins with a collection of laws that govern the construction of altars (20:24–26). The collection is prefaced by a prohibition of "gods of silver" or "gods of gold" at the altar (20:23); this probably covers the worship of other gods and the worship of YHWH. Later in the code, sacrificing to any god but YHWH is placed under the *ḥerem*, or lethal ban (22:20). There is an exhortation in 23:13 not to invoke the names of other gods in any capacity.

The collection governing the altar commands that Israelites build an altar wherever YHWH reveals himself; this will stake claims on the land for YHWH and his people. The altar itself is supposed to be very simple. The code also ends with collections of laws concerned with the practice of religion. Sacred times are marked off for the whole community and rudimentary regulations for practice are set down. The Covenant Code is distinctly and thoroughly religious.

Within the code we find other provisions that have a theological rationale. Witchcraft and bestiality are made capital crimes (22:18–19). Witchcraft is an effort to manipulate the supernatural, and bestiality violates the image of God. Not eating animals that have died in the field (22:31) is also religiously motivated, as is the requirement to offer firstborn males (22:29–30).

The impact of the first commandment reaches even deeper. Moshe Greenberg discerns a theological rationale in the arrangement and rulings of the portion of the code called "judgments" (Exod 21:1—22:17 [18-20]). This body of "casuistic law" resembles the ancient Near Eastern codes in subject matter and content.[10] However, there are subtle differences that set biblical law apart. In particular, crimes against persons are subsumed under a different category, with different principles operative, than crimes against property. Harm to persons calls for a retaliatory punishment whereas crimes against property require composition with compensation.[11] Persons are created in the image of

---

10. Alt, "The Origins of Israelite Law," 88–103.

11. Greenberg, "Some Postulates of Biblical Criminal Law," 5–28; followed up by Paul,

God, and hence are accorded infinite value (Gen 9: 4–7). This is an important example of how divine law calls for a theological interpretation of its content.

The Book of the Covenant has only one case of marriage law (Exod 22:16–17), too marginal to develop a conceptual scheme on. However, Deut 22:13–29 clearly makes adultery a violation not only of a man's exclusive rights to his wife's sexuality, but of a bond sanctified by God. Adultery cannot be legally forgiven by the husband of an adulterous woman, as it can be in almost all ancient Near Eastern codes, because YHWH's law and oath have been violated, placing the community in jeopardy of divine punishment.

The law of contract is not a regular subject of biblical legislation. The prohibition against taking YHWH's name in vain covers it, for a broken oath would be such a false use of the divine name. In the book of the Covenant, we have a series of paradigms for resolving trials in which the accused denies guilt and no evidence is decisive (22:7–13). In the middle of the series, a general rule is enunciated: "In any case of disputed ownership involving ox, donkey, sheep, clothing, or any other loss, of which one party says, 'This is mine,' the case of both parties shall come before God; the one whom God condemns shall pay double to the other" (22:9). This practice is meant to prod the conscience of the guilty: he either refuses to take the self-cursing oath, or the curses overtake him (or her). Note, no ordeal is specified; how YHWH would render a decision is not described. This is general in Israelite law, for it would confuse judgment and punishment.[12] Israelite law is not unique in its use of oaths, but its weighting of oaths and elimination of ordeals is distinctive.

The corpus includes a healthy complement of injunctions and exhortations to protect the poor and marginalized (Exod 22:21–27; 23:4–5, 9). The precedent in the Decalogue is the expansion of the Sabbath law to ensure that children, slaves, and work animals are allowed a rest (Exod 20:10—11). The addressee is warned not to oppress the resident alien, widow, and orphan (22:21–24). If the addressee lends to the poor, he is not to exact interest or do anything to shame the borrower (22:25–27). The addressee also owes duties to assist in cases of stray animals or work animals down under a load (23:4–5). We even find the provisions of the Sabbath year and Sabbath day portrayed as welfare measures (23:11, 12)

---

*Studies in the Book of the Covenant*; and Finkelstein, *The Ox That Gored*.

12. There is the case of a man who accuses his wife of adultery, discussed in Num 5:11–31; the ritual may be an "ordeal," but it in fact does not really put the body of the accused in danger.

*Redeeming Judgment*

It is common for societies to encourage the well-to-do to help the poor and marginal, but not in legal codes. This is a feature of Israelite codes that is unique. The motive for protecting the sojourner is classic: "You shall not oppress the resident alien; you know the heart of an alien, for you were aliens in the land of Egypt" (23:9). This is an argument from Israel's experience, which resonates with YHWH's gracious action for Israel. Israelite law and exhortation is rooted in their identity and the revelation of God in that history.

Finally, it should be noted briefly that there are injunctions and paranaesis (ethical exhortation) concerning the trial procedure (23:1–3, 6–8). This has a precedent in the ninth commandment (Exod 20:16). If the judges are agents of the divine lawgiver, imposing divine judgment on those who violate the law, and resolving disputes within the community, it is important that they and the witnesses and the defendant all bear responsibility. The judges and witnesses are themselves liable for any injustice that is done in the name of YHWH.

To sum up, the content as well as the form of Israelite law is unique, befitting the people who have been set apart from all other nations to be God's special possession. Whatever is unique in Israelite law, moreover, can be derived from the commandment not to recognize any god but YHWH.

## The Golden Calf

When Moses remains on the mountain to receive the law from God, the people decide that he must be dead, or lost, and to replace him they have Aaron make a "golden calf" from their jewelry (Exod 32:1–4). The calf is said to be the "gods who brought [Israel] up out of the land of Egypt" (v. 4). We are told that this is what the people said, though an individual might be speaking for them. The statement is a strange parody of Yahwism. Why is the reference plural, when there is only one statue? Perhaps this is a polemical wording by the author to indicate that the image belongs to polytheism, though the people may think that it is Israel's one and only God who is being spoken of. To confuse matters further, Aaron tries to worship the idol in "a festival to the LORD" (v. 5). He is evidently endeavoring to absorb "folk religion" into Yahwism.

What offense has been committed? The people have, according to what they say both turned to other gods and made an idol to worship. Aaron, of the other hand, has officially violated only the prohibition of images. Both are capital offenses, and everyone in the camp seems implicated. The Covenant Code really did not make provision for collective judgment, but here we have the mass of people acting as one.

This is the first time Israel has violated this commandment, at least according to the pentateuchal narrative.[13] The commandments had just been promulgated and accepted, and no sooner have they been than we witness a massive violation. Where there is law, there is transgression. The covenant and law have obligated the people to norms that it had not known before.[14] Only now do they realize what they have gotten themselves into by entering the covenant.

The scene changes to the mountain, where Moses is receiving the law from YHWH. Suddenly YHWH warns Moses that his (Moses's) people have violated the commandments he had given them (32:7–8). This is the indictment; it is followed by a prospective sentence: "now let me alone, so that my wrath may burn hot against them and I may consume them; but of you I will make a great nation" (32:9–10). Though this has the place of a sentence, it is a request to Moses to allow him to annihilate the people, and to make Moses a patriarch of a new people. Why does God need permission? It sounds as though he is inviting Moses to intervene. Moses, like Abraham had been, is a "friend of the court." He has the task of pleading the people's case, and that is precisely what he does in response. First, Moses insists that the people are *God's* people, beneficiaries of his grace (32:11). Why would God, after doing these people such good, now turn on them? It will give him a bad image among the nations—it will seem as though the Lord had malicious intent all along. God should remember the people's ancestors, whom he had great affection for, and fulfill the promise he made to them. Moses's intercession is successful, and annihilation is taken off the table.

When Moses sees for himself what the people are doing, he explodes. First, he breaks the tablets of the law, signifying the dissolution of the covenant.[15] The tablets are ground up and mixed into water, which all the people are forced to drink (32:20). This is a symbolic ordeal;[16] those who are guilty will suffer (see 32:33–35). Subjecting the people to an ordeal seems odd because there has been no indication up till now that there were any who abstained

---

13. In tradition, this was Israel's fall, duplicating the fall of Adam; see Anderson, *The Genesis of Perfection*, 205–7.

14. Up until Exodus 20, apostasy and idolatry are hardly mentioned in Genesis or Exodus. No other gods are named or distinguished from Israel's God, and only here and there are images mentioned.

15. Coats, *Rebellion in the Wilderness*, 184–91.

16. See Num 5:1–31 for the use of water mixed with something, symbolizing the offense as an ordeal.

from this idolatry. Now it sounds like some are guilty, but that others are not, so punishment must be distributed appropriately.

Another punishment is administered to the people. Once Moses hears Aaron's dissembling version of the story (32:21–24), he recruits sword-bearing enforcers to kill randomly (32:26–28). The Levites volunteer and earn themselves the priesthood (32:28–29). Although Moses makes the decision for the purge of the people, he announces it with YHWH's authority (v. 27) and designates the Levites ordained as a result (v. 29). The prophet acts and speaks with divine authority.

This is not the end of the story. After this incident, it is by no means certain that the covenant is still in place. The broken tablets suggest that it isn't, though Moses is told to proceed with the conquest (32:30–34). Moses is not satisfied with the promise of only an angel's presence; he insists that YHWH accompany them in person (33:1–6, 12–16). In response, YHWH proposes to show himself visually to Moses (33:17–28). This theophany becomes the setting for an explicit reinstatement of the covenant, accompanied by divine commandments that Moses writes on tablets (34:1–28). The Lord promises to "perform marvels, such as have not been performed in all the earth or in any nation" (34:10). Moses has not only saved the Lord's favor for this wayward people, but the covenant now has forgiveness built into its very foundation (34:6–9).[17]

Forgiveness will first of all be offered individuals when their violations are not so severe that they cannot be atoned for or overlooked. No specifics on forgiveness are set down, but we can observe it operating now and then in narratives (e.g., 2 Samuel 12). We shall discover that forgiveness does not stop the consequences of the action returning to harm the actor; this we observe in the case of David.

How about forgiveness of the people? Well, the restoration of the covenant in Exodus 34 is the first instance. Moreover, the construction of the tabernacle for YHWH to dwell in is also a gracious act of forbearance. The ritual performed in the tabernacle will continually cleanse the community of the buildup of guilt. Now let's explore the tabernacle in greater detail.

## The Tabernacle and the Law

Following the ratification of the covenant (Exod 24:3–8, 9–11), Moses is called to the top of the mountain to receive a written version of the Ten

---

17. I learned this from Rendtorff, *Canon and Theology*, 130–32.

Commandments (24:12–14). He receives the tablets at the end of his long stay on the mountain (31:18). While Moses is on the mountain awaiting the tablets, the Lord reveals a plan for a tabernacle or tent of meeting, and a design for its furniture (Exodus 25–31). This tabernacle will be the earthly dwelling place of the Lord God.

The people become convinced that Moses has met a foul end, and propose to construct a "golden calf" to be their god who will lead them on their way. This plan is broken up by the Lord's judgment through Moses. Now the question is, will the building of the tabernacle go forward, and will the Lord dwell in the holy of holies when it is finished?

At first, the Lord says that he will send an angel along with the Israelites as a substitute, perhaps with the understanding that the angel will be less demanding (see 33:1–6). Moses persuades him to reverse this decision, insisting that he (Moses) will not break camp unless the Lord accompanies them (33:12–16). The Lord relents and even grants Moses a confirmation of his presence (33:17–23). When YHWH allows Moses to see him, he makes a proclamation that he is gracious and merciful, though an enforcer of his law (34:6–7). Moses then pleads with him to "go in the midst of us, although it is a stiff-necked people; and pardon our iniquity and our sin, and take us for your inheritance" (34:9, RSV). YHWH grants Moses's request: "I hereby make a covenant. Before all your people I will perform marvels, such as have not been performed in all the earth or in any nation; and all the people among whom you live shall see the work of the Lord" (34:10). Subsequently the construction and consecration of the tabernacle confirms and implements the new order (Exodus 35–40).

The construction of the tabernacle, thus, is a significant element in the restoration of the covenant. The people can build the tabernacle to restore their relationship, rather like penance. When the tabernacle is complete, the Lord descends into the tent (40:34).

The book of Leviticus begins with a code of sacrificial law (chapters 1–7) to be performed in the tabernacle. First to be covered is the burnt offering or holocaust, in which the whole animal is consumed by fire; cereal offerings accompany the burnt offering. The "peace" or "welfare" offering provides a meal for the offerer. The sin and guilt offerings are focused on cleansing the penitent offender, the people, and sanctuary of the stain left by sin.

Leviticus 8–9 narrate the consecration of the high priest of the tabernacle, and his sons. This is the only formal ordination to an office we have in the Pentateuch (until Joshua replaces Moses at the end of Deuteronomy). The high priest is the most powerful figure in the tabernacle-centered society, except for Moses. In Num 16:1–40, there are accounts of a civil rebellion against Moses (by Dathan and Abiram) and of a challenge to the sacerdotal privileges of the house of Aaron (by Korah). Both rebellions are in the name of democracy, and the Lord sides unequivocally with divinely appointed officials.

Leviticus 11–15 is a code on cultic cleanness and purity. Certain foods and bodily discharges render a person unclean; uncleanness can be remedied by ritual. Leviticus 16 sets out the ritual for the Day of Atonement. Atonement rituals are performed by the priests, for themselves and the people. Sanctuary and altar are cleansed by blood from sacrifices. The people send a goat—the "scapegoat"—into the wilderness, burdened with their sins.

Leviticus 17–26 is frequently identified as an independent legal code. There is no title or commission at the beginning of the code, but there is at the very end: "These are the statutes and ordinances and laws which the Lord established between himself and the people of Israel on Mount Sinai through Moses" (Lev 26:46). The laws cover civil society, the moral life, and religious beliefs and practices. Scholars have named this code the Holiness Code after the motive clause: "You shall be holy, for I the Lord your God am holy" (19:2).

Each of the sections of the code is directed at one specific party—the priests or the people. Chapter 17 addresses both because it concerns the sacrifices at the altar—offered by the laity, slaughtered by the priests. Chapters 18–20 are addressed to the laity, 21–22 to the priests, and 23–25 to the laity.

While in the Holiness Code we would expect the first and second commandments to be highlighted, they are not. Leviticus 19:4 and 26:1 prohibit idolatry, and Lev 17:7 explains that an offerer must bring an animal to the tabernacle to avoid honoring demons. We might note the seriousness with which the code takes profanity (24:10–16), an aspect of the third commandment. This paucity of laws on theological subjects seems to be based on the assumption that a faithful priesthood and a compliant lay community will preserve a pure cultic community.

The commandments of the Decalogue that cover relations between Israelites are made the subject of expanded moral exhortation, e.g., "You shall not steal; you shall not deal falsely; and you shall not lie to one another" (19:11). The series of exhortations continues through vv. 12–16 and reaches a climax in vv. 17–18: "You shall not hate in your heart anyone of your kin; you shall reprove your neighbor, or you will incur guilt yourself. You shall not take vengeance or bear a grudge against any of your people, but you shall love your neighbor as yourself: I am the LORD." Later the duty to love expands to the alien (19:34); it is supported by a recollection of Israel's alien status in Egypt.

Leviticus 25 stands out for its effort to return land once allocated to all members of the people to the original families. This law devises not only a scheme for returning land to the families to whom it was originally allocated, but a scheme for preserving Israelites in freedom, even when they have failed economically. If they have become indentured servants, they are to be redeemed in one way or another.

The Holiness Code is "amended" in Leviticus 27 and at several places in Numbers (e.g., 5:1-4, 5-10, 11-31, 61-21). Later, in Num 27:1-11, we find a ruling answering the complaint of the daughters of Zelophehad; they asked for the inheritance when a man has no sons. Numbers 35 institutionalizes the law dealing with homicide, providing for cities of refuge in the promised land. The law is located at the end of Numbers because the people are about to cross the Jordan and conquer the land of Canaan; this is when the cities of refuge should be established.

## Divine Judgment in the Law

Law not only sets down norms, but it prescribes sanctions for violators. Legal sanctions, imposed by a human court, are the subject of remedial law. The court itself acts on behalf of the divine sovereign, but the procedure would not involve any extraordinary act of God. Divine interventions to punish violators and to liberate the afflicted supplement legal sanctions. Legal sanctions are imposed on individuals or groups within the legal community; divine sanctions are also directed against individuals—oppressors of the widows, orphans, and the poor, and sojourners—who for one reason or another escape legal prosecution (see Exod 22:21-27). Authorities and participants in the judicial process are also subject to divine sanctions (Exod 23:7).

What about events like making and worshipping the golden calf? Nothing in the Holiness Code could defuse a crisis of such proportions, but there is an annual event to keep the people free from the guilt that would end in judgment. The Day of Atonement is added to the calendar in Lev 23:26-32, and Leviticus 16 sets forth the procedures. On this day the high priest, properly washed and attired, slaughters a bull and takes its blood into the holy of holies, where the blood is sprinkled on the "mercy seat" (the covering of the ark of the covenant) to cleanse it of pollution caused by priestly uncleanness and sin (16:14). Blood is also rubbed on the horns of the altar and sprinkled about it,

67

## Redeeming Judgment

again cleansing it of contamination by priests (16:18–19). For the people, two male goats are brought to the entrance of the sanctuary, where one is chosen by lot as a sacrifice, and the other is assigned to "Azazel" (a demon haunting the wild). The sacrificial goat is slaughtered and its blood sprinkled like that of the bull (16:16–19); its blood cleanses the sanctuary and altar of pollution from all forms of the people's sin and impurity.

After the purgation of the sanctuary and altar, the high priest lays his hands upon the live goat and transfers to it the guilt and impurity of the community; the goat is then led into the wilderness and released (16:20–22). The goat evidently bears away the guilt of the community so that the community avoids God's wrath. Individual sinners are not forgiven, rather the community that has contracted guilt by association with the sinners is forgiven.

Even with the focus on sin and absolution in the material about the Day of Atonement the Holiness Code concludes with a table of blessings and curses in Leviticus 26. This table fits the pattern of ancient Near Eastern treaties and some other legal documents. Leviticus 26:3–13 offers blessings and good fortune to the people of Israel if they obey the laws in the Holiness Code, but vv. 14–46 tell a story of mounting judgment if they disobey. Leviticus 26:27–32 forecast devastating defeat, and vv. 33–39 describe the conditions of exile. Leviticus 26:40–45 offer the addressees the chance to repent and be restored. These verses end as follows: "I will remember in their favor the covenant with their ancestors whom I brought out of the land of Egypt in the sight of the nations, to be their God: I am the Lord." Here we have a history of life within the covenant from Sinai to the exile.

We also find collective address in the paraenetic (exhortative) sections of the Holiness Code, viz., Lev 18:1–5, 24–28; 20:22–26. There are warnings of national judgment, e.g.: "Do not defile yourselves in any of these ways, for by all these practices the nations I am casting out before you have defiled themselves; ... But you shall keep my statutes and my ordinances and commit none of these abominations ... otherwise the land will vomit you out for defiling it, as it vomited out the nation that was before you" (Lev 18:24–28). However, the very next sentence gravitates to a distributive formulation: "For whoever commits any of these abominations shall be cut off from their people" (v. 29). Taken literally, this threat assumes that the people of God remain obedient and holy, and deviants simply fall outside the holy people.

These curses and warnings in the Holiness Code read rather like future history. In other words, they are more than warning; the addressees of the extant code knew that they would take place. The Holiness Code and Priestly law of Leviticus can be associated with the book of the law of the God of heaven, brought back from exile by Ezra (Ezra 7:6-7).[18] The incorporation of that Mosaic law into the Sinaitic account elevates it to the timelessness or eternity of the revelation at Sinai.

In this legal material, the people are represented as a religious community that shares a calling, a law, and a tent sanctuary; the priesthood is chosen by the YHWH. He is present among his people in the tabernacle. He agrees to dwell among this people despite their stiff-necked character. He forgives them their rebellion and sets up a sacrificial system that not only provides access but atones for sin and maintains the tabernacle in an uncontaminated state. The priests are the primary officials in the community and are set apart as doubly holy. The Levites are not required to maintain the same level of sanctity and are relegated to service roles in the sanctuary.

Corresponding to the focus on tabernacle, priests, and Levites is the identification of God's attribute of holiness as the primary norm for measuring moral, legal, and religious actions. The code sets a very high moral standard and holds the nation as a whole accountable for compliance.

## Law and Judgment

The terms heading this section are necessary complements. One cannot have judgment without norms for which the actor is responsible. The norms, for their part, must be enforced by sanctions in order to be serious, to be ontologically grounded. This chapter shines its light on those norms that are an explicit part the covenant between YHWH and Israel. The norms make up a network of concepts and principles articulated as paradigmatic rulings, and also as commandments and paraenesis (ethical exhortation).

The covenant is the framework for the entire body of legal teaching. It sets up a relationship between the divine sovereign and the people as his subjects. The covenant sets Israel apart from other nations or peoples as YHWH's special possession and sphere of sovereignty. The law must embody and protect Israel's exclusive relationship to YHWH. The law prohibits the recognition of any deity but YHWH among Israelites, and the use of images to worship him (or any other deity). These two commandments expand to include the misuse of the divine name in divination and witchcraft, and rituals that involve human sacrifice. The law also entails duties to sanctify specific days and weeks,

---

18. The practices described for the celebration of Succoth in Ezra 7 match those commanded in Lev 23:39-43.

and designated places for sacrifice, along with rules for worshipping at such times and places.

Covenant law is not restricted to laws that concern the Lord and his worship, but includes the crimes of homicide and assault, stealing and damaging property, marriage violation, and the duties of oath and contract, and social welfare. Theses are legal subjects common to all humans and are the subject of ancient Near Eastern legal codes. Nevertheless, these laws are transformed by being made the subject of divine commandment and by being a part of the system of laws conditioned by the first commandment. The principle of life for life sets the biblical laws on homicide apart from the ancient Near Eastern environment. Property and theft are governed by quite different principles. Marriage is made an unconditional commitment between two persons of infinite worth. The community, finally, has an obligation to marginal members and outsiders to provide them with the means of life and liberty. The entire network of legal sentences is supplemented by motive clauses and moral exhortation. God's requirements reach beyond those that can be enforced by the judiciary.

Judgment is the process of imposing the proper consequences on violators of law, and negotiating between the aggrieved and those who have caused the grief. The legal codes are concerned with the acts of individuals and groups within the community governed by YHWH. The collective is represented by judges in the place of residence, or perhaps by some appellate jurisdiction. If this procedure is operating justly and responsibly, the peace, order, and justice of the body politic is preserved.

Collective judgment is called for when a collective offense is perpetrated. This occurs on Mount Sinai just a few days after the people have entered into the covenant. The event is the making of the golden calf accompanied by a raucous celebration. This collective breakdown of compliance with the first and second commandments arouses YHWH to propose the annihilation of the people. Moses intercedes, but when he confronts the scene, he subjects the people to an ordeal designed to administer punishment distributively, and also recruits the Levites to slaughter the people at random. We have, thus, both distributive and collective judgment of this act of apostasy and idolatry.

The violent resolution to this collective sin prompts the amendment of the covenant to include forgiveness. The amendment is negotiated between Moses and YHWH. YHWH proposes not to accompany Israel into the land, to avoid a repetition of this explosion; an angel will represent him. Moses will have none of that, so he persuades YHWH to accompany Israel and to forgive its sin.

The tabernacle, which had been revealed to Moses, can now be constructed, and when it is, YHWH will settle in the holy of holies. With the tabernacle, the people can perform the sacrifices required of them. To officiate at the altar, Aaron and his sons are appointed priests, and the Levites are commissioned to perform subsidiary functions around the sanctuary. Laypeople are restricted entrance to the sacred area except at times when a person is ritually clean. When persons become unclean, they must perform rituals for restoration to cleanliness. The community is cleansed annually at the ritual of the Day of Atonement.

The book of Leviticus ends with a body of law known by scholars as the Holiness Code. Many of its chapters deal with civil actions. Chapters 18 and 20 cover proper and improper sexual partners. Chapter 19 expands the commandments to cover moral obligations owed by Israelites to each other and to the outsiders living in their midst. The code ends with a new sacred occasion known as the Year of Jubilee, designed to restore freedom and family estates to Israelites.

In case the Israelites fail to fulfill the law collectively, a series of curses will be imposed on them. Leviticus 26 sets these out as a history, one warning after another, until there is the destruction of the nation and exile of its inhabitants. The text actually ends with words of encouragement to the people who are in exile; if they will repent, God will restore them to their land and national life. This is an event far in the future of those who receive the law from Moses.

Readers should mark the structure that has emerged in these covenant texts. We can term this pattern of covenant law enforcement or collective judgment *the* covenant schema, though the full schema will not appear very frequently.

# 5

## Individuals within the Covenant
(Proverbs, Psalms)

THE NARRATIVE THAT RUNS through Exodus, Leviticus, Numbers, and Deuteronomy focuses on the nation's history. When judgments take place, they are collective or at least general. When the people, for example, make the golden calf, with Aaron playing an instrumental role, Moses calls down two types of divine judgment: one collective and one distributive. The fate of individuals in this event is absorbed, so to speak, into the collective fate.

There are occasional glimpses of the judgment of individuals apart from the nation in the historical narrative. When the daughters of Zelophehad approach Moses to request their father's inheritance, they clear his name of any collective judgment which might disqualify his right to a share in the promised land: "Our father died in the wilderness; he was not among the company of those who gathered themselves together against the Lord in the company of Korah, but died for his own sin" (Num 27:3). This is formulated in such a way that we could call it a divine judgment of a private individual, though it is not certain that we should take "he died for his own sin" literally.[1]

The book of Ruth tells a private story of God's grace; the story of Hannah in 1 Samuel 1–2 also tells a private story. In both cases, their children or great great grandchildren become prominent public figures. Their fates are not punishments, but divine favor. The tragedies in David's household (told in 2

---

1. He was not executed and probably died what we would call a natural death. Perhaps the idea was in circulation that everyone dies for some sin or another, though I don't know of any other instance of it.

Samuel 12–20) would fit the definition of judgment, but they are told because the outcome is an important public event, viz., the succession of Solomon.

If we want to come to an understanding of the judgment of private individuals, we must search elsewhere. The book of Proverbs offers teaching about how to live one's life; its horizon is the private life of the men of the city or village. We will discover that divine judgment is very much within the horizon of daily life as depicted in Proverbs. The second half of the chapter considers times of crisis in the lives of individuals. The individual laments of the Psalter are designed for such crisis moments.

## Proverbs: Instruction in the Moral Life

The book of Proverbs is ascribed to wise men and women, from kings and royal counselors to schoolteachers and mothers. The bulk of this instruction is for living one's life in whatever circumstances one finds oneself in. The persons addressed are young men, probably at an age when he is not yet engaged in making a living with and supporting a wife and children. The instruction focuses on what will lead to success and satisfaction. The subjects are practical and moral—primarily virtues and vices of individuals. Teachers seek to form the character and habits of their students.

Though the instruction concerns the aspirations and conscience of the individual, the content is not individualistic. Humans are social animals, and a satisfying life will be one in which one gets along with one's family and neighbors and contributes to the common good.

The sayings typically describe an outcome for a type of action or character trait. The consequences of unethical or unwise actions fit the description of punishment. Proverbs affirm this punishment to be divine. It is limited to this life; Proverbs has nothing on rewards and punishments after death.

There has been an inclination among biblical scholars to distinguish, occasionally even to oppose, "international wisdom" from/to the particularistic theological tradition centered on sacred history, covenant, and cult. It is true that one can find many parallels between the Proverbs and Egyptian wisdom. Nevertheless, the teaching of youth to live in conformity with communal norms and values locates the teaching within the life of the chosen people—who are called to be a peculiar people. The theological proverbs that we will take up first link the Wisdom tradition and the covenant.

*Redeeming Judgment*

## *Theological Proverbs*

The authors or teachers of Proverbs were conscious of their duty to the Lord. Their thinking is undertaken under the rubric, "the fear of the Lord is the beginning of wisdom" (Prov 1:7; 9:10; 15:33 [RSV], with variations found scattered elsewhere). Fear is best taken to mean respect, reverence; it would include faith. All such thinking should be "obedient reason."[2] Obedient reason takes what is known of God by experience, tradition, and revelation and brings all thought into conformity with it. It is understanding that we gain by thinking through what revelation means for all human knowledge.

Let's now look at some proverbs on the subject of divine judgment: "The good obtain favor from the Lord, but those who devise evil he condemns" (12:2; cp. 11:20). God is the measure of good and evil; what God approves is good, and what God condemns is evil. Every action has a motive, which is hidden from others, and sometimes from the actor. The Lord, however, can observe the depths of the self as well as the underworld. Thus, God may know our motives better than we do:

> All one's ways may be pure in one's own eyes,
>> but the Lord weighs the spirit (16:2; cp. 21:2).

In sum, God has the knowledge of the law and of the human heart sufficient to be a true Judge.

If a person is uncertain about what God wills, he or she can consult the divine law. "Those who keep the law are wise children" (28:7). Even if God's prophetic word, communicating God's living will, is silent, the law remains:

> Where there is no prophecy, the people cast off restraint,
>> but happy are those who keep the law. (29:18)

Proverbs has a great deal to say about God's control of the course of human events. We can only sample a few. There are numerous affirmations that God determines the outcome of human action:

> The plans of the mind belong to mortals,
>> but the answer of the tongue is from the Lord. (16:1)

Here is a similar one: "The human mind plans the way, but the Lord directs the steps" (16:9). Another in the same vein reads as follows: "The human mind may devise many plans, but it is the purpose of the Lord that will be estab-

---

2. See Patrick, *The Rhetoric of Revelation*, 84–87.

lished" (19:21). Here is one that teaches us to be reserved about what we can know of our own behavior:

> All our steps are ordered by the LORD;
> how then can we understand our own ways? (20:24)

Human power is no match for God's purposes:

> The horse is made ready for the day of battle,
> but the victory belongs to the LORD. (21:31)

A number of sayings affirm that the righteous and wise are right to depend upon God:

> The LORD does not let the righteous go hungry,
> but he thwarts the craving of the wicked. (10:3)

This happens at the religious level too:

> The LORD is far from the wicked,
> but he hears the prayer of the righteous. (15:29)

What is missing in the theological proverbs is teaching on the first and second commandments. There is a saying warning against misrepresenting what God has said: "Do not add to (God's) words, or else he will rebuke you, and you will be found a liar" (30:6). But there is nothing on recognizing YHWH alone or not making any images of YHWH.

Though one might doubt that it is the business of the wise to propagate distinctive Yahwistic doctrine and duty, we do have wisdom passages that do. One of the prime examples is the poem in Jer 10:2–10. It satirizes the making and worshipping of idols (vv. 2–5, 8–9). That YHWH is the true God is demonstrated by the fact that he is no idol. "Among all the wise ones of the nations and in all their kingdoms there is no one like you" (Jer 10:7). The argument really does belong within the orbit of wisdom, though it most often appears in prophetic books and Psalms.[3]

## Proverbs and Law

A proverb is not a law; it is a catchy form of instruction addressed first of all to the young. However, the teacher covers topics one also finds in the law codes.

---

3. Wisdom seeks to explain why YHWH has no images; in the law it is a matter of a divine prohibition, and prophecy usually condemns Israel for breaking faith with her Lord.

There is very little said about crimes; the law with which the teaching overlaps is concerned with subjects that depend on persuasion: the protecting the poor, maintaining justice in the judicial system and marketplace.

Let's begin with proverbs urging proper behavior in the judicial process. Proverbs 14:5 describes witnessing:

> A faithful witness does not lie,
> > but a false witness breathes out lies.

Another underlines the seriousness of false witness:

> Like a war club, or a sword, or a sharp arrow
> > is one who bears false witness against a neighbor. (25:18)

Proverbs 24:23–26 encourages honest judging:

> Partiality in judging is not good.
> Whoever says to the wicked, "You are innocent,"
> > will be cursed by peoples, abhorred by nations;
> but those who rebuke the wicked will have delight . . . (24:23b–25a)

Finally, Prov 22:22–23 seeks to protect the poor and vulnerable from exploitation by judicial means:

> Do not rob from the poor because they are poor,
> > or crush the afflicted at the gate;
> for the Lord pleads their cause
> > and despoils of life those who despoil them.

The proverbs on maintaining just weights and measures parallels the instructions just cited for the court. In the ancient world, unscrupulous businessmen would have two different sets of weights and two different sets of containers, and use the large or the small to suit their advantage. This was a serious enough form of dishonesty to elicit this proverb:

> A false balance is an abomination to the Lord,
> > but an accurate weight is his delight. (11:1; also 20:10, 21)

Another proverb affirms the righteousness of honest weights:

> Honest balances and scales are the Lord's;
> > all the weights in the bag are his work. (16:11)

Proverbs 22:28 and 23:10–11 prohibit the moving of property markers; the implication is that moving them entails property theft:

> Do not remove an ancient landmark
> > or encroach on the fields of orphans;
> for their Redeemer is strong;
> > he will plead their cause against you. (23:10–11)

The proverb just cited (viz., 23:10–11) could also be used as an example of proverbs protecting the poor and vulnerable. This is a subject covered extensively in the law codes. Proverbs 13:23 covers a case similar to 23:10–11. Proverbs 14:31 makes a strong theological point:

> Those who oppress the poor man insult their Maker,
> > but those who are kind to the needy honor him.

Job expands this idea to slaves in his oath of clearance in Job 31:13–15. Proverbs 19:17 promises a reward from God for lending to the poor:

> Whoever is kind to the poor lends to the LORD,
> > and will be repaid in full.

Proverbs 21:13 covers an analogous case: "If you close your ear to the cry of the poor you will cry out and not be heard" by God.

## Virtues and Vices

The instruction of the young may encourage generosity toward the poor, but it is bent on instilling a work ethic that will make sure they will not become impoverished. One of the vices that the teacher inveighs against is laziness: "The hand of the diligent will rule, while the lazy will be put to forced labor" (12:24). You can tell a lazy person by the condition of the path to his house:

> The way of the lazy is overgrown with thorns,
> > but the path of the upright is a level highway. (15:19)

Of course, this may only be metaphorical, but note how 24:30–34 makes a literal case parabolic:

> I passed by the field of one who was lazy,
> > by the vineyard of a stupid man;
> and see, it was all overgrown with thorns;
> > the ground was covered with nettles,
> > and its stone wall was broken down.

> Then I saw and considered it;
>> I looked and received instruction.
> A little sleep, a little slumber,
>> a little folding of the hands to rest,
> and poverty will come upon you like a robber,
>> and want, like an armed warrior.

Finally, the teacher notes that the lazy are not good employees: "Like vinegar to the teeth, and smoke to the eyes, so are the lazy to their employers" (10:26). While laziness may be the most thoroughly covered vice in these proverbs, anger and strife are roundly condemned. The general attitude is stated in Prov 15:18:

> Those who are hot-tempered stir up strife,
>> but those who are slow to anger calm contention.

Proverbs 16:32 commends one who "is slow to anger" and "whose temper is controlled." The addressee is told to avoid friendship with angry persons:

> Make no friends with those given to anger,
>> and do not associate with hotheads,
> or you may learn their ways . . . (22:24–25a)

Some people seem to stir up fights wherever they go:

> As charcoal is to hot embers and wood to fire,
>> so is a quarrelsome person for kindling strife. (26:21)

Of course, it may not be anger that is at work; Prov 10:12 speaks of hate:

> Hatred stirs up strife,
>> but love covers all offenses. (10:12)

Arrogance and pride may also offend and arouse. We have a number of proverbs condemning arrogance and commending humility: "All those who are arrogant are an abomination to the LORD" (16:5). Proverbs 16:18 has become a cliché of our culture:

> Pride goes before destruction,
>> and a haughty spirit before a fall.

The same point is made in 11:2 and 18:12. The humble person is known by his receptivity to counsel:

> By insolence the heedless make strife,
>> but wisdom is with those who take advice. (13:10)

Proverbs 15:32 says that "those who ignore instruction despise themselves, but those who heed admonition gain understanding."

As one might surmise, lying (12:22; 17:4) and bribing (17:8; 19:6) are condemned, while liberality (11:24, 25) is commended. Excessive drinking is once condemned (23:29–35), but there is no evidence that drinking alcohol is taboo. There are numerous sayings about speaking truthfully and appropriately. The general advice is to hold one's tongue:

> When words are many, transgression is not lacking,
>> but the prudent are restrained in speech. (10:19)

Proverbs 13:3 says about the same thing: "those who guards their mouths preserve their lives" while those who "open wide their lips come to ruin." When one does speak, one should consider how to speak: "A soft answer turns away wrath" while "a harsh word stirs up anger" (15:1).

### Consequences

The Proverbs constantly promise a "reward" for godly, moral and wise behavior, and "punishment" for the opposite. Proverbs 10:27–30 is striking for its repetition of this simple message:

> The fear of the LORD prolongs life,
>> but the years of the wicked will be short.
>
> The hope of the righteous ends in gladness,
>> but the expectation of the wicked comes to nothing.
>
> The way of the LORD is a stronghold for the upright,
>> but destruction for evildoers.
>
> The righteous will never be removed,
>> but the wicked will not remain in the land.

This cluster of variations on the same point must be intentional. Moreover, chapter 11 is saturated with the same assertions, and chapters 12, 13, and 14 are liberally sprinkled with them. This is a doctrine that the book of Proverbs seeks to instill and reinforce.

A study by Klaus Koch may help us understand the investment of the teachers of wisdom in this doctrine. He finds a particular conception of deed-and-consequence common to biblical and ancient Near Eastern wisdom. The idea is that a deed has built-in consequences, like taking poison and dying from it. The consequences are frequently termed the "fruit" of the deed. If one acts righteously, the consequences will be desirable; wickedness brings down evil and misfortune on the actor. This cause-and-effect system operates automatically. God does not intervene; at most he assures that the system is operating, like a mechanic servicing a machine.[4]

If we were to subscribe fully to Koch's analysis, we would have to leave Proverbs out of our study of divine judgment. That is, at least, his contention. The system purports to be automatic, so God is not exercising the power of judge in the punishment of wickedness.

Whatever the ideal system, this does not fit the book of Proverbs. There are a host of statements about the Lord's action in bringing judgment on some, salvation to others; overturning human plans and establishing his own purposes. There is no independent system in operation in Proverbs.[5] There is nothing wrong or misleading about using the word *intervention* for making actions boomerang. We could affirm that God is the subject of the action that lead situations and human interactions toward a resolution. Sometimes this leading shatters the expectations of those involved, and even of observers; occasionally these expectation-defying interactions are called miracles. However, there is no reason to restrict divine intervention to a miraculous turn of events. The book of Proverbs glories in the hidden hand of the divine sovereign.

There are several other reasons to hold on to divine intervention in the operation of consequences. The conception of "the hidden hand of the divine sovereign" is rather pervasive in the prophetic messages of judgment, both individual and collective. There is no question but that the prophet speaks with specific divine authority and announces decisions of the divine judge. Whether God's intervention to punish or prevent is hidden or spectacular, it is an intervention.

The idea of divine intervention is not subject to the critique of rewards and punishments. The book of Job in particular raises serious doubts about the believability of the proposition that virtues are rewarded and vices punished. Note this passage from Job's mouth:

---

4. Koch, "Gibt es ein Vergeltunsdogma im Alten Testament?" 65–103. [See also an abridged English version in Koch, "Is There a Doctrine of Retribution in the Old Testament?"]

5. See Miller, *Sin and Judgment in the Prophets* for an analysis of the language of judgment congruent with mine.

*Individuals within the Covenant*

> Why do the wicked live on,
> > reach old age, and grow mighty in power?
> Their children are established in their presence,
> > and their offspring before their eyes . . .
> They spend their days in prosperity,
> > and in peace they go down to Sheol.
> They say to God, "Leave us alone!
> > We do not desire to know your ways.
> What is the Almighty, that we should serve him?
> > And what profit do we get if we pray to him?"
> Is not their prosperity indeed their own achievement? (21:7–8, 13–16a)

Human experience seems to refute the idea that consequences match the character and behavior of actors. Perhaps they match sometimes, but there isn't any consistency. There seems to be no "law of consequences." But it may well be that we can discern God's intervention to punish the wicked and oppressor when he decides to do so and announces his decision by prophets.

## Laments in the Psalms: Pleading with God

The book of Psalms also provides a window on the judgment of the individual. We have more individual laments than any other genre in the book of Psalms. I propose to study a sampling of these individual laments as events of divine "trial," the verbal component of divine judgment.[6] Imagine the lament as the testimony of the accused in a trial.[7] If God is the judge, as he is referred to from time to time (e.g., Gen 18:25; Judg 11:27; Pss 9:5; 50:6; Isa 33:22), the accused has the right to defend himself and accuse others. He may appeal to God as judge against those who accuse or persecute him. He may swear an oath of innocence, calling upon God to confirm his claims. He may even accuse God for misjudging him.

---

6. Some individual laments evoke the judicial model more than others. After all, not all crises—and laments are responses to personal crises—fall neatly into adversarial exchanges. A person who has fallen seriously ill, for example, will usually not engage in blaming. Even if one also feels isolated and shunned, the friends who betrayed the speaker are not the cause of the condition, nor is their retribution a cure.

7. Brueggemann, *Theology of the Old Testament*, 374–85, treats some laments as "negative testimony." Even Brueggemann would admit, however, that a good portion of the individual laments does not even accuse God, but rather seek to recruit him for the supplicant's cause.

Laments were for the times in an individual's life when a person sought a divine intervention to save. These prayers are primarily for times of crisis. They were written for a person suffering sickness or economic, legal, or social distress, in order to gain access to the divine sovereign and judge.

The laments are quite different in kind from Proverbs. Proverbs address the common citizen, or actually the young man who are to become the substantial citizen. Laments are for citizens of all classes and conditions to say as prayers. The Psalter offers these prayers to the Israelites as acceptable, appropriate ways to approach God. Even those laments that accuse God or vituperate against fellow Israelites are authorized by their canonicity.

Some laments are formulated to evoke a trial setting, with God as judge as well as sovereign power. The supplicant evidently regards his rhetorical task to be to persuade God of his innocence and of his enemies' guilt. The psalms frequently reach a resolution in which the supplicant is convinced that God has decided in his or her favor. Thus, the lament psalm traverses the course of a trial in which the supplicant is found innocent.[8]

Modern interpreters may find the assumption that God causes a crisis to be problematic. Actually, the laments only blame the supplicant's suffering on God's action in rare instances; more often it is God's nonaction (his "permission" if you will) that is mentioned. Monotheism cannot avoid some form of divine involvement in suffering and disaster.

We should not, however, envisage God's involvement mechanically. The person in a crisis is provoked by the crisis to seek God's intervention. This might be compared to a civil suit by a person seeking a cease-and-desist order. The crisis is not necessarily God's fault. A majority of the individual laments in the Psalter seek to elicit God's intervention without ascribing the crisis to God. The origin of the crisis is left alone.

Only a few psalms describe the crisis to God's punishment. Psalm 32, which is a thanksgiving for divine forgiveness, is distinctive in this respect. The supplicant admits the he suffered until he confessed his sin; the confession has opened the way to healing and a restored relationship to God. In this case, the suffering has the force of a warning to repent, or even of a judgment for sin. This is not a general assumption, however; the supplicants of the Psalter are not given to blaming themselves for their suffering and demise.

A number of individual laments do blame God for what the supplicant is undergoing. In these cases, the supplicant does not say that God is judging the speaker for sin. God's hostile or indifferent behavior is incomprehensible and

---

8. There will of course be a "reality check" in the life of the supplicant.

sinister. Here is where modern students of the Bible are in for a shock; they will discover rather strong, violent accusations thrown into God's face in the individual laments and especially in the communal laments.

Before we proceed to the analysis of individual psalms, readers may need a short lesson in the form criticism of the laments. Two main movements occur within an individual lament: the complaint (even an accusation in some) and the request or petition. The complaint is subdivided into first, second, and third person. The first person is often a statement of how the speaker is suffering. The second challenges or accuses God for his unfriendly comportment toward the supplicant. Third-person complaints almost always concern the supplicant's "enemies." Requests roughly parallel these three subjects of complaint. In addition, the individual-lament psalm normally contains an address of God, recollections of divine favor in the past ("contrast motif"), confession of trust, protest of innocence, and promise of praise (after the prayer is answered).

## Laments Enlisting the Lord's Intervention

Many individual laments have no complaint against God. They may complain about enemies, or call attention to the speaker's own suffering. The laments without complaints against God fit the subcategory I am labeling as laments that "recruit divine intervention." Let's examine the individual laments in the Psalter that employ the language of trial, in order to distinguish between, on the one hand, psalms that recruit divine favor and, on the other hand, those that accuse the Lord. Psalms 7, 17, 26, 35, 43, 55, and 143 contain the requisite trial language.

### Psalm 7

Psalm 7 begins with a confession of trust attached to a request:

> O LORD my God, in you I take refuge;
> save me from all my pursuers, and deliver me. (7:1)

Verses 3–5 are an oath of clearance supporting the supplicant's denial of doing something wrong. Verse 6 is a request for God's intervention against enemies. Suddenly the supplicant pleads for a trial before the Lord (vv. 7–8) and expresses trust in the outcome (vv. 9–11). The unrepentant will suffer judgment from God (vv. 12–14); their own schemes will bring them down (vv. 15–16). The psalm wraps up with a promise of praise (v. 17).

## Psalm 17

Psalm 17 begins with a call to judge the supplicant's cause:

> Hear a just cause, O Lord!
>     Attend to my cry!
> . . .
> From you let my vindication come! (Ps 17:1–2)

The supplicant believes firmly in his or her righteousness. This is expressed in an assertion of innocence (vv. 3–5), followed by a request for an answer (vv. 6–9). After a description of the wicked that appear to be the enemies in this psalm, the supplicant calls for God's intervention to judge (vv. 13–14).

## Psalm 26

Psalm 26 has similar content:

> Vindicate me, O Lord,
>     for I have walked in my integrity
> . . .
> Prove me, O Lord, and try me;
>     test my heart and my mind. (26:1–2)

Most of the remainder of the prayer consists of assertions demonstrating innocence or righteousness. Again the wicked are the only enemies of the supplicant.

## Psalm 35

It begins in a similar fashion to Psalm 26, but it is much more oriented toward the supplicant's enemies: "Contend, O Lord, with those who contend with me" (v. 1). The following lines portray "contention" as military combat. The supplicant calls down an array of punishments on those threatening the supplicant's life:

> Let them be put to shame and dishonor
>     who seek after my life!
> Let their way be dark and slippery,
>     with the angel of the Lord pursuing them. (35:4, 6)

This segment of the psalm ends with an expectation of deliverance (35:9–10). The psalm starts over in v. 11 with:

> Malicious witnesses rise up:
> > they ask me about things that I do not know.

The psalmist goes on to say that these witnesses once had been on friendly terms, but now they have betrayed the speaker. This portion to the psalm comes to a vow of praise in v. 18. The lament begins again in v. 19. This third psalm is also focused on enemies who have risen against the supplicant from among his neighbors. This psalm has an accusing negative request:

> You have seen, O LORD; do not be silent!
> O Lord, do not be far from me!
> Wake up! Bestir yourself for my defense . . . (vv. 22–23a)

It is not really certain that the psalm intends to blame the supplicant's calamity on his enemies:

> Let all those who rejoice at my calamity
> > be put to shame and confusion! (v. 26a)

It may be that the calamity befalls the supplicant for some unstated reason, but the speaker believes that he or she can move God to act by recruiting God to his or her side against unfriendly neighbors. The penultimate verse actually mentions the supplicant's friends and supporters:

> Let those who desire my vindication
> > shout for joy and be glad,
> > and say evermore,
> "Great is the LORD,
> > who delights in the welfare of his servant." (v. 27)

## Psalm 31

Psalm 31 features a common motif in the individual laments: the appeal to the Lord to save the supplicant so that enemies and scoffers do not get an opportunity to gloat:

> I am the scorn of all my adversaries,
> > a [horror] to my neighbors,
> an object of dread to my acquaintances;
> > those who see me in the street flee from me.

*Redeeming Judgment*

> I have passed out of mind like one who is dead;
>> I have become like a broken vessel.
> For I hear the whispering of many, terrors all around!
>> as they scheme together against me. (vv. 11–13)

Here we have a text that might be a case study in the psychology of suffering and its accompanying isolation. What is so strange is that just a few verses later the psalm changes mood (v. 19) and ends on a note of praise.

## Psalm 55

Psalm 55 begins as a plea to God to take care of the supplicant faced with the oppression of enemies. This sparks an unusual wish to escape from civilization (vv. 6–8). Indeed, in vv. 9–11 it is the urban environment that is threatening. Suddenly the lament takes an unexpected turn: the supplicant notes betrayal by a close friend:

> It is not enemies who taunt me—
>> I could bear that;
> it is not adversaries who deal insolently with me;
>> I could hide from them.
> But it is you, my equal,
>> my companion, my familiar friend. (55:12–13)

This stanza sounds like it was introduced in a subsequent writing because the reference to enemies prior to this stanza is to a category of violent and dangerous persons; the same is true in vv. 15, 18–19, and 23. The friend who has betrayed the supplicant returns in vv. 20–21. The references to friends and kin who conspire against the supplicant make a fairly familiar trope in the individual laments.

Several other psalms mention enemies, even plead for aid against them, yet the supplicant's real concern is the Lord's saving presence. Psalm 143 begins with a request for God to hear and a plea for God not to judge the supplicant, because no human is "righteous before you."[9] We hear of the pursuit of an enemy in v. 3; a request for deliverance from enemies is made in v. 9; and a request that God destroy these enemies comes in the last verse (viz., v. 12). These enemies appear to be perfunctory. The supplicant complains of overwhelming fear and fainting (vv. 4, 7). The speaker in Psalm 143, like the

---

9. This is a sentiment that belongs to penitential piety; cp. Psalm 130. Otherwise, however, the psalm is not penitential.

supplicant in Psalm 77, confesses trust by remembering the Lord's past saving deeds. The speaker pleads for God's presence now as it was shown in the past (vv. 7–8, 9). There are several requests to be taught the right way to go (vv. 8, 10); this desire to be taught the right way to go seems to go along with God's salvation.

## Psalm 42–43

Psalm 42 and 43, an acrostic psalm, is saturated with longing for God's presence:

> As a deer longs for flowing streams,
>     so my soul longs for you, O God.
> My soul thirsts for God,
>     for the living God. (42:1–2a)

In 42:4 the supplicant recalls the joy of being part of a festival throng. Evidently this is no longer possible, and the supplicant repeats that his soul is "cast down" (vv. 5a, 5b, 11; 43:5). There is a request to "vindicate me, O God, and defend my cause against an ungodly people" (43:1); this evokes a trial scene. Despite the speaker's desire to be vindicated in the sight of "ungodly people," these people do nothing more threatening than asking the supplicant, "where is your God?" (42:3, 10). Actually, the supplicant is asking the same question (42:9; 43:2).

It is time to sum up. The individual laments we examined used trial language. Usually, this language pleads for God's intervention against the speaker's enemies, who are at fault or are falsely accusing him. The trial is to end with his acquittal and the condemnation of these enemies.

Enemies are present in most individual laments. The ancient Israelite experienced suffering as involving the community as well as himself and God. Some psalms differentiate the hostile members of the community from those who are friendly, supportive, and righteous. The enemies can be threatening to the supplicant—even the cause of the person's troubles. Alternatively, they can be mere onlookers who show contempt toward the sufferer, or satisfaction at the suffering of the supplicant. The supplicant may mention the enemies to move God to take the speaker's side. A few individual laments do not bother to mention enemies at all: the speaker's troubles arise for other reasons. Rather frequently the enemies fade into the category of the wicked. The wicked are not defined by their enmity toward the supplicant but by a kind of practical atheism (Ps 14:1: "Fools say in their hearts, 'There is no god'") and exploitative attitude toward neighbors. If the supplicant can identify enemies as wicked, then a rewards-and-punishments theologoumenon kicks in.

According to these psalms, God is outside the battle zone, so to speak. That is, the world has been created by God, but it now exercises a good deal of independence. Either humans cause evil, or evil arises without a known cause. The supplicant seeks to recruit God as an ally against the besetting enemies and troubles. If there are complaints against God in these psalms, they note abandonment or indifference.

It is quite noteworthy that the supplicants of these psalms frequently claim to be righteous, but they do not appeal to their righteousness as a reason for God to intervene. In other words, the supplicant does not claim to have earned a right to God's salvation. The primary appeal in all these laments is to the supplicant's need and to YHWH's gracious nature. So the rhetoric of lament is chiefly an appeal to God's pity for the suffering, his care for the powerless, his sympathy for those who cry to him. Whereas the supplicant may declare innocence or righteousness, this declaration isn't designed to gain God's approval but to clear any suspicion or question of whether the speaker deserves the bad situation in which he finds himself. The oath of clearance (Pss 7:3–5; 17:3–5) is actually a call for God to assess one's claim of innocence; it is strong evidence that a judicial analogy is operative in the prayer.[10]

What do the prayers enlisting God's intervention have to do with divine judgment? The prayers were normally responses to trouble or illness. Interpreters of Scripture have often thought such events were understood by ancient Israelites to be divine punishments for sin. Undoubtedly this idea crossed the minds of many ancients, since it has been around from time immemorial. It assumes that God rewards virtue and punishes vice, so serious reversals must be punishment.

The individual laments we have in the Psalter do *not* evidence this understanding of disaster. If they did, we would expect confessions of sin or protests of innocence much more frequently.[11] Another model is operative, and we will seek to divine it at the end of the section.

We have characterized individual laments as testimony in a trial before God. The supplicant has already experienced some sort of trouble or disap-

---

10. Psalm 143 is quite different in many respects. It asks that the supplicant *not* to be brought to trial, because he like all humans is guilty. This psalm belongs to the small group of penitential prayers that we shall examine later in this book.

11. We are going to discuss penitential psalms like Pss 51 and 130 in a later chapter (in part 2).

pointment and seeks to open an inquest, so to speak. The object of the inquest, from the supplicant's viewpoint, is to obtain a remedy for the situation before it is too late. The judgment proper, the decision of the divine judge, will take place in the answer of God to the lament. A favorable answer from God concludes the "trial" stage of judgment.

Most individual laments seek to recruit the Lord to intervene on the supplicant's behalf and against enemies. The Lord is sovereign over human affairs, the authority behind the law and morality, and the power of enforcement. The supplicant can seek to persuade God to intervene to achieve justice and show mercy. The rare protests of innocence simply indicate that there is no impediment to God's gracious deliverance.

## Laments Accusing God

Now we come to the psalms that accuse the Lord either for the trouble or for indifference to the plight of a victim.[12] This is a significantly different rhetorical strategy: to approach the sovereign with accusations rather than sanguine niceties. We will have to consider the question of rhetorical strategy after expounding a majority of the psalms belonging to this category.

*Psalm 13*

I will work through one lament accusing God, one that could be regarded as a model of this type of psalm. The first element of the lament is the address: "How long, O Lord?" (13:1). The address here is embedded in what will be called the complaint:

> How long, O Lord? Will you forget me forever?
> > How long will you hide your face from me?
> How long must I [bear pain] in my soul,
> > and have sorrow in my heart all the day?
> How long shall my enemy be exalted over me? (13:1–2)

The complaint is divided into three persons: a complaint, or accusation, against God; a description of the supplicant's suffering; and a complaint about the attack or gloating of enemies. These may also be called first-, second- and

---

12. Laments with accusations against God are a minority among individual laments, but almost all communal laments have such accusations. See chapter 11, below.

third-person complaints according to the pronouns (*I, you, they*). The interrogative form is nearly as frequent as the indicative.

Corresponding to the complaints are the requests:

> Consider and answer me, O Lord my God;
> > give light to my eyes, or I will sleep the sleep of death,
> 
> and my enemy say, "I have prevailed";
> > and my foes will rejoice because I am shaken. (13:3–4)

Close inspection of these requests shows that they have the same three parts as do the complaint. Corresponding to the accusation against God is the plea that God turn toward and answer the supplicant. The request to "lighten up" the supplicant's eyes matches the description of suffering. The request is supported by a kind of motive clause—lest I die, lest my enemies get the upper hand. The final request corresponds to the third-person complaint.

Now the lament turns toward the relationship between supplicant and God:

> But I trusted in your steadfast love;
> > my heart shall rejoice in your salvation.
> 
> I will sing to the Lord,
> > because he has dealt bountifully with me. (13:5–6)

The first bicola is a confession of trust; the supplicant here places his prayer in God's hands, so to speak. Then the supplicant vows to give thanks to the Lord when deliverance comes. The prayer ends in this hopeful key.

The address may not stand out as a distinctive feature of an individual lament, but it actually does give us the expression for lamentation, "calling on the name of the Lord." In polytheism, what name was uttered distinguished addressees, but that does not hold for the Bible. Both YHWH and Elohim (God) are each invoked. The biblical address is normally as direct, even abrupt, as it is in Psalm 13. It can be embedded in either an accusation or a request.

Complaints are a feature of biblical prayer that is absent from modern prayer. They are not meant to inform God but to bring out in the open what is disturbing the supplicant. Complaints in the Psalms, like contemporary complaints in an argument with a spouse or friend, are formulated to "clear the air," as we say. Like the biblical complaints, ours may be rhetorical questions or assertions. Complaints might also feature "negative requests," as in, e.g., "Be not far away" (Ps 22:19).

*Individuals within the Covenant*

Only some individual laments have accusations against God. That is undoubtedly due to the momentousness of speaking so harshly to one's Creator and Savior. There is indeed a shocking rudeness in these psalms. It betokens an amazing intimacy, for such insults do not belong to formal hierarchical relationships. It would be a mistake to regard such directness as a sign of contempt. I would guess that this directness belongs to a form of exchange that puts the addressee on the defensive. In philosophical terms, this form of speech exposes the discrepancy between what is and what should be in the rawest terms.

The purpose of individual laments is not only to reestablish one's relationship with God, broken by the troubles that come about either by God's doing or abandonment, but to elicit God's intervention in one's behalf. Psalm 13 articulates both purposes: "consider and answer me," and "give light to my eyes." This psalm is also typical for how metaphorical or indirect the request for intervention is. The individual laments were designed for a range of situations; there are none that would fit only one situation. We have Akkadian laments for toothaches and the like, but the Psalter has nothing of that sort.

Psalm 13 has no request to thwart or overthrow enemies; this is expressed indirectly in motive clauses. Other individual laments do request the Lord to disappoint one's enemies, or even to judge them, destroy them, or cause them to be caught in their own traps. The request for God's intervention against enemies may be expanded into a curse. Some of these are rather raw and violent.

Psalm 13 concludes with a confession of trust and a vow of praise. One can imagine a range of motives for confessing trust, not all of them noble. The motives expressed depend upon the person using the psalm. The supplicant does in fact depend upon God, as the lament itself proves. The confession of trust may also counteract the oppressiveness of the situation by calling to mind the power and goodness of the One who is on one's side.

Psalm 13 does not have either a protest of innocence or a confession of sin. Both are found in individual laments, but neither is particularly common. The protest of innocence seems to be formulated to counter actual charges of wrongdoing or perhaps rumors. Protests of innocence do not claim that the supplicant is "spotless," though one could imagine self-righteous supplicants entertaining such ideas in their hearts. Likewise, confessions of sin are probably for supplicants who know where they have gone wrong and desire to clear the slate.

The vow of praise belongs at the very end, and most individual laments end this way. Just as the confession of trust allows the speaker to psychologically escape from the difficult situation by recalling the One who is on one's side, so the vow of praise reaches toward the future when the supplicant is restored to health, social prestige, and safety. Within the Psalter, this element points to the thanksgiving that will celebrate deliverance. The person who relates to the world "commercially," so to speak, might imagine that he or she is striking a bargain, but God does not bargain with worshippers.

We have just surveyed the building materials of the individual lament and meditated on a model psalm. We have in the individual lament a relationship with God in which God is accessed by personal address. God is persuadable by both emotional and intellectual appeals. God's comportment and action can be reversed by persuasion. The events that shape a person's physical, emotional, social, and spiritual well-being derive from God, so prayer reestablishes the broken relationship caused by suffering, and seeks to elicit God's favorable intervention. The world of these psalms is not one in which humans determine their own destiny, nor is it determined solely by the divine sovereign; rather, it is a world in which destiny is determined by the interaction of God and the supplicant. The proper human attitude is to depend upon God and orient one's action toward God's saving intervention.

## Psalm 6

Psalm 6 begins with a muted accusation. The first verse is what is called a "negative request": "Do not rebuke me in your anger/or discipline me in your wrath." This may imply that the supplicant is experiencing the present crisis as "rebuke/discipline." It is set in contrast to a positive plea: "Be gracious . . ." The first strophe ends with an accusing "how long?"—a rather desperate cry for God to intervene before the speaker is devoured by enemies. The second strophe repeats the request for intervention, but the backing has to do with the "interest" of God in having worshippers (v. 5). The third strophe is a first-person complaint, and the fourth strophe confronts enemies. This fourth strophe expresses a change of mood, as though the supplicant had received a divine assurance between vv. 7 and 8. In v. 8, the speaker tells the enemies that God has joined his side, so to speak. Instead of offering a vow of praise, the final verse of Psalm 6 expresses confidence that enemies will be "ashamed."

## Psalm 22

Psalm 22 represents a bridge between psalms seeking to recruit the Lord to one's cause and psalms that blame the Lord for everything that has happened.

> My God, my God, why have you forsaken me?
>> Why are you so far from helping me?
>> from the words of my groaning?
> O my God, I cry by day, but you do not answer;
>> and by night, but find no rest. (vv. 1–2)

Nothing in this psalm blames God for the crisis the supplicant is in; rather, the Lord is accused of not being with the supplicant in the situation, of not intervening to save (see v. 19).

This lament begins as poignantly as any individual lament in the Psalter. It moves just as quickly away from a second-person complaint to a confession of trust: the supplicant's ancestors were delivered when they cried to God in distress (vv. 3–5). The supplicant then returns to complaint, this time to a first-person complaint; it states graphically how degraded he feels, and how even his enemies witness to his dependence on God (vv. 6–8). The alternation between complaint and confession of trust continues several cycles; the section concludes with a desperate negative request:

> Do not be far from me,
>> for trouble is near
>> and there is none to help. (v. 11)

There follows a long complaint against enemies, who are first compared to wild beasts (vv. 12–13), then to a mob out to destroy the supplicant (vv. 16–18). Spliced in between the descriptions of enemies is a first-person complaint about the supplicant's physical distress.

Until v. 19 the only request made in the psalm is that God "be not far off"—the other side of the initial accusing questions. The supplicant returns to this negative request in v. 19a, then expands upon it:

> But you, O Lord, do not be far away!
>> O my help, come quickly to my aid!
> Deliver my soul from the sword,
>> [my life] from the power of the dog!
> Save me from the mouth of the lion! (vv. 19–21a; 21b is corrupt)

The request is very simple and figurative: save me from the people that are seeking to kill me.

Following v. 21, the psalmist vows praise to the Lord when salvation comes, and then begins that praise. We will discuss this abrupt change of

*Redeeming Judgment*

mood in the later chapter, where we take up the topic of oracles and assurances of salvation.

## Psalm 39

It is hard to say what category Psalm 39 belongs to. It begins with a narrative explaining how the lament came to be:

> I said, "I will guard my ways
>     that I may not sin with my tongue;
> I will keep a muzzle on my mouth
>     so long as the wicked are in my presence."
> I was dumb and silent,
>     I held my peace to no avail;
> my distress grew worse,
>     my heart became hot within me.
> while I mused, the fire burned;
>     then I spoke with my tongue. (vv. 1–3)

It sounds as though the supplicant has a strong complaint of some sort, but we don't know what it is. The reference to the "wicked" suggests that it might be about them, but nothing further is said of them. Rather, the supplicant begins to brood over the shortness of human life:

> LORD, let me know my end,
>     and what is the measure of my days;
>     let me know how fleeting my life is! (39:4)

This train of thought continues through v. 6; strangely, it is the human condition that eats at the speaker.

> And now, O Lord, what do I wait for?
>     My hope is in you.
> Deliver me from all my transgressions. (39:7–8a)

This plea seems hypothetical, but then the supplicant speaks very personally:

> I am silent; I do not open my mouth;
>     for it is you who have done it.
> Remove your stroke from me
>     . . .

*Individuals within the Covenant*

> You chastise mortals in punishment for sin,
> consuming like a moth what is dear to them. (39:9–11a)

Finitude is hardly punishment for sin, but the supplicant seems to experience finitude and punishment as having a combined impact. The speaker has been shocked by God's punishment for sin into realizing that life is "a breath." Strangely, the supplicant has no remorse for his sin. The lament ends very cryptically:

> For I am your passing guest,
> an alien, like all my forbears.
> Turn your gaze away from me, that I may smile again,
> before I depart and am no more. (vv. 12b–13)

If I understand the poem correctly, the supplicant seeks escape from God's scrutiny: says the speaker, "Just let me be!"

## Psalm 77

Psalm 77 agonizes over unanswered prayer. It hovers between a prayer and a narrative. It begins speaking of God in the third person:

> I cry aloud to God,
> aloud to God, that he may hear me; . . .
> I think of God, and I moan;
> I meditate and my spirit faints. (77:1, 3)

Only now does the supplicant actually address God:

> You keep my eyelids from closing;
> I am so troubled that I cannot speak. (77:4)

The psalmist then turns from first-person narrative to meditation on what has happened. The speaker delivers an extensive complaint against God, but it is in the third person.

> Will the Lord spurn forever,
> and never again be favorable?
> Has His steadfast love ceased forever?
> Are His promises at an end for all time?
> Has God forgotten to be gracious?
> Has he in anger shut up his compassion? (77:7–9)

*Redeeming Judgment*

This is a shockingly forthright questioning of the continuing goodness of God. There is nothing like it among laments, with the exception of a few passages in Job. The supplicant reserves his or her most dangerous expression of doubt until last:

> And I say, "it is my grief that the right hand
> of the Most High has changed." (v. 10)

I take this to mean, perhaps God no longer has the power to deliver. If God "loses" power, God loses reality. The psalmist turns away from this prospect and meditates on the saving deeds whose memory has been passed down in tradition:

> I will call to mind the deeds of the LORD;
> I will remember your wonders of old.
> You are the God who works wonders;
> you have displayed your might among the peoples.
> With your arm you redeemed your people,
> the descendents of Jacob and Joseph (vv. 11, 14–15).

Note that the second person has returned: the psalmist can pray his or her memory. The story continues with an epiphanic version of the deliverance of Israel from Egypt's attempt to stop the slave escape (vv. 16–20).

*Psalm 88*

Here we have the most desperate cry of all the individual laments. It begins with a conventional address and plea for God to hear. From there it moves to an extensive first-person complaint:

> For my soul is full of troubles,
> and my life draws near to Sheol, . . .
> like those forsaken among the dead,
> like those whom you remember no more (88:3, 5).

The supplicant just slips into second-person, direct address in v. 5, and that initiates a rather harsh set of charges:

> You have put me in the depths of the Pit; . . .
> Your wrath lies heavy upon me,
> and you overwhelm me with all your waves.

> You have caused my companions to shun me;
> you have made me a thing of horror to them. (88:6–8)

Every aspect of the supplicant's distress is blamed on the Lord, including the hostility of neighbors and relatives. The supplicant begins, in v. 9, to plead with God for a change of mind. The speaker's motivation is rather ironic: What good are the dead to you?

Beginning with v. 13, the supplicant begins to communicate a request for deliverance. It is rather subtle; there is no actual request made; it is a series of indicting questions and assertions that are designed to put God in the situation of having to act on the supplicant's behalf; only a sadist would continue to torture one who has been "wretched and close to death from my youth up" (v. 15a).

The oppressive gloom of the Psalm does not break with a vow of praise or confession of trust. Indeed, the Psalm seems not to conclude so much as break off. This is the sort of lament that could continue for days upon days.

At the outset of this study of selected psalms of lament, I divided them into those seeking to recruit God to the supplicant's side in the struggle with enemies or other causes of trouble, and those Psalms that blame God for the disaster and seek to change his mind. We have finished our study of examples of both types. The category just covered must confront a God who has behaved incomprehensibly, who has acted out of character. Implied in *this* lament is that God is implicated in every disaster.

These psalms are rather diverse as to what they accuse God of. Psalms 77 and 88 accuse God of exercising power immorally or incomprehensibly. But then we note that Psalm 77 brings up the opposite possibility, that God has lost power. According to Psalms 13 and 22, God's absence or indifference has allowed evil to get the upper hand, but God is not the cause of evil. God is the source of the supplicant's crisis in Psalm 39, but the references to punishment for sin weaken the complaint. Moreover, the supplicant seems to exercise such a radical independence that it is hard to see how the speaker has any basis of complaint.

## *The Rhetoric of Adversarial Prayer*

Accusing the judge certainly sounds like a dangerous, provocative strategy for procuring a favorable hearing. Readers might well conclude that it is too far-fetched, that we must abandon the judicial analogy for this type of individual lament.

*Redeeming Judgment*

I would contend, however, that the transaction going on between the supplicant and God is in fact a trial; the supplicant is testifying in a process that will result in God's decision as to his or her fate. We simply have to finetune our analogy, so to speak, to account for the odd, provocative approach to authority.

What we have in the accusations against God are arguments presented to God the judge about the comportment of God the sovereign ruler of creation. When the supplicant accuses God, it is as the power who determines weal and woe.

Another way to look at this is to think of the prayer as an appeal to divine justice and loyalty (Heb. *ḥesed*) in the face of what has happened. The supplicant has the option of seeking to recruit God to intervene in his or her behalf, or of accusing God the sovereign of inconsistent governance. The decision whether to accuse God determines the type of lament one will utter.

The dual role of God in lament—as sovereign and as judge—is a uniquely Israelite problem. It derives from the first commandment, prohibiting the recognition of any god but YHWH. Polytheism could divide responsibilities between deities, so any contradiction could be blamed on the cross-purposes of the gods. In addition, the polytheistic supplicant had access to a personal deity who could mediate between the worshipper and the high gods—those with real power. With this guardian deity the supplicant could be very honest, to the point of anger and sarcasm, without offending the gods that determine one's fate. All these roles or responsibilities within the pantheon are united in YHWH. He must, in theory, play all these roles satisfactorily for the religion to remain viable.

There were dangers to the lament lurking in Israelite "monolotry": certain theological ideas could force worshippers into uncritical submission to God. The freedom to accuse God kept the religion from becoming too heteronymous. Hence, when arguments begin to appear that could silence the lament, like those adumbrated by Job's companions, Yahwism was in danger of becoming a theological tyranny. The postcanonical history of Jewish, Christian, and Muslim prayer manifests the sort of tyranny I am speaking of.

If the psalms of lament are evidence, the biblical God welcomes an honest opening of the heart. The blunt statement of the supplicant's point of view is acceptable. One of the striking features of most individual laments is how they open: they get to the point immediately. There are no pleasantries, let alone flattery, before the request or complaint. This fits the honest, open mood of the psalms.

What persuasive strategy is operative in the individual laments, particularly those that accuse YHWH? Tikva Frymer-Kensky offers an insight that is quite helpful in this regard.[13] She compares this accusing style of prayer to a certain type of human exchange, which she calls "nagging Jewish mother." When Sarah, for example, wants permission to make Hagar's life miserable, she speaks to Abram: "'May the wrong done to me be on you! I gave my slave-girl to your embrace, and when she saw that she had conceived, she looked on me with contempt. May the Lord judge between you and me'" (Gen 16:5). Abram is not really to blame for Hagar's attitude; it was really Sarai's strategy that had backfired. Nevertheless, she accuses Abram—to put him on the defensive. He lets her have her way though he should probably have kept the two apart.

The people in the wilderness kept murmuring against Moses and YHWH, and it had a similar accusative character: "'If only we had died by the hand of the Lord in the land of Egypt, when we sat by fleshpots and ate our fill of bread; for you have brought us out into this wilderness to kill this whole assembly with hunger'" (Exod 16:3). This sort of griping was not exactly approved, but it did not lead to judgment. Rather, it led to the feeding of the people with manna.[14] The freedom to accuse God provided space for the Israelites and kept the religion from becoming a closed, tyrannical way of life.

## Review

We began this chapter with proverbs because this type of discourse can be best interpreted as teaching values to youths to make them good citizens. It is practical instruction, which holds out the prospect of respect, satisfaction and success for conformity with the ideal. If the person deviates seriously, failure and shame threaten. Israel's Lord will enforce the norms, so failure and shame will be a case of divine judgment.

When life does go wrong, the Israelite will normally approach YHWH for a remedy. The individual laments of the Psalter represent something of a trial. These laments assume that the individual's case has not been decided, or can be reversed. The complaints, requests, and other parts of the lament are designed to persuade the divine judge to turn the supplicant's fate.

The individual laments of the Psalter have two different approaches to God the judge. Most do not accuse God but complain about enemies, health, or

---

13. Frymer-Kensky, *In The Wake of the Goddesses*, 128–40.

14. Jeremiah's complaints receive a similar, though harsher, answer: Jer 11:22–23; 12:56; 15:19–21.

personal distress to elicit God's justice and mercy. We have called this strategy recruiting God to the supplicant's side. We would expect a response from God that promises to overthrow the supplicant's enemies, to give the supplicant strength to fight the power of death, to provide an antidote to melancholy, and the like. A negative judgment would sound like Ahijah's oracle to Jeroboam's wife (1 Kgs 14:12–13). Of course, God might subject the supplicant to something like an ordeal to test the faithfulness and justice of the supplicant.

The other approach is to accuse God of betrayal, indifference, or antagonism. While this seems like a counterproductive strategy for winning the judge's favor, it can be understood as a way to put God on the defensive. If the supplicant speaks honestly and is committed to God, the God who prizes truth and courage will hear the plea.

The trial dramatized in an individual lament psalm belongs to the sphere of the covenant between the nation and the Lord. The individual comes before the Lord as a member of the people of YHWH, and the individual's enemies are as well. The God of the covenant is sovereign over the whole world, so he is to be credited or blamed for all events and situations. This doesn't mean that every untoward event is regarded as deliberate, meant as judgment. A sovereign is not the agent of most of what transpires in a society, but he (or she) is responsible for what happens—for the repair of the breach, for retribution and reconciliation. Divine sovereignty is the same in this respect.

The window we have into the divine judgment of individuals does not exhibit temporal development. The psalms have a timeless quality, rather like the Sinaitic law. Undoubtedly piety and poetics changed in the period between the exodus and the exile; indeed, scholars have reconstructed something of a history of the lament.[15] But once a psalm enters the authoritative tradition, it becomes an expression for all times, past and future, to its own present. We have treated individual laments at this point in our exposition to correspond to their timelessness. They belong to life in the covenant whenever and wherever that life is lived.

A change in piety comes with the prophets of judgment and exile, and we will examine it in chapters 15 and 16. The change seems to have been caused by the evolving divine judgment of the people. When the people as a whole were put to trial in prophecy, they responded in communal laments protesting God's action. The prophetic answer was no, and the exile erased the northern tribes from history and transformed the people of Judah permanently. We have a chapter on communal laments: chapter 12. In the wake of the exile, a new,

---

15. See Westermann, "Praise and Lament in the Psalms," 266–305.

penitential lament emerges, and this communal piety spreads to individual laments. We will fill in this sketch after we have traversed the history of the wilderness era, the conquest and judges, and the united and divided monarchy.

# 6

## Judgments in the Wilderness
(Exodus 32; Numbers 10–36; Deuteronomy)

It is time to return to the foot of Mount Sinai, where we are about to depart for the promised land. Now the people are pledged to obey YHWH and have received a full system of law to live by. Prior to the covenant at Sinai, the Israelites were only accountable for their compliance with the common morality and law of the ancient Near East. Now, each and every Israelite is under a personal obligation to the Lord, the lawgiver. This is because all the law is summed up in the commandments, which are personally addressed to each and every member of the society. The divinely revealed law also has different content from the common ancient Near Eastern law, viz., each and every provision has been transformed by the first commandment.

The wilderness period is the first long period of time when Israel will live under this new order. They have to work out the kinks, so to speak. In Numbers, we have a variety of laws to fill in the gaps of the codes from Exodus. For example, Num 5:5–31 provides a procedure for handling the case of a jealous, suspicious husband; and 6:1–21 covers Nazirite vows. According to Num 27:1–11, the daughters of a man who had died without male heirs petitioned Moses for the right of inheritance, and received a favorable answer (their rights are restricted somewhat in 36:1–12).

More to the point of our interest, though, are all the divine judgments that take place in the wilderness. Collective offenses and judgments have been foreshadowed by the making and worshipping of the golden calf. In subsequent Israelite consciousness, this is Israel's fall from grace. The covenant and law had been designed to preserve a peaceful, just, and righteous people. No sooner had it been put into place than we have an egregious violation. Indeed, it is the very law against the crafting and worshipping of images that sets Israel off from all other peoples—viz., the first and second commandments—that was flagrantly violated. This judgment foreshadows the event that leads to the delay of the conquest until the following generation (Numbers 13-14); that event in turn casts its shadow over all the other judgments.

The judgment of the people for making the golden calf demonstrates that the Israelites are just as prone to sin as other humans. If they had thought that YHWH's election and covenant would restore them to a state of innocence, they now know otherwise. The covenant and law are designed to be a remedy for the fractious hearts of humans, but now we discover that a rigid enforcement of this "ideal" order would end in the death of the people. So the covenant is amended to allow for forgiveness. The chosen people will exemplify divine sovereignty by concentrating the human struggle with God in the life of one people, who are known by the name Israel, a word meaning, "the one who strives with God" (Gen 32:28).

The wilderness narrative focuses on collective, political offenses and judgments. The people are more capable of collective action when they are living together in this hostile environment than they will be in Canaan, where localism and regionalism will prevail. Several of the offenses violate a specific commandment, like the first (and second). The others are not violations of laws but lack of faith in the promises of the Lord, or dissatisfaction with human leadership—neither of which can be generalized into a law. Nevertheless, they are offenses against God whose will is expressed in law.

We will discover that the judgments imposed on Israel gravitate toward distributive judgment despite the offenses being collective. Some individuals are singled out for punishment or favor; perhaps some are particularly culpable, or God is making an example of them in the hope of reforming the rest.

## Murmuring of the People

The "murmuring" of the Israelites begins before they have passed through the Sea of Reeds (Exod 14:10-14) and continues on until they arrive at Sinai (15:23-25; 16:2-3; 17:2-4). These recriminations of Moses and YHWH would seem to warrant divine censure, but in fact God responds by filling the need that had prompted the complaint.

*Redeeming Judgment*

After the Israelites leave Sinai, they begin to complain again. At this point the Lord begins to chasten them for their doubt and ingratitude. The wilderness is left with monuments to these events in place names like "Burning" (Num 11:3), "Graves of Craving" (11:34), and "Quarrel" (20:13). When the Lord does sentence the people to death in the wilderness, he specifically mentions that they "have tested me these ten times" (Num 14:22); probably the times of murmuring are counted among the ten.[1]

*Scouting the Promised Land*

The narrative up till now has projected a conquest of Canaan, which follows immediately on the ratification of the covenant at Sinai. The newly incorporated band of escaped slaves marches from Mount Sinai to the oasis on the border of the promised land, known as Kadesh Barnea. There they send out scouts, or spies, to check out the land they are about to attack.

Moses recruits a company of scouts, one from each tribe, to pass through the promised land in order to assess its agricultural value and the inhabitants' capacity to defend themselves. One would expect the scouts to map the territory, or at least to form a map in their head, so that the fighters can plan attacks, chart routes, locate water and food, and the like. These subjects, though, are not mentioned in the scouts' report. The scouts proceed through the southern desert into the hill country of Judah.[2] They are quite impressed with the fruits that grow in the Valley of Eshcol, and bring back samples. Their report to Moses, Aaron, and the people affirms the productivity of the land, but also warns that the people living there are strong, their cities large and fortified. Their description becomes more discouraging as the exchange goes on: "And besides, we saw the descendants of Anak there" (13:28). "We are not able to go up against the people, for they are stronger than we" (13:31, RSV). It is "a land that devours its inhabitants; and all the people that we saw in it are of great size . . . to ourselves we seemed like grasshoppers, and so we seemed to them" (13:32–33).

As one can understand, this report arouses consternation in the camp. Indeed, a restlessness verging on rebellion simmers through the night (14:1–3), and then the people began to choose leaders to take them back to Egypt (14:4). Two of the scouts, Caleb and Joshua, speak up to counteract the mood; they

---

1. See Coats, *Rebellion in the Wilderness*, 137–55, 249–54.

2. One strand does say that they went all the way to the "entrance of Hamath," but the other doesn't mention any site north of the Valley of Eschol.

lay out the classic statement of conquest ideology: "'If the Lord is pleased with us, he will bring us into this land and give it to us, a land that flows with milk and honey. Only, do not rebel against the Lord. Only do not fear the people of the land, for they are bread for us; their protection is removed from them, and the Lord is with us; do not fear them!'" (14:8–9). This eloquent speech is to no avail; the people begin to stone the speakers. Then the Lord descends on the Tent of Meeting to speak with Moses; the appearance of the divine glory stops the rebellion in its tracks.

The Lord's address to Moses (in Num 14:11–12) echoes Exod. 32:7–10. It begins with an indictment of the people. Though they have not violated a law, they have shown contempt toward their God, ignoring his power to give them victory over superior foes. The Lord proposes to destroy this recalcitrant people and make Moses a patriarch of a new people. Moses intercedes, with nearly the same strategy that he uses in Exod 32:11–13. The destruction of Israel would give Egypt and other nations a bad impression of YHWH. It would seem as though he wasn't strong enough to pull it off (14:13–16). God has shown this people favor and promised to be merciful as well as just; now is the time for him to demonstrate his mercy in forgiveness (14:17–19).

YHWH is moved by Moses's intercession enough to cancel his death sentence in favor of life in the wilderness until the Egyptian generation dies off (14:20–23, 28–35). This judgment is poetic justice: the people lack faith in YHWH's power to defeat the inhabitants of the land, so they must live out their lives in the wilderness. The next generation will have a shot at conquest (14:24–25).

The scouts receive their own judgments. The ten who report that Israel would not be able to conquer the land are infected with plague and died (14:36–37), while Caleb and Joshua (the two who trusted in God) are allowed to live long enough to participate in the conquest of Canaan. Caleb is given Hebron as a reward as well.

The people continue to act out their faithlessness. Rather than accepting their judgment, they now attack the southern region of the promised land. Evidently they take the divine word of judgment as only a warning; now they would do what the Lord had wanted earlier. But they are too late and are routed on the battlefield: a reenforcement of the original judgment (14:39–45).

This judgment in no way threatens the promise, which remains alive in the two faithful scouts and the next generation. It is also reinforced by laws promulgated by the Lord through Moses to the people (Numbers 15). One statute begins, "When you come into the land you are to inhabit, which I am giving you . . ." (15:2). The Lord puts the judgment behind them: practices are being put in place for the time of fulfillment. The first ordinance concerns cereal offerings, which are to accompany animal sacrifices (15:1–10). In the wilderness the Israelites have herds and offer sacrifices, but they have no grain for cereal offerings; only when they are settled can they grow grain. The next ordinance (15:17–21) is explicit about its relationship to the fulfillment of the promise: "After you come into the land to which I am bringing you and whenever you eat of the food of the land, you shall present a donation to the Lord" (v. 17). The practice commanded is thanksgiving for the produce of the promised land.

## Two Rebellions

The condemnation of the exodus generation to live out their lives in the wilderness is bound to be a source of unrest. The rebellion of Dathan and Abiram is an instance of just such unrest. In Numbers 16, it has been combined with another rebellion, led by a Levite named Korah. We can treat them separately, beginning with Dathan and Abiram.

The challenge issued by Dathan and Abiram is to Moses's leadership. It is a variation on the murmuring motif. Their complaint runs, "'Is it too little that you have brought us up out of a land flowing with milk and honey to kill us in the wilderness, that you must lord it over us? It is clear you have not brought us into a land flowing with milk and honey, or given us an inheritance of fields and vineyards'" (16:13–14). This evidently threatens to stir up some who might, for example, break away and assault the cultivated land on their own. In any case, Moses sets up a contest between them and himself: "If these people die a natural death, . . . then the Lord has not sent me" (16:29). He predicts that they will be swallowed straight into Sheol, and the earth splits open and swallows Dathan and Abiram and their families (16:30–33).

The story paired with it of Korah and the Levites concerns Aaron's claims to exclusive access to the holy areas of the wilderness sanctuary. Their challenge sounds a democratic note: "All the congregation are holy, every one of them, and the Lord is among them. So why do you exalt yourselves above the assembly of the Lord?" (16:3). Moses accuses these rebels, members of the same tribe as the priests, of wanting, not only to approach the holy places of the tabernacle, but to take over duties reserved for the Lord's chosen priest (16:8–10). Moses sets up a contest between the challengers and Aaron that will allow the Lord to decide whose case is right. This contest tests who can approach YHWH, with a burning censer in his hand; the Lord will destroy those who do not belong in his presence.

Korah brings the whole congregation along with him, and Moses and Aaron have to plead for the lives of all but the ringleaders: "O God, the God of the spirits of all flesh, shall one person sin and you become angry with the whole congregation?" (16:22).

Some verses (16:23, 27, 32) say that Korah is swallowed up into Sheol with Dathan and Abiram, but Num 16:35 says that "fire came out from the Lord and consumed the 250 men offering the incense." Whether Korah dies with his supporters or with the other two leaders is uncertain.

These two cases of rebellion have collective judgments, but the nation is protected. Both cases involve a challenge of the leaders, the civil leadership in one case, and cultic in the other. In both a contest is set up to allow the Lord to show whom he approves of. This is analogous to the challenge of Moses's prophetic status by Miriam and Aaron (Numbers 12). In Numbers 16, though, the losing party is executed. These stories teach the lesson that divinely chosen leaders have divine support and protection against self-chosen challengers.

The judgment of Korah and his party actually angers the people (16:41). The Lord sides with his leaders, and threatens to do away with the congregation. Moses tells Aaron to take a censer among the people to stop the spread of a plague (16:46–49), which he does successfully.

Moses designs, at YHWH's direction, a contest that will demonstrate that Aaron and the tribe of Levi have unique access to the sanctuary. Aaron's staff buds (17:1–9) and is placed before the ark of the covenant"] (17:10). But now the people complain that "everyone who approaches the tabernacle of the Lord will die" (17:13). The answer to this complaint seems to be that priests and Levites will mediate, will go into the holy areas on behalf of the people (18:1–7). For their service, the clergy will receive prebends (18:8–32).

The pattern operative in the wilderness judgments is that the judgment is mitigated, and the order adjusted to avoid repetitions. The golden-calf incident leads to the modification of the covenant to provide for forgiveness. The rebellion aroused by the report of the scouts results in a longer sojourn in the wilderness, which prepares the people for the conquest and life in the land. The rebellion led by Korah secures the arrangement of the community around the sanctuary with priests and Levites mediating.

*Redeeming Judgment*

## *Further Incidents*

In the conflicts with Dathan, Abiram, and Korah, the Lord sides unequivocally with Moses and Aaron. Humans cannot nullify God's election. This is a theocratic community in which human officials carry the authority of God and are answerable to God for their exercise of that authority. What happens when they fail is dramatized in Num 20:2–13: Moses calls forth water from a rock as if he was the power performing the miracle, so he and Aaron are condemned to die before the people enter the promised land proper.

There is a good deal of puzzlement over what Moses says or does that offends the Lord. The story begins with the people murmuring about the absence of water at Kadesh. The Lord appears and instructs Moses to strike a rock, perhaps a stone cliff, with the sacred rod. When he strikes the rock, he addresses the people in anger: "Listen, you rebels: shall we bring forth water for you out of this rock?" (20:10). Then he struck it twice and water flowed. The Lord condemns Moses in these words: "Because you did not trust in me, to show my holiness before the eyes of the Israelites, therefore you shall not bring this assembly into the land which I have given them" (v. 12). Striking the rock twice is not serious enough to deserve this condemnation, so the reason for condemnation must be his formulation with "we" bringing forth water rather than YHWH.

This tragic sin by Israel's greatest leader occurs at the very end of the sojourn in the wilderness. Moses sends messengers ahead to procure permission to pass through Edom; Edom refuses, so Israel must bypass it. The people also skirt Moab, but when the Amorite king, Sihon, refuses to let them pass, they attack and win, and conquer the two "Amorite kingdoms" that become the territory of the Transjordanian tribes.

Once these battles are won, they encamp near the River Jordan, ready to cross and conquer the promised land proper. While Israel is encamped there, the Moabite king, Balak, and his elders contact a seer and magician named Balaam; he is hired to travel to the vicinity of the Israelite camp and curse them. There ensues one slapstick event after another. This is a humorous interlude with the serious lesson that YHWH controls blessing and curse. No human craft or ritual can bring evil upon YHWH's people if he does not will it (22:12, 18–20, 35, 38, and so forth).

The people of Israel, unfortunately, are quite capable of bringing evil upon themselves. At Baal Peor the people join locals in an orgiastic worship of the local Baal. Remember, this is the new generation—the one that will go into the land of Canaan. They have not participated in the making of the golden calf or in the rebellion in response to the report of the scouts. They should be capable of resisting this temptation, but they are just as susceptible as their parents had been. This is the type of apostasy, moreover, that they have been warned about, viz., befriending polytheistic neighbors and becoming entangled in their religion (Exod 23:32–33; 34:15–16; Deut 7:3–4).

The story of the event at Baal Peor is told very briefly. Once the people join the locals in their orgiastic worship, divine judgment breaks out: Moses is told to hang the chiefs of the people, to avoid total annihilation (25:4). Then Moses tells the "judges" to slay anyone involved in the worship of Baal (25:5). Phinehas, a priest from Aaron's line, kills one flagrant violator (25:6–8). Despite these efforts, twenty-four thousand Israelites die of a God-sent plague. However we take this rather cryptic and confusing report, the event was important enough for Hosea to refer to it as the "fall":

> Like grapes in the wilderness, I found Israel.
> Like the first fruit on the fig tree, in its first season, I saw your fathers.
> But they came to Baal Peor and consecrated themselves to a thing of shame,
> And became detestable like the thing they loved. (Hos 9:10)

## The Wilderness in Rhetoric

The wilderness period is the most available of the Pentateuch narratives for use in the rhetoric of subsequent eras. Besides the exodus it is probably the most often called upon to make theological points. The exodus had a narrow range of meanings and could be cited whenever the speaker or writer desired to image YHWH's grace and power. The wilderness could not only be cited as a continuation of YHWH's grace; it could be held up as a mirror for the people. It called to mind Israel's stiff neck and wayward heart, and the divine judgments in response. But some interpreters saw a favorable side to these very events.

Several biblical passages construe the wilderness time as a foreshadowing of later sin and judgment. It is as though the people revealed their true character there, and they haven't changed. Psalm 78 rehearses the wilderness events extensively, e.g.,

> Yet they sinned still more against him,
> Rebelling against the Most High in the desert.
> They tested God in their heart
> By demanding the food they craved. (78:17–18)

*Redeeming Judgment*

> Therefore, when the Lord heard, He was full of rage;
> A fire was kindled against Jacob
> . . .
> Because they had no faith in God
> And did not trust his saving power. (78:21, 22)
>
> How often they rebelled against Him in the wilderness
> and grieved him in the desert!
> They tested God again and again. (78:40–41)

This same refractory behavior continues after the conquest and settlement of Canaan (Ps 78:56–66). Then, to the surprise of readers, we do not hear of the exile but of YHWH's rejection of Judah, particularly Jerusalem. Ps 78 ends up glorifying Zion and David at the expense of the northern kingdom.

Psalm 106 uses the wilderness traditions in much the same way as Psalm 78.

> But they soon forgot his works;
> They did not wait for his counsel.
> But they had a wanton craving in the wilderness,
> And put God to the test in the desert. (106:13–14)
>
> They were jealous of Moses in the camp,
> . . . (v. 16)
> They made a calf at Horeb
> . . . (v. 19)
> They exchanged the glory of God
> for the image of an ox . . . (v. 20)
>
> Then they attached themselves to Baal of Peor
> And ate sacrifices offered to the dead. (v. 28)

The psalm continues through the conquest and into the era of the monarchy (vv. 34–46). It seems to end in the exilic period but purposely leaves the present open for later audiences. The last verse pleads for salvation and regathering of the people.

Ezekiel 20 paints the darkest picture of the wilderness era. The chapter begins with the people's apostasy and idolatry back in Egypt (20:5–8). The sins and threats of judgment in the wilderness span vv. 10–26. Here is a sample:

*Judgments in the Wilderness*

"Then I thought I would pour out my wrath upon them and spend my anger against them in the wilderness. But I withheld my hand and acted for the sake of my name, so that it should not be profaned in the sight of the nations, in whose sight I had brought them out. Moreover I swore to them in the wilderness that I would scatter them among the nations . . . because they had not executed my ordinances, but had rejected my statutes and profaned my Sabbaths, and their eyes were set on their ancestors' idols" (vv. 21b–24). Ezekiel seems to think that only complete rejection and devastation counts as judgment. He alludes to Moses's intercessory prayers in describing what the Lord thought to do before reversing himself. Of note is the claim that the Assyrian and Babylonian exiles were announced at this time. However Ezekiel finds such a message, he makes the wilderness judgments a foreshadowing of exile.

Immediately following Ezek 20:21b–24, the Lord says that he has punished Israel by giving them bad laws—firstborn sacrifice in particular (vv. 25–26). This is the only passage in Hebrew Scripture in which God admits to being the source of that practice.[3] This statement, formulated for its shock value, probably claims that the impassioned urge to offer children was (or is) an act of divine punishment. That is, human proclivity to do this is an expression of their sinful condition.

This is not the only interpretive perspective on the wilderness period. The prophets Hosea and Jeremiah look back to it as an idyllic time:

> I remember the devotion of your youth,
> Your love as a bride,
> How you followed me in the wilderness,
> In a land not sown. (Jer 2:2)[4]

The wilderness years, though filled with divine judgments, were a time when people and YHWH bonded, sealed their relationship, experienced a honeymoon.

When Moses looks back on those forty years in the book of Deuteronomy, the image mellows from divine judgment to disciplining:

> The Lord your God has led you these forty years in the wilderness, in order to humble you, testing you to know what was in our heart, whether or not you would keep his commandments. And He humbled you by letting you hunger then by feeding you with manna, with which neither you nor your ancestors were acquainted...in order to

---

3. Jer 7:31 is more typical: "Which I did not command, nor did it come into my mind."
4. Also Hos 9:10a, which was quoted earlier.

*Redeeming Judgment*

> make you understand that one does not live by bread alone, but by everything that proceeds out of the mouth of the Lord ... Know then in your heart that, as a parent disciplines a child, so the Lord your God disciplines you. (Deut 8:2–3, 5)

This change of perspective has important theological implications. In particular, divine judgment may become redemptive in later perspective if understood in a faithful manner. This will be crucial for the doctrine of atonement.

## Moses's Farewell Address

The book of Deuteronomy starts with a review of the events that have transpired since the people departed Sinai/Horeb. The single most important thing was the people's rebellion when they heard the report of the spies; the Lord condemned them to death in the wilderness during a forty-year period of wandering. Moses is the last of that generation; he must die before the next generation can cross the Jordan under Joshua's leadership.

Deuteronomy 4 recalls the revelation at Sinai/Horeb and draws lessons for the people in support of the prohibition against images and worship of any creature. The revelation at Sinai/Horeb is a unique event in history, and it demonstrates YHWH's love of Israel. But Israel must maintain itself in God's grace by obeying his law.

Chapters 7–11 review the pentateuchal story for other theological lessons. The most salient is the doctrine of election: "The Lord your God has chosen you to be a people of his own possession, out of all the peoples that are on the face of the earth" (7:6, RSV). It was not any quality of Israel such as size that prompted the choice: "It was not because you were more in number than any other people that the Lord set his love upon you and chose you, for you were the fewest of all peoples; but it was because the Lord loves you and is keeping the oath which He swore to your fathers" (7:7). In a later chapter Moses denies that "it is because of [Israel's] righteousness that the Lord has brought [them] in to possess this land" (9:4). Israel is a "stubborn people" (v. 6). Election is an amazing and shocking event—a claim that the Creator of all the earth set his heart in love upon this little people (10:14–15).

The word "love" (Heb. *'ahav*) comes to Moses's lips rather frequently in these sermonic chapters. Not only does he affirm the Lord's love of Israel, but he calls upon the people of Israel to love the Lord. The most famous case is the Shema: "Hear, O Israel: the Lord our God is one Lord. And you shall love the Lord your God with all your heart, and with all your soul, and with all your might" (6:4–5). Again and again the people are urged to love the Lord and obey his law (10:12–13).

## The Law

Before we consider the content of Deuteronomic law, it is important to take notice of its style and motivational appeal. We could call the style of Deuteronomy the "rhetoric of reform." It is important to recognize that the book presents its law not as divine commandment but as Moses's interpretation of the Ten Commandments and Moses's inducement to live according to the law given by God. The "you" who is addressed throughout is not only the audience of the narrative world, but the readers as well. This is a law contemporary to all who hear it as God's people (cp. 5:3; 29:14–15). The human-to-human exchange allows for a less formal, more motivational tone.

Motivational clauses and vocabulary make up a larger percentage of Deuteronomic law than of any other biblical code. Moreover, the hortatory style thoroughly penetrates the wording of the rules of law; one cannot draw a firm distinction between the law proper and the urging to obey it. The paranaesis frequently calls upon Israelite memory to support its imperatives; thus, the preacher builds upon and forms Israelite identity. A sense of urgency pervades the law. Israel must live up to its calling or be subject to divine judgment. "Behold, I set before you this day a blessing and a curse: the blessing if you obey . . . the curse if you do not . . ." (11:26–28).

### *The Content of the Law*

One of the most salient aspects of Deuteronomic law is the prominence of welfare and humanitarian legislation. To please God, the community must provide for the welfare of its destitute and vulnerable. This covers credit, harvesting, wages, even festival meals (12:12, 18–19; 14:26–27; 16:11, 14). Every third year the farmer's tithe of grain is to be set aside in one's village for the poor (14:28–29; 26:12–15). Female slaves are accorded the same rights as males (15:12–18). The harboring of runaway slaves is not a crime but a duty (23:15–16). The needy have a right to glean fields after the harvest (24:19–22). Even animals are under a degree of legal protection (22:6–7; 26:4).

A number of rules protect citizens from the courts. Fathers will not be executed for crimes by their children, or children for crimes by their fathers (24:16). Corporal punishment—flogging—is limited to protect the honor of the guilty (25:1–3). Two witnesses are required for conviction in criminal cases (17:4–7; 19:15), and there is a procedure for assessing suspect testimony (19:15–21).

Serious offenses are addressed to the court, which has responsibility for avoiding guilt from the acts of members being transferred to the community. The court executes the guilty to "purge the evil from the midst of you" (24:7, RSV; also 13:5 [cp. v. 17]; 17:7; 19:10, 13; 21:21; 22:22, 24). Any act of worship or service to any deity besides YHWH is deserving of death (13:1–5; 6–11, 12–18; 17:2–7). A person who deliberately takes another's life deserves death, but an accidental killer should be protected (19:1–13). Divination (18:9–11) and kidnapping into slavery are capital offenses, while testifying falsely (19:15–19) results in the death penalty only if the false charge would have brought death on the falsely accused. A rebellious child can be taken before a court by parents, and if the judges' admonitions go unheeded, the child is to be executed (21:18–21).

The Deuteronomic law is known for its alteration of cultic practice. Deuteronomy 12 stipulates that the people of Israel should sacrifice at the one place YHWH chooses to plant his name (vv. 5–7). Moses admits that up till then they have been sacrificing wherever they pleased (vv. 8–9). The danger is that the people will adopt the sites where the Canaanites worship their gods, and will imitate their practices as well (cp. 12:2–4, 29–31). If Israelite worshippers of YHWH limit themselves to the one place chosen by God, and destroy the rest, they can maintain faithful practice.

This central sanctuary provision reverses Exod 20:24, which encourages the erection of altars.[5] At an early period in Israel's history, locating altars wherever there were Israelites was an act of claiming the land for YHWH as well as of providing an accessible place for his worshippers. The Deuteronomic law finds that the plethora of local altars and temples is conducive to heterodoxy; this can be remedied by decommissioning all sanctuaries but one.

The provision will require significant adjustments in the practice of religion. Those living away from the chosen place will have to bring the animals and produce that they are required to offer as holocausts, well-being sacrifices, tithes, as well as firstborn, votive, and freewill offerings (see Deut 12:11, 17–18). Then there are animals that one might simply want to slaughter for meat;

---

5. As Levenson, *Deuteronomy and the Hermeneutics of Legal Innovation*, 23–49, has shown, the author has carefully repeated phrases from the Exodus verse to make the two laws sound the same. Deuteronomy 12:13–15, for example, uses "in every place" three different ways. The citation makes the innovation sound as though it was an application of the old law.

these were offered as well-being sacrifices in the past. Moses alters tradition by permitting the nonsacrificial slaughter of animals in the towns and villages so that residents do not have to journey to the central shrine for a meal with meat (vv. 15, 20–21).

Other adjustments are enunciated in Deuteronomy 14–16. Tithes (14:23) of firstborn of the herd and flock are modified, and Passover is moved from the home to the sanctuary (Deuteronomy 16). Whenever worshippers live too far away from the chosen place to transport their animals, they are allowed to sell them and purchase substitutes.

Despite the importance of cultic reform for this corpus, priests are not mentioned until 18:1–8, a passage that belongs to a series of laws of offices. The priest is described as an official of a local sanctuary (vv. 1–5); then the right of the local priest to practice at the chosen place is added (vv. 6–8). The office of judge is the first mentioned (16:18–20; 17:2–13). The judges are apparently lay elders living in each Israelite settlement. When cases come before them that surpass their knowledge of the law, they are to consult a board of experts at the chosen place (17:8–13).

Deuteronomy is the only pentateuchal lawbook to make reference to a king (17:14–20). To find a place within the definition of Israel for royalty, "Moses" alludes to the people's request in 1 Samuel 8. The king is permitted but is only a figurehead (within Deuteronomy). No powers or roles are assigned him; the law only warns against abuse of power.

The prophet is also listed among the officials (18:9–22). This unit begins with a condemnation of various forms of divination for accessing the divine will (vv. 9–14). The only legitimate source of revelation is provided by God, who calls and communicates with prophets. These prophets stand in the line of Moses, mediators between the Lord and his people (vv. 15–17). The people must heed the prophet as a spokesman for God (vv. 18–19). False prophets are threatened with death (vv. 20–21); a rule is offered to the people for detecting false prophets (v. 22).

Deuteronomy is the only biblical code to systematically sketch the "constitution" of Israel. In fact, this is a rather unusual meditation within the cultural world of the ancient Near East. It is a form of reflection more characteristic of Greek philosophy. It differs substantially from the Greek models, however, in locating ultimate authority above the officials and institutions of the state; divine sovereignty puts human power in the category of obligations for which actors are accountable. Moreover, there is a "democratizing" tendency in the code's view of human power: kingship is instituted at the people's request;

farmers take responsibility for welfare as well as govern at the village level; the army is a levy of the general populace.

The last chapter of the code, Deuteronomy 26, has a number of rituals for the general populace. The last of these, vv. 16–19, read like the ritual act of ratifying the covenant (cp. Exod 19:3–8; 24:38; Deut 27:9–10). Israel has "declared this day of the Lord that he is your God" (v. 17), and the Lord "has declared you today to be his people of treasured possession" (v. 18). The next two chapters have to do with blessings and curses; chapter 28 is the most extensive list of curses in the Hebrew Bible; it is virtually identical to the conclusions of Assyrian suzerain-vassal treaties.[6]

## Divine Judgment

The book of Deuteronomy is located at the end of the wilderness period and just before the conquest of Canaan. At this moment, as Moses prepares to leave the scene, he has the experience of the judgments of Israel behind him; now he warns of judgment in the future. He has reinterpreted the judgments in the wilderness as "disciplining," but he knows that worse things can happen. At the end of the same section where he compares the judgments of God to a parent's disciplining of a child (8:5), he warns: "If you do forget the LORD your God and follow other gods . . . , I solemnly warn you today that you shall surely perish. Like the nations that the LORD is destroying before you, so shall you perish, because you would not obey the voice of the LORD your God" (8:19–20).

Warnings of this sort recur through chapters 7–11. Deuteronomy 28 goes much further: conditional curses are put into force for disobedience, while blessings are promised for obedience. The list of curses in much longer than the list of blessings, projecting prospects of unrelieved suffering. Obviously, the Deuteronomic Moses seeks to frighten his audience into renewed commitment.

To make the curses for disobedience theologically consistent, the code had to be reformulated to articulate collective responsibility for which the nation is accountable before God. Law is designed to govern the acts of individuals, families, and cities within the legal community. We can call this distributive justice. Only wrongdoers should be held accountable for their actions.

Deuteronomy endorses this principle emphatically (24:16): "The fathers shall not be put to death for the children, nor the children be put to death for the fathers; each man shall be put to death for his own sin."

---

6. Weinfeld, *Deuteronomy and the Deuteronomic School*, 116–29.

How then is the nation held responsible for the divine law? It is responsible at a rhetorical level (not by legal doctrine). Deuteronomy draws out the people's responsibility by the way it formulates the law and motivates compliance. Capital crimes, for example, are regularly formulated as addresses to the people. For example, Deut 24:7 reads, "If a man is found stealing one of his brothers . . . and treats him as a slave or sells him, then that thief will die; so you shall purge the evil from your midst." The addressee (the "you") in this formulation is the people; the criminal is referred to in the third person. The parallel provision in the Book of the Covenant is impersonal: "whoever steals a man . . . shall be put to death" (Exod 21:16). The Covenant Code formulation does not mention the community or court action.

The Deuteronomic formulation is repeated in 17:2 and 22:22, and some comparable expressions are found in 13:1–2, 6, 12; 21:18–21; cp. 22:23, 28; 24:1. One also finds the nation addressed as enforcer of the law in 19:1–13, 18:9–11; 23:18–19; cp. 12:29–31; 14:1–2.

The motive clauses attached to the collectivized legal formulations are also concerned with the good of the community. According to one legal scholar, the application of sanctions in Israelite criminal law had the purpose of "atonement" or "expiation" rather than retribution.[7] What the community "purges" itself of is the residual guilt attached to the crime. The community's relationship with God is endangered by the guilt and must be restored to health by rooting out the evildoer.[8] Whether the Hebrew word *ra'* means "guilt," or "evil" (as translated in the NRSV) is hard to say, so it is uncertain whether the community becomes guilty from an offense in its midst or is in danger of becoming guilty if the wrongdoer is not purged. If we construe the word as "evil," the execution of the criminal prevents the transfer of guilt.[9]

Another common motivation for keeping the law is what could be called the preventive force of enforcement: "And all Israel will hear and fear, and never again do any such wickedness" (Deut 13:11, etc.). Again, the appeal is to the collective good.

The judges of each locality represent the people in the administration of law. These judges were drawn from the elders of the city. In Deut 16:18–20, the

7. Preiser, "Vergeltung und Sühne im altisraelitischen Strafrecht," 7–38. Preiser has all Israelite law in mind, but his case depends chiefly on these Deuteronomic motive clauses.

8. Ibid., 35–38.

9. In the prayer over the heifer in the case of the unsolved murder, "forgiveness" is requested, but then it reads, "set not the blood (guilt) in the midst of your people" (Deut 21:8). Deut 19:10 seeks to avoid guilt by giving asylum to the innocent, making the act preventive rather than expiator.

lawgiver speaks to the people collectively in the first verse ("You shall appoint judges and officers . . ."), and then addresses these judges in vv. 19–20. The judges have become identified here with the people, so much so that their performance has collective import. When the judges are specifically addressed in the code, they are acting on behalf of the nation. In Deut 19:1–13, the people provide for cities of refuge, and the judges hear the cases that come to them. In Deut 17:8–13 and 19:15–21, the court is commanded to consult a body of legal experts in Jerusalem in cases too difficult. In 21:1–9, the court is commanded to perform a ritual to absolve the nation of guilt in the case of an unsolved murder. The court is also told to follow certain procedures to avoid ritual pollution of the land (21:22–23) and social humiliation of a wrongdoer (25:1–3).

The Deuteronomic law is the only code with rules for the militia. At the time Deuteronomy was compiled, this democratic military institution was probably being revived after having been for centuries abandoned in favor of professional troops. The militia is addressed personally in these laws (20:1–9, 10–18, 19–20; cp. 23:10–15; 25:17–19). Just as the judges represent Israel at law, the militia troops are the people at war.

The centralization of sacrificial worship had a collectivizing effect. With one national sanctuary officiated by one common set of priests, the nation was drawn together. The sole recognition of YHWH as God was the single most important law; its violation is the subject of an entire chapter of the code, viz., Deuteronomy 13. The cultic duties of the laity, on the other hand, are not collectivized; the effect of violation would affect the farmer and his family and perhaps his village, but not the nation at large.

The collectivization of law in Deuteronomy 12–26 gives a foundation for the threat of national judgment in chapter 28. It also provides a means for avoiding it. In the book of Deuteronomy we have virtually a systematic theology of covenant. The book has stamped its conception on the consciousness of biblical readers indelibly.

## Times to Come

Deuteronomy does not end with the table of curses. There are supplements in chapters 29–31. In chapter 30, the speaker no longer speaks of judgment as a possibility but as an assured occurrence. The basic stock of the book assumes that judgment is the worst thing that can happen, and there is no future for Israel afterward. Deuteronomy 30:1–10 offer a future after judgment. If the people will repent from their heart (vv. 1–2), YHWH will restore them and

## Judgments in the Wilderness

settle them on the land again (vv. 3–5). Moreover, Israel will be purged of the inclination to sin (vv. 6, 7b).

A poem has been preserved in chapter 32 that rehearses the future of the nation, including divine judgment for religious apostasy (vv. 15–27). This poem also looks forward to divine restoration after judgment (vv. 36–38). Thus one might say that the canonical book ends with provisions for going on after the initial reform fails to save the people.

I mentioned "reform" in the preceding paragraph. This leads to the subject of Josiah's Reform. King Josiah of Judah convenes an assembly of "all the elders of Judah and Jerusalem" (2 Kgs 23:1) after a manuscript found in the temple during repairs was confirmed by oracle (22:12–20) to be Mosaic. Gathered in the temple, this mass of Judeans heard the lawbook read to them by Josiah, who then entered into a covenant with the people before God to obey the provisions of the lawbook (2 Kgs 23:3). The unidentified provisions are reflected in what Josiah does to fulfill his pledge: he eliminates persons, places, and things associated with other gods (23:4–14). When he expands his territory, he follows similar policies (23:15–21). Most such actions could be a response to any pentateuchal code. However, one action points in a very definite direction: "And he brought all the priests out of the cities of Judah, and defiled the high places where the priests had burnt incense, from Geba to Beersheba" (23:8a). The only code to command elimination of all sacrificial altars but one is Deuteronomy.

Identifying Deuteronomy as the Mosaic lawbook found in the reign of Josiah and made the basis of his reform became a pillar of the Documentary Hypothesis. In 1805, a German scholar, W. M. L. De Wette, first argued the identification, which provides an absolute date (621 BCE) for publication of one part of the Pentateuch and a criterion for dating other parts.[10]

We need to recognize that this book entered the national tradition not at the time of Moses but near the end of the monarchical era. In its present form, it represents the reflection of centuries of experience and the meditation of devoted Yahwists about how to save the remnant of the nation from disaster. The roots of the book may be much earlier, and may be from the north, but it entered history at a particular time and place and shaped subsequent Israelite history decisively. More than any other lawbook, it taught Israel to understand its relationship to the Lord in terms of obedience to the will and law of their

---

10. Whatever writing is unaware of the illegitimacy of all sanctuaries but Jerusalem is earlier than Deuteronomy; whatever knows such sanctuaries to be illegitimate is later.

sovereign. It also prepared the people to live without a temple and sacrifice, although it did not originally envisage that.

The book failed to help the people avert the divine judgment of Judah known as the Babylonian exile. Exile did not lead to its disposal. Rather, the people of Judah incorporated the experience of exile in its preaching. We see this in Deut 30:1–10 and 32:1–38. Judgment is—curses are—not the last word; repentance in the light of judgment will build toward a national future.

# 7

## Possessing the Land
(Joshua, Judges)

IN THIS AND THE following chapter we return to the narrative sequence of the Primary History. Now we begin the portion of the Hebrew Bible known as the Former Prophets. This portion begins with the conquest of the Holy Land and ends with its "loss" in the Babylonian exile of the Judeans.

This first chapter concerns the accounts of taking possession of the land and living on it as a loose confederation of tribes who recognize YHWH as their God. The subject of divine judgment comes up concerning the dispossession of the indigenous inhabitants of the land, whom we will call Canaanites. Is their displacement by the Israelites divine judgment? We are also concerned about reverses to the Israelites: In what sense are these reverses divine judgment? In Judges we have a recurring pattern of apostasy–punishment–cry-of-distress–deliverance. This is obviously a depiction of divine judgment, but how are we to appreciate the rather anachronistic framing of the crises of the time?

### Overview of the Books

To start we can characterize the content of each book and conceptualize their relationship to each other. The book of Joshua narrates rituals by which the people take possession of the land. The story begins, after Joshua's commission by YHWH, with the crossing of the Jordan River and the setting of the boundary between the Holy Land proper and the "marginal" Israelite territory in Transjordan. The crossing is a divine miracle; it occurs as a part of a ritual

## Redeeming Judgment

procession with the ark followed by the people. Once they pass through the river, they erect a stone monument to remind later generations of YHWH's mighty act. As Passover approaches, all Israelite males are circumcised to remove "the disgrace of Egypt" (5:9), and then celebrate the Passover (at which time manna ceases).

An angel appears to Joshua to inaugurate the conquest of Jericho, which will be the paradigm for all conquests in Canaan. The siege is unlike any military siege: the Israelite warriors are to process around the city each day for six days; this procession will include the ark and seven priests blowing the *shophar* (ram's horn). On the seventh day the procession circumnavigates the city seven times, and then a loud shout by the whole people flattens the city (Josh 6:1–21). The only military action taken by the people is to kill survivors.[1]

This narrative invites a symbolic reading: YHWH conquers, and the people play assigned ritual roles. In Israel's confession, YHWH gives the nation its land; this account of the conquest of Jericho gives him full credit. Israel simply plays roles assigned by the Warrior God.[2]

When a contingent is sent off to attack another city, Ai, which is on the mountain ridge to the west of the Jordan Valley, they are routed (chapter 7). Joshua mourns the defeat, and is told by YHWH that an Israelite has violated covenantal law. The defeat at Ai is not divine judgment, but a warning that someone has committed a capital violation. It turns out that one Achan has plundered some valuables from the ruins of Jericho—a violation of the rule that all booty in wars of YHWH belongs to YHWH. Once he is found out, Achan and his family and livestock are stoned to death.

Once the Israelites have purged this evil from their midst, YHWH grants them victory over Ai; the inhabitants are all wiped out, according to the law of *ḥerem* (chapter 8). Now the people move on to Shechem, but not to conquer it: rather, they make an altar, inscribe a stone with the law of the covenant, and perform a ceremony of cursing and blessing. One has the impression that this covenant renewal ceremony takes possession of that area.

This is not the end of conquest through ritual. As news of the victorious invaders makes it around the land, the Gibeonites devise a ruse to avoid dispossession and extermination; they pretended to be outside invaders themselves and deceive the Israelites into an alliance. This covenant is adhered to even after it is discovered to have been made under false pretenses (chapter 10). So now Gibeon becomes Israelite territory, and when it is attacked by

---

1. And rescue Rahab and her family because this family had hidden the Israelite spies.
2. For this title, see Exod 15:3.

its erstwhile allies, the Israelites come to its aid, and together they achieve a great victory. The sun stands still so that the routed enemy troops can be killed rather than escape back to their fortified cities at night. The Israelites proceed to besiege a ring of these fortified cities in what will be Judah (chapter 10).

The final stage of this conquest takes place in the far north, at a place called "the waters of Merom." The battle is between the Israelites and a coalition of cities headed by Hazor. After routing the coalition by an ambush, Joshua destroys Hazor.

On the one hand, the book of Joshua, in sum, is not concerned to provide a realistic account of the conquest of Canaan. The narrative credits YHWH with the power to bring victory, and Israel has only to perform ritual and ritual-like roles. The book of Joshua presents a divinely staged drama. On the other hand, the account is concerned to depict the rules, so to speak, for Israel's living on this land. The men must be circumcised, the cult objects and valuables taken as booty must be destroyed as YHWH's possession. The indigenous population must be removed—by killing or emigration—so that the Israelites will not be tempted to apostasy, idolatry, and immorality.

The sites conquered do not make up a large portion of the land. Jericho, Ai, and Gibeon fall within Benjaminite territory, and the ring of cities conquered in siege warfare (Josh 10:29–43) are within Judah. These seem to represent the land. The defeat of the coalition at the waters of Merom represents the conquest of the north. Chapter 12 tallies the conquered cities and their kings; it has additional sites but still leaves out the cities of the hill country of Ephraim and Manasseh. After the list of conquests in chapter 12, the remainder of the book of Joshua is devoted to the allotment of territory to each tribe; this too is of a ritual character.

One might regard the book of Joshua as the picture of the ideal conquest, providing a symbolic memory of the conquest of the land, whereas the book of Judges is a realistic account of what happened. This, however, is simplistic. Judges 1 does begin with an account of the conquest of a couple of tribes' territory by the tribes concerned, but then the text becomes a list of allotted areas not conquered.[3] This does not explain how the tribes planted stakes in their territories, but does explain why Israelites were living side by side with non-Israelites, as they are depicted doing in the rest of Judges. Judg 2:3 announces that this incomplete conquest is divine judgment. A similar judgment is pronounced in 2:21. The indigenous people are a "testing" of the loyalty of

---

3. There is one anecdote about Ephraim's conquest: its conquest of Bethel (1:22–26). It doesn't represent a serious effort to account for that tribe's possession of its territory.

Israelites as well (3:4). One must realize that the incompleteness of the initial conquest seems to cast aspersions on YHWH's potency; these oracles tracing the perseverance of non-Israelites on the land were designed to assuage doubts.

Beginning in Judges 3, the narrative switches from the tribes and nation to heroic individual military leaders. We hear the stories of Ehud, Deborah and Barak, Gideon, Jephthah and Samson. Each leads tribes to military victory over non-Israelites, though Samson's story is more individualistic and does not end in victory. The book of Judges also preserves some old lists (10:1–5, 12:8–15), a story of an abortive effort to establish a monarchy over Shechem and surrounding territory (chapter 9), and two accounts of events demonstrating the anarchy that encompassed Israel before the establishment of monarchy (Judges 17–18; 19–21).

In Judges we do not find an account of any conquest except Judah and Rueben, but glimpses of life during the first couple centuries of settled life. Judges is not saturated with ritual, though there are rituals depicted here and there. The book provides a framework for these accounts that will challenge our hermeneutical dexterity.

## Is the Conquest of Canaan a Judgment of God on the Canaanites?

Several passages in the Pentateuch answer the question in the affirmative, claiming that these peoples are being judged for their sin. Deut 9:4–5, for example, insists that Israel is being given the land, not because it deserves it, but because the Canaanites have aroused God's wrath: "It is not because of your righteousness or the uprightness of your heart that you are going to occupy their land; but because of the wickedness of these nations that the Lord your God is dispossessing them before you to fulfill the promise that the Lord made on oath to your ancestors" (Deut 9:5).

A convergence has occurred between God's decision to fulfill the promise at this time and his judgment of the sinful nations. Gen 15:16 also speaks of the timetable of the conquest depends on the "iniquity of the Amorites" being "complete." Leviticus 18:24–25, finally, speaks of the inhabitants' wickedness as the reason for their expulsion: "Do not defile yourselves in any of the [listed] ways, for by all these practices the nations that I am casting out before you have defiled themselves. Thus the land became defiled; and I punished it for its iniquity, and the land vomited out its inhabitants." In this passage, the concept of purity is operative; the sexual immoralities practiced by the Canaanites brought a (spiritual) contamination on the land, and as if it were a natural process the inhabitants are to be "vomited." The reference to the wickedness of the Canaanites is backing for the exhortation.

Several other Deuteronomic passages imply divine judgment. Deuteronomy 12:30 warns the Israelites against imitating the previous inhabitants. Their practices were abhorrent (v. 31)—including child sacrifice. Deuteronomy 18:9 has an identical warning; the passage lists, along with child sacrifice, a host of forms of divination. "It is because of such abhorrent practices that the Lord your God is driving them out before you" (18:12).

If we were in a trial concerning the guilt of the Canaanites, we would have to be careful not to judge their actions by laws revealed to Israel. The Canaanites had not been forbidden from worshipping many gods and relating to those gods through images. They had not been forbidden divination and the sexual practices mentioned in Leviticus 18. For the Canaanites to be accountable, and subject to divine judgment, it must be for moral and religious violations of norms common to ancient societies.[4]

Most of the acts condemned in these judgment texts violate uniquely Israelite norms, and can only be condemned within the covenant community. We cannot sustain the case against the Canaanites, unless child sacrifice alone is deserving of extermination. I think that we should concede that the texts are designed to persuade—to warn Israelites to avoid said practices, and that is legitimate. The audience is under divine law, and warnings not to imitate the previous inhabitants and outsiders are cogent.

Deuteronomy 9:4–5 should be read as a warning against Israelite pride in its righteousness. The Canaanites and Israelites are equally prone to wickedness. If the Canaanites are being judged, that's between them and God. The Israelites have no business inferring their own virtue from their good fortune: this is God's gift, and Israel had better avoid arousing his wrath and losing the land for its sin.

## Treatment of Defeated Peoples

There is another argument for the expulsion of the previous inhabitants. One set of biblical passages warns against making peace with the inhabitants and

---

4. The condemnation for child sacrifice would probably be found on the list of proscriptions common to ancient humans. Those religions that sanctioned child sacrifice probably deserve condemnation.

becoming caught up in their worship, viz., Exod 23:20–33; 34:11–16; and Deut 7:1–16. Each of these promises the power to conquer these people despite their superior military power. The danger is that Israel will spare them, even assimilate with them: "you must utterly destroy them. Make no covenant with them and show them no mercy. Do not intermarry with them, giving your daughters to their sons or taking their daughters for your sons, for that would turn away your children from following me [sic], to serve other gods. The anger of the Lord would be kindled against you, and he would destroy you quickly" (Deut 7:2–4). YHWH's commitment to Israel is evidently so strong that he is willing to sacrifice justice to Israel's enemies. If they practice their own religion and morality, and they meet up to its standards adequately, they should be able to live in peace. However, they are in the way of YHWH's plans for his people, so the indigenous population must be exterminated.

One might also raise the concept of purity. The predecessors of the Israelites lived on the land according to a "natural" religion and morality and law, and did not violate it so badly that they contaminated the land. However, their actions would contaminate it once it had been settled by the chosen people. Again it would seem that divine justice must be abrogated for the sake of the elect people.

We might draw a parallel to model the issue. Conservative religious people often favor suppressing the sources of temptation. Laws against pornography are a good example. These laws are designed to keep sexually explicit material out of the hands of minors, who are thought to lack self-control. Liberals have tended to oppose restrictions, or at least have sought to keep them to a minimum.

Of course, a secular, pluralistic society is bound to leave the enforcement of particularistic norms to the groups concerned, allowing the rest to do as they please as long as they do not encroach on others. Ancient Israel does not aspire to be a society of that sort; it has the calling of glorifying God. The covenant is expected to sustain a society with one religion, one morality, one law. While it is difficult to justify the expulsion and annihilation of the Canaanites, its ideal can certainly meet the test of legitimacy.

Finally, we should remember that many passages speaking about the conquest do not make any reference to the wickedness of the Canaanites, or to the policy of eliminating temptation. When the Lord calls Moses, he promises "to bring [the people] up out of [Egypt] to a good and broad land, a land of milk and honey, to the place of the Canaanites, the Hittites," and the like (Exod 3:8). When Joshua and Caleb try to persuade the Israelites not to act desperately, they say, "'If the Lord is pleased with us, he will bring us into this land and give it to us, a land that flows with milk and honey. Only, do not rebel against the Lord; and do not fear the people of the land, for they are no more than bread for us; their protection is removed from them, and the Lord is with us'" (Num 14:8–9). Not a word surfaces in either of these passages about the guilt of the inhabitants. Likewise, a passage in Psalm 44 looks back to the conquest, a time when the Lord was favorable to Israel:

> thou with thy own hand didst drive out the nations,
> but them thou didst plant;
> thou didst afflict the peoples,
> but them thou didst set free. (44:2, RSV)

The Lord's favor was a boon to Israel that could not be rationalized.[5]

## Judgment of Achan

The initial assault on Ai ends in a rout of the Israelite contingent (7:2–15). According to the doctrine of the war of YHWH, no one should be able to defeat the Israelite army, even when it is outnumbered and poorly armed. Hence, there is great consternation over this reversal. A revelation explains to Joshua that someone has violated the practice of *ḥerem* (7:16–21). This Hebrew word is often translated "ban," but in these texts it designates the status of movables, livestock, and persons belonging to a conquered city: they are to be destroyed. If an Israelite appropriates anything designated for destruction, he has committed a capital offense.[6] So when Achan is discovered to have appropriated valuable objects from Jericho, he and his whole family, and even his livestock, are stoned to death (7:22–26). This is a case of collective judgment, but it extends only to the person and what he "rules."[7]

When the military unit is defeated by Ai's defenders, the Israelites are not being judged for Achan's crime; rather, they are being warned that an offense

---

5. Many peoples have a story similar to Israel's—about the displacement of a previous population. This is theft when individuals do it. Peoples tend to ignore the moral prohibitions when people are being driven from their land. It is left to later generations to deal with the guilt, as Americans must with the "Indians." I have coined the term "creative injustice" to cover conquests of this sort. It doesn't claim justice for such takeovers, but it attempts to be realistic about the common course of history.

6. This may be due to "contamination" or for violation of a divine commandment.

7. Regarding the principle of ruler punishment, see Daube, *Studies in Biblical Law*, 154–86.

*Redeeming Judgment*

has taken place. If they do not apprehend the offender and confirm his guilt, the warning will become the initial judgment.[8] The execution of the offender and his family and livestock is an example of purging evil from the midst of the people (e.g., Deut 13:5).

Can the execution of Achan be justified? He commits theft, but that crime does not bring the death penalty in Israelite law. It is the status of the objects stolen that arouses the divine wrath. They are in some sense sacred, though not temple property.[9] Something about the stolen objects must have communicated contamination to everyone and everything within the orbit of the thief.

It should be noted that the practice of *ḥerem* is old and not distinctively Israelite.[10] It is reported by Mesha, the Moabite king, on the stone celebrating his victory over Israel and confiscation of some Transjordanian territory.[11] In this case it is the god Chemosh who requires it. The rationale is probably similar. Although Israel knows of the practice through divine revelation, it should be classified as a natural norm in ancient Near Eastern religion.[12]

Its use in our conquest literature has been rationalized. Now it is a way of eliminating temptation. Perhaps the practice now does merit the status of revealed law. Nevertheless, it is a problematic rule; it clashes with current moral reasoning. Some theologians have proposed that it be classified as a case of the "teleological suspension of the ethical," a category devised by Søren Kierkegaard.[13] That proposal seems to be questionable, though; for the type of "ethnic cleansing" of which we are speaking serves the good of the perpetrator, whereas Abraham's offering of his son (Kierkegaard's example) does not.

We are back where we were before: the policy of killing (or expelling) non-Israelites to protect the holy people from temptation or contamination cannot be justified. Achan is certainly wrong for stealing banned goods, but not guilty of a capital crime. We are dealing with a practice that once seemed natural and justified but in retrospect does not.

---

8. Cp. David in 2 Sam. 21:1–7. Also Sophocles's *Oedipus the King* begins with a plague and an oracle warning the people of a crime.

9. We have no laws in Scripture making theft of temple property a capital crime, but that is certainly known in the ancient Near East, e.g., see chapter 6, above.

10. Compare Barr's discussion in Barr, *Biblical Faith and Natural Theology*, 156–73.

11. Mesha Stelle, printed in Pritchard, *Ancient Near Eastern Texts*, 320–21. Note the report in 2 Kgs. 1:1.

12. This is a case of a practice shared across ancient cultures, which would not meet the standards of natural law as interpreted in medieval philosophy.

13. Kierkegaard, *Fear and Trembling; Repetition*, 1–123.

## Recurring Judgment and Deliverance: The Book of Judges

The book of Judges begins with what appears to be an alternate version of the conquest, in which the tribes act on their own or in coalition. Judah is chosen by YHWH to go first, and it recruits Simeon to join it (Judg 1:1–3). There follow some reports and anecdotes of the conquest of various cities within their tribal territory (1:4–8). Beginning with v. 19 the topic of the account changes from what was conquered to what could not be: "And the Lord was with Judah, and he took possession of the hill country, but he could not drive out the inhabitants of the plain." Except for the anecdote in vv. 22–26, the rest of the text of Judges 1 is a report of failure or incompleteness. Thus, the chapter turns out not to be an alternate version of the conquest from Joshua, but a transition from conquest to the next period, when the Israelite tribes live alongside other ethnic groups and come into conflict with them periodically.

In Judges the tribes are settled and come into conflict with others; they protect themselves against the efforts of others to rule them or to pilfer their food stocks. Ehud challenges the Moabite ruler who is in control of some Israelite territory (Judg 3:12–30). Deborah and Barak seek to overthrow a king or coalition of kings who dominate the trade routes across the Plain of Megiddo (Judges 4–5). Gideon seeks to stop the annual raids of desert tribes who are after the food stocks of farming communities (Judges 6–8). Jephthah seeks to stop Ammonite expansion in Transjordan (Judges 11–12).

Judgment plays a salient role in the book of Judges, but not quite where we would expect it. The stories are not, with one exception, of sin and punishment; rather, we have accounts of deliverance from oppression and suffering.[14] Judgment is offered as an explanation for the oppression and suffering from which the "judges" deliver the people of Israel. This constitutes a cyclical pattern that frames the stories in chapters 3 through 16.

Each of the stories of deliverance in Judges is introduced with a formulaic account of how the people are being punished for their sin.[15] Let's take the introduction to the whole series, which is the most loquacious of them all, 2:11–23. It starts with a loosely worded charge of disobedience and apostasy: "And the people of Israel did what was evil in the sight of the Lord and served

---

14. An example of a story of sin not punished is Judg 8:24–27. The account ends, "and all Israel played the harlot after [the ephod] (in Ophrah), and it became a snare to Gideon and to his family." We are never told the story of what happened.

15. The transitional statements are: 3:7–9, 11 (Othniel); 3:12, 15, 30 (Ehud); 4:1–3, 5:31b (Deborah and Barak ); 6:1–2, 7–8; 8:33–35 (Gideon); 10:6–16; 12:7 (Jephthah); 13:1; 16:31 (Samson).

the Baals; they forsook the Lord, the God of their fathers, who brought them out of the land of Egypt; they went after other gods, from among the gods of the peoples who were round about them; and they provoked the Lord to anger" (vv. 11–12, RSV). Their sin prompted divine punishment: "He gave them over to plunderers . . . He sold them into the hand of their enemies round about . . . Whenever they marched out, the hand of the Lord was against them for evil" (vv. 14–15). Then the Lord relents and sends a deliverer: "Then the Lord raised up judges, who saved them from the hand of those who plundered them . . . Whenever the Lord raised up judges for them, the Lord was with the judge, and he saved them from the hand of their enemies all the days of the judge; for the Lord was moved to pity by their groaning . . . But whenever the judge died, they turned back and behaved worse than their fathers" (vv. 16, 18–19).

Note that this passage, like the transitional statements, is in the voice of the narrator. There are several passages that are placed in the mouth of the Lord. For example, the Lord's angel condemns the people for failing to drive out the native populations of Canaan (Judg 2:1–3). The judgment the people suffer is that the peoples will tempt Israelites to apostasy (vv. 4–5). In another, a nameless prophet is sent to the people to explain to them why the Lord has punished them with Midianite raiders (6:7–10): they have betrayed YHWH for the "gods of the Amorites." The Lord directly delivers, in a third example, a message to the people, which elicits their confession of sin and ritual putting aside of idols (10:10–16).

These accusations of Israel have a prophetic-speech form. Juxtaposed to Israel's offense is the Lord's gracious deed of delivering Israel from Egyptian slavery. This "contrast motif"[16] confronts the people with the contradiction in their behavior, their ingratitude to the Lord. This contradiction requires resolution—punishment. In Judges, Israel's punishment is always suffering at the hands of an enemy.

## Observations

Now it is time to step back and reflect on the significance of this framework. I once was rather contemptuous of it—it was so artificial and stereotyped. I wondered how a book with such well-wrought narratives could be stitched together so clumsily. Once I thought about the pattern as rhetoric, however, I realized its artificiality and triteness make the teaching memorable. In other

---

16. The nomenclature and its description come from Westermann, *Basic Forms of Prophetic Speech*, 142–60.

words, it inscribes on the readers' minds the pattern of sin and judgment that is going to be used in more subtle ways later on in the history. If the stories simply began with Israel's suffering from aggression by its neighbors, readers will not ask why God had caused it or allowed it to happen. Our narrator makes us think behind the story to the Lord of history.

The use of the contrast motif, borrowed from prophecy, may also be meant to prick readers into recalling the prophetic message from later centuries. These stories in Judges are Israel's history in miniature. It is striking that a prophet actually does appear to deliver the message on one occasion (Judg 6:7–10). The next time prophets appear, they bear a much different message (1 Samuel 2, 3). It will not be until the end of 1 Kgs (19:15–18) that one hears anything like it.[17] Readers of Judges are being led to telescope history, to collapse the centuries, to think of the divine judgment of exile.

## *Joshua's Warning*

The sin and judgment of the period of Judges is the object of Joshua's warning. At the end of the book of Joshua, there are two narratives of a farewell speech by the leader of the tribes during the period of conquest. Evidently Joshua 23 is designed to condition the reading of the much more memorable Joshua 24. In chapter 23, Joshua reminds the people of the victories that occurred on his watch, and urges them to obey YHWH and continue the conquest. If they leave pockets of non-Israelites, they will become friends, spouses, coreligionists, and end up losing their distinctiveness: "they shall be a snare and a trap for you, a scourge on your sides, and thorns in your eyes, till you perish from this good land which the Lord your God has given you" (23:13). A similar warning, with a stronger bite, can be found in Joshua 24: "Joshua said to the people: 'You cannot serve the Lord; for He is a holy God; He is a jealous God; He will not forgive your transgressions or your sins. If you forsake the Lord and serve foreign gods, then He will turn and do you harm, and consume you, after having done you good'" (24:19–20). This warning comes after Joshua has recited the Lord's gracious deeds for this people and challenged them to follow him in taking ownership of this God (24:2–15). The people persist in their decision, and the "covenant" is ratified (24:21–28).

The warning of judgment seems to point to the Assyrian and Babylonian exiles, but the judgments that occur in the two centuries after Joshua's death

---

17. Actually, we don't read a prophecy of communal judgment with a contrast motif in the Deuteronomistic history, though we do read a generalized form in 2 Kings 17.

are good candidates as well. The difference between the early judgments and the later exiles is that the cyclical pattern of Judges does not endanger the continuation of the people of YHWH, whereas the two exiles do. We are probably meant to read the judgments of Judges as warnings and foreshadowing of things to come

The indictment of the Israelites for apostasy, i.e., for defecting to Baal (and Asherah), is itself anachronistic. The author of the framework has a more developed view of the first commandment than the people in the period of the Judges. The story of Gideon has him destroy his father's Baal altar and Asherah pole, and build an altar for YHWH in their place. Gideon was to consecrate this altar with a sacrifice of the animal used to pull it down (6:25–26). He does the deed at night to avoid a confrontation with those who worship at the Baal altar (v. 27). They are angry when they find it destroyed in the morning, and threaten to execute Gideon. His father, Joash, defends his son: Let Baal defend his own interests. If he doesn't, then he is proven to be powerless. That is the way that the matter is left.

Note that the question for these people is, who is the most potent deity? Indeed, they probably think that it is best to keep on the good side of every deity they know of. They probably cannot imagine the possibility that worshipping Baal and Asherah would incur guilt before YHWH. The author knows that violation of the first commandment incurs guilt, but the people in his story do not.

## The Debate over Kingship

The question of whether the people of God should be ruled by a monarch emerges in the period of the judges. It makes its initial appearance at the end of Gideon's career. After Gideon demonstrates his divine calling and effectiveness in ending the Midianite raids, the Israelites said to him, "'Rule over us, you and your son and your grandson also; for you have delivered us out of the hand of Midian.' Gideon said to them, 'I will not rule over you, and my son will not rule over you; the Lord will rule over you'" (8:22–23). The prospect of kingship is put in a negative light from the outset. Having a human king seems to be analogous to apostasy. This understanding is made much more explicit in 1 Samuel 8 and 12.[18]

---

18. For some reason, Gideon initiates the making of some sort of image from the gold taken as booty. The narrator comments, "Gideon made an ephod of it and put it in his town, Ophrah; and all Israel prostrated themselves to it there and it became a snare to Gideon and his family" (8:27). It sounds strange that one so cognizant of the implications of YHWH's

Although Gideon declines the offer of kingship, his son Abimelech does usurp power over Shechem and reign for a short time.[19] The story of Abimeleh's abortive effort is told in Judges 9. It too is very negative toward monarchy. A parable is told at the outset that suggests that those who desire to be king are like briars, useless and parasitic. The action of the story is of reaping the consequences of the treachery one has sown. It is a story of judgment, but God is hidden entirely from view.

Rather surprisingly, the case *for* monarchy is made in the last two accounts in the book of Judges. The narrator of Judges 17–18 and 19–21 makes the viewpoint rather explicit: "in those days there was no king in Israel; all of the people did what was right in their own eyes" (Judg 17:6; 21:25). The first of the stories traces the making of an ephod, and how it and the priest who is recruited to watch over it end in the tribal sanctuary at Dan. Although it is a story with subtle humor, it does depict a lawless, religiously heterodox era. The second narrative ends with a war by the tribes on Benjamin for a crime committed by the men of Gibeah. This is divine judgment, and the people lament: "LORD, God of Israel, why has it come to pass that today there should be one tribe lacking in Israel?" (21:3).

The period of Judges comes to an end when the last judge, Samuel, retires. In 1 Samuel 8, the people request that Samuel, and YHWH, set up a king—actually an institution of kingship—to replace him. "The elders of Israel . . . said to [Samuel], 'Behold, you are old and your sons do not walk in your ways; now appoint for us a king to govern us like all the nations'" (1 Sam 8:4–5). Samuel does not approve of their request, but YHWH resigns himself to their desire: "they have not rejected you [Samuel], but they have rejected me from being king over them" (v. 7). Then YHWH recalls the past: when he was being gracious to them, they were betraying him. We have here an extension of the "contrast motif," the prophetic form so common in Judges. When Samuel does step down as judge, he once more recites the Lord's gracious deeds of salvation, beginning with the call of Moses and Aaron and including the judgments and deliverances during the era of the Judges (12:6–11). This speech concludes with reconciliation between YHWH, Samuel, king and people (12:12–15, 19–25).

---

claims to sovereignty should so thoughtlessly engage in idolatry. Perhaps he thought that having YHWH as king needed some visible sign of his existence.

19. The Judges account has Gideon offered kingship over all Israel, but the story of Abimelech envisages rule over a city and surrounding villages. That is much more realistic.

## Wrap-Up

We asked several questions at the beginning of this chapter, and we can sum up by reviewing the answers. Was the conquest of Canaan divine judgment on the indigenous population? While there are passages that assert as much, none makes a compelling argument for the guilt of the Canaanites. When specific charges are made, few are for crimes condemned by the common or natural law. Aside from child sacrifice, which continues to tempt Israelites and their neighbors, the violations the indigenous population in Canaan is alleged to commit are not known to be wrong. Rather, they are prohibited only to Israel by divine (revealed) law.

The passages about the conquest are not designed to prove the guilt of the Canaanites but to warn the Israelite population that imitating them would mean their downfall. The dispossession of the Canaanites has been an example for those charged with instructing and motivating the laity.

The accounts of punishment for Israelite violation of the *herem* have the same function. Achan's appropriation of booty leads to a defeat in battle and to the execution of the offender, his family, and livestock. That example underscores the severity of the law. Israel cannot afford to be lax about the sacred. It would be difficult to defend the severity of this punishment by contemporary moral standards, but ancient societies accorded holiness much greater deference.

If the conquest of Canaan is not divine judgment for crimes all humans should recognize, then there is no rational justification for the conquest. That is, it is impossible to justify the divine promise of Canaan and its fulfillment before a neutral judge. Only those who recognize YHWH's authority to grant and withdraw territorial possession would acknowledge its legitimacy. Even then, we would have to ask whether "the Judge of all the earth" is acting "rightly" by arbitrarily withdrawing the Canaanites' right to the land and giving it to the Israelites (Gen 18:25).

According to Gary Anderson, "Israel's claim to the land is of a supernatural order."[20] Even when Israel is in exile, it has a claim on the land of Canaan. Anderson, speaking as a Christian, believes that we must renounce supersessionism: "the promises of scripture are indeed inviolable and . . . Israel's attachment to this land is underwritten by God's providential decree."[21] In other words, Israel's eternal claim to Canaan cannot be justified by secular rational-

---

20. Anderson, "Does the Promise Still Hold?" 22. He is expounding Uriel Simon.
21. Ibid., 24.

ity, but it must be recognized by anyone who recognizes the God of Israel, the Father of Jesus Christ, as true God.[22]

We must qualify our acknowledgement, however. We cannot appeal to divine promises to overrule the principles of justice that guide our political decisions. God's promise has not meant that Israel's presence in the land will be continuous and without interruption. Only in the messianic age, the Tanakh promises, will Israel's settlement in the land be secure and final.[23]

Against Anderson's position would be the thinking of the Palestinian Christian theologian Naim Ateek. He speaks for the inhabitants of the land who are dispossessed, because this has been his experience in the twentieth century. If we use the "mind of Christ" as the norm of Christian theology, we would never sanction the dispossession of anyone for the sake of the people of God.[24] Ateek compares the modern state of Israel to Ahab and Jezebel, who engineer the judicial murder of Naboth to obtain his land.[25] I think Ateek would interpret the gift of the land as coming provided that it become a refuge for the oppressed, a pilgrimage site for all who revere the God of Israel and Father of Jesus Christ.

The cogency of these two opposing positions, and the alternatives to both of them,[26] make any simple justification of the conquest uncertain. No secular justification is possible; one must recognize the God of Israel to find the promise valid. However, one must also be careful not to violate the demands of justice in affirming God's gracious election of Israel.

Now let's turn to Judges: How does divine judgment manifest itself in this book? The framework speaks constantly of sin and judgment. The narrator accuses the people of apostasy to Baal and the other gods worshipped by neighboring peoples. This arouses the wrath of YHWH, who delivers them into the hands of enemies. When they cry to YHWH out of their distress, he sends a judge, or deliverer. This framework serves the literary purpose of weaving the narratives of apostasy and deliverance together, and of explaining why the people suffer a particular scourge. The framework is probably designed to provide a proper understanding of the troubles of their own time, and the exiles of Israel and Judah above all.

---

22. What political implications we draw from this are of another order.
23. Anderson, "Does the Promise Still Hold?" 23.
24. Ateek, *Justice and Only Justice*, 92–114.
25. Ibid., 86–89.
26. The *Christian Century* (January 2009), 25–29, published three responses to Anderson, from Walter Brueggemann, Martin Jeschke, and Donald Wagner.

*Redeeming Judgment*

Finally in the course of the Deuteronomstic history we encounter the issue of kingship. While in the book of Judges only the story of Abimlech's effort at monarchy can be said to entail divine judgment on Israelites for usurping the kingship of YHWH, the issue comes to a head in 1 Samuel. Moreover, the final five chapters of Judges offer the promonarchical perspective on political order. The exercise of royal power will be the primary focus of divine judgment in the next era of the people's history.

# 8

# The Judgment of Kings
(1–2 Samuel, 1–2 Kings)

THE NARRATIVE OF 1 Samuel follows smoothly from that of Judges. The issue of whether Israel is to continue to be ruled by YHWH through directly chosen charismatic leaders or to be under a divinely elected king or dynasty of kings continues to drive the narrative. The issue comes to a head in 1 Samuel 8–12, but the permanency of the monarchy is not settled until David's reign (2 Samuel).

The act of judgment from now on is a divine pronouncement uttered by a prophet. Prophets are spokesmen for YHWH, "messengers" who are authorized to formulate God's word to individuals and the nation. They are not themselves leaders or rulers, as Moses and Joshua were; their task is to convey messages to the people in power, whose insider status makes them too self-interested to be a conduit of the divine word.

We have a series of these prophets in 1–2 Samuel, 1 Kings, and 2 Kings 1–10.[1] They exhibit courage and receptivity to the divine perspective, forging an office that the classical prophets later fill with distinction. The series of prophets of judgment against rulers ends when the eighth-century prophets make their appearance about 750 BCE, though the last prophet to pronounce judgment on a king, Elijah, does so a century earlier.

---

1. 2 Kings 13:4 may allude to Elisha, but there is no explicit mention of that prophet after 2 Kgs 9:1.

## Critical History

Readers may well wonder how trustworthy these accounts of prophets are. That is first of all a question of our sources. The theory that one historian, called the Deuteronomistic historian (Dtr), writing in the exile, assembled the narrative from Deuteronomy through the Former Prophets is sound.[2] However, I think that this author should not be credited with the bulk of the narratives of 1–2 Samuel and 1–2 Kings; rather, he assembles and frames preexisting works. One large work is the story of the rise of the monarchy, beginning with the birth of Samuel (1 Samuel 1) and ending with the ascension of Solomon to the throne (1 Kings 2). The Elijah narratives in 1 Kings 17–19 make up a cycle, but the judgments of Ahab (1 Kings 21) and Ahaziah (2 Kings 1) sound like accounts from a different hand. The story of Jehu's rebellion (2 Kings 9–10) is a finely wrought narrative from the era.[3]

Just how accurate these and other prophetic narratives are is not a concern in this study. What we have are accounts that address rhetorical exigencies of the time represented; they have been incorporated into a history of the monarchy that ends with the exiles of Israel and Judah. Thus, we have a dual perspective in each case, and exegesis must take cognizance of this fact.

### Form Criticism

Oracles of judgment prove to be very prominent in the interchange between prophets and kings. These oracles are introduced by the *messenger formula,* "Thus says the LORD." The body of the message states what we might call the *indictment* of the royal addressee, followed by the *sentence* for the specified offense. Since the divine Judge already knows the guilt of the addressee, the message is the decision that has already been arrived at. The prophet may augment this message with persuasive language meant to elicit the addressee's admission of guilt or his contrition, and the sentence may be modified according to the addressee's response.

The narratives of these prophecies of judgment against individuals have their own rhetorical import. I have called them *forensic narration.* They are designed to persuade readers that the addressee is guilty and YHWH righteous

---

2. A good case can be made for two editions of this work—one from the time of Josiah's reform, and the other from the exile.

3. I am aware a very elaborate genetic scheme has been worked out for most of these accounts, but we need not follow the fragmenting type of scholarship they represent.

in his judgments.[4] The narratives belong to the time when the prophecy was delivered, when readers needed to be persuaded of the guilt of their ruler.

## The Accounts of the Founding of the Monarchy

During the monarchy the power to rule was concentrated in one person, though we must realize that ancient kings did not exercise the degree of control of citizen life that a modern government, even a democracy, with its extensive bureaucracy and technological apparatus, does. The king commanded the army, conducted foreign policy, and guarded internal peace and order.

The period of the judges—which purportedly lasted for several centuries—had been very decentralized; charismatic leaders were raised up to meet crises, but when the battle was over, they retired from public authority. According to the last five chapters of the book of Judges, power was so diffuse that it could be called anarchy: "all the people did what was right in their own eyes" (Judg 17:6).

In the biblical narrative the problem posed by royal power is less its extension, its systematic control of the lives of citizens, than its arbitrary exercise. There were no checks and balances in ancient monarchies.[5] In Israel, the prophets were to check the king. When a ruler misbehaved in the exercise of his office, a prophet representing YHWH's transcendent sovereignty intervened to enforce divine law and justice.

There are two competing versions of the founding of the monarchy interwoven in 1 Samuel 8–15. According to the one we meet first, the people of Israel request a king, "that we also may be like other nations, and that our king may govern us and go out before us and fight our battles" (1 Sam 8:20). The expressed desire to be "like other nations" is blameworthy in the mouth of a people who were called to be different. Samuel and the Lord take the request as a rejection of theocracy mediated by judge-prophets like Samuel. The Lord actually accedes to the people's request after they have been warned (1 Sam 8:11–18).

There is a "promonarchical" account as well. According to it, Samuel secretly anoints Saul as chieftain (Heb. *nagîd*) and encourages him to act when the Spirit comes upon him (1 Sam 9:1–10:16). He acts to assemble a militia from all the tribes when he hears of the Ammonite king's ultimatum to the cit-

---

4. See Patrick and Scult, *Rhetoric and Biblical Interpretation*, 57–79.
5. Of course, the army, city rulers, vassals, priests, etc., might well have restrained kings in practice.

*Redeeming Judgment*

izens of Jabesh-Gilead (1 Samuel 11). The Israelite levy under Saul attacks and routs the Ammonites, and as a result the people declare Saul king (11:12–15).

Given the antimonarchical attitude of 1 Samuel 12, one might expect that declaring Saul king would lead to judgment, but in fact the chapter works out a compromise. It reports Samuel's retirement speech. Though the institution of kingship displeases the Lord, who demonstrates this with a thunderstorm (12:16–18), he has been active in choosing a chieftain who will deliver the people from their foes (9:16; 10:1), and he pledges to remain loyal to the people despite their rebellion against him (12:19–24). As the text says, "'the Lord will not cast away his people, for his great name's sake, because it has pleased the Lord to make you a people for himself'" (12:22). The prophets—Samuel and those who come after him—will intercede for the people and king as well as convey God's word to them.

## Judgments Pronounced by Prophets

Since the monarchy originates at the initiative of YHWH, or at least at his favorable response to the people's request, the prophets of YHWH have the Lord's authority to indict a king for wrongdoing and to impose a sentence for his deeds. The prophet intervenes to impose justice where a human court fears to tread. We might speak of "royal immunity" because no human court would have the temerity to judge a king. The prophet compensates for this deficiency in the legal system. The divine intervention to judge a king or high official[6] is an act of grace to the people in that it purges evil from its midst.[7] Prophets even act to modify the institution to correct it. In one case a prophet precipitates the division of the Davidic monarchy into two kingdoms, and in several others prophets spark coups against the reigning dynasty.

For what sort of wrongdoing do prophets condemn kings? We can answer this question in the following exposition of judgments in the books of Samuel and Kings. So let us now turn to those passages.

### *The "Impeachment" of the House of Eli*

The first judgment to be pronounced in the history of the monarchy is not against a king but against a priestly dynasty associated with the ark. This could

---

6. We have accounts of judgment of nonroyal figures: 1 Samuel 2; Amos 7:10–17; Isa 22:15–25; Jer 20:1–6.

7. A formula in Deuteronomy: see Patrick, "The Rhetoric of Collective Responsibility."

be considered the closing of the curtain on the old order, for the house of Eli was a family tracing its election back to the exodus (1 Sam 2:27–28). Their occupation of the prestigious office came to an end when Solomon banished Abiathar from the Jerusalem temple at the beginning of his reign (1 Kgs 2:26–27).

The oracle against the house of Eli is located in 1 Sam 2:27–36. The forensic narrative portraying the offenses that lead to their tale of woe is told in 1 Sam 2:12–17 and 22–25. The sons of Eli have been violating the customary procedure for procuring the priestly share of each "peace offering" (*shalomim*).[8] The offerers take offense at the priests' boorish behavior (see 2:15–17). It is also said that Eli's sons have sexual intercourse with the "serving women" of the shrine at Shiloh (2:22), but this is too isolated a statement to evaluate. Eli is not himself an offender, but his effort to restrain his sons is ineffective (2:23–25).

The oracle is delivered by an anonymous "man of God" (2:27).[9] He begins with a recitation of YHWH's favor toward the house of Eli (2:27–28), which is contrasted to the behavior of the addressee and his heirs (2:29). The promise to the house has been cancelled because the younger generation is irresponsible (2:30). The way they will be removed from office is by the death of Eli's two sons, Hophni and Phinehas, on the battlefield, bearing the ark in a war against the Philistines (2:34). Some of Eli's grandchildren will survive to fall later (vv. 31–32). A great-grandchild will live to be removed from office, with another dynasty (Zadok's) assuming sole authority over the Jerusalem temple (2:33, 35–36).

Obviously the sentence of this prophecy has been expanded in the light of what happened. This expansion integrates the family's history into the larger story of Israel, particularly into the political story. The process of expansion and integration occurs again and again with prophetic narratives.

Another interesting turn is taken in 1 Samuel 3. Already in chapter 2 we have the story of Samuel's progress juxtaposed to the offensive behavior of Eli's sons (cp. 2:11, 18–21, 26). In chapter 3, we read of Samuel's nighttime call to prophecy. His first message is of judgment upon the house of Eli: "'Behold, I am about to do something in Israel that will make both ears of everyone who hears it tingle. On the day I will fulfill against Eli all that I have spoke concerning his house'" (3:11–12). Samuel's message is a powerful reenforcement of the prophecy of judgment spoken by an anonymous prophet.

---

8. This term doesn't translate well. Often it is now translated "well-being" offering, which makes more sense than "peace." It is the type of sacrifice whose flesh was eaten. According to our text, the meat was cooked by boiling, but Eli's sons would prefer to roast or fry it.

9. It is unusual for the prophet to go unnamed; besides our passage only 1 Kgs 20:35–43 has that happen, but the actual actor in 2 Kgs 9:1–11 is unnamed.

## Redeeming Judgment

### Samuel's Condemnations of Saul

Three oracles of judgment are pronounced by Samuel against Saul, viz., 1 Sam 13:8–15; 15:1–35; and 28:8–19. In the last, Samuel speaks from the dead. The other two are from the period after Samuel's retirement from the office of judge, when he adopts a rather solicitous attitude toward the new order. He becomes the defender of the emerging office of prophet as the counterweight to the king. Both judgments of Saul concern the authority of the prophet to command the king.

The first, 1 Sam 13:8–15, is rather laconic, but we can reconstruct what is at issue. Samuel has commanded Saul not to sacrifice at Gilgal after his victory over the Ammonites (cp. 1 Sam 10:8). However, after waiting seven days, and having potential fighters depart, he proceeds to offer sacrifices (13:8–10a). Samuel arrives as he finishes, and condemns him for proceeding on his own. Saul defends his actions, but Samuel continues to condemn him "for not keeping the commandment of the Lord your God" (v. 13a). The sentence is the replacement of Saul's dynasty with another (vv. 13b–14). This is an allusion to David, but he has not been introduced yet.

The second story of judgment against Saul (15:1–35) is an elaborate story with no specific oracle. According to this story, Samuel commands Saul to destroy the Amalekites, a marauding tribe on the southern border of Israel; this is said to be revenge for the tribe's attack on the Israelites when they were coming out of Egypt (15:1–2). Saul attacks and succeeds militarily. He follows orders in killing captives and livestock, but the army saves the best cattle and sheep and valuables, and Saul spares the king, Agag. When YHWH informs Samuel, he checks it out and confronts Saul with his noncompliance. When Saul makes excuses, including to blame his soldiers, Samuel offers a poem rating obedience over sacrifice and condemning Saul for disobedience:

> Has the Lord as great delight in burnt offerings and sacrifices
> as in obedience to the voice of the Lord?
> Surely to obey is better than sacrifice,
> and heed than the fat of rams.
> For rebellion is no less a sin than divination,
> and stubbornness is like iniquity and idolatry.
> Because you have rejected the word of the Lord,
> he has rejected you from being king. (1 Sam 15:22–23)

To no avail Saul seeks to procure forgiveness, or at least a show of support from Samuel (15:24–31). Now, Saul himself has lost legitimacy, and soon his mind will break, and his reign will decline until he leads his army into a disastrous battle with the Philistines. During this time, his successor is secretly anointed by Samuel (16:1–13) and begins to supplant Saul. Saul and David meet in two confrontations in the wilderness (1 Samuel 24, 26), in which Saul is forced to admit that he has sinned against David and deserves to lose his power to his younger competitor (24:8–21; 26:13–25).

Obviously some features of these accounts were added in the light of later events. The allusions to Saul's replacement by David certainly fits that category. These stories give David a legitimate claim to rule as YHWH's anointed, as well as account for Saul's downfall. Samuel's defense of prophetic authority also has a retrospective character. The accounts of his words of judgment have been generalized so that later prophets can appeal to them.

## Nathan's Confrontation with David

While we know Samuel's life story before meeting him as a prophet of judgment, we know nothing of the prophet Nathan until David makes an inquiry of the prophet stationed at the ark (2 Sam 7:1–2). Nathan encourages David's desire to build a temple to house the ark (7:3) but has his judgment overruled in a theophany that night (7:4–7). While Nathan has to reject the king's plan to build a temple, he more than compensates for this negative word with a dynastic promise (7:8–17; also Pss 89:19–37; 132:1–12, 17–18) that legitimizes the Davidic monarchy throughout its history and fuels messianic hopes. This treasured prophecy gives Nathan the authority to pronounce judgment on the king.

The forensic narration of David's offenses is located in 2 Samuel 11. This narrative is subtle and eloquent. It not only portrays the acts that Nathan will condemn in chapter 12, but it explores the mystery of David's behavior. First, David stays in Jerusalem while his troops are besieging Rabbah of the Ammonites (11:1–2), and he invites the sunbathing wife of a soldier, named Bathsheba, to visit him at the palace (11:3–4). When she turns up pregnant (v. 5), David tries to cover up his adultery by recalling the woman's husband to Jerusalem in the expectation that he will have intercourse with her and believe he has fathered the child (vv. 6–8). But Uriah refuses to go home, staying with David's guards because, he says, he feels solidarity with the troops in the field. David even gets Uriah drunk in the hopes that he will give in to a natural desire for his wife (vv. 9–13). To no avail. In frustration, David sends a message (by the victim) to Joab, his commander, to engineer Uriah's death. Joab complies, though he goes through much trouble to conceal the crime.

Yes, David's behavior is mysterious. He evidently thinks that his adultery is secret, though his guard is instrumental and would have fueled the rumor mill. When Uriah returns to Jerusalem, he probably is informed about what is happening and refuses to play his role in David's plan. Why David then thinks it necessary to kill Uriah is utterly mysterious. Even if he thinks that Uriah does not know of the affair, nothing would be gained by Uriah's death. The adultery would come out. Maybe he thinks no one will know that Uriah is not the father of the child. But when he marries her after her period of mourning for Uriah, there can be little public doubt. It is just possible that David falls in love with Bathsheba and finally is willing to eliminate a rival, even if it means being exposed as an adulterer and killer.

Nathan is summoned by YHWH to pronounce judgment on David (11:27—12:1). He approaches the task with care. He might be killed in the king's wrath at being exposed. Moreover, the king could be redeemed if he could be motivated to repent of his crimes. The parable of the rich man's slaughter of a poor man's pet lamb to feed a visitor elicits David's outrage. It has concealed its true application so well that David could not see through it until he is told (12:1–7). The oracle that begins in v. 7 is actually the explanation of the parable. David is charged with murder and adultery.

Some sophisticated legal reasoning is also involved in the murder charge. If one studies the Israelite law governing murder, one finds that the law invariably concerns whether the death of a person caused by another was deliberate or accidental.[10] David has not physically caused Uriah's death; indeed, Joab has not either. Uriah dies fighting a foe. That his death is engineered by Joab at David's request must have been a surmise.

These are crimes not only of Israelite law but of the natural law.[11] Nevertheless, Nathan clearly makes David's act an offense against God: "Why have you despised the word of the Lord, to do what is evil in his sight?" (1 Sam 12:9). Even natural law has the force of divine law, indeed, a word of YHWH, and the prophetic judgment is a divine judgment.

Nathan's prophecy not only has a sentence—actually several—it also has a contrast motif: "'I gave you your master's house, and your master's wives into

---

10. The laws always envisage a physical assault that results in death, but David avoids doing anything of the sort. He asks Joab to "engineer" Uriah's death by enemy fire. The soldiers on the walls of city were unwitting agents of David, Joab a witting agent.

11. Barton, *Understanding Old Testament Ethics*, 4–5, makes much of this fact.

*The Judgment of Kings*

your bosom, and gave you the house of Israel and Judah; and if that had been too little I would have added as much more'" (v. 8). This is formed from conventional language, for David did not take Saul's wives.[12] The point is, YHWH has given him everything he could legitimately desire, and here he is going after the illegitimate. He wants no limits to his will.

The recorded sentences are somewhat strange. The first is that "the sword shall never depart" from the dynasty (12:10). But this is a truism: monarchs must always have military power and use it periodically. This is not really punishment.

The other sentence is rebellion in David's own house. This seems to be formulated after the events reported in 2 Samuel 13–20 have taken place; in other words, they are prophecy *ex eventu*. This has the artistic effect of connecting David's crime with the troubles that he suffers in the years that follow. These troubles are the "working out" of his sin.

Note, David will suffer these despite the fact that he has been forgiven. When David is confronted with the prophecy, he admits his guilt (12:13). Nathan forgives him, and what must have been an implied sentence, death, is commuted to the death of Bathsheba's child. While readers may question the fairness of this sentence to the baby, any family member could be the stand-in for the head of the family in a situation like this. The father can be punished, that is, by losing his child.

David pleads for the child's life. One might think that he is seeking a fair deal for the child, but one suspects that he is seeking to win forgiveness without consequences. When the child dies, David realizes that God will not let him off Scott free. He has not only lost the child, but he will experience a troubled family life the rest of his life. A struggle ensues even at his death over who will succeed him.

### Ahijah's Enacted Prophecy

No prophets are mentioned during the reign of Solomon until we read of a rebellion, or at least the inception of one, in the last chapter devoted to Solomon's reign. First Kings 11 is often called the dark side of Solomon's reign. It begins with a listing of Solomon's foreign wives, who bring their cults to Jerusalem (1 Kgs 11:1–8); and Solomon naturally joins his wives in their religious celebrations. According to the narrator, Solomon's religious laxity arouses YHWH's

---

12. There was a conflict between Abner and Ishbosheth over one of them; see 2 Sam 3:6–11.

anger (11:9), and he is told that the kingdom, including all Israelites, will be divided, leaving the Davidic dynasty only one tribe (11:10–13). But before the division, the king also suffers successful rebellions against his imperial rule in the territories of Edom and Aram (11:14–25).

The account of Ahijah's prophecy begins with the future king of the northern kingdom, Jeroboam. His career begins in Solomon's compulsory labor gangs, where he is made a foreman of the Ephraimite contingent (11:26–28). A prophet from the Ephraimite city of Shilo, Ahijah, then designates him God's chosen leader of the rebellion of the northern tribes against Solomon.

It is Ahijah's symbolic action that stands out as original. He rips up a new robe and hands Jeroboam ten pieces, and explains, "Take for yourself ten pieces; for thus says the Lord, the God of Israel: 'Behold, I am about to tear the kingdom from the hand of Solomon, and will give you ten tribes'" (11:31).

Beginning with 1 Kgs 11:33, the prophet gives the reason for the division: Solomon has proved apostate and lawless. This essentially repeats the narrator's charges in 11:9–10. As we shall see, it is a leading accusation against kings throughout monarchical history.[13] Thus, it ties together Solomon's offenses with the offenses of kings and people throughout the nation's history, which result finally in divine judgment on Israel and later on Judah.

Solomon's offenses, however, do not correspond well to the punishment. Why would the northern tribes break away because the king was too receptive to the religions of his foreign wives? They might have taken offense at his many wives and seemingly decadent lifestyle, but one would not rebel out of disgust and resentment. In the next chapter, 1 Kings 12, we have an account of the rebellion of the northern tribes, if we can call it that, and in that rebellion the people demand a new policy of Solomon's successor, Rehoboam, one that doesn't tax so heavily and force people to work on royal projects for nothing (12:4). This sounds much more like the sort of discontent that would spark a rebellion, and Ahijah's action would fit it well.

There is evidence that Ahijah commissions Jeroboam to begin his rebellion immediately. The text now has him say, in the name of YHWH, "I will take the kingdom away from his son and give it to you" (11:35). However, Jeroboam does not wait until Solomon is dead. According to 11:40, "Solomon sought therefore to kill Jeroboam; but Jeroboam promptly fled to Egypt, to King Shishak of Egypt, and remained in Egypt until the death of Solomon." Solomon would not try to kill Jeroboam unless the latter had made some move to take control of the tribes that had been given him.

13. Note 2 Kgs 17:7–23.

As is so often the case, prophecies are not fulfilled exactly. The division of the kingdom does not come about during Solomon's lifetime. When Rehoboam is selected to succeed Solomon, he evidently needs the acclamation of the northern tribes.[14] The people refuse to recognize him as king because he does not reply favorably to their demands. Rehoboam's effort to suppress what he considers a rebellion fails, and Jeroboam is chosen king after Rehoboam withdraws.

Ahijah later condemns Jeroboam. One might have expected such a condemnation at the dedication of the royal sanctuaries at Bethel and Dan. The historian condemns the "idolatry" of these sanctuaries continually, but strangely the prophetic word reported in 1 Kings 13 does not mention golden calves. Ahijah has occasion to speak when Jeroboam's wife seeks a word of healing for their son from the prophet (14:1–5). She instead hears a word of judgment against her husband along with a no to her inquiry about healing. Jeroboam is accused of idolatry and apostasy: "You have done evil above all those who were before you and have gone and made yourself other gods, and cast images, provoking me to anger, and have thrust me behind your back" (14:9).[15]

## Elijah's Challenges to the Omride Dynasty.

Here we meet a towering figure, the very symbol of Old Testament prophecy. His story is told in 1 Kings 17–19, 21, and 2 Kings 1–2. The first unit, 1 Kings 17–19, should be set aside until later because it is climactic as well as symbolic. First Kings 21 is the forensic narration of the murder of Naboth and confiscation of his land, climaxed by an oracle of judgment addressed to Ahab (21:17–19). Interestingly, the narrative blames Ahab's wife, Jezebel, more than it does Ahab himself, but the prophecy condemns the king alone.

Ahab proposes to buy his neighbor's vineyard, next to Ahab's country palace in Jezreel (21:1–2). Naboth turns down the offer because the land is a family inheritance. Ahab is displeased and retreats to his bedroom in a funk. Jezebel tries to lift his spirits by promising to procure the land for him. She writes some elders in Jezreel to have a fast, honor Naboth, and then have him charged with blasphemy. He can be executed before anyone has second

---

14. David had made a separate covenant with the northern tribes; see 2 Sam 5:1–5. Probably each successive monarch was supposed to be accepted by them.

15. The Deuteronomistic historian views the golden calves as images of other gods, but in fact they were probably pedestals for the invisible YHWH, according to Carl Evan, oral communication, Bethlehem, Israel, 1990.

thoughts. The elders do as they are instructed and report to Jezebel, who informs Ahab that the land is his. As he is taking possession, Elijah confronts him.

The crimes committed under Ahab's authority are the sort of actions that would be condemned in most societies; it doesn't take divine revelation to know that murder and theft are wrong. To be sure, the killing of Naboth is not something the guilty party does physically, as the biblical law envisages. The king (or queen) has recruited others to do the deed, and with the semblance of legality. Likewise, the confiscation of the land seems to have had a semblance of legality. The problem of crimes committed by corrupt officials within the pretense of legality is not "solved" by revelation. No, revelation enters because the criminals are high officials who are immune from regular court intervention; God must act to bring justice where the human institutions fail.

It should be noted that 1 Kings 21 leaves some questions to be answered. If Jezebel is the person who engineered this judicial murder, why does divine judgment fall solely on Ahab? Moreover, why does the king have the right to Naboth's property after he is executed?

The account of the overthrow of the Omride dynasty by Jehu in 2 Kings 9–10 supplements our information, though its trustworthiness is uncertain. After Jehu slays Joram near Jezreel, he casts the king's body on Naboth's plot, explaining, "For remember, when you [his aide Bidkar] and I rode side by side behind his father Ahab how the Lord uttered this oracle against him: 'For the blood of Naboth and for the blood of his children that I saw yesterday, says the Lord, I swear I will repay you on this very plot of ground'" (2 Kgs 9:25–26). So we hear that Naboth's heirs have also been killed, though why and how is left unsaid. If this can be trusted, though, we can explain why the crown could take possession of Naboth's land.

Jezebel is killed a bit later than her husband, and her body is mashed under horses' feet and eaten by dogs (9:33–36). Jehu quotes another prophetic utterance: "In the territory of Jezreel the dogs shall eat the flesh of Jezebel; the corpse of Jezebel shall be like dung on the field in the territory of Jezreel, so that no one can say, 'This is Jezebel'" (9:36–37). This oracle repeats a follow-up oracle in 1 Kgs 21:23. The prophecy and execution of Jezebel would satisfy our sense of justice, but the paragraph beginning in v. 20 sounds like a prophecy *ex eventu*. It could have been composed to justify Jehu's action.

As for 1 Kgs 21:20–26, it would be best to ascribe it to the Deuteronomistic historian. It begins with an exchange between Ahab and Elijah that portrays them as implacable foes, and then the historian pronounces his judgment on the royal couple (vv. 25–26). All this fits into the historian's overall plan for his historical review.

However, v. 27 of 1 Kings 21 reports Ahab's repentance, and v. 29 YHWH's commutation of his sentence. Ahab is a much more sympathetic and redeemable character than the historian would have us believe. Note that this little paragraph delays judgment until Jehu's revolt and purging of Israel (2 Kings 9–10). Here again a passage that is probably *ex eventu* integrates the narrative into the larger work.

### Elijah's Condemnation of Ahab's Son

Ahaziah is not well known. The forensic narration and oracle take only a few verses of 2 Kings 1 (vv. 2–4). The king has a fall on the upper floor of his house, and is seriously injured by it (2 Kgs 1:2a). He commissions messengers to go to the Philistine city of Ekron to inquire of the Baal worshipped there. Perhaps this god or shrine was well known for healing powers.

Elijah intercepts the messengers and delivers YHWH's answer to Ahaziah's inquiry: "Is it because there is no God in Israel that you are going to inquire of Baal-zebub, the god of Ekron? Now therefore thus says the Lord: You shall not leave the bed to which you have gone, but you shall surely die" (1:3–4). This is an exceedingly economic prophecy, much like the one delivered to Ahab. It starts with an accusing question, one filled with irony. Note, though, that the prophet doesn't leap to a universal deity but to a national one. Clearly Elijah regards exclusive loyalty to YHWH to be an obligation for which each and every Israelite is accountable. One here can glimpse the perspective on the first commandment of the most theologically aware thinkers of the ninth-century-BCE Israel.

The series of exchanges between Elijah and Ahaziah's messengers (1:5–16) is a rather distracting extension of our story; it really doesn't maintain the focus or the characters. Elijah has become a "man of God" who exhibits supernatural power.

### The Drought and Pilgrimage to Horeb (1 Kings 17–19)

This account is the climax of the events of Elijah's tale. There are no pronouncements of judgment, though the last narrative in this cycle announces a future one. The story begins with an oracle-like announcement of a three-year drought (17:1). There is no accusation given to justify this divine trial. It becomes clearer in chapter 18 that YHWH has caused and brought an end to the drought to prove that he, not Baal, exercises power over natural processes.

The remainder of chapter 17 dramatizes the severity of the drought. At first Elijah lives in a wadi fed by ravens, but the brook dries up. He moves to the territory of Sidon, where he lives with a destitute widow and her son. The food supply is maintained by divine miracle, and the son dies, only to be resuscitated by Elijah. These wonder-working stories demonstrate Elijah's power and prophetic status.

When it is time to end the drought, Elijah seeks out king Ahab to set up a contest between YHWH, represented by Elijah, and Baal, served by 450 dervishes. Elijah first meets Ahab's servant Obadiah, who fills him in on the persecution of YHWH's prophets by queen Jezebel (18:3b–4, 13). This establishes the seriousness of the crisis for faithful Yahwists. It is that that Elijah intends to remedy.

The contest between these gods and their representatives concerns who has the power to light their sacrificial fires miraculously. Before the contest begins, Elijah challenges the assembly: "How long will you go hobbling between two [gods]? If the Lord is God, follow him. If Baal, then follow him" (18:21 my translation). The people cannot answer. The prophet could have subjected them to judgment without further ado. Later prophets will. The people are under obligation to recognize YHWH alone. They should recognize that one cannot have him and another. YHWH insists on either/or. However, this sort of either/or is foreign to polytheism, and the people seem to have settled into a polytheistic mindset. Even Ahab acknowledges YHWH as Israel's deity; he gives his children Yahwistic names. However, he does not think that that precludes worshipping his wife's gods. Enough people in Israel practiced this sort of tolerant mixing of religions for there to be a temple devoted to Baal and his consort in the capital city (16:31–33).

But Elijah doesn't condemn the Israelite people; he sets up a contest between the competing gods. Since neither Baal nor YHWH can appear in person, so to speak, cultic personnel perform rituals to elicit the deity's response—the lighting of the sacrificial fire. The prophets of Baal—more like dervishes—spend their allotted time imploring their god, dancing around their altar, finally gashing themselves with knives. The storyteller has Elijah begin to ridicule them.

When Elijah's turn comes, he repairs the Yahwistic altar on Cape Carmel and prepares it by pouring water all over it. Then he prays a very simple but sophisticated prayer, requesting God's demonstration to recover the Israel that is losing its identity, and to confirm Elijah's commission to engage in this contest. The answer of YHWH wins the Israelites over, at least temporarily. The contest ends with the killing of the Baal personnel.[16]

Often overlooked is the scene ending the drought (18:41–46). Who has power over the weather, and fertility, has been the real issue between YHWH and Baal all along. Now that YHWH has demonstrated his cultic power, so to speak—the sacrificial fire is cultic, if anything is—, he shows that he can cause it to rain. Somehow Elijah participates in the summoning of a storm cloud and races ahead of Ahab's chariot to Jezreel.

First Kings 19 is a strange yet profound appendix to our story. When Jezebel hears of Elijah's victory, she does not acknowledge defeat but redoubles her effort to suppress her enemies. Elijah escapes through Judah to the south of Beersheba into the wilderness. Suddenly he becomes weary with living and tries to sleep himself to death. An angel will not allow him, but feeds him and propels him on a forty-day pilgrimage to Mount Horeb.

When Elijah arrives at Horeb, he settles in a cave, probably the very one Moses hid in when YHWH showed him his back (Exod 33:17–23). Then Elijah is questioned as to why he has come, and he answers, "I have been very zealous for the Lord, God of hosts; for the Israelites have forsaken your covenant, thrown down your altars, and killed your prophets with a sword. I alone am left, and they are seeking my life, to take it away" (19:10). This answer obviously expresses the prophet's despairing mood and his sense of isolation. It completely ignores the contest on Cape Carmel, which Elijah won, and that has turned the Israelites back to YHWH. The only altar we hear of being in disrepair is the altar that Elijah rebuilt on Carmel (18:31–32). And only Jezebel is seeking to kill Elijah. In other words, we cannot take this outcry at face value; it is the utterance of a desperate person.

YHWH's answer rather changes the subject. He has a new task for Elijah, because he is about to bring judgment on his people (19:15–18). This is rather shocking, given the people's confession in response to YHWH's lighting of the sacrificial fire on Carmel. One has to fill in that conversion was superficial, and that only a small remnant—"six thousand"—are really loyal Yahwists. The people will be "refined," and the half-hearted will fall, leaving a faithful remnant.

Although YHWH charges Elijah with the task of anointing three agents to carry out God's judgment of Israel, Hazael of Damascus, Jehu of Israel, and Elisha as Elijah's successor, Elijah actually has contact only with Elisha (19:19–

---

16. This is the requirement of Israelite law, according to Exod 22:20 and Deuteronomy 13. It is also revenge for Jezebel's killing of the prophets of YHWH.

*Redeeming Judgment*

21). It is Elisha who has an audience with Hazael (2 Kgs 8:7–15) and sends an underling to anoint Jehu (2 Kgs 9:1–10). Though Elijah does not anoint Jehu, Jehu is inspired by Elijah's prophecy against Ahab to bring down that dynasty and then, conspiring with Jehonadab ben Rechab, destroy the temple of Baal in Samaria, with thousands of worshippers in it (2 Kgs 10:18–27). Whether such a violent purge of the kingdom was true to Elijah or a fanatical distortion, there is little question that Elijah is the inspiration for Jehu's action.

Elisha, by the way, has been regarded as the true heir of Elijah, but his prophetic ministry is quite different. He does not pronounce oracles of judgment over anyone, even when he promises the downfall of Israel's enemies. For this reason, I have not included him in this exposition of the prophets of judgment against individuals.

## The Prophet and His Royal Audience

The story told in 1 Kings 22 seems to be passed on as a paradigm of the peculiar relations of prophets and kings. The hero of the story, Micaiah ben Imlah, is otherwise unknown. He stands out for his courage, toughness, and irony. The two kings, though named, seem to be performing typical or archetypical roles. If one were attempting to locate the story in history, it would fit J(eh)oram's reign better than Ahab's. A struggle is going on between Israel and Aram for control of Transjordan, and Aram has the upper hand. Ahab's son has been engaged in such a struggle, and is seriously injured in the fighting (see 2 Kgs 8:28–29).[17] I will simply call the kings, King of Israel and King of Judah.

The action begins in the capital of the northern kingdom, in the city gate, where the kings are deliberating over whether to go to battle to recover the city of Ramoth in Gilead. Once the Judean king agrees to support Israel, he asks for the word of the prophets. Why do they need prophets? It was important to ancient rulers to have divine backing for their enterprises, and prophets were one way to determine whether they had such backing.[18] Kings evidently employed a number of prophets who could deliver an answer as to whether a proposed course of action would please or displease the deity. The court prophets were evidently known to say what the royal inquirer wanted to hear.[19]

17. While this doesn't match the death of the king told in 1 Kings 22, it comes as close as any event we know of.

18. Other ways would take various forms of divination, but prophecy was the only way to know YHWH's decisions.

19. That is not only assumed in our story, but it is mentioned by classical prophets, e.g., in Micah 3:5.

The Judean king asks for another prophet, suspicious about the objectivity of these court prophets. Of course, it sounds odd to ask for one more when the place is already overrun with them shouting out slogans supporting the king.

The Israelite king immediately thinks of a prophet who does not formulate his message to suit his audience. As the king puts it, "I hate him, for he never prophesies anything favorable toward me, but only disaster" (1 Kgs 22:8). The Judean king wants to hear from such an independent voice, so he is summoned (v. 10). The court prophets feel their message under challenge, so they intensify it by demonstrations. They seem to think that enthusiasm and vividness can persuade the skeptical.

The messenger who summons Micaiah tries to corrupt his message, and Micaiah pretends to go along. One suspects that Micaiah delivers his answer in such a mocking way that the kings can detect that it is insincere. One has to laugh at the Israelite king's admonition: "How many times must I make you swear to tell me nothing but the truth in the name of the Lord?" (22:16). In response Micaiah reports a "vision" of defeat due to the death of the king(s). The Israelite king, then, turns to the Judean king and says, "Did I not tell you that he would not prophesy anything favorable?" The prophet of judgment is damned if he does and damned if he doesn't.

Now the other prophets challenge Micaiah's claim to superior access to the will of God. Micaiah tells a story to account for their false word: they are inspired by a spirit sent from God to misguide the kings. This story is not to be taken literally: it is an ironic comment on Micaia's prophetic opponents. Their leader, Zedekiah, slaps Micaiah and expresses contempt for his "spirit"; Micaiah says that the truth will be known when his prophecy is confirmed by events. The king takes him at his word and imprisons him until the battle is over.

Micaiah does not indict the king of Israel; there is no explanation of the judgment. It is a special case, however; if the king proceeds despite the divine no, he is guilty of disobeying the word of YHWH. In our story, the king does just that and is killed in battle. The attitude of the kings of Israel and Judah is ambivalence toward the prophets of judgment, because such prophets probably are honest spokesmen for God, but they say what the kings do not want to hear. The kings can ignore their advice to their peril, but they desire to silence them. The people as a whole exhibit much the same ambivalence.

## What We Learn from the Judgment of Kings

The following theses can be derived from this study:

a) The monarchy was instituted because Israel needed a concentration of power to maintain internal peace and order to protect the people from outside aggression.

b) The danger of the concentration of power was also recognized in the story of the founding of the monarchy and various traditions of resistance.

c) The prophets of YHWH are credited with the founding of the original tribal monarchy and with the periodic strategic modification of its constitution.

d) The prophets are credited with designating all the ruling dynasties, save the house of Omri.

e) The primary means of limiting the misuse of power by kings was through the prophets of judgment; Saul, David, Solomon, Rehoboam, Jeroboam, Baasha, Ahab, Ahaziah, and Jehoram were all subjected to divine judgment by the prophets.

What do we learn about divine judgment from these judgments of individual kings?

a) The kings are condemned for violating both revealed and natural law. Both of Saul's judgments are for disobedience of prophetic commands. Jeroboam violates religious law in the construction of the state sanctuaries of Bethel and Dan, and Ahaziah commits apostasy. David and Ahab violate laws that are common to human society, though they are given a new dimension by being commanded by YHWH. Solomon oppresses his subjects, and Rehoboam continues in the arrogant attitude of his father. Jehoram suffers for the sins of his fathers.

b) God intervenes in the person of the prophet to judge persons immune from regular courts. Sometimes the prophet institutes the process of judgment—anointing a new king, for instance. At other times, the Lord brings a person's deeds back to haunt him; this sort of punishment is often portrayed as poetic justice. It was, we might say, "rough and ready" because there were no judicial authorities nor procedures involved.

c) Judgment is for the common good, just as normal trials are. The application of sanctions against wrongdoers purges evil from the body politic, and thereby appeases the wrath of God. The judgment of a king, however, can be experienced as a blow to the nation. The people, after all, are closely identified with the country and its rulers. Hence, they have to be persuaded of the king's guilt; forensic narratives have that purpose.

d) We have some cases where forgiveness is sought, but not always with the same result. Saul besought Samuel, but receives no mercy. David admits his guilt and is forgiven by Nathan, but his punishment is "softened," not cancelled. The child of adultery dies, and David suffers the rest of his life in a deeply troubled household. Ahab is personally forgiven, but his wife and son suffer the full brunt of the law. We will need to return to questions of atonement, forgiveness, and suffering of consequences in subsequent chapters.

e) It should be noted that these judgments are not warnings or calls for repentance. The judgments take place in the pronouncement of the prophet. How the accused responds might affect the nature of the punishment, but it does not cancel it. When we come to the judgment of the nation, we should construe the pronouncements of the prophets as belonging to the same order as do these judgments of individuals.

## The Judgments of Kings and National Exile

The accounts we have been examining are incorporated into what might be termed a super-forensic narration. From the warning of Joshua on (Josh 24:19–27), and especially from the establishment of the monarchy (1 Samuel 8–12), the history of Israel has moved inexorably toward the exile of Israel, and subsequently of Judah. The history of the people of God certainly includes the actions and suffering of the common people, but most of the narratives of 1–2 Samuel and 1–2 Kings cover the acts and suffering of rulers, their households, and counselors. Thus, the political history of the country, including its religious history, bears the weight of the action that results in national judgment. The actions of individual rulers not only come under the scrutiny of God and precipitate judgment, but they also contribute to the nation's judgment.

The significance of these individual kings is brought out by the Deuteronomistic historian, who grades every one of them. For example, "In the twenty-third year of King Joash . . . , Jehoahaz, son of Jehu began to reign

*Redeeming Judgment*

over Israel in Samaria; he reigned seventeen years. He did what was evil in the sight of the Lord, and followed the sins of Jeroboam son of Nebat, which he caused Israel to sin" (2 Kgs 13:1–2). This is the typical pronouncement on northern kings. We read of the moral failures of the individual king, and also of his contribution to the nation's sin and judgment.[20]

The historian has a fixation on the "sin of Jeroboam," which was perpetuated by all his royal successors. This sin is the construction of state sanctuaries with golden calves. It is very unlikely that Jeroboam really intended his calves to represent the "[other] gods who brought you out of the land of Egypt." He was trying to create substitute sanctuaries to the Jerusalem temple for the citizens of his kingdom to attend. These citizens were Yahwists.[21] His decision to substitute "golden calves" for the ark (Jerusalem's possession) is fateful; these calves become the target of zealous aniconic prophets, who effectively define them for all history as idols. The historian not only accepts this prophetic view, but it becomes the primary measure for the faithfulness of northern kings.

Nevertheless, the Deuteronomistic history as a whole does not dwell on this "sin" to the exclusion of many others. All the kings but Jeroboam are guilty of other offenses. Though we need to be aware of the historian's rather narrow vision, we should read the history for the larger picture.

*Judgment as the Explanation of Exile: 2 Kings 17*

This chapter recounts the coup de grâce to the northern kingdom (2 Kgs 17:1–6), and then explains the reasons for the fall of the northern kingdom. The explanation takes the form of a litany of its sins: "This occurred because the people of Israel had sinned against the Lord their God, who had brought them up out of the land of Egypt . . . They had worshipped other gods and walked in the customs of the nations whom the Lord drove out before the people of Israel and in the customs that the kings of Israel had introduced" (2 Kgs 17:7–8). Then the historian begins to enumerate particular violations of God's will: high places in towns, pillars and *asherim* in these high places, and offerings according to Canaanite custom. Also, the people make and worship idols. They reject the warnings of prophets, and disobey divine law, and even sacrifice their children. Most of these are cultic offenses, though the history

---

20. The historian's assessments do not always strike one as fair or even germane, but the principle is certainly in line with the work's argument.

21. Evidence of this is the fact that he was anointed by a prophet of YHWH and made king by elders of the northern tribes of YHWH's people.

tells of crimes and oppressions that loom at least as large. The classical prophets of judgment against the people will bring these out eloquently.

The Deuteronomistic historian has to tell not only the stories of the death, but also the details of burial. At the time of the Assyrian exile of Israel, many are deported—probably primarily the leadership classes (17:6), and survivors of other defeated nations are settled in northern territory (17:24–25). The new settlers adopt YHWH after they experience some judgments that suggested that they should appease the local god (17:26), and an Israelite priest is brought back from exile to teach them the ways of YHWH (17:27–28). They continue to worship their own gods as well (17:29–34).

Judah continues to survive as a vassal state throughout the period of the Assyrian empire. The Deuteronomistic historian has only a few verses in chapter 17 about Judah (17:19–20). We would expect an essay at the end of 2 Kings, explaining the judgment of Judah in the Babylonian exile, but we do not have one. The essay on Israel has to apply for Judah as well. As 2 Kgs 17:19 says, "Judah also did not keep the commandments of the Lord their God but walked in the customs that Israel had introduced."

## The Presage of This History in Deuteronomy 32

Though Deuteronomy belongs to a previous chapter of this book, the thirty-second chapter of Deuteronomy surveys the nation's future history down through the exile. This poem, which some scholars have labeled a "covenant lawsuit,"[22] resembles the oracles of the prophet of judgment. Although the narrative line is rather dense and allusive, it announces the judgment of Israel. Readers are to understand this judgment to be the Assyrian and Babylonian exiles that bring Israel's tenure on the land to an end. Thus, before we are told the story of conquest, we are told that the people will lose what they conquered in an event of great suffering. Readers are being instructed in why Israel incurred divine judgment so that we readers can repent of our own unfaithfulness.

The cause of judgment is a specific violation of the covenant: apostasy. Actually, apostasy is so closely tied to idolatry in this rhetoric that we can subsume them under a common heading.

> They sacrificed to demons, not gods,
> To deities they had never known,
> To new ones recently arrived

---

22. So named in Wright, "Deuteronomy."

> ...
> You were unmindful of the Rock that bore you,
> And you forgot the God who gave you birth. (32:17–18)
>
> They made me jealous with what is no god;
> provoked me with their idols. (32:21)

The Mosaic prophecy of judgment comes about in the Assyrian and Babylonian exiles.

The story in the poem does not end with the Lord's judgment of Israel. After it comes the judgment of the nations and the "vindication" of Israel (32:34–43). This is a promise that remains unfulfilled in the history that follows. Although nothing is said in Deuteronomy 32 about how the people can prepare for and hasten God's salvation, Deut 30:1–10 exhorts the people "to return to the Lord your God . . . and obey His voice in all that I command you this day, with all your heart and all your soul; then the Lord your God will restore your fortunes . . ." (Deut 30:2–3, RSV). Thus, readers are incorporated into the story as exiles who can receive the salvation to come by repenting.

# 9

# Four Eighth-Century Prophets of Judgment
(Amos, Hosea, Micah, Isaiah)

HERE WE ARRIVE AT the climax of the prophetic pronouncement of divine judgment. The new message is so significant that the form of the literature changed. Up till now we have been finding our prophetic messages embedded in national history. Now we have whole books containing prophetic oracles, with only scattered, supplementary narratives; these books bear the names of the prophets whose oracles are preserved in them. Since the books were collections of oracles addressed to the people prior to the Assyrian exile, while the readers would come afterward, these collections were designed to draw lessons from the words whose literal application is past. The ordering of the books of prophets, then, had a postexilic audience in mind.[1]

The original significance of these eighth-century prophets is that they pronounce judgment upon the whole people of God. The offenses for which the addressees are condemned are of a different order from the sins of individuals: they are either collective behavior or institutional acts that represent the collective will. The sentence is disaster or at least a national crisis.

When the prophet pronounces judgment, he has to persuade his audience that they are guilty as charged. The prophet could not just tell them, I got this from God, so believe it. The task of the prophet was to convince the people that what they had done and were doing deserves condemnation. This meant that the prophet had to call attention to practices and attitudes that their au-

1. This audience at first was pre-Babylonian exile. The original words of the prophet were supplemented; in the books of Isaiah and Micah, the supplementation is more extensive than the oracles belonging to the named prophet.

dience could confirm from their experience. If the prophet charged that the court system was stacked against the poor, the people should be able to recall events of that sort. What the prophet had to do was to force his audience to pay attention to things they normally ignored or even suppressed.

The prophecy of judgment is unconditional. In other words, the pronouncement itself is the judgment proper. In serious prophecy, we do not have sermons against sin. In YHWH's commission, the prophet is given the authority "to pluck up and to pull down, to destroy and to overthrow, to build and to plant" (Jer 1:10). The calls to repentance and offers of escape from judgment have to do with the sentence. If the accused are willing to admit guilt, they may be open to reform and renewal. Judgment can have a redemptive effect; it can stop oppression and unfaithfulness, and set the guilty on the path to reform and transformation.

This is possible, but the prophets are realists. Amos sees very little possibility of avoiding defeat and exile.[2] Hosea is certain that the kingship must cease and the people either be exiled or enter the desert (at least figuratively). Isaiah's call vision is of utter destruction (Isa 6:11–13); revival must be a virtual resurrection of the dead.

It should be remembered too that the prophets had witnessed ancient Near Eastern warfare. All one has to do is look at Assyrian reliefs of their battles to see how violent and cruel a victorious power could be. Moreover, the Israelites and Judeans had few illusions about their power to defeat the Assyrian army. These tiny states were involved in a delicate diplomatic game trying to appease Assyria and to be supported enough by Egypt to maintain their independence. Israel lost disastrously, and Judah only survived by a miracle. The eighth-century prophets were interpreters of these events.

## Canonical and Historical Exposition

Up until this chapter, I have interpreted the final form of the Old Testament text. I have noted composite authorship and discrepancies between the historical era and the textual representation of it but have not gone behind the text to history or to the author's context and interests. Theological exposition[3] should be built on the text in its final form because that is the text passed on to the church, and the text church teachers have interpreted. Yet, we cannot ignore the gains of the critical era. Critical scholars have sought to identify the

---

2. The only people in the Bible to repent and have judgment canceled is Nineveh.
3. At least biblical theology for teaching and preaching in the church.

actual words of our prophets, separating out the additions of others, and to reconstruct the event about which the prophets speak. This historical perspective is also valuable.

I could have composed this chapter by taking up each prophetic book in turn. In order to focus on the message of judgment, not the full message of each prophet, let alone the subsequent contributions to the book, my strategy is to identify the event of judgment as the subject of the chapter. Canonically speaking, all the prophets of judgment are speaking of the same judgment. One could make the case, though, that Jeremiah and Ezekiel are speaking about such a different phase of judgment that they should be treated separately; that is in fact what I intend to do.[4]

What I am going to do is expound the accusations, sentences, and rationale of judgment attributed to the four eighth-century prophets of judgment, viz., Amos, Hosea, Isaiah, and Micah. Here we will see how each prophet engages the events of his time and the actions of his people. The message of salvation found in each prophetic book will be reserved for later chapters, as will the study of the final form of prophetic books.

## Changes in the Form of the Prophecy of Judgment

The prophecy of judgment against the people expands and complicates the form of judgment prophecy. We can increase our capacity to read the judgment passages of the prophetic books by noting the changes in the elements.

Since prophecy continues to be modeled on messenger speech, we find commissions of the prophet ("go and say to . . .") in many books of prophecy, and the messenger formula ("Thus says the Lord") is located at the head of many prophecies. The messenger formula is well preserved in Amos, and when it is lacking, there is some formal type of address: e.g., "Hear this word." A series of oracles can be strung together with, "on that day." The book of Hosea lacks the messenger formula where we would expect it. It may be that Hosea stands in some other prophetic tradition, or it may have to do with the formation history of the book. Amos, Isaiah, and Micah also have a formula at the end of oracles, often translated, "says the Lord."

The *accusation* or *indictment* is the name I use for the statement of the reasons for the Lord's judgment. The term *accusation* is too tentative for the element because YHWH's accusation amounts to proof of guilt. However, the charges would be heard by the audience as accusations because the audience

---

4. It is difficult to locate Zephaniah, so I am leaving him out of the discussion.

would not know whether the prophet was true or false. Hence, I will use *accusation* or *charge*, or occasionally *indictment* for this element.

In the judgments of individuals that we studied in the last chapter, the accusation was quite specific. "Have you killed and also taken possession?" (1 Kgs. 21:19). "You have struck down Uriah the Hittite with the sword, and have taken his wife to be your wife" (2 Sam 12:10). The addressee knows that he is guilty, so the prophet has no persuading to do. Readers of the narrative do need persuasion, but this is provided by the narrative telling of the crime.[5]

To heighten the addressee's sense of guilt, the prophet often recounts what the Lord has done for the guilty, offering an implicit contrast between divine grace and human sinful response.[6] David, for example, is told, "I anointed you king over Israel, and rescued you from the hand of Saul . . . and if that had been too little, I would have added as much more" (2 Sam 12:7-8). We shall find similar contrast motifs in the prophecy of national judgment.

The judgment of the people must modify the accusation to fit the nation. Claus Westermann divides the accusation against the people into a general and specific accusation. The general accusation can be a bit bombastic or clichéd. The specific accusation or accusations are meant to be evidence, or perhaps symptoms of the guilt of the people. Amos's oracle against Israel in chapter 2 begins with the refrain running through the first two chapters, "For three transgressions of Israel and for four" (v. 6a). It then enumerates a number of particular offenses: "because they sell the righteous for silver, and the needy for a pair of shoes[,] . . . father and son go into the same girl, so that my holy name is profaned" (vv. 6b, 7b). The Hebrew participial phrase, "they who trample the head of the poor into the dust of the earth, / and push the afflicted out of the way" (v. 7a) sounds general enough to be a second general accusation.

Another modification of the accusation from individual to national judgment is the different status the specific accusations have. In judgments of the people the accusations are not enumerated so that trials could be instituted against the guilty; they are meant to characterize the society as unjust, corrupt, immoral, unfaithful, and the like. The prophet is establishing the guilt of the nation. Usually, this judgment is not for acts in the past but for repeated acts. The acts under judgment are, one might say, symptoms of an underlying malignancy or at least malfeasance.

---

5. I have given these the title "forensic narration" in Patrick and Scult, *Rhetoric and Biblical Interpretation*, 57-80.

6. Westermann, *Basic Forms of Prophetic Speech*, 142-48, 181-89.

The addressees in collective judgments do not know that they are guilty, as does the addressee in the judgment of the individual. The prophet has to convince the people that they are guilty. Or, at least to try, for the people will not easily accept this characterization of their society. Their refusal to accept the prophetic characterization compounds their guilt. The ultimate object of prophecy is to touch the conscience of the people, so that they can be changed—redeemed. Although God may use the language of retaliation, God's judgment goes way beyond the measure of *lex talionis*. It is aimed at changing the heart and character of the people.

If the prophet were to convince his or her addressees of their guilt, they would be moved to repent and reform, and the Lord might cancel his decree of punishment. This in fact happens in the parabolic story of Jonah. His message convicts the Ninevites, and they repent with all their hearts. The Lord, then, repents of his message of doom, a decision that offends the prophet. Lest we think Jonah a fantasy, we have a passage in Isaiah that offers Judah forgiveness if it will admit its sin: "Come now, let us argue it out, / says the Lord: / though your sins are like scarlet, / they shall be like snow ... If you are willing and obedient, / you shall eat the good of the land" (Isa 1:18–19). The hearers' refusal to admit their guilt and undergo reform will lead to destruction (v. 20).

With so much riding on convincing the people that they are unjust, unfaithful, unmerciful, immoral, prideful, or decadent, one would expect constant calls to repentance in the prophetic books. This is indeed how the postexilic prophet Zechariah characterizes the message of the prophets of doom: "Do not be like your ancestors, to whom the former prophets proclaimed, 'Thus says the Lord of hosts, Return from your evil ways and from your evil deeds'" (Zech 1:4). Actually, our eighth-century prophets of judgment put very little emphasis on repentance. Only now and then is an exhortation heard, such as Amos's "seek me and live" (5:4). These prophets, at least, speak as though the people would have to undergo drastic punishment before their stubborn hearts would be shattered. The prophets' primary rhetorical goal is to plant seeds in the people that will grow in and after judgment. The people must suffer to be broken of their penchant for wrongdoing. They must also be instructed in what pleases God, because their sin distorts their understanding as well as their will. Hence the prophets engage in torah—"prophetic torah," e.g., "I desire mercy [*ḥesed*] and not sacrifice, the knowledge of God rather than burnt offerings" (Hos 6:6).

The sentence of the judgment prophecy against individuals is an imitation of legal punishment. The individual offender should undergo suffering proportionate to the deed. This is what we mean be retribution. The punishment or execution of the individual offender is to benefit the society, for the deed could infect the society and the unjust or unfaithful ruler wreak harm on the body politic.

The offender could, to be sure, be forgiven if he admitted his wrongdoing and showed remorse. David and Ahab both repent and are forgiven. However, neither has the consequences of his action completely wiped away. David is allowed to live, but his and Bathsheba's son dies. Moreover, his household is plagued by monstrous behavior—rape, murder, rebellion, usurpation—among David's sons. The fall of Ahab's dynasty is delayed until his grandson's reign; nevertheless, his dynasty is overthrown and wiped out, his widow killed. The effect of malicious deeds cannot simply be canceled; the deeds will come back upon the evildoer sooner or later.

The judgment of the people, like the judgment of the individual, may be retaliatory. The action of the people is just as capable of returning to haunt them as are the acts of individuals. However, the prophecy of judgment is not aimed at retaliation to balance the books, so to speak. No, judgment is meant to bring the behavior to an end and shatter the stubborn hearts of the people, opening the way to contrition and reform. It is hard to recognize this *telos* in Amos, who paints what seems to be a dismal picture of the future. The final promises of salvation in Amos seem out of character. Despite appearances, though, Amos hides seeds for renewal in his judgments. Hosea, Micah, and Isaiah are quite explicit about salvation arising out of the ashes of judgment.

Amos announces military devastation to Israel and its neighbors. Thus, it will be a manmade disaster, though God is the judge who recruits the human agent who carries it out. Amos seems to have foreseen the Assyrian empire acting as the agent of divine judgment, though it is not mentioned by name. The military reversal will be the "physical" manifestation of the encounter with the Lord threatened in Amos 4:12. In Amos 4:6–11, a series of troubles are mentioned as God's warnings to Israel—none of which is heeded. Many of these are natural events, "acts of God"—perhaps drought and pestilence too are agents of judgment. However, full-scale judgment calls for a disastrous military defeat.

Amos's vocation as a prophet seems to have been short. He was not active when Israel and Judah came under Assyrian suzerainty, so he had no occasion to incorporate the exchanges between Israel, its neighbors, and the empire in his accusations. Hosea and Isaiah did. Hosea comments on the parties to the Syro-Ephraimite War between 734 and 732 BCE, and the period of submission to Assyria that followed. He may have commented on Hoshea's alliance with Egypt that led to the fall of the remaining territory of the northern kingdom.

Isaiah is called to prophecy after Judah submitted to Assyrian vassalage, is active during the Syro-Ephraimite War, watches Samaria flame out, witnesses Hezekiah's enthronement, and condemns the rebellious policies of his regime. At the very last, he declares the deliverance of Jerusalem from Sennacherib's siege, but afterward calls for penitence rather than rejoicing.

I have sketched the careers of these prophets to explain the point I am about to make. The sentence of Israel and Judah, defeat and forced submission to Assyria, was a testing as well. Isaiah calls Assyria "the rod of my anger" (Isa 10:5). How Israel and Judah take this punishment or disciplining will determine how severe judgment will be. Isaiah 28:22 reads, "Now therefore do not scoff, or your bonds will be made stronger." My reading of this verse is, if you resist and plan rebellion against Assyrian rule, your punishment will be intensified. The Lord's punishment of his people is to subject them to a serious crisis, the response to which will determine their fate.

The crisis is not only a measure of the people's guilt; it is also a transforming experience. That is, it will purify the nation, refine it, shatter the paralysis of will that makes the people anxious. anxious about the status quo but unable to let go. This is spelled out explicitly by Isaiah, who begins a prophecy against Jerusalem, "How the faithful city has become a whore! She that was full of justice . . . but now murderers!" (1:21). In v. 24, the Lord announces judgment ("Ah, I will pour out my wrath on my enemies"), but then changes the metaphor to refining: "I will smelt away your dross" (v. 25). The strophe ends, "you shall be called the city of righteousness, the faithful city" (v. 26). The sinful city has been subjected to God's wrath, which has been a fire to burn away the impurities.

We will discover other forms of speech in the prophetic books: some variations on the prophecy of judgment (e.g.: "woe to those who . . . "),[7] others designed to instruct and persuade the audience. Since they serve the message of national judgment, we do not have to trace their changes.

## The Calls and Commissions of the Eighth-Century Prophets

The books of Amos, Hosea, and Isaiah include accounts of encounters between the prophet and the Lord that set the prophet apart and sent him on his mission. These provide insight into the nature of prophetic authority and action.

7. "Ah" in the NRSV.

Let's start with Amos's call to prophecy, and then expound his pronouncements of judgment, beginning with the cycle against the nations. Chapters 7–9 have accounts of visions, which can be taken as sequential. In the first two visions, Amos is shown a destructive scene—locusts and fire—that he divines to be foreshadowing of judgment of the people of God. He intercedes with YHWH, basing his plea on the vulnerability of the people, and wins a stay of judgment (7:1-6). The third vision (7:7-9) is of YHWH himself assessing the verticality of a wall with a "plumb line."[8] This time YHWH initiates the exchange, telling Amos that the time for forgiveness is past. Obviously YHWH has found the wall to be leaning, for he pronounces doom. In 8:1-3, YHWH shows Amos a basket of summer fruit, and when Amos names it *qayits* ("summer fruit"), YHWH puns upon Amos's word (saying *qëts*, ["end"]). With this vision, the fate of the nation seems to be sealed. Amos 9:1-4 may be a further vision; in any case, Amos hears YHWH pronounce a devastating sentence, which concludes, "I will fix my eyes on them for evil and not for good" (9:4).

It is noteworthy that Amos is told *that* divine judgment is in store for his people, but not *why*. Since God is a just judge, there must be a reason. Amos now has the task of "discovery," of identifying the offense or offenses that have prompted divine judgment. Here his own social class shapes his perception. He identifies himself as a herdsman and dresser (lit.: snapper) of sycamores—a working-class man if there ever was one.[9] He sees economic and legal injustice rampant in Israelite society, and raises that as an indictment. The task then is to convince his audiences that this injustice is deserving of divine judgment.

It seems that Hosea is called to prophecy by being told to marry a prostitute and father children by her (1:2). The command is explained with reference to the nation: "for the land commits great prostitution by forsaking the Lord." The story unfolds in the rest of chapter 1, then resumes a first-person viewpoint in chapter 3.[10] The skeleton of Hosea's life story is that he finds a loose woman named Gomer, has three children, whose names are symbolic of judgment, and then Hosea divorces Gomer, forcing her to sell herself into

---

8. So translated by tradition; the meaning of Hebrew word is uncertain: see Paul, *Amos*.

9. Some scholars are skeptical, given the evidence of his education and writing skills. Even if they are right, he doesn't think or present himself in that way. I had a colleague at my university who was a Marxist and who always wore the clothes of a laborer, and effected other marks of the working class.

10. It could be that chapter 3 is about another woman or is a parallel to c. 1; still, the simplest reading is that it follows up chapter 1. To connect the two, one has to include 2:2 as an allusion to a divorce.

slavery. Next Hosea is told by YHWH to find her, buy her, and enter into marriage again.

Interpreters have found many gaps and suspicious features to this story, but these need not distract us. This is the story the book of Hosea invites readers to consider as a background to his message. When we hear of Israel's infidelity to YHWH, its attraction to the gods known collectively as Baal,[11] we should feel the pain of a cockled husband. This, according to Hosea, is how YHWH feels. Hosea has struck a new image for the relationship between YHWH and Israel. Before his call to prophecy, the covenant was understood as a political arrangement, that of a sovereign to citizenry over whom he ruled. Hosea gives apostasy a new poignancy, a subjective immediacy. Apostasy is not only treason; it is now betrayal of the most intimate personal relationship. His image touches such deep nerves that it is picked up by later prophets (viz., Jeremiah and Ezekiel).

Isaiah recounts his call to prophecy in Isaiah 6. We will take it up in chapter 13. While Micah does not relate a call, he does state:

> But as for me, I am filled with power,
>> with the spirit of the LORD,
>> and with justice and might,
> to declare to Jacob his transgression
>> and to Israel his sin. (3:8)

This has the purpose of substantiating the prophet's authority, much as the call narratives.

## The Prophetic Accusation of Injustice

While the prophets of judgment are not systematic thinkers, it is possible to discern a conceptual whole to each prophet's accusations. In the exposition that follows, the accusations of Amos, the prophet of justice, will be expounded as a consistent set of iniquities. Likewise, the indictments of Hosea, the prophet of faithfulness, will be examined. Isaiah and Micah follow up on both Amos and Hosea, so we can add their voices to the two primary accusations.

---

11. Master or Lord.

## Redeeming Judgment

### Amos: The Prophet of Justice

Amos 1–2 features a cycle of oracles against nations bordering Israel, and concludes with an oracle against Israel itself. Each prophecy begins with the same formula: "Thus says the Lord: For three transgressions of x, and for four, I will not revoke [punishment]."[12] There follows in each an indictment, then a sentence with YHWH as subject judge.[13] The indictments are for international crimes—except for the oracles against Judah and Israel. The oracle against Judah is abstract, a litany of terms for breaking the covenant.[14] The one against Israel is for domestic wrongs: oppressing the poor, desecrating the sanctuary with incestuous sex and in other ways (2:6–8). Before the sentence, a contrast motif occurs, reciting Israel's sacred history and Israel's perversion of God's gifts (2:9–11). The sentence (2:12–16) is quite different from the destruction by fire in store for the rest of the nations.

Aram (Damascus), Gaza, Tyre, Edom, Ammon, and Moab are guilty of international crimes. Aram pursued a ruthless military campaign in an effort to conquer Gilead. The Ammonites committed atrocities in the same region, probably in the same war (1:13).[15] The Philistine cities and Tyre were engaged in the slave trade; the Edomites were the caravanners who transported the slaves to population centers, like Egypt, with an appetite for slaves. Amos, however, accuses the Edomites of Esau's effort to obtain revenge on Jacob (1:11). Moab is condemned for desecrating the body of the Edomite king, probably killed in battle (2:1).

Much of the argument of John Barton in his "Amos's Oracles against the Nations"[16] concerns the norms to which Amos appeals in these oracles. Barton observes that there is no reason to categorize these as oracles against enemies. These neighboring nations had been at peace with Israel for some time. There may well have been pent-up resentment toward Aram and the Ammonites for the brutality toward Israelite tribes living in Transjordan, but just a few decades later Aram and Israel were allied.[17] When the Israelite audience hears

---

12. Literally "it."

13. In all but the judgment of Israel, the sentence is "sending fire."

14. Critical scholarship agrees on the assessment of the Judah oracle as secondary, and those against Tyre and Edom are questioned by many. There is no call for a decision on our part.

15. I take Aram and the Ammonites to be allied.

16. Barton, *Understanding Old Testament Ethics*, 77–129.

17. They were allied in the Syro-Ephraimite war; originally, Judah was a part of that coalition.

these pronouncements of judgment on its neighbors, it may welcome them, but Amos's words are not really good news to them; all these people would suffer alike at the hands of an eastern empire.

The accusations cataloged by Amos are not for crimes that the audience is neutral about; Amos's audience likely considered them atrocities, and judgment for them would have been what the people expected. The offenses "are thought of as a part of the common moral sense of all right-minded people, . . . God shares this moral sense . . . since he is the very epitome of right-mindedness. But there is no real suggestion that the rightness of the moral norms actually derives from God . . . Israel's neighbors are not denounced for sins which they could not have been expected to recognize as such (e.g., idolatry) but for offenses against common humanity; not for disobedience to God but for failure to follow the dictates of their own moral sense."[18] We might call these norms an inchoate international law, though many nations violate it when to do so is advantageous. Any enforcement is ultimately up to the transcendent Sovereign who governs human affairs.

The prophecy of judgment against Israel appeals to a much different set of norms. The leading indictment is the oppression of the poor:

> because they sell the righteous for silver,
> and the needy for a pair of sandals—
> they trample the head of the poor into the dust of the earth
> and push the afflicted out of the way. (2:6b–7a)

The second couplet is rather general; the first is the specific one of selling debtors into slavery to pay off their debt. The other accusations have to do with violating the sanctity of the sanctuary with cultic prostitution (2:7b), misuse of pawns (2:8a) and ill-gotten wine (2:8b).

Why does Amos move from international to domestic offenses in the oracle against Israel? I believe it is because Israel is elect, as the contrast motif indicates in 2:9–11. Israel is under a divine law because its election is to live according to a law with a higher, more exacting standard than the common law of nations (or natural law). Amos would not have indicted Moab or Tyre for the offenses with which he charges the people of God.

Why should we ascribe to revelation the law to which Amos appeals here?[19] Because Amos's sensitivity to the plight of the poor and vulnerable is

---

18. Barton, *Understanding Old Testament Ethics*, 113.

19. Of course, the cultic indictments would derive from revelation; it is the oppression of the poor that could go either way.

*Redeeming Judgment*

not characteristic of wisdom— Israelite or ancient Near Eastern.[20] Israelite law raises the bar of justice under the pressure of the first commandment.

One other passage in Amos speaks directly about the oppression of the poor, even of enslaving humans to pay off debts (8:4–6). To this indictment another specific charge is added, viz., impatience with holidays and the Sabbath because they interrupt business. It is also suggested that the falsification of weights and measures is common in the marketplace. This is definitely a society in which the slogan "Let the buyer (or seller) beware" is prudent advice.

Israelite society also oppresses the poor, and any honest person, in the courts. In Amos 5, we have a woe against the courts, beginning in v. 7:

> Woe to you who turn justice to wormwood,
> and bring righteousness to the ground. (v. 7)[21]

The indictment is interrupted by two verses praising the Creator, but one portion of what is known as the "doxologies of Amos." Then it continues:

> They hate the one who reproves in the gate,
> and they abhor the one who speaks the truth. (v. 10)

Then the text returns to a general charge in v. 12:

> For I know how many are your transgressions,
> and how great are your sins—
> you who afflict the righteous, who take a bribe,
> and push aside the needy in the gate.

One could not ask for a more sweeping description of the corrupt, oppressive judicial system than this prophecy.

Again and again Amos links the oppression of the poor with the luxury of the rich, e.g.:

> Hear this word, you cows of Bashan
> who are on Mount Samaria,
> who oppress the poor, who crush the needy,
> who say to their husbands, "Bring something to drink." (4:1)

---

20. Wisdom originated in aristocratic circles, as collections of ancient near eastern proverbs show. Not even our book of Proverbs, which has been transformed by Yahwism, is very sensitive to the plight of the poor and vulnerable.

21. One has to emend the text to yield "woe," but there is a compelling reason to do so: the verse begins with a participle.

There could be no law against living like this or obtaining wealth, but Amos charges that the procurement invariably is at the expense of the honest and the poor. Whether the appropriation had the semblance of legality or was strictly criminal, Amos condemns it in the name of YHWH. Amos's ideal community would not have discrepancies of wealth, and those with enough should forgive the debts of the poor and needy.[22]

Amos also condemns the wealthy for their extravagant, wasteful, and often decadent lifestyle. Amos 6:4–7 is the prime example:

> Woe to those who lie on beds of ivory
>
> ...
>
> and eat lambs from the flock
>
> ...
>
> who sing idle songs to the sound of the harp,
> and like David improvise on instruments of music;
> who drink wine from bowls
>
> ...
>
> but are not grieved over the ruin of Joseph! (vv. 4–6)

This is a vivid picture of a cocktail party with live music and plenty to eat and drink. This is the luxurious lifestyle that the common people in ancient Israel could not aspire to. Note too that it involves a forgetfulness—really an indifference to the fate of the nation or the suffering of the poor. This is a life lived according to the motto, "Eat, drink and be merry..."

The wealthy do not, however, turn their backs on religion; rather, they take over the cult and make it an image of their lifestyle:

> On the day I punish Israel for its transgressions,
> I will punish the altars of Bethel
> and the horns of the altar shall be cut off
> and fall to the ground.
> I will tear down the winter house as well as the summer house. (3:14–15a)

Note that the altars of the sanctuary are set parallel to the residences of the wealthy. How common it is for the wealthy to be patrons of the cult and reproduce a replica of their way of life in the religion of the society. This seems to be the point of Amos's ironical urging of the audience to perform religious actions:

---

22. Deut 15:1–11 tries to require such charity, though it would hardly be enforceable.

> Come to Bethel—and transgress;
> > to Gilgal—and multiply transgression;
> 
> bring your sacrifices every morning,
> > your tithes every three days . . .
> > for so you love to do, O people of Israel! (4:4–5)

Bethel is the royal sanctuary for the tribes in the central hill country. It is the place where Amos delivers these oracles, and from which he is banished. Bethel, along with Gilgal and Beer-sheba, come in for another ironic condemnation in 5:4–6.

Amos does not believe that cultic actions have any efficacy with YHWH; he formulates a deservedly famous prophetic torah that contrasts justice to cultic practices:

> I hate, I despise your feasts,
> > and I take no delight in your solemn assemblies.
> 
> Even though you offer me your burnt offerings and grain offerings,
> > I will not accept them . . .
> 
> Take away from me the noise of your songs;
> > I will not listen to the melody of your harps.
> 
> But let justice roll down like waters,
> > and righteousness like an ever-flowing stream. (5:21–24)

Scholars have debated whether Amos really advocates a religion without sacrifices and ceremonies. This is probably beside the point, though Amos's prophecy has an effect in later anti-temple literature: Amos is not a reformer, he does not institute rules for practice; he is pronouncing judgment on the nation, including the cult. He condemns the courts; he also condemns the Bethel cult in particular, and probably all cultic activity within the northern kingdom of Israel.

Amos attacks those in the kingdom who deny the judgment he proclaims, probably because they do not think the injustices in the society are serious enough to deserve it. Those who reside in the capital cities are condemned for their confidence and complacency:

> Alas for those who are at ease in Zion,
> > and those who feel secure on Mount Samaria,[23]

---

23. This pairing of the capital cities is decisive evidence that Amos regarded his message of judgment as addressed to the people of both kingdoms. It was because only the northern kingdom was completely destroyed by the Assyrians that Amos's message was narrowed to

> the notables of the first of the nations,
>> to whom the house of Israel resort . . .
> O you that put far away the evil day,
>> and bring near the reign of violence. (6:1–3)

Finally, there is a statement in the midst of a sentence that singles out those who deny the coming of judgment:

> [I will] shake the house of Israel among all the nations
> as one shakes with a sieve,
>> but no pebble shall fall upon the ground.
> All the sinners of my people shall die by the sword,
>> who say, "Evil shall not overtake or meet us." (9:9–10)

## Micah and Isaiah

Several accusations in the book of Micah cover the same territory as Amos. One is directed against conspirators who are devising ways to appropriate others' land. Since land cannot be stolen as one would steal a moveable, one has to purchase it or win it by court action.

> Alas for those who devise wickedness
>> and evil deeds on their beds!
> When the morning dawns, they perform it, . . .
> They covet fields, and seize them;
>> houses, and take them away;
> They oppress householder and house. (Mic 2:1–2)

Micah, like Amos, is from a rural area in Judah. He had a particular animas for the ruling class in the city of Jerusalem. Micah 3:9–11 is the prime example:

> Hear this, you rulers of the house of Jacob
>> and chiefs of the house of Israel,
> who abhor justice
>> and pervert all equity,
> who build Zion with blood
>> and Jerusalem with wrong!

---

the northern kingdom by editors and readers.

> Its rulers give judgment for a bribe,
>> its priests teach for a price,
>> its prophets give oracles for money; . . .
> Therefore because of you
>> Zion shall be plowed as a field,
> Jerusalem shall become a heap of ruins
>> and the mountain of the house a wooded height.

Micah has several prophetic oracles against prophets who trim their message to satisfy their audience or patrons:

> Thus says the LORD concerning the prophets
>> who lead my people astray,
> who cry "Peace"
>> when they have something to eat,
> but declare war against those
>> who put nothing into their mouths. (Mic 3:5)

Like Amos, Micah has prophetic torah that contrasts sacrificing to doing justice, showing mercy, and living according to a humble faith (6:6–8). This has been the most popular passage out of the Micah corpus, and a fitting epitaph for a humble servant of YHWH.

The book of Isaiah is a collection of prophecies from several identifiable prophets and their disciples from a number of centuries. Only Isaiah of Jerusalem, the person for whom the book is named, pronounces judgment on the people of Israel and Judah. This makes our task easy in this chapter: we can concentrate on the prophecies of judgment against the people of God, and against the Assyrian empire and Egypt. These are found in Isaiah 1–11, 28–32, and scattered through Isaiah 13–23.[24]

Let's examine chapter 5, a series of woes (Heb. *hoy*) that single out the unjust and unrighteous for judgment.[25] The chapter begins with a parable. Isaiah sings a song about his "beloved," who turns out to be none other than YHWH. The beloved planted a vineyard, with watchtower and wine vat; but the vineyard produced "wild" grapes—presumably sour, useless grapes. Isaiah invites his audience to decide what to do with the vineyard, then quotes the beloved's decision to destroy the vineyard. In the last verse of the song about the vine-

---

24. See the introductions and commentaries. There are also a few embedded in the narrative in Isaiah 36–37.

25. Actually, the chapter has passages pronouncing national judgment, so the people singled out aren't punished distributively.

yard (5:7), the singer identifies the figures: the planter is YHWH, the vineyard is Israel and Judah, and the sour grapes are "bloodshed" (Heb. *mispak*) and "outcry" (*ze'aqah*ʿ); the good wine would have been "justice" (*mishpaṭ*) and "righteousness" (*tsedakah*). This sets the subject of the chapter.

We have a series of woes running from 5:8 to 5:24. The first is the concentration of farmland in the hands of a few landowners:

> Woe to those who obtain house upon house,
>> who add field to field,
> until there is no more room,
>> and you are made to dwell alone
> in the midst of the land. (5:8)

There is no indication whether the large landowners accumulated their property legally or illegally; the point is, concentration of land ownership in the hands of a few is itself bad for the country; concentrated land ownership runs contrary to the ideal distribution of the holy land among the people. The system of land ownership condemned by Isaiah renders large portions of the population landless laborers or even slaves. It also makes the landowners lonely, depopulating the countryside. Moreover, the interests of landowners will hardly coincide with the mass of the people; there will be (or is) a polarization between the rich and powerful, and the dependent and vulnerable.

The next woe condemns a lifestyle available to the well-to-do: heavy drinking and elaborate feasting. This woe is quite close to Amos 6:4–7; it even has an identification of what the partygoers do not observe: "the deeds of the Lord, . . . the work of his hands" (v. 12b, RSV).[26] Interwoven into this chapter is what might be called a litany of punishment (cp. Isa 5:14–17); it integrates the punishment of those singled out into the national judgment. We have a later passage that condemns the injustices in the judicial system:

> Ah, you who make iniquitous decrees,
>> who write oppressive statutes
> to turn aside the needy from justice
>> and to rob the poor of my people of their right,
> that widows may be your spoil. (10:1–2)

The judicial system is the agent of the rich and powerful exploiting the vulnerable members of society. The patrimony of the vulnerable may be appropriated

---

26. Amos said, "the ruin of Joseph".

by fair means or foul, but whichever it is, it harms those who need the land for a living, and benefits those who least need it.[27]

Like Amos and Micah, Isaiah offers prophetic torah; in it he denies that worshippers will please God and be heard by him by ritual activities when they are guilty.

> What to me is the multitude of your sacrifices?
>> says the Lord.
> I have had enough of burnt offerings of rams . . .
> bringing offerings is futile;
>> incense is an abomination to me . . .
> I cannot endure solemn assembly with iniquity
> . . .
> When you stretch out your hands,
>> I will hide my eyes from you;
> even though you make many prayers,
>> I will not listen:
>> your hands are full of blood. (Isa 1:11–15)

The passage goes on to counsel a change of life:

> Cease to do evil,
>> learn to do good;
> seek justice,
>> rescue the oppressed,
> defend the orphan,
>> plead for the widow. (1:16–17)

Isaiah has added his support to the prophetic stance that cultic activity cannot be substituted for genuine righteousness and justice. Indeed, the ritual life that sustains the religious life seems to carry no weight with God, and to be a positive offense when the worshipper is guilty.

Isaiah's passion for justice even makes its appearance in passages concerned with political issues. In the midst of a prophecy of judgment against the anti-Assyrian policy of Hezekiah, Isaiah inserts a sign of salvation:

> Therefore thus says the Lord God:
> "I am laying in Zion a foundation stone,
>> a tested stone,

---

27. For a discussion of the strategies the land grabbers could use to procure land, consult Davies, *Prophecy and Ethics*, 65–89.

> a precious cornerstone, a sure foundation:
> "One who believes will not be in panic."
> And I will make justice the line,
> and righteousness the plummet;
> hail will sweep away the refuse of lies,
> and waters will overwhelm the shelter. (28:16–17)

The faith that is cool under pressure, and relies upon God rather than armament and alliances, will be known for its justice and benevolence, whereas falsity will not stand in the time of trouble.

## Prophetic Accusations of Unfaithfulness

This type of accusation can be subsumed under apostasy and idolatry, but it extends to marital faithlessness and self-salvation through military preparedness and foreign alliances. The latter belongs here because both Hosea and Isaiah hold political leaders to a standard of trust in YHWH. In terms of natural and revealed law, then, the subjects gathered here are governed by revealed law.

### Hosea: Prophet of Faithfulness

Hosea is the only writing prophet from the northern kingdom. This is exhibited in his identification of the northern kingdom frequently as Ephraim, which would be more characteristic of citizens of the hill country of Ephraim than of outsiders.[28]

Hosea's ministry begins in the reign of Jeroboam II (at about the time of Amos's visit to Bethel, viz. ca 750 BCE) and lasts at least to the end of the Syro-Ephraimite war in 732 (commented on in Hos 5:8–15), and perhaps until the nation's violent death in 721 (perhaps commented on in Hos 13:13–15). Hosea describes the chaotic period of rival rulers and incessant coups in 6:7–10, 11–7:7.

The book divides unevenly into chapters 1–3 and 4–14. The first three chapters tell the story of Hosea's marriage and family, and draw prophecies of judgment from the experience. No further explicit references are made to Hosea's marriage, wife, and children in the book. The issues of apostasy and

---

28. The verse that identifies him—viz., 1:1—names his patronymic, but not his nation or tribe. Indeed, given the list of kings, one might think that he was Judean, since the editor only names one northern king, Jeroboam (the second). The editor was probably Judean and did not know the names of the last kings of Israel.

marital infidelity do continue. There are some fuzzy divisions within 4–14, but they are not sharp enough to build much on. Chapter 4 deals with religious and sexual infidelity; chapter 14 is a concluding repentance ceremony. Chapters 5–8 focus on political failures; chapters 9–13 review Israel's history from numerous angles.

The book of Hosea probably comes from the northern kingdom, perhaps brought by refugees from the Assyrian assault. The text is rather difficult to recover at times, and this may be due to the travail undergone by the refugee bearers of Hosea on their journey to Jerusalem. Nevertheless, the brilliant poetry and meditative voice of the prophet comes through. The book almost sounds like a diary; it does not sound like the public jeremiads of Amos and Isaiah.

Hosea 2 is the poetic application of Hosea's family situation to YHWH and Israel. In vv. 2–13, we have a quasi-narrative of what has happened or will happen to Gomer and her children / to Israel and the Israelites. Verse 2 begins as Hosea's address to his children, but the punishment suddenly shifts to YHWH's punishment of the land:

> I will strip her naked
>   and expose her as in the day she was born,
> and make her like a wilderness
>   and turn her into a parched land. (v. 3)

It is in this way that Hosea establishes and maintains the analogy. It is his wife Gomer who "played the whore" (v. 5a), but when she pursued lovers, she wanted bread and water, wool and flax (v. 5b)—hardly the gifts a woman would seek from a lover. Rather, this is what Israel seeks from the Baals, who were known for providing the necessities of life. Then YHWH pledges to frustrate Israel's effort to make contact with her "lovers."[29] The nation will realize then that it has been YHWH all along who provided these necessities (vv. 7b–8). YHWH's "punishment" of Israel will be depriving it of its necessities and wealth to teach it who is their true source (v. 9).[30] As for the Baals, they will see the nation exposed before their eyes, unable to stop it (v. 10). This will "expose" their powerlessness. Perhaps this is the rubric under which the festivals that she was dedicating to the Baals are put an end to (vv. 11–13).

---

29. It is hard to say whether Hosea did this with his wife, or how he could accomplish it.

30. This reminds me of 1 Kings 17–18: The drought announced by Elijah, which was also ended through actions of the prophet.

But now there is a surprise. The punishment of Israel, which makes a wilderness of the land, now becomes the wilderness of the exodus—or of a new exodus, a second honeymoon, a new start (2:13–14). In this turn of events, judgment becomes one side of a coin that has salvation on the other side. This reversal takes place again at the end of the chapter, when the names of Hosea's three children are resymbolized: Jezreel, a name indicting the house of Omri (1:4–5), takes its Hebrew meaning, viz., "God sows" (2:21–23a); Lo-Ruhammah, a name declaring the end of divine mercy toward Israel,[31] loses its *lo*, now symbolizing God's love of the unloved; and Lo Ami, a name renouncing the nation's election, also loses its *lo* (23b). With Hosea, God's salvation begins in judgment, and builds upon it as well as reverses it.

Chapter 4 begins a collection of oracles that continues without any narrative break through the rest of the book. From here on we must imagine context and reaction. The first three verses of chapter 4 are called a *rib* for the poetic scene of trial that it evokes. The indictment is worth quoting:

> There is no faithfulness or loyalty
> > and no knowledge of God in the land.
> Swearing, lying, and murder,
> > and stealing and adultery break out;
> > bloodshed follows bloodshed. (4:1b–2)

This indictment has the comprehensive scope of the Ten Commandments, which it may well be echoing. Instead of the prohibitions against recognizing other gods and bowing to idols, this passage states duties owed YHWH that are not being fulfilled. With the absence of the proper foundation, every prohibition covering human relations is violated. As a result, the land itself is dying.

The next prophecy singles out religious leaders, primarily priests. They have failed their calling of teaching the people the "knowledge of God" and his law (v. 6), and the people have lost their way. The priests have actually been cultivating the people's sin-consciousness so they will sacrifice more (vv. 7–8). The people want progeny, so they "play the whore," but God will give them none. This prophecy links the perversion of religion, if not apostasy in particular, with sexual laxity, as does the next. In the next, the people are engaged in idolatry ("consult a piece of wood," v. 12) and apostasy "on the tops of the mountains" (v. 13), and promiscuity results:

> Therefore your daughters play the whore,
> > and your daughters-in-law commit adultery. (v. 13b)

31. Cp. Amos 7:8c, 8:2c.

*Redeeming Judgment*

The ironic twist of this prophecy is that YHWH will *not* punish the women because the men are the ones who have intercourse with them (v. 14). These two prophecies in Hosea 4 accuse Israelites of violating marriage literally as well as linking up with the Baals in spiritual infidelity. The same indictment may come out in 4:18 and 5:4, but nowhere else.[32]

The subject of apostasy and idolatry does come up often, especially in the chapters that review the history of Israel as God's people (chapters 9–13). A lot of these have very appealing images:

> Like grapes in the wilderness
> > I found Israel.
> like the first fruit on the fig tree,
> in its first season,
> > I saw your ancestors.
> But they came to Baal-Peor,
> > and consecrated themselves to a thing of shame
> > and became detestable like the thing they loved. (9:10)

This is a contrast motif with a twist. It does not recount God's deeds for Israel but rather the beautiful condition the people were in during the exodus.[33] It was on the edge of the land they were settling that they went rotten, so to speak. That rottenness was due to contact with a foreign deity.

Hosea 13:4–8 tells a similar story. YHWH was Israel's only God from the exodus from Egypt onward; and he provided them with food. Then they became satisfied and proud of their accomplishments, and forgot their true God. It sounds like this defection took place in the wilderness, though when may not be as important as what happened over time.[34]

Hosea 11:1–9 is a favorite passage of Bible readers. The people are the Lord's "son," brought from Egypt, but they have a stubborn, rebellious streak (11:1). The closer YHWH seeks to get to them, the more they go after Baals and idols (11:2). YHWH describes how he taught his people (Ephraim) to walk and cared for it as it was growing up—all to no avail. They went their own way. They will have to relive their history, so to speak, returning to "Egypt," which is the cipher for Assyria (note v. 5). However, the Lord's love for them is too great to permit him to destroy them (vv. 8–9). Their judgment itself seems to arouse the Lord's love for them.

---

32. Hosea is not as "hung up" about sex as naïve readers often think.
33. Rather striking for its positive character, given the stories of rebellion.
34. Cp. Deuteronomy 8.

Hosea 13:1–3 is rather specifically about Ephraim, not the whole nation of Israel:

> When Ephraim spoke, there was trembling;
> > he was exalted in Israel,
> > but he incurred guilt through Baal and died. (13:1)

Exactly why this one tribe—or is it the northern kingdom?—is singled out for its apostasy is hard to say. The prophecy does go on to specific sins of idolatry, climaxing in an allusion, probably, to the golden calf (v. 2). Hosea also condemns the golden calf (or calves) elsewhere (8:4–6).[35]

Finally, it is worthwhile to glance at 10:1–2. It begins:

> Israel is a luxuriant vine
> > that yields its fruit.
>
> The more his fruit increased,
> > the more altars he built;
>
> as the country improved,
> > he improved his pillars.[36]

This does not condemn apostasy or idolatry per se, but rather the deleterious effect on religious sanctuaries, and practice, that prosperity brings. Perhaps Hosea ascribes at least an impulse toward making idols to prosperity and sophistication; this would be a case of adornment to show off the community's wealth and culture.

Despite Hosea's condemnation of his people and their priests for not knowing God, he certainly expects his audience to know the sacred tradition thoroughly. His prophecies are steeped in allusions to events in the sacred history of the people.[37] If the hearers or readers understood them, they were not as ignorant as Hosea's accusations make them out to be. Perhaps Hosea is cultivating historical consciousness in his saturation of prophecies with allusions that the audience has to fill out.

The anthropological dimension of the offense of apostasy is loss of national identity. Israel is a people whose identity has been formed in relationship to one deity, and to fall back into polytheism is to lose the well-grounded

---

35. This is strong evidence that the negative assessment of the golden calf or calves was northern, not a pro-Jerusalem polemic.

36. Ultimately pillars and Ashera are going to be condemned as idols (so Deut 16:21–22), but here the reference is parallel to altars, which are always legitimate.

37. The same holds for the judgments of kings and royal policies.

*Redeeming Judgment*

identity that comes with faithfulness to God and to all the members of one's people.

Hosea 14 is the capstone of the book. It speaks to contemporary readers as much as to the original Israelites. What should our response be to the pronouncements of judgment on monarchical Israel? Hosea provides words for us:

> Take away all guilt; . . .
> accept that which is good,
>     and we will offer
>     the fruit of our lips.
> Assyria shall not save us;
>     we will not ride upon horses.
> And we will say no more, "our God,"
>     to the work of our hands.
> In you the orphan finds mercy. (14:2b–3)

In this confession, the people do admit their sin as much as their dependence on the Lord

Let's go back to the confession of sin because it leads us into Hosea's other indictment of this people. Hosea offers two couplets that summarize much of his indictment:[38]

> Assyria shall not save us;
>     we will not ride upon horses.
> And we will say no more, "Our God,"
>     to the work of our hands. (14:3)

The second couplet renounces idolatry. Note that for Hosea it is wrong because humans are seeking thereby to save themselves. Idols are so-called gods that humans make, yet they are relied upon as though they were independent and capable of lending power to humans. This is not only foolish; it is a disruption of the proper relationship of God and creation.

Now to the other couplet: It offers two parallel lines—one involving an alliance with the dominant imperial power of the age, the other military build-up. One has to generalize from the mention of Assyria, for Israel and Judah are also allied with Egypt.[39] Indeed, this is probably the provocation that weights

---

38. Gottwald, *All the Kingdoms of the Earth*, 140, 143–44, connects this to "double iniquity" in 10:10.

39. Cp., e.g., 11:12—12:1.

the balance against Israel in the eyes of the Assyrians. Hosea is critical of all these alliances. He only condemns militarism once (10:13); one wonders why it gets equal billing with idolatry. On the other hand, the alliances certainly required Israel and Judah to be prepared to fight alongside allies.

Why do I subsume political matters under apostasy and idolatry? The parallelism in 14:2 is a good warrant. Hosea believes that seeking to save oneself by alliance and military power are violations of the security provided by trust in YHWH. Trying to save oneself is sin, whether by idolatry or political machinations. Ancient societies did not separate religion very sharply from politics, and Hosea offers a monotheistic—or better, a first-commandment—political vision for Israel. I offer the analogy of a sect for Hosea's program: Israel should withdraw from the world of power politics just as certain religious groups seek to cut off significant contact with the nonbelieving environment.

Now let us turn to prophecies that indict Israel for political offenses. Among the reviews of Israel's history, we have a number that condemn Israel for the monarchy, e.g.:

> Every evil of theirs began at Gilgal;[40]
> there I came to hate them. (9:15)

> Since the days of Gibeah you have sinned, O Israel;
> there they have continued.
> Shall not war overtake them in Gibeah? (10:9)

There is also one in chapter 8:

> They made kings, but not through me;
> they set up princes, but without my knowledge. (8:4)

This could be a pronouncement against some of the recent kings who arose in coups, but it could just as well be directed at all monarchs in Israelite history. I say this, in addition to the above statements, because Hosea has a passage recalling the antimonarchical tradition in 1 Samuel 8 and 12:

> Where now is your king, that he may save you?
> Where in all your cities are your rulers?
> Of whom you said,
> "Give me a king and rulers."
> I gave you a king in my anger
> and I took him away in my wrath. (13:10–11)

40. See 1 Sam 11:15.

## Redeeming Judgment

In this version of the tradition, YHWH is not reconciled to the people's decision for a monarchical form of government. He granted their request to punish the people, and now their removal is judgment as well. The monarchy, human rule, is incompatible with YHWH's rule.

Hosea's view of the monarchy may have grown on him as the disintegration and suicidal policies of the northern kingdom progressed. His first child was named Jezreel, to indict the dynasty of Jeroboam II for the murderous actions of its founder, Jehu. Jeroboam was at least a stable and successful ruler. When his son was killed, the game of "king on the mountain" began. Hosea tells this story in 7:1–7. The passage begins with a general charge against the kingdom:

> The corruption of Ephraim is revealed,
>   and the wicked deeds of Samaria.
> For they deal falsely—
>   the thief breaks in,
>   and the bandits raid outside. (7:1)

But then it begins to zero in on its rulers:

> By their wickedness they make the king glad,
>   and the officials by their treachery. (7:3)

Officialdom is evidently associated with the underworld. The overheated condition of the rulers is visible in public ceremonies:

> On the day of our king the officials
>   become sick with the heat of wine. (7:5a)

The story comes to a close with evidence that God's judgment is making the deeds of rulers boomerang:

> All of them are as hot as an oven,
>   and they devour their rulers.
> All of their kings have fallen;
>   none of them calls upon me. (7:7)

The most fateful events in the last years of the northern kingdom involve the conflict known as the Syro-Ephraimite war. The name is a misnomer, for Syria and Ephraim were allies, who were seeking to force Judah to join with them in resisting Assyria. When Ahaz of Judah would not, the allies besieged Jerusalem. Hosea's prophecy in 5:8–15 dramatizes the course of events: "Blow the horn in Gibeah, / The trumpet in Ramah . . ." This alludes to the border skirmish when the allies approached Jerusalem. Hosea forewarns, "Ephraim shall become a desolation in the day of punishment" (5:9). A little later he says: "Ephraim is oppressed, crushed in judgment, because he was determined to go after vanity" (v. 11).[41] This must belong to a later moment in the story. Judah enlists Assyria's support against the allies, and the empire wrecks the two "rebels." Ephraim loses about two-thirds of its territory—everything north of the hill country of Samaria. Judah seems to have taken advantage of Israel's vulnerability to expand its territory north: "The princes of Judah have become like those who remove the landmark" (v. 10a). The upshot of these events is that both kingdoms are now vassals of Assyria:

> When Ephraim saw his sickness
> and Judah his wound,
> Ephraim went to Assyria
> and [Judah] sent to the [great king]. (5:13a–b)[42]

Then Hosea issues his evaluation: "But he is unable to cure you or heal your wound" (v. 13c).

Now the Lord declares that he will become the people's enemy and ravage them like a wild beast, then leave them to examine themselves. It is to that situation that the people respond with their inadequate confession in Hos 6:1–3.

Hosea continues to follow events, though it is uncertain as to when chapter 7:8–13; 8:1–3, 4–10; and 12:1 were written. They condemn the royal policy of entering into alliances with the great powers.

> Ephraim mixes himself with the peoples
> . . .
> foreigners devour his strength,
> but he does not know it. (7:8–9)

> Ephraim has become like a dove,
> silly and without sense,
> calling to Egypt, going to Assyria. (7:11)

This is Hosea's poetry at its most eloquent. It is a powerful image of a fruitless, self-defeating foreign policy. In the effort to save itself, the northern kingdom,

---

41. "Enemy" is thought to be a better reading than "vanity."
42. That last line needs some emendations.

*Redeeming Judgment*

under its foolish kings, has effaced the identity of Israel and will soon cause it to be cast off as trash.

Both idolatry and power politics are Israel's effort to save itself. Israel has been called to be different. When the people violate their calling by idolatry or monarchical politics, they are in for divine judgment. This is Hosea's message to the people of God.

## Micah and Isaiah Again

The first part of chapter 1 of Micah begins with the assembling of a cosmic court to judge the two kingdoms into which the people of YHWH are divided. The indictment begins with the capital cities, Samaria and Jerusalem. In the pronouncement of the sentence, the objects to be destroyed are idols:

> All her images shall be beaten to pieces, . . .
>    and all her idols I will lay waste,
> for as the wages of a prostitute she gathered them,
>    and as the wages of a prostitute they shall again be used. (Mic 1:7)

Very little is said about the idols, nothing about why they are sinful; the prophet simply assumes their illegitimacy. The lines about the "wages of a prostitute" could be an allusion to apostasy. If so, then we have evidence of the use of the image of prostitution for apostasy apart from and perhaps before Hosea. Micah's reference, however, is too laconic to build much on. Even the condemnation of the idols may evidence the prophet's animosity toward big-city culture. Places like Samaria would be "corrupted" by commerce with other cultures, and would imitate practices that faithful rural Yahwists would know to avoid.

Isaiah is already the subject of study because of his indictments of Israel and Judah for injustice and oppression and decadence, but his message overlaps with Hosea's as well as Amos's. He has very pointed accusations to make regarding the foreign policy of Ahaz and Hezekiah. His position on alliances is similar to Hosea's, though arrived at by a different route. He also prophesies against foreign nations, particularly against Syria when it allies with Israel, against Egypt when Judah counts on its support against Assyria, and against Assyria itself as it assaults the capital city. Isaiah's theology provides him with a tower, so to speak, from which to observe the entire landscape of international politics during his era.

Strangely Isaiah has no indictments of Israel or Judah for apostasy. This is strange because Hosea sees apostasy everywhere. It is not our assignment to explain this anomaly, simply to call attention to it. We can definitely say that Isaiah's hermeneutic does not derive from the first commandment, as Hosea's does. There was no eighth-century prophet such a thoroughgoing monotheist as Isaiah,[43] but this monotheism functioned in a different way for Isaiah from the way the first commandment functioned for Hosea.

Isaiah does condemn idolatry in chapter 2. Beginning with v. 6, we have a judgment of "the house of Jacob" for religious and spiritual offenses. Idols are mentioned in vv. 8, 18, and 20; only the first of these is an indictment:

> Their land is filled with idols,
> > they bow down to the work of their hands. (2:8)

This is bundled together with other forbidden practices: divination and soothsaying, accumulation of wealth, and of armaments. What do these have in common? A few verses later we have a statement of the fundamental sin:

> The haughty eyes of people shall be brought low,
> > and the pride of everyone shall be humbled,
> and the Lord alone will be exalted
> > in that day.
> For the LORD of hosts has a day
> > against all that is proud and lofty,
> > all that is lifted up and high. (2:11–12)

The sin at the root of all others is hubris, pride, haughtiness, self-salvation. Here we read of Jacob's fall and the Lord's exaltation. Note that this day of judgment has suddenly expanded: it is no longer only for the house of Jacob, now it includes all elevated creatures—even trees, mountains and towers. The prophecy ends with this counsel:

> Turn away from mortals,
> > who have only breath in their nostrils.
> > For of what account are they? (2:22)

---

43. Hosea restricted his horizon to Israel; no judgment of foreign nations, no larger divine design; the relationship of YHWH to Israel filled Hosea's horizon.

## Redeeming Judgment

Obviously, the prophecy has left behind the measure of revealed law, and probed for norms applicable to all human beings.[44] Even idols are condemned for their embodiment of human pride.

Although Isaiah doesn't indict Israel and Judah for apostasy, he does pronounce judgment on the quality of the people's faith. A number of passages refer to the blindness and dullness of religious leaders, e.g.:

> The priest and the prophet reel with strong drink,
>> they are confused with wine,
>> they stagger with strong drink;
> they err in vision,
>> they stumble in giving judgment. (28:7)

It is hard to say whether the language about alcohol is to be taken literally or metaphorically for misjudgment and distorted understanding. The images are often realistic enough to suggest a literal reading, e.g., "tables covered with filthy vomit" (v. 8). Yet errors in vision and judgment sound like intellectual and spiritual malaise. Misguided leaders and teachers will condemn the people to foolish and perverse policies and practices. However, the people often get the leadership they ask for:

> For they are a rebellious people
>
> . . .
>
> who say to seers, "Do not see,"
>> and to the prophets, "Do not prophesy to us what is right;
> speak to us smooth things,
>> prophesy illusions,
> leave the way, turn aside from the path,
>> let us hear no more about the Holy One of Israel." (30:9–11)

This is, of course, Isaiah's caricature of his countrymen, but it undoubtedly brings to light what is going on below the surface.

In a passage in which Isaiah seems to be instructing his disciples, he counsels them to avoid divination: "Now if the people say to you, 'Consult the ghosts and the familiar spirits that chirp and mutter. Should not a people consult their gods, the dead on behalf of the living, for teaching and instruction?' Surely those who speak like this will have no dawn!" (8:19–20). Although Isaiah condemns this as foolish, as leading people to ignorance and as misguided, he does not draw out its apostate character.

---

44. So Barton, *Understanding Old Testament Ethics*, 131–35.

Isaiah also condemns the religion of his time for its shallowness, perhaps even emptiness.

> Because these people draw near with their mouths
> > and honor me with their lips,
> > while their hearts are far from me,
> and their worship of me is a human commandment learned by rote... (29:13)

There follows a punishment appropriate to their condition. The condition itself sounds modern. It is holding on to inherited religion that the heirs no longer understand or believe.

A few verses later Isaiah exposes the thoughtless theology of such shallow religion:

> Ha! You who hide a plan too deep for the LORD,
> > whose deeds are in the dark,
> > and who say, "Who sees us? Who knows of us?"
> You turn things upside down!
> > Shall the potter be regarded as the clay?
> Shall the thing made say to its maker,
> > "He did not make me"[?] (29:15–16)

This accusation is aimed at those who are oblivious to the judgment of God, which is always taking place. Rather than a sentence, Isaiah offers a polemic—analogies exposing the people's nonsensical reasoning.

Readers may have noticed that every one of Isaiah's accusations of religion derives from wisdom, or at least from a scale of measurement that the majority of the human race would recognize. These are not revealed norms. What is revealed is that these foolish behaviors are taken so seriously that divine judgment is in store. It is the one God, known to Israel by revelation, who takes umbrage at shallow religion manipulated to make people feel good.

Looming much larger in Isaiah's message are indictments of rulers and counselors for wrongheaded policies. While Isaiah may have made pronouncements on royal policy before the Syro-Ephraimite war, beginning with that war we start to get a coherent picture of Isaiah's political theology. Isaiah 7 tells the story of Isaiah's message to Ahaz during the siege of Jerusalem by Syria and Israel. Isaiah prophesies:

> It shall not stand
> > and it shall not come to pass

## Redeeming Judgment

> ...
> If you do not stand firm in faith
> you shall not stand at all. (7:7b–9)

For Ahaz this should be an oracle of salvation. His enemies who are besieging him will fail.[45] However, it will depend upon Ahaz's comportment in this crisis whether salvation is in store for Ahaz. When Ahaz rejects the Lord's invitation to ask for a sign (7:10–12), Isaiah offers his own sign, and then pronounces judgment on Ahaz: "The Lord will bring on you and your people and on your ancestral house such days as have not come since the day that Ephraim broke away from Judah—the king of Assyria" (7:17). Why does Ahaz's pious refusal to ask for a sign elicit such a harsh judgment? Because Isaiah believes royal policy should depend on faith—a quiet, cool-headed confidence based on trust in God. Any effort to save oneself by military means is doomed to be thwarted by YHWH:

> In returning and rest you shall be saved,
> in quietness and in trust shall be your strength.
> But you refused, saying,
> "No, we will flee upon horses"—
> therefore you shall flee!
> and, "we will ride on swift steeds"—
> therefore your pursuers shall be swift! (30:15–17)

Ahaz takes care of his enemies by submitting to Assyria and calling them to his aid. Isaiah's condemnation of this policy is found in 8:5–8: "The Lord spoke to me again: 'Because this people has refused the waters of Shiloah that flow gently, and melt in fear before Rezin and the son of Remaliah; therefore, the Lord is bringing up against it the mighty flood waters of the River, mighty and many, the king of Assyria and all his glory; and it will rise above all its channels and overflow all its banks; and it will sweep on into Judah.'" In other words, when Ahaz brings the Assyrians in to destroy his enemies, they will not stop at the border—Judah will be swamped as well.

The irony of Isaiah's struggle with Ahaz is that Ahaz succeeds by his own measure. He saves his own position by submitting wholeheartedly to the dominant power of the day. The country survives, as the northern kingdom goes under. Isaiah's dire predictions do not come true, at least not politically and

---

45. We find the same message again in Isa 17:1–6.

militarily. Judah may absorb too much Assyrian religion and culture, but Ahaz does not seem to care; he is not a committed Yahwist, only a "cultural" one.[46]

Isaiah confronts royal counselors who are also cynical about divine interventions that rulers could trust in; Isaiah's counsel of faith seems to have encountered this skepticism, even ridicule:

> Woe to you ...
> who say, "Let him make haste,
>    let Him speed his work
>    that we may see it—
> let the purpose of the Holy One of Israel hasten to fulfillment,
>    that we may know it! (5:18–19, RSV)

The counselors are telling Isaiah, "We will believe it when we see it. Until then, we will design our policy on what is probable and calculable." Isaiah offers a parable to explain his conception of the plan of God. In Isa 28:23–29, he compares God's working to that of a farmer, who does each operation of plowing, planting, and harvesting in its season.

What does Isaiah mean by God's plan? It is obviously not the sort of wisdom that the wise men of the time would have access to. The royal counselors exhibit typical pragmatic thinking. Isaiah's wisdom is based on revelation. What he sees is Assyria serving the Lord's judgment of his people (10:5–6), and in the process bringing all the nations of the Near East under one sovereign; but then that sovereign, a tyrant, will be overturned by God (10:16–19; 14:24–27) and a new order, one that looks to the prophets of Jerusalem to resolve all international conflicts (2:1–5), will come into being.[47]

Hezekiah succeeded his father Ahaz in 715 BCE. He is the opposite his father in many ways. He is a fully committed, pious Yahwist, inclined to resist Assyrian power with the expectation of divine aid. Isaiah is held in esteem by the king, but he struggles against Hezekiah's rather nationalistic religion and pro-Egyptian alliance policy.

We find evidence of this struggle between king and prophet just a few years after Hezekiah's ascension to the throne. Evidently a number of rulers in Syro-Palestine began discussing rebellion against Assyria—Egypt egging them on with pledges of support. Isaiah dramatizes his opposition by going about naked (Isa 20:2–6). He pronounces judgment on the Egyptians, ruled by the

---

46. He at least named his son Hezekiah, a Yahwistic name.

47. This paragraph is dependent on Gottwald, *All the Kingdoms of the Earth*, 183–84, 233, 36.

*Redeeming Judgment*

Ethiopian dynasty. His pronouncement of judgment is calculated to discourage counsels of war.

We have woes in 30:1–5 and 31:1–3 that pronounce judgment on both Egypt and Judah:

> "Woe to the rebellious children," says the Lord,
> "who carry out a plan, but not mine;
> and make an alliance, but against my will,
>     adding sin to sin;
> who set out to go down to Egypt,
>     without asking for my counsel,
> to take refuge in the protection of the Pharaoh,
>     and to seek shelter in the shadow of Egypt!" (30:1–2)

It is very improbable that Hezekiah has not solicited and gained prophetic approval of any mission to Egypt. The point must be that the YHWH, who speaks through Isaiah, would not approve or bless such a conspiracy.

This prophecy goes on to condemn the alliance to failure and shame. In the next oracle (30:6–7), Egypt's help is declared to be "worthless and empty"; it would be called "Rahab who sits still" (30:7). In the woe in 31:1–3, Isaiah offers another reason not to trust Egypt:

> The Egyptians are human, and not God;
>     and their horses are flesh, and not spirit.
> When the Lord stretches out his hand,
>     the helper will stumble,
>     and the one helped will fall,
>     and they will all perish together. (31:3)

Note how effectively Isaiah appeals to a monotheistic contrast between God and world. This may be the most monotheistic utterance in the eighth century.

There are several chapters of judgments of Egypt in the collection of oracles against foreign nations. The oracle against "Ethiopia" seems to be a condemnation of the anti-Assyrian alliance (18:1–6). The other one lists idolatry and divination (19:1, 3) as features of Egyptian culture, but it is not clear that they offend the divine majesty (19:5–10). Perhaps the country's downfall is the foolishness of the wise (19:11–15). What one yearns for is a condemnation of Egypt for arousing expectations of military and political aid against Assyria only to withhold it when the small, exposed states of Syria and Palestine are under assault.

## Four Eighth-Century Prophets of Judgment

In 705 BCE, Sargon II died and Sennacherib ascended the Assyrian throne. Judah and Babylon withheld tribute, and Sennacherib spent the next five years subduing them, beginning with Babylon. Hezekiah had a few years to prepare to meet the Assyrian onslaught. There are a few Isaianic prophecies that describe these preparations, e.g., 22:8b–11: "On that day you looked to the weapons of the House of the Forest, and you saw that there were many breaches in the city of David, and you collected the waters of the lower pool. You counted the houses of Jerusalem, and you broke down the houses to fortify the wall. You made a reservoir between the two walls for the water of the old pool. But you did not look to him who [brought this on you,[48]] or have regard for him who planned it long ago."

This passage may come from after the Assyrian siege of Jerusalem, but it does allude to measures taken before. Several of the woes condemning alliances with Egypt might come from this period of waiting. I would like to locate here the prophecy that says the ruling elite of Jerusalem "have made a covenant with death" (28:15). If this indictment is to be taken literally, the ruling elite is either dabbling in the occult or making a cynical bargain with chance. Neither really seems to be in step with Hezekiah's piety and moral seriousness. It is possible that Isaiah has made a caricature of the covenant or alliance that the rulers have made, to express his estimate of their policy.

When Sennacherib struck in 701 BCE, he wiped out all resistance in the countryside and besieged Jerusalem. Isaiah's words of judgment were being fulfilled all too thoroughly. The Assyrians offered Hezekiah and the inhabitants of the city terms of surrender. The story is powerfully told in Isaiah 36–37. In the midst of the siege, Isaiah begins to pronounce judgment on the Assyrians for their arrogance and self-sufficiency (37:22–29). One of his oracles of judgment on Assyria is packed with sophisticated theology, viz., 10:5–19. Assyria is an instrument of YHWH's purpose:

> Ah, Assyria, the rod of my anger,
>    the staff of my fury!
> Against a godless nation I send him,
>    and against the people of my wrath I command him,
> to take spoil and seize plunder,
>    to tread them down like mire in the streets. (10:5–6, RSV)

Assyria has, therefore, been assigned the task of punishing Israel and Judah. This is not because they are better; no, they are a vicious and arrogant super-

---

48. The Hebrew reads, "did it," rather cryptic for me.

power, but their will to power has given the will and capacity to do the job. However, they are not doing the will of God purposely:

> But this is not what he intends,
>> nor does he have this in mind;
> but it is in his mid to destroy,
>> and to cut off nations not a few. (10:7)

After describing Assyria's basic intent, Isaiah cites things the Assyrians have said that demonstrate their arrogance and sense of unlimited power. Moreover, they take full credit for their conquests:

> By the strength of my hand I have done it,
>> and by my wisdom, for I have understanding;
> I have removed the boundaries of peoples,
>> and have plundered their treasures. (10:13)

The contradiction cannot last; Assyria must be punished, indeed overturned. We have already seen the larger plan of YHWH, as Isaiah represents it. Isaiah's hope does not fully materialize, but Assyria does relieve the siege of Jerusalem and allow the monarchy to continue for a bit more than a century.

The Jerusalemites are jubilant at the lifting of the siege, and celebrate vociferously. Isaiah does not approve. Several of the prophecies in chapter 22 castigate them for their celebrating (22:1–8, 12–14). Isaiah probably would have them thanking God for his forgiveness, mixed with expressing sorrow over the great loss. That, at any rate, is how I read Isa 1:4–9. Isaiah must have felt that the people learned the wrong lesson from the seeming divine intervention that saved the city.

The root of all political sin for Isaiah is pride and self-sufficiency. His one guiding principle for politics would be the one he enunciates in his oracle to Ahaz: "If you will not believe [stand firm], surely you will not be established [stood firm]" (Isa 7:9b). Though Isaiah elevates wisdom, his ultimate measure is God's will known in faith.

# 10

# Refining Fire
(Amos, Hosea, Micah, Isaiah)

THE PROPHECIES OF JUDGMENT, individual and communal, have no distinct statement of guilt.[1] That is why I have not used the word *verdict*. The prophecy *is* the decision of God, so the accusation specifies the offense or offenses the addressee is guilty of, and the sentence is the divine decision as to what the consequences will be.

*Sentencing* may sound too formal for the actual transactions of prophetic utterance and audience. That is true, because God's decision is conveyed by a human, the prophet, and the audience may be skeptical of the prophet's message. Moreover, the communal prophecy of judgment seeks to persuade the people of their guilt and the inevitability of divine chastisement. Thus, prophecy shades over into deliberative discourse.

Several purposes may be served by the sentence. It may punish felons, making them suffer to the same degree as they caused others to suffer.[2] It may also be designed to instill fear in the rest of society so the crime will not be repeated. It may seek to remove the felon from the society so that the felon cannot repeat the crime. It may seek to reform the offender into a contributing member of society. All these motives are still in play. Ancient Israel worried about incurring collective guilt from the serious crimes by members, so punishment purged the society of guilt (cp. Deut 17:7; 19:13).

---

1. See Westermann, *Basic Forms of Prophetic Speech*, 169–75, 186–87.
2. This would work only for crimes with victims.

## The Term *Sentence* for the Declaration of Divine Chastisement

Now we come to applying the term *sentence* to an element within the prophecy of judgment. The only question is whether the prophecy of judgment against the people is close enough to a trial to use the noun *sentence* for the declaration of consequences. We have been arguing that the prophecy of judgment against the whole people is an expansion of the prophecy of judgment against individuals. If this argument is sound, it is logical to apply the same nomenclature in discussing both types of judgment. Some other advantages accrue to the application of the word *sentence* to the consequences to be imposed on the accused.

The word *sentence* is better than some alternative terms that interpreters have used over history. One is *prediction*. This is understood to be a description of what will happen in the future, known either by rational or by supernatural means. A sentence is *not* a prediction; it is an authoritative pronouncement of a judicial authority about what will be done to the guilty.

Although to speak of cause and effect is not appropriate to the connection between the two parts of prophecy, prophets must establish some connection between what will happen and why. Prophets do draw frequently on images that suggest poetic justice. They may turn a sin into a punishment. They may remind the people of the threat of the great empire that more and more dominates their lives and consciousness. The audience must be persuaded not only of its injustice and unfaithfulness and the vanity of efforts at self-preservation; hearers must be persuaded that they face great dangers, and that these dangers are YHWH's agent of punishment.

Amos seems to have confronted an audience that was not particularly worried about being destroyed and exiled. He reserves some of his harshest judgments for those who deny that judgment is coming.

> For lo, I will command,
>> and shake the house of Israel among all the nations
> as one shakes with a sieve,
>> and no pebble shall fall to the ground.
> All the sinners of my people shall die by the sword,
>> those who say, "Evil shall not overtake or meet us." (9:9–10).

Amos announces numerous times judgment by military defeat, and has virtually no "escape hatches" for his audience. He is driving home that the nation is doomed. However, he does not identify the power who will do this, indicating that imperial Assyria is not a threat dominating the citizens' minds.

*Refining Fire*

Hosea begins to name Assyria, but more as a temptation to leaders—a potential alliance partner. It is frequently paired with Egypt, as though the threats to national existence come equally from both directions. Nevertheless, Hosea does not have the persuasive task that confronts Amos; Assyria became an oppressive power and threat fairly early in Hosea's ministry, and exiled large portions of, if not the whole of, the country. Hosea's persuasive challenge is to convince his audience that those threats were divine chastisement, that YHWH is putting his people through a trial or ordeal that will change their direction.

Isaiah sees quite clearly that Assyria is the dominant power of the Near East in this era. Egypt is a danger because it tempts the little nations between the empires to resist, but does not intervene to save them when Assyria acts to suppress rebellion. Isaiah's audience does not need to be persuaded of the threat of Assyria, but it does need to be persuaded to keep cool and let YHWH do something about it. The instinct of the pious is to expect YHWH to support the efforts of the country to resist the dominance of the empire, though the prophet Isaiah is saying no.

## *Types of Punishment*

Let's survey the eighth-century prophets for their depiction of judgment. It is a general rule that natural disturbances, uncanny events, and catastrophes could be identified as signs or warnings, but destruction and exile were the result of armies and governments. Amos 1:3—2:5 tells that the neighboring nations will be destroyed by military assault. Israel will too, though the images of battle are from open-country engagements (2:14–16). In 3:11, the country is going to be stripped of its fortifications; in 4:1, the women of Samaria will go into exile; in 5:3 there will be the loss of most soldiers; in 6:9–10, there is a picture of catastrophic depopulation; in 8:3, we hear of mass deaths, probably in battle; 8:10 also describes mass death; 9:9–10 describes exile.

Amos does refer to natural disasters and wonders. In one striking passage, he recounts a series of events, each of which should have prompted the people to repent: "cleanness of teeth"; "lack of bread" (4:6); spotty rains during rainy season (4:7), leading to shortages of drinking water (4:8); "blight and mildew" (4:9); deaths of soldiers from several causes (4:10); also an obnoxious stench in the camp; and some indefinite threat that is compared to the destruction of Sodom and Gomorrah (4:11). All these events should have been understood, according to Amos, as warnings from God to return to the just ways of

*Redeeming Judgment*

YHWH. Since they are not heeded, now there will be a full-scale confrontation with God, the Judge (4:12). Amos seems to have announced an earthquake and a solar eclipse (8:8, 9), each as punishment for sin.

The book of Hosea is not as easy to categorize as Amos. Hosea's sentences tend to be driven by his poetic imagery so that we do not have a description of how punishment will come about. For example, in chapter 2 he speaks of turning the land into a wilderness, and then turning the wilderness into the scene of a new exodus (2:12–13, 14–15). The symbolic significance of wilderness, not its impact as a condition to be suffered as punishment, seems to drive the depiction. In Hos 4:3, the land "mourns"—it probably suffers drought, but Hosea has transformed this into a symbolic picture of nature's death. Here natural catastrophe is punishment for sin. In the political prophecies in chapters 5–8, the crimes that can be set forth as an indictment can also be divine punishment for that the nation's sinfulness (5:11, 13; 6:7–10; 7:1–7, 13, 16; 8:8b–10). One unusual twist in the way Hosea pictures divine punishment is that the future exile in Assyria is typologically identified with the past enslavement in Egypt (9:3, 11:5).

Isaiah clearly sees judgment coming by the hands of a great power, namely, Assyria. He uses the image of military defeat and its aftermath frequently. Isaiah 1:7–8 describes the aftermath of war; 3:1–5 depicts the breakdown of society; 5:13–17 portrays exile and the desolation of the land; 5:26–30 pictures the assault of an army from afar. The oracles about the Syro-Ephraimite war (Isaiah 7–8) describe military defeat and overthrow for the allies besieging Jerusalem, and for Ahaz calling for imperial aid against his enemies. The northern kingdom faces internal chaos and military assault (Isa 9:11–12, 14–15, 20–21). Chapter 10 comes to an end with the marching of soldiers toward Jerusalem (vv. 27b–32). Chapter 10 also includes descriptions of the assault of nature: e.g., in vv. 16, 18, and 19.

Finally, we should point out that our prophets often describe rather gruesome events. While prophets may have resorted to these descriptions to arouse pathos in their audiences, the prophets were also realists; warfare during the era of the Assyrian empire was incredibly violent and inhumane. Captives were systematically tortured and mutilated, the masses were enslaved, and cities were looted. The shocking thing is that the Lord God was on the side of the enemy in these judgments.

## Poetic Justice

Frequently the prophets do not bother with how judgment will be executed but depict an appropriate reversal of an unjust action. For example, Amos offers a judgment of thwarted intentions:

> Therefore because you trample upon the poor
>     and take from him levies of grain,
> you have built houses of hewn stone,
>     but you shall not dwell in them;
> you have planted pleasant vineyards,
>     but you shall not drink their wine. (5:11)

Those who love to feast to the sound of music "shall be the first to go into exile, and the revelry of the loungers shall pass away" (6:7). In a sentence that could well be designed as a punishment for the effort to silence prophets of judgment, Amos says:

> The time is surely coming ...
>     when I will send a famine in the land;
> not a famine of bread, nor a thirst for water,
>     but of hearing the words of the LORD. (8:11)

Probably Amos's most famous inversion of (false) expectations is what he has to say about the Day of the Lord":

> Woe to you who desire the day of the LORD! ...
> It is darkness and not light,
>     as if someone fled from a lion,
>     and was met by a bear;
>     or went into the house and rested a hand against the wall,
>     and bitten by a snake. (5:18–20)

This is filled with the irony of one obtaining what he or she thinks is safety, only to discover that it is just as dangerous as what one escaped from. This woe is, of course, entirely analogical; we are never told what the audience actually hoped for or what Amos thought would happen.

If Amos has a healthy savoring of these images of poetic justice, Hosea has a very spicy dish. One meets images of every description. Examples of thwarted intentions include the sentence of unsatisfied eating and fruitless sex (4:10). In the next prophecy, punishment is lack of punishment (4:13b–14). In

*Redeeming Judgment*

6:11b—7:7, the offenses are also the punishment—total disintegration of order and effective political power. Foreign alliances result in the loss of national identity (8:7-10); this prophecy seems to announce the end of monarchical rule. The golden calves are destined for being broken and stolen for their value as a precious metal (8:6, 10:5). Since the idols are false or unreal deities, their worshippers will be like mist, chaff, or smoke blown away in the wind (13:3).

Another interesting set of images in Hosea is those he applies to God:

> I will become like a lion to them,
>> like a leopard I will lurk beside the way.
> I will fall upon them like a bear robbed of her cubs,
>> I will tear open the covering of their heart.
> There I will devour them like a lion,
>> as a wild animal would mangle them. (13:8)

This type of image must have been shocking, for it drew on images that supplicants used to describe their enemies. In prophecy covering the Syro-Ephraimite war, Hosea employs the same imagery—of a lion—in 5:14, but earlier in the prophecy YHWH uses the images of "maggots" and "rottenness" to describe himself (5:12). YHWH becomes a fowler when Israel acts like a silly dove (7:11-12), and an arsonist in numerous prophecies (e.g., 8:14).

Isaiah also employs poetic images to dramatize the people's sin and judgment. He uses drunkenness frequently, but it is uncertain as to whether the references are to be taken literally, e.g., in 28:1-4. Since the people are seemingly not willing to be taught, they will be taught by those speaking an alien language—a reference to the Assyrians (28:9-11, 13). Again and again Isaiah condemns the wise for their lack of vision, so they will drag the nation into self-destructive actions (29:14; 31:1-3). The leadership of the country will pass from the mature and wise to petulant youth (3:1-5, 12). The people will depend on their army as well as alliance partners to deliver them from the Assyrian empire, but the soldiers will be defeated, killed, and scattered (30:15-17). In one strange prophecy, Isaiah compares Jerusalem's fall to a horror image of ghosts speaking from the dust; then their enemies become figments of nightmares who disappear on waking (29:1-8).

Isaiah is not inclined to extravagant images for God, as Hosea is. He does regularly speak of divine intervention: e.g., in 1:24-25; 2:10-12, 19, 21; 3:1, 13-14, 17, and the like. These interventions often occur to bring about some reversal or frustration; most of the judgments have a close relation to the offense. The judgment may be the sin itself or some rather natural consequence.

The close relation of the sin to the judgment does not warrant the theological assumption that God really plays no active role in the outcome. Since the course of events is seldom so inevitable that no alternative is possible, divine intervention in these cases means the resolution that brings judgment on the people of God. When an unlikely event occurs, then the divine intervention is called a miracle, though many people would not speak of a miraculous judgment (unless it was of one's enemies).

As one reflects on the use of poetic images in the prophecies of national judgment, one might have second thoughts about the use of the word *sentence* for such passages. In judicial usage, *sentence* is quite prosaic; how can it be maintained that the poetic rendition of judgment in our prophets still functions judicially? Obviously, the prophets feel called to strengthen the decree of punishment beyond any institutional judicial setting, and even beyond the sentence of the judgments of individuals. There is a rhetorical need to persuade the audience of the coming of national judgment and to elicit a religious response to the God who is coming in it. Amos concludes his recitation of chances to repent with, "Prepare to meet your God, O Israel" (4:12). The language of prophecy has the task of evoking such response. The challenge releases some urge to speak of God in elevated and shocking language.

## Instruments of Divine Action

Let's conclude this discussion of the sentence with the instruments by which God brings about judgment. Our prophets differ on this question. One can see among the eighth-century prophets an evolution of sophistication. Amos describes the judgment of Israel as military defeat and exile. However, he does not name the power that defeats Israel (and its neighbors), and Amos does not think about the imperial power as serving YHWH's purpose. Micah has the same rather apolitical view of judgment that Amos does, although Micah can envisage the route of an Assyrian military campaign (1:10–16).[3]

Hosea names the empire that will wipe the northern kingdom off the face of the earth, viz., Assyria. He also names Egypt, sometimes as a temptation and sometimes as a typological figure to interpret Assyrian exile. In 7:11–12, the two countries are mentioned as competing tempters:

---

3. Mic 5:5–6 does mention Assyria, but this is a prophecy of salvation. Micah 5:7–15 may involve judgment of Jacob, though vv. 7–9 are salvation. I am quite puzzled by this segment of the text.

> Ephraim has become like a dove,
>> silly and without sense,
>> the call upon Egypt, they go to Assyria.
> As they go, I will cast my net over them;
>> I will bring them down like birds of the air. (7:11–12a).

Hosea 12:1, seems to refer to the same confused foreign policy:

> Ephraim herds the wind
>> and pursues the east wind all day long;
> they multiply falsehood and violence;
>> they make a treaty with Assyria,
>> and oil is carried to Egypt.

It may well be that there was a period in which the two superpowers had equally deleterious effects on Ephraim. Hosea could formulate the following judgment (self-inflicted on Ephraim) without naming the foreign nations:

> Ephraim mixes himself with the peoples;
>> Ephraim is a cake not turned.
> Foreigners devour his strength,
>> but he does not know it. (7:8–9)

In another exquisite image, the northern kingdom's foreign policy is compared to "sowing the wind":

> For they sow the wind,
>> and they shall reap the whirlwind. (8:7)

Judgment follows with dramatic inevitability from the foolish policy of Israel's rulers.

Notice, however, that YHWH intervenes regularly in Hosea's account of the Syro-Ephraimite war: "Therefore I am like a moth to Ephraim, and like dry rot to the house of Judah" (5:12, RSV), "For I will be like a lion to Ephraim, and like a young lion to the house of Judah. I myself will tear and go away, I will carry off, and no one shall rescue" (5:14). Assyria is not portrayed as the dangerous power that will subjugate and destroy the small western states; it is an attractive source of power to each of them; it is YHWH who will execute judgment. Assyria is not an *agent* of YHWH in this or any other prophecy of Hosea.

Hosea does recognize that Assyria may be the country that carries the Israelites into exile: "Ephraim shall return to Egypt, / and in Assyria they shall eat unclean food" (9:3). Egypt is a country to which the Israelites *return*, meaning they are recapitulating their history; Assyria is the actual place of exile.

Hosea does not address any prophecy to a foreign nation. All prophecy concerns Israel (and Judah), for sin is against YHWH and punishment by him. Thus, nothing is said about the role of these peoples in YHWH's plans, or whether they will be judged or saved. Hosea's categorization of the great powers as temptations is consistent. His ideal would be nonengagement with other nations, avoidance of international conflicts.[4]

Isaiah's policies converge with Hosea's—to avoid alliances and military involvement; but his reasoning is world's apart. He not only names Assyria, but he regards it as the dominant power of the day and as servant of YHWH. In Isa 10:6 Assyria is addressed as "the rod of my anger" that the God is using to whip "a godless nation . . . the people of my wrath." The idea is quite simple: YHWH is using this foreign empire to punish his own people. Later in the same prophecy Isaiah offers a metaphor that displays his idea further, and construes its contradiction as grounds for indictment:

> Shall the axe vaunt itself over the one who wields it,
> or the saw magnify itself against him who handles it?
> As if a rod should raise the one who lifts it,
> or as if a staff should lift the one who is not wood. (10:15)

He is using the metaphors to dramatize the contradiction of the Assyrian empire exceeding its mandate and boasting of its power. This is, of course, exactly what Isaiah charges Assyria with doing (10:7–14). Assyria is in fact driven by its own motives (10:7–11)—its lust for power, wealth, and glory. YHWH is using its actions for purposes Assyria does not know about. But when its brutality and vainglory overstep bounds (presumably determined by natural law), it is acting like a weapon and wielding the person using it. This contradiction or paradox will turn against the weapon—the agent of judgment itself comes under judgment (10:16–19).

In another passage, Isaiah says that it had been YHWH's intention all along to destroy the empire in the land of Israel:

> As I have designed, so shall it be
>
> . . .

---

4. Perhaps on the model of Switzerland.

*Redeeming Judgment*

> I will break the Assyrian in my land
>
> . . .
>
> his yoke shall be removed from them
>
> . . .
>
> This is the plan that is planned
> concerning the whole earth. (14:24–26)

Assyria has not only executed judgment on Israel and Judah; it has subdued much of the civilized world. If Assyria were to be broken, that would release the countries of the empire to become a new international order.

Isaiah is truly an interpreter of his era. The other eighth-century prophets have urgent words for their own people, and Hosea has a view of judgment performing the work of redemption. Isaiah certainly has that message, but he sees the entire Near East—the known world for him—as participating in and receiving the action of God. Human powers now serve the divine purpose. This idea catches on, later: Jeremiah employs the idea to interpret the rise of Nebuchadnezzar, king of Babylon, to his generation (Jeremiah 27–29), and the anonymous prophet of the exile borrows the idea to interpret the rise of Cyrus of Persia (Isaiah 41, 44, and 45). The prophets become the interpreters of their age.

It must be admitted, however, that Isaiah had God's perspective on Isaiah's own time. He invested the course of events of his generation with the capacity to transform the human condition—at least, to put an end to enmity between nations and war.[5] The issue for us in this chapter is whether he was right in judging the policies of Ahaz and Hezekiah according to this absolute norm. To maintain that Isaiah was right from a theological perspective, one has to reconcile his transcendent measure of the actions of the leaders of his nation with the realistic possibilities and impossibilities of history. Isaiah is engaged in the seemingly impossible task of interpreting our temporal, limited, fallen reality from the standpoint of God's eternal, unlimited and righteous reality.

## The Theological Rationale for Judgment

To bring this exposition of the four eighth-century prophets to a close, let's examine the theological rationale behind the decision of God to take such drastic action. Each of our prophets has passages that defend the action rather

---

5. Isa 2:1–4; also Mic 4:1–5.

## Amos's Theological Reasoning

Amos's theological reasoning can be drawn out from the organization of the first two chapters of the book as well as from the disputations in 3:1–2 and 9:7–8.[6] The nations neighboring Israel are indicted for violating an international law—a law that most civilized human beings would share. Amos expects his audience to know that what these nations have done is wrong. The charges against Israel, however, are based on legal norms that the people had accepted as a part of their covenant with YHWH. The covenant is not mentioned, nor is the lawgiving at Sinai. The laws that Amos highlights—those protecting the poor and marginalized—were nevertheless obligations imposed by YHWH and should have been known by all of his people. Violations of these would never be the basis of indictments of foreign nations that did not know YHWH.[7] The contrast motif (Amos 2:9–10) manifests the elect status of Israel; v. 11 names two gifts of YHWH (prophets and nazarites) in their performance by the recipient nation. Israel is judged because it does not fulfill the obligations imposed on it as God's chosen.

Amos 3:1–2 explicates the rationale of judgment on the elect nation:

> Hear this word that the Lord has spoken against you, O people of Israel,
> > against the whole family that I brought up out of the land of Egypt:
> You only have I known
> > of all the families of the earth;
> therefore I will punish you
> > for all your iniquities.

The addressee is identified not only by name but by reference to YHWH's gracious deliverance, the outstanding, identity-forming event of Israel's history. This is the event in which God "knew" Israel, became intimate with her, chose her as his own. Knowledge of God was imparted to Israel in the same event; otherwise the threat of God's punishment of Israel would make no sense. Being God's elect and entering into an intimate relationship that no other people has

---

6. Westermann, *Basic Forms of Prophetic Speech*, 201, identifies these as disputations.

7. Even if those nations had such laws, violation of them would not be brought up by prophets before an Israelite audience, and there would be no prophet of YHWH going to foreign nations to pronounce YHWH's judgment on people who did not accept his authority. Jonah is an exception.

## Redeeming Judgment

with the universal God imposes unique responsibilities on the people, and makes them accountable in a way no other people would be.

Amos 9:7–8 seems at first reading to contradict 3:1–2, but it actually reenforces it. Amos 9:7 runs as follows:

> Are you not like the Ethiopians [Heb.: "Cushites"] to me,
> O people of Israel? says the Lord.
> Did I not bring Israel up from the land of Egypt,
> and the Philistines from Caphtor [Crete] and the Arameans from Kir?

To paraphrase this passage, Israel is no more precious to God than the most distant nation known to Israelites, and the gracious saving action of God can also be seen in the origins of neighboring peoples. The point of the argument actually comes in the following verse (Isa 9:9):

> The eyes of the Lord God are upon the sinful kingdom,[8]
> and I will destroy it from the face of the earth. (9:8a)

Israel's election does not privilege it; it will be judged like everyone else.[9] Does election mean anything then? Israel knows that God brought them out of Egypt, but the Philistines and Arameans do not. The Ethiopians are precious to the Lord, but they have not heard of the Lord. Israel is not only vulnerable to judgment like other nations far and near; it is responsible for obligations unique to it.

Both these disputations (Amos 3:1–2; 9:7–8) state judgment not as a possibility but as a certainty. In fact, the trial takes place in the prophecy itself. The prophet conveys God's *verdict*. The act of speaking, of pronouncement, brings about a new state of being for the addressee.[10] The nation is judged guilty and under sentence of death. The audience is in denial, but Amos singles out those who say, "evil shall not overtake or meet us" (9:10).

Many interpreters cannot believe that Amos would pronounce judgment and doom as a certainty. Amos's frightful vision of the destruction and pursuit of the people in 9:1–4 seems to be blocked out of the interpreters' consciousness. They assume that Amos at least hopes a remnant survives to carry on, despite his black humor about remnant: "Thus says the Lord: As the shepherd rescues from the mouth of a lion two legs, or a piece of an ear,

---

8. Note the third-person formulation; I don't know why it is used here.

9. Israelites would know that other nations are vulnerable to divine judgment.

10. I am drawing on J. L. Austin's theory of performative language; see Patrick, *The Rhetoric of Revelation*.

so shall the people who live in Samaria be rescued—with a corner of a couch and part of a bed"(3:12).[11] Only if the people can accept their sentence, and turn around before disaster hits that they might receive mercy. The response of the Ninevites to Jonah's message is the right attitude: "Who knows? God may relent and change his mind; he may turn from his fierce anger, so that we do not perish" (Jonah 3:9). If the people of Israel will "hate evil and love good, and establish justice in the gate, it may be that the Lord . . . will be gracious to the remnant of Joseph" (Amos 5:15). Israel may have its sentence commuted—but not canceled.

## Micah's Theological Reasoning

Micah records a judicial contest in 6:1–5. This passage has an apologetic thrust. There is no indictment or sentence, though YHWH is said to have "a controversy with his people" (v. 2). The Lord challenges the people to say how he has "wearied" them (v. 3). This is followed by a recitation of his saving deeds—the exodus and conquest—, concluding with a thesis statement: "that you may know the saving acts of the Lord" (v. 5). The purpose of the passage seems to be to renew the people's loyalty and obedience to their God.

This is the second judicial scene in Micah. The first is 1:1–7. In it the people's offenses are enumerated and destruction is pronounced. Perhaps 6:1–5 is meant to counterbalance the judgment. While the second juridical scene is not an oracle of salvation, it seems to reach out to the people in their time of crisis, to bring the people to a position where they can be transformed and saved. The editors of the book certainly feel that the message of judgment should be balanced by oracles of salvation (in Micah 4, 5, and 7).[12]

The prophecy of judgment does not seek to be the "last word." Even Amos has hope—judgment of the nation would not serve any purpose if there were no hope. Micah is still committed to leading his people back to YHWH once judgment has purged and transformed them. The disputation in 6:1–5 is an example of such leading.

## Hosea's Rationale for Judgment

Hosea has a lot to say about the rationale for judgment. His understanding of his commission is quite distinctive. He speaks only to Israel; the nations may

---

11. This may be directed specifically at the capital city, and not apply to the whole country.
12. Some could be by Micah; that others are by Micah is quite doubtful.

be tempters, but they are not in relationship with God—at least not so as to receive a message from him.

The call of Hosea includes the content of his message much more than our other eighth-century prophets. Indeed, he is called to do something, to perform an act explained as an analogy to God and Israel (1:2). When he and Gomer have children, YHWH tells him what name to give each child. The first child's name, Jezreel, is a message to the reigning dynasty. It is the second and third children whose names carry heavy theological freight. The daughter, Lo Ruhamah—No Mercy, has a name that conveys a message, but the name also resonates with the declaration YHWH made to Moses on Sinai:

> I will be gracious [*ḥanah*] to whom I will be gracious,
>     and I will show mercy [*ruḥamah*] to whom I will show mercy.
> (Exod 33:19)

A bit later YHWH proclaims his nature in these words:

> The Lord, the Lord, a God merciful [*raḥum*] and gracious [*ḥanun*]),
> slow to anger, and abound in steadfast love and faithfulness . . . (Exod 34:6)

Thus, Hosea's daughter's name announces the withdrawal of the Lord's most caring quality; one might even say his motherly quality, for the root is also used in the word *womb*.

Hosea's second son is named Lo Ami—Not my People—to declare the end of Israel's divine election. Perhaps the name is first of all descriptive: the people are no longer devoted to YHWH alone, which means they are not longer his at all, since marriage (presented in Hosea as an analogy of divine election) involves exclusivity. When they are under judgment, the people of Israel will (in a sense) no longer be the Lord's people, though the experience they undergo will lead to their being taken back and shown mercy (2:21–23). This is parallel to the buying back of their mother, and her "redemption" (3:1–3).

Hosea has more reviews of Israel's history with YHWH than any of his fellow prophets. Many of these speak of how Israel corrupted God's grace:

> I am the Lord your God
>     from the land of Egypt;
> you know no God but me
>     and besides me there is no savior.
> It was I who knew you in the wilderness,
>     in the land of drought;

> when I [fed] them, they were satisfied...
>> and their heart was proud;
>> therefore they forgot me. (13:4-6)

The people not only respond ungraciously to the Lord's grace, but they seem to turn what was given to them into the basis of betrayal. Hosea's reviews, thus, are researches into the origins of the sinful practices endemic to the people. Hosea traces the apostasy of the people as well as their political rebellion. A number of his reviews refer to events involving Saul (9:15; 10:9; 13:9-11), and of course he condemns more recent rulers and wars in chapters 5-8.

There are several indications in the book that judgment is a step on the way to a renewed relationship with YHWH—indeed to an unconditional salvation. This is certainly the affirmation of 2:16-20. The prophecy in chapter 11, though, has the most poignant expression of this theme: The prophecy tells the story of a rebellious child who has to be seriously punished (vv. 1-7). Just when we might expect "death," the Lord cries out in anguish that he cannot doom his people as He doomed Sodom. The prophecy ends with a theological paradox:

> I will not execute my fierce anger;
>> I will not again destroy Ephraim;
> for I am God and no mortal,
>> the Holy One in your midst,
>> and I will not come [in wrath]. (11:9)

This sounds as though judgment has been called off, but in fact the book of Hosea has no other indications of that. Indeed, the verses following this passage (vv. 10-11) are predicated on an exile that has scattered the people among the nations.[13]

Not only does YHWH turn to Israel; Israel turns toward YHWH. Actually, Hosea composes the penitential ceremony for the people to speak (in 14:1-3). If the people will pray this prayer, and mean it, the Lord will promise to "heal their disloyalty, I will love them freely" (14:4). Their inner transformation, their redemption, will be accompanied by an explosion of fertility (14:5-7).

---

13. While this may well be a passage from a later time, it is a good reading of our prophecy in the light of events.

*Redeeming Judgment*

## Isaiah's Theological Roots

Isaiah has different theological roots than the other three eighth-century prophets do.[14] He makes few if any references to the exodus or Sinai or the wilderness—the events of the sacred history told in the Pentateuch. His roots are in the distinctively Jerusalemite traditions of Davidic kingship and Zion. Despite this, he has several prophecies that review the sacred history, viz., 1:2–3 and 5:1–7. The first of these tells the people's story very briefly.

> Hear, O heavens, and listen, O earth,
>   for the LORD has spoken:
> I have reared children and bought them up,
>   but they have rebelled against me.
> The ox knows its owner,
>   and the donkey its master's crib;
> but Israel does not know,
>   my people do not understand.

This passage compares Israel's—or Judah's—misbehavior to that of rebellious offspring. To show how "unnatural" their behavior has been, they are compared unfavorably to work animals. Isaiah seeks to elucidate the divine election by a comparison with family, a natural relationship. Nevertheless, the rebellion stands out as "unnatural."[15]

Isaiah 5:1–7 reveals more deeply the significance of judgment. The poet-prophet's "friend" planted a vineyard of fine grapes and prepared everything for the harvest, but, alas, the crop yielded sour grapes. After the audience is invited to decide what it would do with the vineyard, the vintner declares his intention to let it go to waste. Then the prophet identifies the vintner as the Lord, the vineyard as Israel and Judah, and the sour grapes as injustice and violence. The parable explains the purpose of God for establishing the people of God—to "produce" justice and righteousness—and what went wrong, and why the people are being judged. The rationale for judgment stands out starkly.

There are strong indications that judgment was not the last word for Isaiah. There are two prophecies centered specifically on Jerusalem that pronounce judgment, but then the city arises phoenix-like out of the ashes. One of these is Isa 1:21–28 (RSV):

---

14. Von Rad, *Old Testament Theology*, 2:155–69, was very impressed with this thought.
15. Though a lot of families have experienced it, it is fairly "unnatural."

> How the faithful city has become a harlot,
>> she that was full of justice!
> Righteousness lodged in her,
>> but now murderers . . .
> Therefore the Lord says . . .
> Ah, I will vent my wrath on my enemies,
>> and avenge myself on my foes.
> I will turn my hand against you
>> and will smelt away your dross as with lye
>> and remove all your alloy.
> And I will restore your judges as at the first,
>> and your counselors as at the beginning.
> Afterward you shall be called the city of righteousness,
>> the faithful city.

Isaiah 29:1–8 has a similar pattern: the sinful city is judged, indeed brought down to Sheol, but then the besieging enemy will disappear like a dream upon awakening.

Isaiah has one disputation that explains God's plan for history by reference to a farmer's seasonal pattern of working a cultivated field—plowing, working down, planting, harvesting. This concept of plan was important to Isaiah's theology of history. The judgment of Israel and Judah were a part of God's plan for reforming the people of God and transforming the civilized world.

According to Isaiah, Assyria has been drafted, so to speak, to be the "rod of [the Lord's] anger" (10:5). Assyria does not know the role it is playing; indeed, it acts as if it were the supreme power of the world, the master of its own destiny, harvesting the "fruits" of all its conquered peoples. However, after it finishes chastising the people of God and uniting all the nations of the Near East, it will be brought down in judgment for its arrogance and violence. This will have ramifications not only for Judah. It will be a liberating event for all those Assyria assaulted and robbed (so Isa 14:24–27). A new international order will arise in which the nations of the Near East will forego war, submitting their grievances to the prophet who speaks for YHWH (Isa 2:1–4). All the nations are undergoing a time of judgment, but a new order will arise out of it. Judah will continue to be the chosen people, a mediator of the knowledge of God and His grace.

*Redeeming Judgment*

For Isaiah, the events to which God has subjected Israel are both judgment and testing. Many of his accusations concern the response of the king and his counselors to political crises. Ahaz's summons of Assyrian aid against Aram and Israel, and Hezekiah's alliances to throw off the Assyrian yoke, are failures of faith. The proper way to respond to crisis is to stay cool and wait for the Lord. The crisis has been brought on by God, and the effort to control one's destiny is resistance to the divine will. Rather than arming the nation for battle with Assyria, the leaders should be "giving rest to the weary" (Isa 28:12). The foundation stone the Lord is laying in Zion is, "[One] who believes will not be in haste" (28:16, RSV); in the midst of crisis, do what you can do to foster justice and righteousness, and leave international political events to God.

The theological rationale of judgment for each of the four eighth-century prophets contributes to a comprehensive theological conception. All our prophets apply both common human norms and norms applicable only to the people of God. Divine election entails added responsibility and stricter accountability. The judgment takes place in the pronouncement of the prophet; hence, it is unconditional. God can forgive offenses or commute sentences. The response of the addressees to the pronouncement of judgment may shape God's final disposition. Judgment is not meant to be the last word, but it holds up high standards and should transform the people subjected to it. Finally, though Israel is at the center of the prophecy of judgment, other nations are a part of the action. Israel's destiny is wedded to the world of which it is a part.

# 11

## Prophecy for a New Generation
(Jeremiah, Ezekiel)

THE TITLE OF THE chapter was coined to suggest the overall thesis of the chapter: It was the challenge of Jeremiah and later Ezekiel to revive the message of judgment first proclaimed by the eighth-century prophets. The message of judgment had been absorbed into the consciousness of Judeans. Eighth-century prophets communicated effectively, but also the exile of the northern kingdom had been accepted as confirmation of that message, reinforced by a wave of refugees from the north. The people had been conditioned to think in prophetic categories. Such conditioning might, unfortunately, dull the reception of a new generation of prophets; it would sound old fashioned and repetitious. Jeremiah and Ezekiel had to devise ways to puncture their defenses.

As time went on, Jeremiah began to realize that the people were in fact beyond reform and were destined for judgment. His mood becomes mournful; prophecy is clothed in lament. Now the task is to prepare the people to survive exile, to retain their identity and loyalty to YHWH, in the hope of a return to their land and reconstruction. Ezekiel carries an equal burden in this task. For these prophets, judgment is a necessary ordeal for the transformation of the people, but it is hardly the last word.

This chapter will be organized chronologically. Jeremiah prophesied in the reigns of several kings, and his message accommodated to the political, cultural and religious climate of each reign. Under Josiah, Jeremiah seems to have dovetailed his message with the reform. His message of judgment becomes much more irreversible under Jehoiakim. Zedekiah lacked authority, and policy drifted toward the disaster that occurred in 587 BCE. Jeremiah enjoys the window of peace and tranquility under the governor Gedeliah, but that is all too brief, and Jeremiah is finally forced to accompany to Egypt a band of Jews escaping the Babylonians. While there is no nation to condemn any longer, he aims barbs at his abductors and at Egypt.

We can take the structure of the book as reflecting these reigns. Jeremiah 2–6 would fit well into the prophet's message during Josiah's reign. Jeremiah 7 clearly belongs to the beginning of Jehoiakim's reign. The question is, how many of the following chapters belong to this reign and how many to Zedekiah's? We will treat all of chapters 7–20 as belonging to Jehoiakim's reign. Chapters 21–23 cover kings and prophets, and break the sequential pattern. We will limit ourselves to narratives from Zedekiah's reign. Since Ezekiel began to prophesy during Zedekiah's reign, we can survey his prophecies of judgment against his people. After the fall of Jerusalem, Ezekiel turns to other nations as subjects for judgment; we will include Jeremiah's judgment of foreign nations in that last section in the chapter.

It should be noted that large portions of Jeremiah are prose. The critical tradition of scholarship has distinguished layers in the book based on whether a passage is poetry or prose. The poetry has been generally ascribed to Jeremiah himself, the prose either to his scribal friend, Baruch, or to Deuteronomistic authors/editors (because of the style and thought).[1] According to chapter 36, Jeremiah dictated a healthy number of prophecies to Baruch, who read them in the temple and left them in the hands of a royal counselor. They were read to king Jehoiakim, who burned them. Jeremiah dictated another scroll to preserve what was on the burnt scroll and to add to it. These would have been poetry. The prose accounts of his prophecy, known as "prose sermons," simplified his message for laity to comprehend. Baruch's narratives are thin on content, heavy on story.

## During the Hiatus in Prophecy

The eighth-century prophets of judgment attained "classical" status and pretty much inscribed for all time to come what judgment means for biblical monotheism. They had their eyes focused on the political world around them, and as the century drew to a close it was clear that the Assyrian empire threatened the existence of Israel and Judah; indeed, by the end of the century we can forget Israel altogether. It should be noted, though, that these prophets did not

---

1. Consult, for example, Clements, *Jeremiah*, 1–12.

consider the crisis of their time to be the threat of a foreign nation. For them, Israel was its own worst enemy—there was the breakdown of the mutually exclusive relationship between YHWH and Israel, and foreign and domestic policies had perverted civil society and exposed the country to the predation of foreign powers.

The exile of Israel and the destruction of the Judean countryside were certainly, and quite cogently, interpreted as the fulfillment of the messages of the eighth-century prophets of judgment (viz., Amos, Hosea, Isaiah, and Micah). The doctrine of judgment, honed by these prophets, had proven itself. But now we have the problem, what shall be done with their oracles? Once the word has been fulfilled, of what use is it? Well, to our good fortune, the oracles were collected and made into books that conveyed a message to readers.[2] The books were much more than a collection of words once delivered to a live audience; they were designed to have an impact on the new audience—the reading audience.

In the cases of Amos and Hosea, the book was made up predominantly of the prophet's words. It was the arrangement of each book that conveyed the message of the editors.[3] Amos's own corpus of prophecy consists of messages of unrelieved doom. Readers was bound to wonder whether he left any room for hope. Consequently, a couple oracles of salvation, designed for a Judean audience, were attached at the end; this not only answered readers' questions, it located the readers in exile, under judgment, in hope of restoration of the Davidic kingdom and a period of prosperity (Amos 9:11–15).[4]

Hosea's book is designed to highlight his marriage and its application to Israel; devoting the first three chapters to it did this. If readers have no other recollection of the work, they will remember Hosea's life story. At the end of the book we are told to repent and are given the words to say (14:1–8).

The book of Isaiah has a much different story from Amos or Hosea; Micah has a similar story to Isaiah but on a much smaller scale. These books continued to be supplemented, edited, and rearranged over centuries. The result, in the case of Isaiah, is a book with much more material in it by others than by the eighth-century prophet. We may say that it is the response of the "Isaianic tradition" to a host of exigencies from 742 to some time after 500 BCE. Recent studies have shown that the book is deliberately and subtly designed.[5]

2. See Patrick, *The Rhetoric of Revelation*, 156–61.
3. Disciples of the prophet, most likely.
4. This is a position I presented in Patrick, *Rhetoric of Revelation*, 156–61.
5. Rendtorff, *Canon and Theology*, 146–69, 170–80, 181–89.

*Redeeming Judgment*

The response of kings and people to these prophetic messages—perhaps already preserved in book form, though not in their current edition—took extreme forms. First of all, we must realize that after 721 Judah alone maintained and developed Yahwistic religious tradition.[6] King Hezekiah lived about a dozen years after Isaiah's last datable oracles, and undoubtedly he adhered to Assyrian dictates after getting burned. His son, Manasseh, certainly made a concerted effort to satisfy his Assyrian masters, and he was fairly successful at it.[7] He is reported by the Deuteronomistic historian to have adopted the grossest form of polytheism and left a bloody record. One is reminded of the post–World War I era, which saw Europe succumb to cynical hedonism trying to escape the memory of the war, and enacting a nihilism learned from the trenches.

During that cynical period of fifty-five years, there were some ardent Yahwists preparing a religious and cultural reform beyond anything any had ever heard of. They may well have been immigrants from the northern kingdom who brought covenant,[8] legal, narrative, and prophetic traditions (including Hosea) with them, and these writings were revised to fit their new homeland. Deuteronomy was one of their works; it was apparently planted in the temple to be found during the reign of Josiah. He was convicted by the book and initiated an implementation of its provisions. A salient provision was centralization of the sanctuary—the prohibition of sacrifice at any altar but the one in the Jerusalem temple. This required radical changes in the ways people lived and performed their religious duties. The book instituted other changes in the cult and the judiciary as well. Its overall impact was to make obedience to law more important than ritual for the religious life. It prepared Judeans for life in exile, a fate that befell many of them just thirty years after the reform.

The reform met with enthusiastic acceptance by the populace, but unfortunately events overtook it. Josiah was killed by the Egyptian army when he tried to impede their reenforcement of the Assyrian army at Carchemish. The Egyptian-Assyrian coalition lost the battle and the empire to the Babylonians, but Egypt continued to exercise power over Judah for several years. To assert its authority, Egypt took into captivity the son of Josiah who had been chosen

---

6. The Samaritan wing of Yahwism depended on Judah; the Samaritan Pentateuch is proof of that.

7. Second Chronicles 33:10–13 says that he was punished once for unacceptable behavior.

8. This is hardly the most popular hypothesis about Deuteronomy's origin; it just happens to be one that I find very congenial. I would not invest much in any theory of Deuteronomy's origin.

as his successor, and put their lackey, Jehoiakim, on the throne. Needless to say, Jehoiakim did not continue the reform (see Jer 22:13–17).

## During the Reign of Josiah

According to Jer 1:2, Jeremiah begins his vocation as a prophet in the thirteenth year of the reign of Josiah, ca. 627 BCE; Josiah lived until 609, when he was killed by an Egyptian army at Megiddo (2 Kgs 23:29–30). Josiah's reform is dated to 621, hence about six years after Jeremiah's call. In this section we will begin with Jeremiah's call to prophecy, and then take up a few passages related in one way or another to Josiah's reform. The balance of the section will be concerned with the accusations made by Jeremiah, and with his task as detective, and will conclude with his threatening portrayals of the assault of an unknown army.

Jeremiah's call (Jer 1:2–10) has left a deep impression on our understanding of what it means to be a prophet. He is predestined to be a prophet, so no objection on his part can reverse his call. He will, however, object and struggle against it for much of his life. Any shortcomings that he may have can be compensated for by YHWH, who will supply the words. In fact, God touches Jeremiah's lips to sanctify them for his word. Jeremiah is then

> appoint[ed] . . . over nations and over kingdoms,
> to pluck up and pull down,
> to destroy and to overthrow,
> to build and to plant. (1:10)

Jeremiah is the ruler of the world! Wherever the Lord rules, his spokesman rules. Of course, this is hyperbole, but it does indicate what authority a prophet exercises. One might want to object, God gives him the message. Yes, that is said. Yet Jeremiah must discover the message himself. In the visions that follow his call to prophecy (1:11–19), the prophet is told that the judgment of Judah is coming, but he is not told the indictment or the divine reasoning and purpose. The prophetic message will be a human message with divine authority and perspicacity. The message chiefly concerns the people of God, but the good of the world is wrapped up in their destiny, so YHWH's prophet can pronounce judgment or promise redemption to others.

The visions that supplement the call promise to the prophetic word the power to endure and conquer, and divine protection to its bearer. This fills in for the powerlessness of the prophet: the prophet has no capacity to actualize

*Redeeming Judgment*

what has been promised (or threatened) and has no body guard to protect him from the attacks of those who desire to silence the prophet.

Jeremiah begins to prophesy during an optimistic time. The Assyrian empire is crumbling, and Judah has a young king with the vision and piety to revive the country and its religion. In 721, a book of law is found in the temple and read to king Josiah, who is smitten by its provisions and curses. After its authenticity is vouched for by the prophetess Huldah, Josiah convenes an assembly in the temple, at which the book is read and a covenant is made between king and people to put its provisions into effect. A host of heterodox practices in the temple and city are suppressed, and all other altars within the kingdom are decommissioned.[9] This is Josiah's reform.

Jeremiah does not have a major role in this event; the question is, did he play any role at all? According to Jer 11:1–14, Jeremiah is told by YHWH to remind the people of their long history of rebellion against him. YHWH had a covenant with them that threatened curses for disobedience. Since the people are still breaking the covenant, disaster is in store; when it comes, let the people seek help from the gods they have been worshipping. "For your gods have become as many as your towns, O Judah; and as many as the streets of Jerusalem are the altars you have set up to shame, altars to make offerings to Baal" (11:13). Although one could imagine this prophecy as a call to reform, its wording has been colored by the dismal course of later events.

Jeremiah 3:6—4:2 begins with a "dating": "The LORD said to me in the days of King Josiah . . ." (v. 6). The following four verses are a story of sisters: the first, Israel, acted like a common prostitute, so the Lord divorced her. But Judah only *seemed* better: "Yet for all this her false sister Judah did not return to me with her whole heart, but only in pretense" (v. 10). It would seem that this allegory pronounces Josiah's reform a failure. However, the prophecy does not end in judgment, but in a call to "return" (3:12–13). It is addressed to Israel; has Judah been left out? The rest of the passage—between vv. 14 and 25 and chapter 4, vv. 1 and 2—has a number of shifts of direction but consistently holds out the prospect of return and healing. This fits well into Josiah's reform: even if the reform has failed to reach the soul of the people, they can still turn their fate, so to speak.

Finally, just to confirm that Jeremiah is well disposed to Josiah's efforts to reform the people, let me call attention to his praise of Josiah in a prophecy condemning the king's son:

---

9. The story is told in 2 Kgs 22:3—23:25.

> Are you a king
> > because you compete in cedar?
> Did not your father eat and drink
> > and do justice and righteousness?
> > Then it was well with him.
> He judged the cause of the poor and needy;
> > then it was well.
> Is not this to know me?
> > says the Lord. (22:15–16)

It is rare to find a prophet expressing such high regard for a king.

## Apostasy

Jeremiah's prophecy can best be described as a revival of Hosea. What the exact reason for this is unknown. It does mean that the book of Hosea is now in circulation in Judah. Perhaps the fact that Hosea was a northerner (Jeremiah came from a town in the tribe of Benjamin—a Rachel tribe like Ephraim and Manasseh) attracted Jeremiah to the prophecy of Hosea.

Just how does Jeremiah imitate Hosea? The people are frequently symbolized as a loose woman—an apostate nation. Let's look at chapter 2, which resembles Hosea most.[10] It begins with a comprehensive look of the people's history (2:1–13). Like Hosea, Jeremiah regards the wilderness sojourn as a time when the relationship was right:

> I remember the devotion of your youth,
> > your love as a bride,
> how you followed me in the wilderness,
> > in a land not sown.
> Israel was holy to the Lord,
> > the first fruits of his harvest.
> All who ate of it were held guilty. (vv. 2–3)

Then an accusation is leveled at Jacob/Israel—an indicting question: "What wrong did your ancestors find in me / that they went far from me, / and went after worthless things and became worthless themselves?" (v. 5). They did not keep their hopes focused on the God who led them out of Egypt, through

---

10. Note that it uses feminine second-person singular pronouns: hence, addressing the people as a woman.

the wilderness, and into the promised land. Once they entered the land, they defiled it. All their leaders let them down.

In v. 9, we have a "therefore" to signal the sentence. Here comes a surprise: their punishment is to remain in a debate, a legal contest, called a *rîb* in Hebrew. This is a promise as well as a punishment: YHWH will never give up on them. Verses 10–11 are an argument against the people:

> Has [any] nation changed its gods,
> > even though they are no gods?
> But my people have exchanged their glory
> > for something that does not profit. (2:11)

The prophecy concludes with a parable comparing YHWH to fresh spring water, and other gods to cisterns (leaking, with foul water).

The rest of the chapter depicts the behavior of the nation, invariably in images. The images keep changing, but the thrust remains much the same. Here are some examples:

> For long ago you broke your yoke
> > and burst your bonds;
> > and you said, "I will not serve!"
> On every high hill
> > and under every green tree
> > you sprawled and played the whore. (2:20)[11]

> Yet I planted you as a choice vine,
> > from the purest stock.
> How then did you turn degenerate
> > and become a wild vine? (2:21)[12]

> How can you say, 'I am not defiled,
> > I have not gone after the Baals?
> Look at your way in the valley;
> > know what you have done—
> a restive young camel interlacing her tracks,
> > a wild ass used to the wilderness,

---

11. Cp. Hos 4:13.
12. Cp. Isa 5:1–7.

*Prophecy for a New Generation*

> in her heat sniffing the wind!
> Who can restrain her lust? (2:23-24a)

When we come to chapter 3, there is an argument to the effect that it would be unlawful for Israel, the adulterous people, to return to YHWH; it would amount to a remarriage after the woman had married someone else. That practice is prohibited in Deut 24:1-4, part of the law code that Josiah based his reform on. Jeremiah simply leaves us wondering whether there can be a reconciliation between YHWH and his people.

Before we go on, we need to consider the propriety of Jeremiah's indictments. Chapters 2-3 blame the people, whether Israel or Judah, for apostasy and occasionally idolatry as well. One can certainly hear the echo of Hosea, but can one transfer the indictment of one nation at one time to another at another time? Remember, Isaiah had little to say about apostasy or idolatry. Did he simply overlook it, or were those offenses not prevalent in Jerusalem and Judah? If Isaiah did not find religious defection to be a serious problem among his people, what changed the situation so that Jeremiah finds it pervasive? Is it a serious problem in the last decades of the seventh century? Or is Jeremiah hypersensitive due to ideology?

The historian who wrote 2 Kings blames the situation on king Manasseh. Here is what he says:

> [Manasseh] did what was evil in the sight of the LORD, following the abominable practices of the nations that the LORD drove out before the people of Israel. For he rebuilt the high places that Hezekiah has father had destroyed; he erected altars for Baal, and made a sacred tree, as Ahab king of Israel had done, worshipped all the host of heaven, and served them. He built altars in the house of the Lord ... for all the host of heaven in the two courts of the house of the LORD. And he made his son pass through fire, he practiced soothsaying and augury, and dealt with mediums and with wizards. (2 Kgs 21:2-6)

Later he adds crimes against humans: "Manasseh shed very much innocent blood, till he had filled Jerusalem from one end to another" (21:16). One can imagine that the kingdom inherited by Josiah after fifty-five years of Manasseh's rule had become accustomed to religious practices and ideology that provoke Jeremiah's condemnation. The story of Josiah's actions to suppress non-Yahwistic practices also supports the surmise (see 2 Kgs 23:4-14). Perhaps Jeremiah is actually supporting the reform in these prophecies. However, he does not say that this is just a thing of the past; the feminine figure representing the people says things like, "It is hopeless, / for I have loved strangers, / and after them I will go" (Jer 2:25).

We should also consider another possibility. Jeremiah may be using apostasy as a comprehensive category. In other words, other offenses may be incorporated in it. For example, Jer 2:34 seems to combine "prostitution" (presumably apostasy) with violation of the poor:

> Also on your skirts is found
> > the lifeblood of guiltless poor;
> you did not find them breaking in.

And like Hosea, Jeremiah considers turning to imperial power for military aid to be apostasy:

> Is Israel a slave? Is he a home born servant?
> > Why then has he become a plunder?
> The lions have roared against him,
> > they have roared loudly.
> They have made his land a waste;
> > his cities are in ruins, without inhabitant.
> Moreover, the people of Memphis and Tahpanhes
> > have broken the crown of your head ...
> What then do you gain by going to Egypt,
> > to drink the waters of the Nile?
> Or what do you gain by going to Assyria,
> > to drink the waters of the Euphrates?
> Your wickedness will punish you,
> > and your apostasy will convict you. (2:14–18)

Jeremiah may want those who hear him to think about a whole range of evils under the concept of apostasy.

## The Task of Discovery

The focus of Jeremiah's prophecy changes after the call to repentance at the beginning of chapter 4. The rest of chapter 4 and parts of chapter 6 portray the assault on Judah of an army from the north. We shall take up these "foe-from-the-north" depictions at the end of the section; first I want to survey passages in chapter 5 and 6 that I would subsume under the concept of discovery.

## Prophecy for a New Generation

Several times I have mentioned that prophets are commissioned to pronounce YHWH's judgment on his people, and to discover the offenses for which the people are being judged. Jeremiah is the only prophet who mentions examining the people to discover their guilt. Actually, he searches for evidence for forgiveness as much as evidence for judgment. Jeremiah 5:1–5 begins with a commission to search for a righteous person:

> Run about through the streets of Jerusalem,
> > look and take note!
> Search her squares and see
> > if you can find one person,
> one who acts justly
> > and seeks truth;
> that I may pardon her Jerusalem. (5:1, RSV)

When Jeremiah goes out on this mission, he discovers that people swear by YHWH but do so falsely (v. 2). These people should know that God holds absolutely to the ideal of truthfulness. Unfortunately, they are too stubborn to take correction anyway (v. 3).

Jeremiah observes then that he has only checked "the poor" (v. 4);[13] "the great" (or rich) should be better (5a). Unfortunately, they are just as bad:

> But they all alike had broken the yoke,
> > they had burst the bonds. (v. 5b, RSV)

A bit later Jeremiah is told to "go up through her vine-rows and destroy—but do not make a full end; strip away her branches, for they are not the Lord's" (5:10, RSV). He is to prune the vineyard. How this is to be applied literally is hard to say. The passage begins to indict Israel and Judah for faithlessness; unfortunately, the people do not believe that there are any consequences for their offenses:

> "He will do nothing, no evil will come upon us,
> > and we shall not see sword or famine." (v. 12b, NRSV)

It is the prophets' fault for this sense of complacency (v. 13). Now judgment will come because people must realize that there are consequences (vv. 14, 15–17).[14]

Just prior to this commission a few verses remind us of Hos 13:4–8:

---

13. Perhaps this actually means the common people.
14. Here we find one of the few "sentences" in these chapters.

223

## Redeeming Judgment

> How can I pardon you?
> Your children have forsaken me,
> > and have sworn by those who are no gods.
> When I fed them to the full,
> > they committed adultery,
> > and trooped to the houses of prostitutes . . . (Jer 5:7, RSV)

It is hard to say whether adultery is meant literally or is a stand-in for apostasy. The sexual language of these passages is vivid, whatever the exact meaning. Indeed, one wonders whether Jeremiah wants the language restricted to any one offense.

Jeremiah 5:20 commissions Jeremiah to preach to the people (to both Israel and Judah).

> Hear this, O foolish and senseless people,
> > who have eyes, but do not see,
> > who have ears, but do not hear.[15]
> Do you not fear me? says the Lord.
> > Do you not tremble before me? (vv. 21–22a)

There follows a parabolic comparison: the sea knows its boundary, but the Lord's people do not. In vv. 26–28, Jeremiah blames the condition of the people on leaders and "scoundrels" (v. 26). Unfortunately, the whole people will suffer (v. 29). The last strophe (vv. 30–31) condemns prophets and priests, but adds, "My people love to have it so, / but what will you do when the end comes?" The people get the leaders they deserve, and the consequences too.

Jeremiah 6:27 is a report of the Lord's commission of Jeremiah:

> I have made you a tester and a refiner among my people
> > so that you may know and test their ways.

This is the role for Jeremiah that I have identified from the start: to discover whether the people are guilty of offenses deserving of defeat and exile. Verse 28 seems to summarize his findings:

> They are all stubbornly rebellious,
> > going about with slanders;
> they are bronze and iron,
> > all of them act corruptly.

---

15. Cp. Isa 6:9–10.

The Lord has subjected them to a refiner's fire, but so far they are not "purified" of the wicked.

### Depictions of War

So far we have noted a strong emphasis on the indictment, including on the unrepentant attitude of the people; there are occasionally declarations of punishment, but these are secondary to the references to the people's offenses. Alongside these indictments, however, are long poems depicting the assault of an army from the north. Clearly these pictures belong to the "sentence," though only now and then is this made explicit: "your ways and your doings / have brought this upon you. / This is your doom; how bitter it is!" (4:18). The main emphasis is on the assault, the terror of battle, the horror of death and defeat. One of the most poignant passages is spoken by an *I* who is suffering this in the present:

> My anguish, my anguish! I writhe in pain!
>   Oh, the walls of my heart!
> My heart is beating wildly;
>   I cannot keep silent;
> for I hear the sound of the trumpet,
>   the alarm of war. (4:19)

This could be the prophet responding to the vision, or it could be someone who undergoes the assault in the future. It doesn't really matter for the power of the poem.

In the very next stanza (4:23-28), the *I* comes back to see the devastation after the assault. The scene recalls the condition of the world before creation, and foreshadows scenarios in apocalyptic literature. The vision ends with YHWH's explanation: "For thus says the Lord, 'The whole land shall be a desolation; yet I will not make a full end. Because of this the earth shall mourn / and the heavens above grow black; / for I have spoken, I have purposed; / I have not relented nor will I turn back'" (4:27-28).

The frightening images of God's judgment are actually realistic for ancient Near Eastern warfare. For a sense of how awful defeat and destruction were, examine the pictures from the walls and doors of Assyrian palaces.[16] Jeremiah employs them, probably, for their shock value. They are not "predic-

---

16. Yadin, *The Art of Warfare in Biblical Lands*, 2:380-463.

tions," for he doesn't even identify the army that will attack.[17] He may actually still be hoping against hope that his people will repent and avoid this fate. We might compare Jeremiah's words and images here to the "hellfire" sermons of an earlier era of Protestant preaching.

## During the Reign of Jehoiakim

The decade of Jehoiakim's reign (609–598 BCE) overturned much of what Josiah had done, and steered the ship of state in an entirely new direction. When Josiah was killed by the Egyptian army, the people of Judah chose one of his sons, Jehoahaz, to succeed him, but the Egyptian pharaoh removed him from the throne and installed another son, Jehoiakim. Their objective was to place a friendly ruler in an adjacent state—indeed one that provided a buffer between them and the Babylonian Empire. Jehoiakim only reluctantly transferred his loyalty to Babylon in 605 when it asserted its hegemony, and he went back to Egypt when that country stopped a Babylonian advance on their territory. The Babylonians reasserted their authority over Judah in 598; Jehoiakim died before the Babylonian army arrived at the gates of Jerusalem, so his son Jehoiachin had to face the music. Judah did not resist Babylon, and received mitigated punishment. The young king, his mother, and several thousand artisans and leaders were taken into exile, more as hostages than in a permanent population transfer. Another son of Josiah, Zedekiah, was enthroned as a substitute for the legitimate ruler.

Jeremiah has occasion to pronounce judgment on each of these royal figures. He calls for lamentation for both Jehoahaz and Jehoiachin. Of Jehoahaz he says,

> Do not weep for him who is dead [i.e., Josiah],
>    nor bemoan him;
> weep rather for him who goes away [i.e., Jehoahaz],
>    for he shall return no more
>    to see his native land. (22:10)

For Jehoiachin the lament runs as follows:

> Record this man as childless . . .
> For none of his offspring shall succeed

---

17. For many years, the enemy was identified with the "Scythians," which Herodotus mentions as ruling the known world for a short period. Now there is a great deal of skepticism regarding the historicity of this episode in Herodotus.

> in sitting on the throne of David,
> and ruling again in Judah. (22:30)

Since neither reigns long enough to establish a record, neither is indicted.

Jehoiakim is another matter. Jeremiah makes him the subject of a prophecy of judgment against an individual. It runs from 22:13 to 19. It begins:

> Woe to him who builds his house by unrighteousness
> and his upper rooms by injustice,
> who makes his neighbors work for nothing,
> and does not give them their wages. (v. 13)

The king is having a new palace built in Ramat Rachel by forced Judean labor. He is a good example of a ruler who puts his own prestige and pleasure above the good of the citizens. Jeremiah generalizes:

> But your eyes and heart
> are only on your dishonest gain,
> for shedding innocent blood,
> and for practicing oppression and violence. (v. 17)

Jehoiakim's sentence is to die an unlamented death (vv. 18–19).

Jeremiah has other occasions to condemn the successor of Josiah, who undid much of what his father did. We have already mentioned that Jehoiakim burned Jeremiah's scroll of prophecies; Jeremiah utters another prophecy of judgment of an individual for that action (see 36:29–31). The king's offense is his refusal to heed the prophetic word.

## The Temple Sermon

Jeremiah is commissioned to deliver a word of judgment against the Jerusalem temple, at its gate, in the first year of Jehoiakim's reign (see 26:1). This is a prose sermon, known as the temple sermon. The words of the oracle are presented in 7:1–15, a story of what happened afterwards is told in 26:1–24. The sermon begins as a call to repentance: "Amend your ways and your doings, and I will let you dwell in this place" (7:3). This exhortation is backed up by a conditional promise in vv. 5–7. The prophecy sounds like a continuation of Jeremiah's reformist preaching in chapters 2–6. However, the weight seems to shift toward the certainty of punishment. In v. 4, Jeremiah warns the people not to trust in the presence of the temple to guarantee salvation. His words are satirical: "Temple of the Lord, temple of the Lord, temple of the Lord." In v. 8 he begins accusing worshippers of just such false trust. The people break every one of the Ten Commandments (v. 10). The popular belief in the inviolability of the temple has made it a good hideout, a "den of robbers" (v. 11). But YHWH is quite capable of abandoning his house: He did so long ago at Shiloh. He has decided to do so again: "I will cast you out of my sight, just as I cast out all your kinsfolk, all the offspring of Ephraim" (v. 15).

We might compare this oracle in Jeremiah 7 to Amos 4:6-12. The Amos passage recalls numerous warning events that should have prompted repentance but did not. So now the people must face the full judgment of God. In the case of Jeremiah 7, the prophecy begins with the possibility of repentance and avoidance of punishment. Once we arrive at v. 8, the indictment is stated as a fact, and the sentence is presented as a certainty. Once the inviolability of Zion is refuted, that settles the matter. The chance given by the reign of Josiah is over; now a king who has no commitment to the divine calling of Israel has taken the reins of government; Judah's fate is sealed.

Perhaps Jeremiah's fate is paradigmatic. According to chapter 26, he is put under arrest and tried for a capital offense. Before he can be executed, some royal officials arrive from the palace and convene a trial. His self-justification is simple and direct: the Lord commanded me to say what I said. If you condemn me, you will add to your guilt: you will bring innocent blood upon yourselves. Then some witnesses speak out in his behalf: there is a precedent for what Jeremiah has said, viz., Mic 3:12. The proper thing to do is repent, and we may be saved like our grandfathers and grandmothers were. The verdict of innocence might indicate that Judah is not doomed. However, there is a note at the end indicating that Jeremiah has a patron, Ahikam ben Shaphan, that saves the day.[18] Innocent blood had been shed in the case of another prophet, Uriah ben Shemeiah (see 26:20-23).

## Other Oracles from Jehoiakim's Reign

In the remainder of Jeremiah 7 we find more passages concerned with prayer and ritual. The first has to do with Jeremiah himself (7:16-20). He is told not to intercede for the people because the Lord is fed up with them. Prophets had an obligation to intercede, but God was not obliged to grant their petitions. In Amos's third and fourth visions, he is told that the Lord would not longer

---

18. The whole family protects and supports Jeremiah and Baruch; they had been important members of Josiah's cabinet and were sympathetic to the prophetic perspective. Jeremiah may have helped them by counseling the Babylonians to select Gedeliah, a third-generation member of the family, as governor after 587.

forgive Israel (see Amos 7:8, 8:2). I take this to be the import of God's prohibition against intercession.

Jeremiah 7:16–19 is the first of a series of prohibitions against intercession. The prohibition occurs again in 11:14 and 14:11–12. In the case of chapter 14, Jeremiah has just uttered a prayer of communal lament for relief from a drought (14:1–10). The prohibition is YHWH's no to Jeremiah's petition. Jeremiah then complains that the people are encouraged in their complacency by false prophets (14:13). He does not cease interceding; he utters another communal lament in 14:17–22. It actually conveys Jeremiah's message, while seeking forgiveness and pardon:

> Let my eyes run down with tears night and day,
>> and let them not cease,
> for the virgin daughter—my people—is struck down
>> with a crushing blow, with a very grievous wound.
>
> . . .
>
> Have you completely rejected Judah?
>> Does your heart loathe Zion?
> Why have you struck us down
>> so that there is no healing for us?
> We look for peace, but find no good;
>> for a time of healing, but there is terror instead.
> We acknowledge our wickedness, O Lord,
>> the iniquity of our ancestors,
>> for we have sinned against you.
> Do not spurn us, for your name's sake;
>> do not dishonor your glorious throne;
>> remember and do not break your covenant with us.

The Lord's answer is, even if Moses and Samuel were interceding, instead of you, I would have to say no; the people must suffer the consequences of their deeds (15:1–4).

Let's return to Jeremiah 7. In agreement with the eighth-century prophets, Jeremiah is told that sacrifices cannot take the place of obedience.[19] God does not care about rituals designed to please him. He desires obedience. Unfortunately, the people prefer the cultic route. Among the misdirected practices of piety, the worst is the sacrifice of children. This is taking place on the

---

19. Jeremiah's actual contrast has 1 Sam 15:22–23 as it closest precedent.

outskirts of Jerusalem: "And they go on building the high place of Topheth, which is in the Valley of the son of Hinnom, to burn their sons and their daughters in the fire—which I did not command, nor did it come into my mind" (7:31). For such abominations there is no excuse, and they are pounding nails in their own coffin. The end result will be a valley filled with unburied dead bodies.

## Enacted Prophecies

Jeremiah practices "street theater" from time to time—as had Isaiah. According to Jer 13:1–11, Jeremiah is told to buy and wear a loincloth, and then to hide it in a cleft in a rock. This is an image of what the Lord plans to do to his proud and stubborn people.[20]

According to Jer 17:19–27, Jeremiah stands in the gate of the city exhorting people not to carry burdens on the Sabbath. This message would have special force if he delivered it on the Sabbath. According to Jer 19:1–13, Jeremiah is told to buy a jug and then go to a gate facing out on the Valley of ben Hinnom where he is to shatter it to symbolize the coming fate of the people for offenses occurring in that place. He ends up a bit later in stocks—an involuntary enacted prophecy (19:1—20:6).

Jeremiah's visit to a potter working his wheel (18:1–11) is a suggestive image. The comparison of God to a potter who makes creatures as the potter makes earthenware is common the world over. The twist that Jeremiah gives it is to consider how the potter reshapes a vessel that is spoiled or even unpleasing. YHWH uses this process as an analogy: "Can I not do with you, O house of Israel, just as the potter has done?" (v. 6). He goes on in v. 7: "At one moment I may declare concerning a nation or a kingdom, that I will pluck up and break down and destroy it, but if that nation . . . turns from its evil, I will change my mind about the disaster I intended to bring on it" (vv. 7–8). This certainly corrects any theology that considers God's decrees to be unchangeable. Given the explanation in v. 7, we could fill in the potter analogy by attributing the change in the nation to the divine potter's reshaping of his vessel. However, the passage also affirms the reverse: if a country has been destined for good and slips into evil, God may change his mind (v. 10). Few interpreters would want to say that God purposely changed the country so that it would come to judgment. Hence, there are oddly mixed signals coming from this story. With its present

---

20. It is hard to know what to think about this story, since it is unlikely that Jeremiah took long journeys to the Euphrates.

wording, though, the lesson is clear: "Turn now, all of you from your evil way" (v. 11). Alas, v. 12 cites the people's defeatist response.

Perhaps the most poignant enacted prophecy of all is the Lord's prohibition against Jeremiah's marriage and socializing (16:1–9). The prophet loses control even of his personal life. Just as in the case of Hosea, so with Jeremiah God takes marriage and family as a symbolic language. The coming generation will die, and all social networks will disappear in judgment; Jeremiah must live this out proleptically.

## Doom and Lamentation

Before we proceed, let me remind you that judgment—the trial—takes place in the prophecy. When an indictment is issued, the offender—individual or nation—is judged guilty. The sentence may be decreed as well, but a contrite and compunctious response can elicit a commutation of the sentence. This is what is meant by forgiveness.

Now the early chapters of Jeremiah seem to be rather conditional. Forgiveness and renewal seem possible, and the prophet urges seizing the time. He never says that the people are now pleasing to the Lord, nor does he actually offer forgiveness. There is no "assurance of pardon." My interpretation is that he supports Josiah's reform and seeks to motivate the people beyond pretense. When Jehoiakim is placed on the throne by the Egyptians, hope for Judah vanishes. I think we can actually see a shift in Jeremiah chapters 8–20. I will begin, however, with a prophecy, 13:15–26, that starts out conditionally but becomes more a declaration of certain doom. It is hard to say whether all these strophes come from the same time, or grew as further events occurred. Verses 16–17 sound as though repentance and reform are still possible:

> Give glory to the LORD your God
>   before he brings darkness,
> and before your feet stumble
>   on the mountains in the twilight
> . . .
> But if you will not listen,
>   my soul will weep in secret for your pride. (RSV)

The next few verses address the young king, Jehoiachin, and his mother, as they prepare to go into exile (597 BCE):

## Redeeming Judgment

> Take a lowly seat,
>> for your beautiful crown
>>> has come down from you head. (13:18)

Not only the royalty are going into exile; they are accompanied by others (v. 19). They will be ruled over by neighboring countries that once were Judah's allies (v. 21). Verse 22 reminds them why these judgments are overtaking Judah. Yet, they cannot seem to change: They are compared to black Africans and spotted leopards: both might want to change their color but can't. The juridical sentence resumes in 13:24, which warns them that God will scatter them like chaff, and in v. 26, he will shame them like a jealous husband.

These words come at the end of Jehoiakim's reign. By now it is evident to Jeremiah that doom hangs over the nation. The exile of 598 was only the beginning. Jeremiah 15:5–9 has a similar message: The Lord has "stretched out [his] hand against you and destroyed you" (v. 6); God has "winnowed them with a winnowing fork" (v. 7a) and "bereaved them" (7b). The language of assault and loss pound readers remorselessly.

Given Jeremiah's growing conviction that national judgment is inevitable, it should not surprise readers that he clothes a number of prophecies in lamentation. Jeremiah 8:18—9:1 is the most memorable of these. Readers must understand that the poem has voices speaking to and by each other.

> My joy is gone, grief is upon me.
>> my heart is sick.
>
> Hark, the cry of my poor people
>> from far and wide in the land.

This sounds like the prophet speaking, though it could be YHWH.[21] Verse 19b quotes the people: "Is the Lord not in Zion? Is her King not in her?" Then we hear the Lord responding with a complaint:

> Why have they provoked me to anger with their images,
>> with their foreign idols?

Does this mean that the Lord is not in Zion, whatever the people think? In any case, the people await God's intervention to save them; they sound desperate:

> "The harvest is past, the summer is ended,
>> and we are not saved." (v. 20)

---

21. If one is willing to accept the anthropomorphic language.

Now an *I* speaks, probably the prophet, but it could be the Lord:

> For the hurt of my poor people I am hurt.
>   I mourn, and dismay has taken hold of me. (v. 21)

There follows a plaintive cry for medical aid, or for a divine intervention because medicine is ineffective.

> Is there no balm in Gilead?
>   Is there no physician there?
> Why then has the health of my poor people
>   not been restored? (v. 22)

The poem comes to an end, in my judgment, in 9:1,[22] which is a self-description of sorrow:

> O that my head were a spring of water
>   and my eyes a fountain of tears,
> so that I might weep day and night
>   for the slain of my poor people!

One of the amazing things about this poem is that it is decentered to an extreme. Normally, prophecy is spoken in the name of God, but in this poem God is simply one speaker—ultimately the decisive one, but one among many. The perspective of the people is also expressed, poignantly if incompletely. The prophet seems to be all feeling, torn apart by the event that he knows is coming. We are not certain, though, whether only the prophet speaks in these cries.

We find calls for humans to lament the fall of Jerusalem and Judah. Jeremiah 9:10 calls mourners to lament the destruction and depopulation of the land. According to v. 18, the living ("us") are to be mourned; according to vv. 20–21, what is to be mourned is the presence of death everywhere.

YHWH laments the fate of his people in 12:7–13. He admits what he has done in the first of these verses:

> I have forsaken my house,
>   I have abandoned my heritage;
> I have given the beloved of my soul
>   into the hands of her enemies. (v. 7)

---

22. Jeremiah 9:2–9 is hard to classify. Verses 2–6 sound like a misanthropic description of human society. It does *not* sound like divine discourse; the speaker would like to be a hermit. However, we do get a juridical sentence in vv. 7–9. This encourages readers to look back at vv. 2–6 to see if these could function as an indictment.

## Redeeming Judgment

There can thus be no question of YHWH mourning for something done by someone else. In the next couple verses, it seems that the holy land has been taken over by wild animals, or humans depicted as animals. With an ironic twist, "shepherds" are said to have destroyed the vineyard (v. 10). If the shepherds were Israelite leaders of the past, this is an indictment. However, shepherds could be a figure for foreign rulers who have destroyed Judah. In either case, in v. 12 it is YHWH's sword that destroys, and the final verse describes judgment as the frustration of expectations:

> They have sown wheat and have reaped thorns,
> > they have tired themselves out but profit nothing.
> They shall be ashamed of their harvests
> > because of the fierce anger of the Lord. (v. 13)

One might prefer a lamentation that expresses greater sympathy for the object of mourning, but this one will not permit any deflection of blame.

### Jeremiah's Confessions

A series of passages distributed fairly evenly between chapters 11 and 20 go by the name of confessions. They take the form individual laments, complaining specifically about the suffering that befalls the prophet. They do not complain about the message God has commissioned Jeremiah to deliver but of the enmity and isolation God's message generates. They are relevant to us for what they say about the fate of an individual caught up in a national crisis. In such times, the individual's destiny has little or no relationship to his or her own actions; yet the individual's destiny still has its own meaning and value.

Jeremiah 11:18—12:6, the first confession, features a set of laments and divine answers. In the first (11:18–20), Jeremiah describes the plots of the people of his own town of Anathoth; the Lord pronounces doom on them (11:21–23). Then Jeremiah broadens the scope of his lament—really, he offers a question regarding the fairness of life (12:1–4); the Lord's answer is to dismiss the question:

> If you have raced with foot-runners and they have wearied you,
> > how will you compete with horses? (12:5)

In other words, God's asks the prophet, if your question about life's fairness is bothering you, what are you going to do when judgment is everywhere?

*Prophecy for a New Generation*

The next confession—15:10–21—begins with a general complaint about life (v. 10). Jeremiah laments earnestly in 15:15–18. The lament begins with a confession of trust and request for retribution. It is in vv. 16–17 that we hear a complaint distinctive to a prophet:

> Your words were found, and I ate them,
>   and your words became to me a joy . . .
> For I am called by your name,
>   O Lord, God of hosts.
> I did not sit in the company of merrymakers,
>   nor did I rejoice;
> under the weight of your hand I sat alone,
>   for you filled me with indignation.

The first of these verses reviews history in a positive light; the second describes the negative effect of isolation. In v. 18, Jeremiah moves toward an accusation of God:

> Why is my pain unceasing,
>   my wound incurable,
>     refusing to be healed?
> Truly, you are to me like a deceitful brook
>   like waters that fail.

The accusation is clothed in an image that modern readers may miss: a deceitful brook would be a *wadi* that is filled during the rainy season but dries up in hot weather. One may think there is water available when there is not.[23] This Lord doesn't come through in the time of crisis. The Lord's answer in 15:19–21 is, repent; what you are saying is worthless.

Jeremiah 17:14–18 has a plea for salvation (v. 14); the prophet complains about those who taunt him (v. 15) and threaten him (v. 18). He also makes a negative request to the effect that the Lord not also become a "terror" (v. 17). Jeremiah 18:19–23 also focuses on Jeremiah's opposition; his request for revenge is quite harsh (see v. 21–22). It is hard to understand how his protest of innocence, "Remember how I stood before you to speak good for them, to turn away your wrath from them" (v. 20), can be said with a good conscience when Jeremiah is now vehemently requesting collective disaster on their families. In neither 17:14–18 nor 18:19–23 does the Lord answer Jeremiah's prayer. Jeremiah 15:19–21 seems to be the Lord's final answer.

---

23. This image is developed by the Job poet in 6:15–20; it makes its import clearer.

*Redeeming Judgment*

But Jeremiah continues to lament. Chapter 20 has two laments, and they are probably the strongest of all the confessions. In v. 7, Jeremiah opens with a charge against God that hints at rape, or at least seduction. In vv. 8–9, he describes the experience that has elicited this charge.

> For whenever I speak, I must cry out,
> I must shout, "Violence and destruction!"
> for the word of the LORD has become for me
> a reproach and derision all day long. (v. 8)

When Jeremiah tries to keep his mouth shut, he begins to burn inside and finally explodes (v. 9). This does not make him any friends: rather, he becomes the object of plots (v. 10). Jeremiah does find confidence in the Lord's willingness to pass judgment on his persecutors.

Jeremiah's final confession is not a lament proper, but a "curse of the day of his birth" (20:14–18). The import of such an utterance is that nonexistence is better than existence. There is an implied charge against the Creator.[24]

Jeremiah had been promised in his call to prophecy that the Lord would protect him from his enemies. Nothing was said about the emotional toll and melancholy that aggravates his suffering. Jeremiah does survive the attempts on his life, and he does not succumb to despair. By the end of his life, he seems reconciled to the role he was assigned. Baruch also seems to have lamented about his troubles, and Jeremiah delivers YHWH's answer: "I am going to break down what I have built, and pluck up what I have planted—that is, the whole land. And you, do you seek great things for yourself? Do not seek them, for I am going to bring disaster on all flesh, says YHWH; but I will give you your life as a prize of war in every place to which you may go" (45:4–5). This oracle can be an epithet for both of them.

## During Zedekiah's Reign

The legitimate heir's uncle is selected by the Babylonians to preside over the last decade of Judah's existence. We have already noted how the young Jehoiachin is taken into exile with his mother and several thousand Jerusalemites. They are hostages to keep Judah from rebellion. The effect of the policy is the opposite its intention. There is great pressure to rebel in hopes that YHWH will overturn Babylon and liberate the exiles—as well as the temple treasures. Zedekiah does not have the authority based on legitimacy, so his capacity to

---

24. Job has a similar, more extended curse of the day of birth in chapter 3.

resist the Zeitgeist is minimal. He himself seems to have lacked leadership qualities: in several stories of the last days, Jeremiah counsels him to do one thing, and he expresses fear that his own officials will kill him (38:19). It seems that a pro-rebellion party rules the government, and the king is forced to go along with it.

Jeremiah has a new message, indeed a new calling, once the young king Jahoiachin and the Jerusalemites are taken into exile. According to chapter 24, he has a vision involving two baskets of figs—one good and one rotten. The Lord explains this vision: the good figs are those taken into exile; the bad those left behind (24:3–10). The Lord will treat them accordingly. Jeremiah then takes it upon himself to teach those in exile to adjust to the new situation and to await their deliverance in about seventy years: "For thus says the Lord: Only when seventy years are completed will I visit you, and I will fulfill to you my promise and bring you back to this place. For surely I know the plans I have for you, says the Lord, plans for your welfare and not for harm, to give you a future with hope" (29:10–11). The rest of chapter 29 indicates that the exiles are not ready to take the long view. Jeremiah must fight the same false hopes among the exiles as he has to fight in Jerusalem.

The story of the battle against false hopes is told in chapters 27–28. Jeremiah is told by YHWH to construct a "yoke" and wear it about in Jerusalem. It so happens that envoys of neighboring nations are visiting Jerusalem to discuss prospects for a revolt against Babylon. Jeremiah has a message for all of them: "'It is I who by my great power and my outstretched arm have made the earth, with men and animals that are on the earth, and I give it to whomever I please. Now I have given all these lands into the hand of King Nebuchadnezzar of Babylon . . . All the nations shall serve him and his son and his grandson, until the time of his own land comes; then many nations and great kings shall make him their slave'" (27:5–7).

The conspirators are warned: "If any nation or kingdom will not serve this king, Nebuchadnezzar of Babylon, and put its neck under the yoke of the king of Babylon, then I will punish that nation with the sword, with famine, and with pestilence, says the Lord, until I have completed its destruction by his hand. You, therefore, must not listen to your prophets, your diviners, your dreamers, your soothsayers, or your sorcerers, who are saying to you, 'You shall not serve the king of Babylon'" (27:8–9). It is noteworthy that Jeremiah believes that even Jerusalem and Judah, despite their status as bad figs, could survive the period of Babylonian rule by submitting to it.

## Redeeming Judgment

Jeremiah chapter 28 tells the story of a confrontation between Jeremiah and another prophet over this policy. A man named Hananiah ben Azzur directly contradicts Jeremiah in his presence: "Thus says the LORD of Hosts, the God of Israel: I have broken the yoke of the king of Babylon. Within two years I will bring back to this place all the vessels of the LORD's house . . . [and] Jeconiah the son of Jehoiakim, king of Judah, and all the exiles from Judah who went to Babylon, says the LORD, for I will break the yoke of the king of Babylon" (28:2–4, RSV).

Jeremiah pretends to support his message (v. 6) but offers a test of its veracity: "The prophets who preceded you and me from ancient times prophesied war, famine, and pestilence against many countries and great kingdoms. As for the prophet who prophesies peace [Heb. *shalom*], when the word of that prophet comes true, then it will be known that the Lord has truly sent the prophet" (28:8–9). Hananiah then breaks Jeremiah's yoke and wins the rhetorical contest. The audience probably goes away with renewed hope of a speedy restoration of monarchy and temple. Jeremiah holds his peace until YHWH speaks to him again: Make an iron yoke and tell Hananiah he will die for proclaiming a false prophecy.

If we take a step back, we can draw lessons about the criteria of true, and false, prophecy.[25] Obviously the party for rebellion was driven by nationalism and a kind of theism that sees the nation's good as the single focus of God's attention. They were Yahwists, but they could not see that the nation was broken, so to speak, and needed to be fixed.

In Jer 23:9–40, Jeremiah expands on the criteria of true and false prophecy. Verses 13–14 tell the story:

> In the prophets of Samaria
>    I saw an unsavory thing:
> they prophesied by Baal
>    and led my people Israel astray.
> But in the prophets of Jerusalem
>    I have seen a more shocking thing:
> they commit adultery and walk in lies;
>    they strengthen the hands of evildoers,
>      so that no one turns from wickedness. (23:13–14a, RSV)

---

25. At the time of Jeremiah, citizens would not have the benefit of canonization to decide the contest. They would have to know by their relationship with God. We have the power of hindsight; the canonical process has settled who was legitimate prophet.

You can tell false prophets, he is saying, by their own moral integrity and whether they hold the people to a high standard. "They keep saying to those who despise the word of the LORD, 'It shall be well with you'; and to all who stubbornly follow their own stubborn hearts, they say, 'No calamity shall come upon you'" (23:17).[26]

We might add one more criterion that Jeremiah may not have noticed: Jeremiah's message is realistic to the core, whereas the policy represented by Hananiah is predicated on miraculous intervention. Not only does he believe falsely that YHWH *should* overthrow Babylon to save Judah, but he is willing to put YHWH to the test.

Jeremiah had to live through the Babylonian slaughter and destruction of Jerusalem and the deportation of many more citizens into exile. We read of these events in chapters 37–39. Jeremiah exhorts resisting soldiers to defect to the Babylonians (38:2-4). King Zedekiah does not seem to have much to say in the nation's foreign and military policy, but neither does he have the fortitude to follow Jeremiah's counsel. Jeremiah seeks the king's protection, but some officials conspire to kill him. Jeremiah is placed in a cistern to die, but then is rescued by an Ethiopian slave (38:7) and ushered secretly to the king. If chapters 37 and 38 are sequential, this is the second interview: "Jeremiah said to Zedekiah, 'If I tell you, will you put me to death, will you not? And if I give you advice, you will not listen to me.' So King Zedekiah swore an oath in secret to Jeremiah, 'As the LORD lives, who gave us our lives, I will not put you to death or hand you over to these men who seek your life'" (38:15-16).

Jeremiah offers Zedekiah the following advice—in the name of YHWH: "If you will only surrender to the officials of the king of Babylon, then your life shall be spared, and this city shall not be burned with fire, and you and your house shall live. But if you do not surrender to the officials of the king of Babylon, then this city shall be handed over to the Chaldeans, and they shall burn it with fire, and you yourself shall not escape from their hand" (38:17-18). Then Zedekiah expresses his fear of his own people (v. 19). Alas, Zedekiah does not have the willpower to take advice that he knows is wise, so the city is destroyed and he is captured, forced to watch his sons slaughtered, and then blinded and taken into exile.

Jeremiah, on the other hand, survives, is captured and released by the Babylonians and allowed to return to Benjamin, where he hopes to live out the

---

26. For a perceptive study of the measure of truth in prophecy, see Moberly, *Prophecy and Discernment*.

rest of his days on the land he purchased from his cousin at the height of the siege. What happens to overturn his hopes is another story.

## Ezekiel: Prophet of Judgment among the Exiles

Jeremiah hears that prophets have arisen in the exile community, and condemns them because they have been fanning the embers of rebellion (Jer 29:15-23, 24-32). But there was another prophet who arose among the exiles, one whom Jeremiah would have affirmed had he heard of him. I am speaking of Ezekiel, who receives his call in Babylonian exile in 593 BCE—in the middle of Zedekiah's reign.[27]

Ezekiel does confront those prophets who promise "shalom" when there is none (Ezek 13:10). These prophets have not stood, he says, "in the breaches" or "repaired the walls" (13:5). They have "false visions and utter lying divinations" (13:9). Of course, these mantics believe that they have received revelation and therefore are speaking truth. They should realize, though, that when they offer "shalom" to the Israelites, they are "whitewashing" the defective wall built by the people (13:11). The true prophet will be known on the Day of Judgment.

Ezekiel also opposes the policy of king Zedekiah's administration—a policy the prophets like Hananiah were encouraging. In Ezekiel 17, Ezekiel is told to propound a fable, an allegory. He tells the story of an eagle that took a twig of cedar and planted it in good soil; then another eagle plucked it up and replanted it. What will the first eagle do? Pull it up and let it die. The first eagle represents the Babylonian emperor, the second the Egyptian ruler, and the plant is Judah. In the explanation, Ezekiel says, "As I live, says the Lord God, surely in the place where the king resides who made him [Zedekiah] king, whose oath he despised, and whose covenant with him he broke—in Babylon he shall die" (17:16). The Egyptians will not intervene to save their ally, so Judah will fall. Since Zedekiah is under oath, in a covenant—with YHWH as witness—it would be contradictory for YHWH to support the perfidious Judean king.[28]

The book of Ezekiel is well organized. The first twenty-four chapters are judgments over Jerusalem and Judah. They are all dated to the years between Ezekiel's call in 593 BCE and the fall of Jerusalem in 587 BCE. The remainder of the book is divided between prophecies of judgment against foreign nations

---

27. According to Ezek 1:1-3; it says the fifth year of the exile.
28. Verses 22-24 are a messianic passage.

*Prophecy for a New Generation*

(Ezekiel 25–32) and prophecies of salvation for Judah (Ezekiel 33–37, 40–48). Both these sections are dated after 587.

Ezekiel's style is quite distinctive. His prophecies are largely prose; they are usually lengthy, repetitious, and exaggerated. The prophet seems to make great efforts to gain the people's attention. Yet some narratives indicate that he has enough standing among the exiles that "elders" consult him (e.g., 8:11; 11:25; 17:1–4; 20:1–4).

One recurring theme in the prophecies in the early chapters is that the Lord is about to bring judgment on Israel so that the people "shall know that I am the Lord" (e.g., 6:7, 10, 14; 7:4, 9). This must mean that the event of judgment will expose false conceptions of God, as well as distorted affections, and replace them with true knowledge, knowledge of the sovereign Lord that evokes trust and obedience.

Ezekiel's message of judgment concerns the homeland directly—the exiles in so far as the homeland is in their heart and their future is its future. In any case, the land, the city, the temple all stand condemned. We read sentence after sentence concerned with their fate. When Ezekiel believes that his audience is practicing idolatry or contemplates apostasy, he refuses to answer any inquiry, and gives instead a command to repent (see 14:1–8; 20:1–4, 32, 33–39?). The exiled community represents the "remnant," the nucleus of the nation that by the Lord's grace will be revived and restored; it is the audience, along with the exiles created by the fall of Jerusalem in 587, who will receive the promises of Ezekiel 33–37.

*Reviewing History*

There are many similarities in subject matter as well as perspective between Ezekiel and Jeremiah. It is possible that Ezekiel had heard Jeremiah prophesy before he was exiled. In any case, I will survey Ezekiel with frequent comparisons to Jeremiah's prophecies.

In Jer 2:1–13, Israel is figured as a woman who becomes YHWH's wife; and the history of the two of them is reviewed to discover what went wrong with their relationship. Ezekiel 16 does the same thing for Jerusalem. At first she is an abandoned baby of mixed parentage, whom the Lord saves. When she is grown, he marries her—"enter[s] into covenant with [her]" (16:8). The young woman, unfortunately, trusts in her beauty and begins to have affairs with others—with gods (and goddesses). She even lavishes the Lord's gifts on these lovers, and sacrifices the Lord's children. Not only is she apostate; she

*Redeeming Judgment*

also finds lovers among the nations (cp. 16:23–34). The juridical sentence begins in chapter 16, v. 35. All Jerusalem's lovers will turn against her, bringing destruction and exile (vv. 36–43).[29]

Ezekiel 23 rehearses history with the figuration of two sisters, one representing Israel and the other Judah. This resembles Jer 3:6–14, though the outcome is judgment; no repentance and restoration are mentioned.

Ezekiel 20 reviews history without figuration. It addresses the elders who have come to inquire of Ezekiel: he is told to "let them know of the abominations of their ancestors" (v. 4). The story begins in Egypt. When YHWH promises to free Israel from Egyptian slavery, he commands the people to rid themselves of idols, but they do not; YHWH becomes angry but decides to deliver them "for his name's sake." The same thing happens several times in the wilderness, and after the conquest. The oracle in chapter 20 comes to a conclusion not with a sentence, but with a question—perhaps an indicting question:

> Therefore say to the house of Israel, Thus says the Lord God: Will you defile yourselves after the manner of your ancestors and go astray after their detestable things? When you offer your gifts and make your children pass through fire, you defile yourselves with all your idols to this day. And shall I be consulted by you, O house of Israel? As I live, says the Lord God, I will not be consulted by you. What is in your mind shall never happen—the thought, "Let us be like the nations, like the tribes of the countries, and worship wood and stone." (20:30–32)

This is followed by a promise of redemption (vv. 33–44).

It should be recognized that Ezekiel 20 departs from all the accounts of the exodus and even of the wilderness by its emphasis on the Israel's sinfulness throughout its history.[30] The mood of this review is almost the opposite of Jer 2:1–3. It foreshadows a development in postexilic penitential literature.[31]

## The Temple

Jeremiah's temple sermon is one of the most memorable in his book. In it the people are indicted for relying on the existence of the temple in its midst to protect the city and even the nation; the Lord, they think wouldn't allow his

---

29. This chapter continues, but the subject shifts; it ends with restoration.

30. See Patrick, "The First Commandment in the Structure of the Pentateuch," 107–18; and Rendtorff, *The Canonical Hebrew Bible*, 52–68.

31. Cp. Psalm 106.

*Prophecy for a New Generation*

residence to be destroyed by foreigners. So the people go about their sinful ways and hide out in the temple.

Ezekiel is a member of the Jerusalem priesthood, and shares the priestly conception of the temple as the throne of YHWH.[32] So how can he proclaim the temple's destruction? The vision in chapters 8 through 11 of Ezekiel provides an answer. He is "transported" by the Spirit to the temple. He is first shown the depredations going on in the temple. First he sees an "image of jealousy," a euphemism for a sacred pole devoted to the goddess Asherah (8:3). A full complement of elders is offering incense to images of animals and idols in a secret gatehouse chamber (8:7–13). Women are weeping for Tammuz in the north gate (8:14–15). In the inner court, a group faces east, worshipping the sun (8:16–18). Then Ezekiel is shown a company of "executioners" approaching to destroy the desecrated temple and to punish those doing the desecrating. The city is purged along with the temple. Then the Lord, manifested in "glory," begins to exit the temple. The cherubim bearing the throne move with him. The Lord leaves the temple to the east, and seems to settle on the Mount of Olives. The temple can now be destroyed without infringing on the holiness and majesty of God. Ezekiel has arrived at the same message as Jeremiah, but the route has been different.

*Intercession*

Right after the temple sermon, the book of Jeremiah tells how the Lord prohibits the prophet from interceding for the people of Israel (Jer 7:16–20). While Ezekiel is not so commanded, he himself seems to refuse to intercede for persons who are betraying YHWH. In 14:2–6, the Lord seems to replace intercession with a call to repent:

> And the word of the LORD came to me: "Mortal, these men have taken their idols into their hearts, and placed their iniquity as a stumbling block before them; should I let myself be consulted at all by them? Therefore speak to them, and say to them, Thus says the Lord GOD: Any of those of the house of Israel who takes their idols into their heart and place their iniquity as a stumbling block before them, and yet comes to the prophet, I the LORD will answer those who come with the multitude of their idols, in order that I may take hold of the hearts of the house of Israel, all of whom are estranged from me through

---

32. Jeremiah was also from a priestly family, but his family was attached to one of the outlying sanctuaries that were decommissioned by Josiah. If Jeremiah is any indication, the family did not buy into the "high" doctrine of the sanctuary held by the Jerusalem priests.

*Redeeming Judgment*

> their idols . . ." Thus says the Lord God: Repent and turn away from your idols . . . (14:2–6)

Just a bit later (14:12–23), Ezekiel is told that the intercession of even Noah, Daniel, and Job—three legendary righteous men—would not turn judgment aside. It seems that each person or group will be judged for wrongdoing belonging to the person or group, and no one else's merit can make up for a deficiency.

Ezekiel confronts the issue of individual and collective accountability in 18:1–32. What provokes his discussion is a popular saying making its rounds among the people: "The parents have eaten sour grapes, and the children's teeth are set on edge" (18:2).[33] This is a bit of dark humor about their suffering for the wrongdoing of their ancestors. Ezekiel objects to the saying. If you are judged, you deserved it. So he sets up an ideal judicial system: a person is punished only for one's own actions, though there may well be a continuation of what one's ancestors did. If the person repents and begins again, the threat of judgment will be removed. Guilt will not be inherited.

The irony is, Ezekiel not only sets forth his ideal, but he assumes that this is in force. I draw that conclusion from his final accusation: "Yet you say, 'The way of the Lord is unfair.' Hear now, O house of Israel: Is my way unfair? Is it not your ways that are unfair? When the righteous turn away from their righteousness and commit iniquity, they shall die for it; for the iniquity that they have committed they shall die'" (18:25–26). This assertion seems to ignore the collective dimensions of guilt. Institutions, practices, and moral norms are passed on from one generation to the next; the later generation often is stuck with what it has inherited, and if that is guilt producing, then the later generation is guilty despite the fact that it did not choose to do what it continues to do. Moreover, some individuals may keep clean but the society continues to follow past evils.[34] Which is to say, Ezekiel's scheme of individual accountability may well be an ideal to aspire to, but it cannot defeat the popular proverb.

## Enacted Prophecies

Let's return to Ezekiel's judgments against Judah. Ezekiel is just as inclined toward street theater as Jeremiah. We have several enacted prophecies at the beginning of the book. In Ezek 4:1–8, the prophet is told to imitate child's play—to portray a battle against a city symbolized by a brick. He is then to lie

---

33. Cp. Jer 31:29–30.
34. Racism is a good example in American society.

on his left side for 390 days, symbolic of the years of Israel's exile; then to lie on his right side for forty days—one for each year of Judah's exile. During this period he will be tied up so that he cannot turn. As if this were not enough, he is told to make a bread of mixed grains, of which he can only eat about eight ounces a day (4:9–15). His water is also rationed.

Ezekiel 5 has him commanded to shave his head and beard (5:1–4); the hair is to be disposed of symbolically. All these actions are meant to proclaim the destruction of Jerusalem and exile of the rest of its inhabitants. In the next chapter, viz., chapter 6, Ezekiel is told to prophesy against the mountains of Israel; this expands his message beyond Jerusalem to all Judah. The mountains are chosen because they have heterodox sanctuaries on them (6:4–7).

In chapter 12, Ezekiel is told to pack up for exile, and "go into exile by day in their sight" (v. 3). The symbolism is transparent. Later he is told to "eat your bread with quaking, and drink your water with trembling and fearfulness" (12:18). This action is meant to foreshadow the condition of the people after defeat and destruction (12:19–20).

The most poignant enacted prophecy comes at the end of the period of judgments: "With one blow I am about to take away from you the delight of your eyes; yet you shall not mourn or weep, nor shall your tears run down. Sigh, but not aloud; make no mourning for the dead" (Ezek 24:16–17a). The death of Ezekiel's wife comes during the siege of Jerusalem, and the answer he is to give to any inquiry is that the sanctuary is about to be destroyed, and the inhabitants of Jerusalem put to the sword. The event will be so devastating that the exiles will be numb (24:19–24). When word of the city's fall reaches the exiles, Ezekiel is permitted to speak, and weep, as normal (24:25–27).

## Prophecies against Foreign Nations

We have had occasion to attend to prophecies against foreign nations now and then, but we have not addressed the category systematically. As we conclude our discussion of the prophecy of national judgment, we have the opportunity to do so. We are following the order of the book of Ezekiel by locating this discussion after the study of the prophecies of judgment against Israel.

By what rationale do Israelite prophets pronounce judgment on foreign nations? Isn't the role of the prophet to deliver messages to the people of YHWH from YHWH? This is how Deut 18:15–22 presents the office. The prophet is called to be a living Moses, so to speak. Of course, Moses addressed the pharaoh as well; perhaps that is the rationale for the prophets addressing foreign nations. That is to say, the prophet speaks to other nations because the nations have wronged, or are wronging, the people of YHWH. This, however, would limit the prophet to a partisan role. The standing of foreign nations in YHWH's eyes, according to that model, depends solely on how they treat his people.

One of our prophets does not prophesy against foreign nations: Hosea. The fact that there are no such prophecies in his book could, of course, be fortuitous. However, there are good reasons for regarding the absence of prophecies against foreign nations as deliberate. In other words, Hosea does not see it as his calling to pronounce on their fate. Hosea understands prophecy to be a part of the transactions within a mutually exclusive relationship of people to God. By comparing this relationship to a marriage, Hosea compounds the intimacy and exclusivity of the bond. The nations he names, Assyria and Egypt, are powers competing with YHWH for Israel's devotion and trust, but Hosea finds no occasion to condemn them. It is Israel's fault that these nations are eroding their faithfulness to YHWH. Without knowing YHWH, nations like Assyria and Egypt are not under the divine norms by which they could be judged.

Hosea is alone in the restriction of prophecy to Israel. All the other prophets we have discussed have judgments of foreign nations. It is uncertain whether judgments against other nations in Micah 4–5 are by the prophet, but nothing in his theology would keep him from pronouncing judgment on foreign nations. The final form of the book of Micah, which does contain oracles against foreign nations, represents the prophet well.

The book of Amos opens with a cycle of judgments against neighboring nations. The extant text condemns Damascus/Aram (1:3–5), Gaza and the Philistines (1:6–8), Tyre/Phoenicia (1:9–10), Edom (1:11–12), Rabbah and the Ammonites (1:13–15), Moab (2:1–3), and Judah (2:4–5). Some of these oracles may not have been by Amos, but most are in good standing. These judgments are understood to be a rhetorical strategy for gaining an audience and setting them up for a shock. The judgments are nevertheless for offenses that all nations and peoples would condemn, offenses, moreover, perpetrated not only against Israel but also against other nations. The murderous assault by Aram and the Ammonites on Gilead was a crime in which Israel was a victim. The slave trade in which the Philistines, Phoenicians, and Edomites engaged may have included Israelite victims, but hardly only these. Finally, Moab's desecration of the body of the king of Edom is an offense between two foreign countries.

## Prophecy for a New Generation

What is Amos's rationale for delivering judgment against foreigners? His theology is sensitive to international moral norms that are as much under YHWH's oversight as the revealed norms governing Israel. Amos can single out his people as being under a different, more demanding standard (3:1–2), but he can also say that Israel is not different from other nations when it comes to judgment (9:7–8). If Israel is a sinful kingdom, it can be judged; likewise, other nations can also be judged.

Now we come to Isaiah. His call commissions him to speak to Israel and Judah, not foreign nations.[35] Nevertheless, his book has numerous prophecies against foreign nations.[36] Some of these are directly relevant to his message to Israel and Judah. Aram comes in for condemnation because it is allied with Israel to dethrone Ahaz and replace him with a more pliable Davidide (see Isaiah 7–8; 17:1–9). Assyria plays a central role in the divine plan, according to Isaiah. It is a tool, a "rod," for punishing Israel and Judah (10:5–19; cp. 37:22–29). It also has a role for the "whole world" (14:24–27). But note, it has itself incurred guilt for its violence, greed, and pride of power (10:7–14, 15). When that empire has fulfilled its role, it will be destroyed—in the holy land itself, according to 14:24–27. Assyria's elimination will usher in a new order for the known world, one that will look to Jerusalem to resolve international disputes (2:1–4).

Egypt comes in for judgment when Hezekiah begins to rely on it in his plans for breaking away from the Assyrian Empire. Isaiah goes about naked to demonstrate how the Assyrians will treat the Egyptians (20:1–6). There are a number of woes in Isaiah 30–31 and related passages that speak of Egyptian defeat and Judean disaster for opposing the Assyrian empire. Egypt also comes in for judgment in the collection of oracles against foreign nations. Isaiah 18 condemns the Nubian dynasty, though its offense is not stated. Isaiah 19:1–15 speaks of civil war in Egypt, and a breakdown of the irrigation system. Their offense is "becoming fools" (vv. 11–15), though this could just as well be punishment as offense.

Isaiah has occasion to speak to the nations bordering on Israel and Judah. Conspiracies against Assyria were frequently afoot: e.g., 20:1–6, perhaps 14:28–32. Since Isaiah was adamantly opposed to human efforts to overthrow the Assyrian yoke, he calls down judgment on the conspiratorial rulers.

Isaiah had an amazingly expansive view of the civilized world and what was happening to it. He also was inclined to utopian hopes. It is hardly surpris-

---

35. This is also implied by the call visions of Amos in chapters 7, 8, and 9.
36. Most of Isaiah 13–23, and scattered passages elsewhere.

ing that his book attracted anonymous prophecies about nations like Babylon (chapters 13–14), Elam and Media, (chapter 21) and Tyre (chapter 23), and the apocalypse involving the judgment of all nations (chapters 24–27).

Jeremiah is called to function as a prophet "over nations and over kingdoms, to pluck up and to pull down, to destroy and to overthrow, to build and to plant" (1:10). One might think that he would have a lot to say about nations other than Judah, but there is less than one would expect. Jeremiah has taken over Isaiah's view of a great empire being a tool of YHWH. Speaking words for YHWH, the way Jeremiah puts it is, "It is I who by my great power and my outstretched arm have made the earth, with the people and animals that are on the earth, and I give it to whomever I please" (Jer 27:5). Note that Jeremiah does not speak of Babylon being a tool of punishment; it simply is the appointed ruler for the foreseeable future. Actually, it is the emperor, Nebuchadnezzar, whom YHWH favors. The nations of the western Levant had better grant this figure his rights, or they will suffer.

In his letters to the Judean exiles living in Babylonian, Jeremiah tells them to settle down, build houses, raise gardens, marry and produce children (29:5–6), seek the welfare of the city, and pray for it (29:7). It will be several generations before Babylon ceases to rule the world. He actually offers a time frame—seventy years (29:10).[37] The people can move back when a new power replaces Babylon.

There are other indications that Jeremiah prophesies the downfall of Babylon. According to 51:61–64, Jeremiah tells a messenger named Seraiah to throw a scroll of judgments into the Euphrates after reading it aloud. Whether the long set of prophecies in 50:1—51:58 derives from Jeremiah or a later prophet, they fit the bill fairly well. The text is repetitious and rather conventional. It does start out explosively:

> Declare among the nations and proclaim,
>> set up a banner and proclaim,
>> conceal it not, and say:
>
> Babylon is taken,
>> Bel is put to shame,
>> Marduk [Heb. *Merodach*] is dismayed.
>
> Her images are put to shame,
>> her idols are dismayed (50:2)

---

37. Which turned out to be fairly accurate: from ca. 598 to 538.

The gods of Babylon fall along with the city and empire. This will be at the heart of the message of Isaiah 40–55.

Echoing a salient theme of Jeremiah's early prophecy and a descriptor for Babylon itself, late in Jeremiah Babylon's destruction is said to be coming from an assault of an army from the north (e.g., 50:3–5). Babylon is repeatedly taunted, and then lamented. Repeatedly it is said that YHWH is taking vengeance.

> Because of the wrath of the Lord she shall not be inhabited,
>   but shall be an utter desolation. (50:13a)

> For this is the vengeance of the Lord:
>   take vengeance on her,
>   do as she has done. (50:15b)

Occasionally it is said explicitly that Babylon's suffering is payback for its treatment of Jerusalem and Judah, e.g.,

> For Israel and Judah have not been forsaken
>   by their God, the Lord of hosts;
> but the land of the Chaldeans is full of guilt
>   against the Holy One of Israel. (51:5)

While this is rather nationalistic, it can be justified from divine election.[38] Once the Judeans are invited to testify against Babylon:

> "Nebuchadrezzar the king of Babylon has devoured me,
>   he has crushed me;
> he has made me an empty vessel
>
> . . .
>
> The violence done to me and to my kin be upon Babylon,"
>   let the inhabitants of Zion say.
> "My blood be upon the inhabitants of Chaldea,"
>   let Jerusalem say. (51:34–35, RSV)

The Lord gives this testimony a positive hearing (51:36–37). The Judeans, who are frequently portrayed in these chapters as residing in Babylon, are told to exit the city to avoid falling with it (e.g., 50:8; 51:6). Other passages promise salvation to them (e.g., 50:33–34).

---

38. "Anyone who curses you I will curse" (Gen 12:3).

## Redeeming Judgment

There are few indications of what occasioned the other pronouncements of judgment against foreign nations in Jeremiah. The judgment of Egypt (chapter 46) is quite understandable. Just as in the days of Isaiah, Egypt was recruiting Philistine city-states and Jerusalem-Judah to resist the Mesopotamia-based empire. Egypt wanted a buffer between it and these Mesopotamian powerhouses. Jehoiakim had been placed on the throne by Egypt, and when he had reason to trust in Egypt's strength and reliability, viz., after Egypt fought the Babylonians to a standstill in 601 BCE, he withheld tribute (see 2 Kgs 24:1–7). Several times during Jehoakim's reign, Jeremiah would have had occasion to pronounce judgment on Egypt for encouraging Judah into suicidal rebellion. Jeremiah would have similar occasion when Zedekiah courted Egyptian support for rebellion (from 593 on). Some of his prophecy against neighboring nations—Gaza chapter 47), Moab (48), Ammon (49:1–6), Edom (49:7–22), and Damascus (49:23–27) may be connected to one of these same conspiracies against Babylon, egged on by Egypt.

Many oracles against foreign nations do not mention what the addressee has done against Israel or Judah. That is, they do not have a nationalistic rationale for judgment. Ezekiel has a number of these, and we will give them our attention. Ezekiel's oracles against foreign nations constitute a collection of materials in chapters 25–32. A considerable number of Judah's neighbors are condemned, but most rather perfunctorily, viz., Ammon, Moab, Edom and Philistia; each receives only a few verses of chapter 25. Tyre, on the other hand, is singled out for three full chapters. Egypt is also singled out for a large section: chapters 29–32. It will be worth our while to look closely at the judgments of Tyre and Egypt.

The oracles against Tyre begin with an account of how the Babylonian army will besiege the island city.[39] Little is said about the reasons for Tyre's sentencing.[40] Chapter 27 is a dirge over the destroyed city; it is uttered proleptically of course. One gets the impression that Tyre must fall because it had been such a successful, wealthy commercial center.[41] It had trading partners around the known world (27:12–25). The city is portrayed as a ship, and in vv. 26–36 it sinks and is mourned by many.

---

39. Nebuchadnezzar besieged Tyre for thirteen years but failed to take it; see 29:17–21.

40. Ezek 26:2 (RSV) sounds like the sort of thing that would offend a Judean prophet: "'Aha, the gate of the peoples is broken, it has swung open to me; I shall be replenished, now that she is laid waste.'"

41. Perhaps we have the Greek idea of nemesis here.

If the descriptions of sentencing occur in chapter 27, the series of oracles finds its indictment in chapter 28. The first oracle of this chapter cites words of the ruler of Tyre which indicate how proud and insensitive he is:

> Because your heart is proud,
>> and you have said, "I am a god,
> I sit in the seat of the gods,
>> in the heart of the seas." (28:2)

This ruler has great wisdom, the kind of wisdom a successful trader has; he has acquired great wealth for himself and his nation. But his wealth has inflated his ego. YHWH declares his sentence:

> Therefore thus says the Lord GOD:
> "Because you consider yourself as wise as a god,
>> therefore, behold, I will bring strangers upon you, ...
> They shall thrust you down into the Pit." (28:6–8)

The ruler who imagined himself a god will be stripped of his false consciousness when he faces his killers and after his death.

The second unit of the chapter employs myth to describe the condition and the fall of the ruler, now called the king, of Tyre. Ezekiel 28:11–19 is called a lament or dirge (v. 12). It tells the story of the original man.

> You were in Eden, the garden of God;
>> every precious stone was your covering ...
> On the day that you were created
>> they were prepared.
> With an anointed guardian cherub I placed you;
>> you were on the holy mountain of God;
> in the midst of the stones of fire you walked. (28:12–14)

The fall occurs in v. 15:

> You were blameless in your ways
>> from the day you were created,
>> till iniquity was found in you.

This myth is then applied to Tyre's commercial activity:

> In the abundance of your trade
>> you were filled with violence, and you sinned;
> so I cast you as a profane thing from the mountain of God ... (28:16)

*Redeeming Judgment*

Divine punishment for this sin is described as being "cast to the ground" (v. 17b; cp. v. 16b). This could be comparable to the "death" imposed on the original couple in Genesis 3. However, as a punishment for Tyre, it becomes a sight for others to see (v. 17b). In v. 18, the addressee burns up and becomes ashes for others to see. This, presumably, would fit the fate stipulated for Tyre in chapter 26, viz., destruction by the Babylonian army.

Ezekiel's use of royal citation in 28:1–10 and myth in 28:11–19 allows the oracle of judgment against Tyre to take on paradigmatic force.[42] Above all, the story characterizes the sinful inclinations of all nations. Reinhold Niebuhr draws out this theological lesson from the oracles against Tyre:

> These words of the prophet Ezekiel to Tyrus are a succinct interpretation of the whole Biblical approach to the destiny of nations. Men seek in their collective enterprises, even more than in their individual life, to claim an absolute significance for their virtues and achievements, a final validity for their social structures and institutions and a degree of power which is incompatible with human finiteness. Since the collective achievements of men are more imposing than those of individuals, their power more impressive and their collective stabilities less subject to the caprice of nature, the idolatrous claims which are made for them are always more plausible than the pathetic pretensions of individuals.[43]

It is surprising that Tyre was chosen to represent the pride and limitless desire of nations because it was not an empire that had slaughtered the inhabitants of the lands it sought to conquer or had pillaged their cities. If it was an imperial power, then trade and commerce that extended its power over others. It was perceptive of Ezekiel to bring a seemingly benign nation to judgment.

The next chapters of Ezekiel focus on a more typical imperial power: Egypt. Chapters 29–30 announce and portray the destruction of Egypt at the hands of Babylon. The prophet explicitly says that Egypt is compensation to Nebuchadnezzar for his fruitless effort to conquer Tyre. In actual fact, Babylon did not conquer Egypt either.

The mythical material is located in chapters 31–32. The first of these chapters tells the story of a great tree that grows toward heaven, fed by the waters of the deep (Heb. *tehom*). In v. 10, YHWH speaks a word of judgment because the tree has exceeded the limits of a creature, and "its heart has become proud of its height"; the tree will be felled by foreigners, and all those

---

42. Zimmerli, *Ezekiel*, 2:77, 95, says as much.
43. Reinhold Niebuhr, *Faith and History*, 218.

animals that depended upon it will abandon it (v. 12). Then beginning in v. 15 of chapter 31, the image changes to a "tree" relocated in the underworld, in Sheol. The chapter ends with a foreshadowing of scenes from Sheol in chapter 32. This story is said at the beginning and end to be about "the Pharaoh and all his pomp" (31:2, 18); otherwise, it could be the allegory of any empire. Walter Zimmerli says aptly, "In the comparison with the magnificent tree which acquires its size and beauty from the rich waters of the primeval deep, it is shown with the boldness of mythical terminology that mysterious, primeval forces are at work in earthly power complexes."[44]

Ezekiel 32 has two dated oracles, viz., vv. 1–16 and 17–32, each termed a lament. The first is actually a series of declarations of divine intention to distress and destroy the pharaoh and Egypt. The pharaoh is compared to a "dragon" who lives in the waters of Egypt's rivers (v. 2). Some scholars have identified this dragon as a cosmogonic Leviathan of myth. However, there is very little left of its mythic power. The judgments describe how God will capture and kill this creature and "strew [its] flesh upon the mountains [and] valleys" (vv. 4–5). The oracle ends with a land purified and emptied of inhabitants (vv. 13–15).

The second oracle concerns the mass of Egyptians, who are to be sent to Sheol. The nation is proud of its beauty, but that does not save it from death. The nation will join past empires—Assyria, Elam, Meshech and Tubal; Edom, Phoenicia and "rulers of the north" are added later. These nations are buried in ignominy. Though all humans come to the grave, those who "spread terror in the land of the living" (vv. 23, 25, 27) will be shamed. In particular, rulers of empires are separated from "the mighty men [of old] who went down to Sheol with their weapons of war, whose swords were laid under their heads, and whose [shields] are upon their bones" (v. 27). Evidently this passage means to contrast the age of heroes to that of the rapacious empires.

These oracles against Egypt and its pharaoh, like those against Tyre and its ruler, are not really judgments with specific indictments, and sentences that rectify the scales of justice. They are so generalized that they can be applied to all human rulers and powers—at least to a significant extent. This is what happens when humans gain power by military means, commerce, or culture. They become prideful and defensive of their privileges. They begin to imagine that they are the captains of their destiny and will live forever. How perfectly symbolic it is that the pharaoh was deified and immortalized in Egypt; that is, he was considered a deity during his life and became an immortal deity

44. Zimmerli, *Ezekiel*, 2:153.

*Redeeming Judgment*

at death. Mesopotamian rulers were said to become gods when they died. Ezekiel's oracle "demythologizes" these pretentious claims: all will go down to Sheol, and the imperial powers will be shamed in death.

Walter Zimmerli notes that Ezek 32:1–16 has an apocalyptic flavor: "The main point of this oracle is the description of the judgment. God is able to remove from his element the one who is apparently all-powerful in his own waters. And what is he then? A rotting, stinking corpse at whose putrefaction the whole world will be shrouded in darkness because God has extinguished its light. In these apocalyptic features there is expressed the truth that where God raises up the terror of his judgment, even among the great leaders of the created world . . . there are no areas of aristocratic exclusion."[45]

This is a sufficient sampling of the prophecy of judgment against foreign nations to understand its thrust and justification, and the direction it is tending. We could have examined Isaiah 14, which has many similarities with Ezekiel's "mythical" oracles. That chapter, directed against Babylon, calls upon a myth associated with "the day star, son of dawn" (v. 12). It is the story of the failed attempt of an angelic being to usurp the sovereignty of God, resulting in banishment from heaven. The figure, in Latin, was named Lucifer, and from this text a midrash grew about the rebellion of the devil against God at the beginning. Within Isaiah, however, it is meant to indict the Babylonian empire. This empire became a cipher in apocalyptic literature; that could be the topic for another chapter.

---

45. Zimmerli, *Ezekiel*, 2:162.

# 12

## Communal Lamentation and the Prophet's Answer

(Psalms, Lamentations, Hosea, Jeremiah)

THE PROPHECY OF COMMUNAL judgment has reached its fulfillment in Jeremiah and Ezekiel. The two eras of prophecy of communal judgment—the eighth century, and the seventh and sixth centuries BCE—have stamped an understanding of the Assyrian and Babylonian exiles as divine judgment on the people of God. Indeed, later generations will see that this was a turning point in their history. Sacred history is, as it were, suspended in expectation of a reversal of judgment. Judgment is not intended as an end of sacred history, but the people of Israel do not escape its burden within the time frame of the Hebrew Bible.

The next logical step in our study of judgment would be to turn to the prophecy of salvation. That is what we propose to do. However, we need to hear the cries of the people in the midst of judgment. It is for the redemption of the people that God has been driven to subject them to judgment. The response of the people to their judgment must be incorporated into God's action. Their cries in fact call forth both his pity and his polemic. It is this movement from the people's cry to the prophetic answer that we propose to trace in this chapter. The chapter will begin with the lamentation of the people as recorded in the Psalms and Lamentations, and then take up the answer given by Hosea and Jeremiah.

## Our Study of Communal Lament

What will we be after in our study of the laments of the people? We should first of all regard the communal lament as a counterpart of the individual lament. When a person experienced a serious crisis in life, he or she complained to God about it and petitioned for relief. When the people experienced trouble, either weather related or political, they too complained to God about it and petitioned for relief.

Whatever the original occasion for the composition of the communal laments we have in the Psalter, they naturally gravitate to the fall of Jerusalem and Judah in 598/587 BCE. That is how at least five communal lament psalms are best read now. So we can examine them for their perspective on the events of divine judgment and *what* the people sought from the Lord and *how* they seek to persuade YHWH to act.

Besides the communal laments in the Psalter, we have the book of Lamentations bewailing the fall of Jerusalem. Only parts of the book are communal lament in form, but these can be compared to those in the Psalter. The other portions of the book are dirge and individual lament; these too have become vehicles of mourning their fall and seeking to persuade YHWH to give them a future.

## Communal Laments of the Psalter

Like the individual laments we discussed in chapter 6, the communal lament has address, usually integrated into an initial request or complaint; complaints against God (in the second person), enemies (in the third person) and about one's suffering and distress (in the first person). Accusations against God are even more frequent and intense here than in individual laments. Often the community recalls God's past saving deeds with which to contrast his present behavior.

As in the individual lament, the request also divides into three parts: for God to turn, to intervene to save the people, and to overturn or frustrate the enemies. There may be a vow of praise at the end, but not as regularly as in the individual lament.

Something else happened that shaped the preservation of the communal laments of the Psalter. Five of them centered on a military reversal of great magnitude, and they gravitated to the fall of Jerusalem and Judah. One of them, viz., Psalm 89, was written for this event, but the others do not come so well marked. Psalms 44, 74, 79, and 80 could have been composed for this catastrophe, but could have derived from earlier events, including the fall of the northern kingdom.[1] Now, however, these psalms can be read with the Babylonian defeat and exile as their reference.

The Babylonian exile curtailed the need for the form of lament concerned with national catastrophe; the exile was not only the most salient subject of national lamentation, but it was the last one Israel experienced as an independent political actor.[2]

## What the Communal Laments Say

Rather than expound each of the five Psalms serially, I will work through Psalm 44 and draw in the corresponding elements in Psalms 74, 79, and 80. We will work our way through Psalm 89 at the end.

Psalm 44 begins with a rehearsal of the tradition of YHWH's saving activity in the conquest of Canaan.

> You with your own hand drove out the nations,
>> but [our ancestors] you planted;
> you afflicted the peoples,
>> but them you set free;
> for not by their own sword did they win the land,
>> nor did their own arm give them victory;
> but your right hand, and your arm,
>> and the light of your countenance;
>> for you delighted in them. (vv. 2–3)

Verses 4–8 continue in the same vein, confessing the Lord's empowerment of the Israelite victories. Then in v. 9 we encounter a reversal:

> Yet you have rejected us and abased us,
> and have not gone out with our armies.

This opens the door to a series of accusations against God:

1. Psalm 80 describes YHWH as the God of northern tribes; that could indicate that it originally lamented the fall of the northern kingdom. As for the other three communal laments, Psalm 83 has Transjordan in view, Psalm 60 has an oracle in it declaring various areas in Canaan and Transjordan to belong to YHWH; it is not entirely clear what it is about. Psalm 85 could be read as a lament over a drought.

2. During the canonical period, the people were in diaspora. Whatever happened to Jerusalem or the temple was of concern to all Jews, but new forms of prayer would have to develop to express the people's anguish.

> You have made us turn back from the foe
>
> ...
>
> You have made us like sheep for slaughter
>
> ...
>
> You have sold your people for a trifle
>
> ...
>
> You have made us the taunt of our neighbors
>
> ...
>
> You have made us a byword among the nations (vv. 10–14)

Interspersed among these second-person complaints are some first-person ones. The blame for defeat and suffering and humiliation lies squarely on the Lord.

Several other of our laments have a similar contrast motif. Psalm 80 has the most beautiful one. The psalm begins with a series of requests for the Lord's attention and intervention (vv. 1–3). This is followed by accusations that the Lord has not listened to the people and has allowed others to rejoice at their downfall. These complaints are still rather subdued. Then a long parable is told, the sacred history rehearsed under the image of a vine grower and vineyard:

> You brought a vine out of Egypt;
>> you drove out the nations and planted it.
>
> You cleared the ground for it;
>> it took deep root and filled the land (vv. 8–9).

Just as the vine is flourishing and expanding, the Lord decides to destroy the vineyard:

> Why then have you broken down its walls,
>> so that all who pass along the way pluck its fruit?
>
> The boar from the forest ravages it,
>> and all that move in the field feed on it. (vv. 12–13)

This accusation exposes the seeming irrationality of the Lord's behavior. It seems that he has taken his mind off his job, so to speak. The people cry out to catch God's attention:

> Turn again, O God of hosts!
>> Look down from heaven, and see;
>
> have regard for this vine,
>> the stock that your right hand planted. (vv. 14–15a)

## Communal Lamentation and the Prophet's Answer

This passage rehearsing sacred history under the image of a vineyard recalls the famous prophecy by Isaiah (chapter 5). In it, the Lord prepares the ground, and plants and cares for his vineyard, but it yields "wild grapes," perhaps sour grapes. The bad grapes are decoded as injustice and violence (Isa 5:7). We can see something of an argument going on between YHWH, represented by the prophet, and the people over the interpretation of the exile (or the two exiles).

Psalm 74 also has a contrast motif. This lament begins bluntly:

> O God, why do you cast us off forever?
>> Why does your anger smoke against the sheep of your pasture? (v. 1)

Verses 4–8 offer a detailed account of the destruction of the sanctuary. Then the people lament their sense of lostness:

> We do not see our emblems;
>> there is no longer any prophet,
>> and there is no one among us who knows how long. (v. 9)

Verses 10 and 11 are second- and third-person complaint. The question in v. 11 suggests the complaint has to do with God's power. This leads directly into a recollection of God's mastering of the power of chaos at the beginning of time.

> Yet God my King is from of old,
>> working salvation in the earth.
> You divided the sea by your might;
>> you broke the heads of the dragons in the waters.
> You crushed the heads of Leviathan . . . (vv. 12–14a)

The recitation of the demonstrations of power once performed by the Lord seems to provide the confidence to request his attention and intervention (vv. 18–23).

Psalm 44 has an adamant protest of innocence. After recalling the disgrace the people feel, the psalm insists that the people have fulfilled their half of the covenant:

> All this has come upon us,
>> yet we have not forgotten you,
>> or been false to your covenant.
> Our heart has not turned back,
>> nor have our steps departed from your way . . . (vv. 17–18)

## Redeeming Judgment

This is then reinforced by an oath of clearance.[3]

> If we had forgotten the name of our God,
> or spread out our hands to a strange god,
> would not God discover this?
> For he knows the secrets of the heart. (vv. 20–21)

The people then turn their protest against the Lord: not only have we not done anything to deserve this treatment, but we are suffering *because* we are loyal to you (v. 22). The requests and accusations appear outrageous: God is accused of sleeping, or of hiding his eyes from trouble. This psalm seeks to *provoke* the Lord to answer.

The other communal laments do not protest the people's innocence. Psalm 74 does remind the Lord that those who are suffering are those who confess his "name" (v. 18); they are the "oppressed" and "poor and needy" (v. 21). It also calls attention to the contempt Israel's enemies show YHWH (vv. 18b, 22b–23). These references are calculated to move YHWH to act in the people's behalf, for they are his charges, they worship in his temple, and the like. Psalm 79 uses a similar strategy; v. 1 mentions the nations defiling the temple. The plea to God is that wrath be poured out on nations "that do not know you," that "do not call on your name" (v. 6). The psalm does ask that God forget the sins of previous generations; this is not a serious confession of sin, since the speakers do not include themselves among the sinners.

Psalms 79 and 80 have promises of praise at the end. Actually, Psalm 80:18 promises to be loyal to the Lord rather than to praise him. Psalms 44 and 74 end with pleas for God to intervene; one might ask whether this lack of resolution signals a lack of hope.

### Psalm 89

Psalm 89 remains to be examined. This psalm differs markedly from the other four. This lament concerns the dethronement and suffering of the Davidic king, not the downfall of the nation as a whole. Of course, the king may represent the nation in the psalm—but he is not in any of the other psalms of communal lament. It is hard to imagine any other disaster to the Davidic kingship that fits the description in Psalm 89 besides the Babylonian exile.[4] In any case, once the

---

3. A person directs conditional curses at him- or herself for the misbehavior specified.
4. It is even hard to fit it into the fall of Zedekiah.

## Communal Lamentation and the Prophet's Answer

Davidic monarchy was brought to an end by the Babylonians, the psalm would certainly migrate to it (if it wasn't composed for it).

The psalm is actually three psalms that have been fused together to give extra power to the lament in vv. 38–51. Verses 1–4 introduce the first two psalms—the first of which praises the Creator, and the second of which presents an etiology of the Davidic monarchy. The psalm is a declaration of an individual, probably a worship leader; he declares his intention to praise.[5] It identifies the divine attributes of faithfulness and mercy as praiseworthy, and cites the covenant with David as evidence.

The first psalm calls the divine beings to join Israel in praise of YHWH because he is supreme over all of them, and he subdued the powers of chaos to create the earth (Ps 89:5–13). This God of overwhelming power and majesty is also known for what could be called moral virtues: righteousness, justice, mercy (*ḥesed*), and faithfulness. It is these attributes that guarantee his trustworthiness to his people (vv. 14–18). Exemplifying these virtues, YHWH promises David through a prophet that David and his offspring will rule forever over his people Israel. God will bestow great power on David, authorize him to mediate between himself and his people, and pass on his office to David's own offspring (vv. 19–37). Davidic rulers might fall under YHWH's judgment, but the dynasty will endure (vv. 29–37). This last promise is crucial, for it is the one that current events disconfirm.

The lament breaks out abruptly in vv. 38–39:

> But now you have spurned and rejected him;
>   you are full of wrath against your anointed.
> You have renounced the covenant with your servant;
>   you have defiled his crown in the dust.

There follows a description of what the king has suffered, with YHWH as the subject of practically every sentence. This is a serious accusation. What is happening contradicts the promises of YHWH, and calls into question either YHWH's superior power or his faithfulness and mercy. The barrage of accusations ends with an indicting question:

> How long, O Lord? Will you hide yourself for ever?
> How long will your wrath burn like fire? (v. 46)

This is followed by a generalization about human finitude, perhaps meant to warn God that the supplicant will die before the Lord gets around to reversing

---

5. An alternative to a call to praise; we find it, e.g., in Psalms 103, 104, 108.

## Redeeming Judgment

the situation. The lament concludes with an accusing question, followed by an indirect plea for intervention:

> Lord, where is your steadfast love,
> > which by your faithfulness you swore to David?
> > Remember, O Lord, how your servant is taunted . . . (vv. 49–50a)

These last verses make the humiliation of the king very palpable; YHWH himself should feel it vicariously. This is where the psalm leaves us—without any vow of praise or other hint of resolution. The lament, as readers know, reflects accurately later history.[6]

### The Theology of Communal Lament

What stands out most for modern readers about communal laments is that these laments place the blame for what has gone wrong squarely on YHWH's shoulders. None of them has a confession of sin, and one—Psalm 44—has a vehement protest of innocence.

God is to blame for what has gone wrong. Almost every psalm had some contrast motif, contrasting not what God has done to what Israel has (as the prophets did), but what God once did with what God is now doing. Psalm 80 reviews the sacred history, and then describes YHWH's current action as a contradiction to what he has done. Psalm 44 reviews the Lord's empowerment of his people's army in the past but his abandonment in the present. Psalm 89 makes a quasi-legal case for the Lord's obligation to save the Davidic king. If God is as powerful as the creation psalm affirms, the king's current suffering is a betrayal by God. Psalm 74 also recalls the Creator's demonstrations of power, which then rule out a lack of power as an excuse for God's failure to act.

Readers may well wonder how ancient Israelites could be so direct, even rude, in a petition to the sovereign judge they were trying to persuade. One would expect much greater deference, indeed no accusations. However, we have to realize that the Lord's election of Israel permitted the people to speak honestly, forthrightly, even angrily. The rhetorical strategy is the same that a husband or wife might use with the other: to lead with an accusation that puts the other on the defensive.[7] Moreover, our communal laments appeal to traditions of the past that the people take still to be in force. So the people are not upsetting "orthodoxy" but seeking to restore it when a breach has occurred.

---

6. Verse 52 is not a part of the psalm; it is a doxology for the third book of Psalms.

7. An alternative to a call to praise; we find it, e.g., in Psalms 103, 104, 108.

The people are pleading for the Lord to remain true to his character and the promises he has made.

This theological question can be pursued on another level. Biblical monotheism transformed lament in profound ways. Laments within ancient Near Eastern polytheism encouraged a servile stance in the presence of superior power. The gods were jealous of their power because that power was limited; the god had to compete with other gods, demons, and even humans to achieve what they desired. Power was a zero-sum game; each deity and each human had to guard privileges and seek to enhance potency. The supplicant had the freedom of bargaining with gods to find the most effective divine helper, but ultimately the success of one's prayer depended upon finding the right source of aid and submitting to it.

In the case of YHWH, the supplicant had no freedom to access the "right savior," because there was only one. Freedom was introduced into the transaction of prayer itself.[8] The God worshipped by Israel did not have to guard his power, because it was not limited. He allowed his worshippers to negotiate with him because his power over them depended upon their willingness to belong to him. It was a world of persuasion, including charges and countercharges.

## The Inconclusive Disputation

A perusal of biblical theologies will reveal a strange silence among biblical theologians on lament—individual and communal. Communal lament gets even less recognition than individual lament—if any distinction is made. One of the few biblical theologies that takes lament seriously is Walter Brueggemann's.[9] He has given a liberation thrust to the accusation against God: in the lament, we are allowed to confront power critically, to protest against injustice, to cry out when we are in pain.[10]

In his *Theology of the Old Testament*, Brueggemann categorizes laments—actually called complaints—as "counter-testimony," indeed as countertestimony of the most damning kind. Brueggemann has carefully constructed the category of countertestimony as the shadow side of Israel's "core testimony." It is subversive of system, maintaining incompleteness against all threat of clo-

---

8. See the essay that I wrote with Ken Diable: "Persuading the One and Only God to Intervene," 19–32.
9. Cp. Brueggemann, *Theology of the Old Testament*, 373–403.
10. Ibid.

## Redeeming Judgment

sure. It is a specifically Jewish form of thinking, where the particular and the incongruous are acknowledged.

Brueggemann places laments—both individual and communal—in the category of "negativity." They accuse YHWH of failure to live up to his covenant and promises. In other words, actual life diverges rather sharply from the "core testimony." Of course, the people's testimony confronts the prophetic interpretation of the catastrophic events. It is a matter of who is to blame. Neither side capitulates to the other, so the debate goes on.[11]

I would propose another model for incorporating communal laments into the theology of the Old Testament. Jeremiah 2:1–13 has planted the seed for my model. In v. 9, the Lord declares, "therefore I will contend with you . . . and with your children's children I will contend." The Lord's sentence of the people is not punishment—at least not in this passage—but a continuing debate or legal tangle. The word "contend" translates the Hebrew word *rîb*, a word that frequently refers to the argument phase of a trial.[12] The Lord issues his accusations through his spokesmen, the prophets, and the people respond with lament protesting what God is doing. The debate will go on until there is a convergence of the two. This is both a judgment and a promise: Israel cannot escape the dispute with YHWH, but the dispute will tend toward reconciliation and salvation. That, at least, is the secret hope.

We could, of course, compare what the people say to what the prophets accuse them of. Take the protest of innocence in Ps 44:17–22. Jeremiah contests similar protests (Jer 2:23–24). Perhaps the people themselves may suddenly wake up, so to speak, to what they are doing (Jer 2:25). Of course, they may have counterevidence to offer to the Lord. Obviously, this sort of discrepancy has to be reconciled.

If the communal laments are to be interpreted as responses to the experience of judgment, it would seem that the issue was settled. However, the people are not yet persuaded that God is in the right. The preservation of these psalms invites a continuation of the debate—even to the present day. What is right about the communal laments is that they insist on being heard by God, insist on life, are willing to struggle for a saving hope, will not give up. These psalms do not evoke a sense of resignation, defeat, and shame. The people must keep talking to avoid being silenced. There can be no reconciliation and redemption until there is an uncoerced convergence between God's view and the people's view.

---

11. Brueggemann, "The Costly Loss of Lament," 98–111.
12. See Isa 3:13 57:16; Ps 103:9; Amos 7:4; Job 10:2; Isa 27:8, etc.

## The Book of Lamentations

This book is attributed to Jeremiah in later tradition, but the association has no scholarly foundation. The book does come from the era, viz., from 586 BCE or shortly afterward. It has the sound of someone who has suffered through the fall of the city of Jerusalem and is living in its ruins.

The five chapters of the book are five poems of lamentation. There is no narrative thread, the poems are not in a necessary sequence, and there is variation in their genre. The first four chapters are predominately dirge over the dead "daughter of Zion," Jerusalem represented in the figure of a young woman. The last chapter is communal lament. We shall begin our exploration of the book with the last chapter, because it is easiest to compare it to the communal laments of the Psalter.

### Lamentations 5

One can identify the chapter as a communal lament by the first-person plural pronoun used throughout. There is evidence that the countryside is included within the plural, first-person pronoun (see v. 11). The structure of the lament is distinctive—even distorted. The initial request calls upon the Lord to take note of the condition of the people. This condition is described thoroughly, if anecdotally, in vv. 2–18. If one were seeking to classify the elements of lament found here, most of these verses would be first-person complaint. The enemy is only mentioned here and there, e.g., "our inheritance has been turned over to strangers / our homes to aliens" (v. 2), "slaves rule over us" (v. 8). The people are destitute, their customary forms of life have ceased, and they suffer from depression.

Scattered through the description of their suffering are confessions of sin, viz., "Our ancestors sinned; they are no more, and we bear their iniquities" (v. 7). Although the speakers admit that their condition is due to divine judgment for sin, they really deny personal responsibility for incurring God's wrath. The entire chapter could even be taken as an indictment of God for punishing the wrong generation. However, they do own up to their own contribution to their fate in v. 16b: "woe to us, for we have sinned!"

The lament ends with a description of the temple mount, which has been taken over by jackals. The people then turn their minds to the one who was enthroned in the temple. He is still enthroned, though in a transcendent realm:

*Redeeming Judgment*

> But you, O LORD, reign forever;
>> your throne endures to all generations. (v. 19)

Now comes the only second-person complaint:

> Why have you forgotten us completely?
>> Why have you forsaken us these many days? (v. 20)

It is as though the Lord's invulnerable throne makes him indifferent to what happens to his people. The people feel abandoned and request a renewal of relationship:

> Restore us to yourself, O LORD, that we may be restored!
>> Renew our days as of old! (v. 21)

This would make a fit conclusion to a typical communal lament, perhaps followed by a vow of praise. However, instead of praise they express the fear that the Lord has completely discarded them:

> unless you have utterly rejected us
>> and are angry with us beyond measure. (v. 22)

This is a people that has lost its confidence and is losing its desire to struggle with the Lord for a future.

## Lamentations 1

The dirge form predominates in chapters 1–4. Dirge is lamentation for the dead. Two dirges attributed to David exemplify the form, viz., 2 Sam 1:19–26; 3:33–34. They celebrate the life and death of worthy public figures—Saul, Jonathan, and Abner. There is little or no address of God in the dirge, neither as complaint nor as request. Since ancient Israel had no hope in immortality, there was nothing to pray for at the death of a person.

Using the dirge form for the downfall of a city or kingdom is metaphorical.[13] The city or kingdom is represented by a human figure. In the book of Lamentations, Jerusalem is represented as a young woman, called the "daughter of Zion." One can still recognize the elements of lament behind the dirge. The depiction of the destruction and shame of the "daughter of Zion" reflects first-person complaint. The first poem starts out with it:

---

13. There are a number of ancient Near Eastern precedents for this metaphorical extension of the dirge, viz., Ur, Sumer, and Nippur.

> How lonely sits the city
>> that was full of people!
> How like a widow has she become,
>> she that was great among the nations!
> She that was a princess among the cities
>> has become a vassal.
> She weeps bitterly in the night,
>> with tears on her cheeks;
> among all her lovers
>> she has none to comfort her;
> all her friends have dealt treacherously with her,
>> they have become her enemies. (Lam 1:1–2)

This sort of description recurs through the chapter—in vv. 3, 4, 5, 6, 7, 10, 11a, 12a, 16, 17, 19, and 21. I have left out the verses that ascribe the action of judgment to YHWH, and those that confess the people's sin. In chapter 1, depictions of YHWH's hostile actions toward his people are attached to acknowledgements of sin:

> Because the Lord has made her suffer
>> for the multitude of her transgressions;
> her children have gone away,
>> captives before the foe. (v. 5b–c)

In several verses, the confession of sin precedes the mention of the act of the Lord:

> My transgressions were [bound] into a yoke;
>> by his hand they were fastened together;
> they were weight on my neck,
>> sapping my strength;
> the Lord handed me over
>> to those whom I cannot withstand. (v. 14)

Jerusalem is said to be punished in vv. 8 and 9, but this punishment is not ascribed explicitly to God:

> Her uncleanness was in her skirts;
>> she took no thought of her future;
> her downfall was appalling,
>> with none to comfort her. (v. 9b–c)

*Redeeming Judgment*

Verse 18 is a doxology of judgment:

> The LORD is in the right,
>     for I have rebelled against his word.

Occasionally, YHWH is addressed; in vv. 9c, 11c, and 20 he is called to take cognizance of the suffering of the people, and the last verse of the chapter (v. 22) pleads for reprisals against the people's enemies.

## Lamentations 2

Chapter 2 is very striking for how many verses are devoted to YHWH's assault on the people. Though the passage is in the third person, it exhibits much of the vigor of the second-person complaint of the communal lament.

> How the Lord in his anger
>     has humiliated daughter Zion . . .
> The Lord has destroyed without mercy
>     all the dwellings of Jacob . . .
> He has cut down in fierce anger
>     all the might of Israel . . .
> He has bent his bow like an enemy,
>     with his right hand set like a foe . . .
> The Lord has become like an enemy,
>     he has destroyed Israel . . .
> He has broken down his booth like a garden . . .
> The Lord has scorned his altar,
>     disowned his sanctuary . . .
> The LORD determined to lay in ruins
>     the wall of daughter Zion. (vv. 1–8)

It is noteworthy that this section has no confessions of sin. Thus, it breathes the spirit of the communal laments of the Psalter. Following this section we have eight verses describing the people's suffering as a result of YHWH's intervention. Chapter 2 concludes with a call to the people to plead with YHWH, and then offers a prayer describing how severe their suffering is (vv. 19–22).

There are two verses within the chapter that represent the prophetic perspective on the event, viz.,

> Your prophets have seen for you
>     false and deceptive visions;

> they have not exposed your iniquity
> > to restore your fortunes,
> but have seen for you oracles
> > false and misleading. (v. 14)

A number of oracles in Jeremiah and Ezekiel are directed to false prophets; this verse represents their accusations perfectly. Verse 17 assures the people that YHWH's intervention to destroy was planned:

> The Lord has done what he purposed,
> > has carried out his threat;
> as he ordained long ago,
> > he has demolished without pity;
> he has made the enemy rejoice over you,
> > and exalted the might of your foes.

This doesn't sound like judgment so much as a predestined act in conformity with some hidden purpose. That it was judgment is known from elsewhere.

## Lamentations 3

Chapter 3 is noteworthy for its mixture of forms. The first twenty verses are an individual lament by a figure who speaks as a personification of the city. The accusations against God predominate—with a smattering of first-person complaints and virtually nothing about enemies. As in chapter 2, so in chapter 3 the second-person complaints do *not* mention the speaker's sin. The mood changes in v. 21, and the new mood continues through v. 39. This is a confession of trust, a meditation on how suffering can purify and strengthen character. Based on vv. 32–39, it seems that the acceptance of one's judgment is a step toward rehabilitation.

In the next section of chapter 3 (vv. 40–47), the poem takes the form of a communal lament. Actually, the section begins as a declaration of intent to repent (vv. 40–41), followed by a short confession of sin (v. 42). Then it veers off into second- and first-person complaint. Evidently, the anger and despair of the present overwhelm the intention to repent.

Beginning with v. 48, and continuing to the end of the chapter, is an individual lament. Again it hides a surprise: after two strophes of first-person complaint, it becomes a thanksgiving, though the deliverance is more a recognition of YHWH's control of events, empowering one to survive.

*Redeeming Judgment*

*Lamentations 4*

Chapter 4 divides into two sections: vv. 1–16 is a dirge over the suffering of the city, with poignant portraits of the children. A couple of these verses accuse YHWH of violence against his people (vv. 11, 16). The second section, a communal lament that concludes the chapter (vv. 17–22) dwells on the suffering of the nation. This lament concludes with a warning to Edom to prepare to suffer, for its turn is coming (vv. 21–22).

## The Distinctive Voice of Lamentations

Readers' first impression of the book of Lamentations is that the people who speak in it are still in shock. They are a people who have suffered devastating physical blows, and the survivors—those not killed or deported—suffer deprivation and the disintegration of their worldview. There are numerous, recurring depictions of their suffering. This is how chapter 1 begins, and it pervades chapter 5. Nor are we allowed to forget it as we read through chapters 2–4. Quite appropriately, there are frequent requests to YHWH simply to take a look. It is as though the Lord has not seen what has happened, or that he has averted his eyes because it is too painful. The aim of the book, I would suggest, is to move YHWH to pity.

Chapter 1 has altered the typical accusations of divine antagonism. Every mention of YHWH's hostile action toward his people is accompanied by a confession of sin. Verse 8 announces the reason for the defeat and exile: "Jerusalem sinned grievously; / so she became a mockery." Whatever punitive action YHWH performed, it was as a righteous judge punishing a wayward nation. The many divine passives in the chapter suggest that YHWH's role is even bigger than explicitly said. Chapter 1 stands in some tension with chapters 2–4; the implied accusations in chapters 2–3 must be qualified now, but the people's smoldering anger has not been extinguished.

Chapter 2 does ascribe many destructive acts to God, but in the third person. In other words, it is as much description of the people's condition as it is a complaint. A few verses allude to the guilt of various parties, but the nation itself is not held responsible. Chapter 3 does not have much self-blame either; in fact, it has the most unencumbered accusations against God in the book. That chapter also strikes out in a novel direction in searching for purgative and strengthening effects of suffering. Chapter 4 is designed to arouse God's pity, preparing the way for the communal lament in chapter 5.

Lamentations is struggling for a voice. The primary persuasive strategy is to appeal to YHWH's pity. In the first chapter the speakers also take blame for what has befallen the city and nation. Otherwise, only a verse here and there expresses contrition. We have not yet adopted the voice of penitential piety.[14] There are accusations against God, but the speakers are too uncertain of YHWH's favor to speak out as in the communal laments of the Psalter.

## The Prophets' Answer: Hosea and Jeremiah

The title of this section is predicated on the thesis that the prophetic message of salvation is formulated to answer the people's lament. There is a scholarly theory that communal laments were "answered" by prophets.[15] Second Chronicles 20:15–17 is taken as an example of what typically happened. The king delivers the communal lament in an assembly at the conclusion of a fast, and then Jahaziel ben Zechariah, a Levite, is inspired to provide a divine oracle of salvation: "Do not fear or be dismayed at this great multitude; for the battle is not yours but God's" (2 Chr 20:15). Whether or not this kind of transaction was a regular occurrence in Judah, this account displays a ritual embodiment of a paradigm of lament and answer. The prophecies of salvation do in fact answer the people's lament, whether the answer occurs in a ritual or not.[16]

The prophet is turning the experience of judgment into an occasion for God to save, and making judgment itself into a stage or step in God's redemption of his sinful people.[17] The words of judgment are preserved and inculcated so that the people will recognize who their ancestors and they themselves are, and will submit to the divine reformation. If the words of judgment have had their proper effect, the words of redemption and salvation will draw the people into a new, hopeful future.

The prophecies of salvation in Hosea and Jeremiah will be examined in this chapter. In both books, the message of salvation is to the people of God, not to Gentiles. Both sets of prophecies are answers to the people's lament. For both prophets, the pastoral concern of comforting the afflicted seems to be primary. The divine promises they communicate are not theological abstractions but words that have the power to heal, sustain, and redeem the people.

---

14. See chapters 17 and 18.
15. Westermann, "Sprache und Struktur der Prophetie Deuterojesajas," 92–170.
16. Cp. Hezekiah and Isaiah in Isaiah 36–37.
17. I am using the word *redemption* for the transformation of faithless and unjust people into faithful and just. *Salvation* is used for the rescue of humans from suffering and death.

The prophetic responses to the people's suffering and despair are calculated to arouse hope, to comfort in loss, to elicit repentance, to satisfy longing.

Hosea and Jeremiah do provide theological concepts for the thoughtful, though their messages are not driven by systematic impulses. We would expect some teaching on how the plan of God is moving forward, how events are transforming the people that God judges sinful into people pleasing to God. Eschatology vies with realism in their messages. We find hopes that exceed the capacity of history—utopian hopes, if you will. These are usually mixed with more practical, everyday prospects. Full-scale eschatology enters in visions with a mythological flavor, and progressively purges the penultimate from the ultimate.

## Hosea

We can begin simply by locating the prophecies of salvation in each book. Hosea 2 is a series of interconnected oracles. These announce judgment on Hosea's wife, Gomer, and their three children, who are representative figures for Israel. Judgment is pronounced in vv. 2–13. Beginning with v. 14, the message changes to salvation, and this message continues to the end of the chapter. Hosea 3 is a kind of echo of the salvation oracles in chapter 2. Hosea, at YHWH's command, buys Gomer back and remarries her under a reform discipline. We have no full-scale prophecy of salvation again until chapter 11. Chapter 11 begins as a prophecy of judgment, based upon a contrast motif under the image of a parent (YHWH) and a child (Israel or Ephraim). The child is so rebellious that he must be harshly punished. Suddenly YHWH is overwhelmed by compassion, and renounces annihilation, if not judgment. The chapter ends with a promise of the return from the diaspora. Finally chapter 14 urges the people to repent and provides a confession of sin, followed by an oracle of salvation.

Beside these full-scale salvation messages there are scattered verses promising Judah a happier fate: 1:7; 6:11a; cp. 3:5. Whether 1:10–11 belong here is uncertain. The mention of Judah in contradistinction to Israel probably belongs to the editing of the book for a southern audience.

### Hosea 14

All but the last verse of Hosea 14 makes up one unit, a liturgy created by the prophet, or those who preserved the book, to lead readers in the right direction. It makes a perfect conclusion to the book. Having read and appropriated the judgments in the first thirteen chapters, readers are ready to follow the prophet's lead in the last chapter.

Hosea 14:1–2a is a call to repent spoken by the prophet in his own voice:

> Return, O Israel, to the LORD your God,
>> for you have stumbled because of your iniquity.
> Take words with you
>> and return to the LORD.

The prophet then provides the people with a confession of sin in vv. 2b–3. It begins with a plea for divine acceptance:

> Say to him,
>> "Take away all guilt;
> accept that which is good
>> and we will offer
>> the fruit of our lips. (v. 2b)

The actual sins of the people are specified in a statement of intent to cease doing them:

> Assyria shall not save us;
>> we will not ride upon horses;
> we will say no more, "Our God,"
>> to the work of our hands. (v. 3)

I take the first couplet as a renunciation of political alliances and war-making; the sin involved in these is trying to save ourselves. The second couplet renounces idolatry. In earlier chapters, Israel's primary sin is apostasy—loyalty to the lovers in chapter 2—but here we learn that Hosea recognizes that the Baals are the products of human projection.[18] The sin in idolatry would be seeking to save ourselves.[19] Perhaps all of Hosea's indictment of Israel can be subsumed under idolatry/apostasy and self-reliant foreign policy.[20]

The confession in chapter 14 concludes with a self-identification as an "orphan," because the Lord has a particular affection for the vulnerable. The Lord's response is an oracle of salvation. It begins with a promise to instill faithfulness in the people and to show his love for them in a direct way rather

---

18. Actually, idolatry is the subject as early as Hosea 4.
19. If the parallel to alliances and war making holds up.
20. Cp. 10:10, which uses the expression, "double iniquity"; cp. Gottwald, *All the Nations of the Earth*, 140–44.

## Redeeming Judgment

than indirectly through anger and punishment. The oracle then portrays this salvation as the power to grow and flourish:

> I shall be as the dew to Israel;
> > he shall blossom as the lily...
> His shoots shall spread out;
> > his beauty shall be like the olive tree,
> > and his fragrance like Lebanon. (vv. 5–6)

This language may be reminiscent of language describing Baal, but now YHWH appropriates it to make lovely poetry.

Verse 8 suddenly changes focus, as though an afterthought: it starts out sounding like an indicting question: "O Ephraim, what have I to do with idols?" But this question is not for the purpose of indicting; rather, it's for persuading readers that YHWH is the caregiver.

The oracle of salvation is an answer to a prayer of the people. To be sure, the prayer has been composed by the prophet. This is a case of the prophet "creating" the people that YHWH can answer with a promise of salvation. If the people can recognize their sin, they can be reformed. The book of judgments should have brought readers to this state of mind. YHWH offers redemption as well as salvation. If the people know their sin, he can heal them. Salvation can grow out of healing.

### Hosea 5:8—6:6

This exchange between YHWH, the people, and the prophet confirms the suspicion that YHWH's promise of healing cannot be made until the people have undergone judgment. The passage begins with an impressionistic dramatization of the Syro-Ephraimite war (5:8–15). The people respond to the crisis by resolving to "return" to YHWH (6:1–3), but YHWH sees through their falsity (6:4–6). No judgment is spelled out, but the prophets will have to "slay them" with words until they learn that YHWH desires loyalty and "knowledge" of him.

### Hosea 11

This chapter is one prophecy of judgment expanded by a divine soliloquy and a promise of salvation. The prophecy of judgment (vv. 1–7) is an extended contrast motif, figuring God as parent and Israel as son.

> When Israel was a child, I loved him,
>> and out of Egypt I called my son.
> The more [I] called them,
>> the more they went from [me]; . . .
> Yet it was I who taught Ephraim to walk,
>> I took them in [my] arms;
>> but they did not know that I healed them. (vv. 1–2a, 3)

The story itself contains the accusation as well as a reference to the Lord's saving deeds. The son is rebellious to the point that he must be fought and deported.[21] This harsh punishment could be the end for the people of God, but to our surprise the Lord begins to reflect upon what he is about to do, and he rejects the worst outcome:

> How can I give you up, O Ephraim?
>> How can I hand you over, O Israel?
> How can I make you like Admah?
>> How can I treat you like Zeboiim?
> My heart recoils within me;
>> my compassion grows warm and tender. (v. 8)

The cities named Admah and Zeboiim were destroyed along with Sodom and Gomorrah (Genesis 19). Hosea 11:8 evokes the burning compassion that the Lord feels for his people. This sounds like the mirror image of a lament; this state of mind is what supplicants seek to arouse in God. It has prepared the way for God's decision:

> I will not execute my fierce anger;
>> I will not again destroy Ephraim;
> for I am God and no mortal,
>> the Holy One in your midst,
>> and I will not come in wrath. (v. 9)

Verse 9a renounces full-scale destruction of Ephraim. One might conclude that the Lord has changed his mind entirely, and will not judge Ephraim at all. The decision is justified by an appeal to divine freedom. The justification hints at YHWH's transcendence beyond finite categories—a transcendence that exceeds the grasp of the human mind.

---

21. Verse 5 drops the parent-child figuration.

## Redeeming Judgment

The prophecy ends (vv. 10–11) with a promise of ingathering for the diaspora. The promise tells us that the Lord does not entirely renounce judgment; the Lord's decision in Hosea 11 must have been to commute the sentence.

There are other hints in Hosea's prophecies of judgment that the Lord has a saving future in mind. In chapter 11 itself, the reference to "returning to the land of Egypt" has to be read typologically: When the people go into Assyrian exile, they will be recapitulating their period of slavery in Egypt. A promise of a new exodus is not made explicit, but the ingathering of the diaspora (vv. 10–11) echoes it. The same typological reference to Egypt is found in Hos 9:3, 6, and 7:16.

### Hosea 2

The pastoral motive has been quite evident in the passages discussed so far, but the chapter to which we are turning is more theoretical, though the mind that produced it was more poetic than logical. The change of the event of judgment into an event of salvation depends upon the capacity of one image—wilderness—to signify both destruction and beginning.

The best reading of this chapter is as one action: a series of judgments have been sequentialized to communicate judgment (vv. 2–13), then another series tells of a reversal and renewal. Judgment produces the situation (wilderness) that is then transformed into a place of reform, replenishment, and reconciliation.

The verses communicating judgment are complex poetry themselves. We begin with Hosea's family, which is breaking up because of the unfaithfulness of Hosea's wife, Gomer. This is a carryover from chapter 1. However, Gomer is progressively juxtaposed with and identified as Israel; her and Hosea's children represent the Israelites. The Lord is endeavoring to prove to Gomer/Israel that her produce and wealth, which she ascribes to and lavishes on the Baals, are really the Lord's gifts. The Canaanite deity Baal, who can become a plurality by the multiplication of sanctuaries, seems to be a personification of the forces of natural productivity and fecundity. YHWH wants to show that these "forces" are not sources. Judgment will consist of withholding the gifts, and bringing the harvest festivals and the like to an end; this will prove that it was YHWH who provided them in the first place. Israel will return to the wilderness:

> And I will lay waste her vines and her fig trees,
>   of which she said,

> "These are my hire,
>> which my lovers have given me." (v. 12, RSV)
>
> And I will punish her for the feast days of the Baals
>> when she burned incense to them
>> and decked herself with her ring and jewelry . . . (v. 13)

Now that the country is a wilderness, Gomer/Israel will recapitulate the wilderness sojourn during the exodus:

> Therefore, behold, I will allure her,
>> and bring her into the wilderness,
>> and speak tenderly to her.
> And there I will give her her vineyards,
>> and make the Valley of Achor a door of hope.
> And there she shall respond as in the days of her youth,
>> as at the time when she came out of the land of Egypt. (vv. 14–15, RSV)

In Hos 2:17–20, we have a series of "amendments," so to speak, to the covenant of the human community with animals; and other nations will also be peaceful. The section ends with reconciliation with YHWH, who adopts the language of marriage. Hosea etches the image of marriage on the healthy relationship of YHWH and Israel, just as he has done for the "unhealthy," i.e., adulterous. This indicates that he has a deeper purpose in applying this language than touching his people's sense of repulsion at adultery: the relationship between YHWH and Israel is more than a political one; it is a passionate connection, driven by *eros* and *philia*. The conclusion of the section suggests this deep personal connection: "And I will take you for my wife forever; I take you for my wife in righteousness and in justice, in steadfast love, and in mercy. I will take you for my wife in faithfulness; and you shall know the Lord" (vv. 19–20).

The prophecies end (2:21–23) with a change of names for Hosea's three children. The name Jezreel is reinterpreted, while Lo-Ruḥama (Not Pitied) and Lo-Ami (Not My People) have the *Lo* (the negation) dropped. This brings the prophecy full cycle.

The series of prophecies in Hosea 2 make the prophecies of Hosea virtually eschatological. The judgment of Israel is once for all, and results in a radically new era. The renewal of their marriage vow is "for ever." There will not be cycles of judgment and salvation. It exceeds the realistic possibilities of history,

*Redeeming Judgment*

where wars recur, nature revolts against humans, and marriages go through hard times. We might call Hosea's vision utopian.

It is also noteworthy that Hosea's vision is restricted to the people of Israel. He does not pronounce judgment on other nations, and does not offer them salvation. Their fate is beyond Hosea's horizon; he isn't responsible for them; they do not belong to the sacred history. The promise of peace to Israel does imply a new international order, but one must look to other prophets, particularly Isaiah, for divine promises concerning international peace and justice.

*Hosea 3*

Along with the series of prophecies in chapter 2 that juxtapose Hosea's family life to sacred history, we have the narrative of marriage, of the birth and naming of children, of an implied divorce, and of the restoration of the marriage. The simplest way to read chapter 3 is as the story of the restoration of the marriage between Hosea and Gomer, though the name of the woman is not given in the chapter. Remarriage seems to be the parallel we expect, given Hos 2:14–23.

So Hosea is told to "buy back" his wife—a rather mysterious way of putting it. Had Gomer been sold or sold herself into slavery? The language implies something along those lines. In any case, Hosea buys her back—with the price duly recorded! Gomer is put under restrictions. The point is then applied to Israel. Hos 3:5 looks beyond the horizon of Hosea to an emerging "messianism" (or at least the restoration of the Davidic monarchy).

# Jeremiah

This prophet, who appeared about 130 years after Hosea began to prophesy, seems to have been under the latter's influence. Again and again we hear echoes of Hosea in Jeremiah. That is one reason we are treating their messages of salvation in the same chapter. Hosea's saving message was probably an important precedent for Jeremiah; it was important that the message of salvation not be unfounded in tradition. The prophet known as Second Isaiah went so far as claiming that the coming of Cyrus had been "declared to Zion" in the distant past (41:26–27; 44:7–8; 45:21). The rather skeptical, hardheaded realist, Jeremiah, would have just as much reason to desire a precedent for his hope.

We shall discover that there were other striking convergences between Hosea and Jeremiah, but we should wait to point those out until after we have explored the texts.

The primary location of Jeremiah's prophecies of salvation is the "Little Book of Comfort" (Jeremiah 30–31). Some narratives have gravitated to this collection: letters to the exiles in Jeremiah 29, and Jeremiah's purchase of a cousin's field in Jeremiah 32.[22] Jeremiah 27–28 seems to be associated with chapter 29. That gives us a fairly independent unit in the book of Jeremiah. The whole of it is clearly separated from the other collections of poetic prophecies.

The prophecies in the Little Book of Comfort have some oddities. Many of the oracles are addressed to the northern kingdom, or figures representing the tribes within that kingdom; Zion seems to be mentioned frequently enough, but Judah is marginal. Perhaps Jeremiah, whose hometown was in Benjaminite tribal territory, regarded the exile of the southern kingdom as an equalizer. That is, now that both kingdoms had experienced full-scale judgment, they were in the same position; salvation would come to the people of both.

## Jeremiah 14

Before I engage the prophecies of the Little Book of Comfort, I want to recall an earlier occasion where the people approach YHWH in communal lament, and receive a negative answer from him. We find a complete exchange in Jeremiah 14. Jeremiah seems to be on both sides of this exchange: he composes the lament for the people and then receives YHWH's negative answer.

> Though our iniquities testify against us,
>   act, O Lord, for your name's sake;
> our apostasies indeed are many,
>   and we have sinned against you.
> O hope of Israel,
>   its Savior in time of trouble:
> Why should you be like a stranger in the land,
>   like a traveler turning aside for a night?
> Why should you be like a someone confused,
>   like a mighty warrior who cannot give help?

---

22. Chapter 33 is also devoted to prophecies of salvation, written in prose. We shall not concern ourselves with them, however.

*Redeeming Judgment*

> Yet you, O Lord, are in the midst of us,
>   and we are called by your name;
>  do not forsake us! (vv. 7–9)

The Lord's answer is straightforward and negative:

> Truly they have loved to wander,
>   they have not restrained their feet;
>  therefore the Lord does not accept them,
>   now he will remember their iniquity
>   and punish their sins. (v. 10)[23]

Then an exchange takes place between Jeremiah and YHWH in which YHWH tells Jeremiah not to intercede for Judah, and Jeremiah blames their condition on the complacency of the prophets. YHWH insists that he did not send the prophets. Then Jeremiah is told to mourn the people in a dirge, but the poem continues on into accusations against YHWH (v. 19, in the first person, spoken as Judah), followed by a confession of sin (v. 20), a request for the Lord's favor (v. 21), and a confession of trust (v. 22). The Lord then rejects their prayer again (15:1–3).

The tenor of this exchange is that the Lord will reject his people's prayer until judgment takes place. Even though the people, prompted by Jeremiah, have expressed remorse for their sin, YHWH is not convinced. Judgment seems to be a necessary step in the reformation of the people.

## Jeremiah 30–31

The Little Book of Comfort begins with a divine commission to write this series of prophecies. The book is for the future, or for the present to prepare the people for that future.

The first poem is not a promise but a description of the suffering of the people addressed in the book:

> We have heard a cry of panic,
>   of terror, and no peace.
>  Ask now, and see,
>   can a man bear a child?

---

23. The contradiction between the messenger formula and the third-person formulation of the message is unsettling but common in this book.

> Why then do I see every man
>> with his hands on his loins like a woman in labor?
>> Why has every face turned pale?
> Alas! that day is so great
>> there is none like it;
> it is a time of distress for Jacob
>> yet he shall be saved from it. (vv. 5–7)

The people are assured that the Lord will sustain them through the trial ahead and will revive them in the future:

> But as for you, have no fear, my servant Jacob, says the LORD,
>> and do not be dismayed, O Israel;
> for I am going to save you from far away,
>> and your offspring from the land of their captivity.
> Jacob shall return and have quiet ease,
>> and no one shall make him afraid. (v. 10)

From this point on we read at least a half dozen oracles, introduced with the messenger formula, "thus says the Lord." The first begins with YHWH articulating the people's lament:

> Your hurt is incurable,
>> your wound is grievous.
> There is no one to uphold your cause,
>> no medicine for your wound,
>> no healing for you. (vv. 12–13)

Not only is the people badly wounded; it has no friends to comfort and sustain it.

> All your lovers have forgotten you;
>> they care nothing for you;
> for I have dealt you the blow of an enemy,
>> the punishment of a merciless foe,
> because your guilt is great,
>> because your sins are flagrant. (v. 14, RSV)

The final couplet slips into an assertion of sin, a surrogate confession of sin. The next verse repeats the diagnosis, and YHWH accepts full responsibility for the wounded condition of the people:

## Redeeming Judgment

> Why do you cry out over your hurt?
>> Your pain is incurable.
> Because your guilt is great,
>> because your sins are so numerous,
>>> I have done all these things to you. (v. 15)

Despite the incurable nature of Israel's wounds, YHWH will in fact cure them:

> For I will restore health to you,
>> and your wounds I will heal, says the Lord,
> because they have called you an outcast:
>> "It is Zion; no one cares for her!" (v. 17)

The following oracle (vv. 18–22) deals more with the physical restoration of the nation. The infrastructure will be rebuilt, and the land will be repopulated. A ruler from the people will replace foreign rulers; he will be invited into an intimate relationship with YHWH. The oracle ends with what is known as the covenant formula: "You shall be my people, / and I will be your God" (v. 22).

Jeremiah 31 begins by recalling precedents in the past for salvation after judgment:

> The people who survived the sword
>> found grace in the wilderness;
> when Israel sought for rest,
>> the LORD appeared to [him] from far away.
> I have loved you with an everlasting love;
>> therefore I have continued my faithfulness to you. (vv. 2–3)

This assurance leads to the promise of restoration: "Again I will build you, and you shall be built, / O virgin Israel!" (v. 4a).

The next oracle begins with a call to praise:

> Sing aloud with gladness for Jacob,
>> and raise shouts for the chief of the nations;
> proclaim, give praise, and say,
>> "The LORD has saved his people,
>> the remnant of Israel." (v. 7, RSV)

The ingathering of the diaspora is depicted to explain the call to praise. It ends with a powerful declaration:

> For I have become a father to Israel,
>> and Ephraim is my firstborn. (v. 9c)

The following oracle (vv. 10–14) extends the theme of rejoicing and feasting.

Now we step back to the moment of lamentation again. This time we hear a woman weeping: Rachel, the mother of Joseph (Ephraim and Manasseh) and Benjamin (v. 15). The Lord offers her words of comfort:

> Keep your voice from weeping,
>> and your eyes from tears;
> for there is a reward for your work, says the LORD,
>> and they shall come back from the land of the enemy.
> There is hope for your future, says the LORD
> and your children shall come back to their own country. (vv. 16–17, RSV)

Our focus suddenly shifts to the moaning of Ephraim, who is in a profound state of compunction, confessing his sin and shame:

> Indeed I heard Ephraim pleading,
> "You disciplined me, and I took the discipline.
>> I was like a calf untrained.
> Bring me back, let me come back,
>> for you are the LORD my God.
> For after I had turned away I repented;
> ...
> I was ashamed, and I was dismayed
>> because I bore the disgrace of my youth." (vv. 18–19)

The Lord, moved by his son's remorse, is inspired by love to take him under his care:

> Is Ephraim my dear son?
>> Is he the child I delight in?
> As often as I speak against him,
>> I still remember him.
> Therefore I am deeply moved for him;
>> I will surely have mercy on him, says the LORD. (v. 20)

Evidently Jeremiah regards this period following the fall of Jerusalem and Judah as a *kairos* when the people will recognize their guilt and helplessness, moving YHWH to intervene to save. Again we see how judgment plays an

283

essential role in God's redemptive action. Judah and Jerusalem are in bondage to their sin as long as they cling to the old regime. It must come to an end. Monarchy as the people had known it is past; it had after all been a moral and spiritual encumbrance. In exile the southern kingdom was united, as it were, with the northern kingdom. Hence the promises of chapters 30–31 are addressed to both of them.

## New Covenant

Toward the end of chapter 31 we find what is undoubtedly the most famous oracle in these two chapters: "The days are surely coming, says the Lord, when I will make a new covenant with the house of Israel and the house of Judah" (31:31). There is nothing explicit in this passage about the exile and lament, but it fits well in such a context. The new covenant involves forgiveness of the people for their sinful past (v. 34). It will not require forgiveness in the future because the hearts of the people will be transformed so that they will perform the covenant without having to be told and coerced: "But this is the covenant which I will make with the house of Israel after those days, says the Lord: I will put my law within them, and I will write it on their hearts; and I will be their God, and they shall be my people. No longer shall they teach one another or say to each other, 'Know the Lord,' for they shall all know me, from the least of them to the greatest, says the Lord; for I will forgive their iniquity, and remember their sin no more" (vv. 33–34).

It has been the stubborn, impulsive, unruly human heart that has thrown salvation away; now the people will be converted, transformed. Yes, this sounds utopian. However, something amazing will come of it. Jeremiah might have had trouble recognizing it, but a new piety—a penitential, inward piety—will be born in this period to fulfill his ideal. That piety will be the subject of a later chapter.

## Jeremiah 29

This chapter is quite instructive because it shows how Jeremiah's prophecy of salvation plays in the last days of the Judean monarchy. He sends a letter to the exiles in Babylon with a promise of eventual return and restoration, and counsels the people to settle down for a long wait. The address, "to all the exiles whom I have sent into exile from Jerusalem to Babylon" (v. 1) is a subtle reminder that it is the Lord who sent them into exile; the Babylonians are only agents of the deity. The people are tempted to think that their exile is due to a failure of their God to protect their interests, but Jeremiah's wording disputes such reasoning. Moreover, the people are told to settle down: "Build houses and live in them; plant gardens and eat what their produce. Take wives and have sons and daughters; take wives for your sons, and give your daughters in marriage, that they may bear sons and daughters; multiply there, and do not decrease" (vv. 5-6). This is such reasonable advice that one almost wonders why it needs a prophet's authority. Now he takes another step: "But seek the welfare of the city where I have sent you into exile, and pray to YHWH on its behalf, for in its welfare you will find your welfare" (v. 7). Now we have a strategy for members of a religious community living in a nation ruled by others and devoted to different religions. One can live a faithful life in such a nation, devoting oneself to its good despite its alien quality.

Now Jeremiah tries to silence some prophets—any prophets—who would tell the people otherwise. The prophets he opposes are promising an overthrow of the Babylonians and quick return of exiles and temple treasures. Jeremiah offers a greater hope, but one requiring patience and toughness. The exiles are hoping for a victorious uprising of Jerusalem, so Jeremiah throws cold water on such expectations (vv. 16-19). Far from delivering the exiles, the pitiful forces in Jerusalem are bent on throwing away what little they still have.

Our story shows how the prophecy of salvation can become just as controversial as the prophecy of judgment. The future of a nation is at stake. Who the people believe and follow will determine its fate. Jeremiah's message not only comforts the exiles; it produces realism and patience. His opponents produce suicidal schemes and virulent nationalism. Unfortunately, the people in charge in Jerusalem are swayed by false prophets, though King Zedekiah knows in his heart that Jeremiah is right. The king does not have the courage to be cautious and realistic, and so he causes the city to be destroyed and its institutions to fall with it. Jeremiah, however, seems to have been more successful among the exiles, who follow his counsel and save Judaism and cultivated the biblical tradition.

## Hosea and Jeremiah

In this section we can identify significant similarities between these prophets from the northern tradition.[24] Our interest is not in their shared images, expressions, and doctrines, but in the theology of judgment that emerges in each.

---

24. Note the use of "Ephraim" in Jeremiah 30-31.

Both prophets respond to laments. Their prophecy of salvation is meant to respond to the people's complaints and petitions. The oracles make their prayers "answered prayers." This is most evident in Jeremiah's Little Book of Comfort; in it we can hear the people's wailing and moaning in the distance. Hosea's prayers are less direct and emotional, and in one he has "created" the people that could receive the divine answer of salvation. The most poignant lament in Hosea is the Lord's soliloquy (Hos 11:8–9).

Both prophets reject laments by the people in the period before judgment. In the prophet's judgment, the people must undergo punishment before reconciliation can take place. Only the experience of suffering, death, institutional breakdown, and the disintegration of their worldview can impress on them how serious their sinfulness and guilt is. Divine judgment is an essential ingredient in the redemptive action of God.

Both prophets have the Lord respond to the people's condition with deep emotion. The people's suffering and helplessness arouses God's passion and love. He is no longer acting in his role as overthrower of the mighty; now he is the one who raises up the lowly. In Hosea, the people come before God as orphans.

Neither prophet depicts the Lord as saving Israel because it is righteous, faithful, or even penitent. Nineveh does reverse the Lord's decree by their earnest repentance (see the book of Jonah), but never does the Lord congratulate Israel on their reform or their resolve to reform. However, both prophets do have the people admit their guilt and declare their intent to change. They approach the Lord in a state of compunction. This is a necessary first step in the people's rehabilitation under the Lord's tutelage.

Jeremiah employs the prophecy of salvation in his struggle against prophets who are instilling false, suicidal expectations in the people. He promises reconciliation and restoration in seventy years—a long enough time to require the generation being addressed to live under the straitened conditions. Though the prophecy of salvation is usually thought to be a comforting, appealing word, with our prophets it is controversial and demands a strong faith and patience in order to be appropriated.

Both prophets evidence a pastoral concern. The message of salvation is evoked by those in pain and despair who need comfort and hope. I think that this accounts for the fact that both prophets only address their promises to Israel (and Judah). Hosea is consistent in this restriction: his judgments fall only on Israel, the people of God. Jeremiah, however, has been "set over nations and kingdoms," both to "destroy and overthrow" and to "build and plant"

(1:10). He pronounces judgment on foreign nations, but only the people of God are promised salvation in his book. This was not a theoretical, theological decision; his oracles of salvation are occasioned by specific situations. In the Little Book of Comfort, he is in fact "comforting the afflicted."

The occasion for the prophecy of salvation is pastoral need, but we should not conclude that the message is invented on the spot to make people feel good. Skeptics probably regard divine promises as manufactured consolation, but the community that acknowledges the divine authority of the prophets should insist that they have theological foundations and the precedents of the past prophets in support of his message of judgment (Jer 28:6–9); the same could be said about his prophecies of salvation.

If these two prophets promise salvation to Israel, does this mean that divine election somehow guarantees Israel preferred treatment in the divine counsel, so to speak? In fact, the Jewish community debated that prospect for centuries. However, our prophets are not chauvinists. Hosea and Jeremiah certainly understand Israel and Judah to be vulnerable to divine judgment. Hosea may regard Israel to be the only people who have the sort of relationship with the Lord that would result in his judgment. In any case, without revelatory history, covenant, and law, divine judgment would mean something quite different from what it does for Israel. Jeremiah would certainly concur with that model. Israel is held to its own standard; it will be held accountable to that standard, and will be transformed by judgment until it does play the role divine election assigned it. For a message of salvation to Gentiles, we have to look to the book of Isaiah.

## Postscript: The Prophetic Books

Books like Amos, Hosea, Isaiah, Micah, Jeremiah, and Ezekiel are preserved on the assumption that reading and appropriating these words of judgment has a salutary effect on readers. As announcements of judgment, the prophetic words become superfluous once the judgment has worked its way through punishment. In other words, the exiles of Israel and Judah fulfill the function of the prophecies. The collection and preservation of these words assumes that a "remnant," at least, of the people will survive to read them and learn why they suffered as they did, and still do. Moreover, the prophets expected the survivors to learn the lesson of judgment and be transformed.[25] This expectation is

---

25. *Remnant theology* is often taken to mean that judgment will purge the worst offenders but spare the faithful. This idea is highly suspect; even Job finds it false: see 21:28–32.

disappointed in the reconstruction period, but there were significant changes in national life and piety.

The books of prophecies were designed to persuade the reading audience that Israel was guilty and deserving of divine punishment. The majority of the oracles in most of these books are judgment. However, every one of these books has promises of national restoration and reformation. Judgment is not the last word. We might say that judgment will purge the people, or apply shock therapy, make matters fluid again. Whatever its exact effect, it should deliver the people to YHWH to reform them and reconstruct the institutions of national life. In fact, the latter did not happen, but Israel was refounded on a new, non-national basis. The prophetic books, though, left the people with utopian political images that sustained them in diaspora.

# 13

# Restoring Judgment to Theology

OUR INVESTIGATION OF THE text of Scripture was designed to confirm the relevance of the doctrine of divine judgment to all aspects of Old and New Testament theology. On the one hand, the argument should be judged on its soundness as exegesis and exposition. On the other, it should persuade readers of the pervasiveness of divine judgment in the biblical story. Readers should be convinced that anyone who aspires to take the promises of redemption and salvation seriously must incorporate the judgment of God. Indeed, one should recognize that judgment provides depth and realism to the church's message. Anyone who presumes to come before God must have absorbed the attitude of humility and compunction.

What did our study show us about the reasons, the means, and the purposes for judgment? First, judgment requires that those subject to it are responsible and accountable. When it is divine judgment, humans must know the norms of behavior expected of them by their Creator. They should in principle be capable of recognizing the justice of their judgment.[1] Divine judgment cannot be capricious or impetuous, but deliberate, modulated, and purposeful.

The sentence of God's judgment must be mediated through natural forces or human actions, including the acts of those who have been sentenced. The biblical narrative depicts many judgments as the "intervention" of God in the course of events. The contemporary theologian is not obliged to adhere to the concept of direct supernatural intervention. All that is required is to accord certain events the status of divine punishment or interdiction.

---

1. Unfortunately, evildoers can become so hardened that they cannot in fact recognize their guilt.

*Redeeming Judgment*

As to the purpose of judgment, it is intended to enforce the will of God, to protect and deliver those who suffer unjustly, and to deter further aggression, or to rescue those who are destroying themselves, and to set humans on the path of redemption, i.e., to convert them away from sin to a life of faithful obedience. We can summarize the purpose of divine judgment as prevention, deterrence and/or retribution, and restoration and reform. We will explore this subject more in the review that follows.

We approached the concept of divine judgment as a *leitmotif* running through the biblical story. Each act in the biblical drama comes as a consequence of prior action. Each act incorporates a revision of the divine law-and-enforcement strategy. Despite the constant revision of God's strategy for dealing with sin, no past act or law is rendered false or anachronistic. Each remains relevant to subsequent events. Each action brings a resolution of some crisis or tension, but a new manifestation of sin arises in its wake. All historical judgments bring temporary resolution but are incomplete and flawed. They all point toward a final judgment, which resolves the contradictions and conflicts of history.

## What the Biblical Story Reveals about Divine Judgment

If we go back to the first chapters of Genesis, where we are presented with a representation of the human condition, we can grasp why this condition will persist as long as humans inhabit the earth. When humans make the transition from innocence to responsibility and accountability, they become subject to temptation and the attraction of sin. The transgression of the first couple is not a deliberate act of disobedience, but in satisfying their curiosity they fall into disobedience. From now on, the human race will succumb continually to such sins as envy, pride, greed, sloth, and lust. The sons of the first couple, for example, end up competing for the Lord's favor, and Cain kills his brother out of envy. Cain succumbs to the power of sin and cannot resist the urge to act.

By the time of Noah, the Lord has seen enough. He admits that "the wickedness of men was great in the earth, and that every imagination of the thoughts of their hearts was only evil continually" (Gen 6:5). The text actually says that the Lord regretted the creation of humans and was ready to put an end to this blotch on the face of creation. At the last moment, he changes his mind and calls Noah to build an ark, and the rest is history. Nevertheless, the Lord acknowledges that this new start will not put an end to the perverseness of the human heart. Indeed, he uses this observation as the rationale for a new policy: "I will never again curse the ground because of humankind, for the imagination of human heart is evil from their youth" (8:21). God promises never to destroy the world, but to deal with human sin through law (9:1–17).

## Election, Covenant, and Law

Following the dispersion of the human race to thwart a collective assault on heaven (Gen 11:1–9), the Lord calls Abraham out from the world of nations.[2] Abraham is consecrated to know and live according to the will of God and to intercede for others. Those who encroach on the people of the Lord are subject to judgment.

The people become a nation under Egyptian slavery; the pharaoh and his army are subjected to divine judgment when he does not assent to the Mosaic request for permission to leave the land. Once the Hebrews are delivered, they enter into covenant with YHWH and accept his will as law. The provisions of that law set a higher standard than common human law. This standard is conditioned by the first and second commandments.

No sooner have the people entered into covenant than they collectively break its law. The judgment for making a golden calf on Mount Sinai begins a series of judgments in the wilderness. In retrospect these judgments are regarded as disciplining; the people are being prepared to live faithfully in the promised land. In Moses's benedictory address, he pleads with the people to live according to the divine law, and warns them that failure to do so will lead to severe judgment.

## Life with Territory and under a King

Israel receives Canaan as a gift. The victories of its fighting forces are empowered from above. The Lord urges the conquerors to drive out or slaughter the previous inhabitants to protect the Israelites from corrupting influences. Note that Israel itself is subject to judgments for apostasy and idolatry in the period of conquest. These infractions are not serious enough to endanger the people's future; rather, they teach the people to recognize YHWH alone and to cling to him.

The Israelite monarchy is inaugurated to stand up to the aggression of the Philistines and their allies. David succeeds in suppressing the forces around Israel and constructs a petty empire. Beginning with the very first king, Saul,

---

2. The world of nations is governed by God by means of a balance of power.

*Redeeming Judgment*

the Lord's anointed is subject to God's judgment imposed by prophets. The punishment of kings for serious offenses maintain the nation in good standing before God. The judgment of individual kings does not, however, save the kingdoms of Israel and Judah from their day in court.

*Prophecy of National Judgment*

The eighth-century prophets of judgment conduct trials in their oracles. Since they are speaking for YHWH, the Judge, the trial is aimed not at persuading the judge of the guilt or innocence of the accused, but at persuading the accused of their guilt and inevitable punishment. The decision has already been made, and the only open question is whether the accused will acknowledge the truth of God's decision. Punishment is also somewhat open ended: the severity of punishment depended upon the response of Israel to her condemnation. Aggressive empires were bent on taking control of Israel and Judah; this put the kingdoms to the test.

These prophets are specific in their accusations against the kingdoms or their rulers. Amos stresses the oppression of the poor and powerless, and inordinate wealth and luxury of the upper classes. Hosea focuses on national idolatry and apostasy, and a foreign policy dependant on allies and armament. Micah and Isaiah have accusations along both lines. Isaiah is particularly critical of Judean royal policies.

The eighth-century prophets realized that serious repentance would not take place without judgment and punishment. Several of them faced the possibility of national annihilation, though all expressed hope against hope. Hosea witnesses the fall of the northern kingdom—a fall from which it would never rise. Isaiah attempts to guide Judah through its hour of judgment, but the people stubbornly resist contrition and repentance.

Seventy-five years after Isaiah, Jeremiah was called to revive the message of judgment. Only Judah remains as a political entity, and the Assyrian Empire has been replaced with the Babylonian. Jeremiah's rhetorical challenge is to persuade his contemporaries that the accusations of the eighth-century prophets still hold, and only repentance can save them. With the death of Josiah, the hope of repentance dies, replaced by a mood of unrelieved doom. He begins to place his hopes on the survival and revival of the first wave of exiles. Ezekiel reinforces Jeremiah's message of judgment until Jerusalem falls.

## A Prophetic Nevertheless

No prophetic book pronounces judgment without promises of salvation after judgment. Not all of these promises belong to the same prophet, but those who pass on the tradition believe that judgment would be balanced by salvation. Hosea, Isaiah, Jeremiah, and Ezekiel all adhere to that coupling themselves. Hosea looks forward to the repentance of the people after their judgment—or at least pleads for it in the concluding exhortation addressed to readers. Jeremiah's message of salvation is the answer of the God of the powerless and suffering to his people, who have been reduced to abject conditions.

## The Uniqueness of the Prophecy of Judgment

Although arguments for the uniqueness of the Old Testament are currently passé, I contend that there is nothing like the prophecy of judgment against the people of God in the ancient Near East. It is unique to Israelite Yahwism, for only the Yahwistic tradition could produce it. YHWH, who is the exclusive power in heaven and on earth, speaks unconditional judgment against his own people (before and during the prophesied events).

Israelite prophecy of judgment against the people betokens radical transcendence of the prophet; he (or she) transcends the parties and passions of the time, and the institutional interests and political machinations of the era. Prophecy looks at the people from a perspective that allows the evaluation of the national life "from above," so to speak. The prophet does not speak for any particular interest and so is able to measure what is happening against eternal values.

One might say that prophecy is a proof for the existence of God, though one who does not believe in the theology of the prophet would have to deny it. In other words, prophecy is revealed knowledge of God. The prophet knows that the truth of what is spoken requires YHWH's call authorizing the message; indeed, speaking of one's own authority about what God's judgment is, is false prophecy.

I am attracted to Abraham Heschel's proposal that the prophet is clued into God's "pathos," God's emotional response to the world. The prophet can experience this pathos by "sympathy" to the divine mood. The prophets' intimacy with God teaches them to experience events as though they shared in

*Redeeming Judgment*

God's experience of the events. We can even say that the prophets participate in the divine pathos.[3]

The prophets are also thinkers. They know from their calls that their people are under the wrath of YHWH. Now it is their task to discover what they have done to incur God's wrath, and how they can persuade the people that they are guilty and heading for disaster.

Thus, prophecy is rhetorically driven: the prophet had to persuade the human audience that it is hearing God and not the prophet's own heart or some party's interest. The prophet must persuade the people that they indeed are guilty as charged. The people must be persuaded without the benefit of the revelation that the prophet has experienced. The people have not been convinced until they repent. Unfortunately, their guilt will prevent them—at least according to Isaiah's call (Isa 6:9–10)—from acknowledging their guilt and repenting. However, the ideal audience will know the truth of the prophet's arguments.

We are going to discover in part 2 that the prophetic books are designed for an ideal audience living after the original event of prophecy. Now the truth the prophet had to say to contemporaries has to be reapplied to readers in whatever time and historical conditions they happen to exist in.

## The Application of the Biblical Teaching on Judgment

We have discovered that divine judgment is pervasive in the Old Testament. Every generation experiences some form of judgment—not necessarily judgment that they suffer, but at least judgment that impinges on their lives. No serious reader of the Bible can escape the recurring announcements or reports of judgment.

The issue for us is how these texts, indeed the whole ongoing story of judgment, can continue to be relevant to twenty-first-century Christians. Despite its prevalence in the Bible, there are high barriers to the employment of the idea of divine-judgment events in our lives. Most conservative Christians think that only the Last Judgment matters, though a few find it advantageous to trace catastrophes to the immorality of the body politic. Divine judgment has become a tool in the conservative polemic against "liberal" social norms.

The liberal wing of the church tends to dispense with judgment altogether. The very idea of divine wrath seems primitive and rather repulsive to them. Moreover, they use the rantings of the likes of preachers such as the late

---

3. Heschel, *The Prophets*, 2:307–23, 426–46, 472–74.

Jerry Falwell to discredit any idea of contemporary divine punishment. The result is, of course, that God is not an active agent in human events but only an inspiring idea.

## Conservative Objections

A first objection from conservative Christians to the notion of judgment is that the New Testament so diminishes the more and less of history that we can no longer speak of divine judgment within history. Once the kingdom of God has been inaugurated in the ministry of Jesus, the rise and fall of nations and cultures is irrelevant to believers. The only salvation worth our desire is the unconditional salvation of the kingdom. It would be materialistic or unspiritual to invest our energy and imagination in the ups and downs of historical existence.

This objection is rather otherworldly and out of step with modern sensibility. Nevertheless, it has the weight of classical Christian orthodoxy. Often those who espouse it have a modestly progressive view of history and revelation. That is to say, the human understanding of God matures as humans grow more sophisticated and spiritual. Christ is the climax of this history of revelation; now progress is limited to the interpretation of Christian revelation.

My objection to this progressive view of revelation is that it renders earlier revelation obsolete and overvalues the new. I contend that God doesn't speak or act for a limited time; revelation is true to the eternal, unchanging God. Although God has changed his strategy for dealing with sin, sin is a persistent factor in human history. When the Lord decides to save Noah from the flood, he does not count on Noah and his family improving morally and spiritually. "I will never again curse the ground because of humankind, for the inclination of the human heart is even from youth" (Gen 8:21). Every confrontation between God and human sin manifests the one Lord and can be used for our edification.

The judgments of God in the history of Israel and elsewhere continue to be relevant to the church not only in its understanding of the Last Judgment, but also its interpretation of the course of human events. Thus, there is every reason for faithful people to invest the crises and opportunities of their era with great seriousness. We are not involved in history secondhand.

I would agree that the kingdom of God transcends time and history in a way that judgment does not. The Final Judgment is analogous to the United States Supreme Court's review of earlier court decisions; they are of a piece.

*Redeeming Judgment*

Both the Supreme Court's ruling and the Last Judgment continue and perhaps correct earlier judgments. The same cannot be said of unconditional salvation. Though we can live proleptically in the kingdom, we live in a fallen era whereas sin, evil, and death will be things of the past when Christ hands over the redeemed creation to God (cp. 1 Cor 15:27–28).

Nevertheless, we need not take such a pessimistic view of history that we condemn it to endless, unrelieved judgment. Rather, history is a mixture of good and evil, joy and sorrow, creativity and oppression, life and death. Redemption may not be available in history, but we can enter onto the road toward the redemption that is on the horizon.

It should be noted that one strain of twentieth-century conservative theology is not as otherworldly in its eschatology. I am thinking of those apocalypticists who interpret events of the present and project events in the near future that are bringing history to its final judgment and salvation. Many of these eschatologies followed by these Christians involve the state of Israel, which plays a decisive role in their end-time drama. These Christians are enthusiastic supporters of the state of Israel, and their interpretation of events does not correspond to realistic analysis of what is happening in the Near East or around the world. This sort of theology of history is a dangerous confusion of the penultimate and the ultimate.

## Liberal Objections

Now let us consider what the liberals of the church have against divine judgment in human history. There are two aspects to the liberal rejection of divine judgment: (1) Though I have shown judgment to be a pervasive theme in the Old Testament, liberal Christians may nevertheless reject the continuing relevance of this teaching. They do not believe that everything the Bible says is true; it is up to believers to exercise discernment. (2) Ascribing judgment to God, particularly ascribing wrath to him, is unworthy of the God revealed in Jesus Christ. At most judgment is self-inflicted (i.e., when one knows what is good and true, but chooses otherwise and reaps bad consequences). Such self-inflicted judgment is not the will of God, not what he desires for the sinner.

### The Question of Scriptural Authority

Not too many generations ago the idea of dismissing such a pervasive doctrine as divine judgment would have been unheard of among the faithful. After all, the Bible authorized the Christian message, and the church was subject to it. However, rationalism progressively ate away from this heteronomy, in favor of an autonomy of the individual conscience. The churches that I am calling liberal are most seriously affected by the rationalist, Enlightenment spirit.

The tendency of the liberal churches, both in the pulpit and the pew, is to formulate beliefs on the basis of cultural consensus and personal attitudes, and only then to locate scriptural texts that support them. If certain texts contradict one's position, they must be neutralized. Of course, religious teachings are often derived from Scripture, but the pick-and-choose style of interpretation elevates the individual's judgment above the Scripture.

In the current intellectual climate in the liberal churches, then, scriptural authority is a vacuous slogan. The argument we have made will have little force if we cannot support its wisdom. I will endeavor to do so in the next sections, but I think the issue of authority needs to be addressed as well.

## Why Authority Is Necessary

Protestant churches were founded on very high doctrines of Scripture, so it is hard to dispense with scriptural authority altogether without undermining the legitimacy of the church. After all, authority is not only the exercise of force, but even more authorization. A church that invests final authority in individual or collective conscience has no authorization to proclaim redemption and salvation.

All essential components of the Christian kerygma have the force of *performative* utterances. That is, they are promises, commandments, judgments—speech acts whose truth depends on the speaker and the pronouncement itself.[4] When the Lord recruits Moses to lead the Hebrew people out of Egypt, Moses's commission is based upon an unconditional promise of God to act in the people's behalf and bring about the desired outcome. Later Moses mediates the commandments to the people at Sinai; the people are obligated to obey because they have sworn to obey this God.[5] When the prophets declare judgment, their word is not a prediction or a conditional warning, but a decree of the divine judgment.

The *deeds* of the Lord that make up the balance of the biblical story, such as the exodus from Egypt and the death and resurrection of Jesus, have permanent significance because they too bear performative force. Compare, for

---
4. This is the argument of Patrick, *Rhetoric of Revelation*.
5. Not because they approve of the content!

example, Paul's statement in Romans 4:24–25: "[Righteousness] will be reckoned to us who believe in him that raised from the dead Jesus our Lord, who was put to death for our trespasses and raised for our justification." Simply put, the acts of God have power for those who receive them by faith.

Obviously, the authority of the text is essential to the church's existence in as much as its teaching and ritual are authorized by God's speech-acts and deeds. They are the source of our knowledge of God. The words were formulated by humans, but they only bear the force needed for their truth by virtue of God's authorization. There is a place for reason and experience in our knowledge of God, but these are dependant on and subordinate to God's revelation.

## The Wisdom Revelation Affords

Liberal Christians want to be convinced of the truth of any religious teaching. Historically, this has meant an apologetic theology; revelation was only the means by which humans learned a truth that could be known by reason.[6] Unfortunately, this rationalistic assumption has impoverished those churches under its sway and has misrepresented the human situation.

The rationalist perspective denies the fallenness of human reason and the doctrine of original sin. It seems to me that the believing community cannot afford such an easy conscience, such a Pollyannaish conception of humanity. As Reinhold Niebuhr has stated, probably in jest, original sin is the one empirical doctrine, i.e., the one doctrine that can be proven by experience.

If one does recognize the sinfulness of the human heart and mind, revelation is necessary if we are to come to the truth. That is, God must break through our falsehood. We cannot know this breakthrough by fallen reason; rather, it must be apprehended by faith, which is inspired by the Spirit.

On the basis of faith, a wisdom can be founded. Anselm is known to have said, "faith seeking understanding" (*fides quaerens intellectum*). That is, we begin with faith, and we gain understanding of life and history, as well as of God and his kingdom, by thinking through the tradition that has been provided to instruct us, and the implications of these traditions for the mysteries that confront all humans. This is Christian wisdom.

Finally, even liberal Christians usually accept the legitimacy of law, law enforcement, judicial procedures, and punishment. They may argue for greater mercy than do conservatives, but they seldom reject the use of law

---

6. This formula goes back at least as far as Maimonides's *Guide to the Perplexed*.

and coercion to maintain the justice, peace, and integrity of society. Why then should God not be the ultimate ground of such practices, and the one who supplements human actions? That is what is involved in the doctrine of divine judgment.

## The Application of Divine Judgment to Contemporary Events

Now let me introduce a number of theologians who can provide the wisdom we seek for applying the doctrine to our times. The first is Dan Via, who argues that the events known as 9/11 be regarded as a warning for our nation's pride, injustice, and violence. Then we shall take up the thought of H. Richard and Reinhold Niebuhr about World War II. The unit will end with a discussion of Desmond Tutu's idea of "restorative justice," a practice meant to bring a degree of justice and reconciliation after civil war.

### *Dan Via's* Divine Justice, Divine Judgment

Via's argument is that the Al-Qaeda assault on the Twin Towers in New York City, known as 9/11, is divine judgment on the United States for injustice and imperialism. He draws primarily on the Old Testament prophets of national judgment for his norms. These prophets prophesy against Israel's neighbors and the imperial powers of the day as well as against Israel. Since America is not a "chosen" people, it would be judged according to norms recognized by all civilized peoples.

Via rejects the condemnations of America by the Reverend Jerry Falwell, who initially proposed that the attack was God's judgment on our society for condoning homosexuality and sexual immorality. Via dismisses Falwell's values as "disvalues."[7] He rather accuses the United States of serious injustice in its domestic life and imperialism on the international stage. He sets out his evidence for his accusations quite methodically.

The real issue is whether catastrophic events like the Al-Qaeda assault can be blamed on God. Numerous voices oppose the idea rather explicitly, and Falwell's initial support made it even less palatable to liberals. Via clears the air by disabusing moderns of a misconception. When one says that God judges a nation, one is not saying that God is the cause of the event. No; in this case, Al-Qaeda is the cause, the perpetrator, and its terrorism deserves the harshest condemnation. However, God could still be using this terrorist organization

---

7. Via, *Divine Justice, Divine Judgment*, 4.

to punish or warn America. In a similar way Isaiah understands the Assyrian Empire to be God's weapon of judgment: the empire is driven by its own will to power and wealth, and will be judged by God for its sin. The aggressive actions of the empire against Israel and Judah serve God's purpose of judging his people for their sin.

Via is himself uncomfortable speaking of divine intervention. He insists that we not make God an additional cause of action alongside the human agent. The agent acts on its own, with its own motives. God does not even provoke or "harden the heart" of the human actors. God does not intervene to compel them to do something they had not planned to do.[8]

Let me introduce an alternative model of divine action in human history. God's will is invariably in tension with human desires and purposes. Since the capacity to act is a gift of God, the exercise of power serves the purposes of God despite what humans intend. Al-Qaeda resents decadent and imperialistic Western nations, the United States in particular. Its enactment of its resentment was a dastardly deed, but the World Trade Center appears to have been an expression of arrogance, greed, and vanity—qualities that drove the Rockefeller who built it and the business culture he represented.[9] September 11 brought guilt on Al-Qaeda and judgment on the builders and agents of international commerce. We have, according to my proposed model, an action involving various independent agents, interacting with each other but also serving the judgmental purposes of God.[10]

Via rejects the idea that the United States is an elect nation,[11] and rightly so. However, nations recognize standards and values peculiar to them. We should be able to speak of their judgment for failure to live according to their standards. They have been "called" to exemplify these values among the nations. Abraham Lincoln named the American calling this way: "a nation conceived in Liberty, and dedicated to the proposition that all men are created

---

8. I disagree with Via on this point; provoking or hardening the heart of a human is compatible with "free will." I also think that we can speak of divine intervention, especially when the prophetic word interprets an event as God's intervention. When God and humans are interacting in the course of events, God may well shape the outcome—roughhew them how we will.

9. Via, *Divine Justice, Divine Judgment*, 89–92 (I cannot locate reference to Rockefeller).

10. Reinhold Niebuhr, *The Irony of American History*, vii–viii, spoke of seemingly fortuitous events that on closer inspection exhibited an ironic connection between purposes and consequences.

11. Via, *Divine Justice, Divine Judgment*, 24–26, 107–9.

equal."¹² He rephrases this later in the same speech: "that government of the people, by the people, and for the people."

Lincoln understood the Civil War as a judgment on the nation for living the contradiction of slavery: "If we shall suppose that American slavery is one of those offenses which, in the providence of God, must needs come, but which, having continued through His appointed time, He now wills to remove and that He gives to both North and South this terrible war as the woe due to those by whom the offense came, shall we discern therein any departure from those divine attributes which the believers in a Living God always ascribe to Him?"¹³ This subtle statement articulates the concept of divine judgment as well as any that one will find among great public orations.

Finally, Dan Via wants to classify 9/11 as a warning. One could just as well say that it was a significant event in a series of judgments around the world. These judgments certainly did not bring America down in the manner of the exiles of Israel and Judah. What these events did is test our nation. Perhaps George W. Bush's presidency was the nation's initial response to that testing; Barak Obama's presidency is another response, perhaps repairing the initial one.

## *The Advantage of Via's Application*

What Via has done so nicely is to recover a biblical teaching that is seemingly at odds with modern consciousness and shunned by the American middle class. He defends it from such detractors as Jean Bethke Elshtain.¹⁴ He clarifies the natural mistakes of one-dimensional thinkers, for whom Al-Qaeda are heroes or villains, and their act welcomed or revenged. Via has shown that events can have two meanings at once.

Via has shown the heuristic value of the judgment paradigm. One can evaluate his use of the concept as one could a judicial case. The reasons he gives for the judgment amount to accusations. The accusations are evils that are their own punishment and yet subject to retaliation. Punishment is testing as well as retribution; the outcome depends on the response of the accused. At each point, the interpreter must convince readers of the truth of his interpretation, just as the ancient prophets had to do.

---

12. Quoted in Wills, *Lincoln at Gettysburg*, 263.
13. Quoted in ibid., 186.
14. Via, *Divine Justice, Divine Judgment*, 64–66.

## Redeeming Judgment

### H. Richard Niebuhr

Outstanding theologians within the last century have argued that God's redeeming action is active in present history. Indeed, the very action of God experienced as divine judgment is also a redeeming force. H. Richard Niebuhr held that "God . . . is always in history, he is the structure of things . . . He is the rock against which we beat in vain, that which bruises and overwhelms us when we seek to import our own wishes, contrary to his upon him."[15] "But this very same structure in things which is our enemy is our redeemer; 'it means intensely and means good— . . . the good which we would desire if we were good and really wise.'"[16] It is unclear whether Niebuhr recognized a discontinuity between history and the kingdom of God. For him "the kingdom of God comes inevitably, though whether we shall see it or not, depends on our recognition of its presence and our acceptance of the only kind of life which will enable us to enter it, the life of repentance and forgiveness."[17]

When Niebuhr takes up the question of war, he does not regard it as judgment so much as "crucifixion." The participants are being crucified. "The believer should realize that China [in the Japanese war to conquer China] is being crucified (though the term is very inaccurate) by our sins and those of the whole world."[18] Though he equivocates on the use of the term *crucifixion*, Niebuhr repeats it a decade later of the innocent millions in World War II.[19] Evidently Niebuhr was willing to ascribe atoning value to innocent suffering in the midst of events of judgment.

If I understand Niebhur's theological reasoning, both judgment and redemption are aspects of one and the same divine action. So World War II could be a judgment on the political powers of Europe, America, and Asia and an atoning work of those innocent victims of power politics.[20]

---

15. As quoted in Fowler, *To See theKingdom*, 77.
16. Ibid., 78.
17. Ibid., 77.
18. Ibid., 75.
19. Ibid., 75 n. 55.
20. One has to wonder whether the populations of Germany, Italy, and Japan were simply innocent victims, for they supported their rulers and basked in the glory of the nation. Note the argument of Daniel Goldhagen, *Hitler's Willing Executioners*. The guilt of the populations of the Allies was less evident, but there is our pride and prejudice.

## Reinhold Niebuhr

H. Richard's brother, Reinhold, viewed the war as divine judgment.[21] It was not solely a judgment on Germany but on European and American civilization. His challenge was to justify supporting the Allied cause without aggravating American self-righteousness. We are guilty and suffering God's judgment, but it is necessary to distinguish between Hitler's evil empire and the capitalist West.

After the war, Reinhold Niebuhr addressed the First General Assembly of the World Council of Churches in Amsterdam in the summer of 1948. The title of the address was "The Christian Witness in the Social and National Order."[22] In it, he returns to this question of making distinctions: "It is true that the human situation is such that repentance is always required even as evil always flourishes. But it is wrong to preach this Gospel *sub specie aeternitatis* as if there were no history with its times and seasons, and with its particular occasions. Nor is our preaching of any avail if we only persuade men and nations to acknowledge the original sin which infects us all but not the particular sins of which we are guilty."[23]

His advice to the assembly was to proclaim a word to each party:

> Must we not warn victorious nations that they are wrong in regarding their victory as a proof of their virtue, lest they engulf the world in a new chain of evil by their vindictiveness, which is nothing else than the fury of their self-righteousness? And is our word to the defeated nations not of a different order, reminding them that their warfare is accomplished seeing that they have received at the Lord's hand double for all their sins, and that the punishment is really at the Lord's hand even though it is not nicely proportioned to the evil committed? Must we not warn powerful and secure nations and classes that they have an idolatrous idea of their own importance and that as surely as they say, "I sit as a queen and shall never know sorrow," so surely shall "in one moment her sorrow come?" And must we not remind those who

---

21. Reinhold Niebuhr did not, as far as I know, address the metaphysical question of how God acts to conduct the course of human events. He did assume that all countries were "under pressure," so the speak, for their particular manifestations of sin. H. Richard observed that for Reinhold, God is outside the historical process, in a position that H. Richard regarded as overly supernaturalistic. He also disagreed with Reinhold's eschatology, which he described thusly: "'the history of mankind is a perennial tragedy,' which can derive meaning only from a goal which lies beyond history" (quoted in Fowler, *To See the Kingdom*, 77). The position I have been developing in these pages is closer to Reinhold's.

22. Reinhold Niebuhr, *Christian Realism and Political Problems*, 105–17.

23. Ibid., 112.

> are weak and defrauded and despised that God will avenge the cruelties from which they suffer but will also not bear the cruel resentment which corrupts their hearts?[24]

One can see from this quotation how Niebuhr discerned the judgment of God in the outcome of World War II but endeavored to balance the judgment with mercy to the defeated and warnings to the victorious. In his theology, divine judgment is not the only action of God. As we have said throughout this book, judgment serves a redemptive purpose, and forgiveness and reconciliation should arise from the ashes. The end of World War I was vindictive toward the defeated parties and fed their resentment and desire to retaliate. After World War II, the Allies prosecuted the worst war criminals but otherwise sought to restore the defeated countries and revive the economies and establish democracies. This act was not pure magnanimity; it served the interests of the capitalist victors; it also was designed to quell the appeal of the Communist East. Whatever the motives, though, the divisions of Europe were healed so successfully that the European Union has emerged to be an equal to the great powers East and West. Reinhold Niebuhr would have welcomed the outcome as a grace beyond anyone's expectations.

However it is to be defined theologically, it is important for theology not to abandon the doctrine of divine judgment of nations. Without it we cannot understand the rugged realities of human history or take up our responsibilities with both confidence and humility. While history will never overcome the need for a last judgment, and no movement in history should be entrusted with the power to redeem, forgiveness and reconciliation belong together with judgment within as well as at the end of history. That is clearly the teaching of the Niebuhr brothers, as well as many other theologians in the history of the church.

## Judgment and Forgiveness

The archbishop from South Africa, Desmond Tutu, has advanced the argument for redemptive measures to temper and build upon events of judgment. His thought arose in a particular setting and is most relevant to that setting. When the apartheid regime in South African abdicated, allowing the black and colored populations to assume power, Nelson Mandela and the African National Congress (ANC) made a great effort to avoid retaliation against the whites. Their object was to create a multiracial society. The black African lead-

24. Ibid., 113.

ership sought to keep the whites, who were the primary ownership and commercial class, from emigrating to avoid confiscation or worse.

The civil war that preceded the transfer of power in South Africa had involved many heinous "crimes against humanity," both by the white regime and the black revolutionaries. Since the revolutionaries had come into power, they could have exonerated all freedom fighters and condemned all illegal and unjust acts of the apartheid regime. This would have completely alienated the white community, and would have prompted it to rebel against the new government or exit the country. The black and colored populations have a just cause in a retributive sense, but confiscation would have ruined the economic foundations of the country and would have failed to develop a truly multiracial society.

The alternative could have been to "let bygones be bygones," as they say. That is, a general amnesty might have been declared, allowing everyone to make a new beginning. This would have pleased the whites, but the families of victims, and surviving victims, would not have received the dignity of having their lives valued as equal to the lives of perpetrators. Retribution affirms the value of victims; judicial power is designed to bring closure to their suffering.

A compromise was devised by Mandela and the ANC: a tribunal that would hear cases of "crimes against humanity" not to prosecute the perpetrators but to know the truth of what happened. Hence the tribunal was known as the Truth Commission. The chair of the tribunal was archbishop Desmond Tutu, who was also its theological exponent. Perpetrators were offered amnesty if they confessed their deeds in public, in the presence of the families and friends of victims. By receiving amnesty, the perpetrators had less reason to remain silent or to lie about what they did. They received the protection of the state against prosecution or suit by telling their story.

The tribunal was also called the Reconciliation Commission. Ideally, those who confessed would express remorse for what they had done and renounce the racist ideology that justified it.[25] The victims or their loved ones could relive the events, experience a catharsis, and forgive the perpetrator. The state itself sided with those who suffered; Tutu often sang songs or prayed to facilitate reconciliation and closure.

There are objections to the Truth and Reconciliation Commission. The main issue is whether the exposure of crimes really renders justice to victims; retribution should be enforced against perpetrators. One can defend the commission as a compromise to elicit confessions, but one should not, it is said,

---

25. Revolutionary violence should also prompt feelings of guilt.

take that as a rendering of justice. This criticism rang especially true when perpetrators exhibited no remorse and continued to believe that apartheid was a good policy.

Tutu, however, defends the characterization of these "trials" as rendering justice. He calls it "restorative justice." The perpetrator is restored to fellowship with the community and with God. His book's title is, *No Future without Forgiveness*.[26] Forgiveness allows wrongdoers back into the community, hopefully to contribute to its good. The victims are vindicated in their righteousness and are made into vicarious sufferers for the health of the body politic.

Tutu's application of the doctrine of forgiveness builds on the African idea of *ubuntu*, which means something like "our common humanity," and presumes that individuals become human by belonging to a community. Tutu has modified the African concept by identifying it with the image of God, which grants each individual unconditional worth. Another word, *umuntu*, supplements *ubuntu*; it means the "intelligence and vitality that encompasses the living, the dead, and spirits."[27] When any part of the web of life is wounded, the whole is weakened.[28]

This is not the place to debate all the issues raised by the Truth and Reconciliation Commission and Tutu's "restorative justice." I have expounded Tutu's thinking as an example of how historical judgment can be resolved by confession and reconciliation. Of course, neither judgment nor reconciliation is final in history; they are approximations and earnests of the final judgment and redemption.

## Where We Go from Here

In part 1 we have followed the story of divine judgment through the Old Testament. We discovered that judgment was seldom an isolated act, never an action of God with no purpose besides retribution. It always served some larger good, though the one judged might not experience anything but the wrath of God. Sometimes judgment actually was meant to turn the convict's life around.

Once the one to be judged was warned of coming judgment, usually by a prophet, it became unavoidable. Some prophets hoped for reform and re-

---

26. See bibliography.
27. Tutu, *No Future without Forgiveness*, 161–62.
28. Ibid., 159–65.

newal, but only Jonah experienced his addressees' conversion and renewal. For the people of God, judgment was unavoidable.

Among our prophets there are hints of postjudgment redemption.[29] Indeed, the prophets of judgment were uncomfortable proclaiming salvation without a change in the people who had been judged. The prophets were not willing to inaugurate a future that would repeat the past. History cannot be a cycle of judgment-salvation-sin-judgment . . . Judgment must break the inclination to sin, or it should simply be the end of the affair.

During the exile—where we left our history of judgment—it would not yet be clear that the people of God would still be under the grip of sin when judgment had run its course. When the exile was over, the people would be restored but not truly redeemed. However, the restoration was not to the status quo ante; there was a new configuration, and the continued sin of the people of God would require another antidote; there would not be a repetition of the judgment of exile.

Out of the experience of restoration would arise a transcendent hope of redemption. Beyond the judgments of history there would have to be a final judgment that brought an end to the history of sin, and the establishment of the kingdom of God. That awaits the second part of this theological exposition of judgment.

The second part will begin with the book of Isaiah: it preserves the messages from the eighth century, of the prophet Isaiah of Jerusalem, along with anonymous contributions from prophets of the following three centuries. The best known of these is called Second Isaiah, writing from Babylon at the end of the exile, and his disciples, who returned to Jerusalem. The message of Isaiah of Jerusalem left room for the Babylonian prophet who would announce the end of the exile—an end to the judgment that Isaiah had announced in the eighth century. So the two prophetic messages were synthesized in the final form of the book. Not only synthesized, but supplemented and applied to the conditions of reconstruction.

Our exposition of judgment and redemption in the prophets of the eighth through sixth centuries BCE has concerned the nation. We have had very little to say about the individual. As we saw in the case of Jeremiah and Baruch, the individual's destiny was intertwined with the nation's; at best individuals could survive and tell the tale. At the end of the book of Isaiah, there is a hint of a

---

29. It should be recalled that we have reserved the word *redemption* for an irreversible transformation of a sinful nation (or individual) into a penitent and faithful and just society (or individual). To be redeemed, one must now belong exclusively to God.

personal destiny distinct from the nation's. A fissure runs through the community, with the truly penitent, pious "servants" of the Lord on the one side, and unrepentant priests and their allies on the other.

These servants exhibit a different piety, one that can be called penitential. Actually the mood of compunction is one of several strains. It is an inward piety that prizes the movements of the heart and despises mere external cultic actions. It is earnest in its obedience to God's commandments. Indeed, it corresponds to the qualities of the people of Jeremiah's new covenant. We might say that the servants of the Lord have internalized the prophetic message of judgment, making a consciousness of guilt their mark of identity.

This piety can also be found in a number of penitential psalms—above all, in Psalms 51 and 130. These psalms are not only for times when one feels guilty, but are meant to be a way of life. The piety displayed in these psalms is a piety open to the reform of the spirit of the Lord. The focus of prayer is the movement from sin to faithfulness and righteousness, a movement that is never completed in this life.

Unfortunately, this new piety clashed with the classical lament. It would silence any complaint against God because the supplicant was always in the wrong. God is always righteous, so the supplicant should blame him- or herself whenever things go wrong. This clash of pieties is dramatized in the book of Job.

The servants of the Lord have appropriated the title of the figure depicted in Isaiah 42; 49; 50; and 52:13—53:12. This mysterious figure is called by the Lord to bring justice and righteousness to the nations, beginning with Israel. His ministry leads to his rejection and even his murder. His suffering and death are said to be vicarious both by an anonymous group of humans and by the Lord. The figure seems to be the correlative of penitential piety: he bears the sins of those who admit their sin.

These new beliefs and lifestyles call for an ultimate, once-for-all quality. God should not have to designate a servant of the Lord, one who suffers vicariously, more than once. While repentance can be repeated, it becomes a meaningless ritual if each confession does not push one further on the journey toward true righteousness. Yet sin remains a power as long as one lives, and as long as history goes on.

If the promise of true redemption, of an irreversible change, is true, a final judgment and salvation must be on the horizon, so to speak, and temporal passage must be a journey on the way toward this horizon. We find a few affirmations of this horizon, and the action of God toward it, in the Psalms.

It is with this hope and expectation of a final judgment that we conclude our exposition of judgment in the Old Testament.

The New Testament is going to take over the final judgment on the horizon and bring it into the present, the "now" of proclamation. The Last Judgment and the kingdom of God are "near," even among us. Both John the Baptist and Jesus proclaim this invasion of the eschaton, though with different accents. The Gospels also proclaim Jesus as the one who fulfills the figure of the servant of the Lord, who carried out his call faithfully and suffered for the cause of God. His death and resurrection become the heart of the message of Jesus Christ. Penitential piety takes the form of faith in the redemptive power of Jesus Christ, who both convicts and justifies sinners. The individual has become the center of concern, national identities (along with gender and class identities) are to be transcended in the believing community.

In the second part of this book, we hope to show convincingly that judgment continues to be an essential part of the Bible's message. Moreover, it is not only retributive but also redemptive. Atonement does not supplant judgment but transforms it into a force for change, reform, conversion, faith, hope, and love.

# PART TWO

# 14

# Resuming the Argument

DIVINE JUDGMENT IN ANCIENT Israelite theology was not meant to be an end in itself. To be sure, the application of *lex talionis* could bring an end to a killer's life—likewise for an idolator, adulterer, or kidnaper. Nevertheless, the perpetrator could still be brought to remorse for the deed and accept death as the just outcome. The perpetrator would, thus, die in a state of reconciliation.

Even less was divine judgment the end for the people of God. Remnants of the community would survive judgment. The prophetic hope was that the remnant would take their judgment to heart and be restored to a vibrant, faithful life. In a word, judgment is to serve a redemptive purpose. The people had to be redeemed—transformed, converted—in order to receive salvation; otherwise, they would again abuse their privilege. Judgment was intended to inaugurate that transformation.

It was imperative that the action not become a cyclical pattern of judgment and salvation. Judgment would not be repeated, or at least not be repeated at the same level. The book of Isaiah starts with judgment of the nation but ends with judgment of a unredeemed portion of the nation. Accountability passes from the nation to individuals. Indeed, it is Isaiah that brings us to the threshold of the New Testament. Our argument for this contention is complex; the reader must attend to it closely.

## The Message of the Prophets to Their Contemporaries

Practically all the prophets who announce judgment on Israel and Judah regard it as penultimate. That is, the people of God will be restored after judgment.

When they are restored, the people will also be transformed in such a way that they will never have to undergo judgment again. Although judgment may not have been logically necessary for the nation's redemption, in fact its sinful ways required purgation or refinement and the instilling of a penitent heart.

We find oracles of salvation in the books of the prophets of judgment. Those of the book of Amos may be by anonymous prophets, but those by Hosea, Isaiah, Jeremiah, and Ezekiel are traceable to the prophet. We expounded those of Hosea and Jeremiah as answers to laments; they are exemplary of the prophets of judgment. The Lord would answer the cries of his people when they were suffering under judgment. All that was needed was repentance for the guilt that had brought them under judgment.

We can say, on the basis of the juxtaposition of judgment and salvation oracles, that judgment contributes to the redemption of the people of God. Judgment purges and transforms; it touches the conscience to instill recognition of guilt and to arouse sorrow and a humble awareness of a propensity to sin. Only with such a state of mind can Israel be saved with an unconditional salvation.

## The Prophetic Book and Its Readers

Up to this point, we have been characterizing the message of the prophets to their contemporaries. Now we have to take into account the message of the books of prophecies to its readers. What is the effect of the publication of prophecies as books for later audiences?

Isaiah and his fellow eighth-century prophets composed and delivered their prophecies to various audiences during their careers. Their oracles were preserved by disciples. When the consequences of judgment had overtaken the addressees, disciples collected the prophet's words. Over time a book of prophecies took shape, designed not for the original audience, but for the descendants of that audience who were suffering the effect of past judgment. Each prophecy, thus, gained a second meaning: besides what it meant in its original setting, it now had import for the reading audience as well. All subsequent readers had access to the prophet's message through the published collection. By then, additional oracles and sayings of anonymous origin had been included among the prophet's words, and the whole had been arranged to support the message which the preservers of the book had discovered in the oracles which received their authority from the prophet's commission.

## Resuming the Argument

In our previous chapters on prophecy (in part 1), we were attuned to the original message—the prophet's message to his contemporaries. Thus we expounded the four eighth-century and two seventh- and sixth-century prophets of judgment as messengers to their preexilic audience, and the oracles of salvation as words of consolation to the audiences that had experienced the judgment. I downplayed the distinctive message of each prophet and ignored the editing and presentation of the books. It is my belief that the original transactions between prophet and audience is a constituent moment in the history of the text. This is the moment when the words had performative force; i.e., when a judgment was pronounced on the society, the audience became guilty and faced the consequences of their deeds. This sort of transaction will not happen with later readers of said prophecy; one might say that the prophecy "spends" its judicial force in the utterance.

Once the prophecy is past and the word has taken shape in event, the prophecy becomes precedent and paradigm for later audiences. We have already seen how Jeremiah and Ezekiel revived the prophecy of the eighth century. The same sort of appropriation and adaptation took place between the prophet's words and other audiences. The later reading audience can use the authoritative texts as a measure of its own condition and as a precedent for what is in store for the community.

It takes a prophet to apply the words of an ancient prophecy to a contemporary audience. All preachers, however, are authorized to teach their congregations the actions of previous generations of the people of God. The people of God need to understand their propensity to break faith with God and take advantage of their neighbors. Even more, the people of God need to recognize that their election does not mean they are more righteous than those outside; indeed, the religious community is representative of the whole human race. We learn the human propensity to sin by witnessing the sinfulness of those who have been favored by God.

The prophetic books also explain why the people of God no longer have the title to the land of promise. Nor is there a Davidic king, a temple, priesthood, or many other institutions promised by God. These are missing because the people of God still live under the sign of judgment.

The prophetic books also make promises to their readers. The book of Isaiah, in particular, sets out the "divine plan" that links the past with our present and the eschatological future. A plan is enacted as a drama with one comprehensive action toward an ultimate resolution. We have already observed the unfolding drama that led from creation and fall to the exiles of Israel and

Judah. The same action is embodied in a distinctive configuration in Isaiah. The book is the unfolding of God's plan from the moment of prophetic judgment through the purgation of the people to their return from exile. The future holds the redemption of the people of God, and the conversion of the nations.

Despite this future, the people remain unredeemed at the end of the book of Isaiah; an eschatological transformation is still a matter of promise and hope. Even though humans remain the same sinners as they were declared to be before and after the flood, God continues to modify the conditions of life toward redemption. The political embodiment of the people of God is radically altered in the course of Isaiah, and they receive a new calling corresponding to this alteration.

## Toward the New Testament

The turning point in Israel's history—the one that leads toward the New Testament—occurs in the book of Isaiah. Isaiah spans the history of the people of God from the first proclamation of national judgment through its execution; the announcement of the end of judgment and the beginning of salvation; and the interpretation of the ambiguities left by the restoration of Jerusalem and Judah. By the end of this action, readers look forward to an eschatological judgment that holds out hope to those who are humble, contrite, and deeply reverent. The New Testament will announce the fulfillment of these promises in an inaugurated eschatology.

Half of part 2 explores the New Testament. It will be our contention that both John the Baptist and Jesus bring what is on the horizon of the Old Testament into their present. John's hellfire preaching locates the Last Judgment in the present or immediate future of the audience. Jesus's draws out the reverse side of John's eschatology, viz., that the kingdom of God is at hand. These motifs of realized or present eschatology are juxtaposed with futuristic judgment in the Gospels. The result of this dialectic is "inaugurated eschatology," that is, the final events of judgment and salvation begin with Jesus—the "first coming"—and will be completed at the parousia, or return of Christ.

In the present age the kingdom of God can only enter history incognito. That is, the kingdom is hidden. The norm for the kingdom is nonviolence and nonretaliation. While not strictly powerlessness, this means nonparticipation in the ambiguous power struggles of history. Here again a qualification is needed: those devoted to the kingdom must participate in the life of the world, but they renounce the use of coercive power to attain justice and peace.

Jesus's victory over the powers of this world is by his suffering and death. It is the resurrection that turns those defeats into victory. Jesus suffers for others. We can find a paradigm for vicarious suffering in the figure of the Servant of the Lord (Isaiah 40–55). Those for whom he suffered receive its saving benefit by recognizing that he suffers for them and with them.

The resolution of history will be thematized in different ways by different apostolic authors. Jesus's atonement for sin has become the most prominent. Paul works this out in the most universal and comprehensive exposition of the New Testament in the Epistle to the Romans. We will conclude the expository portion of our argument with an exegesis of Romans 1–11.

## In Search of a Strategy for Interpreting Isaiah

It is our intention in the following three chapters to follow the plan of God as it is represented in the book of Isaiah. The book presents serious obstacles for a "final form" reading. There are three prophetic books within the one book, First, Second, and Third Isaiah—Isaiah 1–39, 40–55, 56–66. The first thirty-nine chapters proclaim the judgments that Isaiah was commissioned to speak, and some promises that he and others contributed to the mix. Second Isaiah can be read as the work of one author, but not as the work of Isaiah of Jerusalem. Third Isaiah probably represents a collection of oracles composed by a number of anonymous prophets. If we were to take meaning to be what the original author meant to convey to his audience, the book could not be interpreted as one message. Our task is to justify reading it as one and devising a strategy for doing so.

Let's begin by describing the critical picture of the book of Isaiah. The first verse of the book is a fine place to start: "The vision of Isaiah son of Amoz, which he saw concerning Judah and Jerusalem in the days of Uzziah, Jotham, Ahaz, and Hezekiah, kings of Judah." Let's assume that this sentence describes the literary remains of Isaiah correctly, viz., that his message was derived from a vision, that he spoke about Judah and Jerusalem, and that he ministered during the reigns of the kings listed.

If the statement is taken literally—as it was for most of the interpretive history of the book—it calls for an attribution of every word in the sixty-six chapters of the book to Isaiah of Jerusalem. Passages that pronounce on the fate of nations and rulers who lived much later than Isaiah would have to have been communicated to the prophet supernaturally; at least that has been the explanation readers have adopted over the centuries.

*Redeeming Judgment*

How would historical critics question these authorship claims? First, we would raise questions about the understanding of prophecy as predicting occurrences in the distant future, far after the time that the prophet and audience existed. Any interpretation of a passage to this effect must be held suspect. Any passage that requires such an interpretation must be held suspect. As a rule, prophets speak to their own generation about events and situations that immediately involve them. Claus Westermann applies this view to the hypothetical author of Isaiah 40–55 nicely: "Deutero-Isaiah in his day had to speak the word appropriate to a different situation [than the prophets of judgment]. It is quite impossible to dissociate the prophetic word from the time at which it was uttered."[1]

How has Deutero-Isaiah been distinguished from Isaiah of Jerusalem? This is actually so widely accepted that the arguments often are perfunctory. Usually one starts out by calling attention to the naming of Cyrus in Isa 45:1. Then one can identify passages scattered through Isaiah 41–48 that describe him without naming him. Could Isaiah of Jerusalem have learned his name and role by supernatural means? One answers that according to one's theological predilections. However, the prophecies in this book address the Judean exiles living in Babylon. It would have made no sense to the people of Isaiah's own time, so the scroll of Isaiah 40–55 would have had to be stored away, taken into exile, and proclaimed to the exiles once Cyrus had conquered the Medes and perhaps Lydia.

Chapters 40–55 speak to an audience living in Babylon. In fact, at the end of chapter 48 they are urged to leave (48:20). Chapters 56–66 speak to conditions in Jerusalem after the return of the exiles from Babylon. The language is similar enough to Isaiah 40–55 that one could ascribe these chapters to the same prophet. Perhaps Second Isaiah returned. However, a closer reading of Isaiah 56–66 has compelled most scholars to hypothesize a different author or, more likely, several, who were disciples of Second Isaiah. Thus, we have reason to believe that the book of Isaiah belongs to at least three different eras, with different venues and different prophets.

If we adhere to a classical view of textual meaning, each prophet's message is limited to what he himself intended and his audience could or at least should be able to understand. Mixing and harmonizing of messages is forbidden.

---

1. Westermann, *Isaiah 40–66*, 9.

## Brevard Childs

Now let's turn to the approach of canonical criticism as practiced by Brevard Childs. Childs shocks the historical-critical sensibility and changes the paradigm of scholarly interpretation. His guiding principle is that "canonical shaping" is the unconditional key for interpretation. To understand his view, let's begin with a modest claim for canon: interpret all texts within the Bible as God's word for the people of God. This is compatible with historical criticism; all that it requires is that after one has subjected the text to whatever criticism that seems to shed light on the origin and meaning of the discourse, one take the results as God's word (or at least containing it).

Childs seeks in canonical criticism a principle that will literally save us from the impoverishment of the biblical message by overzealous scholarship. Here is his critique of the statement by Westermann quoted above: "In my judgment, this exegetical principle reflects a misunderstanding of what the Old Testament means by the living word of God . . . Westermann's exegetical rule renders virtually impossible the task of taking seriously the canonical shape of the biblical text. Specifically in terms of Second Isaiah, the final form of the literature provided a completely new and non-historical framework for the prophetic message which severed the message from its original historical moorings and rendered it accessible to all future generations."[2]

Readers must attend to his point carefully: the specific historical import of the text must be suppressed for the text to mean anything for later generations of readers. Knowing that Second Isaiah was addressed to the Judean exiles in Babylon actually undercuts the import of Isaiah 40–55 within the book of Isaiah. To quote Childs,

> By placing the message of Second Isaiah within the context of the eighth-century prophet his message of promise became a prophetic word not tied to a specific historical referent, but directed to the future. A message which originally functioned in a specific exilic context . . . has been detached from this historical situation to become fully eschatological. In its new context its message no longer can be understood as a specific commentary on the needs of exiled Israel, but its message relates to the redemptive plan of God for all of history. The announcement of forgiveness to downtrodden Israel . . . is not confined to a specific historical situation . . . in its canonical context it is offered to sinful Israel as a promise of God's purpose with his people in every age.[3]

2. Childs, *Introduction to the Old Testament as Scripture*, 337.
3. Ibid., 326.

## Redeeming Judgment

Childs would dismiss any conclusions about the failure of Second Isaiah's message to materialize in the period of return: "The discrepancy between what happened after the exile and the prophet's eschatological description of God's will is not a criticism of the truth of the promise, but rather an indication of how little the exilic community partook of the promised reality."[4]

What about First Isaiah? Doesn't it retain its historical reference? No, says Childs. The message of Isaiah 1–39 has been modified by the attachment of this message of forgiveness and return from exile. Second Isaiah adds a whole new dimension to the promises of eschatological redemption and a new world order scattered through Isaiah 1–39. The oracles against foreign nations culminate in chapters 24–27 "in which one hears the liturgy of the redeemed community."[5] Chapters 34–35 foreshadow the message of Second Isaiah and even imitate its poetic style, while chapters 36–39 are edited to provide "a historical context for Second Isaiah's message of hope."[6]

If we were to adopt Childs's understanding of the impact and intent of the collections of prophecies, what strategy should we take toward interpretation? Rolf Rendtorff, P. R. Achroyd, R. F. Melugin, and Christopher Seitz have conjoined the canonical principle with "rhetorical analysis" of the final form.[7] We can explore an example of this type of interpretation.

### Rolf Rendtorff

I am taking this Heidelberg scholar as representative of the canonical strategy. He traces networks of words and phrases connecting the three parts of the book, viz., chapters 1–39, 40–55, and 56–66. ʿAwon, "guilt," is such a word; it first occurs in 1:4 and again in 40:2, where it is pardoned. The same is true of the matching word, ḥataʾ (1:4; 40:2). The word naḥam, "comfort," with which Second Isaiah begins so dramatically also occurs in Isa 12:1, a part of a psalm that concludes Isaiah 1–11 with praise for deliverance. The same word returns several more times: in Isa 51:12 and 66:13, and in the embedded hymns in Second Isaiah—49:13; 51:3; and 52:9. Another important word in this network is kabôd, "glory," usually in the construct phrase, "glory of the Lord." This expression occurs in Isaiah's call vision (Isa 6:3) and in Isa 35:2 and 40:5. It also occurs in 60:1 and 66:18. All these involve humans seeing the divine glory.

4. Ibid., 327.
5. Ibid., 332.
6. Ibid.
7. Trible, *Rhetorical Criticism*.

Rendtorff is convinced that Isaiah 12 and 35 are important linguistic links in the network that unites the major divisions of the book. In a different way Isaiah 1 and 33 provide links as well.[8]

These words often point to conceptual links between divisions. The people who are burdened with guilt (Isa 1:4) have that guilt pardoned in 40:2. A number of other passages in Isaiah 1–39 employ "guilt" in a manner similar to 1:4, viz., 5:18; 22:14; and 30:13. There are also references to forgiveness in these chapters, viz., 6:7; 27:9; 33:24. In Second Isaiah, forgiveness of Israel recurs in several passages, viz., 43:24–25; 50:1; and the fourth Servant Song, 53:5, 6, 11. In Third Isaiah, forgiveness is the dominant subject in Isaiah 59; see verses 2, 3, 12, and 20; also Isa 64:5, 6–7, 9.[9]

Rendtorff also traces a number of broader themes through the three divisions of the book. *Zion/Jerusalem* is found in all three divisions. In the very first chapter Zion is a remnant, and it is barely surviving; but later in the chapter is its reconstitution, and in the first verses of Isaiah 2, Zion is the pilgrimage center of a new world order. In the following chapters the city must face God's judgment, but a remnant will survive to start again. It is less prominent in Isaiah 13–35, and almost entirely hopeful. *Zion/Jerusalem* is quite prominent in Second Isaiah; Isaiah 49–55 could be said to be "the Zion-Jerusalem section."[10] "The sayings about Zion/Jerusalem in the second part of the book of Isaiah are extremely unified in theme; they are directed entirely toward consolation and the assurance of divine help for ruined and depopulated Jerusalem."[11]

Another expression that Rendtorff highlights is the divine epithet *qadôsh yisrael* ("Holy One of Israel"). Commentators have long been struck by the use of this epithet in both First and Second Isaiah, and nowhere else in Hebrew Scripture. The uses of the expression differ, according to Rendtorff, rather systematically. In First Isaiah, all the passages "have to do with the question whether and how the people who are being talked about in each case worship 'the Holy One of Israel.'"[12] In Second Isaiah, the epithet is either claimed personally by YHWH or referred to him in an expanded messenger formula. "We therefore meet the phrase 'the Holy One of Israel' in the second part of the book of Isaiah in speeches touching on and promising salvation, but never

---

8. Rendtorff, *Canon and Theology*, 149–53.
9. Ibid., 153–55.
10. Ibid., 157.
11. Ibid., 158.
12. Ibid., 160–61.

in disputations or judgment speeches."[13] Isaiah 12 tries to bridge the uses in First and Second Isaiah. The phrase recedes in Third Isaiah, appearing only in 60:9, 14.[14]

First and Second Isaiah divide sharply over the use of *tsedeq(ah)*. In First Isaiah, the word is used in parallel with *mishpaṭ* ("justice") and as the object of the verb "to do"; in these formulations it calls for a translation of "righteousness." In Second Isaiah, the word is paired with *yashaʿ* and *yashuaʿ*, "salvation"; in these formulations the word is translated "victory" or "deliverance."[15] First Isaiah's usage belongs to sin and judgment, Second Isaiah's usage to the Lord's saving power. Third Isaiah begins (56:1) with a juxtaposition of the two contrasting usages. Subsequently Third Isaiah tends to transfer victory from YHWH to Israel or Zion.[16]

This list by no means exhausts the network of links, antitheses, subjects, and themes that constitute the book of Isaiah in its final form. However, it is enough to establish the internal linkage of the parts of the book. The question is, what sort of reading strategy is suggested by the evidence and how would one build up a theology?

### H. G. M. Williamson

This scholar represents an effort to synthesize the older source-critical approach to analysis and the final form strategy of Childs, Rendtorff et al. Williamson has set out an argument in *The Book Called Isaiah* for Second Isaiah interpolating passages into chapters 1–39 that made the book a precedent and prologue of his own writing.[17] Williamson holds himself to stricter standards of proof than someone simply showing the general unity of the book; he demands that verbal connections be exclusive to the book of Isaiah.[18]

He begins his argument with evidence that Isaiah 6, the call narrative, exercised influence on Second Isaiah. "High and lifted up" (v. 1) is used not only in other passages in chapters 1–39, but also in 52:13 and 57:15. "Holy One of Israel," as we already noted, is found in both Isaiah 1–39 and 40–55. "Blindness" and "deafness" (6:9–10) are taken up in 42:16, 18–19, 21–25; 43:8;

---

13. Ibid., 161.
14. Ibid., 162.
15. God is the subject in these cases.
16. Rendtorff, *Canon and Theology*, 163–64, also 181–89.
17. Williamson, *The Book Called Isaiah*.
18. Ibid., 19–29.

45:18. "Hearing but not understanding" is found in 40:21; 41:20; and 52:15. The desolation and depopulation of the land (6:11–12) is found in 49:14–21 and 54:1–3.[19] The use of the word "king" for YHWH (6:5) is also found in 41:21; 43:15; 44:6; and 52:7.[20]

Other passages in Isaiah 1–39 are echoed in chapters 40–55. The woe in Isa 29:15–16 is only slightly reformulated in 45:9. The signal (*nes*) that the Lord raises in Isa 5:26; 11:10, 12; 13:2; 18:13; 30:17; 31:9; and 33:23 is mentioned in 49:22 (and in 62:10). The change from dark to light (9:1, 2) is reflected in 42:16; 45:7; 49:6; 50:10; and 51:4; and the inspiration for "first and last" (44:6, 48:12, etc.) and "announced of old" (44:7b; 48:12). The expression "fading flower" in 28:4 is echoed in 40:6–8. The use of imperfect with ʾ*amar* in the expression, "The Lord says . . ." is found in Isa 1:11, 18; 33:10; and 40:1, 25. Rahab, a mythical dragon, is equated with Egypt in 30:7; and in 51:9–10. Finally, a distinctive use of *torah* occurs in Isa 30:8 (8:16; 30:8) that is repeated in 42:4, 21, 24; and 51:4, and 7.[21]

Williamson believes that Second Isaiah "associated the written presentation of his oracles with the literary deposit of Proto-Isaiah from the start as part and parcel of the same 'book.'"[22] He argues that Second Isaiah contributed transitional passages to summarize and foreshadow portions of the text. In chapters 2–12, Second Isaiah composed the psalm (Isaiah 12) that ends the first eleven chapters and separates it from what follows. One hears in its themes of exodus and divine exaltation telltale features of the message of chapters 40–55. Isaiah 11:11–16 also belong to Second Isaiah, as does the related text, 5:25–30; the latter has only one verse composed by Second Isaiah (v. 30), but it was transposed to its current position from elsewhere. Isa 8:22 has been transposed from elsewhere too. Finally, Isa 2:5 is by Second Isaiah, who probably interpolated 2:1–4 and composed verse 5 as a bridge.[23]

Williamson believes that the oracles against Babylon in chapters 13–14 were inserted by Second Isaiah, but that otherwise there are no traces of Second Isaiah in chapters 13–27. Chapters 24–27, the Isaiah Apocalypse, were inserted by someone after Second Isaiah's editing. The same is true of Isaiah 36–39 and 34–35. Williamson thinks that Second Isaiah's version of First

---

19. And in Third Isaiah as well.
20. Williamson, *The Book Called Isaiah*, 30–56.
21. Ibid., 57–93.
22. Ibid., 114.
23. Ibid., 126–55.

Isaiah ended with chapter 33, which is linguistically and theologically congruent with Second Isaiah, though it was not necessarily authored by him.[24]

## A Reading Strategy

It would seem that we are caught in a dilemma. If we want to read the book as a whole, we have to abandon actual history as well as the particular audience to which a given passage was addressed. If we want to preserve historical reference and audience, we have to retain the atomistic ideology of source criticism. How can we read the book as one whole yet preserve the relevance of history? How can we appropriate the contributions of Childs, Rendtorff, Melugin, and Williamson without adopting Childs's entire scheme?

I propose to adopt a modified version of Hugh Williamson's thesis as a reading strategy. We cannot follow him in tracing particular passages of Isaiah 1–39 as contributions of Second Isaiah and others to other authors or editors. Rather, let's read all of Isaiah 1–39 as designed to be completed by Isaiah 40–55 and 56–66. We want to test our expectation that divine judgment is aimed at redemption, and that redemption presupposes and incorporates the effects of judgment. We can begin with Isaiah's call, which announces divine judgment. The effect of the announcement will be to harden the people's hearts, preparing them for judgment. Where in chapters 1–39 is this message delivered? Isaiah 1–11 is chiefly judgment of Israel and Judah before or during Ahaz's reign; chapters 13–27 chiefly judge the nations; chapters 28–39 judge Judah during Hezekiah's reign, and juxtapose an equal number of oracles of salvation. The question we are asking is whether the proclamation of judgment envisages redemption arising from it.

## Interpreters of the Isaianic Prophetic Heritage

We can continue along the same lines in our analysis of the next eleven chapters of Isaiah, viz., to read chapters 56–66 as the product of the disciples of the Babylonian Isaiah. That the prophet or prophets who composed Isaiah 56–66 were disciples of the Babylonian prophet is perfectly reasonable. The book retains features of the style of Isaiah 40–55, and its content is congruent.[25] Moreover, the chapters locate the prophet and audience in Jerusalem. If the prophet who wrote Isaiah 56–66 was indeed a disciple of the Babylonian

---

24. Ibid., 184–239.
25. See Hanson, *The Dawn of Apocalyptic*, 32–78.

Isaiah, he would have composed the contribution to the book between 535 and 510 BCE.

Following this reading strategy, we can construe Isaiah 56–66 as an effort by a disciple of the Babylonian Isaiah to adapt the master's promises to the reality experienced in the return, or ʿ*aliyah*. The prophet who had Isaiah 1–39 as well as 40–55 available in written form evidently rediscovered the message of judgment proclaimed by Isaiah of Jerusalem. In particular, we again meet accusations against members of the prophet's society. Isaiah's sentence of national judgment could not, however, be revived, because the Babylonian Isaiah had promised, not only the end of exile, but also no repetition of judgment. Salvation is unconditional. So the sentence of the postexilic prophet is the *delay* or *postponement* of the promised salvation.

The prophet begins to differentiate between groups within the postexilic society of Jerusalem. The one the prophet belongs to is named the "servants" of the Lord, echoing the title of "servant" depicted in the Servant Songs of Isaiah 40–55. Their piety is distinctive: they are deeply conscious of the sinfulness of the society to which they belong. They describe themselves as humble and contrite. Moreover, they are opposed to the rebuilding of the temple and resumption of sacrifices on its altar.

Over against the servants are those who now claim the title of Israel. This amorphous group exemplifies the sinful behavior that has caused the delay of salvation. In the last two chapters of the book, the arrival of salvation will be judgment on those who had sinned grievously. How this division will be effected is not depicted, though the portrayal of salvation raises the event to eschatological proportions.

The last two chapters of Isaiah, along with chapters 24–27, provide a horizon for every other act of judgment and salvation performed in the book. All history has become an action leading to a culmination, a resolution of the contradictions of history and a full realization of the divine intent in creation.

## The Piety of the Servants

Why couldn't our argument simply move from the book of Isaiah to the New Testament? Actually, it could. However, there is a story to follow about how the inward piety of the servants spreads out to encompass much of Second Temple Judaism. The New Testament community inherits a piety very much abroad in the Judaism of the era. We will trace a strand of this "penitential piety"—the strand that cultivated humility and compunction among individuals. We find

*Redeeming Judgment*

in certain psalms the same penitential language as Isa 66:1–4. These psalms, which are quite eloquent and profound, were the vehicle for the dissemination of the piety that began among the disciples of the Babylonian Isaiah.

This piety was (and still is) the proper inward appropriation of the prophetic message of judgment. The exile is interpreted by Third Isaiah as the Lord's execution of the sentence pronounced by the earlier prophets. The Babylonian Isaiah had insisted that the exiled people accept the fact that their unhappy condition as due to their sin. Only if the people become conscious of their propensity to sin could God redeem them from its power.

One can observe the appropriation of the judgment of God in a number of contrite communal laments and rehearsals of national history. We discover one of these in Isaiah 56–66, viz., 63:7—64:12. Among the Psalms, Psalm 106 incorporates the story of Israel's constant rebellion into the story of God's saving history. Such passages demonstrate that a national consciousness of sin is linked to the prophecy of judgment.

We do not need to prove that the penitential psalms for individuals derive from the prophetic message of judgment against the community; it is enough to note the congruence of the piety of the "servants" with that of the penitential psalms. Moreover, their piety was (and still is) a valid theological conclusion to draw from the prophetic message as it is conveyed to us in the prophetic books.

This new piety collides with the piety of the classical individual laments. We examined these laments in part 1 of this book. The classical laments have little or no confession of sin, and some have adamant protests of innocence. We identified two rhetorical strategies within individual laments for persuading God to intervene in the supplicant's behalf: to seek to recruit YHWH against enemies or natural threats (the majority), or to accuse God of abandonment or worse (the minority).[26]

The penitent worshipper would not think of accusing God. The worshipper blames the self for the current trouble. The requests focus on forgiveness and power to overcome one's sinful proclivities. The whole drama of life has changed from, on the one hand, the quest for a happy, productive life and protection from the threats to it to, on the other hand, sin and redemption.

We could simply flesh out a comparison of the psalms representing classical piety and those representing the new, prophetic piety. However, we have the dramatization of the clash between these pieties in the book of Job. That is why an exposition of the book of Job has been included in the chapter on peni-

---

26. The accusations were, I think, to shame YHWH into acting.

tential piety. It so happens that the resolution of the drama can be interpreted as either the affirmation of the classical lament or the legitimation of the new piety of humble, contrite submission.

## Final Judgment as the Horizon of History

Isaiah 65–66 introduces us to a full-scale eschatology. It is an event of judgment that divides the servants of the Lord from the unworthy, and establishes a new order in which the negative conditions of life are overcome. These chapters provide an ultimate horizon against which the scenes within the book are played out.

Can we discover this type of eschatology in the psalms? The answer is yes; a few psalms look forward to a final judgment.

Most of the psalms that refer to divine judgment do not mean a final, culminating judgment. Judgment is praised and pleaded for as a resolution to the troubles humans experience in their day-to-day lives. The attitude of the people who wrote and prayed these poems was virtually opposite that of modern, liberal churchgoers. Readers who are repulsed by the prospect of divine judgment need to realize just how out of step with the piety of the Bible they are.

Our chapter on final judgment (chapter 19, below) will begin by sampling psalms that praise or plead for God's judgment. We will then locate those psalms that look forward to a future judgment that will culminate and correct the judgments of history.

The dominant image of the Last Judgment is that of a trial. One finds such an image in apocalyptic literature. The trial scene does not necessarily imply that the cases are not yet decided. Often the "books are opened," or something to that effect. God (or the one exercising judgment for God) does not need to hear testimony in order to learn the facts of the case. Just as the prophets of judgment announce the judgment and sentence, so the divine decision is announced and the sentence follows without further deliberation. If we follow the scenario of the prophets, the ultimate destiny of the accused depends upon the person's response to the decision.

Another common image of the Last Judgment can occur, namely, of a great battle in which the powers of evil are defeated. This image is found in the Isaiah Apocalypse (Isaiah 24–27).

The eschatological denouement of history is on the horizon of the Old Testament; it becomes the event which is "at hand" in the New.

## Judgment in the New Testament

Readers should be surprised by the division of the biblical text in pursuit of the doctrine of redeeming judgment. We did not limit the treatment of the Old Testament to part 1 of this book and devote the second part entirely to the New. Nor did we fall into anything like, the God of the Old Testament is a wrathful God while the God of the New is gracious and merciful. It is our contention that both testaments depict a God of judgment and redemption. There is no difference on that score.

We do witness a subtle change in the situation of the people of God in the book of Isaiah. By the end of the book, the national judgment proclaimed by the eighth-century prophets is no longer a theological possibility. It has been ruled out by the announcement of the end of judgment by the Babylonian Isaiah. Now judgment takes the form of the delay of salvation, or of the exclusion of some from the salvation offered to the people. Only those who acknowledge their propensity to sin and welcome God's inspiration can be redeemed.

Now we are ready for the New Testament message. The Christian kerygma is an answer to the pervasiveness and persistence of human sin. The message is that the person and work of Jesus Christ overcomes the power of sin, and sets believers on the way to salvation. The servants of Isaiah 56–66 become the disciples of the Servant and the apostles of a new age embodied in the person of its Lord.

What do we have to discover in the New Testament to confirm its essential continuity with the book of Isaiah and fellow prophets, and witnessed to throughout the Old Testament? Quite simply, we have to find the message of divine judgment. Without this basic teaching, the New Testament does not represent sufficient continuity with the Old to affirm that the God of Jesus is in fact the God of Israel, or that the promises of the Old Testament are fulfilled and renewed in the New.

We do indeed find judgment in the New Testament. All readers need to do to confirm this claim is to recall the message of John the Baptist. Jesus never renounces John's message but actually builds upon it. He himself threatens judgment upon those who do not seize the chance to repent before the coming of the Final Judgment. His message is in fact very close to that of Isaiah 56–66.

The Gospel of John periodically denies that Jesus came to judge humans yet insists that the response of those who meet Jesus determines their destiny. This is not too far removed from the message of the Synoptics.

In the Revelation of John, judgment is primarily imposed upon principalities and powers. Nevertheless, individual humans will fare as do the powers that control their lives. The victory of Christ over the powers of the world is nonviolent—indeed the sacrifice of the cross. I would suggest that it is the victory of persuasion over coercion.

The book of Romans brings together the major themes of Paul's theological teaching. To the embarrassment and discomfort of many interpreters, Paul begins his exposition of the gospel with the wrath or judgment of God hanging over all humanity. The whole effort of humans to establish their righteousness, their worthiness to be saved is doomed to failure. There is no hope for those unwilling to acknowledge their sinfulness and to plead for God's mercy and grace.

## The Good News of the New Testament

If the New Testament does not renounce divine judgment but in fact affirms it in an eschatological key, what makes the gospel "good news"? Of course, one can answer, the person and work of Jesus Christ. One still needs to explain how Jesus changes the human situation. In particular, how does Jesus rescue humans from the certainty of judgment? This questions thrusts us into the meaning of the cross. What did Jesus's suffering, death, and resurrection do to our common situation under divine condemnation?

We have found a precedent for God's acceptance of a human's suffering and death as a source of mercy and forgiveness of those who despised and even persecuted him. This is the servant of the Lord depicted in Isaiah 40–55. There are allusions to the servant in the Synoptics, though one cannot say for sure how deliberate they are. In any case, this would not be decisive for determining whether Jesus was in fact the servant of the Lord. What is essential is that God impute the righteousness of his messiah designate to all humans or at least to those who acknowledge him as savior.

The course of the Synoptic accounts of Jesus's life, viz., Mark, Matthew, and Luke, begins with Jesus's announcing the in-breaking of God's kingdom but leads toward the identification of the kingdom with the One announcing it. Jesus's death and resurrection facilitate the introduction of the Kingdom into history. How so? This is what we must answer.

The Gospel of John leaves readers with much the same perplexity. Jesus is introduced as the "Lamb of God who takes away the sins of the world" (John 1:29, 36). How does Jesus accomplish this? We shall seek clues to the answer.

The Revelation of John provides additional clues, for it too identifies Jesus as the sacrificial Lamb (Rev 5:6). How does sacrifice atone for sin committed and at the same time overcome the propensity to sin?

Romans offers Jesus's suffering and death as the remedy for the judgment facing sinners. The letter employs several metaphors to explain what happens, though none amounts to a full-scale doctrine of atonement. This has encouraged various theologians in the history of the church to complete what Paul began. Paul not only sought a theological explanation for how Jesus's death facilitates the forgiveness of sin—of all sin of all humans, but how it could also overcome the propensity to sin.

The atoning power of the cross may be the deepest mystery of the gospel. There has never been a conciliar decision to settle what orthodoxy demands. Some Protestant churches have spelled out particular doctrines in their confessions, but these were never accepted beyond the denomination. This lack of final definition suggests that we make the best of the plurality of metaphors.

# 15

## The Book of Isaiah I
(Isaiah 1–39)

THE TOPIC OF THIS chapter is the effect of publishing prophecies as books for later audiences. Isaiah and his fellow eighth-century prophets composed and delivered their prophecies to various audiences during the prophets' careers. Their oracles would have been preserved by disciples. When the judgment had overtaken the addressees, the disciples collected the prophet's words. Over time a book of prophecies took shape, designed not for the original audience, but for the descendants of that audience who were suffering the effect of past judgment. Each prophecy, thus, gained a second meaning: besides what it meant in its original setting, it now had import for the reading audience as well. All subsequent readers had access to the prophet's message through the published collection. By then, additional oracles and sayings of anonymous origin had been included among the prophet's words and the whole had been arranged to support the message the preservers of the book had discovered in it.

In the past few chapters, we have been attuned to the original message—the prophet's message to his contemporaries. Thus we expounded the four eighth century and two seventh-sixth century prophets of judgment as a message to their preexilic audience, and the oracles of salvation as words of consolation to the audiences that had experienced the judgment. I downplayed the distinctive message of each prophet and ignored the editing and presentation of the books. It is my belief that the original transaction between prophet and audience is a constituent moment in the history of the text. This is the moment when the words had performative force, i.e., when a judgment was pronounced on the society, the audience became guilty and faced the consequences of their deeds. This sort of transaction will not happen with later readers of said prophecy; one might say that the prophecy "spends" its judicial force in the utterance.

Once the prophecy is past and the word has taken shape in event, the prophecy becomes precedent and paradigm for later audiences. We have already seen how Jeremiah and Ezekiel revived the prophecy of the eighth century. The same sort of appropriation and adaptation takes place between the prophet's words and other audiences. The later reading audience can use the authoritative texts as a measure of its own condition and what is in store for the community.

Preserving precedents and paradigms is not all the prophetic books do. When God speaks and acts, his action is once for all. The book of Isaiah, in particular, sets out the "divine plan" that links the past with our present and the eschatological future. A plan is enacted as a drama with one comprehensive action toward an ultimate resolution. We have already observed the unfolding drama that led from creation and fall to the exiles of Israel and Judah. The same action is embodied in a distinctive configuration in Isaiah. The book is the unfolding of God's plan from the moment of prophetic judgment through the purgation of the people to their return from exile. The future holds the redemption of the people of God, and the conversion of the nations. Despite this future, the people remain unredeemed at the end of the book; an eschatological transformation is still a matter of promise and hope. Even though humans remain the same sinners as they were declared to be before and after the flood, God continues to modify the conditions of life toward redemption. The political embodiment of the people of God is radically altered in the course of Isaiah and they receive a new calling corresponding to this alteration.

It is our intention in this and the next two chapters to follow the plan of God as it is represented in the book of Isaiah, following the sequence of: Isaiah 1–39, 40–55, 56–66.[1]

## Isaiah 1–12

The story of Isaiah's call is told in chapter 6. YHWH appears to Isaiah in all his glory, surrounded by angelic beings. Isaiah cries out, fearful that he will die, but he is graciously purified so that he can be a messenger of God. After he has volunteered to accept the commission, he is told:

---

1. See p. 317 above.

> Go and say to this people:
> "Keep listening, but do not comprehend;
> > keep looking, but do not understand."
> Make the heart of this people dull,
> > and stop their ears,
> > and shut their eyes;
> So that they not look with their eyes,
> > and listen with their ears,
> and comprehend with their minds
> > and turn and be healed. (Isa 6:9–10)

This is a shocking commission, suggesting that the people are predestined to judgment. As Craig Evans puts it, "It would seem that Isa 6:9–10 means that it is God's intention to render his people obdurate through the proclamation of his prophet. The purpose of this obduracy, it would appear, is either to render judgment certain, as is implied in vv. 11–13, or perhaps to make it more fully deserved. It is possible that both ideas are in view."[2]

My reading is that YHWH knows that the people are predisposed to their sinful behavior, so the prophet's truthful word will not prompt repentance but rather stubbornness and retaliation. Nevertheless, they have a putative right to be offered a chance to repent. If they were to do so, God would grant them a new lease on life. Note the offer made in Isa 1:18–20:

> Come now, let us argue it out, says the Lord:
> Though your sins are like scarlet,
> > they shall be like snow;
> though they are red like crimson,
> > they shall become like wool.
> If you are willing and obedient,
> > you shall eat the good of the land;
> but if you refuse and rebel,
> > you shall be devoured by the sword.

This sounds like a conventional offer of rewards for obedience, punishment for disobedience. However, since the offer begins with their situation, one of sinfulness and guilt, the offer probably concerns the people's willingness to change their ways and renew their faith.

---

2. Evans, *To See and Not Perceive*, 19.

*Redeeming Judgment*

It is noteworthy that Isaiah is not told in his call of what the people are guilty and should repent. Like Amos, he must discover the subject of the indictment. Whether he was familiar with Amos's prophecies or not we do not know. If he happened to be, he could have proceeded on the assumption that his predecessor had a true understanding of God's will. If not, he rediscovered what Amos had discovered a decade before him.

We can use this call as a landmark. Isaiah has been commissioned to pronounce judgment to harden his Judean audience. Some critical scholars have taken this restrictively, viz., that Isaiah only speaks of judgment and all words of salvation in the book belong to other authors.[3] I think they are being too literal. None of the classical prophets of judgment regard judgment to be the final word. Judgment has redemptive force, and therefore we would expect promises of salvation woven into the judgments. Our strategy will be to locate the prophecies of judgment—which Isaiah was commissioned to speak—and then take note of how salvation emerges from judgment.

Isaiah 1–12 is a collection of prophecies of judgment from before or during Ahaz's reign. Virtually nothing in these chapters calls for dating in Hezekiah's reign; very little in Isaiah 28–32 derives from before or during Ahaz's reign. Thus, the distribution of judgments is relatively chronological.

The judgments in chapters 1–5 are addressed to the people and perhaps royal advisors, but not the king. Chapter 5 is an epitome of Isaiah's prophecy against the nation. It begins with a parable that dramatizes Israel's and Judah's failures (failures in justice and righteousness). The rest of the chapter is a set of woes against the wealthy, indolent, and cynical for the harm they are dong to the body politic. The woe in Isa 10:1–4 takes up a similar offense—injustice in the judiciary. It is for these types of offenses that YHWH has appointed Assyria as his instrument of punishment (10:5–6).

Chapter 1 of Isaiah is an overview of the prophet's message. It begins with a brief parable exposing how unnatural Israel's refractoriness is (1:2–3). Following that is a general accusation against the people. It is sinful, corrupt, and unfaithful, and has been punished severely for its misbehavior. The countryside is desolate: "Zion is left like a booth in a vineyard" (v. 8). The section ends with a reference to Sodom and Gomorrah. They have suffered because their behavior is comparable to these ancient cities (v. 10).

The prophet dramatizes God's rejection of temple rituals to pacify him (vv. 11–17). What will please him? To turn away from their evil:

---

3. Consult Eissfeld, *The Old Testament*, 317–28.

> Your hands are full of blood.
> Wash yourselves; make yourselves clean;
>> remove the evil of your doings from before my eyes;
> cease to do evil—
>> learn to do good;
> seek justice—
>> rescue the oppressed,
> defend the orphan,
>> plead for the widow. (vv. 15–17)

Immediately following this teaching is an offer of forgiveness to the people (vv. 18–20). If they are willing to admit their sinfulness and then make efforts at reform, they will be forgiven; but if they insist on remaining as they are, they will suffer, even to the point of destruction. Given Isaiah's commission, this offer of forgiveness seems rather unreal. The people seem to be doomed to make the wrong choice. Nevertheless, this type of conditional promise seems to accompany the pronouncements of judgment throughout Isaiah.

A pronouncement of judgment follows on the city of Jerusalem:

> How the faithful city has become a whore!
>> she that was full of justice,
> Righteousness lodged in her—
>> but now murderers!
> . . .
> Your princes are rebels
>> and companions of thieves.
> Everyone loves a bribe
>> and runs after gifts.
> They do not defend the orphan,
>> and the widow's cause does not come before them. (1:21, 23)

This contrast, incorporating the indictment, leads to the sentence: "Ah, I will vent my wrath on my enemies, / and avenge myself on my foes" (1:24). Now the prophecy takes an unexpected turn: instead of collective judgment, we have a "sifting or refining":

> I will turn my hand against you
>> and will smelt away your dross as with lye
>> and remove all your alloy. (1:25)

## Redeeming Judgment

This is balanced with a promise of salvation to the city itself:

> And I will restore your judges as at the first,
>    and your counselors as at the beginning.
> Afterward you shall be called the city of righteousness,
>    the faithful city. (1:26)

In case we have missed it, there is an "appendix," speaking again of the division among the people:

> Zion shall be redeemed by justice,
>    and those in her who repent, by righteousness.
> But rebels and sinners shall be destroyed together,
>    and those who forsake the Lord shall be consumed. (1:27–28)

This is the end of the prophecy; vv. 29–31 are an indictment for a heterodox cultic practice that does not fit well here,[4] but it can be read as a further indictment or description of the wicked.

Several things are noteworthy about this prophecy. First, it combines judgment and salvation. Judgment, in fact, has a purgative effect on the city. Thus, the prophecy ends with the division between those who are willing and able to live in and support a just city, and those who would undermine its order. Second, it builds its image of the future on an image of the past; salvation is restoration after corruption. Third, we already observe another characteristic of Isaiah's prophecies of salvation: they involve the restoration or transformation of officials—here judges and counselors. The prophecy does not mention the king, perhaps to encourage the king not to interfere in the city's affairs.

Isaiah 2:2–4 is a promise of salvation of another order. Now it is a bit hard to see its connection with 1:21–28; the condemnation of sacred gardens and the heading in 2:1 separate them. They do make a fine pair, though: the first promises a redemption of the city and the second a central role for the city in a new international order. The best way to read of the elevation of Mount Zion is as a symbol of its new status. It will become a pilgrimage site for the nations; they will worship YHWH in the temple and receive torah from him. The city, through its priests and prophets, will disseminate this teaching to peoples from around the known world. There will also be an international judicial function: international disputes will be arbitrated by YHWH's spokesmen. Weapons can be reforged as farming implements. It is quite in keeping with this passage that a statue of a blacksmith reforging swords into plowshares stands in the United

---

4. It sounds like it belongs to Third Isaiah; perhaps it gravitated here to form a precedent.

Nations building in New York City; our passage is one of the profoundest expressions from antiquity of the peacemaking ideal of the UN.

## Isaiah 7:1—9:7

This seems to be an independent section; it has been dubbed the Isaiah Memoir by scholars. Within these chapters, only 9:2–7 are an unconditional promise of salvation. However, 7:1–9 is a promise of salvation with a conditional ending. It is directed to king Ahaz, though it concerns the kingdom of Judah as a whole. The promise is that the Lord will thwart the efforts of Aram and Israel to oust Ahaz and place one Ben Tabeel on his throne (7:6, 7–9). What exactly will happen to these nations and their rulers is not said.

This could be a saving message to Ahaz, but if he doesn't believe ("stand firm"), he will fall with them. When he is offered a sign to confirm the authenticity of the prophecy, he declines to ask for one. His reason sounds pious, but Isaiah sees it as a rejection of the divine promise. So a sign is given: the birth of a son to a "young woman" (or virgin), whose name will be Immanuel ("with us is God"). This sign will not be a confirmation of hope for Ahaz, who will in fact suffer as badly, as the Davidic king did when the nation divided: this time the cause of suffering will be the ruler of Assyria. Ahaz has already been courting Assyria's intervention; now he will get what he wants, but he will either drown or barely survive (see Isa 8:5–8).

Immanuel *is* a sign to those who do believe, who trust in the Lord and do not try to take their fate into their own hands. We do hear Immanuel addressed in 8:8, 10. Otherwise, he is a mystery figure. We don't know whether he is Isaiah's child, Ahaz's child, someone else's child, or a symbol who did not actually exist. To be a sign, of course, we would expect an actual birth and an actual child. Why then is nothing further said about him?

As we move forward in the Isaiah Memoir, we do meet a promise of an ideal Davidic king. If one is looking for some follow-up to the promise of Immanuel, the birth of this royal child comes as near as anything to fulfilling our expectations. Not only does Isa 9:2–7 promise a royal child; the child has a set of symbolic names: "Wonderful Counselor, Mighty God, Everlasting Father, Prince of Peace" (v. 6). These would certainly fit a child bearing the name Immanuel.

The promise in Isa 9:2–7 is focused as much on the people as on the royal figure. The people are not named, but since the king is a Davidide, one would assume that we are speaking of Judah. However, in the verses just preceding

## Redeeming Judgment

the promise, we have the area of the north mentioned: "But there will be no gloom for her that was in anguish. In the former time he brought into contempt the land of Zebulun and the land of Naphtali, but in the latter time he will make glorious the way of the sea, the land beyond the Jordan, Galilee of the nations" (9:1). Perhaps we have an implied promise of a Davidic king who rules the north as well as Judah (cp. Isa 11:13–14).

The prophet describes the situation into which the royal child comes as "darkness" and "gloom" (v. 2, also 8:22). The birth of the child is a divine gift of light and joy:

> You have multiplied the nation,
>> you have increased its joy;
> they rejoice before you
>> as with joy at the harvest,
>> as people rejoice dividing plunder. (9:3)

Now we have hints of deliverance from an oppressive foreign power:

> For the yoke of his burden,
>> and the bar across his shoulder,
> the rod of their oppressor,
>> you have broken as on the day of Midian.
> For all the boots of the tramping warrior in battle tumult
>> and all the garments rolled in blood
>> will be burned as fuel for the fire. (9:4–5, RSV)

Note that war seems to be over now. The child is only a baby, not a conquering hero; he comes to power as an heir to a throne:

> For a child has been born for us,
>> a son given to us;
> authority rests upon his shoulders. (9:6a)

With the bestowal of names hinting at divinity or divine kingship, the child's authority is clearly from God. As time goes on, this young king will assume greater power and extend peace to all who are under his authority:

> His authority shall grow continually,
>> and there shall be endless peace
> for the throne of David and his kingdom.
>> He will establish it and uphold it

> with justice and with righteousness
> > from this time onward and forevermore. (9:7)

This is the ideal Davidic monarch. He will earn his reputation in the eyes of his subjects by the quality of his rule of the kingdom over which he presides. The temporal extension of this rule into the eternal future is indicative that the ideal king bursts the limits of history.

The promise is now designed to be unidentified, to be open. A Davidic king will someday reign who meets all the hopes and obligations that the Davidic dynasty bore. The accounts in Isaiah 7–8 indicate that these hopes and demands are not being met by the occupant of the throne. Ahaz is driven by his desire to stay in power by hook or crook. He actually avoids the most foolhardy policies—those followed by the northern rulers to their destruction, and by Ahaz's successor Hezekiah, to his near destruction. According to Isaiah's perspective, Ahaz's policy was a case of doing some of the right things for the wrong reasons, and "playing with fire" by embracing Assyria.

In the passage immediately following the promise in 9:2–7, the rulers of the northern kingdom are also condemned:

> The Lord sent a word against Jacob,
> > and it fell on Israel;
> and all the people knew it—
> > Ephraim and the inhabitants of Samaria—
> > but in pride and arrogance of heart they said:
> "The bricks have fallen,
> > but we will build with dressed stones;
> the sycamores have been cut down,
> > but we will put cedars in their place." (9:8–10)

It so happens, then, that the promise of an ideal Davidic ruler is juxtaposed to defective Ahaz, and the pathetic rulers of Israel. Isaiah calls the latter prideful and arrogant, but one wonders whether theirs isn't bravado in the face of a desperate situation.

Before we take up the other major Davidic promise in chapter 11, we should note some ideas in chapter 10. The prophecy beginning in 10:5 is directed against Assyria. It begins with a claim that Assyria is an instrument of YHWH:

> Ah, Assyria, the rod of my anger—
> > the club in their hand is my fury!

> Against a godless nation I send him,
>> and against the people of my wrath I command him,
> to take spoil and seize plunder,
>> and to tread them down like the mire of the streets. (vv. 5–6)

The Assyrians have their own notions, their own motives:

> But this is not what he intends,
>> nor does he have this in mind;
> but it is in his heart to destroy,
>> and to cut off nations not a few. (v. 7)[5]

This is an instructive statement of what Isaiah means by YHWH's plan. Assyria, driven by its own lust for power and wealth, is serving a quite different purpose. However, it has exceeded its commission, so to speak. We find an instructive set of analogies in v. 15:

> Shall the axe vaunt itself over the one who wields it,
>> or the saw magnify itself against the one who handles it?
> As if a rod should raise the one who lifts it up,
>> or as if a staff should lift the one who is not wood!

Because it is driven by sinful desires and has exceeded its divine commission, it will be judged by God:

> Therefore the Sovereign, LORD of hosts,
>> will send wasting sickness among his stout warriors,
> and under his glory a burning will be kindled,
>> like the burning of a fire. (v. 16)

This sentence continues to v. 19, at which point we meet what appears to be an "appendix." It begins with an allusion to an indictment of Judah and Israel known in Hosea: "In that day the remnant of Israel and the survivors of the house of Jacob will no more lean upon the one who struck them, but will lean upon the Lord, the Holy One of Israel, in truth" (v. 20). The next few verses promise an ingathering of the diaspora (vv. 21–23). This prophecy of salvation is followed by another; it begins with an assurance: "O my people, who live in Zion, be not afraid of the Assyrians when they beat you with a rod and lift up their staff against you as the Egyptians did. For in a very little

---

5. The Assyrians do not know that they are serving YHWH; they do have the promise of victory from their own gods.

while my indignation will come to an end, and my anger will be directed to their destruction" (vv. 24–25). This sequence establishes a pattern: the defeat of the empire which has served as YHWH's instrument of punishment; it will be subjected to judgment in its turn, and that judgment will entail salvation for the people of God.

For some reason, the rest of chapter 10 reverts to judgment of Israel and Judah.[6] It ends with a very general declaration of the Lord's judgment of that which is lofty (using the image of tall trees). This is the background to the announcement of a new Davidic king (11:1–5). This prophecy too emphasizes that the ideal ruler belongs to the family of David.[7] It will be another branch of the family from the one that has reigned. The emphasis falls on his divine endowment:

> And the spirit of the LORD shall rest on him,
>> the spirit of wisdom and understanding,
> the spirit of counsel and might,
>> the spirit of knowledge and the fear of the LORD. (11:2)

This endowment now manifests itself in a particular pattern of behavior:

> He shall not judge by what his eyes see,
>> or decide by what his ears hear;
> but with righteousness he shall judge the poor,
>> and decide with equity for the meek of the earth. (vv. 3b–4a)

It is quite noteworthy that the one royal act that is mentioned is judgment. This is re-enforced by the characterization of the ruler in v. 5:

> Righteousness shall be the belt around his waist,
>> and faithfulness the belt around his loins.

The ideal is constructed, thus, by reference to the judicial activity of government.

Isaiah 11:1–5 is designed to reinforce the promise in Isa 9:2–7. The two are similar in their characterization of the figure, and both seem to put a good deal of emphasis on birth. In Isa 11:1, it is a king deriving from a new branch of the family. That seems to break the pattern of "bad" Davidic kings. The king

---

6. The locations mentioned are on a route from north to south, arriving at Jerusalem.

7. Actually the lineage of Jesse could mean another line from David's, but it is only naturally to trace the lineage to David, though not through the reigning line (Solomon, Rehoboam, and so forth).

will exercise power to establish a just order which entrusts its salvation to the Lord.

The verses that follow up this prophecy of a new, faithful Davidic ruler promise a radical transformation of the natural order. In particular, predators will cease to kill other living creatures to eat, and poisonous creatures will no longer kill to protect themselves. Humans are inserted into the idyllic scenario as children, innocent and defenseless. This is a measure of the reign of peace, instituted in the natural order. This ideal is associated with the "holy mountain" in v. 9:

> They will not hurt or destroy
> > in all my holy mountain;
> for the earth will be full of the knowledge of the LORD
> > as the waters cover the sea.

Despite the location of this peace at the holy mountain, the idyllic order seems to reign in all the earth.

This set of verses is a "portrayal of salvation"[8] that has a striking effect on the promise of a new Davidic ruler. It locates the latter in an eschatological age because this transformation of nature transcends what is possible in the Darwinian world that we know. This elevates the office of the Davidic king to an eschatological office.

The passages have been inscribed in Isaiah 1–12 to bear the weight of hope. After Isa 1:25–28 and the prose reassurance in 4:2–5, the messianic oracles and associated passages are the only full-scale divine promises in the first twelve chapters. The overthrow of Assyria will release Judah to experience salvation, but the new order is portrayed as a revived Davidic monarchy. This new order belongs to an eschatological age.

Chapter 11 continues in the promissory mode. Verse 10 seems to be a bridge to a promise of national restoration and military might (vv. 11–16). What is significant about this passage is the hope of the reuniting of the northern and southern territories into one nation again. They will, because of their new strength, be able to subdue neighboring countries. There is also the hope of an ingathering of the diaspora. These are the sort of hopes that one might associate with a new Davidic king, though they lack the ideal character of eschatological vision.

---

8. Mentioned in Westermann, *Sprache und Struktur der Prophetie Deuterojesajas*, 92–117, 117–24.

The first third of First Isaiah is rounded off with a praise of the Lord for his saving work. This is the thrust of chapter 12. It starts as an individual thanking the Lord for saving him. Then in v. 4 the speaker calls the people of YHWH to give thanks to him for his saving work for the nation. It is a simple, stark call to praise: "Give thanks to the Lord / . . . / make known his deeds among the nations / . . . / Sing praises to the Lord, for he has done gloriously" (12:4, 5). The effect of this psalm is to characterize the judgments and promises in chapters 1–11 constituting salvation—salvation to come, which can already be celebrated.

## Isaiah 13–27

A salient feature of these chapters is the repeated heading, "oracle concerning": Babylon (13:1), Moab (15:1), Damascus (17:1), Egypt (19:1), the "wilderness of the sea" (21:1), Dumah (21:11), the "valley of vision" (22:1), and Tyre (23:1). The material under these headings is not as systematic. The chapter referring to Damascus also concerns Israel, its ally in the Syro-Ephraimite War. Isaiah 18 concerns Egypt, though the heading is a chapter later. Isaiah 21:1 has a cryptic title ("The oracle concerning the wilderness of the sea"), maybe a cipher; vv. 1–10 are about the destruction of Babylon by Elam and Media. "Dumah" (21:11) may be a code name for Edom. The "valley of vision" (22:1) is not a known place name, and the material is judgment against Jerusalem and Judah. Closer inspection reveals even more anomalies, e.g., the stories of Isaiah's prophesying in chapters 20, and in Isa 22:15–25. Thus, the organization of the section must be regarded as somewhat artificial and inaccurate.

This final ordering, however, does seem to lead toward the piece called the Isaiah Apocalypse in chapters 24–27. This drama begins with judgment on the entire earth (24:1–13). For some reason, in the midst of the carnage a song of divine praise arises (24:14–16a), but the destruction continues (24:16b–23). The author praises the Lord in 25:1–5 (and again in 25:9–12; 26:1–6). The praise is followed by the announcement of a "feast of rich food, a feast of well-aged wines" for "all peoples" (25:6). The passage ends with, "he will swallow up death forever," and "the Lord God will wipe away tears from all faces," and "the disgrace of his people he will take away from all the earth" (25:7–8). Isaiah 26:7—27:1 is a psalm expressing a yearning for God's justice. The speaker's beliefs about judgment are stated in vv. 9b–10:

> For when your judgments are in the earth,
> > the inhabitants of the world learn righteousness.

> If favor is shown the wicked,
>> they do not learn righteousness...
>> and do not see the majesty of the LORD.

Later the supplicant comes to the belief that the dead, though gone and forgotten (26:14), will rise from their graves:

> Your dead shall live, their corpses shall rise.
>> O dwellers in the dust, awake and sing for joy! (26:19)

Isaiah 27:1 speaks of the monster known as Leviathan being slain in the sea. That may symbolize a victory over the forces of evil in creation. The rest of the chapter looks forward to the restoration of the people of God after their judgment for their false worship.

While this "apocalypse" promises the end to evil among humans and a paradise of sorts for the peoples, it does not have a last judgment in a judicial sense, and it really leaves open the question of individual retribution. The primary focus is on the judgment of nations. This is the fulfillment of the judgments of individual nations pronounced in chapters 13–23.

The oracles addressed to the nations are not very time specific. The aim seems to be to look at human history from a rather synoptic point of view. To be sure, the first set of chapters introduces us to the horizon the editors seek to evoke. However, note that most of Isaiah 13 has to do with the judgment of the whole earth. It forms an *inclusio* with chapter 24 (25–27). Only in 13:17, 19 do we have Babylon identified, and there is nothing about why this particular empire is in for the Lord's wrath. Only in chapter 14 do we hear an indictment:

> The LORD has broken the staff of the wicked,
>> the scepter of rulers,
> that struck down the peoples in wrath with unceasing blows,
>> that ruled the nations in anger with unrelenting persecution. (vv. 5–6)

The fall of Babylon is depicted as an event in Sheol; this is a "wisdom" motif, viz., all humans end up in the land of the dead. In 14:12–21, we have another judgment against Babylon—this time employing a myth about the morning star, which is expelled from heaven because it sought to "ascend to heaven... make myself like the Most High [Elyon]" (vv. 13, 14). This indictment is now placed in the mouth of contemporaries:

> "Is this the man who made the earth tremble,
>> who shook kingdoms,

> who made the world like a desert
> and overthrew its cities,
> who would not let his prisoners go home?" (vv. 16b–17)

The rulers of Babylon not only will be brought down to the earth; they will not be honored in burial.

This event does have saving significance for the people of God. At the beginning of chapter 14 we hear a promise of salvation: "The LORD will have compassion on Jacob and will again choose Israel, and will set them in their own land, and aliens will join them and will attach themselves to the house of Jacob. And the nations will take them and bring them to their place, and the house of Israel will possess the nations as male and female slaves in the LORD's land; they will take captive those who were their captors, and rule over those who oppressed them" (vv. 1–2).[9] The context suggests that salvation will come as a result of the overthrow of Babylon.

In Isa 14:24–27 we encounter a very powerful theological statement. We have already discussed the passage in the chapter on the eighth-century prophets of judgment; it has significance for the message of salvation as well. The prophecy begins with a theologically charged declaration that what God is about to do is according to plan:

> As I have designed,
> so shall it be,
> and as I have planned,
> so shall it come to pass. (v. 24)

Now God declares his intention to destroy the Assyrian force in the land of Israel:

> I will break the Assyrian in my land,
> and upon my mountains trample him under foot;
> and his yoke shall depart from them,
> and his burden from their shoulders. (v. 25)

This is the specific prediction in the passage. Now the Lord returns to the fact that this was planned before hand, but with a twist: the defeat of Assyria will not only benefit Judah, it will benefit the whole known world.

---

9. The vindictive strain of this passage can be justified as "reparations," though it falls below the highest moral standard.

## Redeeming Judgment

> This is the plan that is planned
> > concerning the whole earth;
> and this is the hand that is stretched out
> > over all the nations. (v. 26)

It would seem that the nations will enter an era of salvation; that is only implied here, but it is fully stated in Isa 2:2–4. The final verse is something of a challenge to anyone who doubts this message:

> For the LORD of hosts has planned,
> > and who will annul it?
> His hand is stretched out,
> > and who will turn it back? (14:27)

This short prophecy is out of place in the chapters devoted to Babylon. Nevertheless, we can regard the current context of the passage as deliberate. The people who passed on and edited Isaiah reapplied his message of judgment. Assyria did fall, but it didn't bring salvation to the nations. That fact would have encouraged the editors to reapply the prophecy.

### Judgments of the People of God

Within the central section of First Isaiah are several prophecies against the people of God and even one narrative of an enacted prophecy. The judgment of Aram and Israel (Isaiah 17) comes from the Syro-Ephraimite War. These two kingdoms are a temptation to Judah because they counsel rebellion against Assyria. They oppose the divine plan. When Ahaz prudently withdraws from the conspiracy, they seek to force Judah to go along. This too represents a danger, but Isaiah promises Ahaz that YHWH will protect him. However, his lack of trust in YHWH leads to an alliance with Assyria that threatens to swamp Judah.

Ahaz's son Hezekiah breaks with his father. He begins to conspire with surrounding kingdoms to ally with Egypt against Assyria. He seems to have pursued this policy over a decade. We find Isaiah prophesying the demise of Egypt in Isaiah 20; this is designed to warn Hezekiah and his counselors not to trust in Egypt. We find a number of prophecies against this alliance in Isaiah 28–32. The truth of Isaiah's warnings is confirmed when Sennacherib brings Judah to its knees in 701 BCE (see Isaiah 36–37).

*Universalism*

Isaiah's universalism is of great importance to the book and to the biblical theological tradition. Now and then scholars dispute the ascription of such universalism to this prophet, but there is no other way to take Isa 14:24–27. When God acts for Israel, it is for the good of all humanity. If there is judgment, it serves one common good. The editors of the book did not invent this universalism; they did, though, expand it and deepen it.

There are few promises of salvation between Isaiah 15 and 24, but one of them is quite noteworthy for its universalism: Isa 19:16–25. This passage begins with a depiction of the Egyptians as fearful of YHWH (vv. 16–17). But then it prophesies the appearance of Hebrew-speaking cities in Egypt (v. 18) and a Yahwistic altar (vv. 19–20). The Lord will reveal himself to Egypt and elicit their worship (vv. 21–22). A highway will link Egypt and Assyria, and both nations will worship YHWH together (v. 23). Israel will join them under the banner, "Blessed be Egypt my people, and Assyria the work of my hands, and Israel my heritage" (19:25). The seed that Israel has planted has grown into a giant tree.

## Isaiah 28–39

With chapters 28 through 32 we have returned to the horizon of the eighth century, while the next three chapters verge on the eschatological. Aside from the first four verses of chapter 28, the only prophecies that can be easily pinned down to a specific time are in chapters 30 and 31, viz., when Judah under Hezekiah was allied with Egypt against Assyria. The other prophecies would fit into the reign of Hezekiah fine, so we can regard them as such.[10]

*Chapter 28*

Only two furtive verses of promise appear in this chapter: after the condemnation of Ephraim's rulers, called a "proud crown" (RSV) or "proud garland" (NRSV) for their decadence. The charge of drunkenness and gluttony probably are to be taken literally. Verses 5–6 reverse the judgment: YHWH will be the "crown" or "garland" "of glory" and "diadem of beauty" to the "remnant of his

---

10. Isaiah 28:1–4 belongs to the last decade, probably, of the northern kingdom. Williamson, *The Book Called Isaiah*, 162–64, 186–87, suggests that Isa 14:28, "the year King Ahaz died," was once the heading for the original collection of Isaiah's prophecies from Hezekiah's reign. Aside from the anomalies like 28:1–4 and 17:1–9, this thesis sounds plausible.

## Redeeming Judgment

people." Verses 7–8 revert back to drunken officials, with priest and prophet singled out. They could be Judean rather than Israelite. Whether the image of drunkenness is literal or figurative, the charge is that they "err in vision, / they stumble in giving judgment" (v. 7).

We have a couple of prophecies of judgment in 28:9–22. Each contains a declaration of how Judah can be saved. Verse 12 states, "This is rest; / give rest to the weary; / and this is repose," but they would not hearken. Therefore they are going to be "taught" by those speaking an alien tongue (v. 11).

Verse 16 is another one of these "saving alternatives":

> See, I am laying in Zion a foundation stone,
>  A tested stone,
> a precious cornerstone, a sure foundation:
>  "One who trusts will not panic." (v. 16)

We might characterize this "foundation" as a principle for behavior. The measure of whether the people follow it is the quality of their life together: "I will make justice the line, / and righteousness the plummet" (v. 17a). The rulers of Jerusalem have evidently entered into a pact "with the devil," so to speak (see v. 15). They are called "scoffers" (v. 14, also v. 22).

Perhaps the parable in vv. 23–29 is meant to instruct these scoffers. The farmer cultivates his land in a reasonable sequence—plowing, harrowing, and seeding. Each kind of crop is located in its own plot, presumably calibrated to its needs for sun, water, fertility, and protection from wind. When it comes to harvest, each crop is harvested in its own way. Twice the farmer is said to be taught by God (vv. 26, 29). This is an argument in favor of divine providence. Taken in context, it would indicate that the Lord's judgment serves his purpose, it is according to plan.

### Chapter 29

Isaiah's prophecies are typically rather transparent and down to earth, but he also has a poetic, visionary side. Isaiah 29:1–8 is one of those passages. In v. 1 the prophet identifies Jerusalem, called Ariel, as the city "where David encamped." Of course, he actually settled there and made it the capital city of the kingdom. Isaiah, however, wants "encamped" because in v. 3 he says, "I the Lord will encamp against you; I will besiege you with towers and raise siege works against you." (YHWH has identified himself with the army assaulting

Jerusalem.) The people will be in such desperate straits that they can be described as ghosts speaking from the ground:

> Then deep from the earth you shall speak,
> > from low in the dust your words shall come;
> > your voice shall come from the ground like the voice of a ghost,
> > > and your speech shall whisper out of the dust. (v. 4)

Then suddenly, as an answer to the moaning and lamentation of the people, the besieging army becomes like dust and chaff caught by the wind:

> You will be visited by the LORD of hosts
> > with thunder and earthquake and great noise,
> > > with whirlwind and tempest, and the flame of a devouring fire. (v. 6)

Then the image changes again: the nations which fight against Ariel "shall be like a dream, a vision of the night" (v. 7). Then in the next verse it is no longer the besieged that are waking from a bad dream, but the besiegers:

> Just as when a hungry man dreams he is eating
> > and awakes with his hunger not satisfied, . . .
> > so shall the multitude of all the nations be
> > > that fight against Mount Zion. (v. 8, RSV)

In content, this visionary prophecy recalls Isa 1:21–28. First the city experiences judgment, but this turns into salvation. What 29:1–8 lacks is an indictment explaining why YHWH is bringing judgment on his people, and a portrayal of the transformation of the city into the place it ought to be. These lacunae are filled by surrounding prophecies.

In Isa 29:9–16 there are what appears to be a series of short prophecies of judgment, though the divine punishments tend toward the ironic. Two of these offer a sharp critique of Judean religion at the time:

> Because these people draw near with their mouths
> > and honor me with their lips,
> > while their hearts are far from me,
> > > and their worship of me is a human commandment learned by rote. (v. 13)

Isaiah sees the officially orthodox religion going "through the motions," as we say. This is custom, not conviction. The next woe condemns the people, who are creatures, for thinking they can hide their motives and plans from God, their Creator (v. 15). Instead of a sentence, Isaiah teaches his audience theology: "Shall the potter be regarded as the clay? / Should the thing made say of its maker, 'He did not make me'"? (v. 16). The people subject to judgment are precisely those who think they can hide their devious ways from God as well as humans.

These short judgments are followed up with an assurance of a day when things are set to right (vv. 17–21): the deaf shall hear the words of the scroll, the blind shall see, the meek and needy will experience joy, while tyrants and scoffers shall disappear.

## Isaiah 30–32

The first two of these chapters begin with Hebrew *hoi*, best translated "woe." In each case the woe is directed against Judean leaders for allying with Egypt and even purchasing its military support. The Judean rulers are warned: "everyone comes to shame through a people that cannot profit them" (30:5a). The attached prophecy ends:

> For Egypt's help is worthless and empty,
> > therefore I have called her,
> > "Rahab who sits still." (30:7)

When the crisis comes, Egypt will refuse to intervene because in doing so risks its own independence.

The people want to hear only prophecy that comforts and encourages (30:9–11). Such a body politic will reap what it deserves, collapsing of its own falsehood. The policy approved by YHWH is well known:

> In returning and rest you shall be saved;
> > in quietness and in trust shall be your strength,"
> but you refused. (v. 15)

Their punishment will be humiliating defeat. The city of Jerusalem will end up "a flagstaff on the top of a mountain, / like a signal on a hill" (30:17b).[11]

Isaiah 31:1–3 are Isaiah's final condemnation of the pro-Egyptian policy of Hezekiah's reign. It is noteworthy that he does not single out the king, as he does Ahaz. Perhaps he attributes the policy of the pious Hezekiah to the counselors and officials around him. In any case, these woes and regular condemnations of the policy give us a perspective on Sennacherib's destruction of

---

11. Isa 1:8 uses a similar image to describe the result of Sennacherib's assault on Judah.

the countryside and siege of Jerusalem, told in Isaiah 36–37: the condemned policy leads the people to brink of annihilation.

Isaiah also provides a profound theological perspective on this policy:

> [Woe] to those who go down to Egypt for help
> and who rely on horses,
> who trust in chariots because they are many
> and in horsemen because they are very strong,
> but do not look to the Holy One of Israel
> or consult the LORD. (v. 1)

Of course, Hezekiah's administration would have "consulted the Lord," but it was a spokesman for him who prophesied "smooth things" (30:10). The very focus of the policy was cursed: it built up as much power as it could, then called upon YHWH to support it. The policymakers should recognize that they have things upside down:

> The Egyptians are human, and not God;
> and their horses are flesh, and not spirit.
> When the Lord stretches out his hand,
> the helper will stumble, and he who is helped will fall,
> and they will all perish together. (31:3)

Here a powerful monotheistic vision flashes before our eyes.

Isaiah 30:19–33 is a collection of prophecies of salvation. It begins with an assurance that YHWH intends to show grace to his people. Verses 19–22 state the meaning of judgment: "Though the Lord may give you the bread of adversity and the water of affliction, yet your Teacher will not hide himself any more, but your eyes shall see your Teacher. And when you turn to the right or . . . left, you ears shall hear a word behind you, saying, 'This is the way; walk in it'" (30:20–21). Nature's bounty is promised in vv. 23–26. Verses 27–28 are a poetic depiction of a divine epiphany; God comes to judge the nations. The set comes to a close with judgment of Assyria over which the Israelites rejoice (vv. 29–33).

Isaiah 31:4–9 promise salvation. The Lord is like a lion guarding his kill (v. 4); Jerusalem is the "kill" in this strange analogy. Then YHWH becomes a raptor circling the city (v. 5). The last two verses of the chapter promise the destruction of Assyria and deliverance of Jerusalem in uncanny terms:

> And the Assyrian shall fall by a sword, not of mortals;
> And a sword, not of humans, shall devour him. (v. 8a)

*Redeeming Judgment*

This foreshadows the account of deliverance in chapter 37.

It would seem that chapters 30 and 31 are composed analogically, beginning with judgment for a misguided foreign policy, and ending with salvation. Chapter 31 continues into the following chapter, which offers a portrait of salvation. The first line sounds as though we are being offered another "messianic" vision, but then the king is joined by the leadership cadre:

> Behold, a king will reign in righteousness,
>> and princes will rule with justice.
> Each will be like a hiding place from the wind. (Isa 32:1–2a)

These officials are compared to shelters from storms. The prophecy then promises the reversal of the call of Isaiah:

> Then the eyes of those who see will not be closed,
>> and the ears of those who hear will hearken.
> The mind of the rash will have good judgment,
>> and the tongue of the stutterers
>> will speak readily and distinctly. (vv. 3–4, RSV)

The passage is a prophecy of healing not of the handicapped, but of those who willfully refuse to use their senses. When he is called, Isaiah is told "to make the heart of this people fat, and their ears heavy, and shut their eyes" (Isa 6:10). That will be undone now.

This will be the "healing" of the citizens upon which the nation depends for sound policy and performance. Those who are by nature or disposition irresponsible or self-centered—the "fools" and "villains"—should not (and will not) be given honor and power (32:5). The rest of this prophecy becomes a lesson in the depredations of fools and villains, and the virtues of the noble (vv. 6–8).

The rest of the chapter can be read as one prophecy. It starts out as a prophecy of judgment "clothed" in a call to lament (vv. 9–14). The women are called to mourn in vv. 9 and 11, and what they are to mourn is described in vv. 10, 11, 12, and 13a. Agriculture will decline and the cities be depopulated. Then the spirit of God will be "poured out" and the wilderness will become fruitful, and justice and righteousness will pervade the community. The last verse that makes much sense promises peace and security:

> My people will abide in a peaceful habitation,
>> in secure dwellings, and in quiet resting places. (v. 18, RSV)

This final prophecy, indeed the whole chapter, falls within the kind of hopes that people frequently entertain. They are within the possibilities of history, though such ideal conditions seldom last for long periods of time. The king is a fallible human, but one who rules well and has the support of the leadership class. I mention this fact because the book of Isaiah promises a future king that transcends historical possibility and international judgment, and restoration that also exceeds the historical. The passages we have looked at so far are much more sober and realistic. But note, the section has not come to a conclusion; chapters 33—35 do venture beyond the promises offered in chapters 29—32.

## Isaiah 33-35

The section begins with a woe against an unidentified "destroyer." The woe doesn't seem connected to what went before or comes afterward. If we take it as referring to one of the two empires that have been condemned in the book of Isaiah (Assyria or Babylon), we could say that the destruction of the tyrannical empire is a prelude to a new saving order.

The rest of chapter 33 has been identified as a liturgy. It begins with a prayer (vv. 2-4), spoken by "us"—including the reading audience. Without any indication of a change of speakers, there is a praise of the Lord's power to save (vv. 5-6). The speaker must be a prophet who speaks to us as "you." Then we hear a cry of lamentation over the decadence and decay of the times (vv. 7-9). To this lament the Lord answers, "Now I will arise" (v. 10); the next two verses seem to be the Lord's assessment of human efforts (vv. 11-12). The Lord's promise of salvation begins in v. 13 with a call of those both far and near to hear. The "sinners" in Zion are afraid, but those who live an upright life should take refuge in it (vv. 14-16). Being in the temple city, one will "see the king" (v. 17). Foreign oppressors will no longer be around to disturb the life of the citizens of Jerusalem (vv. 18-19). Now the people enjoy a secure, festive city in which the divine majesty will dwell (vv. 20-21). The people will be able to affirm, indeed the readers can do so now—

> For the LORD is our judge, the LORD is our ruler,
> the LORD is our king; he will save us. (v. 22)

Chapter 34 comes as something of a shock after we have arrived at the idyllic conclusion of chapter 33. In chapter 34 the nations are summoned to court. The first four verses describe a violent scene of retribution. Beginning in

v. 5, Edom seems to be singled out for divine assault. Much of the violence is against domestic animals. By the end of the chapter, the country has returned to the wild.

Chapter 35 returns to the message of salvation. Its similarity to Isaiah 40–55 in style and mood has struck many scholars; if it is not composed by the same poet as is Second Isaiah, it at least functions to foreshadow the chapters to come. The poem begins with a preparation for the appearance of God. The natural environment will break out in spring-like verdure, while humans must be strengthened to endure God's presence (vv. 1–4). The saving work of God will be manifested in the healing of the blind, lame, and speechless (vv. 5–6a) and the watering of the desert (vv. 6b–7). A highway—the Holy Way—will run through the newly watered desert—a highway reserved for those who are ritually clean (v. 8); dangerous animals will be kept away (v. 9). This way is for the people of the Lord to return to Zion by v. 10.

One might debate whether the portrait of salvation in chapters 33 and 35 reach eschatological dimensions. We are in the realm of poetry, and the style of these chapters may magnify rather natural, ordinary expectations. Nevertheless, the mood created soars above the everyday, and intimates a radical change in the human condition. Statements like, "everlasting joy shall be upon their heads; / they shall obtain joy and gladness, / and sorrow and sighing shall flee away" (35:10b) fit the description of eschatological vision. These chapters reach forward to the message to come in Isaiah 40–66.

## Isaiah 36–39

These four chapters are a somewhat different rendition of the narrative of Sennacherib's invasion, Hezekiah's illness and recovery, and Hezekiah's reception of Babylonian envoys that is told in 2 Kings 18:13—20:19. It makes no difference to our interpretation of the chapters whether the Kings version is the original.[12]

Chapters 36–37 play an important role in the book of Isaiah. They provide an historical context for many of Isaiah's prophecies from the reign of Hezekiah. These chapters could be said to match the role of Isaiah 7–9, the "Isaiah Memoir." In particular, they indicate what the condemnations of the alliance of Judah with Egypt (30:1–7, 15–17; 31:1–3; also chapter 20) is about, and what Isaiah fears. Their alliance and Hezekiah's withholding tribute to

---

12. See Williamson, *The Book Called Isaiah*, 189–211, for a discussion of the evidence.

Assyria at Sennacherib's ascension to the throne nearly brings about the elimination of the nation.

The same narrative also explains why Isaiah reverses his message of divine judgment by the agency of Assyria. Actually he does not reverse it so much as commute the death sentence on Jerusalem. Ultimately, that is a necessary step in the Lord's plan: there has to be a remnant to carry on as the people of God. This is not stated in so many words, however.[13] Rather, Assyria is condemned for its arrogance and blasphemy:

> Whom have you mocked and reviled?
> ...
> The Holy One of Israel!
>     By your servants you have mocked the Lord
> ...
> Because you have raged against me
>     and your arrogance has come to my ears,
> I will put my hook in your nose
>     and my bit in your mouth;
> and I will turn you back
>     on the way by which you came. (Isa 37:23, 24, 29)

The judgment of Assyria is not, however, an ad hoc decision of YHWH; according to Isa 37:26, it is a part of the divine plan: "Have you not heard / that I determined it long ago? / I planned from days of old / what now I bring to pass, / that you shall make fortified cities / crash into heaps of ruins" (Isa 37:26). This verse evidences the same thinking as Isa 14:24–27, which states emphatically that "as I have planned . . . I will break the Assyrian in my land" (vv. 24–25).

How the Assyrian army is said to have been "overthrown" (Isa 37:36–37) explains the description of judgment in 31:8–9: "Then the Assyrian shall fall by a sword, not of mortals; / and a sword, not of humans, shall devour him" (v. 8a). The use of dream imagery in 29:7–8 also fits the accounts well. Isaiah has been condemning military armament (30:15–17); this deliverance seems to confirm him.

The two chapters that follow the account of Sennacherib's siege of Jerusalem seem to fit better in the years before it. Christopher Seitz argues that the story of Hezekiah's healing from leprosy is a parallel to the deliverance

---

13. I think it is alluded to in the expression, "it is in his mind to destroy, and cut off nations not a few" (10:7).

*Redeeming Judgment*

of Jerusalem: Hezekiah is condemned to death, but he is delivered in answer to his prayer. Jerusalem too seems condemned to death but was delivered in answer to the king's prayer.[14]

Chapter 39 tells the story of the visit of a delegation from a Babylonian ruler named Marduk-apal-iddina. Isaiah condemns Hezekiah for showing the envoys his storehouses. It probably is a gesture sealing an alliance to withhold tribute from Assyria. That would indicate that the transaction took place before Sennacherib's attack on either rebel city.

Why it is located after the Assyrian siege is anyone's guess, but in the book of Isaiah the chapter is a preface to Isaiah 40; that is, it predicts the Babylonian exile: "Behold, the days are coming, when all that is in your house, and that which your fathers have stored up till this day, shall be carried to Babylon; nothing shall be left, says the Lord. And some of your own sons, who are born to you, shall be taken away" (39:6–7). Hezekiah, oddly, takes comfort from Isaiah's prophecy, but that does not detract from the importance of the prediction for the reading of the book.

## Review of the Argument

When Isaiah is called (chapter 6), he is commissioned to pronounce judgment until the land is desolate and the people gone. It is important to see that his numerous individual oracles of judgment are simply embodiments of one message. Judgment is what Isaiah was authorized to speak, and all that he speaks contributes to that one message. Even the oracles promising salvation are extensions of his message of judgment if they are delivered with divine authority.

The call itself states that the message could produce repentance and healing (that the hearers might "turn and be healed"). The people would have had to admit their guilt and have undergone a conversion of heart. This is precisely what Isaiah offers them in 1:18–20. They will have to, by the aid of Isaiah's message, see, hear, and comprehend rightly.

Yet Isaiah is commissioned to dull their minds, stop their ears, and shut their eyes. Why would YHWH commission him to seal them in their sin? It cannot be that Isaiah is to deliberately mislead them: God would not use falsehood to entrap his people. Isaiah can only "tell it like it is." His message will have a deleterious effect because the people are in such bondage to their

---

14. Seitz, *Zion's Final Destiny*.

sin that the truth only hardens their hearts. Their instinctive response to the prophetic message of judgment is the opposite of what it should be.

## *The Phoenix:* Redeeming *Judgment*

An element running through the judgments indicates what Isaiah's audience should be doing, and contrasting it to their comportment (leading to judgment). I just mentioned Isa 1:18–20, which states clearly that Judah could be redeemed if only it could admit is guilt. Isaiah 5:7 deciphers the parable thus: the sour or wild grapes yielded by the vineyard are bloodshed and cries of anguish; the Lord had expected justice and righteousness. During the siege of Jerusalem by Aram and Israel, Ahaz is promised their defeat, but what happens to him depends upon his response to their threat: "If you do not stand firm in faith, you shall not stand at all" (7:9). The sign given—the birth of Immanuel—will be hope for those who do trust in YHWH (see 8:13–14). Isaiah 22:11 indicates what the people didn't do when they fortified their city: "But you did not look to him that did it or have regard for him who planned it long ago." Isa 28:12 counsels those in crisis to do what they can do: "This is rest; give rest to the weary." Let God take care of the military crisis; do not try to control events. Isaiah 28:16 has the most elaborate promise of all: "I am laying in Zion a foundation stone / . . . / 'One who trusts will not panic.'" The test of people's clinging to this saving certainty is whether they maintain justice and righteousness (28:17a). A flood will sweep through, drowning all who are not anchored to the rock. Isaiah 30:15 reminds us that Isaiah counsels his people to avoid alliances and military conflicts at all costs: "In returning and rest you shall be saved; / in quietness and trust shall be your strength." The people, however, insist on "riding on horses," which will result in their being routed.

We could add to this list of rejected truths, but we have located enough to establish our point: in every crisis, there is a course of action that would lead to salvation, but Isaiah's people insist on taking their fate into their own hands. Isaiah's faithful Judean would learn to wait, to allow God to shape history, but to do what could be done to give rest, supply need, show kindness, end exploitation.

Though judgment is inevitable, YHWH's saving purpose cannot be thwarted, even by human sin. If the people of God insist on their own way, they will have to suffer. Yet, this judgment will purge the community of its wicked, transform those indifferent or timid, and give leadership to the inspired. The scenario of redemptive judgment is offered in the very first chapter of Isaiah. The once lovely city of Jerusalem is pervaded with violence, corruption, and exploitation (1:21–23). The Lord will judge the city, purge it of evildoers, and restore trustworthy judges and counselors (vv. 24–26). Isaiah sums up: "Zion shall be redeemed by justice, / and those who are in her who repent, by righteousness" (v. 27).

On the one hand, Isa 29:1–8 tells much the same story, but there is less interest in the redemptive force of judgment, and more in the miraculous reversal itself. On the other hand, a little later in the same chapter we find a promise of hearing to the deaf, sight to the blind, and supplies to the needy (29:17–19); the tyrants and scoffers will be purged (vv. 20–21). In Isa 30:19–24, we read an explanation for God's judgment within his plan of salvation. Isaiah 32:1–8 would fit nicely right after 1:28: from king to princes to counselors, the leadership of the people will be a shelter from the storm, while fools and villains will reap the harvest of their deeds. The very next prophecy (32:9–20) begins as a call to lament (vv. 9–14), but then heaven sends its spirit, and nature and society are healed: "The effect of righteousness will be peace, / and the result of righteousness, quietness and trust forever" (v. 17). Finally in Isa 33:17–22 we find the hope of restoration and more for the people who have known hardship for a long time. The section begins: "Your eyes will see the king in his beauty." They will remember their oppression as a thing of the past; now they will be independent and enjoy the fruits of their labor (33:18–20). YHWH himself will be their judge, ruler, and king (33:22).

Redemption arising out of judgment seems to be an important component of the composite message of Isaiah 1–39. The prophecies hover between realism and utopianism. Will judgment purge the country of those who would corrupt and exploit it? Certainly not permanently, probably for no more than a generation or two. Humans remain inclined toward evil from their youth (Gen 8:21). Yet we should not abandon the effort to bring justice and peace to our time; at least the configuration of evil will change. Judgment is a necessary component of this fallen world because a victory over wrong serves the divine plan, even if full redemption always remains an unrealized hope.

## Portrayals of Salvation

Now we come to the other type of prophecy of salvation—the portrayal of salvation. These promises are of a different order: there is little about the transition to the new, and a good deal about the configuration of the ideal order. The judgment that entered into the inauguration of the new order is only hinted at. Hence, such promises would have no place in a book about judgment if it were not their part in the message as a whole.

Isaiah 2:1–4 concerns the future role of Jerusalem. Nothing explains how it will achieve this status, but the preceding unit in 1:21–28 prophesies judgment leading to redemption of the holy city. Isaiah 2:2–4 now completes the story of salvation. Verse 2 describes the city's elevation to greatness as an elevation in altitude. All nations will now "go up" to this exalted city. Their objective will be to learn the ways and law of YHWH (v. 3), the God who dwells in the midst of Jerusalem. YHWH will also arbitrate conflicts among nations (v. 4). The peoples of the world will renounce war and pound their weapons into agricultural implements.

This beautiful little passage articulates a number of characteristic Isaianic themes: Zion, universalism, law, and peace through arbitration. The book of Isaiah offers the most universalistic message of any Israelite prophet. Moreover, its sober images of peace-making and governing by intrinsic authority are also hallmarks of the book.

Isaiah 19:16–25 exhibits the themes of universalism and peacemaking. It begins with a description of Egypt at some future date, but then speaks of the conversion of that nation to YHWH (19:19–22). The passage concludes with an "alliance" between Egypt and Assyria, both of which now share the status of election with Israel (vv. 23–25).

*Messianic Prophecies*

Hugh Williamson observes that Isa 7:1–17; 8:23—9:7; and 11:1–10 are well integrated into their contexts in Isaiah and are mutually reinforcing. Christians have always taken these texts as messianic. Various efforts have been made by critical scholars to deny the passages' messianic character or Isaianic authorship.[15] Whatever their original meaning, they now invite a full-scale eschatological interpretation. Isaiah 9:7 promises a reign lasting forever. Of course, one could "fill in" in the idea of a dynasty, but the text itself invites an attribution of endless life to this ruler. Isaiah 11:6–9 associates a transformation of nature with the reign of the Davidic king. Taken together, the three passages (Isa 7:1–14; 9:1–7; 11:1–9) fuel the eschatological imagination.

It is worth repeating that these passages leave the identity of the Davidic king a mystery. He will come, evidently, from another line of the family from

---

15. E.g., Mowinckel, *He That Cometh*.

*Redeeming Judgment*

the one that has ruled Judah since David. This allows interpreters to look in many directions, for the royal blood was probably flowing in the veins of thousands by the end of the monarchy.

The context of these promises is a series of judgments on rulers. Ahaz will suffer for his lack of faith and cynical subordination to Assyria (see chapters 7–8). The rulers of the kingdom of Israel are trying to save themselves by bravado (see 9:8–21). The Assyrian ruler is arrogant, brutal, and insatiably avaricious (see 10:5–19). The king of the Lord's choosing, who will replace these human powers, will be faithful, righteous, and just, with a divinely illuminated mind. He will not only be named Prince of Peace, but he will exercise authority without using force. Perhaps that goes beyond the evidence: the passages simply do not depict him using force, and the activity that he is described as exercising is, according to Isa 11:3b–4, judicial. I would read v. 4b as a judicial sentencing (Isa 11:4, RSV):

> And he shall smite the earth with the rod of his mouth,
> > and with the breath of his lips he shall slay the wicked.

There is no reason to believe that he needs to be violent to have a sword-like effect by speaking judgment.

There are hints, perhaps, of a lawgiving power in, "of the increase of his government and of peace / there will be no end" (Isa 9:7a, RSV). However, in Israelite theology, the law is given in divine revelation; it is not even mediated by a king, but communicated by Moses.[16]

## Concluding Reflection

It surely is a mistake to divide the message of Isaiah rigidly between judgment in chapters 1–39 and salvation in 40–55. True, Isaiah of Jerusalem was commissioned to proclaim judgment. This is the message that predominates in large parts of Isaiah 1–39. However, again and again we see judgment transformed into redemption. The people of Israel may face a harsh future, but it is a future that fulfills YHWH's original purpose in calling the nation. Moreover, the salvation slated for Israel is time and again inclusive of the nations. The destruction of the great empires dominating the Near East during the eighth through fifth centuries BCE is for the good of subject populations. Yet, even the empires have a future in the eschatological denouement of history.

---

16. In an office all his own, but more prophetic than royal.

One can see that the message of Isaiah 1–39 has the potential for completion in the message of salvation and release from exile. The message of Second Isaiah will be another act, as it were, in the drama that began with the call of Isaiah.

# 16

## The Book of Isaiah II
(Isaiah 40–55)

SETTING ISAIAH 40–66 OFF from chapters 1–39 seems rather contradictory to the thesis that the book was designed to be read as one message of God. I have not changed my opinion that it was designed to be one message. Dividing the chapters is for practical purposes. A chapter on the whole book of Isaiah would have been too long in proportion to our other chapters; it had to be split in thirds.

Even if we had kept them together, it would have been necessary to characterize chapters 40–55 and 56–66 separately. Our position is not "precritical." We regard it as beyond serious need of argument that chapters 40–55 belong to a prophet located in Babylon among the Judean exiles between 550 and 538 BCE,[1] and that chapters 56–66 derive from the disciples of the Babylonian prophet; the disciples (but not their master) returned to Judah after Cyrus assumed control of the Babylonian Empire.

The unity of Isaiah must be discovered by interpretation, rather like a judge in the common law tradition must discover the collective force of that legal tradition vis-à-vis a particular subject. The Isaianic authors and editors aspired to a greater degree of unity than the rulings of common law, but the interpretive task remains much the same.

The prophet who authored what is known as Second Isaiah aspired to pass on Isaiah's message to a new generation; the author thought that YHWH's

---

1. Actually, Seitz, *Word without End*, 130–49, and elsewhere, raises questions about the Babylonian location of the prophet; hence, our description as "beyond serious argument" is an overstatement.

word spoken through Isaiah had the capacity to be applied to a new exigency. Isaiah of Jerusalem, in a sense, foresaw that exigency. After all, the eighth-century prophet pronounced the judgment, which was understood to have been fulfilled in the Babylonian exile. He had also promised salvation as the culmination of judgment. Other prophets, to be sure, had "updated" the message of the eighth-century prophets, but Isaiah had a message that still lived on. Second Isaiah was an heir to the prophets of the Judean exile, Jeremiah and Ezekiel, but the heir chose to hide his or her message in the book of Isaiah.

The chapters that have been passed on to us from the prophet have distinctive literary and intellectual qualities. We have already discussed Williamson's linkages between Second and First Isaiah. Now we should look at the literary qualities of the chapters themselves. Several of my teachers argued that the chapters are deliberately, elaborately designed.[2] They are not a collection of independent oracles but one "epic-length" work. The only passage in the classical prophets like it is Ezekiel 40–48, though those chapters are prose and linked together much less elaborately.

Within Isaiah 40–55, there is one major division, viz., chapters 40–48 are to be separated from chapters 49–55. Within these units Muilenburg and Westermann found "poems," units like Isa 40:12–31 with a connected sequence and a beginning and ending.[3] Westermann took the scattered calls to praise as indications of breaks, e.g., 42:10–12. We will break up our analysis along these lines, though adjacent units, which cover similar material and have a similar form, will be combined.

We are going to discover that the poems have recurring scenes and subjects; they resemble what might be called leitmotifs, or themes (like a musical theme), which are varied when repeated. When we come across a theme for the first time, it can be examined and related to later variations; subsequent mentions should be primarily for recall. That at least seems to be a reasonable way to work our way through Second Isaiah.

Chapters 56–66 are not as deliberately designed as Second Isaiah. There are poems of chapter length, but no overall structure. Indeed, one of our tasks will be to discover why the chapters are in the order that they are.

---

2. Muilenburg, "The Book of Isaiah, Ch. 40–66," 381–773; and Westermann, *Isaiah 40–66*.

3. Muilenburg, ibid.; and Westermann, ibid.

*Redeeming Judgment*

## Isaiah 40–48

The first eleven verses of chapter 40 are commonly identified as the prologue. It has characteristics that suggest that we have a "hidden" prophetic call. The first two verses address a plurality—messengers of God, divine or human,[4] and the announcement of a world-wide epiphany of the Lord (40:3–5) is meant for the whole nation, but then the prophet—presumably—is commissioned to speak the "word" of the Lord:

> A voice says, "Cry!"
>     And [I] said, "What shall I cry?"
> "All flesh is grass . . .
> The grass withers, the flower fades;
>     but the word of our God will stand for ever" (vv. 6, 8)

This is indeed rather elliptical; the prophet is not told at this time to pass on the message in 40:1–5, but rather how secure the word of the Lord is. By implication, human words die along with their speakers, while the divine word is as permanent as the eternal God. A similar affirmation is made at the end of Second Isaiah, viz., 55:10–12. In the latter passage, the efficacy of the divine word is highlighted.

We already learn from the first two verses that the prophet's message is the end of the exile. The people have undergone the appropriate punishment, and now they will be liberated from the "incarceration" of the exile. This isn't exactly forgiveness; the people have "paid" for their sins. Where forgiveness comes in—and it does—is restoration to full relationship to YHWH. The covenant is reinstated, election is reaffirmed. Such things will come later in these chapters.

The freeing of the exiles will not only concern them; their return to their homeland will be a worldwide epiphany of YHWH. We actually don't learn that the way through the desert is for Israel as well as YHWH until chapter 41. Isaiah 40:3–5 focus on the universal scope of YHWH's work for Israel; this is a subject that will be developed in subsequent chapters: we will call it the "new exodus."

With vv. 9–11, we encounter an interpretive problem. The RSV and NRSV have the message addressed to Zion/Jerusalem:

---

4. If we follow Seitz in discerning an address of the "divine council"—see Seitz, *Word without End*, 179–82.

> Get you up to a high mountain,
> > O Zion, herald of good tidings.
> Lift up your voice with strength,
> > O Jerusalem, herald of good tidings.

I prefer the translation mentioned in the footnotes to the NRSV: "O herald of good tidings to Zion . . . O herald of good tidings to Jerusalem." In this case, it would be an address to the prophet. The message of the herald, in either case, is a subtle theological dialectic:

> See, the Lord God comes with might,
> > and his arm rules for him;
> his reward is with him,
> > and his recompense before him.
> He will feed his flock like a shepherd;
> > he will gather the lambs in his arms,
> and carry them in his bosom,
> > and gently lead [the ewes with lambs]. (vv. 10–11)

The first of the two verses describes the power of God in his intervention. This is not a description of a divine attribute, viz., omnipotence, but of the divine intervention; he has the power to reward and recompense. In the case at hand, the "reward" is not merit, but simply that the city/nation has served its time. The second verse dramatizes YHWH's compassion and tenderness. On the flock's way back through the desert, it will need more than "freedom."

Williamson notes a number of links between the verses of the prologue and Isaiah 1–39.[5] Second Isaiah believes that the message of salvation proclaimed by Isaiah of Jerusalem, a message that was indissolubly connected with judgment, was now taking place. Now is the time promised long ago. The prophet did not, however, simply conclude this by rational deduction; he or she had been empowered by YHWH to announce it. This is the basis of the unity of the book.

## Isaiah 40:12–31

The subject and mood of the chapter change in v. 12: the prophet addresses a question to the people. It is actually a rhetorical question, because the answer is in the nation's religious creed. Indeed, the question itself belongs in the realm of descriptive praise. It is God the Creator who is being described. The

5. See Williamson, *The Book Called Isaiah*, 30–93.

question is, why does the prophet seek to elicit a confession of YHWH from his exilic audience? The answer comes in v. 27:

> Why do you say, O Jacob,
>> and speak, O Israel,
> "My way is hidden from the Lord,
>> and my right is disregarded by my God"?

The people are complaining in their communal laments that YHWH hasn't protected them the way he should. Either he did not see what had happened to them, or he had ignored their plight. It isn't quite articulated, but they may also be doubting his power to do much. I suggest the latter because the praise in vv. 12–26 affirms YHWH's power and incomparability. The prophet has sought to assuage any doubts of divine power by his celebration of YHWH's power in and over creation: Everything that is has YHWH as its source, and his power and glory surpasses it all. The nations—that loom so large to the exiles—are insignificant to him. The Lord overthrows human power at will.

The praise of the Creator has two special passages. One rejects idols because they do not measure up to him (vv. 18–20), and the other rejects any analogy between God and the host of heaven (vv. 25–26). Stars are as much the Lord's creatures as animals or mountains.

In response to the people's complaint against God, the prophet affirms God's eternal power and its availability to humans. We know that this prophet does not believe that the people have suffered because of some failure of YHWH. He is going to argue that the suffering is an expression of divine concern—of divine judgment. But the Lord is still a source of strength, of endurance and hope.

> The Lord is the everlasting God,
>> the Creator of the ends of the earth.
> He does not faint or grow weary,
>> his understanding is unsearchable.
> He gives power to the faint,
>> and strengthens the powerless.
>> . . .
> those who wait for the Lord shall renew their strength,
>> and they shall mount up with wings like eagles,
> they shall run and not be weary,
>> they shall walk and not faint. (vv. 28b–29, 31)

This is an assurance of ongoing support, not divine intervention.

The prophet has incorporated the creation faith and given it prophetic power, something our prophets of judgment did not do.[6] Creation has to do with the permanent conditions of life, and the prophets of judgment are concerned with specific situations. However, the exilic prophet could see the need for a foundation of certitude for the people.

In chapter 45, the prophet is able to draw on creation to support his specific message. After the Lord announces his "anointment" of Cyrus to do his purpose (vv. 1–6), he asserts the monotheistic principle:

> I form light and create darkness,
>> I make weal and create woe;
>> I the LORD do all these things. (45:7)

The Judean exiles must accept the fact that the Lord is free to employ a world conqueror as his instrument of salvation for his people. This conqueror doesn't even know YHWH (vv. 4, 5), though the prophet believes he will (v. 3). A few verses later, the Lord confronts the resistance of the Israelites with a woe:

> Woe to [you] who strives with [your] Maker,
>> an earthen vessel with the potter
>
> . . .
>
> Woe to anyone who says to a father, "What are you begetting?"
>> or to a woman, "With what are you in travail?" (vv. 9, 10, RSV)

Then the prophet addresses the issue directly:

> Will you question me about my children,
>> or command me concerning the work of my hands?
>
> . . .
>
> I have aroused him[7] in righteousness,
>> and I will make all his paths straight;
>
> he shall build my city
>> and set my exiles free,
>
> not for price or reward . . . (vv. 11, 13)

Just for good measure, the prophet draws on the creation message again in 45:18–19. It is clear that the prophet expects, not only that the doctrine of

---

6. Von Rad, "The Theological Problem of the Old Testament Doctrine of Creation," 131–43.

7. NRSV "Cyrus."

creation will assure his people that their life is secure in God's hands, but also that they allow God to do "new things."

## Isaiah 41:1—42:12.

This poem shifts from creation to history—Near Eastern history of the sixth century BCE, to be exact. The poem begins with the call of a trial or debate:

> Listen to me in silence, O coastlands;
> > let the peoples renew their strength;
> let them approach, then let them speak;
> > let us together draw near for judgment. (41:1)

Although Israelite prophets did not have the power to convene international assemblies, they did evoke such settings in their poetry.[8] Isa 41:1 extends that sort of scene painting to include all humans. This will be a recurring scene in chapters 40–45. It calls to mind the philosopher Hegel's dictum that "world history is the world's court of justice." YHWH convenes a debate or trial to determine who has empowered the world conqueror—unnamed as yet—to succeed. It is actually a debate with other gods, but that does not come out yet. YHWH claims to be the sovereign ruler of history:

> Who has performed and done this,
> > calling the generations from the beginning?
> I, the LORD, am first,
> > and will be with the last. (v. 4)

This claim seems to be unsubstantiated, though the One who can call himself "the first . . . with the last" is a good candidate. But before the debate can be joined, the humans respond to this conqueror. First we get a glimpse of the nations, near and far. These peoples see the need for supernatural intervention. So they build idols. Somehow the image will be the body for a god. The makers must exhibit courage and strength; they must believe in their project and invest their deity with qualities that persuade others.

The Israelite exiles are not engaged in that sort of enterprise. The Lord takes the initiative to reassure them:

> But you, Israel, my servant,
> > Jacob, whom I have chosen,

---

8. Micah 1:2–4 and 6:1–2, for example, have trials with heaven and earth acting as judges.

> the offspring of Abraham, my friend;
>> you whom I took from the ends of the earth,
> . . .
> saying to you, "You are my servant, I have chosen you
> and not cast you off";
> do not fear, for I am with you,
>> do not be afraid, for I am your God;
> I will strengthen you, I will help you,
>> I will uphold you with my victorious right hand. (vv. 8–10)

These are very reassuring words, words meant to keep the exiles calm and patient. The Isaianic tradition has had powerful counsel for believers under pressure. Second Isaiah calls on that in the new situation. These words, and the oracles to follow, take the place of the images the nations are making.

Let's turn to the three oracles of salvation. Why was the assurance not enough? The assurance brings us to the same place we were at the end of chapter 40. This chapter seeks to locate Israel in the movements of history. The promises in vv. 11–13, 14–16, and 17–20 do so. The first is a promise to thwart the efforts of hostile peoples. The divine answer to Israel is,

> For I, the LORD your God,
>> hold your right hand;
> it is I who say to you, "Do not fear,
>> I will help you." (v. 13)

The second oracle is a promise to make the powerless "worm" into a weapon. Actually, the term used is an instrument for threshing; in an odd turn of phrase, the mountains and hills will be made chaff to be blown away by the wind (v. 15). This is about as removed from literal language as one can imagine. The exiles are not a military force, and the metaphor of mountains or hills for enemies alerts the reader to the figurative nature of the statement. Perhaps the mountains are barriers to returning home. If so, that would feed directly into the third oracle, a "new exodus" passage. It begins with a promise to answer the "poor and needy," who become in vv. 18–19 the mass of Judean exiles returning through the desert to their homeland:

> I will open rivers on the bare heights,
>> and fountains in the midst of the valleys;
> I will make the wilderness a pool of water,
>> and the dry land springs of water.

## Redeeming Judgment

> . . .
> I will set in the desert the cypress.

The miraculous transformation of the desert for the returning exiles has a revelatory purpose:

> That all may see and know,
>   all may consider and understand,
> that the hand of the LORD has done this,
>   the Holy One of Israel has created it. (v. 20)

This verse recalls the epiphanic announcement in Isa 40:3–5. Now the human subjects on the pilgrimage, Israel, are located in the picture. This epiphany should demonstrate to the world that YHWH is the one and only God.

The court scene returns in 41:21–29. The calls for testimony come from the gods/idols: "Set forth your case[,] . . . / bring your proofs" (v. 21). The Lord then explains to a third party ("us") what their testimony should consist of:

> Tell us the former things
>
> . . .
>
> that we may know their outcome
>
> . . .
>
> Tells us what is to come hereafter,
>   that we may know that you are gods:
> do good, or do harm,
>   that we may be afraid and terrified. (vv. 22b, 23)

These are the criteria that the Lord proposes for demonstrating a reality claim. Does the candidate for deity have a record of interpreting past events accurately, and announcing the events taking place now and in the future? Just for good measure, let the candidate do something—anything—as a sign. The strophe ends with his negative judgment:

> Behold, you are nothing,
>   and your work is nought;
>   an abomination is [anyone] that chooses you. (v. 24, RSV)

Now YHWH sets forth his own case for being God. He repeats the claim he made in Isa 41:4. How do we know that his claim is true? He claims to have declared it beforehand:

> Who declared it from the beginning, so that we might know
> ...
> There is none who declared it, ... none who heard your words. (v. 26)

Only YHWH has declared it: "I first have declared it to Zion, and I give to Jerusalem a herald of good tidings" (v. 27). This proof from prophecy has been appropriated by Christian apologists. It requires greater care, and less rigidity, than is often given it. Did Isaiah of Jerusalem really predict the coming of Cyrus? Not in any prophecy in Isaiah 1–39. What one can find are promises of salvation following judgment. The prophetic tradition shapes the perception of life and history in such a way that the nation has a framework to interpret this turn of events. Indeed, it has a category for the Persian conqueror—the instrument of God (earlier filled by Assyria).

The chapter ends with a further assessment of the gods:

> But when I look there is no one;
> > among these there is no counselor
> who, when I ask, gives an answer.
> > No, they are all a delusion. (vv. 28–29)

Gods, images, and human devotees fuse into one another. The idols made by workers in 41:5–7 are probably the "gods" of this trial, while the workers are an "abomination" (v. 24).

The Lord continues to speak in 42:1–4, but the subject has changed. The exposure of the unreality of the gods/idols is finished with 41:28–29. Now the Lord introduces his servant—to the court, which includes all the nations. Whoever this servant is intended to be, he is represented as an individual in this song. The Lord first "takes ownership" of him and describes his calling:

> Here is my servant, whom I uphold,
> > my chosen, in whom my soul delights;
> I have put my spirit upon him,
> > he will bring forth justice to the nations. (42:1)

One might still imagine a king at this point, perhaps even Cyrus. However, the description of the way the servant is going about establishing justice shows him not to be the conqueror, and not any typical ruler:

> He will not cry or lift up his voice,
> > or make it heard in the street;
> a bruised reed he will not break,
> > and a dimly burning wick he will not quench. (vv. 2–3)

*Redeeming Judgment*

In modern times, he would be called a nonviolent activist. Since he does not take recourse to coercion, he constitutes a counterimage to Cyrus.[9] How can YHWH be identified with both? That is the question we must continue to ask as we proceed through this study of Second Isaiah.

The song ends with an assurance that the servant will not quit but continue until successful:

> He will faithfully bring forth justice.
> He will not fail or be discouraged
>> till he has established justice in the earth
>> and the coastlands wait for his law. (vv. 3c–4, RSV)

This is mysterious, because it is unlikely that the servant's crusade will be realized in history; it would certainly not be in the course of one person's life.

The servant song is over in v. 4, but now there is an oracle addressed to the servant, or so it seems. Scholars have frequently relegated the "excurses" at the end of this servant song and those in chapter 49 and 50 to the status of editorial addition.[10] That identification does point out the imperfection of the fit; nevertheless, we can make sense of the final form of the text. Isaiah 42:5 introduces YHWH with hymnic predications of the Creator, and 42:6–9 addresses the servant. The latter section begins with an affirmation of divine election; note how expansive it is:

> I have appointed you a covenant of [the] people,
>> a light of [the] nations. (v. 6)

His mission is aimed at the "imprisoned" (v. 7), which could refer to the Israelite exiles. In any case, that is all that is said about the servant, for now the oracle takes up the identity and purposes of YHWH:

> I am the LORD, that is my name;
>> my glory I give to no other,
>> nor my praise to graven images.
> See, the former things have come to pass,
>> and new things I now declare;
> before they spring forth,
>> I tell you of them. (vv. 8–9)

---

9. Credit goes to Millard Lind for bringing this out: Lind, "Monotheism, Power, and Justice," 153–70.

10. Westermann, *Isaiah 40–66*.

Perhaps the oracle is intended to tie the servant's mission together with YHWH's purpose.

The call to praise (42:10–12) can be taken as the concluding strophe of the poem. Note how broad its vision is; it is a fitting conclusion to the trial involving the ends of the earth.

## Isaiah 42:13—44:23

This long passage contains several poems and a prose satire of idol making. I am putting them together because they have a lot in common. The focus of 42:13—44:8, 22–23 is the relationship between YHWH and Israel. Neither the nations nor their gods come in for more than a casual mention. The trial that ran through the previous unit is absent; it will return in chapter 45. Here the issue is Israel's judgment and deliverance, and its role in the world.

Let's list the units and their subjects:

1. New Exodus (42:13–16)[11]
2. Disputation over the Exile (42:18–25)
3. Oracle of Deliverance from Exile (43:1–7)
4. Appointment of Israel as Witness (43:8–13)
5. New Exodus (43:14–21)
6. Disputation over the Exile (43:22–28).
7. Oracle of Deliverance from Exile (44:1–5)
8. Oracle regarding YHWH's deity (44:6–8)
9. Satire of idol making (44:9–20)
10. A Final Word to People (44:21–22)
11. Call to Praise (44:23)

The strophes just before and after the prose satire do not fit any apparent pattern, but the material in 42:13—44:5 is clear. There are two cycles, if you will: a new-exodus passage, followed by a disputation over the reason for the exile, followed by a promise of deliverance from exile. A passage recruiting the people as witnesses on behalf of YHWH's deity falls in between the two cycles.

Let's examine the two new-exodus passages first. I have associated 42:13 with 42:14–16, though some strophic divisions attach it to the end of the call to praise. In it the Lord compares himself to a soldier who works himself into a frenzy as he engages in battle. In v. 14, he compares himself to a woman in

---

11. Verse 17 is a stray bit of condemnation of idolaters.

labor—also a noisy, frenzied state. There are very few parallels to this imagery in the rest of Hebrew Scripture. It suggests an urgency and tension, even suffering, that will soon explode into a divine intervention. The first verse of this intervention is negative, out of step with all other new-exodus passages:

> I will lay waste mountains and hills,
> > and dry up all their herbage;
> I will turn the rivers into islands,
> > and dry up the pools. (42:15)

The next verse returns to the positive action of facilitating the return home:

> And I will lead the blind
> > by a road they do not know
> . . . .
> I will turn the darkness before them into light,
> > the rough places into level ground. (42:16)

A new exodus is promised again in 43:14–21. This is in fact the most elaborate new-exodus passage in Second Isaiah. The oracle begins with a rather literal message of divine intervention:

> Thus says the Lord,
> > your Redeemer, the Holy One of Israel:
> For your sake I will send to Babylon
> > and break down all the bars. (v. 14, RSV)

In Isa 43:16, we have a new messenger formula ("Thus says the Lord"), with a hymnic account of the original exodus:

> Thus says the Lord,
> > who makes a way in the sea,
> > a path in the mighty waters,
> > who brings out chariot and horse,
> > > army and warrior;
> > they lie down, they cannot rise,
> > > they are extinguished, quenched like a wick. (vv. 16–17)

Then comes the surprise: The Lord says, "Do not remember the former things." The audience, rather, should be looking to what is about to happen: "I am about to do a new thing; / now it springs forth, do you not perceive it?" (v.

19a). The prophet then launches into a beautiful description of the transformation of the desert:

> I will make a way in the wilderness
> and rivers in the desert.
> ...
> The wild beasts will honor me,
> the jackals and the ostriches;
> for I give water in the wilderness, rivers in the desert,
> to give drink to my chosen people ... (vv.19b–20)

The new-exodus passage ends with a purpose clause that points us in the direction of the people's assignment as witnesses: "The people whom I formed for myself / that they might declare my praise" (v. 21).

Now that we have surveyed a number of new-exodus passages, we need to reflect on their importance to the message of Second Isaiah. That message is that the Judean exiles have paid their debt to the divine law, so to speak. Their punishment is over. The prophet, and many of the people, will not be satisfied with a mere declaration. Living conditions have to change. Indeed, the people should return to their homeland and restore their civilization. The return home requires a long, arduous journey. Before that, the empire that has deported them will have to either change its policy or be overthrown. Our prophet announces the latter, and designates the Persian conqueror as agent of YHWH. He will facilitate the return home. This return will have transcendent significance and manifest the one sovereign God for the nations of the world to see. This will be such a momentous event that the exodus from Egypt will pale in comparison.

Two important disputation passages appear in this section: 42:18–25 and 43:22–28. It is essential to YHWH's claim to be sovereign Lord of history that the deportation of the ruling classes of Jerusalem and Judah not be a defeat of YHWH, as ancient Near Eastern polytheism would understand it. If YHWH is supposed to protect his people, and the Babylonians and their gods overwhelm his protection, they must be stronger than he is. To affirm his power to save Israel, he must demonstrate that he sent them into exile.

This argument is only half the story, of course. The prophets of judgment did not wait until Israel was defeated and exiled before pronouncing judgment. That would have been an ex post facto justification, not a judgment based on Israel or Judah deserving what came to them. The exile demonstrates, in the prophetic mind, the truth of its message. Now it is necessary for the judgment

## Redeeming Judgment

to be appropriated by the people who are slated for salvation. Second Isaiah has the task of stamping the lesson of judgment on the hearts and minds of the elect so that they can be redeemed.

The first of the disputation passages (Isa 42:18–25) begins by characterizing the exiles as "blind" and "deaf":

> Listen, you that are deaf;
> > and you that are blind, look up and see!
> Who is blind but my servant,
> > or deaf like my messenger whom I send?
> Who is blind like my dedicated one,
> > or blind like the servant of the LORD? (42:18–19)

These people are blind to and deaf to the lesson of judgment:

> [He] sees many things, but does not observe them;
> > His ears are open, but he does not hear.
> The LORD was pleased, for his righteousness' sake,
> > to magnify his law[12] and make it glorious. (42:20–21, RSV)

Unfortunately, the people are too beat down to appropriate the lesson:

> But this is a people robbed and plundered,
> > they are all of them trapped in holes
> > and hidden in prisons;
> they have become a prey with none to rescue,
> > a spoil with no one to say, "Restore!" (42: 22)

The prophet finally inscribes the lesson of the judgment on their ears, so to speak:

> Who gave up Jacob to the spoiler,
> > and Israel to robbers?
> Was it not the Lord, against whom we have sinned,
> > in whose ways they would not walk,
> > and whose law they would not obey?
> So he poured upon him the heat of his anger
> > and the fury of war . . . (42:24–25a)

The second disputation (Isa 43:22–28) calls to mind the torah of the prophets of judgment:

12. NRSV "teaching."

> Yet you did not call upon me, O Jacob,
>> but you have been weary of me, O Israel!
> You have not brought me your sheep for burnt offerings,
>> or honored me with your sacrifices.
> I have not burdened you with offerings,
>> or wearied you with frankincense (vv. 22–23).

It is sin that arouses the Lord's anger:

> But you have burdened me with your sins;
>> you have wearied me with your iniquities. (v. 24)

This assertion is supposed to close the book on the debate, but now the disputation takes an odd turn: the one who has passed judgment on Israel now declares that he is the one who forgives them:

> I, I am He
>> who blots out your transgressions for my own sake,
>> and I will not remember your sins. (v. 25)

This does not, however, silence the discussion of the nation's guilt. The people are invited to renew their accusation against God (v. 26), and then he divulges how he will answer it:

> Your first ancestor sinned,
>> and your interpreters transgressed against me.
> Therefore I profaned the princes of the sanctuary,
>> I delivered Jacob to utter destruction
>> and Israel to reviling. (vv. 27–28)

It does not sound like the Lord is going to make good on his promise to "not remember your sins" (v. 25). The people must appropriate their guilt before it can be put in the past.

It is noteworthy that this disputation is followed up by "but now" and a promise. That is also how the first disputation was followed up (in 43:1). Isaiah 44:1–5 centers on fertility of land and humanity. This may be a mirror image of "your first ancestor sinned," and it certainly fits "who formed you in the womb" (44:2). Isaiah 43:1–7 centers on the repopulation of the Holy Land too, but the emphasis is on the return from diaspora. Both these promises of salvation begin with strong affirmations of the value of Israel in God's eyes, in his heart:

> But now thus says the LORD,
>> who created you, O Jacob,
>> he who formed you, O Israel:
> Do not fear, for I have redeemed you;
>> I have called you by name, you are mine. (43:1)

> But now hear, O Jacob my servant,
>> Israel whom I have chosen!
> Thus says the LORD who made you,
>> who formed you in the womb and will help you. (44:1–2)

Perhaps forgiveness has more to do with this reestablishment of intimacy between YHWH and his people. While the people can "pay for" their sins, they cannot claim the privileges of election. Their behavior could have made God suspicious and unwilling to place much trust in them again. Perhaps the forgiveness of God heals the alienation that accompanied guilt.

Finally there is the commission of Israel as the Lord's witnesses (43:8–13). The passage begins by identifying the Judean exiles as "blind, though they have eyes, / who are deaf yet have ears" (v. 8). This echoes the first disputation (42:18–20). It sounds as though the people are going to be accused or reminded of their guilt. But no, the Lord calls a trial—or arranges for one (because we have no proceedings until chapter 45). The nations are summoned, to be witnesses to divine knowledge (v. 9). Israel then is designated YHWH's witnesses; they are to witness to YHWH's sole deity:

> Before me no god was formed,
>> nor shall there be any after me.
> I, I am the LORD,
>> and besides me there is no savior. (42:10b–11)

How is this to be proven? The people are to remember their history with him:

> I declared and saved and proclaimed,
>> when there was no strange god among you;
>> and you are my witnesses, says the Lord.
> I am God, and also henceforth I am He;
>> there is none who can deliver from my hand;
>> I work and who can hinder it? (vv. 12–13)

This strong affirmation leads into a new-exodus passage. The trial will take place later.[13]

What is Isa 44:9–20 doing in Second Isaiah? A lot of scholars have asked that question. I think it offers comic relief. It certainly would discourage any Israelite from assimilating too thoroughly into Mesopotamian culture. The three poetic verses that precede the prose satire proclaim the Lord's uniqueness and incomparability, a perfect contrast to the gods made from firewood.

## Isaiah 44:24—45:25

In this portion of Second Isaiah's prophecy, we return to the Persian conqueror, who is named for the first time; it ends with an invitation to the Gentiles to convert. In between, the objection of Israelites to YHWH's "anointment" of a stranger as his agent of salvation is addressed, and a promise is made that the nations will reward the holy city to procure favor with its God.

It should be evident to any serious reader that the oracle to Cyrus in Isa 45:1–6 is a dramatic highpoint. Cyrus is the subject of the debate between YHWH and the gods of the nations in chapter 41. Now Cyrus is named and addressed. The prophet confronts a skeptical audience and takes pains to justify the message; before the Cyrus oracle there is a long preamble: 44:24–28. This starts out as though an oracle will be delivered, but it is a long praise of YHWH:

> Thus says the LORD, your Redeemer,
>   who formed you in the womb:
> I am the Lord, who made all things,
>     who alone stretched out the heavens,
>     who by myself spread out the earth. (v. 24)

This is followed by judgments of non-Israelite diviners:

> Who frustrates the omens of liars,
>     and makes fools of diviners;
> who turns back the wise,
>     and makes their knowledge foolish. (v. 25)

---

13. While this is only a poetic figure for Second Isaiah, it prepares the way for the Israel of the future, the Israel that is dispersed among the nations and called on to live their faith, obey their law, in distinction from all those around them.

*Redeeming Judgment*

Then there are promises to Israelite prophets, and the reconstruction of the holy land. In the prophet's mind, the latter is the fulfillment of the message of the former. Then the prophecy moves to Cyrus:

> Who says of Cyrus, "He is my shepherd,
> and he shall carry out all my purpose." (v. 28)

Readers are now prepared for the oracle that follows:

> Thus says the LORD to his anointed, to Cyrus,
> whose right hand I have grasped
> to subdue nations before him
> and strip kings of their robes,
> to open doors before him—
> and the gates shall not be closed.

Calling Cyrus messiah ("anointed," 45:1) is quite a shocker. For the Judean audience, that would mean someone in the Davidic scion. Second Isaiah actually has abandoned dynastic hopes for restoration; that is the implication of Isa 55:3. The prophet seems to mean no more than that Cyrus will serve YHWH's saving purposes. The promises made to Cyrus in 45:1b–3 reflect the description of his conquests in 41:2–3. In chapter 41, YHWH claims to be the power behind Cyrus's military conquests; here he promises them to the emerging emperor.

There is some unusual dialectic in the purpose clauses. YHWH empowers Cyrus so that "you may know that it is I, the LORD, the God of Israel, who call you by your name" (45:3b). In v. 4, the Lord says, "I call you by name, / I surname you, though you do not know me." In the very next verse, YHWH empowers Cyrus so that men and women may know, "from the rising of the sun and from the west, that there is none besides me; I am the Lord, and there is no other" (v. 6). This world-historical purpose, which culminates at the end of this chapter, does not cancel the special purpose for Israel: "For the sake of my servant Jacob, / and Israel my chosen" (v. 4a).

Isaiah 45:7 is an expansive thesis about the God who is sovereign over all:

> I form light and create darkness,
> I make weal and create woe,
> I am the LORD, who do all these things. (RSV)

This thesis has shocked some commentators, for it implies that the Creator is the source of evil as well as good. However, it would not require that we give equal ontological status to evil as to good. It would be quite compatible with Joseph's affirmation in Gen 50:20: "Even though you intended to do harm [evil] to me, God intended it for good." Cyrus's conquest of the Near East may be no less evil than the expansion of any other empire, but it serves YHWH's saving purpose for Israel and for the world.

After the call to praise (45:8), YHWH engages in a disputation with his people over the choice of Cyrus. Actually, the passage begins with woes for anyone who would deny God the freedom to anoint Cyrus (vv. 9–10). One should not take the condemnatory force of these woes too seriously; their objective is to persuade the Israelites to accept what the prophet ascribes to YHWH. That is, the prophet's audience is denying the prophet's message; if they knew that it was YHWH's word, they would probably submit to it without protest. The prophet uses the argument to teach the audience some theology, and then to reiterate YHWH's plans for Cyrus:

> I have aroused Cyrus in righteousness,
> and I will make straight all his ways;
> He shall build my city
> and set my exiles free,
> not for price or reward. (v. 13)

Now, in vv. 14–17, the prophet turns from Cyrus to the peoples of the Near East. The content is surprising:

> The wealth of Egypt and the merchandise of Ethiopia,
> and the Sabeans, tall of stature,
> shall come over to you and be yours,
> they shall follow you;
> they shall come over in chains and bow down to you.
> They will make supplication to you, saying,
> "God is with you only, and there is no other,
> no god besides him." (v. 14)

Not a few scholars have seized on this verse to argue that Second Isaiah is not genuinely universalistic. This is a serious charge. I would take the statement in this verse as a kind of reparations for the years when others thrived while Jerusalem and Judah were in exile.[14] The image of "coming in chains" is a bit excessive, but the idea that these peoples besought the Israelites to mediate

---

14. We should not forget, by the way, that many Judean peasants remained in the national territory while the upper classes were deported.

between them and their God seems to be a natural and healthy consequence of election.

The speaker of "Truly, you are a God who hides yourself" is hard to identify but probably represents a polytheist's perception of a God who rejects all images (cp. Isa 45:16). To Israel the Lord can say:

> I did not speak in secret,
> > in a land of darkness;
> I did not say to the offspring of Jacob,
> > "Seek me in chaos."
> I the Lord speak the truth,
> > I declare what is right. (v. 19)

Perhaps this claim is best justified by identifying the Lord as Creator (see v. 18).

Now we come to the second major trial scene of these chapters. The Lord calls together the "survivors of the nations"—perhaps those who have survived Cyrus's onslaught. The Lord dismisses the devotees of idols as unknowing, though they are invited to state their case:

> They have no knowledge—
> > those who carry about their wooden idols,
> and keep on praying to a god
> > that cannot save.
> Declare and present your case;
> > let them take counsel together!
> Who told this long ago? (vv. 20b–21a)

But YHWH answers his own question: "Was it not I, the Lord? / There is no other god besides me" (v. 21b). That is as close as we are going to come to a "decision" in this trial. There is a circle here: to concur with the Lord's verdict on the gods/idols, a person has to accept him as true God. Hence, the Lord issues an invitation to the people to abandon their worthless deities and attach themselves to him:

> Turn to me and be saved,
> > all the ends of the earth!
> > For I am God, and there is no other. (v. 22)

The decision has become self-involving, because the choice of a god is also a judgment as to who has the power to save, and what salvation is from and to.

*The Book of Isaiah II*

Though humans have the freedom to decide their own fate, the Lord will not cease from seeking to persuade them until the whole world of humans has become his:

> By myself I have sworn,
>> from my mouth has gone forth in righteousness
>> a word that shall not return:
> "To me every knee shall bow,
>> every tongue shall swear." (v. 23)

It may be the Lord's persistence that makes the question objective. That is to say, a person's decision against the reality of the Lord does not end the matter; one will not be able to put it behind one.

The two concluding verses are the observation of the prophet.[15] The peoples of the world will be reconciled to the one God: "all who were incensed against him / shall come to him and be ashamed" (v. 24b). The converts to the Lord will evidently attach themselves to the people of God: "In the Lord all the offspring of Israel shall triumph and glory" (v. 25).

This chapter is the climax of the first six chapters of Second Isaiah. We have been building up to the commission of Cyrus and the conversion of the nations. Of course, the latter is ongoing. The Lord insists on being everyone's god, and he will not cease until all acknowledge him. Acknowledging him is also being saved by him. And the acceptance of the Lord's salvation means "joining" with the people of God.

## *Isaiah 46–47: The Judgment of Babylon*

Readers may not be aware of it, but Babylon has not been mentioned up till now. Even now it is not mentioned by name until chapter 47. First comes the Babylonian gods, a father and son duo, carried in a procession on the backs of animals.

> Bel bows down, Nebo stoops,
>> their idols are on beasts and cattle;
> these things you carry are loaded
>> as burdens on weary animals.

---

15. Actually, the first pair of lines is in the first person and belongs to YHWH, but the rest are in the third person. I don't know whether this was deliberate or accidental.

> They stoop, they bow down together;
>> they cannot save the burden,
>> but themselves go into captivity. (46:1–2)

Then we are told that they are being carried into captivity—either the idols or their bearers. If the lesson is not already obvious, the Lord makes it so:

> Hearken to me, O house of Jacob,
>> all the remnant of the house of Israel,
> who have been borne by me from your birth . . .
> even to your old age I am He . . .
> I have made, and I will bear;
>> I will carry and will save. (vv. 3–4, RSV)

From this comparison another is made:

> To whom will you liken me and make me equal,
>> and compare me, that we may be alike? (v. 5, RSV)

As we have grown to expect, there follows a satire on idol-making.

As we read on, we discover that the prophet is confronting an audience that isn't receptive to the message. In 46:8, the prophet calls the people "transgressors," and follows this with a "recollection of former things." In v. 12, the audience is called "you stubborn of heart," and "you who are far from deliverance"; but the word delivered to them is reassuring.

The first couple verses of this chapter arouse our expectations of oracles on the fall of Babylon and its gods, but the chapter wanders off to the recalcitrant Israelites. It is possible that some of the exiles are assimilating to Babylonian religion, eliciting the prophet's harsh words. Alternatively, the audience is not yet willing to accept Cyrus as the Lord's anointed.

Isaiah 47 does condemn Babylon. It is a prophecy against a foreign nation, the only one in Second Isaiah. For the Judean exiles to be freed from their forced resettlement and be permitted to return to their homeland, the Babylonian Empire will have to be overturned. There is one reference to the Lord's purpose in the first strophe:

> I will take vengeance,
>> and I will spare no one.
> Our Redeemer—the LORD of hosts is his name—
>> is the Holy One of Israel. (vv. 3–4)

The rest of the strophe is an address to the "virgin daughter of Babylon" (v. 1), which is a corporate figure for the city, like the "daughter of Jerusalem/Zion" in Lamentations. Indeed, this chapter resembles Lamentations; only, it is spoken by an outsider who regards Babylon's fate as well deserved. The daughter of Zion will be mistreated like a female prisoner of war. The second strophe also has a verse about Israel, spoken by the Lord:

> I was angry with my people,
>> I profaned my heritage;
>
> I gave them into your hand,
>> you showed them no mercy;
>
> on the aged you made your yoke
>> exceedingly heavy. (v. 6)

This adds to the indictment of Babylon. Verse 7 introduces a motif that recurs through the chapter:

> You said, "I shall be mistress forever,"
>> so that you did not lay these things to heart
>> or remember their end.

When Babylon was at the height of its power, it did not act as though it would have to suffer in proportion to its deeds. The people did whatever they desired (v. 8a) without any sense of restraint: "I am, and there is no one besides me; / I shall not sit as a widow / or know the loss of children" (v. 8b). This is precisely what is in store for Babylon (v. 9).

The same theme of lack of restraint, a lack of a sense of finitude, or moral and social limit, recurs in v. 10. A new subject comes up in vv. 12–13: a strong attraction to divination and astrology. This was a distinctive feature of Neo-Babylonian culture. The issue is, can these diviners predict, and perhaps warn them, of what will come upon them?

The poem ends with a depiction of the abandonment of Babylon by its allies:

> Such to you are those with whom you have labored,
>> who have trafficked with you from your youth;
>
> they wander about in their own paths;
>> there is no one to save you. (v. 15)

The chapter assumes that Babylon will be defeated and brought low. There is no exact description of defeat, but also no awareness that the Babylonians capitulated without a fight. Babylon capitulated to Cyrus without a battle, and he was welcomed into the city as a hero.[16] One can say that Babylon "falls," becoming a subject city within the Persian Empire, but it did not suffer appreciably, and there was no disruption of religion and culture. In this case, the fulfillment of the prophecy was "inexact."

## Isaiah 48

This chapter ends the first half of the "book" of Second Isaiah. The poet takes the opportunity to reiterate some important aspects of his message and to underscore some themes integrated into other contexts previously. The first strophe of the chapter (vv. 1–2) provides an elaborate identity description of the people, and in the middle of the chapter we find an identity description of YHWH.

The chapter concludes dramatically with a command to leave Babylon:

> Go out from Babylon, flee from Chaldea,
>> declare this with a shout of joy, proclaim it,
> send it forth to the end of the earth;
>> say, "The LORD has redeemed his servant Jacob!"
> They did not thirst when he led them through the deserts;
>> he made water flow for them from the rock;
>> he split open the rock and the water gushed out.[17] (vv. 20–21)

This is a variation on the new exodus; it of course calls to mind Moses's summons of water from the rock.

Two strophes are devoted to the exile as divine judgment. Verses 9–11 begin as through Israel has not been punished:

> For my name's sake I defer my anger,
>> for the sake of my praise I restrain it for you,
>> so that I may not cut you off.

Despite that statement, v. 10 (RSV) refers to judgment:

> See, I have refined you, but not [like] silver;
>> I have tried you in the furnace of affliction.

---

16. Consult a history of Israel, e.g., Miller and Hayes, *A History of Ancient Israel and Judah*, 437–43.

17. Verse 22 is a reader's comment, probably meant to signify the end of the section.

YHWH judged Israel, according to v. 11, to protect his honor and glory.

Verses 17–19 return to this subject. The Lord introduces himself as Israel's teacher, and then indulges in a "might have been":

> O that you had paid attention to my commandments!
>> Then your prosperity would have been like a river,
>> and your success like the waves of the sea;
> your offspring would have been like the sand. (vv. 18–19a)

This is a counterimage to the exile, probably to underscore the need to learn the lesson of the exile.

Off and on in chapters 41 through 43, YHWH speaks of his having "declared former things," which can be taken as prophecy and fulfillment in the past. Isaiah 48:3–5 repeats the point, but a new reason is given:

> Because I know that you are obstinate,
>> and your neck is an iron sinew
>> and your forehead brass,
> I declared them to you long ago,
>> before they came to pass I announced them to you,
> so that you would not say, "My idol did them." (vv. 4–5)

In other words, the Lord prophesied events beforehand so Israel could not interpret them as the work of some other divinity. The correspondence of prophecy and fulfillment may not prove that God is active, but it confirms it at a pragmatic level.

The next strophe (vv. 6–8) brings up the present; the people are hearing new things (v. 6). They are being "created now." Israel cannot claim that it knew that these things would happen (v. 7). No one had ever heard what the Lord was telling them (v. 8).

Now, doesn't this contradict chapter 41, vv. 25–27 ("Now who declared it from the beginning, so that we might know, / and beforehand, so that we might say, 'He is right'?")? Either the events unfolding in the present were prophesied in the past, or they are being declared now for the first time. My take on this is that it takes a prophet in the present to recognize that the prophecies of the past encompass the events unfolding before us. The logician might find this too circular, but that seems to be the way prophecy operates. The people must await the prophet's interpretation of the tradition, but if they are faithful, they can recognize the truth of the prophet.

Finally we have the strophe that begins with the summons of an assembly (vv. 14–16). Whether the call is to all peoples or to the Judean exiles is uncertain. It actually sounds like an appeal to the exiles. The thrust is to claim once again that Cyrus is the Lord's chosen agent:

> The LORD loves him;
>> he shall perform his purpose on Babylon,
>> and his arm shall be against the Chaldeans. (v. 14b)

This statement is very strong—the Lord loves him. It is backed up with an oracle:

> I, even I, have spoken and called him,
>> I have brought him, and he will prosper in his way. (v. 15)

Verse 16a seems to confirm the oracular word. Then v. 16b takes us by surprise: "And now the Lord God has sent me and his spirit." We have not heard first-person speech from the prophet since chapter 40. The prophet is suggesting that his existence, and the coming of the spirit to inspire reception, clinches the truth of this controversial message.

## Isaiah 49–55

It is striking that Isaiah 48 has no reference to the servant of Isa 42:1–4, but it does defend YHWH's call of Cyrus. This situation is reversed in chapters 49–55. Cyrus is not mentioned again after chapter 48, but the servant is quite prominent. There are three Servant Songs and two attached passages in chapters 49, 50, and 52–53. That means that the human bearer of the sovereign power of God is configured in opposite ways in these two halves of the "book" called Second Isaiah.

Yet despite the prominence of the servant in these chapters, it is not clear what role he plays in the story of the nation's liberation and return and restoration of Zion—the other story being followed in chapters 49–55. Connecting the role of the servant to the larger story will be one of our biggest challenges in this portion of the study of Isaiah.

I propose to start at the end—at chapter 55. If the book is rhetorically coherent, the last chapter will round off the whole message, or at least chapters 49–55. We shall not expound chapters 49–53 except for the three Servant Songs and their attachments, 49:1–6 (7–11); 50:4–9 (10–11); and 52:13–53:12.

## Isaiah 55

This last chapter is designed, from beginning to end, to move the readers to act. To show that, let me consider each strophe carefully for its rhetoric.

The very last strophe (55:12–13) promises a new exodus in the audience's return from exile. Thus, it conforms to the pattern set by Isaiah 48. The latter, however, began with an imperative; this one is a promissory statement. It is also noteworthy that the epiphany of the Lord early in chapter 40 is a new exodus. If readers or hearers get no other message from the prophecy of Second Isaiah, they cannot miss the promise of a new, world-transforming exodus.

> For you shall go out in joy,
>     and be led back in peace;
> the mountains and the hills before you
>     shall burst forth into song,
>     and all the trees of the field shall clap their hands. (v. 12)

Plants will spring up in the desert—plants that have never been able to grow there (v. 13a). This change will be "to the Lord a memorial, / . . . an everlasting sign" (v. 13b).

Just preceding the new-exodus promise is an affirmation of the trustworthiness of the Lord's word. What makes it trustworthy is its power to bring about what it announces. The prophet compares the word to rain and snow, "which do not return [to heaven] until they have watered the earth, / making it bring forth and sprout" (v. 10). The word of the Lord "shall not return to me empty, / but it shall accomplish that which I purpose" (v. 11). This word is the promise of the new exodus delivered by this exilic prophet.

The chapter begins with an offer of salvation. It imitates a salesperson selling food. But this food and drink is free:

> Come, buy wine and milk
>     without money and without price.
> Why do you spend your money for that which is not bread? (vv. 1b–2a)

This pitch concludes with the offer of life: "Incline your ears and come to me; / listen so that you may live" (v. 3a).

So far the real subject matter is hidden. The audience must pay attention. Now there is an offer made:

> I will make with you an everlasting covenant,
>     my steadfast, sure love for David. (v. 3b)

*Redeeming Judgment*

The audience knows of the covenant made with the house of David. This promise will be revived in the years ahead—it will be the promise of a revived Judean kingship under a descendant of David.[18] Second Isaiah, however, reinterprets the promise to David to apply it to all Israelites:

> [Behold,] I made him a witness to the peoples
>
> . . .
>
> [Now behold,] you shall call nations that you do not know,
> and nations that do not know you shall run to you
> because of the LORD your God. (vv. 4–5)

The promise made to David now goes to the whole nation.[19] The prophet probably has abandoned the idea that the people of God will be political kingdom in the future.

This verse is one of the few allusions to the conversion of the nations in Isaiah 49–55. The prophet has now tied the two halves of his message together.

Following this reinterpretation of the promise to David, the chapter's audience is urged to seize the opportunity of salvation: "Seek the Lord while he may be found, / call upon him wile he is near" (v. 6). The audience will need to examine itself and repent:

> Let the wicked forsake their way,
> and the unrighteous their thoughts;
> let them return to the Lord, that he may have mercy on them,
> and to our God, for he will abundantly pardon. (v. 7)

The prophet now seems to wander off into theology:

> For my thoughts are not your thoughts,
> nor are your ways my ways, says the Lord.
> For as the heavens are higher than the earth,
> so are my ways higher than your ways,
> and my thoughts than your thoughts. (vv. 8–9)

What is this argument about? Like a similar argument in Hosea 11:9, it justifies showing mercy and granting forgiveness. The Lord is capable of both judging and forgiving. How can he do both? That transcends human understanding. What we do know is that he will do whatever he needs to in order to redeem his fallen, rebellious creatures—both his own people and all peoples.

---

18. Found in Haggai and Zechariah.
19. Frequently called democratization.

## Isaiah 54

If Isaiah 55 is designed to persuade the people to receive the promise of the new exodus and all that is attendant on it, we must look to chapter 54 for the completion of the promise giving. The best way to read chapter 54 is to locate yourself in Jerusalem at the end of the new exodus; the new exodus is behind you, now, so to speak.

The chapter begins with an exhortation to an unidentified female addressee, described as "barren one," to celebrate the multitude of children she has—so many children the living quarters will have to be expanded. These children are not born to her, at least she did not "labor" for them, yet they are members of the family (vv. 1–2). With these numbers, the people will be able to repossess the tribal land grant of the past (v. 3).

Now this unidentified addressee is assured that she need not feel ashamed. "The shame of your youth, and the disgrace of your widowhood you will remember no more" (v. 4). The Lord, "your Maker," is also her husband (v. 5). He "abandoned" her for a brief while, but now he feels great compassion (v. 7). There is only an allusion to the reason for this abandonment:

> In overflowing wrath for a moment
> > I hid my face from you,
> but with everlasting love I will have compassion on you. (v. 8)

The poet wants the people to surmount both their anger and their sense of guilt for the exile. The past should not be denied, but it should not tether the future either. YHWH will never again subject them to judgment:

> This is like the days of Noah to me:
> > Just as I swore that the waters of Noah
> > would never again go over the earth,
> so I have sworn that I will not be angry with you
> > and will not rebuke you. (v. 9)

The promise is rephrased in v. 10:

> For the mountains may depart
> > and the hills be removed,
> but my steadfast love shall not depart from you,
> > and my covenant of peace shall not be removed.

The remainder of the chapter amplifies this promise. Jerusalem will be rebuilt with precious stones, the "children" will prosper and secure their wealth with justice; external foes will not be able to harm them, since God will thwart the forging of weapons.

The promise of an everlasting covenant is essential to the message of Second Isaiah. The great prophets of judgment—Amos, Hosea, Isaiah, Micah, Jeremiah and Ezekiel—did not think in terms of cycles of judgment, restoration, judgment, and so on. Israel's judgment was once for all, and her salvation will never be interrupted by divine judgment.

## The Servant Songs

Between Isaiah 49 and 53, promises to Zion are interspersed with three Servant Songs. Most of the nonservant material is concerned with the restoration and repopulation of Zion, subjects that reach their climax in Isaiah 54. We have no need to pursue these subjects further here.

A number of reasons converge to justify a separate section of the Servant Songs. They stand out and attract our curiosity. They are even more important to Christian believers. They are analogous to the "messianic" promises of First Isaiah. They call for theological reflection because they challenge the pragmatic view of political power and what counts as victory and defeat. Other dimensions of meaning may lay hidden by these questions. The effort should prove worthwhile.

The first Servant Song does describe the servant as called to "bring forth" and "establish" justice (42:1, 3, 4). This does sound rather judge-like; the Davidic king exercises judicial power, especially according to Isa 11:3b-4. The servant does not use coercion but extends the reign of justice and torah nonviolently. He sounds a bit like a gardener in 42:3: "a bruised reed he will not break, / and a dimly burning wick he will not quench." This corresponds to an ideal judicial process—one that so convinces contending parties that they accede to the judgment without resistance.

The servant's authority reaches to all humans. This should remind us of Jeremiah's call, in which he is told, "I appoint you over nations and over kingdoms" (1:10). The prophet in principle exercises his office over all the peoples the Lord rules. The servant, however, has a bigger task than Jeremiah or any other prophet: he is "to establish justice in the earth . . . and the coastlands" will come under "his torah" (v. 4). This is a truly eschatological condition. It is also too big for any one prophet to attain in his lifetime; indeed it encompasses all history.

The calling of the servant is juxtaposed to passages describing the ruler and general who was conquering the world at the time of the prophet. Cyrus will extend his rule over many nations, though hardly all. He will establish his rule by defeating armies and militias defending their lands and cities. Some nations will capitulate without a fight because they know that resistance is useless and counterproductive. If he is welcomed as a hero, he might reward the welcomer. This conqueror has the backing of YHWH too! It sounds as though the Lord is duplicitous, supporting the winner in the game of power politics, and calling a figure who eschews the game. How do we reconcile these "contradictions" in the Holy One of Israel?

There is no explicit resolution in the text. All we can say is that each is playing a role in the divine economy. The oracle addressed to the servant in 42:5–9 tells him that he has a particular calling:

> I have called you in righteousness,
>> I have taken you by the hand and kept you;
>> I have given you as a covenant to the people,
>>> a light to the nations. (v. 6)

The oracle then specifies a specific task, one that evidently provides light to the nations:

> To open the eyes that are blind,
>> to bring out the prisoners from the dungeon. (v. 7)

God's mission of mercy is the servant's focus.

The second and third Servant Songs (Isa 49:1–8; 50:4–10) are autobiographical in form. They can be read as the report of the prophet of the Babylonian exile to the world. He begins in chapter 49:1 with an account of his call. It is said to have been given in his mother's womb. That makes very little literal sense, though it echoes the words of the Lord to Jeremiah (Jer 1:5). According to Isa 49:3, the prophet of the exile is told, "You are my servant, / Israel, in whom I will be glorified." This sounds as though the servant is a collective image. That idea is contradicted, however, in v. 6, where the prophet is told, "It is too light a thing that you should be my servant, / to raise up the tribes of Jacob." When he is addressed as Israel, he must be a representative—like a sports star whose victory or defeat gives the nation glory or shame. Since Israel is the Lord's elect, and a source of divine prestige, the servant could bring glory to the Lord as well as to Israel.

## Redeeming Judgment

The most striking point of the second Servant Song is that the prophet's scope of responsibility is expanded to the nations:

> I will give you as a light to the nations,
>> that my salvation will reach the end of the earth. (49:6)

The prophet who tells his story in 49:1–6 does not start out as the servant described in 42:1–4. He is sent only to his people; now in this oracle he is assigned the task given the servant in 42:1–9.

The oracle attached to this song also tells the servant that he has been given "as a covenant to the people" (49:8; also 42:6). Perhaps this means that he is some sort of mediator. Again his is a task of mercy, "saying to prisoners, 'Come out,' / and to those in darkness, 'Show yourselves'" (Isa 49:9). This assignment does lead into the task of initiating a "new exodus" (vv. 9b–11). However, nothing said in these verses suggests a role restricted to Judean exiles.

The third Servant Song (Isa 50:4–10) is the first to mention persecution. The second mentions the prophet's disappointment (49:4), a form of suffering but not necessarily due to hostility: "But I said, 'I have labored in vain, I have spent my strength for nothing and vanity.'" But now we hear of physical and verbal assault (v. 6). This persecution has occurred despite the fact that the Lord has been teaching the prophet pastoral skills: "that I may know how to sustain the weary with a word" (v. 4).

The challenge for the servant/prophet is not to interpret his suffering or the motives of his attackers but to remain obedient to the Lord and to allow the Lord to vindicate him.[20] This is how he can fulfill his calling, and the role of the servant described in 42:1–4. If he were to retreat from his calling to avoid persecution, he would betray his commission. If he were to retaliate, he would fail to exemplify the nonviolent figure of 42:1–4. The introduction of the servant in 42:1–4 doesn't mention suffering and persecution, but it does set narrow parameters if it arises.

Of course, it is mysterious why persecution should arise. The servant has done nothing to provoke it; even his message is comforting. Let me share a personal experience that may shed light on the question. I had a pacifist friend who went to prison rather than register for the draft during the Vietnam War. Even a deferment for conscientious objection was, in his opinion, too much cooperation with the military system. I had this friend explain his stance to a class of seminary students, and within an hour of exchanges almost every

---

20. This should caution scholars to pause when they insist that Jesus consciously modeled himself after the suffering servant.

member of the class of preministerial students was hostile to him. Nothing that he said was calculated to offend them, but his principled pacifism offended their sense of manhood.

The fourth Servant Song (Isa 52:13—53:12) brings all the themes of the series to a climax. The issue of power is quite salient. The servant is introduced as very powerful, but in the course of his life he has been despised and persecuted and finally murdered; his exaltation is a divine gift after death. The suffering and death of the servant was not accidental. It seems that inevitably the person who seeks to establish justice, enforce divine law, and bring this about without coercion is going to be defeated, and may well be victimized. Those who live by power sense the vulnerability of the powerless and exploit it; they take offense at those who are powerless by choice as a matter of principle. The suffering of the servant seems the probable destiny of anyone embarked on the servant's narrow path.

Skeptical readers will regard the exaltation of the Suffering Servant by God to be a fantasy, a *deus ex machina*. The exercise of violence will always win out, and the only way to achieve justice and peace is to possess or gain more power than the "bad guys." This is often futile and even tragic, for the oppressed can easily become the oppressor, coercion can generate counterforce, and so forth. However, one who can live with proximate justice and a degree of uncertainty can be satisfied by a rough-and-ready peace of balanced powers.

Our passage is eschatological. More than a tolerable balance of power is promised. Cyrus has his role, but it produces only temporary "salvation." The God who has called the servant and introduces him as exalted from the dead has taken a decisive step to bring about something beyond the possibilities of history as we have known it. Whether this new situation will come about in the course of human events or at the end of all historical sequences is a matter for systematic or philosophical theology. Our passage does not say how or when, and it leaves us in limbo about the status of the language of this poem.[21] But what it does say is unsurpassable.

For many interpreters, the most difficult or problematic teaching of the poem is vicarious suffering. That the servant has suffered in place of others is unavoidable. The "we" who speak in Isa 53:1–6 say it four times in three successive verses:

> Surely he has borne our infirmities
> and carried our diseases;

---

21. The second and third songs made sense as the autobiographical account of the prophet of the exile, but the fourth exceeds anything that could have happened to him.

> ...
> But he was wounded for our transgressions,
> > crushed for our iniquities;
> upon him was the chastisement that made us whole,
> > and with his stripes we are healed
> ...
> and the Lord has laid on him
> > the iniquity of us all. (Isa 53:4–6, RSV)

The language may be metaphorical, but it is certainly transparent enough to understand. The philosophical and theological problems that the poem raises has made some readers deny its understandability.

Of course, one could object that we have only heard from the humans; perhaps God has some other take on the servant's ordeal. Unfortunately, the Lord seconds the testimony of the "we":

> By his knowledge shall the righteous one, my servant, make many to be accounted righteous;
> > and he shall bear their iniquities.
> Therefore I will allot him a portion with the great
> ...
> because he poured out his soul to death,
> > and was numbered with the transgressors;
> yet he bore the sin of many,
> > and made intercession for the transgressors. (vv. 11–12, RSV)

The import of these statements is impossible to escape: the servant suffers for others.

## The Interpretation of Bernd Janowski

The Old Testament scholar Bernd Janowski focuses our attention on the rhetorical effect of the passage rather than its doctrinal content. Daniel Bailey puts this nicely: "The concern that Janowski highlights in the text focuses not so much on theodicy or atonement theology as on problems of religious epistemology, how Israel comes to recognize both her guilt and its cancellation so as to be changed and ultimately saved."[22]

This statement calls for clarification. Janowski takes the servant to be the prophet of the exile, and the story of his demise to be an historical account.

---

22. See Bailey, "Concepts of *Stellvertretung*," 246.

The "we" who speak in Isa 53:1–6 is the congregation of Israel, the Judean exiles in Babylon. For the reasons I have already given, I would not take the servant in this passage to be the prophet of the exile. It portrays the servant as exalted by God after his death, and it is doubtful that anything like that happened to Second Isaiah.[23] As for the "we," the mention of nations and kings in Isa 52:15 makes them the best candidates for the "we." Of course, one has to ask how these persons could speak as though they knew the prophet while he was alive (Isa 53:2, 3). This leaves their identity rather mysterious. I think the poet has deliberately left their identity open—so that readers could insert themselves into the song.

Isaiah 52:13 should be taken quite seriously. Janowski does say that this oracle (52:13–15) together with the one at the end (53:11–12) have revelatory force, changing the perspective of "we" on the servant and on themselves.[24] I would go further. The whole scene is set by the first verse: The Lord announces his newly exalted servant, and those who are "in the audience" are startled and prompted to tell their story. They tell only of the early years, and how they view him. Notice their summary in 53:4b: "we accounted him stricken, / struck down by God, and afflicted." They may have thought that he was being punished; Janowski thinks that ancient Israel inevitably fit experience into that scheme.[25] I have serious doubts.[26] The language in v. 4b could indicate that "we" felt pity for an unlucky compatriot. Moreover, the speakers had no idea that he was suffering *for* them, even *instead of* them.

According to Janowski, vicarious suffering has become a dimension of the servant's "bringing Jacob back to [God] . . . that Israel might be gathered to him" (49:5). The servant voluntarily surrendered his life as an *asham*, a "means of wiping out guilt."[27] In Janowski's words, "Israel, which is in no position to take over the obligation arising from its guilt, must be released from it in order to have any future."[28] What is said of Israel must be applicable to anyone who reads the passage with religious intent.

---

23. That still leaves us with the unsettling problem of according redemptive power to a fictional personage. We need some actual person who was despised, and then revealed to us as one who was called by God. We have people like that in our experience, and perhaps they are to have the text applied to them.
24. Bailey, "Concepts of *Stellvertretung*," 247–48.
25. Ibid., 247.
26. See my argument in chapter 5 above.
27. Bailey, "Concepts of *Stellvertretung*," 247.
28. Janowski, "He Bore Our Sins," 69.

*Redeeming Judgment*

It took the Lord's revelation of the true identity of the servant for the "we" to realize what he had done for them and what they owed him. In a role reversal, the servant suffers what the people should have suffered, so they are confronted by their own guilt. Seeing the servant shatters their complacency, prompting them to change. They now know that their own status before God, and their good life, are based upon the Lord's acceptance of the servant's suffering in lieu of theirs. They cannot but respond in gratitude.

In other words, the "we" see in retrospect that the servant's suffering and death was "substitutionary." The servant has suffered so that the people can recognize their sin and guilt and repent. His suffering is also "representative" because he has shared the people's suffering by choice, because he did not deserve it.

## *Biblical Parallels to the Fourth Servant Song*

There are some parallels: one is the story of Moses's intercession on Mount Sinai for the apostate Israelites (Exod 32:11–14). The Deuteronomic retelling of the story includes an additional forty days of fasting and pleading with the Lord (Deut 9:18–19, 25). Although this is a ritual action, not suffering forced on the person, yet it is performed by one person for the good of others.

An even closer parallel is found in Job 42:7–8. Job and his companions engage in a long, painful dialogue in which Job's companions charge him with sin and impiety. His lament is answered by the Lord (Job 38–41), and Job "confessed" his newfound faith in God (42:1–6). Following that resolution, the Lord turns to Eliphaz: "My wrath is kindled against you and your two friends; for you have not spoken of me what is right, as my servant Job has. Now therefore take seven bulls and seven rams, and go to my servant Job, and offer up for yourselves a burnt offering; and my servant Job shall pray for you, for I will accept his prayer not to deal with you according to your folly" (42:7–28).

Job plays the role of servant for his friends. He suffers the slings and arrows of outrageous fortune. The friends have nothing to do with that. Indeed, they are exercising their responsibility to console the afflicted. But they are trapped by their own doctrine and piety into persecuting him; they become his enemies. According to a standard of strict justice, they would have suffered divine judgment for their false and harmful theologizing. The Lord insists that they recognize that they were in the wrong. They had aggravated the suffering of the righteous. They have to humble themselves by requesting that Job intercede for them. Their sacrifices could cleanse their sin's negative physical or metaphysical effect, but the prayer will be essential to allowing them into God's presence again. The prayers of the righteous carry a special weight, while those of the unrighteous are not "heard."

Neither of these parallels to the fourth Servant Song have the righteous victim die, so the sufferer has not had "victimhood" consume life. In Job's case, his primary suffering has nothing to do with his friends; he does not suffer for or because of them. It was their aggravation of his suffering that involves this vicarious exchange. Within this limited parallelism, we can see that the friends being forgiven requires that they be reconciled with their victim. This parallels the practice of the Day of Atonement in Jewish ritual. Before the Day of Atonement, one has to procure the forgiveness of all those one has sinned against during the year; only then will God offer his forgiveness of sins against other humans. I see in this practice the logic of the servant passage.[29]

## Concluding Reflections

Readers hardly need reminding that we are reading Isaiah 40–55 as an integral part of the book of Isaiah. The corollary is that our account of the message readers of this portion of the book must be congruent with what we said about Isaiah 1–39.

The message that the Babylonian Isaiah designed for the Judean exiles between 550 and 538 BCE has performed its function and is no longer in effect. His words were preserved for later readers in other times and places. The highly poetic formulation of this message and its elaborate structure may seduce us into construing his own message as timeless and placeless, but we must remind ourselves of the difference between the original utterance, calculated to meet a particular exigency, and its reapplication in the book of Isaiah. Something of its original rhetorical force must be retained in any reading of the book of Isaiah in its final form.

The original message had the performative force of declaring the end of divine judgment and promising a return to the homeland and reestablishment

---

29. Once we view the story in this way, we will find numerous instances of vicarious suffering in our lives. Others have suffered (or now suffer) because of us, for us, even instead of us. If we recognize this, we should be changed by it. I remember attending a memorial service for Martin Luther King Jr. right after his assassination. The text that was read was Isaiah 53. Not only did it seem to say exactly what needed to be said at that sad but celebrative moment, it has illuminated the passage for me since that time. Martin Luther King Jr. lived his life and died his death on the frontlines of a racial conflict that white America had maintained for hundreds of years; he suffered for our sin and led us in the struggle to repent of it.

## Redeeming Judgment

there. It is our challenge to discover a performative exchange with readers of Isaiah comparable to that of the original utterance. If judgment is taken to be imposed upon all readers, indeed all humanity, by Isaiah of Jerusalem, what would the declaration of the end of judgment mean for us? It cannot be that the wrath of God that overshadows all human history has been removed and replaced with salvation.

The original message was a problem for those who came after it was delivered. The disciples of the Babylonian Isaiah had to overcome disappointment with the return and reestablishment of the exiles in Jerusalem. They had to face the continuing reality of sin—of sin in the people who had been promised that there would never again be judgment of the whole people of God. They were forced to think through a message that somehow combined the judgment of Isaiah 1–39 and the irreversible salvation of 40–55.

The message that endures for Jews is that the people of God will continue and never face collective divine judgment again. Moreover, they are called to witness to YHWH among the nations. As we shall see in the next chapter, judgment had to be reactivated in a new key to fit the new situation.

I suggest that we Christians take another look at typology.[30] In particular, there are significant structural analogies between the Babylonian Isaiah's declaration of the end of the exile and his promise of new exodus, and Jesus's proclamation of the kingdom of God (in Mark 1:15 and so forth). They both have the structure of "already" and "not yet." Both too are at the initiative of God but invite humans to participate in the saving event. Although the kingdom of God is not proclaimed as the formal end of judgment, it would place those who enter it proleptically "beyond judgment." On the other hand, the audience that Jesus addresses is not the corporate body of Israel, so we cannot stretch our analogy too far. Each is an independent message from God; their analogical character simply supports the unity of the Old and New Testaments.

It is not clear in Isaiah 49–53 where the Servant Songs fit in—how the servant's activity and fate relates to the declaration of the end of national judgment and return. The Christian kerygma ultimately invests Jesus's being and suffering with the power to bring about repentance, self-examination and purification; in other words, his life and death inaugurate the kingdom. Perhaps this can fill out what the book of Isaiah left unresolved.

---

30. Following von Rad, *Old Testament Theology*, 2:319–409.

# 17

# The Book of Isaiah III: Prophetic Tradition and Penitential Piety

(Isaiah 56–66)

THE LANGUAGE AND THOUGHT of Isaiah 56–66 is reminiscent of Second Isaiah, making it a reasonable surmise that the author of these chapters was a disciple of the prophet of the exile.[1] This prophet (or prophets) was living in Jerusalem.[2] Let's assume that they had followed Second Isaiah's urging to return to Jerusalem once Cyrus permitted them to.

These disciples had a hermeneutical task of applying their master's prophecies to the situations that arose either on the return trip or when they settled in Jerusalem. The powerful, quasi-eschatological promises of the exilic prophet had been confirmed in a general way by Cyrus's ascending the Babylonian throne and permitting exiled peoples to return, but the harsh conditions the returnees experienced along the way and in Jerusalem didn't match the "vision" that the master had painted for them. They had to understand the discrepancy and devise a strategy for resolving it.

We can appreciate how the disciples (who had prophetic powers in their own right) could begin to draw on Isaiah of Jerusalem as well as the prophet of the exile. They needed precedent for accusing their fellow returnees of violating the divine will, and the eighth-century prophet certainly provided it.

---

1. There are enough differences in thought and style to distinguish them: See Hanson, *The Dawn of Apocalyptic*, 32–46.

2. That at least is how we propose to read chapters 56–66.

*Redeeming Judgment*

However, since the Babylonian Isaiah had said that the judgment of the exile was once for all, and there would be no repetition, disciples of the Babylonian prophet had to find an alternative to the prophecy of national judgment.

For the prophets' message of judgment and redemption to have an effective impact on the consciousness of Israel, it had to have a deep and lasting impression on its piety. The piety we are looking for is located in Third Isaiah. We shall find a new, or altered form of communal prayer. Lament becomes penitential prayer of the people. It reviews the history of the people with their God, juxtaposing God's grace with Israel's sin and judgment. The piety of individuals also changes: lament is replaced by penitential prayer, or lament focused on sin and redemption.

## Awaiting Salvation

For a good many years I accepted a reconstruction of the "sociology" of the community in which the prophet known as Third Isaiah prophesied. A relative chronology of prophecies was reconstructed according to an evolution from the message inherited from Second Isaiah to an apocalyptic or quasi-apocalyptic message.[3] It has been criticized over the years, but that is not why I am suspending my use of this hypothesis. Rather, it is my decision to interpret the final form of the text, and to bracket out the historical reconstruction of the literature. All we need to know about the social setting is the image of the era projected by biblical literature.

So our task is to work out the argument embedded in the final form of the text. We can examine the eleven chapters with questions like this: Why are the chapters ordered in the way they are? What does this order convey? How does this order condition our reading of the book of Isaiah? How did this author or these authors apply the received traditions, especially First and Second Isaiah, to its novel situation? How does this help us to read and interpret the whole book of Isaiah?

### The Beginning

One might expect this new set of prophecies to begin like Isaiah 40, namely, with the call/commission of the prophecy of salvation. Isaiah 56–66 does have the report of a commission in 61:1–4, famous to Christians because Jesus cites it in his inaugural sermon in Luke 4:18–19. That report, however, is not cited at

---

3. See Hanson, *The Dawn of Apocalyptic*.

the beginning to validate the authenticity of the prophecies, but in the middle of the book, surrounded by promises of salvation:

> The Lord has sent me to bring good news to the oppressed,
> to bind up the brokenhearted,
> to proclaim liberty to the captives
>
> ...
>
> to proclaim the year of the Lord's favor,
> and the day of vengeance of our God,
> to comfort all who mourn. (vv. 1–2)

This passage seems to be the high point of the book, the climax, to which the early chapters are leading us. It is the divine guarantee of the hope of salvation mediated by a person who recalls the servant of Second Isaiah, particularly the second and third Servant Songs. This rather symbolic identification takes the place of the actual name of the prophet.

While we might have expected the call of the prophet first, we actually get what should be recognized as the thesis of the eleven chapters of prophecy:

> Thus says the Lord:
> Keep justice (*mishpat*) and do righteousness (*tsedaqah*),
> for my salvation (*yeshuʿati*) will come
> and my victory (*tsidqati*) to be revealed (56:1 RSV)

I provided the Hebrew words because I want readers to notice that the same word is used for "righteousness" and "victory." This pun actually signals a synthesis of First and Second Isaiah: First Isaiah means "righteousness" whenever *tsedakah* is used, while Second Isaiah means "victory." *Mishpat* is the regular word for both "judgment" and "justice," and *yeshuʿah* for "salvation."

The verse sounds like a truism, but it is this exhortation or promise that synthesizes the prophecies of Third Isaiah. The disciples of Second Isaiah returned to Jerusalem with great expectations. Those expectations are preserved in Isaiah 40–55; they are also stated and restated in chapters 60–62. However, the returnees experienced a "delay of the parousia," that is, of the salvation that centers on the people of God and reaches to the ends of the earth. In the search for an explanation, they discovered the persistence of sin among those who returned from exile and in their compatriots who had remained in the land during the exile. While the disciples of the prophet believed that Israel would not be subject to judgment again, the people's sin was holding back the promised salvation. The people should redouble their efforts to please God by their justice and righteousness.

The thesis verse (56:1) is followed up with a statement commending those who pursue justice, observe the Sabbath, and avoid evil. This sounds rather individualistic, and may foreshadow the eschatology that comes to the fore in chapters 65–66. At this point it is simply an encouragement.

Now chapter 56 takes a surprising turn. It exhorts birthright Israelites to welcome foreigners and eunuchs into the religious community. It begins with quotes from the outsiders expressing their fear of rejection and exclusion (v. 3). This is answered by an oracle to eunuchs (in vv. 4–5) and foreigners (vv. 6–7). At the end of v. 7 we discover that the Lord intends his temple to be open to all peoples: "for my house shall be called a house of prayer for all peoples." This is followed by a statement that associates the ingathering of the diaspora with the gathering of converts.

Second Isaiah had planted the seed for this gathering of foreigners in the concluding trial in chapter 45. That chapter offers Gentiles salvation: "Turn to me and be saved, all the ends of the earth" (Isa 45:22). Second Isaiah also designated the people of YHWH "witnesses" to him. This probably did not add up to an active mission, but it would be an openness and welcoming of the non-Jewish population in whose midst Jews would live henceforth. Now the disciples of Second Isaiah have become patrons, so to speak, of those who accepted the invitation.

## Apostasy and Injustice in the Sacred Community

The accusations against the people begin in 56:9 and continue to the end of chapter 59. The first unit condemns the leaders, the shepherds, for getting "drunk" while the flock is devoured by wild animals (56:9–12). This is followed by a saying about the death of the righteous that, again, charges the leadership with indifference (57:1–2).

Chapter 57 now covers the subject of apostasy in the community rather exhaustively. The addressees are identified as "children of a sorceress"—who is also an adulterer and whore (v. 3). We then are told one forbidden practice after another:

> You . . . burn with lust among the oaks
> . . .
> [you] slaughter your children in the valleys . . .
> To [spirits?] you have poured out a drink offering

> ...
> Upon a high and lofty mountain
>> you have set your bed,
>> and there you went up to offer sacrifice.
>
> ...
> You journeyed to Molech with oil
>> and multiplied your perfumes;
> you sent your envoys far away,
>> and sent down even to Sheol (from vv. 5, 6b–7, 9)

At the end of this catalogue of apostasies, the Lord addresses the perpetrators:

> Whom did you dread and fear
> ...
> And did not remember me?
> ...
> Have I not kept silent and closed my eyes,
>> and so you do not fear me?
> . . . .
> When you cry out, let your collection of idols deliver you!
>> The wind will carry them off
> ...
> But whoever takes refuge in me shall possess the land,
>> and inherit my holy mountain. (vv. 11–13)

Notice that judgment will soon come, and idolaters will have to suffer the fate of their idols, while the faithful will inherit the holy mountain.

This is the extent of judgment in this chapter. Now we have a promise of salvation. It begins with the encouraging words, "build up, build up, prepare the way" (v. 14). The Lord now describes his true dwelling place:

> I dwell in the high and holy place,
>> and also with those who are of a contrite and humble spirit,
> to revive the spirit of the humble,
>> and to revive the heart of the contrite. (v. 15)

This is revolutionary: we have a piety that is driven by contrition and humility. We are going to return to this subject later in the chapter. The oracle that follows this self-introduction announces the message of salvation by explaining its relationship to judgment:

> For I will not continually accuse,
>> nor will I always be angry
>
> ...
>
> Because of their wicked covetousness I was angry,
>> I struck them, I hid and was angry;
>> but they kept turning back to their own ways
> I have seen their ways, but I will heal them;
>> I will lead them and repay them with comfort. (vv. 16–18)

Note that the persistence of sin among the redeemed has forced God to persist in the healing process.

Now we come to one of the all-time favorite social gospel texts. Isaiah 58 is devoted to the subject of fasting. The prophet speaks about his commission at the outset:

> Shout aloud, do not hold back
> ...
> Announce to my people their rebellion (58:1)

The people pretend to seriously seek the Lord:

> Day after day they seek me,
>> and delight to know my ways,
> as if they were a nation that practiced righteousness
>> and did not forsake the ordinance of their God. (v. 2)

The people do have a complaint: "Why do we fast, but you do not see?" (v. 3a). The Lord has a complaint as well: "You serve your own interest on your fast day / and oppress all your workers" (v. 3b). During their fasts, they quarrel, and make a big show of their contrition (vv. 4–5). Now the prophet seizes the opportunity to teach the people the type of fasting that the Lord would approve of:

> Is not this the fast that I choose:
>> to loose the bonds of injustice,
>> to undo the thongs of the yoke,
> to let the oppressed go free,
>> and to break every yoke?
> Is it not to share your bread with the hungry,
>> and bring the homeless poor into your house;
> when you see the naked, to cover him,
>> and not to hide yourself from your own kin? (vv. 6–7)

We now hear conditional promises of salvation, e.g.,

> If you remove the yoke from among you,
> > the pointing of the finger, the speaking of evil,
> if you offer your food to the hungry
> > and satisfy the needs of the afflicted,
> then your light shall rise in the darkness . . . (vv. 9b–10)

Thus, though the prophecy began as if we would hear of punishment, instead it goes into teaching and offers salvation contingent on the fulfillment of that teaching. A similar promise is made to those who observe the Sabbath (58:13–14).

The beginning of chapter 59 is a sermon explaining why the salvation promised by the Lord has not materialized:

> See, the Lord's hand is not too short to save,
> > nor his ear too dull to hear.
> Rather your iniquities have been barriers
> > between you and your God. (59:1–2)

The next six verses continue in the same vein: "your hands are defiled with blood," "your lips have spoken lies," "no one brings suit justly," "their works are works of iniquity," "their feet run to evil," "the way of peace they do not know, and there is no justice in their paths."

This jeremiad elicits a confession of sin by the people (59:9–15a). The supplicants sound serious about accepting responsibility for the mess they have made. What is striking is there is virtually no sign of hope for forgiveness and restoration. And in fact, the Lord's "answer" is silence, due to displeasure, and he decides to play the executioner, so to speak:

> He put on righteousness like a breastplate,
> > and a helmet of salvation upon his head;
> he put on garments of vengeance for clothing,
> > and wrapped himself in fury as a mantle.
> According to their deeds, so will he repay. (vv. 17–18a)

To our relief, a few verses later God promises to come to Zion as a redeemer, saving those who turn away from their sin (v. 20).

## Redeeming Judgment

### A Time of Salvation

Reading chapters 60–62 is like stepping into a different world from chapters 57–59. There is nothing on the sin of the inhabitants of Jerusalem and the countryside. The focus is the restoration of the city and its religious calling. Each chapter begins with a dramatic introductory strophe. Chapter 60 has a call to awaken at dawn:

> Arise, shine; for your light has come,
>> and the glory of the Lord has risen upon you.
> For darkness shall cover the earth
> ...
> But the LORD will arise upon you,
>> and his glory will appear over you.
> Nations shall come to your light,
>> and kings to the brightness of your dawn. (60:1–3)

The third verse signals the primary message of the rest of the chapter. The nations and rulers will bring gifts to dedicate to the Lord (vv. 5–7). This gift giving will be accepted: "they shall be acceptable on my altar, / and I will glorify my glorious house" (v. 7c). Those in the diaspora will be brought by the peoples; the strophe ends with a reminder of what happened and will happen: "in my wrath I struck you down, / but in my favor I have had mercy on you" (v. 10b). The next strophe promises great wealth from foreigners (vv. 11–13); this ends with the declaration, "I will glorify where my feet rest" (v. 13b). The people's past oppressors will have to do homage to Israel and provide from their wealth (vv. 14–16); this will happen so that the Israelites "shall know that I, the Lord, am your Savior / and your Redeemer" (v. 16b). The next strophe has Peace and Righteousness appointed as supervisors of the city, and Salvation and Praise made the walls and gates (vv. 17–19). The Lord himself will be the city's life "and glory" (v. 19c). The final strophe promises the things necessary for the city to endure (vv. 20–22); at the right time the Lord "will accomplish it quickly" (v. 22).

Chapter 61 begins with the commission of the prophet—a passage we have already discussed. Isaiah 61:5–6 stand out as the word that explains the election of Israel. The people "shall be called priests of the Lord / ... ministers of our God," and other nations will be the laity who bring their offerings. The Lord has put his seal on the people:

> I will faithfully give them their recompense,
>> and I will make an everlasting covenant with them. (v. 8)

Other peoples will recognize them as the Lord's elect. Verse 10 has an Israelite speak: "I will greatly rejoice in the Lord, / my whole being shall exult in my God." (v. 10)

Chapter 62 brings this great collection of promises to a conclusion. The attention-arresting strophe begins:

> For Zion's sake I will not keep silent,
>> and for Jerusalem's sake I will not rest,
> until her vindication shines out like the dawn,
>> and her salvation like a burning torch. (62:1)

The thrust of the chapter seems to be that the people of God will be vindicated before the world and held in honor by the Lord. Note his extravagant promise in v. 3:

> You shall be the crown of beauty in the hand of the LORD,
>> and a royal diadem in the hand of your God.

The relationship between the Lord and his people is then compared to marriage (vv. 4–5). This is followed by a promise of intercessors who will keep the Lord from ever abandoning his people again (vv. 6–9). The chapter ends with a procession through the city, led by the saving God (vv. 10–11). The people and city will be given a name of honor:

> They shall be called "The Holy People,
>> the Redeemed of the LORD";
> and you [the city] shall be called "Sought Out,
>> A City Not Forsaken." (v. 12)

## Pleading for Divine Intervention

I have entitled this section to characterize the communal lament in 63:7—64:12. This lament elicits a reply from the Lord in chapter 65. However, between the lament and the promise of salvation in chapters 60–62 is a prophecy of judgment against Edom: Isa 63:1–6. This passage was made famous in the American hymn from the Civil War, "The Battle Hymn of the Republic." What the prophecy is doing in Third Isaiah is hard to say; nothing has been said about Edom, or any other neighboring people, in Third Isaiah. It may be here

## Redeeming Judgment

because of its vivid depiction of divine intervention—both to save and to punish. Perhaps it is meant to remind readers of YHWH's might, rather like Habakkuk 3—also a portrayal of a spectacular divine epiphany. It functions to bridge the change of mood from the promise of salvation to the communal lamentation.

The communal lament does not begin with lamentation but with recounting praise. The first two verses praise the Lord for his saving actions in the past.

> I will recount the gracious deeds of the Lord,
> > the praiseworthy acts of the LORD,
> because of all that the LORD has done for us,
> > and the great favor to the house of Israel. (v. 7)

This praise continues through v. 9. Suddenly the prayer confesses the people's sin and divine judgment:

> But they rebelled
> > and grieved his holy spirit;
> therefore he became their enemy;
> > he himself fought against them. (v. 10)

This is a "new" element in the communal lament: a confession of past sin that brought deserved judgment. We did not find anything of this sort in the communal laments of the Psalter; only Jeremiah 14 has any sort of confession of corporate sin (v. 7). We have, of course, already heard a confession of sin in Isa 59:9–15a; that is much closer to our passage than any parallel in other writings.

Once the people suffered divine judgment and accepted their responsibility, they began to review the past. We have in vv. 10–12 a question of the people: What happened to the God who has given us power and intervened for us? This recital of the Lord's saving deeds continues through v. 14, which shifts from recounting to addressing YHWH: "Thus you led your people, / to make for yourself a glorious name."

Now, for the first time, the people begin to plead:

> Look down from heaven and see,
> > from your holy and glorious habitation.
> Where are your zeal and your might?
> > The yearning of your heart and your compassion?
> > They are withheld from me. (v. 15)

Notice that the request for the Lord's attention quickly spills over into an accusing question. Verse 17 is subdued accusation, also in interrogative form:

> Why, O Lord, do you make us stray from your ways
>    and harden our hearts, so that we do not fear you?

This is an amazing question, in as much as the people would normally take responsibility for their own actions. Nevertheless, the theology of the book of Isaiah does regard God as a "cause" alongside the human will. In the call of Isaiah (chapter 6), he is told to "make [their] mind dull, / and stop their ears / and shut their eyes" (v. 10).[4]

Verse 16 is an unusual glimpse into the consciousness of this group, which traces itself to the prophet of the exile:

> For you are our father,
>    though Abraham does not know us
>    and Israel does not acknowledge us;
> You, O Lord, are our father,
>    our Redeemer from of old is your name

The people have been "disowned" by the religious community of Jerusalem. Since we read attacks on the priesthood (e.g., 65:5), they probably have been ostracized from the religious community presided over by the priests.

Verse 17b is the first full-scale request of this lament: "Turn back for the sake of your servants, / for the sake of the tribes that are your heritage." Verses 18–19 are first-person complaint; it almost sounds like an explanation for the request for divine help. The people have no temple, and even the divine inheritance is not in their possession. This is no evidence that the people are chosen by the Lord:

> We have long been like those whom you do not rule,
>    like those not called by your name.

Isaiah 64 begins with a wish—a wish for divine intervention. This is a weakened request (or petition). The formulation goes along with the unusual request:

> O that you would tear open the heavens and come down,
>    so that the mountains would quake at your presence—

This image continues into v. 2, which ends in 2b with a purpose clause: "to make your name known to your adversaries, / so that the nations might trem-

---

4. Moreover, the Lord was famous for "hardening the heart" of Pharaoh.

ble at your presence." The people simply desire an epiphanic display so that they and their adversaries would realize that the Lord is "real." This wish is expanded by a recollection of past displays:

> When you did awesome deeds that we did not expect,
> > you came down, the mountains quaked at your presence.

Verse 4 confesses YHWH's sole deity: "No eye has seen any God besides you." This recollection concludes with the idea that the Lord displayed his power because the people "gladly do right, / . . . [they] remember you in your ways" (v. 5a). The supplicants have conveniently overlooked the accounts of sin and judgment in the sacred history.

Verse 5b is a bit of a puzzle: "you were angry and we sinned." One would expect the sequence to be reversed. Is the poet saying something by this order: that the Lord caused Israel's sin by getting angry with them? Whether that is the intent or not, the prayer has broached a difficult question. God's anger is having the opposite effect than it should have, driving Israel away, inviting anger in return, threatening a complete shipwreck of the relationship.

Verse 6 sounds like a confession of sin: "We have all become like one who is unclean, / and all our righteous deeds are like filthy rags."[5] Within the passage, it borders on a first-person complaint; the follow-up begins like a lament over finitude—"we all fade like a leaf"—then moves to sin: "and our iniquities, like the wind, take us away" (v. 6b, RSV). This is a deeply melancholy meditation on a life emptied of meaning and hope. Verse 7 (RSV) exposes the unintended effect of God's judgment:

> There is no one who calls upon your name,
> > or attempts to take hold of you;
> for you have hidden your face from us,
> > and have [delivered] us into the hand of our iniquity.

What can break this destructive cycle? All the people know to do is plead with the Lord to calm his anger:

> Do not be exceedingly angry, O Lord,
> > and do not remember iniquity forever.
> > Now consider, we are all your people. (64:9, NRSV)

---

5. KJV: "But we are all as an unclean thing, and our righteousness are as filthy rags." RSV: "We have all become like one who is unclean, / and all our righteous deeds are like a polluted garment." This verse was made famous by the Reformation.

This plea has been prefaced with a confession of the Lord's importance for the people (v. 8).

This prayer is very reticent in comparison to standard communal laments.[6] The accusations are subdued, toned down, left hanging. The people are deeply conscious of their own sin, and wonder whether God will continue to show them grace. There seems to be a need to build up confidence in YHWH's power and graciousness by recitations of his deeds in the past—in the sacred tradition. Nevertheless, the prayer does confront the actual situation with courage and insight. The anger of judgment has become counterproductive. "While we may deserve our suffering, your anger is driving us away from you and into a kind of heedless cynicism. If you do not reverse course, you may not have a people to be your witnesses, your priesthood."

Chapter 65 is the Lord's answer to this lament. Commentators differ as to how far the answer extends. I draw the line at v. 16. The Lord's answer is something of a denial that he has been indifferent to their prayers:

> I was ready to be sought out by those who did not ask;
> to be found by those who did not seek me.
> I said, "Here I am, here I am,"
> to a nation that did not call on my name. (65:1, NRSV)

The Lord then accuses the people of false and immoral religion. Many of these actions belong in the category of private religious acts, like "sacrificing in gardens," "sit[ting] inside tombs and spend[ing] the night in secret places." The people violate Jewish dietary laws by eating swine and other "abominable" things. One of these sinful practices, though, concerns the official cult:

> Who say, "Keep to yourself,
> do not come near me, for I am too holy for you." (v. 5a)

This separation of the priests from the laity elicits an additional condemnation: "These are a smoke in my nostrils" (v. 5b) There seems to be no stopping the escalating alienation and reprisal.

But now comes a turn, potentially revolutionary. With v. 8 the Lord begins to promise "my servants" a hopeful future:

> Thus says the LORD:
> As the wine is found in the cluster,
>     and they say, "Do not destroy it,
>     for there is a blessing in it,"

---

6. Psalms 44; 74; 79; 80; 85; 89; Lamentations 5; Jeremiah 14.

> so I will do for my servants' sake,
>> and not destroy them all.
> I will bring forth descendants from Jacob,
>> and from Judah inheritors of my mountains;
> my chosen shall inherit it,
>> and my servants shall dwell there. (vv. 8–9, RSV)

In vv. 11–12 (NRSV), the Lord addresses those who continue to practice their occult religion:

> But you who forsake the LORD,
>> who forget my holy mountain,
> who set a table for Fortune
>> and fill cups of mixed wine for Destiny,
> I will destine you to the sword.

And if readers have missed the point, vv. 13–16 vividly underscore the division to take place:

> My servants shall eat,
>> but you shall be hungry;
> my servants shall drink,
>> but you shall be thirsty;
> my servants shall rejoice,
>> but you shall be put to shame;
> my servants shall sing for gladness of heart,
>> but you shall cry out for pain of heart,
>> and shall wail for anguish of spirit. (vv. 13–14)

Names will change their meaning so that the servants will inherit the land and divine election (v. 15). The passage ends with the new truthfulness of the new era:

> Then whoever invokes a blessing in the land
>> shall bless by the God of faithfulness,
> and whoever takes an oath in the land
>> shall swear by the God of faithfulness;
> because the former troubles are forgotten
>> and are hidden from my sight. (v. 16)

As I have already indicated, this division of the people of Israel is potentially revolutionary. While the prophets of judgment recognized the differences between righteous and unrighteous, religious and irreligious, judgment still came upon the nation, the people of the Lord. This passage changes that. The fate of the one party, called the servants, is salvation, while the dominant religious community, many of whom also indulge in occult or syncretistic practices on the side, will be judged. The inheritance, and the dignity of election, and the sacred traditions, will be transferred to this ostracized group.[7]

This division of Israel down the middle gives additional importance to the individual. When we considered the individual laments, we recognized that individuals were in situations involving judgment as individuals. However, now the national or collective fate has an individual component. That is, the individual can decide to become a "servant of the Lord" or continue among the majority religion. The person's decision and faithfulness to that decision now receive divine recognition, so to speak.

This "sect"[8] seems to have consciously adopted the name *servant* from Second Isaiah. Exactly how much of the servant was imitated in this group is hard to say. They certainly do not explicitly cite the vicarious sufferings of the servant portrayed in Isaiah 53. The prophet seems to have appropriated the tasks assigned the servant in the first three Servant Songs. I say this on the basis of Isa 61:1–4, which I take to be the prophet's testimony.

We have the evidence of the communal lament to reconstruct a description of their piety. This is very important. The religious group associated with the prophetic author of Third Isaiah has appropriated divine judgment so thoroughly into its religious affections and practices that we can speak of penitential piety. The ideal that was cultivated in the community has been condensed to what amounts to a slogan. We have already come across a telltale characterization of the ideal:

---

7. This group will also include converts.

8. According to Hanson, *Dawn of Apocalyptic*, 46–202, 211–19. Second Isaiah's disciples, and those attracted to them, were becoming a "sect," that is, a group that shares doctrine with the dominant religion of a society, but is more intensive in its commitment and practice, and withdrawn from the "world." The prophet who speaks in these writings conforms to 'orthodoxy" to the degree that it was defined; we know from the catalog of religious sins condemned that the sect aspired to purity of belief and practice. The prophet found his contemporaries—those outside the circle of servants—lax in their religion and exploitative as slave owners and businessmen. They were the powerful and wealthy—at least relative to the prophet and his associates. They embraced the privileges of the priests and civil authorities, and were indifferent or oppressive to the landless. This is the picture the prophet himself paints, though he may be making a caricature of the opponents of the servants.

> I dwell in the high and holy place,
>> and also with those who are contrite and humble in spirit,
> to revive the spirit of the humble,
>> and to revive the heart of the contrite. (57:15b)

We come across the same characterization, indeed the same dialectic, in 66:1–2:

> Heaven is my throne
>> and the earth is my footstool;
> what is the house that you would build for me,
>> and what is my resting place?
> All these things my hand has made . . .
> But this is the one to whom I will look,
>> to the humble and contrite in spirit,
>> who trembles at my word.

In chapter 66, the saying is a part of an antitemple polemic. God's throne is not in the temple but in heaven *and* in the heart of the humble, contrite person. This is the revolution that this group is articulating and promoting.

Isaiah 66:1–5 sounds as though it originated as a polemic against the rebuilding of the Jerusalem temple in 520–515 BCE. This explains why the prophet goes on to ridicule the sacrificial cult.

> Whoever slaughters an ox is like one who kills a human being;
>> whoever sacrifices a lamb, like one who breaks a dog's neck;
> whoever presents a grain offering, like one who offers swine's blood;
>> whoever makes a memorial offering of frankincense, like one
>> who blesses an idol. (66:3)

The unit ends with an address to the pious:

> Hear the word of the Lord,
>> you who tremble at his word:
> Your own people who hate you
>> and reject you for my name's sake
> have said, "Let the Lord be glorified,
>> so that we may see your joy";
>> but it is they who shall be put to shame. (v. 5)

Those who "tremble at the Lord's word" are precisely those in whose hearts YHWH reigns. This verse singles out "enemies" who cast aspersions on the pious. Isaiah 65:1–16 divides the society between those who despise the Lord, and the pious. The one group will be punished; the other—the "servants of the Lord"—will be rewarded (vv. 11–12, 13–16). The salvation depicted in 65:17–25 and 66:7–14 is destined for the pious. These are not defined by ethnicity or social class, but by the spirituality they exhibit, the kind of people they are. The fate of the individual has now become distinguished from that of the nation.[9]

## A New Heaven and New Earth

The final two chapters of Isaiah sketch an eschatological horizon for the salvation of the servants, and condemnation of the members of the community at large. Isa 65:17a states God's intention to "create new heavens / and a new earth." What follows this is a saying affixed to the new exodus in Second Isaiah: "the former things shall not be remembered / or come to mind" (v. 17b; cp. Isa 43:18). The remaining eight verses provide poetic images of what this new state of existence will be like. The new is first of all characterized by joy and the cessation of sorrow (65:18–19). Examples are given regarding length of life (v. 20), building and planting (vv. 21–22), and children (v. 23). The Lord will answer prayer without fail (v. 24). Nature will be transformed by ending predation (v. 25, cp. Isa 11:6–9).

Chapter 66 also has an eschatological vision, beginning in v. 7. Verses 7–9 introduce the new age as a miraculous birth: "Before she was in labor / she gave birth; / before her pain came upon her / she delivered a son." This is applied to the repopulation of Zion. Isaiah 66:10–14 are based on the idea of consoling those "who mourn over Jerusalem" (v. 10). Jerusalem is symbolized as a mother breastfeeding her children (vv. 11, 12) and taking care of them as they grow up (v. 13). The unit concludes with an opaque reference back to the division of the people between servants and opponents:

> And it shall be known that the LORD is with his servants,
>     and his indignation is against his enemies. (v. 14)

---

9. The group associated with Third Isaiah seems to have returned eventually to the dominant religious community and accepted the temple. The very fact that we have their writings in the canon is evidence of that. But it is also to be noted that some passages in these chapters assume a legitimate temple cult, above all 56:6. The verse combines the revolutionary universalism of this group with rituals of the temple cult: "I will bring [foreigners] to my holy mountain . . . their burnt offerings and their sacrifices will be accepted on my altar."

There follow two verses describing how his indignation will annihilate those enemies (vv. 15–16).[10]

The chapter concludes with what might be called an appendix. Only here do we find a promise to include the nations in this denouement (vv. 18–21). Verse 21 is quite striking: "I will take some of them [viz., Gentiles] as priests and as Levites, says the Lord." The promise continues into vv. 22–23. This poetic fragment recalls the introduction statement:

> For as the new heavens and the new earth . . .
> shall remain before me, says the Lord;
> . . .
> so shall your descendants and your name remain. (vv. 21, 22)

This is the closest the passage comes to offering immortality: the immortality of progeny and remembrance. The next verse promises that all flesh will join in the worship of the Lord.

This eschatological vision is surprisingly down to earth. As Marius Reiser states, the passages do not describe the new heavens and new earth as "*totaliter aliter*, not a new creation after the destruction of the old, but a marvelous renewal of the world through God's removal of all evil from it."[11] It is a greater break with history than the promises of salvation in First and Second Isaiah, but it remains "in touch" with the earlier hints of eschatology. I would say that precisely because of its this-worldly character, it can perform an important rhetorical function. It provides an ultimate horizon for all the judgments announced and performed in the book, and also the announcements and earnests of salvation; each had its particular moment and horizon, but as these become past, there needs to be a horizon, a future, in which these still have prophetic force. The final two chapters of Isaiah provide such a horizon, one that still deals with the realia of life but looks forward to transformation.[12]

The new age is introduced directly by divine intervention.[13] The text is actually left open for readers to supply a concept of what is going to happen. Most apocalyptic works do have scenarios of the transition—usually battles or a final trial. The fact that Isaiah 65–66 does not provide any scenario is an

---

10. Isaiah 66:6 may also belong here; the judgment of the wicked comes back in the last verse, viz., 66:24.

11. Reiser, *Jesus and Judgment*, 30.

12. Ibid., 30, n. 23, quotes Augustine as saying, "For this world shall pass away by transmutation, not by absolute destruction" (*City of God*, 20, 14).

13. Hanson, *The Dawn of Apocalyptic*, 34–60.

advantage for the use of the book in religious communities; the absence of a final scenario allows interpreters to fill it in or remain silent as they see fit.

The book of Isaiah not only depicts the idyllic new age but also judgment, "perdition." Invariably this is an event of death and destruction. Since there is no eternal heaven, there is no eternal hell. Those ideas will emerge in apocalyptic, but they are beyond the horizon of Isaiah. For the visionary who wrote Isaiah 65–66, the worst fate a person could suffer is a gruesome, shameful death, and consequent exclusion from the joyful, fruitful world of the saved.

The division of the people is not between good and bad but between the "servants of the Lord," characterized by humility and contrition, and those who despise and exclude them. This is quite this-worldly, centering on a conflict within the Jewish religious community. The sectarian exclusivism in evidence in the prophecy of Third Isaiah would have been relaxed when the prophet's community was absorbed into the wider community and their piety taken up by others. The criteria for salvation were undoubtedly loosened so that that anyone whose comportment was pleasing to God would not be excluded, perhaps even Gentiles.[14]

## Drawing Things Together

Third Isaiah begins as a follow-up on the promises of Second Isaiah and ends with a comprehensive eschatological vision. The promise itself is restated by a new, anonymous prophet in Isaiah 60–62. The chapters that precede this proclamation explain the delay of the fulfillment of the promise; this explanation entails accusations of oppression, arrogance, and idolatry. Following the proclamation of the promise, we find a communal lament saturated with penitential piety. It is a plea for God's saving intervention, the fulfillment of the promise. The Lord's answer is that he has yearned to save them, but the people were turning their backs on him. Then a new prospect is announced: God will save a particular group, his "servants" but punish those who are in control of the temple and city. This division will occur as a part of the creation of a "new heaven and a new earth."

---

14. Reiser, *Jesus and Judgment*, 145–50, 157–58, believes that Gentiles were excluded in principal, viz., they did not know the law.

## The Travail of Second Isaiah's Promise

There is very little in Second Isaiah's prophecies that deals with the "reversion" of the people of God to the behavior that brought the divine judgment of exile. The prophet is very clear that Israel and Judah had brought judgment on themselves by their sin. However, what they will do once they return to Zion and are restored is left out of account. The impression is left that they will be cured of the propensity to sin. That allows the prophecy to bear eschatological weight, but it forces the disciples of the exilic prophet to adjust to reality.

Brevard Childs dismisses any conclusion about the failure of Second Isaiah's message to materialize in the period of return: "The discrepancy between what happened after the exile and the prophet's eschatological description of God's will is not a criticism of the truth of the promise, but rather an indication of how little the exilic community partook of the promised reality."[15]

While I concur with Childs that the discrepancy between the prophetic promise and the events that followed doesn't discredit the promise, he detaches the promise from its transactions with history. The appropriation and modification of this promise by the prophet's disciples as they struggle to understand the vicissitudes of their history should belong to the promise.

I would remind readers of the story of Noah and the flood. The Lord is motivated to wipe out the human species because "every inclination of the thoughts of their hearts [is] only evil continually" (Gen 6:5). His motivation for forbearance at the end of the flood is, "for the inclination of the human heart is evil from youth" (Gen 8:21). The destruction of all humans but Noah and his family does not make any progress toward converting or transforming the human heart and will. The change of policy announced in Gen 9:21–22 is instituted by God to allow the human race to continue despite its penchant for evil.

This same conclusion can be applied to Israel. The people undergo the judgment of exile and experience the sustaining grace that leads them to their new, postexilic mode of existence. These traumatic events have a deep, transforming effect of the people, but the people remain as inclined as ever to oppression, arrogance, and idolatry. The postexilic situation, like the postflood situation, is less collective, and the people have been given new laws and institutions, but they remain sinful.

The exile inscribes a strong sense of national guilt on the consciences of the disciples of Second Isaiah and their sympathizers. This consciousness

---

15. Childs, *Introduction to the Old Testament as Scripture*, 327.

humbles them and keeps them open for the guidance of the Spirit. We find this penitential piety articulated in the communal lament in Isaiah 63–64. It is also named several times: "a humble and contrite heart/spirit" (57:15, 66:2). According to Isa 66:1–2, this is the spirituality that provides a throne for God. Those who share it are the party named "servants of the Lord" in our chapters. They are contrasted to unrepentant Judeans—those who indulge in various forms of idolatry and snobbery (65:2–7). The unrepentant claim title to the heritage, but the servants will receive it. The servants will be rewarded, the unrepentant punished on the Day of Judgment.

## Looking Back at Isaiah from the Perspective of the Final Chapters

The book of Isaiah is rather like a monumental building to which wings have been added by different architects at later times.[16] Viewers invariably ask whether the additions are in harmony with what preceded them. Likewise, readers of Isaiah must inquire after the harmony of the added parts. Indeed, we would like to affirm that the sequence is of vital importance: the book "progresses" toward its eschatological conclusion.

The best way to regard Isaiah 56–66 is as the appropriation and application of the first two parts of the book. It is not the climax but more like the fifth act in Shakespearean tragedy, in which the consequences of the climax are worked out. Most readers of Isaiah would probably locate the climax in Isaiah 40–55, though in many ways the exile itself needs to be recognized as a turning point.

The book of Isaiah is rooted in Isaiah's call in chapter 6. After all, the truth of the prophet's message is its authorization by God. Isaiah is commissioned to convey a message to the people, a message of divine judgment for the people's sin. The exact content of this message is unspecified; rather, Isaiah is told of the contradictory effect the message will have on the people. If the people would attend to his message, and repent, they could be pardoned and healed. They will not, probably they cannot, and that is further evidence of how deeply they are in the grip of their sinful condition.

Isaiah fulfills his commission in chapter after chapter. However, only a few chapters are unrelieved judgment; e.g., chapter 5. Chapter 1 is pervaded with judgment, present as well as imminent, but also sets forth hope

---

16. The Des Moines Art Center is on this order: the original core building was designed by Eliel Saarinen, added to by Richard Meier and I. M. Pei.

## Redeeming Judgment

for restoration and redemption. It appears that Isaiah regarded judgment as a transforming event—an event that punishes and purges evil, resulting in a purified community inhabited by humble, penitent citizens. Hence, under his authorization to put the people of God on trial he can promise Zion that it will become the capital of an international order, the residence of a messianic king, and so forth.

The door has clearly been left open to the announcement that Israel's time of punishment is over, and its sin is pardoned, so salvation is at hand. This new message is also divinely authorized in the first verses of chapter 40. It requires such validation for its authority, its truth.

Although the message of Isaiah 40–55 addresses Israel—actually Judean exiles—150 years after the death of the Isaiah of Jerusalem, it sounds like a direct follow-up to the message of Isaiah 1–39. The prophet speaking in Isaiah 40–55 repeatedly characterizes the exile not as due to the power of a human empire but as the active intervention of Israel's God to make the people of God "pay" for their sin. When Israel laments her condition, she should not blame her enemies, though those enemies may well have carried out their divine calling too harshly. Israel should acknowledge that God brought about the suffering and should be praised for his justice and righteousness. If Israel insists on blaming someone, she should blame herself—in other words, show remorse and repent.

Now the people of God should turn away from the tragedies of the past and look forward in expectation to the new exodus. This message too has its roots in the message of Isaiah of Jerusalem. That at least seems to be alluded in such declarations as Isa 41:26-27: "Who first declared it from the beginning . . . / beforehand . . . ? / [I] first to Zion . . . / and I give [or gave?] to Jerusalem a herald of good tidings."

Cyrus is God's instrument; he will conquer Babylon and release those who were settled in "political detention." Notice that Cyrus plays a similar role in Isaiah 40–55 to the one Assyria plays in Isaiah 10 and 14. Now, however, the foreign power is an agent of salvation, not judgment. It was this claim, evidently, that sparked opposition from the prophet's audience.

The servant is a mystery character in Isaiah 40–55. When he is first introduced (Isa 42:1-4), his mode of conquest is persuasion, a sharp contrast to Cyrus. He does not destroy or coerce, yet he will spread his law around the world. When we next meet him (49:1-4), the servant is speaking, describing his calling and the aid he receives from God. He is already expressing discouragement. In the third Servant Song (50:4-9), he describes persecution but puts his trust in the Lord to deliver him. The climatic song (52:13—53:12) depicts a life of suffering, persecution, and death, followed by a mysterious "resurrection" allowing the servant to continue his role of atoning for others' sin.

It is hard to locate the servant in the scenario of pardon and new exodus. Nevertheless, we do get a glimpse of the people's reaction to the message and a new perspective on the people's judgment and forgiveness. Perhaps the prophet's suffering is meant to transform the hearts of those for whom he suffered.

To understand Isaiah 56–66, we need to hypothesize that the disciples of the Babylonian prophet returned to Judah among the first wave of those who made *alli'ah*. The message opens (56:1) with a statement that indicates that the prophet (or prophets) intends to "combine" Isaiah 1–39 and 40–55. The book unfolds in such a way that we hear new accusations against the society. The message of Isaiah of Jerusalem has been revived, but in a new key. The divine punishment takes the form of a delay of the promised salvation.

The task of the prophet is to "announce to my people their rebellion, / to the house of Jacob their sins" (58:1) on the one hand, and to arouse hope: "he has sent me to bring good news to the oppressed, / to bind up the brokenhearted, to proclaim liberty to captives, / and release to the prisoners— / to proclaim the year of the Lord's favor" (61:1–2). It is these two poles that the prophet must reconcile for a discouraged, destitute and mean-spirited community. The prophet cannot "return" to Isaiah of Jerusalem's message because the Babylonian Isaiah's salvation is once for all. He initially explains the delay of salvation as the mode of God's punishment.

A new message begins to emerge in the later chapters of Isaiah 56–66. We hear of a group of servants—perhaps a "sect"—who are humble, penitent, "broken spirited." These are ready to be saved, but the powerful, landowners, and probably commercial businessmen, along with the temple priesthood, are displeasing to God. There will soon be a Day of Judgment, a day when the sinners are removed and the servants take over. This event will be so dramatic that it can be described as the creation of "new heavens and a new earth" (65:17; 66:22).

We are now on the verge of a theological vision that will take over postexilic Judaism. We have a new piety that internalizes the prophetic message and its fulfillment in the exile, and a new understanding of the future, viz., a final judgment in which the wicked will be punished and the righteous (those who exemplify penitential piety) saved. Salvation will be a transformation of the character of humans and of the conditions of human existence.

It is legitimate, I believe, for Christian readers to adopt this appropriation and application of Isaiah's message of judgment and salvation. Christians must accept that Isaiah's message of judgment applies to all the people of God, throughout their history, and the whole human race as well. For Christians, the message of salvation will invariably be linked typologically with the person and work of Jesus Christ. Isaiah 56–66 lays down an appropriate piety and eschatology for this vision of life.

Before we turn to the New Testament, however, we should trace the impact of this new piety and full-scale eschatology have on the book designed for the use of the people in worship, viz., the Psalms. This is the internal canonical evidence of the spread of these new teachings into the postexilic Jewish community.

# 18

## A Debate over Piety
(Psalms, Job)

THE TASK OF THIS chapter is to follow the footprints, so to speak, of the servants' piety. There are certain slogans in common between Isaiah 56–66 and a few psalms. These seem to indicate that the passages derive from the same circles. We are not, however, seeking to establish some causal relationship. A final-form reading need only recognize that the piety of the disciples of Second Isaiah appears elsewhere. Moreover, one could not ask for a better "pulpit" for spreading a new spirituality than the community prayer- and songbook.

How is the spread of this piety relevant to the theme of divine judgment? It is my contention that the piety is the appropriation and internalization of the prophecy of judgment, which was fulfilled in the exile.

Readers should immediately recognize penitential piety because it pervades the New Testament. Jesus's parable of the tax collector and the Pharisee (Luke 18:9–14) teaches it, as do the beatitudes in Matthew 5.

What the reader may not realize is that penitential piety clashed with the piety expressed in the individual laments of the Psalter. This sort of piety we can call classical. It was, probably, the norm among the people of God until the postexilic period.

We could simply compare classical and penitential piety, and leave it at that. However, I think we have a dramatization of the clash of pieties in the dialogue of the book of Job. Job defends the right to accuse God and protest his fate, and his friends believe that the appropriate response to all untoward events is to acknowledge that one deserves this fate and repent. The upshot of the divine resolution of this clash is that there is a tension between two legitimate pieties.

## Prayers of Individuals

Now we turn from the communal penitential prayers to the piety of individuals. There are no prayers of individuals in Third Isaiah, but several passages characterize their ideal; e.g.,

> But this is the person to whom I will look,
>   the one that is humble and contrite in spirit,
>   and trembles at my word. (Isa 66:2b)

We have quoted this description earlier, but I wanted to remind readers of the language used. Isaiah 57:15b is also relevant:

> I dwell in the high and holy place,
>   and also with him who is of contrite and humble spirit,
> to revive the spirit of the humble,
>   and to revive the heart of the contrite.

This characterization is, I think, something approaching a slogan of those aspiring to live according to this ideal. We can follow it to other passages that express the piety of the humble, contrite person.

### Psalms 51

I will examine Psalm 51 first, and then take up 50. Psalm 51 has a close link to Isa 66:2:

> The sacrifice acceptable to God is a broken spirit;
>   a broken and contrite heart, O God, you will not despise. (v. 17)

I would call this a variant of the slogan that best characterizes penitential piety. Let's explore the form and content of psalms with penitential characteristics. Psalm 51 begins with a request for forgiveness and cleansing.

> Have mercy on me, O God, according to thy steadfast love;
>   according to thy abundant mercy blot out my transgressions.
> Wash me thoroughly from my iniquity,
>   and cleanse me from my sin! (vv. 1–2, RSV)

*A Debate over Piety (Psalms, Job)*

In Old Testament piety, sin was both a broken relationship with God (specifically an act of disobedience to the express or evident commandment of God) and a "fouling" of one's being—hence, the language of cleansing.

The next strophe explains why the supplicant seeks forgiveness and cleansing:

> For I know my transgressions,
> > and my sin is ever before me.
> Against you, you alone, have I sinned,
> > and done what is evil in your sight,
> so that you are justified in your sentence
> > and blameless when you pass judgment. (vv. 3–4)

The supplicant wants to state publicly, before God and the human community, that he or she owns up to the wrongdoing. Verse 4 has a strong theological thrust—at odds, I might say, with much piety: all sin is against God. When one violates oneself or another human, one breaks a divine commandment. This acknowledgment that one has acted against the divine majesty opens the door to a justification of God's judgment; some call this a "doxology" of judgment. Verse 5 seems to be a commentary on the supplicant's propensity to sin: "Indeed, I was born guilty, / a sinner when my mother conceived me." This sounds like a statement of the doctrine of inherited sin, a doctrine rarely attested and atypical of Old Testament thinking. We could construe it thus: at no point in the supplicant's life has he or she been free from sin.

The next couple of strophes (viz., vv. 6–7, 8–9) are requests all directed to personal transformation.

> You desire truth in the inward being;
> > therefore teach me wisdom in my secret heart.
> Purge me with hyssop, and I shall be clean;
> > wash me, and I shall be whiter than snow. (vv. 6–7)

Verse 6 begins with a confession concerning God's character. It forms the basis of the request in the second line. Here the focus is on inwardness. The supplicant wants not only to know "wisdom" with the conscious mind but absorb it into the "secret" places. Parallel to this inwardness are the images of external cleansing.

Verses 8–9 request good effects from this transformation:

> Let me hear joy and gladness;
> > let the bones that you have crushed rejoice.

> Hide your face from my sins,
>> and blot out all my iniquities. (vv. 8–9)

The request for the capacity to rejoice has the strange image of broken bones, and some commentators take it as proof that the supplicant has suffered physically, and it was this that prompted repentance. That is quite out of keeping with the rest of the psalm, and since the psalm is not a personal expression but a liturgical text to be used by many worshippers, it would be quite inappropriate to narrow its application to such an odd selection of people. This is the wrong way to read psalms.

Verse 9 is the other side, so to speak, of joy: the supplicant enjoys receiving not only forgiveness but also a clear conscience.

Verses 10–12 seem to repeat the requests of vv. 6 and 8:

> Create in me a clean heart, O God,
>> and put a new and right spirit within me.
> Do not cast me away from your presence,
>> and do not take your holy Spirit from me.
> Restore to me the joy of your salvation,
>> and sustain me with a willing spirit. (vv. 10–12)

If there is a difference between v. 10 and v. 6, it is that v. 10 asks for a new will or spirit. The supplicant desires what we call a "conversion"—not a conversion to a new belief, but a change of heart that can be called "being led by the Spirit." Linguistically, at least, this sounds very Pauline. Verse 11, though stated negatively, is a request for the infusion of the divine spirit. The strophe ends with another request for joy, but note that this mood is also "generous."

Verses 13–14 are a vow to teach other members of the people how to live the penitent life:

> Then I will teach transgressors your ways,
>> and sinners will return to you.
> Deliver me from [bloodguilt], O God,
>> O God of my salvation,
>> and my tongue will sing aloud of your deliverance. (vv. 13–14)

Those familiar with the individual lament will recognize that the vow to teach has taken the place of the vow of praise that frequently concludes laments, e.g.,

> My heart shall rejoice in your salvation. I will sing to the Lord,
>> because he has dealt bountifully with me. (Ps 13:5b–6)

# A Debate over Piety (Psalms, Job)

One can still hear that vow of praise in 51:14b. Verse 14a has puzzled commentators, for nothing has been said about the crime of murder, and it seems doubtful that the supplicant thinks he will be tempted to murder in the future. The line would read better if it includes "bloodguilt" (not "bloodshed," as the NRSV has), and this were taken metaphorically. After all, the psalm is for the use of many people in all sorts of situations.

Verse 15 repeats the vow to praise but is accompanied by a request for the power to do so: "O Lord, open my lips, / and my mouth shall show forth [your] praise" (RSV). The strophe now offers another type of explanation:

> For you have no delight in sacrifice;
> > if I were to give a burnt offering, you would not be pleased.
> The sacrifice acceptable to God is a broken spirit;
> > a broken and contrite heart, O God, you will not despise. (vv. 16–17)

The praise promised in v. 15 will not be accompanied with sacrifice, as it so often is in individual laments. Verse 16 articulates a teaching of the prophets of judgment:

> What to me is the multitude of your sacrifices?
> > says the Lord;
> I have had enough of burnt offerings of rams
> > and the fat of fed beasts;
> I do not delight in the blood of bulls,
> > or of lambs, or of rams. (Isa 1:11; see also Amos 5:22;
> > Hos 6:6; and Jer 7:22)[1]

At one level, the polemical statement in Psalm 51 explains why the supplicant offers praise without sacrifice; at another, it is offering, according to v. 17, a "broken spirit" and a "broken and contrite heart" *instead of* animals. These two verses, I maintain, generalize the psalm as a whole. The psalm supplies the words for someone who desires to please God. The psalm is not composed for persons who feel guilty for some action, some misbehavior; it provides words for one to say continually. Whatever one feels like, it gives you words with which to come before God, and could also be a paradigm for other prayers.

I have not forgotten vv. 18–19. In v. 18 we have a prayer for Zion—one might say, a request at home in communal laments:

> Do good to Zion in your good pleasure;
> > rebuild the walls of Jerusalem

---

1. A slight alteration of the RSV.

*Redeeming Judgment*

> then you will delight in right sacrifices,
>> in burnt offerings and whole burnt offerings. (vv. 18–19)

The plea dates itself and the psalm. It requests the rebuilding of Jerusalem, specifically its wall. That would date the verses as before Nehemiah; however, the rebuilding of the temple, not city fortifications, might be implied, since not having walls does not impede sacrifice, but ruins for a temple might well.

Why did readers or editors have to refute the teaching of the psalm? Obviously, the rejection of sacrifice is contrary to the temple cult, and the psalm might well have been left out of the Psalter if the psalm's teaching had not been neutralized. Surely the priests did want to keep it; it is one of the most beautiful, powerful psalms in the tradition.

## Form and Piety

Psalm 51 was categorized as an individual lament by Claus Westermann, my mentor for form criticism.[2] However, form critics have not been comfortable with that categorization.[3] More recently a program unit was added to the annual meeting of the Society of Biblical Literature devoted entirely to penitential prayer. Several books have come out of that unit and from its members.[4] I have not been a part of this group, but I was delighted to discover their work because of dissatisfaction with the form-critical categorization of this type of prayer as individual lament.[5] It is good to have a number of people working together on a problem.

Let's note some of its odd form-critical features. Psalm 51 has no complaint (German *Klage*). It does have request, but note that the supplicant does not seek deliverance from an external foe or from any sort of calamity the supplicant has suffered.[6] All requests have to do with the supplicant him- or herself—for forgiveness of sins committed by the supplicant, and for the power to avoid sin in the future. Sin is like an addiction in this psalm, and the requests have to do with deliverance from a condition one has brought on oneself.

---

2. Westermann, *The Praise of God in the Psalms*, 41, 76.

3. Note, for example, Miller's special treatment of the Psalm in his book *They Cried to the Lord*, 244–61.

4. Boda et al., *Seeking the Favor of God*, vol. 1.

5. I had the odd experience of having to write on this psalm in my doctoral examination on form criticism. I gave it a Westermann-style analysis, but was unhappy with the result. However, I didn't begin thinking seriously about what to do about it until recently.

6. With the possible exception of "the bones thou hast broken."

*A Debate over Piety (Psalms, Job)*

This psalm aspires to be used not just when one is feeling bad about something one did, or beset upon by God for guilt. The editors of the Psalter may have kept it for this niche, but it offers a new piety, which would at least stand in tension with the vast bulk of individual laments in the Psalter. Psalm 51:16–17 have the function of legitimizing a "broken spirit and contrite heart" as the approved way of approaching YHWH. We have in the psalm, and a few others, a piety that promises to "infuse" the lives of Jews. It did in fact slowly permeate Jewish piety and largely silence the classical individual lament.

*Psalm 50*

Now I want to call attention to another psalm that seems to be designed to legitimize penitential, inward piety. Psalm 50 begins as a temple theophany:

> The Mighty One, God the Lord,
>> speaks and summons the earth
>> from the rising of the sun to its setting.
> Out of Zion, the perfection of beauty,
>> God shines forth. (vv. 1–2)

Here we have a picture of God's appearance before his people. It seems rather strange, even ironic, that a temple theophany should communicate an anti-sacrificial message. To add to the irony, the addressees are identified as those "who made a covenant by sacrifice" (v. 5).

The divine address, which takes up the bulk of the psalm (vv. 7–23), begins as a trial. YHWH says he will "testify against you" (with heaven and earth playing the role of witnesses). The accusation begins with a negative: the people are not sinning by failing to sacrifice (vv. 8–9). Indeed, YHWH does not need sacrifices; if he were hungry, he could eat wild animals (vv. 10–13). This is an argument against sacrifice; it is intended to render sacrifice absurd.

Verses 14–15 offer an alternative to sacrifice, or an alternative form of sacrifice.

> Offer to God a sacrifice of thanksgiving,
>> and pay your vows to the Most High.
> Call upon me in the day of trouble;
>> I will deliver you, and you shall glorify me.

Beginning in v. 16, we have accusations; however, unlike classical prophecy this oracle singles out "the wicked." The accusations against the wicked continue until v. 22; the last verse of the psalm (v. 23) returns to the right way to approach God, regarding thanksgiving as a substitute for animal sacrifice, indeed an act of sacrifice of another order.

While this psalm doesn't have the slogan "broken spirit and contrite heart," it does teach an inward piety and ridicule the ideology of sacrifice. I am inclined to take this psalm as a preparation for Psalm 51; it provides the divine authorization for inward piety and the ideal of humility.

## Psalm 130

In this short psalm we find a subtle expression of penitential piety. It lacks the telltale slogan. It also lacks any explicit expression of remorse or compunction. Indeed, the psalm is a marvel of indirection, of indicating the unsaid.

It begins with a haunting cry: "Out of the depths I cry to you, O Lord" (v. 2). In a standard lament we would classify this statement as first-person complaint. It describes, metaphorically, the emotional mood of the supplicant. The speaker is in deep melancholy. This autobiographical statement is followed up with a plea to be heard, for the Lord to hear one's anguished cry. Notice that this is stated twice, in different words, to emphasize its importance; it implies a desperate mood.

We might expect a complaint, a lament, about one's troubles, or a request for deliverance. Not so. Rather, we find a meditation on the guilt of all humans. Even this meditation is indirect: it is hypothetical. If God kept tabs on the behavior of all humans, it is doubtful (expressed as a question) that anyone would pass the test. Hidden in this meditation is the supplicant's admission of guilt.

The anxious thought about guilt—personal and universal—is answered by a confession of trust. God would not keep a record of a person's misdeeds, because he is forgiving. Here again we have an indirect statement, an assurance of pardon to the supplicant's indirect confession of sin.

At this point we can say that the supplicant is—that we ourselves are, if we are praying the Psalm—overwhelmed by guilt, deserving of divine judgment, but relying on God's forgiveness. We are in the depths of despair due to our guilt, and are staying afloat by the hope for divine relief.

One might expect a request at this point, but we find the psalm expressing trust, or rather describing an attitude of trusting. We are waiting in hope of a divine answer. What will the answer be? Is it an act of God or a word of God?

*A Debate over Piety (Psalms, Job)*

Not only are we waiting in hope, but our waiting is compared to a watchman waiting for dawn. The mood of waiting is evoked by the repetition of the metaphor. Yet we are never told what we are waiting for, what would count as a divine answer. Salvation must have something to do with forgiveness, but it seems to imply more than that. We want, it seems, to be released from our guilt and the sin that has us in its grip.

In the very last strophe (vv. 7–8) we encounter one final surprise. Despite the fact that we receive no resolution in the prayer up till now, the supplicant becomes an evangelist, so to speak, for the Redeeming God. "Israel" is told to put its trust and hope in its God. This God is known for his *hesed*, his "steadfast love," for his own. Hence, he will "redeem" them. This is a new term within the psalm. It suggests taking care of one's own. However, we have no hint yet as to what one needs to be redeemed from. In the very last verse, this is spelled out: YHWH "will redeem Israel from all its iniquities." This is a new use of the word *redemption*. The power that has taken over the people is its own actions, and probably its addiction to sinful actions. It takes God to free his people from their own willfulness.

I would suggest that the last strophe of Psalm 130 enacts the promise made in Psalm 51:13 to "teach transgressors your ways [that] sinners will return to you." That is another reason to call the final strophe evangelistic.

It is clear that Psalm 130 as well as Psalm 51 embody a robust, profound penitential piety. They represent a view of life that regards sin and guilt as the worst dangers to Israel's or the individual's good, and deliverance to take the form of forgiveness and redemption.

## The New Piety and the Classical Lament

The supplicant in penitential psalms regards sin and guilt as the all important issues of the moral or religious life. The enemies have disappeared, and even problems of health and well-being have retreated. Complaints against God have been largely silenced, though they are still heard in the communal lament of Isaiah 63–64. There is a passionate desire to be purified of the impulse to sin—this is what redemption is about. The supplicant never protests his or her innocence; no, sin is undeniable, and it pleases God when one admits one's particular sin.

The next step toward redemption, according to Psalm 51, is being inspired by God's Spirit to act in accordance with God's will (51:10–12; also v. 17). The penitential spirit is one that admits its shortcomings and awaits God's regeneration. Sin is too deeply rooted in the self to be eradicated by an act of will. The supplicant "surrenders" to God and allows God to take over. Grace is not only forgiveness; it is power to change.

There seems to be no expectation that sinners will overcome their propensity to sin. Redemption, one might speculate, is being set on the path toward faithfulness, righteousness, and holiness—not arriving at the goal.

Psalm 130 gives us the expression, "redemption from [our] iniquities/sin." This is the meaning of *redemption* that will take over Christian theology. Not only have the issues of social conflict and health become secondary, but the social and political issues of poverty and oppression have been demoted. These must be integrated into the scheme of sin, guilt, forgiveness, redemption, and salvation if they are to be preserved.

### The Contrasting Spirituality of the Classical Lament

The most obvious difference between penitential piety and the classical piety is the virtual absence of confession of sin in the latter. Indeed, it is much more likely to find a protest of innocence or righteousness. It is even shocking to find the situation over which the supplicant prays to be pictured in black and white.

At a deeper level, the issues that concern the supplicants of the classical laments are life and death, social conflict and shame, judicial trouble—in a word, the common problems of daily life. The supplicant has experienced a crisis prompting him or her to go to God, the sovereign over life and death. The supplicant most often seeks to recruit God, to enlist his aid against whatever problem threatens well-being. A few individual laments accuse God of betrayal or even animosity. The rhetorical strategy of these seems to be to shame God into acting appropriately.

When divine judgment is brought up in individual laments, the supplicant appeals to God as judge. The crisis calls for a "trial" of sorts; the supplicant hopes that God will condemn the enemies. It hardly occurs to the supplicant that God might condemn. How different from Psalm 130!

## Job: A Dramatized Lament

The title of this section is more the presupposition of the argument than the point of it. All my scholarly studies of Job over the decades have been premised on this characterization of the book. I learned it from Claus Westermann's *The*

*Structure of the Book of Job*,⁷ and anyone who seeks a demonstration of this form-critical analysis may consult it.

I have been reading the book as an apologia for the kind of individual laments that accuse God. This will be the thrust of this chapter. It is quite relevant to the subject of divine judgment, because the theological position that silences accusations against God proposes to make all disasters and disruptions into warnings or judgments. Eliphaz states the thesis forthrightly at the beginning of his first discourse:

> Who ever perished who was innocent? . . .
> Again and again I have seen those who cultivate injustice
> And sow trouble harvest it. (4:7, 8, AT).⁸

Initially this assertion is meant to encourage Job to take his suffering as a warning to straighten out his life (5:8–27), but later he says it is simply to silence Job's blasphemy.

So the issue is, when are disasters divine judgment, and when are they not? Job, however, only argues this issue explicitly in a late speech (21:1–34; 24:1–12, 22–25). Up until then he works himself into a direct challenge of God to demonstrate his (i.e., Job's) guilt (13:13–27). When this challenge is not immediately answered, Job displaces his hope into the future (14:13–17; 16:18–21; 19:23–27; cp. 23:3–17). So the dynamics of the prayer of accusation come to the fore in this book.

We can bracket out the prose prologue (Job 1–2) and epilogue (Job 42:7–17) for our purposes. They would be an essential part of the exposition of the book, but we are interested solely in the dramatized lament articulated by the main character in the poetic drama. Thus, Elihu is not within our scope. The dialogue between Job and his three companions is front and center because it dramatizes the clash between pieties. The answer of God will bring the clash to a mysterious resolution, so it will also be attended to.

## *The Structure of Job*

The poetic drama takes up chapters 3:1—42:6 of the book. Within that, we have the dialogue between Job and his three companions between chapters 3 and 27. Within this, there is an initial utterance of Job and a curse of his birth (chapter 3), which provokes one friend, Eliphaz, to respond (chapters 4–5).

---

7. The title in German: *Aufbau des Buches Hiob*.

8. Throughout this chapter, I will be drawing on my own translation of Job, published in Patrick, *Arguing with God*, 16–61.

## Redeeming Judgment

Job responds in turn (chapters 6–7); followed by the speech of a second friend, Bildad (chapter 8); Job again (chapters 9–10); the third friend, Zophar (chapter 11); and Job wraps up the first cycle with a long speech (chapters 12–14). This sequence is followed in a second cycle, with speakers in the same order; the speeches are shorter. At the end of the second cycle Job openly disputes the doctrine his friends have been trying to foist upon him (chapter 21, cp. chapter 24). To this, Eliphaz responds with a direct accusation against Job (chapter 22). According to Westermann, whose analysis I am following, Job turns away from the friends after Eliphaz's accusation.[9]

Job 28 is a poem that doesn't fit into any character's mouth; it does make a profound commentary of the action, so I would not regard it as an intrusion.[10] The next three chapters are a concluding lament by Job, which makes a good transition between the dialogue and the Lord's answer to Job.

When we speak of accusations against God, these include third- and second-person discourse. There is actually something to be learned by noting the patterns of distribution for second- and third-person discourse. Job's curse of the day of his birth has only three verses referring to God in the third-person. In Job's response to Eliphaz (chapters 6–7), there are 15 verses accusing God, 11 of which are in the second person. In his response to Bildad (chapters 9–10), 49 of 56 verses of the discourse are accusations against God, 21 of which are in second person. Job's response to Zophar, which climaxes the first cycle, has 41 verses of accusation, 18 of which are in second person. Within each of these discourses, the third-person statements come at the beginning, but once Job addresses God, he continues to do so to the end of that discourse.[11]

### Job's Curse of His Existence and Eliphaz's (Chapter 3)

This chapter plays a crucial role in the plot of the poetic drama. First, it sets the drama off violently from the story. This is a different Job, one who speaks to shock readers into recognizing his angry mood. He does not accept his suffering piously. No effort has been made to bridge his change of mood from the

---

9. Westermann, *The Structure of the Book of Job*, 131–34; the chapters that follow, viz., 24–27, are disturbed by almost everyone's estimation, and Westermann surmises that they are displaced fragments which belong earlier in the dialog. This hypothesis yields better sense than the current arrangement, but we will stick to the final form.

10. When my students dramatize this drama, a narrator handles the poem on the inaccessibility of wisdom as well as prolog and epilog: see Patrick, *Arguing with God*.

11. There is one contradiction of this thesis: 9:32–35.

previous chapter; indeed, the poet's object is to force the audience to notice the discontinuity.

Job's curse of his day is an expansion of the first-person complaint. However, it reaches a higher level of generality. It amounts to the proposition that it is better to not be than to be; the best of all would be to have never been. Once one exists, one becomes attached to being and afraid of dying, so to have never been, or to die in the womb, is preferable. One cannot imagine a harsher accusation of the Creator. In chapter 3, that accusation is only implied; later it is spelled out:

> Why did You deliver me from the womb?
> Why wasn't I stillborn before an eye had seen me? (10:18, AT)

Here we have an ancient version of a very modern question: Does life have any meaning or value?

Eliphaz realizes immediately that Job is out of control—that he has allowed his emotions to master his mind, and that he needs to be brought back to the tried-and-true response to suffering. This response is associated with the cultural tradition known as wisdom. Eliphaz leads with the argument that those who perish deserve their fate:

> Who ever perished who was innocent?
> Where were honest men swept away? (4:7, AT)

Later in the speech he goes farther, claiming a law of action and consequences:

> For despair does not simply spring up from the dust
>   nor does trouble just sprout from the soil.
> Rather, a man gives birth to his own misery,
>   just as sparks from a fire fly upward. (5:6–7, AT)

A second argument is put forward by Eliphaz—an argument introduced with great fanfare:

> Can mere man be righteous before God?
> A man be blameless before his Maker? (4:17, AT)

Eliphaz seems to employ this argument to warn Job against protesting his innocence. It simply supplements the argument that all events are under the control of the all-powerful and righteous God and therefore should be understood as "instruction" and perhaps warning or punishment.

*Redeeming Judgment*

*Job's Response to Eliphaz and Bildad's Response*

Job certainly refuses to comply with the prescriptions of his companions. In his first response, he appeals to the proportions of his suffering:

> If only the full weight of my suffering were measured
> > and my numerous causes of anger laid on the scales,
> they would outweigh the sand on the seashore.
> > That's why my words are savage. (6:2–3, AT)

It is not only the quantity of his suffering but its duration, its seemingly unending character. He even expresses the wish that God would put an end to his life so that suffering will come to an end (6:8–13). He feels abandoned by friends, even his three companions (6:14–30). As far as the deity is concerned, Job describes God as a violent opponent, using military imagery:

> My blood sucks in the poison arrows flung by a God of war
> > and He readies His torture chambers for me. (6:4, AT)

At this point, the deity is an impersonal force that has intruded arbitrarily in his life.

As the discourse continues, Job works his way into his first personal address of God. The first second-person pronoun is found in a meditation on the shortness of life:

> Remember [2nd pers.], my life is but a breath . . .
> While Your eye is on me I will vanish forever. (7:7a, 8a, AT)

This is furtive, and would only be a "slip," but for the fact that it opens a floodgate, so to speak. In 7:11 Job works up the courage to express his complaints to God. His complaints are rhetorical questions: "Am I the Sea, am I Tannin, that You should put me under guard?" (7:12, AT). Job is not a threat to cosmic order, as is the monster from myth, so why does God subject him to constant scrutiny and punishment? This idea is expressed in the parody of Psalm 8:

> What is man that You take him so seriously . . .
> examine him every moment? (7:17–18, AT)

This complaint could be called "big brother is watching you." It is noteworthy that Job does not insist on his innocence in this discourse, as he will later. Here he is speaking for all humans; God is an unjustified, oppressive presence.

This discourse outrages his companions, and ignites a rather hostile series of exchanges. Bildad's extant speech is rather short and lackluster. Westermann believes that 25:2–3; 26:5–14; and 25:4–6 (in that order) belong to it. That order would explain Job's response, which is to the thesis that all humans are guilty before God. As it is, we have to have to regard Job as offering a delayed response to Eliphaz (4:12–21).

### Job's Response to Bildad

Job begins his discourse agreeing that no human is righteous before God (9:2).[12] However, he does not mean the same thing as his friends: for him, it is that no human is able to *prove* that he is righteous. To dramatize this perception, he imagines a trial:

> Do I really want to argue with him? How would I choose my words?
>> Though I am in the right I could not refute him.
>
> I would have to implore mercy from the One I accuse.
>> If I summoned him to court and he responded,
>
> I could not be sure that he would listen to my voice . . .
> Is it a trial of strength? He is strongest.
>> Is it a matter of law? Who can arraign him?
>
> Were I to prove my innocence he would condemn me.
> (9:14–15a, 16, 19, 20a; AT)

Job evidently believes that God's monopoly on power allows him to rule arbitrarily, and that any challenge to his rule will result in the elimination of the upstart, no matter the legitimacy of his case. Yet Job, either a romantic or a fool, shouts out: "I plead innocent! I accept the risk! I despise my life!" (9:21).

While Job is into imagining a trial before God, he adumbrates an idea that will grow on him. "If only there were an arbiter with power to decide the dispute between us" (9:33, AT). This prospect is going to grow into the "redeemer" that Job pins his hope on in the second cycle.

For now, Job begins to formulate his case against God. If I understand 10:2a correctly, he states an accusation hypothetically; that is, this is what he plans to say when they meet. The challenge he proposes is, "Do not condemn me! Give the legal grounds of Your verdict" (10:2, AT). Job's present suffering is taken evidently as a divine judgment that Job wishes to challenge. In the verses that follow, he questions God regarding His constant surveillance (10:3–7), the contradiction of destroying the creature He made personally

---

12. Westermann inserts 26:2–4 before 9:2, again with good reason: Westermann, *The Structure of the Book of Job*, 132–34.

(10:8–13), and the catch-22 situation of the person who has been charged with guilt (10:14–17).

## Job's Response to Zophar

This discourse at the end of the first cycle is the climax of Job's accusations against God, or challenges of God to justify his judgment. Job 12 is a distorted praise of God the ruler of history: it is fixated on God's destructive actions. While this activity might be understood as divine judgment, Job views it more as the arbitrary action of a tyrant who tolerates no rivals.

Then Job turns to his own defense. He accuses his companions of false witness, standing up for God in a trial whose verdict should not be a foregone conclusion.. He prepares for his challenge of God with a rather elaborate confidence builder:

> Keep quiet and let me speak,
>> and let come what may!
> I will seize my flesh in my teeth
>> and take my life in my own hands.
> Though he slay me—and I have no hope[13]—
>> yet I will argue my case before Him!
> This itself may be my salvation
>> for the unrighteous cannot appear before Him. (13:13–16, AT)

Job takes responsibility for his actions; if God slays him, he alone is to blame. But note that Job does see a glimmer of hope, though a paradoxical one, in the prospect of simply getting to argue his case before God.

His accusation or challenge is very simple: "What great evil am I guilty of? Expose my sin before my eyes" (13:23, AT). God has treated him as though he were guilty of some horrendous offense, but Job insists that the charges be "made public," so to speak. Job's conscience does not condemn him (so 27:6).

Job's climactic discourse ends with another imaginary resolution:

> If only You would hide me in the underworld,
>> conceal me there until Your wrath has passed,
>> and appoint a time to meet me. (14:13, AT)

---

13. The translation of this clause is much discussed; mine is a literal translation of the words on the page; the KJV had "yet will I trust him."

Job has no belief in life after death, at least not in a positive sense, so this hope of reconciliation after death seems to contradict what he "knows." Yet this prospect refuses to die, but returns in the second cycle.

*Job's Discourses in the Second Cycle*

Job's friends grow harsher in the second cycle of discourses. Job has not only refused to humbly repent and plead for mercy, he has spoken blasphemously of God. The friends pretty much abandon their effort to return him to the righteous path of wisdom; now they try to frighten him with descriptions of the fate of the wicked and impious.

Job for his part loses his capacity to pray in the second cycle. It is as if his great challenge to God for an explanation of his condemnation has exhausted his capacity to pray. Or he simply becomes convinced that he will not receive a hearing before he dies. He does begin to formulate the hope that his death will itself prompt a hearing of his case, and that he would be represented by an ombudsman. He only returns to lament in his concluding lament in chapters 29–31.

In place of prayer Job utters a hope of a reconciliation between God and himself after death. This raises the question of eschatology. Let's review some passages that expose Job's take on the common conception of death among Israelites during the biblical period.

In the dialogue, Job speaks repeatedly of death—his death and the death of all humans. Remember, this is to be distinguished from dying. Job does feel that he will soon die, but it is the annihilation of human consciousness and vitality that weights most heavily on him. Despite his wish that he had died a newborn, he bemoans the shortness of life. At the end of each discourse in the first cycle, he images how Sheol will be like, e.g.,

> Straightway I will go and not return,
> > to a land of dark and shadow,
> A night land, gloom, dead-black,
> > black shining in black. (10:21–22, AT)

Though one retains a degree of consciousness, it is like being so laid up by an injury or fever that one's

> Sons are honored, but he does not know it,
> > or they are humiliated, but he is not conscious.

> He feels only the pain of his decaying flesh,
> > and his soul mourns over itself. (14:21–22, AT)

It is really strange that Israel should have retained such a hopeless, dismal image of the afterlife when every theological doctrine pointed in the other direction. The fact that the soul was totally cut off from God, not able to render praise, was exploited by supplicants to motive God:

> What profit is there in my death,
> > if I go down to the Pit?
> Will the dust praise you?
> > Will it tell of your faithfulness? (Ps 30:9)

This sort of appeal is rather absurd, but it is available because ancient Israel did in fact understand the dead to be cut off from the Creator. About all one can say in favor of this conception is that YHWH is the God of the living, not the dead.[14] A God for whom the dead are dead is not the Creator, nor would he be the Judge of the whole earth (e.g., Ps 98:9).

In the second cycle of discourses, Job begins to consider his death to be a potential source of hope. The idea is first planted in the last discourse of the first cycle:

> If only You would hide me in the underworld,
> > conceal me there until Your wrath has passed,
> and appoint a time to meet me.
> > But how can a dead man still be alive? (12:13–14a, AT)

This is only an imaginary possibility here, one forced on Job by the contradictions in his situation. God's wrath seems to have mastered the Lord temporarily, but sooner or later his mercy and justice will take charge again. However, the absurdity of finite creatures coming back from the dead—a fact Job has brooded over several times (6:8–10, 14:7–12)—explodes this idea, and he falls back on the unrealistic, but reasonable hope of holding out until God changes (14:14b).

But Job does not give up on his absurd hope. In his next discourse he expresses it in melodramatic terms:

> O earth, do not cover my blood!
> > Do not let my outcry find a resting place!

---

14. Jesus says this, according to Mark 12:27.

*A Debate over Piety (Psalms, Job)*

> Even now I have a witness in heaven,
>> on high there is one who will testify. (16:18–19, AT)

This strophe requires the tracing out of a number of themes. The address of the earth to not cover his blood recalls the story of the first murder: after Cain has slain Abel, and has denied having anything to do with his disappearance, the Lord says, "The voice of your brother's blood is crying to me" (Gen 4:10). Job wants to be sure that his blood testifies to his murder: his cry should effect that. The killer is, by implication, God himself. This is the reason that Job suddenly expresses belief that there is a witness in heaven who will stand up for him once he is dead. Someone other than God, yet one who represents divine justice, must hold God to account.

Now where did this figure come from? Again we find the seed of it in a previous discourse, this time 9:33 (AT): "If only there were an arbiter with power to decide the dispute between us." Nothing more is made of this until the discourse in chapters 16–17. It is amazing the Job can suddenly speak with such conviction with so little to support it. Yet we, the audience, can come to his aid: the whole idea that YHWH lost contact with the dead and that nothing could be done to rectify an unjust death contradicts genuine monotheism. That there needed to be a second figure who represents divine justice over against divine power is a sign that this is doctrine still in a rough state.

No sooner does Job articulate this hope than he is swept over with a wave of doubt:

> If I accept Sheol as my home and make my bed in the darkness,
>> then where will my hope be? who will watch over my hope?
> Will it descend with me into Sheol?
>> Will we sink into the dust together? (17:13, 15–16, AT)

This is where the discourse ends: in Sheol again, but with questions rather than images.

The next discourse articulates the same hope under a different image:

> O that my words were written down!
>> O that they were inscribed on copper!
> Engraved by iron styles on lead!
>> Chiseled in stone for all time!
> For I know that my vindicator exists,
>> one who will someday testify on this spot.

## Redeeming Judgment

> After my skin has decayed away,
>> from (or without) my flesh I shall see God—a God who is on my side. (19:23–27a, AT)

Job's words, inscribed for permanence, or remembered from this dramatic outcry, will be put in evidence by his heavenly ombudsman, and God will be changed, reconciled to him. This time the expression of hope in vindication precipitated by his death is the last word: Job's faith has survived the tests of reason and awaits its fulfillment.

This is the end of Job's search in the dialogue; he does not return to it. Chapters 29–31 represent a recapitulation of Job's lament, especially chapter 30. Chapter 29 rehearses Job's idyllic past, before tragedy overtook him, and then chapter 30 depicts his reversal of fate. From that a lament arises that breaks into addressed accusations against God (30:20–23), then sinks into first-person complaint. Chapter 31 introduces something new: Job swears an oath of clearance. This is a poetic offshoot of a judicial procedure in which the accused denies his guilt in self-curses—if I have done $x$, let me suffer $y$. This poetic offshoot covers a whole range of offenses and impieties, since Job does not know what he might be accused of. At the end he challenges God to review his life and either sustain a charge or change his judgment (see 31:35–37).

### The Position of Job's Companions

The friends, perhaps rightly, regard what Job says to be blasphemy. Having avoided directly accusing Job of wickedness and faithlessness, Eliphaz responds to Job's challenge (in chapter 21)[15] with direct charges (chapter 22). Their reasoning seems to be: if he speaks so blasphemously, Job must be blameworthy in every way.

Job's companions' leading argument is that God is in complete control of all events, and perfectly righteous in all his dealings, so humans should consider events, particularly untoward events, as messages about divine displeasure. Events are either to warn or to punish. The better part of wisdom is to repent and submit to God's disciplining.[16]

The friends bring up another argument in favor of penitential piety. This is the proposition that no creature, certainly no human, is righteous before

---

15. And parts of chapter 24, according to Westermann's rearrangement: see Westermann, *The Structure of the Book of Job*, 132–34.

16. Frequently, suffering is pictured as the boomerang effect of one's deeds, with no reference to divine intervention; see Koch, "Gibt es ein Vergeltungsdogma im Alten Testament?"

*A Debate over Piety (Psalms, Job)*

God. Eliphaz introduces this argument in his first discourse. He prefaces the teaching with an account of how it was revealed to him (4:12–16). This means that he does not consider it a truth that can be known by observation and reflection. He heard an angel in a night vision say,

> Can mere man be righteous before God?
> > A man be blameless before his Maker?
> No even in his servants does He trust and He finds fault with His angels.
> > How much more the creatures of mud houses with dirt foundations.
> (4:17–19, AT)

He appeals to the same teaching in the second cycle:

> What in human nature is worthy of purity?
> > How could a creature born of woman be righteous?
> He does not even trust His holy angels
> > and the heavens are tainted with sin.
> How much more a being which is profane, even foul,
> > Mortal man, who drinks imperfection like water! (15:14–16, AT)

A third statement of the teaching is attributed to Bildad:

> How then can a man be righteous before God?
> > How can one born of woman be clean?
> Even the moon does not shine brightly
> > nor are the stars spotless in His eyes.
> How much less man, a worm,
> > one of the human race, a maggot! (25:4–6, AT)[17]

These add up to a very powerful statement of human guilt and unworthiness. It is not clear, however, what the argument does for the friends' counsel. One might think that it would undercut their doctrine of rewards and punishments: if no human can satisfy God, what sense does it make to promise to reward virtue?

It may well be that the argument is to be taken independently of the other: it is meant to support the teaching that the way to come before God is in humility and contrition. Accusing God, as one does in classical lamentation, is out of the question. It evidences an arrogance unworthy of a pious believer. When you go before God, always admit that you are unworthy of his attention

---

17. This is a part of the disturbed section. Job 26:2–14 could also belong to Bildad, since his discourse in chapter 25 is too short and truncated.

and favor, that your sins are foul and deserve punishment, and that you are completely dependent on God's mercy.

Are the three passages a version of penitential piety? At first glance, they sound like our penitential literature. However, a closer look shows that the friends argue from creatureliness; the "fall" is ontological, not one which humans were able to avoid.[18] That would work havoc with the concept of responsibility and guilt.

The question can still be asked, is penitential piety compatible with the classical lament? In the history of the synagogue and church, I think penitential piety, in conjunction with other ideas and practices, did undercut the classical lament.[19] Penitential piety tends to accept blame and concentrate on inner conversion. Even if it differs somewhat from the proposition of Job's friends, it may well have discouraged classical lamentation. Indeed, the most common translation of Job's response to the Lord's discourses from the whirlwind reads: "Therefore I despise myself, and repent in dust and ashes" (42:6, RSV). This standard translation assumes that Job has been shown to be in the wrong in what he said, and so he has to acknowledge that wrongness in the response—which is otherwise a confession of faith and thanksgiving. If one adopts the viewpoint of penitential piety, it would only seem right for Job to repent of what he has said.

## The Answer from the Whirlwind

The greatness of the Lord's answer to Job from the whirlwind is its unpredictability, though many readers find it non sequitur. A best-text interpretation of the Lord's discourses would discover dramatic continuity; the answer should suit the issue and resolve the conflict, but in such a way that the audience must make an effort to make the connection. If the supplicant is in the wrong in some way, the Lord's discourses should either correct or condemn him, according to how he responded. In other words, the discourses should continue the trial rather than simply terminate it with a decision. No new information should be introduced, or the issue of accountability will arise; what will be new is a perspective that only God could provide on what the humans already know.

---

18. According to Reinhold Niebuhr, Paul Tillich's understanding of the fall was of an "ontological" fall: see Kegley and Bretall, *Reinhold Niebuhr*, 433.

19. Cp. Morrow, *Protest against God*, 43–45, 54–55, 106–46.

## A Debate over Piety (Psalms, Job)

The Lord adopts Job's metaphor by employing judicial language at the beginning of each discourse: "Take your stand like a man!" (38:3, AT). "I will interrogate you and you will testify!" (40:7, AT). Accompanying each challenge is a question designed to put the addressee on the defensive:

> Who is this who eclipses deliberation
>     with words without knowledge? (38:2, AT)

> Will you impugn My justice?
>     Condemn Me to prove your innocence? (40:8, AT)

The first of these questions Job's competence to criticize the workings of the world, the second Job's motive for criticizing.

The questions that follow each introduction do not follow upon anything Job or his friends have said in the dialog. It seems that the judicial metaphor has broken down. The Lord is indulging in non sequiturs. Neither Job nor his friends had expressed any doubt about God's creating the world, yet the whole first discourse challenges Job to affirm that it is God, not Job, who creates. The second discourse sounds somewhat more germane: Can Job overthrow the mighty and tyrannical? The Lord says, ironically I'm sure, that if Job can do that, he can save himself.[20]

There are more surprises in store: the second discourse veers away in midcourse from human history to describe two monsters, Behemoth and Leviathan, which fall somewhere between identifiable species and mythical creatures. There is one section, 41:1–11, that challenges Job, indeed a corps of humans, to attempt to domesticate Leviathan. It ends with the mysterious profound reflection:

> No man is so courageous as to arouse [Leviathan].
>     Who then can take his stand before Me?
> Who has confronted Me and survived?
>     Who under the broad sky? (41:10–11, AT)

This would make a dramatically brilliant conclusion to the second and last theophanic discourse. As it is, we have 22 more verses of description that do not concern Job's situation in the least.

Does the Lord's barrage of questions constitute a judgment? By Job's own criterion, receiving any answer is an affirmation of his righteousness (13:15–16). This is probably a valid surmise. But the Lord is not only appear-

---

20. The effort to save yourself is the root of sin; cp. Hos 14:3.

447

ing to Job and acknowledging Job's integrity; he is seeking to persuade Job to acknowledge him as his Creator and Savior. Let's examine each discourse and Job's responses more closely.

The first discourse is focused on the subject of creation. The act of creation is covered at the beginning, but most of the discourse explores the cosmos and the meteorological processes of our environment, and comes to a conclusion with an impressionistic survey of animal life. The discourse is a mixture of questions, challenges, and descriptions. The questions and challenges are aimed at forcing Job—and readers, of course—to acknowledge that humans do not possess the requisite wisdom, power, and know-how either to be or to rival the Creator.

How does this constitute judgment of Job? The Lord ends the first discourse with a forensic question:

> Will this critic continue to dispute with the deity?
> Let the one who accuses God answer these questions. (40:2, AT)

I would take it that Job's answer, "I have spoken once, and I will not answer", to this question and challenge determines the course the trial will take from now on. Job still withholds his praise; he is not fully "converted." The God of creation can impress us with his majesty and grandeur, with his power and wisdom, but we do not know whether he governs with justice and mercy, whether the human good is served.

The second discourse of the Lord seeks to persuade Job to praise him; silence is not enough. The discourse is concerned with the Lord's governance of history. The inquiry begins with a question about the "disinterestedness" of Job's accusations: "Will you impugn my justice—condemn me to prove your innocence?" (40:8, AT). This is germane to Job's testimony, though it does not address its substance. It does not even refute Job's accusations against God, but it does raise doubts. Moreover, it could be construed to deny the logical either/or: either God is to blame for mistreating an innocent person, or God is rightly punishing a wicked and impious person (or one who is suffering from pride). Job and his companions think one or the other of these propositions is true, but the Lord could deny the either/or. If he does so, however, God must admit that the world either is absurd or is ordered by principles that transcend human wisdom.

The challenge to Job to take on the mantle of Lord of history (40:9–14) could well illuminate our quandary. We humans do not rule history any more than we rule nature, but in this case the issue of justice is implied: overthrow despots and tyrants. Humans are in fact capable of doing so, indeed do so rather frequently. Does that give us the power to save ourselves? Invariably, the power that seeks to create justice becomes a threat to justice. The only true sovereign of history must be outside the competition for power.

Now we are surprised by the description of two powerful, semimythological creatures. Only one section, 41:1–11, concerns the position of humans in the created world. If these beasts belong to the natural world, we could say that the Lord has returned to the topic of the first discourse. However, they are on the borderline. In any case, 41:1–9 cover a range of activities relating to Leviathan: Can you capture him? Can you kill him? Can you tame him? Can you make him your servant? Leviathan is too "wild" to be mastered by humans in any of these ways. The point of the argument comes next: if you are afraid to confront this creature, why do you think you can confront its Maker and survive?

Job does in fact respond to the second discourse with praise:

> Now I know that You can do anything!
>     Nothing You propose can be thwarted! ...
> I had heard of You by the hearing of the ear,
>     but now my eye sees You.
> Therefore I repudiate
>     and repent of dust and ashes. (42:2, 5–6, AT)

According to a best-text interpretation,[21] Job is speaking in good faith. That the Lord has granted him a theophany is as important as what the Lord says: Job has experienced a reality that heretofore he only knew by the teaching of tradition (42:5). However, what the Lord has said must reinforce the impact of his presence; otherwise, we cannot make sense of Job's "second" conversion, viz., from silence to praise. Yet the Lord has not said anything that Job does not already know from the praises (at least those known to the reading audience). The Lord has shown Job, though, that his power is a source of life in creation, and of salvation for humans. The latter is hidden in the challenge to take on Leviathan:

> Who has confronted me and survived?
>     Who under the broad sky? (41:11, AT)

---

21. See Patrick and Scult, *Rhetoric and Biblical Interpretation*, for an exposition for this hermeneutical principle.

Commentators are afraid to make much of these words: the translation is difficult, and the result seems to be too profound and subtle for its obscure placement.[22] Nevertheless, these words may be the clue to Job's conversion. The question sounds at first like a rhetorical one expecting the answer, "no one." However, in fact Job has.[23] Rather, I should say, Job has, if he can receive the gift and perform his duty, viz., praise.

According to my translation, Job does not "confess" that he had spoken sinfully before.[24] Many translations read v. 6 as a confession of fault: "Therefore I despise myself and repent in dust and ashes."[25] The Hebrew of the verse is quite ambiguous, and the decision regarding how to translate it comes down to one's judgment as to dramatic propriety. I do not think that Job's lament is condemned by God; the reader's sympathy for Job's viewpoint has been cultivated throughout the drama and is affirmed by the Lord in 42:7–9.[26] Thus, there is no reason for Job to "repent." Since he has been covered by dust and ashes throughout the drama, I think that he cleans up and puts on new clothes; His time of mourning is at an end, the Lord has lifted him up.

So, in my opinion, Job was not judged and censured for his lament. So why does the Lord censure him at the beginning of each discourse? My answer runs thus: though Job has not been wrong to lament, the Lord must bring it to an end, and he does so by forcing Job to decide whether he will accept his status as the Lord's creature, or will seek to be the Lord's equal and rival. The latter choice would result in a much different denouement to this trial.

## Final Reflections

What does Job have to contribute to our understanding of God's judgment of individuals? Job has conceived of his argument with God as a judicial contest. This metaphor begins when he takes up the friends' thesis that no human is righteous before God (9:2). His response is to meditate on what would happen if he did join legal arguments with God (9:14–20). From that point on, it becomes Job's fixed idea to confront God in court. He is still doing so in chapter

---

22. E.g., S. R. Driver (*Job*), and anyone else who would support this contention—namely the contention that Job has wrestled with God and has for all intents and purposes won.

23. Cp. Jacob's wrestling match, Israelite elders seeing God on Horeb, etc. These people see God but don't die; they wrestle with God and "win."

24. See Patrick, "Short Note," 369–71 and Patrick, "Job's Address of God," 268–82.

25. So RSV; consult Morrow, "Consolation," 211–25.

26. Which is not a part of the poetic drama, but I suspect it was composed by the author of the drama.

31 when he swears an oath of clearance and concludes with a challenge to God to pass judgment. When YHWH replies from the whirlwind, he adopts Job's metaphor by employing judicial language (38:3; 40:2, 7–8). The thrust of that reply will be discussed in the next section.

Now our question is, how appropriate is a judicial hearing for individual lament? It depends upon the situation and the supplicant's rhetorical strategy. If Job had focused on physical healing, a judicial inquiry would have made a poor fit. Job was, however, more concerned with God's general assault on his well-being; only two or three verses mention his physical suffering. Moreover, the friends' theology forces Job to judge whether he is guilty of some sin worthy of such an assault on his well being. He adopts the strategy of confronting God as his oppressor and antagonist, not of recruiting God as an ally.[27]

Ultimately, it is God's answer that will settle whether Job's accusations against him are to be judged true or inappropriate. However, we already can judge whether they are compelling. On the one hand, Job has spoken with fierce honesty, has exposed the falsity of the arguments against laments accusing God, and has left open a way to be reconciled with God. On the other hand, Job's accusation of divine injustice cannot be accepted by God; it has to be refuted. The question of the truth of an accusation or challenge of God cannot be judged objectively; its truth must reside in the rhetorical propriety. This type of lament leads to reconciliation with God. That is the message of Job.

The book of Job tells the story of one particular judicial contest between a human and God. The person who speaks here, though fictional, is quite distinctive. He is upright to an outstanding degree, and will insist upon his integrity to this own detriment. Precisely because Job is a unique individual, he becomes a representative of us all. His discourse frequently recalls the conditions all humans share, e.g., shortness of life, the burden of suffering, fear of death, guilt. He can represent the universal because his suffering is not punishment, individual or collective.

Now we come to God's answer from the storm wind. The argument of Job's three companions is disposed of by YHWH; the lament that accuses God has been vindicated. One cannot argue from an untoward event back to the guilt of the victim. In Job 42:7, the Lord clearly sides with Job against his companions: "After the Lord had spoken these words to Job, the Lord said to Eliphaz the Temanite: 'My wrath is kindled against you and against your two friends; for you have not spoken of me what is right, as has my servant Job.'"

---

27. The poet employs military imagery from time to time, but the image doesn't yield as much insight as the image of a judicial opponent.

Yet we must recognize that the Lord is not easy with Job. He censures him, pressing him to change his discourse. The interpretation of Job as repenting is dramatically appropriate to the tenor of the Lord's answer, and it is linguistically just as legitimate as the interpretation I have argued for.[28] Any theological interpretation of Job must justify both translations of Job's answer.

The history of the interpretation of Job 42:1–6 corresponds to Jewish piety. Penitential piety spread out among Second Temple Jews. The members of the consultation on penitential prayer, a program unit of the Annual Meeting of the Society of Biblical Literature, have tended toward the position that penitential prayer displaced, if not replaced, the classical forms of lament.[29] This may be an accurate assessment of what happened in postexilic prayer texts.

However, if one holds to a canonical hermeneutic, what happened to Jewish piety cannot overrule the fact that there are far more laments preserved in the Psalter than there are penitential prayers. The laments could continue to witness to their type of piety. Penitential prayer had to compete with the classical tradition.

So here we are—with a strong witness to the classical lament in the Psalter, but with a history of piety that has largely silenced lament as a practice of synagogue and church. In recent years we have bemoaned the costly loss of lament.[30]

How can the "new" piety, which calls for a new theology revolving around sin, guilt, redemption, and salvation, be kept from silencing the classical lament? The evidence does suggest that it had a silencing effect.[31] Our question, however, is not historical but theological. What we are seeking, I think, is a way to recover the confidence and willingness to wrestle with God in classical lament after acknowledging our own guilt and bondage to sin. We might call this, using an expression coined by Paul Ricoeur, a "second naiveté."[32]

One might actually adopt another Paul's "justification by faith" as a stance: though one is sinful through and through, God permits one to come before him in confidence, as though he or she is righteous. Appealing to Paul at this point may be out of place. However, Paul did believe that his doctrine of justification was deeply embedded in the Old Testament. Perhaps the coexistence of two potentially rival pieties within Hebrew Scripture evidences it.

28. Note Morrow's position in "Consolation," 211–25.
29. Boda et al., *Seeking the Favor of God*, 196–98.
30. For a discussion, see Morrow, *Protest against God*, 201–18.
31. Although not all at once or completely.
32. See Ricoeur, *Essays on Biblical Interpretation*, 119–54, 155–82.

# 19

# Final Judgment on the Horizon

IN THIS CHAPTER WE will trace another emanation from the book of Isaiah: the expectation of a Final Judgment. Such expectations are enunciated in Isaiah 24–27 and 65–66. These provide what I am calling an horizon for the book of Isaiah as a whole.

The concept of a Final Judgment or even a final battle is not found in preexilic texts. It was simply not a part of orthodox Yahwism. The prophets spoke of the unfolding events of their time with a strong sense of finality. They also articulated future conditions that stretch our credulity. However, neither the judgments nor the saving order coming afterwards transcended the temporal framework of the present age. We might say that prophetic judgments and promises prepared the way for a Final Judgment on the horizon of history.

Why does a concept of a final denouement, a judgment that determines the value of all that went before it and sets human history on a decisive new track, make its appearance in the middle and at the end of the book of Isaiah? One might take recourse to the history of religion. Some form of Last Judgment is a common, recurring motif of religion. Humans tend to desire or fear an event that gives what might be called a "final grade" on our lives, our causes, our piety, and our ethical behavior.

Interestingly enough, Israelite religion did not seek such closure until the closing centuries of the biblical era. So why did it arise among the disciples of Second Isaiah during the decades of the restoration? I believe that it met a particular theological need among those disciples. Isaiah 55–56 promised a resolution of a conflict between Jewish parties within Jerusalem and Judah just before and after the rebuilding of the temple. The conflict had a theological dimension. One party held the reins of power, and under its leadership the poor were oppressed, and the priests sought to provide ritual cleansing of guilt. Moreover, the religious practices of the community included many heterodox elements.

In the days of the classical prophets of judgment, a prophet could have formulated these oppressive and apostate communal patterns in accusations against the people. However, the prophet or prophets speaking in the tradition of the Babylonian Isaiah could not return to the classical prophecy of judgment; their master had promised that YHWH would never again subject the people to judgment. A cyclical view of history alternating between salvation and judgment is out of the question. When YHWH judged his people in the Assyrian and then the Babylonian exiles, that was a once-for-all event. The forgiveness and deliverance of the people after the exile was also once for all. So the solution was to interpret the nonfulfillment of the more glorious aspects of the prophecy of the Babylonian prophet as YHWH's punishment; it was a delay of fulfillment.

However, as the delay seemed to continue indefinitely, and the community settled more deeply in its sinful ways, the disciples of Second Isaiah began to look forward to a decisive event that would resolve the situation: a divine intervention to divide the community, rewarding the humble, penitent servants of the Lord with salvation while punishing the wicked and vain establishment with perpetual exclusion from the redeemed community.

What we have said about Isaiah 65–66 doesn't fit Isaiah 24–27. That apocalypse begins with a prediction of worldwide destruction. There follow a few indications that Jerusalem will be saved, probably to be made a center for the reconstruction of the world. A remnant of the nations will join Israel in the eschatological victory and utopia of God. We find universalistic affirmations, such as, "when your judgments are in the earth, the inhabitants of the world learn righteousness" (Isa 26:9b).

This Final Judgment is a resolution to the section (Isaiah 13–23) directed primarily to the nations of the Near East. Isaiah 13–14 is a judgment on the Babylonian empire, fused into an earlier oracle promising the destruction of Assyria and restoration of independent nations. The editors of the book applied to Babylon Isaiah's prediction of Assyria's fall in the promised land. It is assumed that the fall of the oppressive empire will liberate subject peoples. Unfortunately, Babylon takes Assyria's place, requiring this typological identification of the two successive empires. Of course, Babylon is replaced by

Persia, a more enlightened despotism, but hardly an eschatological order. We need a break in the succession of empires; the "Isaiah Apocalypse" provides it.

It should be recognized that imperial politics is not the only evil on the international horizon. There are conflicts in and between smaller independent monarchies. Isaiah singles out Israel, the northern kingdom, allied with Aram (Damascus) and some other minor states, to resist the Assyrian subjugation, for judgment. Both Israel and Judah at one time or another ally with Egypt to resist Assyria; Isaiah also condemns these conspiracies. Isaiah 24–27 would also resolve all such misdirected policies.

So in the book of Isaiah we have the foundations for an eschatological judgment. A number of important dimensions had, of course, been left out. Above all, the servants who are promised salvation are not themselves freed from their propensity to sin. They are open, because of their humility and compunction, to being "reformed" by the Lord, but there is no discussion of the end point, of the qualitative transformation of sinner to saint.

Although chapters 65–66 clearly have a division between those who pleased God and those who aroused his wrath, we do not get a glimpse of the scene in which this takes place. Isaiah 24–27 does have images of war and destruction, but that hardly satisfies our desire for a deliberate, discriminate judgment on individuals and nations. We await the development of images appropriate to the event.

Despite these gaps, we do find in Isaiah the idea of a final event that completes and corrects the judgments that take place within history. This event is not strictly "otherworldly," but rather a culmination of the events of judgment within history. The event is, as it were, a final grade on each and every grouping of humans, on individuals too, and on their causes and retractions, and so forth. It is also a rectification of wrongs suffered in history by the innocent and relatively righteous. The justice of history is "rough and ready" and needs correction.

On the other side of Final Judgment is the fulfillment of the promises of salvation. Both Isaiah 24–27 and 65–66 offer images of the new age. They tend to be extensions and corrections of the bountiful conditions one hopes for in life: long life, many children, food enough, no economic catastrophes, and universal peace. They are still "this-worldly," though utopian. It will take centuries for theologians and poets to envision the conditions of eternal life. A seed has been planted, however, with the expectation "of a new heaven and a new earth" (Isa 65:17; 66:22).

*Redeeming Judgment*

Now in this chapter it is our task to find traces of the idea of a Final Judgment or eschatological transformation of human existence in the book of Psalms. As in the case of penitential piety, we are expecting the Psalms to disseminate ideas restricted to an "outcast" group-—Second Isaiah's disciples. In fact a few Psalms look forward to the Lord's judgment of the world, a truly Final Judgment. The psalms of which we speak are well known and well beloved and undoubtedly performed the task of disseminating the expectation of a Final Judgment.

Like Isaiah, though, the psalms speak much more often of judgments within history. We are going to locate some explicit references to divine judgment in individual laments and penitential psalms; some of these are very positive about the prospect, others fearful. We also discuss some psalms that look back painfully on God's judgments of his people, and others that look forward to the judgment of foreign nations or their gods.

These judgments within history are the drama to which the Final Judgment is something like the last act. Some might regard the Final Judgment as the climax of the history of judgment, others the working out of the climax.

## Divine Judgment in the Individual Laments

Most individual laments approach the Lord confident of the supplicant's just cause and moral standing. Some of these call the Lord judge, or appeal to him to act as one. Psalm 7:11 contains the statement, "God is a righteous judge," paired with, "has indignation every day." The verse is a part of a confession of trust. The strophe begins with v. 9, requesting divine judgment of the wicked, backed up with statements of trust: "You who test the minds and hearts, O righteous God" (v. 9), and "God is my shield, who saves the upright in heart" (v. 10). The supplicant expects to benefit from God's judgment because the world will be set right. Psalm 7 as a whole is an individual lament; the supplicant seems to have been charged with wrongdoing (see vv. 3–5).

Psalm 9:7–8 describes the Lord as sitting on a throne judging the world: "He judges the world with righteousness; / he judges the peoples with equity" (v. 8). The psalm is the first half of an acrostic psalm that continues through Psalm 10. Psalm 9 begins as a thanksgiving, but becomes a lament as it progresses. It has a strong interest in the judgment of nations, and the rectification of the world at large.[1] Again, the supplicant looks to the Lord to straighten out the distortions of human society.

---

1. It pits the wicked against the poor and oppressed.

Psalm 17 appeals to the Lord as disperser of justice. Though the title "judge" isn't used, the supplicant begins, "Hear a just cause, O Lord" (v. 1), and has, "From you let my vindication come" (v. 2). Following this plea, the supplicant utters an oath of innocence (vv. 3–5). All that belongs to a judicial setting or at least to trial as metaphor. The remainder of the psalm is preoccupied with the supplicant's enemies, who are characterized as wicked. If they are overthrown, the supplicant will be saved.

These direct references to God as judge fit the general pattern we discerned in chapter 5 on the "Individual in the Covenant." Individual laments belong to all eras, for individuals experience similar crises in their private lives no matter what national and international conditions obtain. These laments are frequently formulated as trial situations in which the Lord is appealed to as judge. The majority of the laments in the Psalter complain of the assault of enemies, ill health, legal trouble, economic straits, and the like. Most of them seek to elicit the Lord's sympathy, mercy, and justice. A few admit guilt, but most express confidence in the supplicant's righteousness and fidelity. A few individual laments accuse the Lord of betrayal, indifference, or antagonism. This would appear to be a counterproductive strategy; however, they may be designed to put God on the defensive, to force him to reexamine the supplicant's case and change the decision. Moses himself uses this strategy in his intercessions for Israel.

## The Fate of the Wicked and/or Righteous

Psalms describing the fate of the wicked and/or righteous are reflective derivatives of the individual laments. Psalms 1 and 37 fall within this category. Each sets forth the ways of righteousness and wickedness, and describes the destiny of each. Psalm 1:5 mentions a "judgment" that the wicked cannot endure. Although this originally did not refer to a Final Judgment, but simply to some opportune time when a person must face up to what he or she has done, in the Septuagint (LXX) it was formulated as a future event—probably an eschatological one.[2]

Psalm 37 has the same ideological scheme as Psalm 1, but it is quite different in style. It is an acrostic psalm that wanders from subject to subject. The audience is told to trust the Lord and not to fret over the seeming injustice of the world. Sooner or later the wicked will suffer the appropriate fate, while the humble and righteous will be protected by God. There is no actual use of

---

2. See Reiser, *Jesus and Judgment*, 35–37, 43, 47, 68, 136, 177, 211, 252.

the title "judge," but we do have "the Lord loves justice; he will not forsake his faithful" (v. 28).

## Penitential Piety

An inward pity marked by contrition and humility grew up in response to the exile. The prophets of judgment had interpreted defeat and exile as judgment for the people's sin. Those who absorbed the prophetic interpretation were stamped by a sense of guilt and unrighteousness.[3] The disciples of Second Isaiah were clearly attuned to the prophetic message and modified the language for communal lament, suffusing it with confessions of guilt and doxologies of judgment. "We have all become like one who is unclean, / and all our righteous deeds are like a filthy cloth" (Isa 64:6).

This same penitential piety comes to expression in the prayers of individuals. Ps 51 is the prime example. It is offered as the one proper way of coming before the Lord. "You have no delight in sacrifice / . . . the sacrifice acceptable to God is a broken spirit; / a broken and contrite heart, O God, you will not despise" (Ps 51:16–17). The penitent is open to being remade by the spirit of God. A person who is fully compunctious will not cling to settled character but awaits the inspiration of the divine spirit.

Psalm 51 admits guilt and the propensity to sin; v. 4 sounds as though God has already declared his judicial decision: "So you are justified in your sentence / and blameless in your judgment."[4] We do hear the supplicant express apprehension that judgment (now or in the future) would not be favorable in Ps 130:3–4: "If you, O Lord, should mark iniquities, / Lord, who could stand?" The psalmist hopes that God will forego judgment in his mercy: "But there is forgiveness with you, / so that you may be revered." The supplicant knows that God would condemn him, and everyone else, if one were held to a measure of strict justice. God is forgiving, and that compensates for human failure. The purpose is to encourage a renewed effort at faithfulness and obedience.

Psalm 50 depicts the Lord holding court, this time in the temple among his people. The epiphanic description (50:1–6) ends with the affirmation: "The heavens declare his righteousness, / for God himself is judge" (v. 6). The psalm then begins to sound like a prophecy of judgment against Israel:

---

3. Others continued to protest in the vein of Psalms 44; 74; etc.
4. NRSV: "when you pass judgment": the translators have removed it from the past and made it timeless.

> Hear, O my people, and I will speak,
> O Israel, I will testify against you.
> I am God, your God. (v. 7)

However, a close reading reveals that the Lord's proclamation of judgment is not against the people as a whole, but only the wicked (vv. 16–22). It also contains a polemic against the effort to please God through sacrifices (vv. 8–15). This aspect of the psalm connects it to penitential piety. However, Psalm 50 does not express the type of apprehension of divine judgment that one detects in Psalm 130.

## Psalms 105 and 106

We have two recitals of Israel's sacred history in Psalms 105 and 106. They are meant to balance each other. Psalm 105 reviews the sacred history as a story of divine grace. It begins with patriarchs, then progresses through the sojourn in Egypt, sustenance in the wilderness and some short references to conquest. The psalm ends with a statement of God's purpose: "to the end that they should keep his statutes, and observe his laws" (v. 45). The introduction is more explicit about the reason for the recital, namely, to "tell of all his wonderful works" (v. 2, also v. 5). There is also an affirmation of YHWH's loyalty to the "covenant," specifically the patriarchal covenant but also with the nation as a whole (vv. 8–11). Verse 7 includes God's "judgments are in all the earth." Perhaps the "judgments" are meant to refer to the wonders and covenant, though these are restricted to Israel.

Psalm 106 covers the same sacred story, but from a much different perspective. It is a history of Israel's sinful responses along with the Lord's saving deeds. Now God's saving deeds are done "in spite of" Israel's behavior. Occasionally the people do "believe" (v. 12), but they soon "forget" (vv. 13–15). When we arrive at the end of the sacred story, at the conquest, we are told that now YHWH has subjected them to judgment (vv. 40–46). Nevertheless, he continues to keep them alive, and intervenes to preserve them from death (vv. 43a, 44–46). The psalm ends with a plea for salvation (v. 47).

So now we are confronted with a "double-sided" view of the sacred story—the dark side along with the light. For readers, judgment has become an important component in the national identity. It naturally leads to a penitential consciousness. Psalm 106 is on the same track as Ezekiel 20 and Nehemiah

8.[5] It is especially important because the book of Psalms, as the community's prayerbook and hymnal, disseminates this penitential reading of sacred history to the Jewish community at large.

It should be noted that Psalm 106 preserves the theological perspective introduced by the classical prophets of judgment. Virtually no other psalm in the Psalter embodies the radical critique of the people of God.

## The Judgment of National Enemies

Communal laments frequently request that God direct his wrath at the people's enemies. Psalm 79, for example, pleads that God "pour out your anger / on the nations that do not know you, / and on the kingdoms that do not call on your name" (v. 6). Later in the same psalm, the supplicants plead: "Let the avenging of the outpoured blood of your servants / be known among the nations before our eyes" (v. 10b). Obviously the supplicants believe that their enemies deserve judgment and divine justice requires it.

Psalm 82 portrays the Lord as a sovereign judge who holds court in the council of the gods (v. 1). There is no other psalm like it. YHWH speaks in v. 2, accusing the gods of having not ruled the world justly. Verses 3–4 address the members of the council about their duties as rulers; but since they have not performed well, so to speak, they are being eliminated. Verse 5 is idol polemic, suggesting that the whole psalm is intended as an exposé of the gods of the nations and as an affirmation of YHWH's exclusive divine sovereignty. Verses 6–7 are a divine decree demoting the gods to nothings. The psalm ends with a plea to God to "judge the earth; / for all the nations belong to you" (v. 8). This plea amounts to requesting that what has happened in heaven now take place on earth. The psalm is on the verge of being eschatological; the similar judgment of the gods in Isaiah 41, and so forth, from Second Isaiah is also on this threshold.

## In Praise of God's Judgment

I chose this section title, not only to signal that we are turning our attention to praise psalms, but to jar liberal readers who desire to avoid all mention of divine judgment. The Psalms not only mention God's judgment frequently; they plead for it and praise God when it occurs. The classical individual lament pleads for God's intervention on the behalf of the supplicant; we found a num-

---

5. And to an extent, the communal lament in Isa 63:7–64:12.

ber of these that portray that intervention as a judicial act, a judgment. The supplicant assumes that he will prove righteous in any trial, and his enemies will be exposed as evil. The penitential psalms are an exception to this self-understanding. The supplicant is anxious about judgment because the speaker is sure that all humans would be judged sinners in an event of divine judgment.

Communal laments, like classical individual laments, look forward to divine judgment. God will surely dispose of Israel's enemies as godless and perverse. In one psalm we find that the gods of the nations are deposed by the Lord; the psalm ends with the plea that this heavenly judgment be implemented on earth.

We do find one recital of sacred history that portrays Israel as sinning at every juncture, and finally as brought to judgment in the exile. This expresses penitential piety and would not look forward to even more judgment.

While all witnesses acknowledge the judgment of God, there is a mixed attitude. However, even a fearful attitude toward judgment honors God's sovereignty and the finality of his decisions. Thus, even those who fear God's judgment praise him for his judgments. Praise honors power that establishes truth and right; judgments do that. Judgment uncovers hidden evil, sets things right, forces the sinner to acknowledge the harm of sinful actions, and invites repentance. All those acts are worthy of praise.

We find the praise of God's judgments particularly in the "enthronement psalms." Probably all psalms of praise imply God's role as judge, but explicit reference is restricted. So we are going to end the chapter with the psalms that explicitly praise God's judgment. It so happens that it is among these that we find a few explicit mentions of a Final Judgment, a judgment that brings divine judgment to an end.

## Enthronement Psalms

We turn next to a collection of descriptive praise psalms that share the expression, "God is [or: has become] king," viz., Psalms 93, (95), 96, 97, (98) and 99.[6] A few other psalms can be associated with this collection, Psalms 46 and 47 in particular. A once popular thesis went that these psalms were originally a part of a festival that celebrated YHWH's annual ascension to the throne. The thesis no longer seems quite so compelling; in any case, it is not relevant to the "final-form" reading of the texts.

---

6. The Hebrew *malak* (in the perfect aspect) can be translated either way.

Several of these enthronement psalms specifically celebrate YHWH's coming to judge the earth:

> for he comes to judge the earth.
> He will judge the world with righteousness,
> and the peoples with his truth. (96:13)

> Zion hears and is glad, and the towns of Judah rejoice,
> because of your judgments, O God.
> For you, O Lord, are most high over all the earth,
> you are exalted far above all gods. (97:8–9)

> ... at the presence of the Lord, for he is coming
> to judge the earth.
> He will judge the world with righteousness,
> and the peoples with equity. (98:9)

Psalms 96 and 98 portray this judgment as the denouement of YHWH's action among humans. One might surmise that YHWH fully becomes king when he judges the world in a "final" judgment. Both psalms begin with a call to praise YHWH with a "new song" (96:1; 98:1) and invite the nations to join in the praise (96:3, 7, 9; 98:4). Both even expect the natural world to join humans in praise (96:11–12; 98:7–8). Addressees are to declare "his name," "his salvation," "his glory," "his miraculous works" (96:2–5), "victory," "vindication," and his fidelity to his chosen people (98:2). These two psalms are joyous eschatological praise.

Psalm 97 does not speak of one final, future judgment, but rather of "judgments" (97:8); these are associated with the Lord's exaltation above all other beings (v. 9). Notice how the psalm goes on to express trust in God's saving works: "The Lord loves those who hate evil; / he guards the lives of his faithful; / he rescues them from the hand of the wicked. / Light dawns for the righteous, / and joy for the upright in heart" (97:10–11). "He rescues them from the hand of the wicked" is a judicial act.

Psalm 95 begins in the spirit of Psalms 96 and 98, though the powers ascribed to YHWH in 95:4–5 are those of Creator. His relationship to his people is captured in the metaphor of the shepherd, with the people as his flock. No judgment is mentioned in vv. 1–7a, but then the psalm changes abruptly from praise to entreaty. The entreaty is formulated as a wish: let the addressees not repeat their rebellions of the past, particularly those in the wilderness. Note

## Final Judgment on the Horizon

that the speaker is God: this is an oracle. As abrupt as it is, this reminder of Israel's past character introduces judgment into the psalm; past judgments should serve as a warning.

Psalm 99 celebrates YHWH's kingship and associates his rule with judgment (v. 4). This psalm also has an abrupt change in tone: a recollection of the Lord's care of his people through holy leaders, and his revelations during their time. The psalm seems designed as a counterweight to Psalm 95. The time in the wilderness and at Sinai was an ideal time in which "you were a forgiving God to them, / but an avenger of their wrongdoings" (v. 8).

Psalm 93 is an enthronement psalm (see v. 1). Its emphasis is on God the Creator, in particular God's superior power to the seas. His power guarantees the Lord's decrees and calls for worship.

Psalm 94 interrupts the series of enthronement psalms running from Psalms 93 to 99. Psalm 94 is not a praise, nor is it about YHWH's royalty: it is a lament with a distinctive thrust: the enemies are "the wicked," and the speaker is not identified. The first-person speech in vv. 16–19 is singular, and that may tip the scales for individual lament. The psalm is saturated with judgment: God is addressed as "God of vengeance" as well as judge; he is asked to intervene to throw down the evildoers/proud:

> But the LORD has become my stronghold,
>    and my God the rock of my refuge.
> He will repay them for their iniquity
>    and wipe them out for their wickedness;
>    the LORD our God will wipe them out. (94:22–23)

The behavior of the evildoers is described in vv. 4–7. This ends with a quoted suggestion that they doubt that God notices their behavior. The psalmist addresses them with the assurance that God does see them, and hears them and knows what's going on (vv. 8–11). So the supplicant can rely on God in his struggle to survive (vv. 16–23). In this psalm the judgment of God is the central article of faith, and the psalm ends affirming God's final destruction of the wicked.

Psalm 47 is associated with the enthronement psalms we have studied. The exact affirmation, "YHWH is king," is lacking, but he is called king in vv. 2, 6, 7, and 8. The psalm celebrates YHWH's empowerment of his people to conquer other nations; these other nations should now honor YHWH. This theological justification of imperialism is problematic. One would prefer to defend a "spiritual" conquest, viz., conversion.[7] The psalm as it stands reminds one of medieval Christian and Muslim practice.

Psalm 46 is a counterweight to Psalm 47. It is a confession of trust. God is Israel's refuge or fortress. He protects Zion, his "capital," so to speak. The nations may assault the city, but he will guarantee its survival. Rather than defeat the attackers, he makes wars to cease:

> He makes wars cease to the end of the earth;
> > he breaks the bow, and shatters the spear;
> > he burns the shields with fire.
> "Be still, and know that I am God!
> > I am exalted among the nations,
> > I am exalted in the earth." (46:9–10)

This affirmation is cryptic, but it can be read it as a relative to Isa 2:1–4. Universal peace is certainly worthy of eschatological hope.

What can we draw out from these descriptive praises and associated psalms? We certainly confirm the proposition that God is praised for his judgments and for those in prospect. The Lord's judgments manifest his power and communicate it to his creatures. He will bring the world to its destiny by one Final Judgment. The Lord's past judgments in Israel's own history should teach Israel to respect his will.[8] They became redemptive as well—in retrospect. The nations can appropriate these memories as they learn to recognize YHWH alone as God. These nations can also reinterpret their own histories to perceive the divine judgments.

## The Last Horizon

This chapter was titled for the eschatological judgment that culminates the judgments and restorations of history. *Horizon* is, of course, a metaphor drawn from visual experience. It is the background to images on which we can focus our attention; it is most palpable in scenes of out of doors.[9] When we are apply-

---

7. Modern secular critics of Christianity are offended by that as well, but they are hardly disinterested parties.

8. Notice how similar historical and eschatological judgment is in the psalms. When we compare Psalms 96; 97; and 98, for example, we have trouble distinguishing the historical from the eschatological. This demonstrates that historical and eschatological judgments are continuous, so to speak. Final judgment is the culmination, correction, and end of historical judgments; historical judgments are foreshadowings of final judgment.

9. This would fit best if one lived in a place with mountains in the distance, foothills and

ing the term to time and history, we are speaking of the most comprehensive synthesis of all finite perspectives, the denouement of all stories. That's why we qualified this horizon as the *last* one, i.e., one beyond which there is nothing.

It seems that a trial scene is an ideal image for the denouement of history. It is the most common eschatological denouement in biblical tradition and the history of the church. It also appears in many other religious traditions. A trial intends to bring a story to a close and sort out the value of each person's and group's actions. The trial is based on the worldview that the value of human lives is measured by how well each and every human fulfilled or did not fulfill what was expected. Since humans participate in societies, the individual's value is entangled with the society's value. Creativity is the quality of one's performance.

What happens in the trial? Often, the scenario is of an opening of books (cp. Dan 7:10): the destiny of humans has already been decided, and those who are acquitted or condemned have power only to ask when and on what basis the judgment was made (cp. Matt 25:31–46). One wonders whether the response of the judged plays any role at all. It should play some role, I believe, because the judgment is not just a measurement of what has been done but of the character of the actor. Perhaps those who admit their wrongdoing and repent are forgiven (cp. Isa 1:18–20).

The elect are judged according to the revealed law, which is a much higher standard than common human law. The Old Testament and rabbinic halakah should direct the life of a Jew and be the measure of his or her life. The radicalized law of Jesus's proclamation, as found distilled in the Sermon on the Mount and distributed through the Synoptics, is the measure for a Christian. Even Paul, who breaks out of the Old Testament/Jewish legal tradition, still expects a saving faith to yield fruits of the Spirit.

The enthronement psalms, note, do not say anything about who is saved or damned, or any other particular about the Last Judgment. In these psalms, the victory of God is front and center. That is, the sovereign God will banish all that opposes his will, all that destroys the intended harmony of life among humans, and between humans and the natural environment. This is an outcome much desired by all who praise God. God's sovereignty has been compromised by human sin, and his rule has had to be enforced by judgment. The Last Judgment will bring the necessity of judgment to an end.

---

perhaps a city at middle distance, and a residential neighborhood in the foreground. I was born and raised in the Willamette Valley in Oregon, where such picture was available on clear days.

*Redeeming Judgment*

The Last Judgment will not nullify the judgments of history. Retribution is a divine good, as is preventive intervention. Revelation of the truth is much to be desired, and it provides the basis for repentance. Judgment also purges the body politic in order to restore it to a healthy, just society; seldom does the human system meet a divine standard, but it is a legitimate aim of society. The Last Judgment also promises to save those who are redeemable. Whatever is true and good will be preserved in the Final Judgment.

# 20

## Divine Judgment in the Synoptic Gospel Message
(Matthew, Mark, Luke)

I HAVE HEARD LAITY far too often say that the God of the Old Testament is wrathful and harsh while the God of the New Testament is loving and compassionate. The argument of this and the following four chapters is that there is plenty of judgment in the New Testament. The first question to ask of this message is whether it is an unnecessary holdover from a more primitive stage of religion, as many liberals would have it, or an essential stage of redemption. What role does it play in the "divine economy"? Can we testify that the Gospel is falsified when judgment is not taken seriously?

We also have to ask whether the understanding of divine judgment in the New Testament is the same as in the Old Testament. Is there enough continuity to draw on Old Testament passages to expound New Testament texts, and to interpret events in the life of the Christian church and the societies in which it is located? Can we show that the person of Jesus meets the qualifications of a prophet, that is, is he one who pronounces divine judgment with authority? While the answers may be confessional, answering will force the church to consider inescapable questions.

The Old Testament has a message of redemption and salvation as well. Since this message is addressed to the people of God in exile, suffering judgment, it is clearly connected to judgment. The message of salvation, we would say, is a remedy for judgment, and judgment is incorporated into the redemption of the people from their sin. Does the New Testament message of fulfillment also remedy judgment and incorporate it in redemption? Is Jesus the saving figure depicted in the Servant Songs?

I do not claim that the Hebrew Scripture—the Tanak—needs the New Testament to be complete. Judaism has lived a faithful, observant communal life without the New Testament.[1] It ordered its life around obedience to the Lord's Torah; this was an authentic form of religious life. The only claim on Hebrew Scripture that Christians can make is that they worship the same God, honor the Old Testament as Scripture, and regard the New Testament as preserving and advancing the theology of the Tanak.

I do think that the New Testament is dependent on the Old. A few Christians take the sentiment expressed in the first paragraph—viz., God of wrath vs. God of love—too literally and propose divorce from the Old Testament, so to speak. They ignore the connection between love and wrath, they have a sentimental idol for a god, and they see no need for the authority of revelation. This Marcionite position has been dismissed whenever it has arisen in the past, and it should continue to be.

History has put the two testaments together for Christians. There should be no need for an apologetic (unless by *apologetic* one means a demonstration that the New Testament and the church have maintained the substance of Old Testament theology). That is what I will be doing in this and the following two chapters. We need to recognize the existence of divine judgment in the New Testament and realize that it makes an essential contribution to the New Testament message. We will seek to show that the New Testament maintains the basic teaching of the Old and synthesizes its kerygma with the received tradition.

How shall we deal with the changes in theology, sociology, and culture that separate the Israelite and early Jewish eras from the Hellenistic-Roman era represented in the Gospels and Epistles? The eschatological horizon of the New Testament represents the foundation of the theological difference. The Old Testament had an eschatological horizon in the background, but it becomes foreground in the Gospels. Perhaps the eschatological horizon can actually be the solution to the problem of change. Eschatology offers a comprehensive horizon within which the historical drama is played out. The set of events that had the eschatological horizon in the foreground also played out within the larger horizon.

---

1. Perhaps the Talmud "completes" the Hebrew Bible, but it certainly is not equivalent to the New Testament in form or content.

Let me illustrate my point from legal tradition. There are several states of law in the Old Testament. The covenant between God and Noah culminates a development of common human law. Israel receives the revealed law at Sinai, also as a part of a covenant. The actual law codes that spell out this law are introduced at various junctures of history. These codes come into being under specific conditions, but once they become divine law, they partake of the eternity of God. Every provision has authority and calls for interpretation by rabbis. Christians would say that Jesus "purified" the law, so that it led those who accepted it into the kingdom of God.

Where does the eschatological horizon enter the picture? Of course, if one grants authority to Jesus's interpretation of Mosaic law, then his interpretation points to the kingdom. Even if one doesn't accept Jesus's authority, the Talmudic tradition seeks to articulate an eternal, transcendent law drawn from texts that were communicated in time.

To review what has been said, divine judgment will be shown to pervade New Testament teaching and to belong to the New Testament's presentation of the redemptive process. Thus, we will continue to receive the Old Testament texts concerning judgment and redemption as authority for the Christian church. These texts embody in time the will of the eternal God.

## Expounding the Gospels in their Final Form

In my study of the Old Testament, I maintained a "final form" reading of the canonical text. It is the canonical text that is recognized as authoritative in the church, and I am Barthian enough to locate biblical theology in the believing community. My position is similar to that of Brevard Childs and Rolf Rendtorff. Moreover, this entire study is designed as a corrective to the liberal wing of the Protestant church; that means I am building on as well as critiquing the theology of a community. Since the liberal wing of the church does not answer without question to scriptural authority, one has to provide sound reasoning in support of scriptural teaching.

I have not abandoned critical methods, but I have embedded them—some might say buried them. In particular, I have bracketed out critical history: I am taking the narratives, oracles, laws, and the like as "rendering"[2] a particular course of events, and leaving aside the question of accuracy. Questions may be

---

2. I published a theological monograph in the Fortress Overtures to Biblical Theology series, titled *The Rendering of God in the Old Testament*. I use the word *rendering* as a synonym of *depiction*. They indicate the artistic creation of character and action as if the reader were actually present, witnessing events from the "inside."

posed, moreover, that can be answered without recourse to critical methods, though they have been treated critically in contemporary scholarship.

Consistency requires that I continue to expound the final form of the text of the New Testament canon. I will not be endeavoring in this chapter to pin down the historical John the Baptist or the historical Jesus. The focus is on how these figures are rendered in the gospel texts. I will begin the reconstruction of the rendering of a character or action with texts that most critical scholars would regard as the foundations, so to speak, of the gospel accounts. Other accounts can be regarded as dependent on these, though offering valuable insights and perspectives in their own right.

One aspect of a final-form reading that might escape notice is respect for our text's interpretation of its texts. Frequently there is a tension between a gospel author's understanding of a saying and the scholarly interpreter's understanding. Historical Jesus studies try to remove the sayings of Jesus from their gospel settings and consider what they might have meant in an original setting. That procedure is not acceptable in a final-form reading. The gospel writer's interpretation must be given priority, though the interpreter is certainly free to probe "behind" the text to expand the range of possible meanings of a saying.

A canonical reading also leaves aside noncanonical texts of the same era. We have Jewish and Hellenistic cultures contributing to the intellectual and spiritual world of the text. One can incorporate the knowledge of these worlds into the interpretation of canonical texts, but it would be confusing to expound background texts along with the canonical text. Readers, and scholars as well, would be drawn away from the world created by the text to the historical world.

Scholarly readers will notice the paucity of notes on the Greek text. This book is written for an audience that includes many persons who are not familiar with biblical languages and would soon be put off by technical discussions. I have sought to formulate my argument so that it doesn't rely on the nuances and technicalities of Hebrew and Greek.

## The Challenge of the Gospels

The four Gospels present a peculiar challenge to a final-form, canonical reading. It is one thing to read the final form of a composite text and quite another to read four different accounts of one individual's life and times—each with a theological message. In the Old Testament, we covered many composite

## Divine Judgment in the Synoptic Gospel Message

texts—both narrative and poetry; our strategy was to approach the text from an angle that preserved its unity.

How about the four Gospels? Many scholars would demand that each gospel be expounded independently. The critical era has championed this understanding of textual meaning. That would be acceptable but not advantageous. As a canonical text, each gospel has been preserved as a witness to one Jesus Christ. Hence, we need a composite reading that incorporates all the witnesses.

Tradition has usually harmonized the Gospels, but this ignores the distinctive witness of the individual accounts. Usually the minister opts for a reading that is most congenial to his or her piety and the piety of parishioners. This certainly avoids anxiety and offense.

Let me propose an alternative: We can begin with the "bottom layer" of the tradition, then follow its development, clarification, and correction in "later" texts. This is an "embedded" historical-critical form of exposition. In our case, the subject of divine judgment will exercise a gravitational pull, as it were, to texts; we can note how it is presented and subsequently interpreted or ignored.

Let me sketch the agenda for a section on John the Baptist. He is certainly relevant to the subject of divine judgment in the New Testament. John is depicted as a prophet proclaiming the Final Judgment and calling his audience to repent and receive baptism. By honoring and quoting John, the Gospels have put their imprimatur on his message.[3]

This chapter will begin with an exposition of Markan texts depicting John the Baptist, followed by an exposition of the texts in which Jesus speaks about John. I accept the common scholarly inference that Matthew and Luke depend on and diverge from Mark. Then we will take up texts depicting John, and Jesus's teaching about John in the texts shared by Matthew and Luke, though absent in Mark. A passage or two only found in one of these gospels will be expounded as well, but there is not enough space in this chapter to take up the distinctive representations of John in Matthew, Luke, or the Fourth Gospel. It so happens that very little that is distinctive to these three narratives touches on John's message of judgment.[4]

We will not cover the "message about Jesus" in this chapter, but in the next. There is a scholarly formula to the effect that Jesus proclaims the king-

---

3. The church's adoption of baptism implies that it accepts his authority in calling for repentance.

4. We are not concerned with John's christological sayings except as images of judgment.

dom of God, and the apostles and preachers proclaim Jesus. While such scholarly rubrics do not bind a final, canonical form of reading, it is a relatively easy distinction to maintain. The inclusion of christological affirmations requires significant adjustments to the theological scheme received from the Old Testament and filtered through John the Baptist. We can focus our attention on certain christological affirmations found in the Gospels and a sampling of other writings in the next chapter.

Finally, you may notice that I rely heavily on one New Testament scholar, Marius Reiser, whose book *Jesus and Judgment* has guided me through this exposition. I have allowed him to set the agenda, so to speak, and I have adopted many of his theses, but I also go my own way off and on. Not being a New Testament scholar in any strict sense, I am not at all embarrassed by relying on one to lead me through it.[5]

## Mark's Rendering of John the Baptist

John is given great prominence in Mark's gospel; he is literally the first person we meet (see 1:2–11). He is introduced by a Scripture passage that seems to fit him nicely (1:2–3, 4). Thus, before we even meet John, we have the idea that he is the fulfillment of Old Testament prophecy.[6]

Mark reports that John proclaims and practices "a baptism of repentance for the forgiveness of sins" (v. 4). The practice is described in the next verse: the baptism was preceded or accompanied by a confession of sins (v. 5). Whether this confession took the form of a text like Psalm 51 or a recitation of one's known sins is unknown. It is also unknown whether the act of baptism effected the removal of sin, or perhaps the "stain" that one metaphorically ascribed to sin (cp. Ps 51:7), or whether it was a public sign of an "inward grace."[7] It does

---

5. I am not bent on identifying the historical Jesus, whereas Reiser is. Moreover, Reiser did not cover Jesus's sayings about John, and that is important to my argument.

6. The actual verses quoted are from two different prophetic books; the division of Isa 40:3 follows the LXX, which makes "in the wilderness" modify "voice" rather than "way" whereas the MT has the latter.

7. Taylor, *The Immerser*, 49–100, covers the question fairly thoroughly. She urges the view that repentance came first, and then baptism to clean the body in harmony with the soul, which had been cleaned by repentance (98). "John's immersion itself is not identified . . . as conferring any particular exemption from the coming judgment; righteousness born of a repentant heart was the important factor" (99).

seem to have been a one-time ceremony like proselyte baptism, not a repeated ritual like the ablutions performed at *mikvaot* in numerous locations.⁸

The description of John's attire (1:3), along with his desert venue, suggests the norms by which he lived. He definitely was an ascetic. This was an essential element of his message. Within Mark, only the practice of fasting calls attention to the correlation of lifestyle and message (see 2:18-22). In the gospels of Matthew and Luke we will notice that Jesus uses lifestyle to characterize message.⁹

Mark quotes only one saying of John; the first sentence reads, "After me comes he who is mightier than I, the thong of whose sandals I am not worthy to stoop down and untie" (1:7 RSV).¹⁰ This statement describes an "ontological order," so to speak. The one coming is more powerful and more honorable than the speaker. Who is this powerful one? The gospel writers and Christian readers have identified him as Jesus. By implication, John is speaking of a human who has messianic credentials. Marius Reiser, however, has decided that John was speaking of God.¹¹ In other words, he was speaking of a direct divine intervention. This interpretation, however, seems rather farfetched: Who even imagines handling God's sandals? That is simply too anthropomorphic for most readers.¹² If John did have God in mind, the confusion of Christian authors and readers is understandable and justified.

The other statement in 1:7 predicts that this greater figure will complement John's baptism with another: "I have baptized you with [in] water, but he will baptize you with [in] [the?] holy spirit." The parallel in Matthew and Luke adds "fire" to "holy spirit." This is taken by many interpreters to be preferable to Mark's version.¹³ A final-form reading, however, should seek to make sense of Mark's wording. Mark may mean that the coming one will communicate power, God's holy power. Perhaps the newly baptized person will be empowered to live the new life that those baptized have pledged to live by confessing

---

8. Ibid., 70-71, questions the idea that the rite was unrepeatable. She has no evidence to the contrary, though. It was not a regular procedure like baths for ritual purity; whether a person who had fallen back into sin could be baptized a second time is unknown.

9. See the discussion below of Matt 11:7-9//Luke 7:24-26 and Matt 11:16-19//Luke 7:31-34.

10. "Mightier" could also be translated "stronger" or maybe even "more powerful."

11. His argument is found in Reiser, *Jesus and Judgment*, 181-86.

12. Schlatter, *Johannes der Täufer*, 103; Aune, *Prophecy in Early Christianity*, 131-32, also dispatches this interpretation of the coming one.

13. Reiser, *Jesus and Judgment*, 184-86.

their sins. It might, of course, refer to the charismatic phenomena, which are associated with Pentecost and known in Paul's churches.[14] For Mark, the messianic figure brings and communicates spiritual power to those who seek it.

The laconic report of "baptism for the forgiveness of sins" in v. 4 does not indicate what norms John would have applied. That is, what would count as sin for John and his auditors? He does seem to be addressing a Jewish audience. That is indicated by the places from which they came (v. 5). They undoubtedly recognize the God of Israel—the God for whom John spoke—and thus would have acknowledged the authority of the Torah. Whether they followed the Pharisaic interpretation of the law is not stated. Nor is it stated how they squared John's baptism with the temple sacrifices for sin and guilt required by Torah. They did "know" their sins because they are said to confess them.

There is one other pericope in Mark that indicates the norms John applied. John was arrested by Herod Antipas for condemning Antipas's marriage to his brother's wife, Herodias. He is quoted as saying, "It is not lawful for you to have your brother's wife" (6:18). Since the marriage was lawful by civil law, Antipas and Herodias are condemned for violating Torah.[15]

We do not have any evidence of what John thought about the salvation of Gentiles. Reiser thinks that he would have shared the views of many fellow Jews—that without the law, the Gentiles would perish in judgment, or at best would live to serve the Jews.[16] Gentile gospel writers would not have known this, because they would not have held John in such high regard if they did.

## Jesus's Statements about John in the Gospel of Mark

Clearly Jesus respected John enough to submit to baptism. The later church was puzzled and embarrassed by his action. They believed Jesus had committed no sin, so didn't need the rite.[17] Nevertheless, Mark records it unapologetically. For him, the baptism contained the call of Jesus by God, Jesus's designation as

---

14. Cp. Johnson, *Luke*, 66. Also Fitzmyer, *Luke*, 474.

15. Taylor, *The Immerser*, 238–40, cp. ibid., 247–48.

16. Reiser, *Jesus and Judgment*, 180: "The Baptizer does not seem to have given any special attention, in his preaching, to the eschatological fate of the Gentiles. This can only mean that on this question he shared the common conviction of early Judaism: The Gentiles, insofar as they were not converted to the God of Israel, would perish, or else live out their lives as slaves of Israel."

17. Matt 3:14 is the best evidence of this.

God's son. For Mark, this revelation was private, appropriate to the "messianic secret" that Jesus kept until near the end.[18]

Mark's Jesus expresses no reservations about John's preaching and actions. He believes that John has received his authority from God and has exercised it as a true prophet. Mark 11:27–33 is particularly important. When Jesus is questioned by the temple authorities about his authority to do what he has done, he asks them by what authority John baptized (v. 28). This is an amazing reply: Jesus appeals to John's authority to defend his own. Remember, Jesus is regarded by the author and the church as infinitely superior to John in authority. To cover the embarrassment, the author points out how clever Jesus' question was. For us, the passage might well suggest that Jesus regarded John as an equal, and an ally. Jesus did not repeat what John said, but he assumed that it was now known and appropriated. It now belongs to the gospel message, just as his baptism has become a rite of the Christian church.

Jesus accords John great honor; according to Mark 9:11–13, Jesus identifies John as Elijah. Mal 4:5–6 promises Israel that Elijah will be sent back to earth[19] in preparation for the Final Judgment: "Behold, I will send you Elijah the prophet before the great and terrible day of the Lord comes. And he will turn the hearts of fathers to their children and the hearts of children to their fathers, lest I come and smite the land with a curse" (RSV). The idea evidently took hold in the Jewish religious community during the Second Temple period. According to Mark 9:11, the religious scholars—the scribes—are affirming the promise. The role of Elijah would be to convert the hardhearted before they faced YHWH.

Mark 9:11–13 is rather indirect, secretive in a Markan mode. As Jesus, James, John, and Peter descended the mount of transfiguration, the disciples asked Jesus why "the scribes say that first Elijah must come?" The question seems to come out of the blue, as we say in English. Perhaps the disciples were thinking about Elijah because they had just seen him and Moses speaking with Jesus. In any case, they are speaking of the end time, the Last Judgment: that is the only scenario in which Elijah's coming is expected. The "first" in the disciples' question alludes to the one who comes afterward, the Lord himself according to Mal 4:5. Of course, one might regard the "Son of man" as the manifest agent of God.[20]

---

18. Credit for recognition of the importance of this feature of Mark's representation goes to Wrede; I would account for it as a rhetorical theological strategy.

19. According to 2 Kings 2, he was taken up to heaven in a chariot without dying.

20. According to Fitzmyer, *Luke*, 672, there is no evidence that Elijah precedes the mes-

Jesus's response is packed. His first statement sounds like a straightforward answer: "Elijah does come first to restore all things" (9:12, RSV). Though the question is about the scribes, it is legitimate for Jesus to simply affirm their answer. The scribes say it because they are right.

Jesus's next statement, a rhetorical question, is much more mysterious: "How is it written of the Son of man, that he should suffer many things and be treated with contempt?" (9:12b, RSV). This is a passion prediction, seemingly delivered without reason. It seems to be a case of free association.

The passion prediction interrupts the train of thought that runs from v. 12a to v. 13: "But I tell you, Elijah has come, and they did to him whatever they pleased, as it is written of him" (RSV).[21] There are several amazing assertions in this statement. How can Elijah have already come, and no one know? How does Jesus know? One suspects that he is engaged in a bold interpretation of John the Baptist. That is certainly what Matthew thought: "Then the disciples understood that he was speaking to them of John the Baptist" (Matt 17:13, RSV).

If John was the person Jesus was alluding to in Mark, his violent end had to be incorporated into the picture. But where on earth would one find "what is written of him"? Certainly not in Mal 4:5–6. Where else in Scripture might one find a prediction of a suffering Elijah? This is, as I said, a mystery-filled passage. Still, one can say that Jesus expresses great respect for John by identifying him as Elijah.

I can't say that I understand this passage, but it is certainly tantalizing. There are several secrets hidden in it. Not only the unknowns I have just mentioned, but what the passage had to do with Jesus. Assuming that Mark's Jesus was conscious of a messianic calling, he could be identifying John as preparing the way for him.[22] That line of thought is the only way one can find any cogency in the passion prediction. Here he may be coming to the realization that the suffering of John foreshadows his own.

---

siah in Jewish apocalyptic. This is strange because the gospels assume that such an expectation was abroad. Moreover, Jews to this day set out a cup of wine for Elijah during Passover meals; this is in case he should come announcing the end.

21. Matthew recognized that Mark 9:12b interrupts the train of thought; Matt 17:10–12 rearranges Mark to follow the more logical order. This leads me to ask how Mark is to be explained.

22. Fitzmyer, *Luke*, 673, proposes a development like this: Jesus said that John was his precursor. From that grew the identification of John as Elijah, and then the idea that this expectation that Elijah preceded the messiah.

## John's Preaching of Judgment in the Material Shared by Matthew and Luke

We are turning now to gospel traditions that antedate the writing of Matthew and Luke; the evidence for this is, of course, that they are found in both gospels. Assuming that the two gospels were written without knowledge of each other, the shared traditions must have a common source. While this source has acquired a name and has been the subject of intense scholarship,[23] the separate examination of the source seems to be contradictory to a final-form exposition. Therefore, we can treat the shared material as the oldest layer in the text of the gospels of Matthew and Luke without projecting an independent writing.

The collection of sayings found in Matt 3:7–12 and Luke 3:7–17 provides vivid access into the homiletic framework into which baptism was fitted. The fit is snug. John says the time of judgment has come; indeed it is already in progress. The people who heard John are urged to repent in order to avoid the wrath of God. Baptism is mentioned in the sermon, but it is not offered as a prophylactic.[24] To quote Marius Reiser, the "expectation of the final judgment in the immediate future was the basis of his call for repentance and the action that gave him his name: baptizing."[25]

Matthew and Luke identify the audience of John's preaching differently. According to Matthew, the harsh address, "You brood of vipers! Who warned you to flee the wrath to come?" is prompted by the presence of "Pharisees and Sadducees" among those seeking baptism. These are the leading parties in Palestinian Judaism at the time. Given the sorry state of Jewish society, by John's standards, the establishment would bear much of the responsibility (hence, guilt) for the crisis. By implication, John would not have identified an audience of, say, peasants and laborers, in the same harsh terms.

Luke does include everyone: the crowds coming for baptism are simply "the multitudes" (Luke 3:7, RSV). Thus, all the members of the society, from the lowest to the highest, come under the description, "brood of vipers." Luke provides us with another glimpse into the audience in 3:10–15, where he spells out what people should do: share any clothes they can spare, collect only the specified tolls (tax collectors), do not abuse citizens (soldiers). Luke may soften

---

23. The source is known as Q, which is the subject of much critical scholarship; the Society of Biblical Literature has a program unit devoted to this "document."

24. There is no indication that people who were not baptized were in for judgment.

25. Reiser, *Jesus and Judgment*, 167.

his characterization of the audience a bit in the saying "do not begin (*arkeisthe*) to say" rather than Matthew's "do not presume (*doxēte*) to say."[26] Luke may be implying that their appealing to Abraham may be innocent, rather than an act of pride.

## The Day of Wrath

Now we turn to the content of the saying shared by Matthew and Luke. The discourse begins: "You brood of vipers! Who warned you to flee from the wrath to come?" (Matt 3:7b//Luke 3:7b). If the form of John's utterance were prophecy, this address and question would be categorized as "indictment" or "accusation."[27] The question would be categorized as an indicting question, for John is not really asking his audience for information. By the sound of it, the moral or spiritual character of the addressees contradicts their effort to avoid judgment. In Old Testament prophecy of judgment, we would expect a "sentence" next; that is, a no to their quest for forgiveness[28] and a specification of the penalty. This is not classical prophecy, however; instead of receiving a sentence the people are urged to repent—actually, to live a "fruitful life," which should follow the act of repentance.[29] The reason for urging the "fruits of repentance" is that a person might well undergo baptism and return to the old ways. That would not, in John's scheme, save one from divine judgment.

John then identifies a particular danger to his audience. As the people of God, they may begin to take confidence in their elect status. John seeks to puncture any complacency due to a belief that God will overlook the sins of his elect: "Do not presume to say to yourselves, 'We have Abraham as our father'; for I tell you, God is able from these stones to raise up children of Abraham" (Matt 3:9). The point is very much in the spirit of Amos 9:7: "Are you not like the Ethiopians to me, O people of Israel?" Election does not confer divine indulgence, but puts the elect in a position of greater responsibility and accountability.[30]

---

26. Based on the fact that Luke likes to use "begin to," Fitzmyer, *Luke*, 468, believes the Matthew preserves the original Q reading.

27. My form criticism of the prophets is based on Westermann, *Basic Forms of Prophetic Speech*.

28. For example, the answer to the people's lament in Jeremiah 14.

29. Aune, *Prophecy in Early Christianity*, 130–31, outlines John's message and explains the difference between John's preaching and Old Testament prophecy of judgment.

30. See Patrick, "Election."

The next verse—"even now the axe is lying at the root of the trees; every tree therefore that does not bear fruit will be cut down and thrown into the fire" (Matt 3:10)—takes the place of the sentence of the classical prophecy of judgment. God is cutting down trees that fail to bear fruit.[31] According to the image, the divine judgment doesn't occur in one sudden moment but is underway over a period of time. Bad trees are being culled from the orchard all the time. Repentance must bear fruit, or the tree will be destroyed—cut down and used for firewood.

One can link John's message back to the Old Testament prophets of judgment despite the difference in form. Reiser connects the expression "the wrath to come" to the "Day of the Lord" found in Ezek 7:19 and Zeph 1:18; 2:2, 3; cp. Isa 13:3.[32] Fire is used for judgment rather often: Neh 1:6; Ezek 30:14-16; Joel 2:3; 3:3; Obad 8; and Mal 4:1. While the axe at the root of the trees may be original to John, Isa 6:13 uses the image of destroying the tree roots so it won't grow back.

John is nevertheless an apocalyptic preacher: the Day of Judgment is coming, and the people of the present should prepare for it. In the Old Testament prophets, judgment occurs in the prophetic pronouncement; the execution of the sentence is up to God in the course of events. Here, judgment is in the future, and the preacher's task is to exhort the audience to prepare for it.

According to Reiser, John was attempting to save Israel by turning the people around. Reiser goes on to say that John was "certainly aware that he [could] move only a part of the people to repentance. Still, he places his entire hope in that portion, as did the post-exilic prophets, for they will survive the judgment and afterward as the remnant of Israel, will receive the gifts of eschatological salvation."[33] The people who had undergone John's baptism did not form a separate religious community—so far as we know; but they would have been aware of belonging to "the eschatological people of God" in the present.

## The Coming One

In the Matthean narrative, this sermon continues into a description of the one coming after John (Matt 3:11-12), while Luke has John enter into an exchange

31. For the use of this image for judgment, cp. Luke 18:6-9.

32. There are also some occurrences in the Apocrypha and Pseudepigrapha. Fitzmyer, *Luke*, 465, notes that pride in being "children of Abraham" is mentioned in John 8:33-39; Rom 4:16-25; and Gal 3:29.

33. Reiser, *Jesus and Judgment*, 189-90. Fitzmyer, *Luke*, 474, notes a saying in a Qumran document that uses fire as an image of purgation.

with his audience (3:10–15) before he speaks about the "coming one" (Luke 3:16–17). I want to put off the exposition of Luke 3:10–15 until later. Let's finish John's apocalyptic sermon. The prediction of one coming begins with a saying also found in Mark 1:7 (and cp. John 1:30–31). The saying in Matthew and Luke has a different order of words from Mark: the saying about inferior ontological rank is spliced into the saying about baptizing: "I baptize you with water for repentance, but he who is coming after me is mightier than I, whose sandals I am not worthy to carry; he will baptize you with holy spirit [or with the Holy Spirit] and with fire" (Matt 3:11). Matthew's John is not worthy "to carry" the powerful one's sandal; Luke has "untie," like Mark. Both Matthew and Luke pair "fire" with "holy spirit." Some interpreters would give fire the force of judgment in contrast to the work of the holy spirit; nevertheless, fire is later portrayed as a sign of the Spirit (e.g., Acts 2:3–4).[34] Since fire can have either a negative or a positive meaning, the interpreter is left to work out a solution.

The second statement in the unit about the coming one has no parallel in Mark; it depicts his action: "His winnowing fork is in his hand, and he will clear his threshing floor and gather his wheat into the granary, but the [straw][35] he will burn with unquenchable fire" (Matt 3:12). The last judgment is depicted as a farmer's act of threshing cut grain, throwing the material in the air for the wind to blow the chaff away, and separate the seed from the straw. The straw will be burnt to heat the house or cook.

We have already discussed whether the coming one is the transcendent God or a messianic figure. Now we come to his activity. Although the image of threshing grain and burning the straw sounds arbitrary and violent, the act is deliberate and discriminating. The act of threshing is not punishment, but simply separation of what had grown up as one plant. The household burning of the straw (or using it for feed or bedding) is pragmatic and conserving. The image is effective and should not be regarded as an act of vengeance or indiscriminate slaughter. The added phrase, "with unquenchable fire," does sound vindictive; it is what marks the language as an eschatological parable.

The evangelists understood this "prophecy" to be fulfilled by Jesus. This is not obvious, however. The apocalyptic separation of the righteous and wicked really does not match Jesus's activity very well. It is much more in the vein of what Christians expect of the second coming than it is the ministry of Jesus

---

34. Fitzmyer, *Luke*, 474; Reiser, *Jesus and Judgment*, 171–72, believes that John would use "fire" as an image of judgment.

35. See Reiser, *Jesus and Judgment*, 176–80, on the procedure and translation.

recorded in the New Testament gospels. One can understand why John would have had trouble recognizing Jesus as messiah.

Luke 3:10–14 is without parallel. It may be a dialogue composed by the author of Luke-Acts, but I still intend to treat it as if John said it. After hearing John's warnings about the wrath to come, one might well ask the prophet for advice. Interestingly, John does not recommend baptism. This must mean that his hearers have accepted baptism and now are searching for the norms for their new life. John's answers are really rather commonplace. They could be called social welfare measures. People with a surplus of necessities should share their excess with others. Tax collectors should be scrupulously honest, and soldiers not abuse their power to coerce. This type of advice is practical; it should initiate a life oriented toward meeting the needs of others. This advice, by the way, would be just as appropriate to Gentiles as to Jews.[36]

## Jesus's Sayings about John in the Material Shared by Matthew and Luke

Matthew and Luke have a "collection" of John the Baptist materials. With one exception, the material and sequence is the same. It begins with the visit of John's disciples seeking to learn whether Jesus is the one who is coming as prophesied by John (Matt 11:2–6//Luke 7:18–23). After Jesus answers them, he begins to speak to the crowd about John (Matt 11:5–15//Luke 7:24–30). He locates John within the divine plan. The collection concludes with a parable and interpretation linking John's ministry and Jesus's (Matt 11:16–19// Luke 7:31–35). The gospels differ occasionally in wording, and Luke locates the parallel to Matt 11:12–13 in Luke 16:16 (see below).

My understanding of the structure of the unit is as follows: John initiates an exchange by sending his disciples to Jesus, which allows Jesus to indicate the evidence of his messiahship. "Go and tell John what you hear and see: the blind receive their sight and the lame walk, lepers are cleansed and the deaf hear, and the dead are raised up, and the poor have good news preached to them" (Matt 11:3//Luke 7:19). The evidence adduced defines what Jesus considered the calling of the messiah to be. After John's disciples depart, Jesus begins to describe John. This set of sayings is highly metaphorical and cryptic. The collection ends with the parable of the children playing in the marketplace, which Jesus then interprets as applying to John and himself.

---

36. Fitzmyer, *Luke*, 470, makes this observation.

## Redeeming Judgment

What does this set of passages have to do with divine judgment? There is in fact not one explicit reference to God's judgment and redemption. We could just leave it at that; Reiser does. However, one of my contentions is that Jesus puts his "imprimatur" on John's ministry, which includes his preaching of judgment. We will discover that John's message has been transposed, within this collection, to his lifestyle. His message of judgment has been lived out as a wilderness ascetic. When Jesus compares his own ministry to John's, it too is rendered as "lifestyle"—the ascetic life over against the "glutton and drunkard." Despite their difference, however, Jesus regards the two of them serving the divine purpose.

### Jesus and John

John's question of Jesus is rather surprising. Both Matthew and Luke ascribe prophetic knowledge to John, which includes a recognition of Jesus as the one who is to come.[37] Why then does he question Jesus about it? The passage offers no explanation, leaving room for preachers and scholars to venture explanations.[38] One line of interpretation assumes that John does this to teach his disciples; this would fit some passages in the Fourth Gospel (John 1:35–37; 3:25–30). Others wonder whether perhaps John has begun to doubt, and seeks reassurance. Critical scholars take the passage as evidence that according to the earliest traditions John did not know Jesus, and did not know that he was the messiah.[39] The problem with that explanation is that both gospel writers passed on an account at variance with their understanding. I would venture a final-form line of reasoning: John's description of the coming one as a harvester does not match Jesus's list of evidences (Matt 11:5). John is being forced to decide whether his preconceived idea is true, or whether he can acknowledge a healer and consoler of the poor as the saving figure he longed for.[40] John, rather like Simon Peter and the rest of the disciples, must grapple with the discrepancy between Jesus and the tradition. Perhaps Jesus formulates the

---

37. Matt 3:13–14; Luke 1:40–45.
38. Fitzmyer, *Luke*, 664–65, surveys the explanations of John's doubts.
39. One might even go farther and doubt that the earliest tradition even had John ask the question.
40. The images of a healer and a consoler of the poor are quite different from John's harvester. For John to accept Jesus's credentials, he would have to radically revise his understanding of how God will bring salvation. Fitzmyer, *Luke*, 664–65, concurs with this explanation.

final blessing, "Blessed is the person who takes no offense in me" (Matt 11:6// Luke 7:23), for the Baptist's benefit.

John's messianic expectation corresponds to his message of judgment. The one who comes to resolve the contradictions of history must overthrow "the bad guys," burn up sinners "in unquenchable fire." Not only is Jesus not the one "stronger" than John, but Jesus is not proclaiming a message meant to inspire fear of judgment. The concluding passage sets that out clearly. "To what shall I compare this generation? It is like children sitting in the marketplace and calling to one another, 'We played the flute to you, and you did not dance; we wailed, and you did not mourn.' For John came neither eating nor drinking, and they say, 'He has a demon;' the son of man came eating and drinking, and they say, 'Look, a glutton and a drunkard, a friend of tax collectors and sinners!' Yet wisdom is vindicated by her deeds" (Matt 11:16–19//Luke 7:31–35, NRSV).[41] The parable is interpreted by Jesus in an allegorical manner.[42] Jesus played dance music; John sang sorrowful songs. Jesus could have described their messages but instead contrasts their lifestyles. Since they have been presented in parallel, and the people ("they") reject them both, Jesus and John are spoken of as equals. The quotes from the people are about the images the two project—John has a demon, Jesus is a decadent aesthete who hangs around the wrong people.

If this were a prophecy of judgment, the people would be condemned for rejecting two prophets of God. Instead, it ends with a cryptic statement about "wisdom." This has spawned a good deal of scholarly speculation.[43] Given the fact that the statement cannot be a statement of punishment, one might look for an affirmation that the future will confirm that John and Jesus were speaking God's truth. Some interpreters identify wisdom with Christ,[44] but that seems forced since the "son of man" is one of the figures in the parable. Another line of interpretation is that wisdom, an attribute of God, is communicated to the elect, who will recognize God's hand in the prophets' ministries.[45] Surely the

---

41. "Children," according to Luke.

42. The parable itself is open to several interpretations. Does one group want to dance and the other lament, or does one group propose both to dance and lament? I opted for the latter interpretation on the basis that John and Jesus are allied. Fitzmyer, *Luke*, 679, agrees.

43. Cp. ibid., 681.

44. Overman, *Matthew*.

45. Johnson, *Luke*, 124, says: "Those who are children of Wisdom (God) will respond positively to the prophetic visitation."

point to be made is that both prophets are serving God's purposes, though it is uncertain as to the exact meaning of the wording.[46]

## John's Person

How about Jesus's sayings about John in Matt 11:7–15? The first saying runs, "What did you go out into the wilderness to see? A reed shaken by the wind? Why then did you go out? To see a man clothed in soft raiment? Behold, those who wear soft raiment are in kings' houses. Why then did you go out? To see a prophet? Yes, I tell you, and more than a prophet (Matt 11:7b–9, NRSV). Jesus addresses his audience as John's supporters—indeed as people like him, who were baptized by John. John was their spiritual leader. Then in the last verse quoted, Jesus stretches his audience: John was *more than* a prophet. The emphasis on lifestyle alludes to John's message, but this last statement transfers interest to his person—more precisely, to what John is within the plan of God. Jesus now quotes Mal 3:1a to explain what he means by "more than a prophet":

> See, I am sending my messenger ahead of you,
>   who will prepare your way before you. (Matt 11:10)

Oddly, the object pronoun has been changed from "me" (in Malachi) to "you" (in Matthew); the change transfers the statement from a statement of intent, for the sake of the audience, to a promise to whomever comes to preach repentance.[47] The figure of the messenger is not named in Malachi 3 or in Matt 11:10//Luke 7:27. In Matthew, Elijah is named in 11:13b. This verse sounds like a follow-up to v. 10, with vv. 11–13a designed to delay the dramatic disclosure.

Matthew 11:11 turns on "greatness." John is honored as one of the greatest humans who ever lived: "Among those born of women there has arisen no one greater than John the Baptist." This is a bit hyperbolic perhaps, but it makes fairly straightforward sense. The second statement in the verse is more cryptic: "yet even the least in the kingdom of heaven is greater than he." What is this trying to say? It obviously elevates those who enter the kingdom. Why are they greater than John? Is John not great enough to make it? Do not the dead make it as well as the living? Has the meaning of "greater" changed?

---

46. Fitzmyer, *Luke*, 681, summarizes his interpretation to this effect: God's plan seems foolish to the contemporaries of John and Jesus, but it is or will be vindicated. He bases his position on Suggs, *Wisdom, Christology and Law*, 33–61.

47. Both Matt 11:10 and Luke 7:27 have the pronoun *sou* (twice) where the LXX of Mal. 3:1a has *mou*.

## Divine Judgment in the Synoptic Gospel Message

The follow-up verse (Matt 11:12) is also cryptic, but in a different way. John is a timetable of sorts; actually, he is the beginning of the time period that will end with the arrival of the kingdom. This is quite odd, though, because John has not yet died: how can one speak of a time lapse between him and the narrative present. Moreover, the characterization of the time period is also mysterious: "the kingdom of heaven has suffered violence [or has been coming violently], and the violent take it by force" (v. 12). The gospels normally do not speak of the kingdom of God like this. How can a future state of being be the object of human action, and how could anyone successfully force their way in? Well, the one thing we know about the violence of the time is John's imprisonment (and eventual murder). Could Jesus be referring to that? Any interpretation of this passage is quite speculative.

The mysteries keep coming. Verse 13a adds another cryptic utterance to the mix: "For all the prophets and law prophesied until John." The closer one looks at this statement, the stranger it reads. Why does this order run, Prophets and Law; rather than the standard order: the Law and the Prophets? This probably doesn't refer to the two parts of the Jewish canon. What is meant by the notion that "the law prophesied"? Now to "prophets": Is John in the line of the prophets? How is he the pivot of a timetable in which the preparatory era (when prophets *prophesy*) comes to an end, and the fulfillment era begins? Is the identification of John as Elijah an explanation of his pivotal status? Is this the kind of periodization that Luke offers in 16:16?

Luke does not present the material of Matt 11:12–13 in the chapter 7 sequence. In its place, Luke has a remark about reception: "All the people who heard this, including the tax collectors, acknowledged the justice of God [or, praised God], because they had been baptized with John's baptism. But by refusing to be baptized by him, the Pharisees and [scribes] rejected God's purpose for themselves (Luke 7:29–30).[48] Actually, only the first sentence in this passage describes reception. The second condemns the Pharisees and scribes but doesn't say how they took Jesus's saying, or whether they were even in the crowd. The two sentences do divert our attention from the "gap" that Luke (7:28) has left—that is, the gap between (according to Jesus) the greatest man who had ever lived (that is, John the Baptist), and the person least in the kingdom of God.

Luke 16:16 is a part of a disconnected series of sayings. The wording differs from Matt 11:11–13; it is not as dense and cryptic: "The law and the prophets were in effect until John came; since then the good news of the king-

---

48. NRSV, except it reads "lawyers" instead of "scribes."

dom of God is proclaimed, and everyone tries to enter it by force [or, everyone is strongly urged to enter it]." One can understand how people might "try" to enter the kingdom violently, but surely they would not succeed. The time scheme set up by this wording is the sort of evidence that Hans Conzelmann used to construct his thesis that Luke is working with the idea that "Christ is the mid-point" in time.[49]

Jesus puts his imprimatur on the ministry of John the Baptist in this set of sayings. By implication, John's preaching of a threatening Last Judgment, which is either incipient or about to happen, has been authorized to complement Jesus's proclamation of the good news of the kingdom. What Jesus says about John is cryptic but does add up to an intimation that John's coming either inaugurates the era of fulfillment or ends the era of prophecy. We would have to examine Jesus's utterances about divine judgment to determine how faithful Jesus is to John's message, but that is a question for another day.

## Some Synthetic Observations on John's Proclamation of Judgment

When one compares Mark's rendering of John the Baptist to the material shared by Matthew and Luke, one quickly realizes that Mark's is missing the apocalyptic message. On the basis of Mark alone, one could not say that the Baptist's call for confession of sin and baptism was grounded on the prospect of the Last Judgment. After all, the quest for forgiveness of sins may spring from other motivations: to restore a person's relationship with God or to avoid punishment by God in the course of everyday events (not the Last Judgment). These two could also be combined. The penitential piety of Psalm 51 provides another motive: confession of sin opens the self to reform by the spirit of God. All these may be motivating a person without reference to last judgment.

Moreover, John's messianic prophecy (Mark 1:7–8) need not refer to a figure within an apocalyptic scenario. He may, after all, come within this present, fallen age and empower followers to live a different kind of life in time. This is, after all, the Christian interpretation of Jesus as the messiah. Mark's saying is compatible with the Christian kerygma.

We might compare Mark's rendering of the Baptist to that of the Fourth Gospel. In that gospel, the Baptist's message is not at all apocalyptic. In other

---

49. His work is translated into English as *The Theology of St. Luke*. Fitzmyer, *Luke*, in his theological introduction, is critical of Conzelmann's schematic view of Luke's division of time.

*Divine Judgment in the Synoptic Gospel Message*

words, the Gospel of Mark and the Gospel of John agree on this matter, though their actual accounts differ substantially. Where Mark and John differ on apocalyptic is that the Fourth Gospel sublimates or spiritualizes the apocalyptic theological framework while Mark preserves apocalyptic material in Jesus's proclamation.[50]

It is worth adding that Josephus's account of John the Baptist is stripped of the apocalyptic coloring of his message.[51] Since Josephus did not approve of apocalyptic, he may have suppressed this facet of John's rhetoric.[52] It is nevertheless striking that we have three separate accounts of John in which apocalyptic is absent.

The identification of John as an apocalypticist depends entirely on the sermon quoted by Matthew and Luke in Matt 3:7–12//Luke 3:7–9 (10–14), 15–17. The very first verse of the sermon refers to "the wrath to come," and we find two metaphoric depictions of the Last Judgment in the verses that follow. The axe at the root of the trees (Matt 3:10//Luke 3:9) portrays a culling of unfruitful trees going on right now. It definitely thrusts the hearers within the process of judgment.

The harvest to be carried out by the messianic figure (Matt 3:12//Luke 3:17) is clearly a future event, probably occurring in a "moment," so to speak. It would certainly happen so quickly that no one would have time to alter his or her fate.[53] This saying is the only one in John's sermon that hints at a positive reward for the righteous, and it is only a hint: the granary into which is put the seed gathered from the threshing. In this saying, the straw is not only burnt, but the description "unquenchable fire," sounds like hell.

Rhetorically, the force of this apocalyptic language rouses a fear of the pain and suffering of judgment for sin. This is why I call it hellfire preaching. As frontier preachers put it, you would frighten sinners into heaven. This sort of rhetoric is now out of favor in liberal Protestant churches. The message can nevertheless be defended theologically on the basis that it affirms a correspondence between how one has lived his or her life and what it adds up to

---

50. Most obviously in the Synoptic Apocalypse (Mark 13:1–37), but also here and there throughout the narrative.

51. For a translation, see Hollenbach, "John the Baptist," 887–88; also Aune, *Prophecy in Early Christianity*, 382n.

52. See Taylor, *The Immerser*, 94–95; cp. ibid., 215–19.

53. The threshing process does take time, but the separation (by winnowing) occurs at one time, during one action.

*Redeeming Judgment*

in eternity. Providing a vivid image of the outcome should prompt repentance and reformation.

## What Is an Apocalyptic Prophet?

An apocalypse is a literary form, and the characteristics of this literature are those of written discourse. A prophet, on the other hand, speaks; prophetic discourse has the characteristics of oral discourse. Isn't an "apocalyptic prophet" a contradiction in terms? Well, what other name would we give a person who seeks to move people to prepare for the approaching Final Judgment? The framework of the Baptist's portrayal in Matthew and Luke is apocalyptic, the medium is oral discourse, and the spirit is prophetic.[54]

Let's review the characteristics of classical prophecy and show how John's message differs from it. The Old Testament prophet of judgment is told of the divine decision to judge the people, and the prophet has to discover what they are guilty of—what has aroused God's wrath.[55] The prophet's oracle is itself the trial: it states the indictment and pronounces a sentence. Since God is the judge, the prophet does not have to convince him of the people's guilt. Guilt has been decided by God. The rhetorical task is to persuade the accused—the people—of their guilt and its punishment. Their reaction to the message would determine the severity of their punishment.

The punishment is not an end in itself, as if the Lord just wants to balance his books, so to speak. He is seeking to redeem the people, so their judgment is for discipline, purgation, and reorientation. It becomes a death sentence only if they refuse to acknowledge their guilt. Judah, in any case, is granted a reprieve and is restored, though the postexilic Jewish community is hardly the status quo ante. After the Babylonian exile comes a new beginning and the emergence of a new piety, while the diaspora becomes a significant bearer of tradition and the agent of mission. It is in the diaspora that Jews become witnesses to the one true God.

Eschatology becomes the comprehensive horizon of prophecy and history. Remember the formation of the book of Isaiah: the final chapters provide a horizon for all the prophecy and history in the previous chapters. The eschatological psalms also provide a horizon for the transactions within the Psalter. These psalms look forward to the ascension of the Lord to uncontested

---

54. John actually was one of a series of prophets in the first century; see Theissen, *The Shadow of the Galilean*, 29–35, 199–200.

55. They had the benefit of the Yahwistic tradition and intimate rapport with God; on the latter, see R. Abraham Heschel's argument in *The Prophets*, 2:279–308.

sovereignty over the entire world. Apocalyptic extends this eschatology to victory over the power of sin and death in human life. It tends to locate the opposition to God's sovereignty in the supernatural. Historical life is a battleground between supernatural powers. Good will defeat evil once for all and usher in a new age.

Within the Old Testament, the Final Judgment and the salvation of a remnant is on the distant horizon, though now and then it seems to be at hand. The apocalyptic passages of Daniel do date the eschatological event in the proximate future of the author and his original audience. However, one has to decipher a cryptic calendar to arrive at that, and when the original date is past, one can keep the apocalypse current by recalculating the date.

With John the Baptist, the speaker and audience are told that they are or will soon be a part of the event. This prediction makes John's preaching more than a general warning as to the judgment that will come after the audience dies—in the distant future of the earth. It is John's "now" of judgment that requires prophetic authorization. He also warns the audience of their pride, which encourages them to think that they will receive an indulgent judgment because they belong to the people of God. This would be the subject of indictment in classical prophecy, but it has become a warning in John's message. This is because judgment is in the future, though it may already be beginning; in any case, the prophet does not impart judgment in his discourse. Rather, he warns and counsels and baptizes those who come to him.[56]

## Jesus's Proclamation of Final Judgment

Jesus has placed his imprimatur on John's message of judgment and announcement of a messianic judge. John's baptism has the authority of God, symbolizing a person's conversion and commitment to live accordingly. John himself is the prophet Elijah coming to prepare the people of God for the Last Judgment. Although Jesus does not perform the messianic role predicted by John, he does accept the title and assume the authority of the coming one.

---

56. There are several features of classical prophecy that obscure the sharp distinction I am seeking to draw. When Amos took over the hoped-for Day of YHWH and turned it into a day of reckoning, one gets the impression of a future day of judgment. Amos's warning in chapter 4 to "prepare to meet your God, O Israel," also sounds like a future day of reckoning. Ezekiel's image of the prophet as a watchman also fits the idea of a future day of judgment. Despite this "drag," I will stick by my characterization of classical prophecy: the prophet imparts a decision of the Lord about the people.

## Redeeming Judgment

Did Jesus call for the people of God to repent? If so, was his call supported by the threat of apocalyptic judgment? If not, did Jesus proclaim judgment at all? What role did judgment play in his message? Is this role essential to this message? Could Jesus's proclamation get along without any reference to divine judgment?

We will continue to be guided in our exposition by Marius Reiser. Though we are not concerned here with the "historical Jesus"—the Jesus reconstructed by critical historians—we do begin with what critical scholars would most likely regard as the first written texts in the gospel tradition. As we did in the exposition of John the Baptist, so we will begin with Mark, and then take up the texts shared by Matthew and Luke, with an occasional look at a passage found only in one.

### In the Gospel of Mark

This gospel's summary of Jesus's message converges with and differs from the Baptist's. According to Mark 1:15, Jesus proclaims "the good news of God, saying, 'The time is fulfilled, and the kingdom of God is at hand (or near); repent, and believe in the good news'" (RSV). The call to repent corresponds to John's,[57] but Jesus's announcement in Mark does not mention a Day of Judgment, a day of reckoning. Rather, one is to turn around and receive the fulfillment of the promises of old. The kingdom's coming is good news, not a threat of doom.[58]

One might jump to the false conclusion that Mark's Jesus, like Mark's John, does not proclaim judgment. In fact, according to Reiser,[59] there are sixteen pericopés (thirty-seven verses) devoted to divine judgment. This amounts to 22 percent of the oral discourse in Mark. In addition, there are Jesus's actions of cleansing the temple and cursing the fig tree (Mark. 11:11–26). It will be our task in the paragraphs that follow to survey the judgment passages and draw some generalizations.

A number of passages speak of what sort of actions will condemn the doer to hell, Gehenna.[60] In Mark 3:28–29, all sins are said to be forgivable but

---

57. See Matt 3:2, 4:17. Note that Matthew summarizes John's and Jesus's proclamations in the same words, though we have no evidence in the received material that John proclaimed the kingdom.

58. Reiser, *Jesus and Judgment*, 314–16, applies this differentiation to all the traditions about Jesus and John, not only Mark.

59. Ibid., 310–20.

60. A Jewish name for hell derived from the valley west of Jerusalem where children were sacrificed.

"blasphemy against the Holy Spirit"; a person who does that is guilty of an eternal sin (v. 29). This saying was applied to someone who accused Jesus of demonic possession.

Mark 4:24–25 is a proverbial statement: "the measure you give is the measure you get." This is very much in the spirit of the *lex talionis*. It is assumed that "reward" comes in the Last Judgment. Verse 25 adds that the one who has will be given more, and the one who doesn't have will lose what he has. Since v. 24 has announced a reversal of *give* and *receive*, "having" in v. 25 could be read as having a record of giving.

Mark 8:38 announces that "whoever is ashamed of me and of my words in this adulterous and sinful generation, of him will the Son of Man also be ashamed when he comes in the glory of the Father with the holy angels." This saying could be read as distinguishing between Jesus and the Son of Man, but the gospel text has identified them. A Last Judgment scene is assumed in which the Son of Man comes with God's authority to judge the human race, and he will protect those under his care. Those who are "ashamed of him" will not have that protection; indeed, they are betrayers.

Mark 9:43–48 advises those tempted to sin with hand, foot, or eye to cut them off in order to avoid hell. This is hyperbolic, but it does draw upon the threat of eternal suffering to reinforce the gravity of sin. The image has power because it treats the body member as an actor, though the audience knows better. The unit concludes with the mysterious, "everyone will be salted with fire"; this has something to do with judgment, perhaps a process of refining.

Mark 10:25 draws the conclusion that it is harder for a rich person to enter the kingdom than for a camel to go through the eye of a needle. This was an observation based upon the "rich young man's" unwillingness to give away his possessions in quest of eternal life (10:17–22). The "eye of the needle" may be a gate designed to keep animals out. In any case, the attachment of the rich to their possessions makes it virtually impossible for them to give themselves completely to the kingdom. This passage goes on to promise a "return" for giving everything up. At the end, there is an odd remark that "many that are first will be last, and the last first" (10:31, RSV). What sense does it make to speak of a hierarchy in the kingdom?

A few references to the Last Judgment are associated with advice to the disciples or apostles regarding missionary proclamation. At the conclusion of the parable of the Seed (of the kingdom) growing of its own accord, it is harvest time (Mark 4:26–29). This isn't itself a reference to judgment, but it certainly could be taken to imply judgment if one heard an echo of John's messianic prophecy (Matt 3:12//Luke 3:17). Jesus's stipulation of a ritual of "cursing" for towns and cities that do not receive the disciples (Mark 6:11) assumes that the rejection will be "testimony" on the Day of Judgment.

One would expect to find references to divine judgment in the Markan apocalypse (Mark 13:1–37). The apocalypse begins with a prediction of destruction for the temple (vv. 1–4). The prediction is not strictly a proclamation of judgment, but we have already witnessed the cleansing of the temple (in Mark 11:15–18). There Jesus calls it a "den of robbers" (v. 18); this implies divine judgment. Mark 13:1–2 makes that explicit.

Mark 13:5–8, 9–13, and 14–23 describe the "troubles" that will come in the final days, but it is hard to locate any accusations for which these are punishments. The troubles are more on the order of signs to the faithful to prepare for the Last Judgment. The Judgment is depicted briefly in Mk 13:24–27. The "powers of heaven" will be shaken, and all will grow dark, and then the Son of Man will appear in glory. Now one would expect a Final Judgment, a trial. That doesn't happen; rather, the "elect" are gathered by angels, and that is all that is said. No action is taken with the rest of humanity. Nor is heaven or hell described. Thus, we would have to say that judgment is only implicit in the Markan apocalypse.

A few other references to divine judgment appear in the Jerusalem section of Mark. In the interrogation of Jesus by the Sanhedrin, after hearing various accusations against him, the high priest asks point-blank, "Are you the Christ, the Son of the Blessed?" (Mark 14:61). Jesus replies, "I am," a surprisingly forthright statement, given his reticence to reveal his identity throughout the gospel. Then Jesus prophesies, "You will see the Son of Man seated at the right hand of Power, and coming with the clouds of heaven." The high priest and Sanhedrin condemn him for blasphemy (Mark 14:62–64).

Jesus's announcement of the parousia of the Son of Man is mysterious. How does it answer the question from the Sanhedrin? Jesus has to have meant, or to be taken to have meant that he would return soon (after they have killed him?) to overturn the present order. Surely judgment is implied by the setting.

In Mark 12:38–40, Jesus condemns "the scribes" who enjoy the prestige of office, and allow this to go to their heads—an attitude manifested in their pretentious prayers. They actually corrupt the justice system by their rulings ("they devour widow's houses"). Matthew has a much longer list of condemnations of Jewish religious leaders (in Matt 23:1–31).

One of Jesus's parables preserved in Mark proclaims judgment on the Jewish establishment. It is found in Mark 12:1–12. According to the parable, a landowner lets out his land to sharecroppers. When it is time to pay their rent, the tenants drive away the curriers empty handed. After several rounds, the owner decides to send his son, thinking that they will show him more respect. Instead, they decide "to kill the heir," fantasizing that they might take over the farm. But now the landowner will come in person armed to put down their rebellion. New tenants will be found for the farm. The authorities understood that this was a condemnation, and wanted to arrest him. Matthew took this parable and the parable of the banquet as justifications of the rejection of the Jewish people for Gentiles (cp. 21:41, 43; 22:1–14).

This last passage involves judgment against the people of God, as does the cleansing of the temple. The threat of judgment to the scribes and the Sanhedrin involve the leaders of the Jewish people. Shaking the dust off one's sandals as testimony against a whole town or city is also collective. The other passages concern the judgment of individuals. One might think that the generalization about how hard it is for a rich person to enter the kingdom to be collective, but it really concerns the attachment of individuals to their possessions.

About half the condemnations are for the rejection and/or persecution of Jesus himself. That is true of condemning the killing of the son, of the trial of Jesus, and, earlier, of accusing him of being possessed by demons. The towns and cities that spurn his representatives are also rejecting him. The condemnation of those who are "ashamed" of him probably concerns unfaithful followers. Other passages concern judgment for immoralities and crimes that are recognized by practically everyone. The corruption of the temple should be recognized by any Jew.

## In the Gospels of Matthew and Luke

We will be focusing on passages on judgment shared by Matthew and Luke, and occasionally examine a passage found in only one gospel. These passages are covered by Marius Reiser; hence, they probably go back to the historical Jesus, though that is irrelevant to our argument. Reiser divides these passages into those concerned with the Jewish people collectively, and those concerned with individuals.

Matthew 12:41–42//Luke 11:31–32 preserves a saying about the "testimony" of other nations against Israel on the Day of Judgment: "The men of Nineveh will arise at the judgment with this generation and condemn it; for they repented at the preaching of Jonah, and behold, something greater than Jonah is here. The queen of the South will arise at the judgment with the men of this generation and condemn them; for she came from the ends of the earth to hear the wisdom of Solomon, and behold, something greater than Solomon is here." The saying follows up a refusal to provide any "sign" to his contemporaries besides "the sign of Jonah." This calls to mind the repentance of Nineveh, which stands in contrast to Jesus's contemporaries; the Ninevites can expose the hard-heartedness of the present generation, who cannot repent despite the fact that they are being told to by someone greater than Jonah. The parallel about the queen of the South coming to hear Solomon's wisdom is less relevant. "This saying, more than almost any other, reveals Jesus's sense of unity both with the tradition of the Old Testament and with the living tradition of his own time, but on the other hand it shows the supreme ease with which he could give that tradition a twist that was devastating in its impact on his contemporaries."[61] The saying is actually a warning to Jesus's audience that it is in danger of being condemned because "the repentance of the Gentiles will be an accusation against Israel."[62]

Matthew 8:11–12//Luke 13:28–29 is also a comparison of Gentiles and Jews. Here is the unit in Matthew's wording: "I tell you, many will come from east and west and sit at the table with Abraham, Isaac and Jacob in the kingdom of heaven, while the sons of the kingdom will be thrown into the outer darkness." Matthew locates this saying at the end of the curing of the centurion's servant; the centurion had exhibited a level of faith that Jesus had not found among Jews. The image of salvation is a "messianic banquet," though the worthies at the table are not the messiah but the patriarchs of Israel. Instead of by their descendants, however, they are joined by Gentiles, while the descendants suffer in Gehenna. The saying is meant to arouse Jewish "envy" of the outsiders.

Matthew 11:21–24//Luke 10:13–15 pronounces woes on a number of villages around the Sea of Galilee. Luke's wording runs, "Woe to you, Chorazin! Woe to you, Bethsaida! For if the mighty works done in you had been done in Tyre and Sidon, they would have repented long ago . . . It shall be more tolerable in the judgment for Tyre and Sidon than for you. And you, Capernaum, will you be exalted to heaven? You shall be brought down to Hades." These prophetic woes do not address the entire nation, but some towns—indeed, places where Jesus lived or visited frequently. They are rather obscure places. They are compared to two foreign cities, known in the past for their deserving judgment. On the Day of Judgment, these disreputable places will fare better

---

61. Reiser, *Jesus and Judgment*, 220.
62. Ibid., 221.

than towns to which Jesus ministered, because the latter had been favored—mighty works had been performed in their midst—yet they hadn't "repented." Even Jesus's home base, Capernaum, is doomed to hell.

Luke 13:1–5 recounts an exchange between Jesus and his audience about a recent outrage perpetrated by the Roman prefect. Jesus is asked whether this had happened to the Galileans because of their sin. He replies: "I tell you, no. But unless you repent you will likewise perish" (v. 3). He then adds another example of inexplicable disaster—the fall of the tower of Siloam, and again warns his audience to repent. Thus, Jesus refuses to blame the victims, but he is willing to use experiences of disaster as warnings. Note that repentance "is demanded of everyone, without exception, be they great or little sinners, righteous or godless, and it is the same for all."[63] "Judgment is the obverse of salvation, and its necessary precondition."[64] Here Jesus adopts John the Baptist's strategy of appealing to fear of judgment. In general, though, it is "not the fear of judgment that should move Israel to repentance (according to Jesus), but the fascination of the reign of God."[65]

Matthew 23:37–39//Luke 13:34–35 report a lament over Jerusalem. To understand it as judgment, we must identify the speech form carefully. Here is Matthew's wording: "O Jerusalem, Jerusalem, killing the prophets and stoning those who are sent to you! How often would I have gathered your children together as a hen gathers her brood under her wings, but you would not! Behold, your house is forsaken [and desolate]. For I tell you, you will not see me again until you say, 'Blessed is he who comes in the name of the Lord.'" The speaker is God, the only one who could have sought to gather the city "under his protective wings." This is a prophecy of communal judgment clothed in a lament uttered by God.[66] Jeremiah in particular was given to clothing divine judgments in lament (e.g., Jer 15:5–9). Jesus has imitated Jeremiah's prophecy here. The city has persecuted and killed God's spokesmen, and refused to accept the protection offered by God. It prefers to enter into alliances and to take recourse in armaments for protection. Now it is God-forsaken, and will not remain the capital and pilgrimage site of the people of God for long. To return to favor, it must welcome its true (messianic) king.

---

63. Ibid., 248. One might question categorizing this passage as addressed to Jews collectively. It is aimed at Jews in particular, not at Gentiles, given the examples.
64. Ibid., 255.
65. Ibid.
66. See Westermann, *Basic Forms of Prophetic Speech*, 202–3.

## Redeeming Judgment

There are several passages that address the threat of judgment to the Pharisees, a religious party, and the "scribes" who seemed to be closely associated with this party. Mark 12:38–40 condemned the scribes for their oppressive rulings and their pride of position. Matthew expands this "woe" into a full-scale critique of Pharisees and scribes. The Pharisees were a religious party known for their reinterpretation of Mosaic law and their scrupulous observance of this law. They claimed to be the true "teachers"—or rabbis—of Judaism. According to these "woes" of Jesus, they are guilty of overburdening the people with rituals and tithes (Matt 23:1–5). They seek honor for their piety (Matt 23:6–13). They mislead their compatriots in the rules about oaths (23:16–22). Their practices of purification concern external uncleanness, not internal (23:25–28). They honor the righteous figures of tradition but persecute the prophets of their own day (23:29–31). Luke has a number of these condemnations scattered about his gospel (Luke 20:45–47; 11:46; 20:46; 11:52; 20:47; 11:39–51).

Luke's version of the parable of the great banquet (Luke 14:15–24) warns the Pharisees that they are missing out on the kingdom of God. Luke sets the telling of the parable at a banquet in the house of a Pharisee, and Jesus addresses his remarks to the guests (probably Pharisees themselves). There is "testing" going on. One of the guests gets carried away with the prospect of the eschatological banquet, providing an opening for Jesus's parable. When a noble in some town or city throws a banquet for those of his same class, all of them make excuses at the last minute. Now the host has an elaborate meal prepared and no guests to eat it; he invites whoever will come from the streets and even from the countryside. If we assume that the guests who turn the host down are the religious Jews—Pharisees in particular—while the riffraff who enjoy the banquet are "tax collectors and sinners," we have Jesus telling his fellow guests (and his host) that they are missing the party they were looking forward to.

Now we can turn to some sayings that Reiser categorizes as judgment of individuals. Matthew 7:1–2//Luke 6:37–38 prohibit judging others. Luke 6:37 reads, "Judge not, and you will not be judged; condemn not, and you will not be condemned." The passage goes on to urge forgiving and giving as well. Matthew does not have this string of exhortations, but only judging; it does make the second clause subordinate: "Judge not, *that* you be not judged." This could mean that one will be judged by the same norms that one judges others; that would make it an antidote to hypocrisy, and also encourage generosity in one's assessment of others.

Matthew 18:23–35 tells the parable of an unforgiving steward. This farm manager has run up an astronomical debt to his royal landlord, and pleads with him to avoid debtors' prison. He is forgiven and allowed to continue in his job. When someone who owes him money asks for similar treatment, he shows no mercy. When his lord hears, the steward goes to prison—his forgiveness is conditional on being forgiving.

Matthew 5:25–26//Luke 12:57–59 advise the addressee to make peace with a creditor or accuser before a formal hearing. According to Reiser,[67] who has traced back to Egyptian practice the legal proceeding assumed here, the debtor should make whatever deal he can before the hearing because the judge will invariably back up the creditor's claims. This has been offered as an analogy for the way to prepare for the last judgment. We might find an analogy in the Jewish practice of reconciling with those one has offended or injured before the Day of Atonement. Reiser, however, suggests that Jesus is the creditor, and one should seek to satisfy his claims before the Day of Judgment.[68]

Finally, there is he parable of the unjust steward (Luke 16:1–8). This parable has stumped many interpreters because it seems to recommend cheating. It seems to have attracted far-fetched efforts to understand it even before Luke's composition, because there are a number of attachments (16:9–13). According to Reiser,[69] v. 8a is not a part of the parable, but the narrator's report of Jesus's interpretation: "The master commended the dishonest steward for his shrewdness." When the steward is fired by the landlord, he contacts renters or debtors (to the farm) and cuts their obligations down. He expects these beneficiaries of his debt reduction to pay him back by taking him in. The manager is commended for his resolute, resourceful response to the crisis. Likewise, in the face of the Last Judgment, one should do whatever one can to avoid condemnation.[70]

## Conclusions

From his exegesis of these passages, Reiser draws a long list of conclusions. Let's survey the list and assess the validity of his inferences.

---

67. Reiser, *Jesus and Judgment*, 282–86.
68. Ibid., 288.
69. Ibid., 292.
70. Ibid., 300–301.

## Redeeming Judgment

(1) Jesus's preaching of Final Judgment—either pronouncing it or describing it—is pervasive and essential to his message.

(2) The passages yield a clear and consistent picture of Jesus's understanding of the Final Judgment. What "Jesus announces is always the same event, and the decision he demands in the light of that event is always the same. Since all are threatened by destruction, he calls for all to repent."[71]

(3) Jesus makes a provocative contrast between Israel and the Gentiles. While this will ultimately serve the Gentile mission, it is formulated to "shame" the people of God into living up to their creed. This is, of course, only one among several strategies Jesus employs to provoke his audience.

(4) There are a variety of images used to depict the eschatological event; trial imagery is only one among others—e.g., a harvest and the summoning of the elect from their graves. Some sayings presuppose that the decision has already been made, while others regard the decision to arise from the exchange on the Last Day.

(5) Jesus frequently alludes to scriptural passages and motifs, providing continuity and spontaneity to the interpretation of Scripture.

(6) Jesus doesn't explicitly name the judge, but it is clearly God (the Father).

(7) Judgment is determined by the addressee's relationship to Jesus and his message.[72] This thesis seems suspect to me. Jesus's indictment of his contemporaries for failing to repent when someone greater than Jonah and Solomon arrives, conforms to Reiser's thesis; so too do the towns witnessing Jesus's mighty deeds and not repenting. However, some sayings have the people failing to repent in the face of recent disasters. The abuses of the scribes and Pharisees have nothing to do with Jesus and his message. The lament over Jerusalem now calls for receiving Jesus when he comes, but the trouble they have had in the past has nothing to do with him. The warning against judging others and the duty of forgiving others need not involve a relationship with Jesus or his teaching. Mark's eschatological passages also split.

---

71. Ibid., 304–5. I might add that there are a goodly number of passages in Matthew and Luke which have the same pattern: Luke 12:8–9//Matt 10:32–33; Luke 17:26–27//Matt 24:37–39; Matt 7:24–27//Luke 6:47–49; Luke 16:19–31; Matt 12:28//Luke 11:20.

72. Ibid., 310–11.

The remainder of Reiser's conclusions note Jesus's relationship to contemporary Jews. Just as Jesus did, so the Teacher of Righteousness at Qumran also made his teaching and the relationship of others to his person a measure for judgment. Jesus and John the Baptist were alike in employing metaphors and parables to depict the Final Judgment; they also shared a stress on repentance and its fruits. Though Jesus had his own characteristic emphases,[73] he shared the main characteristics of the apocalypticism with the Jews of his era.

"Judgment," according to Reiser, "is not only the precondition for *the final coming of salvation*; to the extent that salvation is already present in Jesus' work, judgment is at the same time *the necessary consequence of salvation rejected or despised*.[74]

We will draw our own conclusions after we have considered the question of the norms according to which people would be judged. This means that we will take up Jesus's teaching of Mosaic law.

## The Law of the Kingdom

Judgment normally entails the imposition of a penalty for the violation of some known norm. The penalty would be an arbitrary assault on a person or group if there were no violation of norms. The person penalized must be obligated to the norms that he or she should have known. Otherwise, the person or collectivity is not accountable for the action, and the imposition of the penalty is not judgment.

In the Old Testament, the norms can be divided into those known by all peoples and societies, and those to which only God's people are obligated. We have been noting this division off and on through this entire book. Jewish tradition ascribes the common human norms to the Noachic covenant. Few would claim that the covenant has specific provisions, but would hold that laws covering killing and assault, marriage and family, ownership and theft, truth telling and promise keeping, can be found in all, or practically all, societies. The common human law is not strictly timeless either; some subjects like slavery and the subordination of women were once universal but have been purged over time, while ownership has been expanded, for example, to include intellectual property and inventions.

---

73. Jesus emphasized repentance in order to enter the kingdom of God, and expressed no hatred or disdain for the godless or Gentiles.

74. Reiser, *Jesus and Judgment*, 323.

*Redeeming Judgment*

Only the people of Israel are under the yoke of Mosaic law, that is, God's law revealed through Moses to the people. The gospels depict a society under revealed law, and Jesus's promulgation of the obligations his audience owes God is an interpretation of Mosaic law. His interpretation is set in opposition to the most popular school of interpretation among Jews at the time—the Pharisees. There are conflicts over "working" on the Sabbath, and whether healing comes under the provision. There are conflicts over purification rituals and eating restrictions. Jesus's claim to authority—to forgive, to revise Mosaic law, even to exorcise demons—was disputed. On many issues, the gospels depict Jesus as an advocate of a more relaxed or less scrupulous interpretation of religious practice.

However, he counterbalanced this "liberal strain" with a radicalization of what might be called the weighty laws. This latter strain is brought to full, dramatic expression in the Sermon on the Mount (Matthew 5–7). I agree that the Sermon constitutes an epitome of Jesus' teaching about his audience's obligations to God. We can examine these teachings to grasp their fundament thrust or thrusts, and supplement the materials of Matthew 5–7 when helpful.

Jesus's interpretation of divine law is contained in Matthew 5–6. It begins with the Beatitudes (6:3–12). These are followed by what we might call heuristic guidelines (5:13–20). The meat of the chapter is a series of interpretations of Mosaic commandments: against murder (5:21–26), adultery and divorce (5:27–32), swearing oaths (5:33–37), retaliation (5:38–42), and loving enemies (5:43–48). All these but swearing have to do with relations between humans. Chapter 6 concerns piety and faith. The first units (Matt 6:1–4, 5–8, 16–18) counsel an inward, theocentric piety; the Lord's Prayer is spliced in here, set in contrast to "heaping up of empty phrases" (v. 7). The next set (Matt 6:19–21, 22–23, 24) stresses a piety that concentrates on the vertical, on communion with and loyalty to God alone. The teaching on piety comes to an end with the counsel, "do not be anxious about you life" (v. 25). This means surrendering control of one's life, putting it in the hands of the providential God (6:25–34).

The Beatitudes commend a particular set of virtues—virtues that will not help one succeed in this life, but that are of eternal value. One can read the list in various ways. Hans Dieter Betz regards the first, "Blessed are those who are poor in spirit," as comprehensive, and the rest as "unfoldings" of this one.[75] One could just as well read them as building a cumulative picture, or of validating a variety of people with different strengths. A person might be a peacemaker, for example, but not be "pure in heart"—a passionate piety with a

---

75. Betz, *Essays on the Sermon on the Mount*, 35.

mystic hope. The problem with this latter reading is the one might have qualities that "cancel" out the virtues. A lot of people who champion just causes—"hunger and thirst for righteousness"—are not particularly "poor in spirit." Indeed, I would hold that without the humility that is commended by "poor in spirit" and "meek," a person is seriously flawed. It is this virtue that links the piety of the Beatitudes to the penitential piety that emerged in postexilic Israel. Only here and there does Jesus indicate that one should be conscious of one's sinfulness (e.g., Mark 10:18//Luke 18:19; Luke 18:9–14), but the allied virtue of humility is essential to the Beatitudes. Jesus's teaching about piety in Matt 6:1–18 speaks of practicing one's piety in secret—and not reaping worldly reward. This inwardness certainly belongs with meekness and purity of heart.

The final two Beatitudes are strictly for Christians; the image of faithfulness in a time persecution epitomizes the Christian life. It is doubtful, however, that one has to be a Christian before one can be said to exemplify these other virtues.

The key to one's obligations to one's neighbors is in the saying, "I have come not to abolish [the law and the prophets] but to fulfill them" (5:17) coupled with the warning, "unless your righteousness exceeds that of the scribes and the Pharisees, you will never enter the kingdom of heaven" (5:20). The first of these explains why Jesus cites Old Testament texts for each of the following teachings. He follows the citations with, "but I say to you . . ." and a more stringent reading: "You have heard it said, 'An eye for an eye and a tooth for a tooth.' But I say to you, Do not resists one who is evil . . ." Jesus is calling for a pacifism that far exceeds the requirements of strict justice. There are various reasons why one should adopt this policy, but the promise that it will win over the attacker would be false. Jesus is calling upon his followers to take up their crosses and follow him. One's victory is in the kingdom, and only sometimes in history. Indeed, one's martyrdom may be the foundation of the victory of one's cause—as in the cases of Martin Luther King Jr. and Mahatma Gandhi.

Jesus's fullest teaching on divorce is not found in Matt 5:31–32 but in Mark 10:1–12//Matt 19:1–12. It is Jesus's stated view in the Markan version that marriage is a bond created and protected by God, so humans have no right to sever it (10:8–9). To be sure, Moses allowed for divorce (10:4), but this was a concession to human sinfulness (10:5). If one wants to live up to the standards of the kingdom, divorce must be renounced.[76]

---

76. Matthew provides for divorce when one party committed adultery; that is a bit of practical wisdom but undercuts the logic of Jesus's statement.

## Redeeming Judgment

The Sermon on the Mount has little on wealth and poverty. There is the saying in Matt 6:19–21 about "laying up" treasures in heaven and not on earth. In Luke 12:33–34, this saying is attached to Jesus's advice to "sell your possessions and give alms."[77] In the same passage we find the parable of the rich fool and the encouragement to rely on providence. In the section, the quest for wealth is an effort to gain security and control life. Elsewhere attachment to wealth makes it well nigh impossible to release attachment to this world to enter the kingdom (Mark 10:17–31 and parallels). There is, by the way, little on the obligation of the wealthy to support the poor.

One other subject is of great weight in the gospel tradition: forgiveness. In the Sermon on the Mount, it is only explicitly addressed in the Lord's Prayer: "Forgive us our debts, as we forgive our debtors" (Matt 6:25, cp. Luke 11:4; Mark 11:25). The command to love one's enemies might well come under the rubric of forgiveness, though Matthew seems to reserve the word *forgiveness* for one's face-to-face community, where persons ask to be forgiven. Thus, Matthew's primary teaching is in chapter 18, where policies and guidelines are offered for church life. The ethical ambiguity that hovers around forgiveness is whether one should forgive a person who has no contrition, and who will probably continue to offend.

The foundation of all Jesus's teaching regarding obligations to God is the dual commandment to love God with all one's being and to love one's neighbor as oneself (Matt 22:34–40//Mark 12:28–34//Luke 10:25–28). This is the reason for the radical thrust, the going farther, which graces Jesus's teaching. Matthew 5 ends with, "you must be perfect, as your heavenly Father is perfect" (v. 48). Luke has the parallel: "Be merciful, even as your Father is merciful" (6:36).

The logic of Matthew 7 is hard to follow, but the last two units clearly challenge the audience to adopt and live out the teaching of the Sermon. Verses 24–47 tell a parable to indicate how "everyone who hears these words of mine and does them" will be proven over time to be wise, while the person who does not will crumble when he or she experiences troubles. The troubles are not portrayed as the Final Judgment but rather the storms of everyday life.

Just prior to this unit is a warning (7: 21–23) that on the Day of Judgment those who have not "done the will of my Father who is in heaven" will not receive Jesus's protection. The unit portrays Jesus not as judge but as one who has the authority to protect his own from judgment.[78] In this pericope, he warns

---

77. This sounds rather like the exchange between Jesus and the well-to-do young man (Matt 19:21//Mark 10:21//Luke 18:22).

78. See Betz, *Essays on the Sermon on the Mount*, 141–51.

that he will disown those who claim to belong to him but have not lived accordingly: "I never knew you; depart from me, you evildoers" (v. 23).

Both these units address Christians. Only those who have "heard these words of mine" could be expected to build a house upon them. Only those who claim Jesus as their Lord can be disowned. Those who claim the privilege of being in Christ are accountable for his interpretation of the Law.

How about those outside this circle? Well, Jews must be distinguished from Gentiles. Jesus is interpreting Mosaic law—the divine law for which Jews are accountable. The issue here is interpretation: that is, can Jews be held accountable for Jesus's interpretation of the law? Several statements in the Sermon on the Mount suggest that they are. The scribes and Pharisees would represent the highest level of righteousness among the Jewish parties. When Jesus says, "unless your righteousness exceeds that of the scribes and Pharisees, you will never enter the kingdom of heaven" (Matt 5:20), he is implying that the righteousness of these rigorous Jews does not meet the standards for entrance. Evidently they are condemned. Some particular examples of their piety are condemned as well (Matt 6:2, 5).

This entire Sermon, of course, is rhetorically driven, and it is not forensic rhetoric. The "righteousness of the scribes and Pharisees" would appear to characterize their teaching and common practice, not the morality and piety of individual scribes and Pharisees. There is another question that should be answered: how can the Pharisees be held accountable for the norms of a prophet they do not know, or whom they reject? There is a conundrum here. Jesus claims to provide the best interpretation of Mosaic law; Jews should have arrived at this interpretation, and they fell short because of sin (cp. Mark 10:2–12).

Paul deals with a similar problem in Rom 10:14–21. He urges that evangelists to preach to the Jews so they can make a deliberate decision (Rom 10:14–17). Then he reverses himself, deciding that there is scriptural testimony to their having already heard (10:18–20). While Paul is certainly stretching his texts to find evidence that Jews have heard the gospel, it could be argued that they have the basis in their tradition to recognize the messiah when he came. Paul believes that they should have in particular recognized that justification is by faith, not by works of law.

Here is another analogy. When modern readers find laws governing slavery, encouraging violent pursuit of power, or subjugating women, we not only reject the authority of these laws, we ascribe them to the sinfulness of the social elite that promulgated them. These "bad" laws are not an accident

503

of nature, they are a collective wrongdoing. Yet these laws belonged to the taken-for-granted world of the whole society. At the very least, responsibility is mitigated, and individuals are not personally responsible for participating in an international consensus.

In this eschatological moment, Jesus is offering entrance into the kingdom of God, and this requires his addressees to repent—not just of personal sins under the regnant regime, but of the interpretations of the law that did not fully embody the unconditional love of God and the love of all human beings equally. The objective was not to condemn Jews but to transform them. However, those who were unwilling to repent did face exclusion from the kingdom.

How about Gentiles? The Gentiles are without Mosaic Law, so the Sermon on the Mount doesn't hold them specifically responsible. This could mean that they had no chance of being saved. Marius Reiser believes that this position was well nigh universal among Jews, including John the Baptist.[79] Jesus, on the other hand, certainly envisaged the possibility of Gentiles being saved. In Matt 12:41–42//Luke 11:31–32, the Ninevites and the queen of the South will testify against Israel on the Day of Judgment. Tyre and Sidon, and even Sodom, will testify against some Jewish villages on the northwest corner of the Sea of Galilee (according to Matt 10:13–15//Luke 10:13–15). The children of the kingdom will watch from Gehenna while Gentiles eat at the messianic banquet with Abraham, Isaac, and Jacob (Matt 8:11–12//Luke 13:28–29). The parable of the Last Judgment in Matt 25:31–46 says that "all nations" will be gathered before the Son of Man; the separation of sheep and goats is not an ethnic but a moral division. As Reiser says, these passages are not promises of salvation addressed to Gentiles; they are meant to arouse Jews to fulfill their calling. However, the Gentiles are not to be excluded, even if the Jews were to be reformed and transformed.

The Gentile mission only began after Jesus's death and resurrection, and then more as a "rebound" when most Jews rejected the gospel. Nothing had been worked out theologically regarding the responsibility of the Gentiles for their condition before encountering the gospel. When they did convert, they provoked a theological debate concerning whether they should be circum-

---

79. See Reiser, *Jesus and Judgment*, 80. On 136–37, various rabbinic interpreters are cited, some of whom envisaged a scenario in which "righteous Gentiles" were saved along with righteous Jews; others thought all Gentiles were condemned because they "forgot God."

cised and be held account for the Mosaic law. If this had been settled by Jesus, it would not have boiled up as a source of conflict.[80]

The Jewish tradition pondered the problem of Gentile responsibility. One example is a parable of *b. Abodah Zarah*.[81] At the Last Judgment, God will invite those who occupied themselves with Torah to step forward and receive their reward.[82] The nations can't do so, but one after another tries to justify itself by how it treated Israel. God blames them all for being motivated by their own sinful inclinations; then the nations object to being judged by a standard they had never known. After a discussion of whether they would have received it, God decides that they can be judged by the Noachic covenant, which has seven fundamental commandments. Unfortunately, they have not kept them either. The dispute takes some more turns, but ends with a rejection of the Gentiles in total.

The New Testament gospels do not attain such a theoretical, abstract level of thought on the subject. They speak a pastoral word: the church needed to know that it was responsible for Jesus's interpretation of Mosaic Law, though Paul eliminated the Mosaic character of the obligation for Gentile Christians. The church also knew that Jew and Gentile alike needed to repent and turn their lives over to the leading of the Spirit.

Thus there is no answer to the question about what happens to Jews who do not accept Jesus as messiah and Gentiles who have no knowledge of Christ. Paul comes to the belief that Jews will convert before Christ returns (Rom 11:11–36). He may have had collective ideas about the Gentiles, though he does not share these with readers.[83] We will discover that he does articulate a theoretical theological view of divine judgment and the norms under which this takes place.[84]

---

80. One reads of these conflicts (in a sanitized version) in Acts, and (in a blunt account) in Galatians.

81. Discussed extensively in Betz, *Essays on the Sermon on the Mount*, 134–41.

82. Ibid., 135

83. Romans 15:8–29 skims over his missionary career and his plans for the future. Why does Paul think it sufficient to establish a few churches around the Aegean Sea, and then say that he "has no room to work in these regions"? Do the churches he has established somehow sanctify the whole province?

84. Paul's position in the New Testament canon is rather analogous to Isaiah's within the prophetic canon of the Old Testament.

## A Synthesis of Our Findings

What remains to be done to draw this chapter together? We have identified a powerful message of divine judgment in support of the call to repent and be baptized. According to the material shared by Matthew and Luke, John the Baptist announced the approach of the Final Judgment, urged his fellow Jews to repent, and held out the expectation of a messiah. This is, of course, John's contribution to the gospel. His message is validated by Jesus's interpretation of John as his precursor. In later texts, John returns the favor. Jesus himself takes up the message of judgment, though with a different emphasis. In any case, both John and Jesus regard their generation to be at the threshold of the final reckoning; indeed both hint that it has begun.

The gospels agree that Jesus regarded John as a true prophet; he was even willing to link his authority with John's. He was also willing to portray his ministry as complementary to John's in the parable of the children in the marketplace. Jesus sought to build on John's message, so the gospels are true to Jesus in reporting John's message and life.[85]

In several sayings Jesus identifies John as the "Elijah" to come. His role seems to be to send out the call to repent to the people of God, and to arouse expectation of a messiah, who will separate the grain from the straw and chaff. He appears, according to Jesus, at a moment of transition between the time of the prophets and the kingdom. Moreover, the Elijah figure is destined for martyrdom, prefiguring the martyrdom of the Son of Man.

According to the gospel writers, the truth of John's prophecy resides chiefly in the messianic component. All four gospels cite it.[86] Once Jesus has been baptized, John's role is eclipsed; his imprisonment symbolizes his completion of his role. John's message of apocalyptic judgment becomes fused, in the Synoptic Gospels, with Jesus's prophecy of the coming of the Son of Man. It is, one might say, deferred.

Jesus does not lead with the threat of the Last Judgment but with the promise and hope of the new age—the kingdom of God.[87] He is forced nevertheless to pronounce judgment. In the Gospel of Mark,[88] Jesus condemns the temple and probably prophecies its destruction. He also condemns the

---

85. So Sanders, *Jesus and Judaism*, 91–93.

86. One is reminded of the Isenheim Altarpiece by Matthias Grünewald, in which Christ hangs from the cross and John the Baptist is on the left side pointing at him, with a book in his hand.

87. A point underscored in Reiser, *Jesus and Judgment*, 304–5.

88. Repeated, of course, in Matthew and Luke.

"tenants" of the vineyard in the parable of the Wicked Tenants; this is an allegory indicting Jewish religious leaders. Again, he condemns the scribes, and continually censures the Pharisees. He seems to allude to the second coming during his trial; this would imply judgment. Finally, he prescribes a procedure for cursing cities that spurn his apostles.

Jesus also has occasion to warn his audience of individual judgment. There are memorable sayings about the unforgivable sin and cutting off hands and feet, or of putting out eyes, to suppress temptation. Jesus observes that wealth seems to enslave a person to worldliness, but promises that giving receives a heavenly reward. Finally, Jesus warns his followers not to be ashamed to him; if they are, the Son of Man will not protect them on the Day of Judgment.

In the material shared by Mathew and Luke but absent in Mark, we find a valuable cache of judgment sayings. A number of sayings compared the behavior of Gentiles to that of Jews. The Ninevites will expose the hard-heartedness of Jesus's contemporaries; they repented in response to Jonah's prophecy, but Jesus's contemporaries have not, though the Son of Man is in their midst. The citizens of Tyre and Sidon will "testify" against Chorizin, Bethsaida, and Capernaum. Gentiles from all nations will join the patriarchs at the messianic banquet table, while those who should be there are excluded. All these are collective. The lament over Jerusalem employs a prophetic form to evoke the city's history of rejecting the will of its God to indicate that it will not be graced with God's presence until it receives his messiah.

Jesus refers to a number of recent disasters as signs that his hearers should repent. The individual is told to avoid a censorious attitude in order to keep from being scrutinized to the same degree. The person who has been forgiven is obligated to forgive those who seek it from him or her; if one will not, as it were, pass forgiveness on, one will not receive it. When one is indebted to another, one should be quick to negotiate, for the judge will side with the creditor. The parable of the banquet warns the Pharisees, according to Luke, that they are missing out on the kingdom of God, while the riffraff are taking their place.

Now we come to the subject of law. John the Baptist measures his contemporaries by Mosaic law; we have no indication of the interpretative tradition to which he belonged, though he was quite rigorous about marriage law. Jesus also accepted, according to Matthew and Luke,[89] the divine authority of Mosaic Law, but he offered a distinctive interpretation of it. We could formulate it thus: when he called his contemporaries to repent, he meant, not only of

---

89. Matt 5:17–20; Luke 16:17.

## Redeeming Judgment

the sins that they would own up to, but of sin due to the compromises made because of the people's hardness of heart. Jesus's own interpretation of the Law was meant to withdraw the compromises.

The call to repentance suggests a penitential piety. Jesus definitely commends a sin consciousness, according to the parable of the Pharisee and the tax collector, and in response to being addressed as "good teacher." In the Beatitudes, however, the emphasis is on humility, spiritual and ethical passion—in the spirit of "going farther." This is rooted in the unconditional, unqualified love of God, which frees a person to love neighbors and enemies and persecutors as God loves them. Violence and retaliation are ruled out of relations with one's fellow humans, and the marriage promise and promises calling for oaths should be unconditional. To be free for God, one must not be attached to worldly possessions or social prestige either.

Jesus's radical teaching about the law is binding on followers. Since it is offered as the divinely intended interpretation of divine law, it is also incumbent on Jews. This does not necessarily mean that Jews who do not accept Jesus as messiah, and therefore do not submit themselves to his interpretation of the law, are condemned to hell. Who knows what stores of grace are laid up? Remember, the gospels provide pastoral guidance, not doctrine.

How about Gentiles? Those who have no knowledge of Jesus and his teaching could hardly be held accountable for it. One might think that Jesus's teaching is an ethic and piety for all humans. This is why Christians are told to reach out to all peoples. But they are not accountable to a revealed law until they have committed themselves to the God in whose name it is promulgated. They are accountable for the provisions of the Noachic covenant, nothing more. This does not, however, make them candidates for the kingdom of God; only those who accept the invitation and commit themselves to the Law are.

### Jesus and Judgment

According to Marius Reiser, "The judgment Jesus announces for Israel as a whole and for every individual . . . [is?] closely *related to himself and his message*."[90] This is loosely enough formulated to allow for some of Jesus's marginal statements. However, Reiser goes further: "The repentance he calls for is not . . . a turning back to Torah, but turning to him and his teaching, in which, of course, he fully affirms Torah and thus sees it simultaneously elevated (*auf-*

---

90. Reiser, *Jesus and Judgment*, 310 (italics original).

*gehoben*) and given its full force."[91] Just how can Reiser support this radical claim? I think he regards all of Jesus's judgment sayings as of a piece. Thus, he takes the sayings about the Ninevites and the queen of the South as evidence that his contemporaries have before them someone "more than" Jonah or Solomon.[92] The towns of Chorizin, Bethsaida, and Capernaum have witnessed greater miracles than Tyre and Sidon. These two judgments correspond to the Beatitude in Matt. 13:16–17//Luke 10:23–24, to the effect that the contemporary generation is especially fortunate. Woe to those who do not repent in the face of such awesome events. "The object of judgment . . . is nothing but the refusal to repent in response to his message."[93] Jesus is making the sort of claim that will elicit the charge that he is usurping Scripture and God himself.

Except for these few statements alluding to his own identity, the Synoptic Gospels do not portray Jesus as "preaching himself" or recruiting "adherents." Of course, he does recruit disciples and expect them to submit to his will, but he is not trying to create a movement or a church. His message is the kingdom. He is its messenger. His works are signs of the kingdom's power. He even answers John that he is the one John is expecting. He shares glimpses of his supernatural stature with his disciples. But in public he is incognito, hidden behind the kingdom. I would say, then, that Reiser has overstated Jesus's claim for himself.

Hans Frei argues in a lean, modest theological monograph that Jesus becomes progressively identified with the kingdom.[94] This is a sound reading of the Synoptic Gospels. The Fourth Gospel, on the other hand, starts where the Synoptics leave off, and reviews the whole life of Jesus through the lens of the exalted Son of God.

---

91. Ibid.
92. Note Matt 12:6: "I tell you, something greater than the temple is here."
93. Reiser, *Jesus and Judgment*, 311.
94. Frei, *The Identity of Jesus Christ*.

# 21

## The Suffering Servant and Son of Man in the Synoptics

(Matthew, Mark, Luke)

THE QUESTION ADDRESSED IN this chapter is: How does the person and life of Jesus contribute to and modify the message John and Jesus proclaimed? Scholars have formulated the distinction between what Jesus himself proclaimed and what the gospels and letters of the New Testament proclaim. Jesus proclaimed the kingdom of God; the church proclaimed Jesus Christ himself.

The gospels disclose the identity of Jesus from the outset. In Mark, Jesus is identified by God very early as "my beloved Son" (1:11). Later in the gospel the voice from heaven tells three of Jesus's disciples the same (9:8). Demons also divulge Jesus's identity but are quickly silenced. Jesus himself demonstrates who he is. In the transfiguration (Mark 9:2–8), Moses and Elijah join Jesus on the top of the mountain. Prior to that, Jesus had stilled a storm (4:35–41) and walked on water (6:45–52)—theophanies that were permitted the disciples but were not to be divulged until he was raised from the dead (8:9–10). Jesus also tells his disciples not to reveal his identity after they rightly identify him as messiah (8:29–30). Jesus wants to carry out his mission incognito, and have his full identity become public after his resurrection—in retrospect. Only once in Mark do we find a forthright messianic claim in a public arena (14:62); he would not have expected the temple authorities to believe his claim, but they deserved to know whom it was they were about to execute.[1]

---

1. The majority of the historians of the life of Jesus think that Jesus did not claim to be messiah, and in fact had no such idea about himself. However that may be, a final-form,

Jesus prophesies his fate in a number of Markan passages known as passion predictions; three stand out: 8:31–33; 9:30–32; and 10:32–34. Each time, there is a narrative associated with the prediction, indicating that the disciples don't understand. Messianic expectations among Jesus's disciples, as well as the Jewish people at large, entailed victory over all that stood in the way of establishing the kingdom of God. If the messianic pretender were captured and killed and his followers dispersed, he was a false messiah. So when Jesus follows Peter's confession with a passion prediction, Peter "rebukes" him. For him, a true messiah who suffers and dies is a contradiction in terms.[2] Jesus rebukes Peter for sharing the views of his compatriots—an all too human perspective. After the second passion prediction readers discover that the disciples had been arguing over who is the greatest (9:33–34). Jesus uses this as a "teaching moment": "If anyone would be first, he must be last of all and servant of all" (v. 35, RSV). That corresponds to a suffering, crucified messiah. After the third passion prediction, James and John request to occupy the most honored positions in the kingdom (10:35–37). When the other disciples hear about this request, they are offended. Jesus then expands on the nature of leadership in his community: "whoever would be great among you must be your servant, and whoever would be first among you must be slave of all. For the Son of Man came not to be served but to serve, and to give his life as a ransom for many" (10:43–45, RSV). This is the fullest statement of the revolutionary view of power embedded in the gospel of Christ. What Jesus accomplishes is to "ransom" many, the ultimate act of service.

The passion predictions are not public proclamations but instructions to Jesus's disciples. The disciples must be prepared for what is about to happen, and they must understand what it means afterward. What happens to Jesus will become the heart of their message, and the kingdom of God will become a subtheme. What Jesus would accomplish by suffering could not be proclaimed until it had moved from possibility to actuality. The gospels now proclaim the life, death, and resurrection of Jesus as an actuality. Matthew and Luke do not retain the incognito of the Son of God as carefully as Mark, but they still retain the centrality of the kingdom of God and its law.

---

canonical reading must bracket this critical thesis. The gospels depict Jesus as conscious of his identity as messiah, Son of God, and as imparting this knowledge to the inner circle. Nevertheless, we can agree with the critical position up to a point: namely, that Jesus discovered what his calling entailed as challenges came his way.

2. They couldn't grasp his prediction of resurrection, though such a hope was alive among the Jewish circles that Jesus moved in.

*Redeeming Judgment*

The subject of our last chapter was the preaching of John and Jesus; now we will consider their preaching as transactions with their audience. Society was impacted by John's message of repentance; large crowds came out into the wilderness to hear him and respond with repentance and baptism. Others were antagonistic or indifferent.

Jesus had a large impact as well. He attracted many followers and sympathetic supporters, and aroused a good deal of antipathy among the Pharisees and Sadducees, as well as among the Galilean ruling elite. The effect of both men was to split the society, adding to the many conflicts and parties. Both were silenced by the power elites. John was executed by Herod Antipas. Jesus was tried and executed by a cadre of Jerusalem religious authorities in alliance with the Roman imperial government.

The authorities will be judged in retrospect by readers as guilty of a crime. Jesus' reaction to his persecution and martyrdom was a test of his faith and his message. God is put to the test, so to speak, by Jesus's cry from the cross; God has abandoned the one he called "beloved son." A judicial event has occurred in which every party acts both as judge and defendant.

If the trial had ended with the burial of Jesus and the dispersion of his disciples, the meaning of the event would have been quite different from the account of the New Testament. Jesus would have been proven to be a false messiah, and the God who called him an illusion of his mind. The authorities would not have been cleared of judicial murder, but the meaning of their injustice would be the cynical "might makes right." The resurrection of Jesus overturns all these judicial outcomes. Now we are faced with the question: what is the theological meaning of his death? Are there Old Testament texts that can interpret it? Was it the fulfillment of an Old Testament prophecy?

The Servant Song in Isa 52:13—53:12 is the best candidate—practically the only one.[3] I am attracted to Roy Melugin's thesis to the effect that even if no New Testament author cited this text, it would be quite legitimate for Christians to use it to gain a "rich understanding of what vicarious suffering—and especially the vicarious suffering of Jesus—is all about."[4] He points out that Isaiah 53 and the New Testament texts about vicarious suffering are "in the Christian *canon* of scripture," which permits and urges us to put them in dialog. In fact, they are components of a comprehensive symbolic world.[5]

---

3. Except for allegorists!
4. "On Reading Isaiah 53 as Christian Scripture," 67.
5. Ibid., 67–68.

Melugin's thesis does not render an earlier type of scholarship completely superfluous, but it may alter its import. We have no reason to cite "promises" that Christ fulfills; that belongs to an outmoded and unconvincing apologetic. Now we can ask whether the Old Testament casts light on the meaning of the texts and events in the New Testament. I will be drawing on arguments that identify certain gospel passages as dependant on Isaiah 53. We can ignore the apologetic element in the argument. We can, rather, assess the match of Isaiah 53 and these passages, and indeed the fit of Isaiah 53 and Jesus's fate.

I have not forgotten "Son of Man" in our chapter title. Jesus uses this expression quite frequently, and others do not use it of him. We will consider only the predictions of suffering and those that refer to the Son of Man coming as a part of the Last Judgment. In the extant text of the gospels, the references to the Son of Man are taken to be predictions of the second coming of Jesus Christ. This connection between the predictions and the references to the Son of Man raises an interesting theological question: can the one who had to suffer become the judge of the world in might without contradiction? The answer has to be yes, but we cannot overlook the fact that Jesus eschewed the use of violent, coercive power during his ministry, but the language associated with the Son of Man has a military sound to it. How can nonviolent, noncoercive, persuasive power "overthrow" its opposite and take sovereignty over all human life? How can Jesus remain true to himself while he "puts all his enemies under his feet" (1 Cor 15:25)?

*Prospectus*

Now let me sketch what we are going to cover in this chapter. We are restricting our study to the Synoptic Gospels. We will locate those sayings that interpret Jesus's suffering and death, and assess how well they conform to the teaching of Isaiah 53. We should be able to anchor the servant in the symbolic world of the gospels. At the end of the chapter, we shall locate "Son of man" passages that challenge theological consistency.

## The Suffering Servant in the Synoptic Gospels

We can begin our discussion of this topic by identifying passages that critical scholars have regarded as quite possibly under the influence of Isaiah 53. Mark's passion predictions are prime candidates, and the follow-up to the third passion prediction purports to explain why Jesus must suffer. Matthew and Luke pass on the passion predictions in somewhat modified form. In addition, the words associated with the Last Supper accord sacrificial significance to Jesus's death.

How well does the concept of vicarious suffering depicted so effectively in Isaiah 53 fit the gospel narratives? How did Jesus ignite tension and conflict in Galilean and Jerusalemite society? Who was for him? Who was against him? What were the motives and institutional imperatives of the authorities? Why did the crowds in Jerusalem turn against Jesus? Why did Jesus' disciples abandon him?

What does the account of the actors in this deadly drama have to do with vicarious suffering? Well, each party played a role in the execution of this person. If he was righteous and holy, the other actors are guilty before God. Is it possible to regard their actions not only as criminal, but as an act of God facilitating atonement for them? Why would God even want to atone for their dastardly deeds?

Why was it theologically necessary for the messiah to suffer? To regard it as necessary, Isaiah 53 must be understood as a prophecy, in which the servant suffers vicariously for other humans, particularly as atonement for their sin. Put another way, the servant's suffering, and exaltation would be taken to be the final resolution of the conflict between God and the human race; the event was prophesied beforehand because it was God's plan to effect the reconciliation of all humans with his sovereignty.

## Markan Passages That Echo Isaiah 53

The three passion predictions (Mark 8:31; 9:30–32; and 10:32–34) and the exchanges that follow each (8:32–9:1; 9:33–37; 10:35–45) are candidates most often mentioned. Mark 10:45, "For the Son of Man also came not to be served but to serve and to give his life as a ransom for many" (RSV), is the most explicit statement regarding why Jesus must undergo the passion. While the statement does not say to whom the price for release (*lutron*) is to be paid, and why it is owed, it does describe Jesus's serving and death as done on others' behalf.

Can this verse be traced to Isaiah 53? Rikki Watts admits that the argument is indecisive: "Taken in isolation, it is true that none of the individual words in Mark 10:45 unequivocally suggests Isaiah 53."[6] In particular, Mark's wording doesn't reflect the Septuagint. To make a connection, one has to ap-

---

6. Watts, "Jesus' Death," 147.

peal to a synthetic allusion, i.e., an allusion to several passages at the same time.

Though the argument is inconclusive, even scholars who are skeptical "admit that Jesus' passion predictions 'correspond broadly' to Isaiah 53."[7] Moreover, Isaiah 53 does support the claim that "it was necessary that the Christ should suffer these things" (Luke 24:26). When the risen Christ finds such a claim in "Moses and all the prophets" (v. 27), the Servant passages of Second Isaiah would constitute his strongest evidence.

The suffering of the messiah or servant should not be isolated. In each of the passion predictions, the disciples are taught an important lesson about God's way in the world. In the first prediction, Simon Peter has just identified Jesus as *messiah*, or *christos* in Greek; he brings his understanding of that title into play when he "began to rebuke" Jesus for predicting his suffering and execution (Mark 8:32). For Peter, the messiah is supposed to conquer, not suffer. Jesus has to rebuke him for thinking of divine power in all too human, diabolical terms. Then Jesus turns to the crowd and warns them that if they want to follow him, they must be prepared to suffer in imitation of him.

After the second passion prediction, Jesus has to teach the disciples that greatness must be calculated differently if you are following a crucified lord. It requires taking care of little ones and little things. After the third passion prediction, the sons of Zebedee (James and John) ask for the most honored places in the kingdom. Jesus reverses their request: "Are you willing to drink the cup that I drink?" This cup is the cup of suffering, perhaps the judgment of God (see Isa 51:17-23; Jer 25:15-31). Later, when the other disciples get wind of the brothers' request, they are offended. Jesus then teaches all of them that his followers are to serve; the more service, the more honor. Power in this community must be the communication of power to those for whom one is responsible. Vicarious suffering is the ultimate dimension of serving others.

*Possible Influence of Isaiah 53 in Matthew and Luke*

Both Matthew and Luke preserve the Markan passion predictions. It is clear, though, that the wording has been modified and the emphasis shifted. Matthew 16:13-23 highlights Peter's confession; indeed, his nickname Peter (or *Cephus* in Aramaic) becomes a basis for a pun: "And I tell you, you are Peter [*Petros*], and on this rock [*petra*] I will build my church" (Matt 16:18). Peter's demotion to being an ally of Satan becomes much less important in Matthew and Luke

7. Ibid., 148.

than it is in Mark. Luke 9:18–22 reports Peter's confession but not his rebuke of Jesus and Jesus's rebuke of him.

Matthew passes on a rather perfunctory version of the second passion prediction, but preserves a full text of the third with the exchange between Jesus and the sons of Zebedee.[8] Luke suppresses the embarrassing question of the brothers, and relocates the teaching on leadership at the Last Supper (Luke 22:24–27).

At Jesus's baptism both Matt 3:17 and Mark 1:11 report that the voice from heaven quoted or alluded to Isa 42:1, the first verse of the first Servant Song ("Behold, my servant, whom I uphold, my chosen, in whom my soul delights"). This could be evidence of the identification of Jesus as the servant of the Lord. Matt 12:18–21 also quotes the first Servant Song. The Evangelist explains why Jesus withdraws from the Pharisees who were conspiring against him: he has his calling, articulated in Isa 42:1–4, to fulfill before he is executed. This suggests a divine agenda on the order of the Gospel of John's "[his] hour had not yet come" (2:4).

Luke has nothing comparable to Mark 9:9–13 and Matt 17:9–17, in which Jesus and the three disciples discuss the coming first of Elijah, and Jesus identifies John the Baptist as the Elijah people are expecting. However, Luke does report the subject of the interchange between Jesus, Moses and Elijah: "[they] appeared in glory and spoke of his departure, which he was to accomplish at Jerusalem" (9:31, RSV). "Departure" should be taken to mean both Jesus's crucifixion and exaltation. This matches the Fourth Gospel's "I, when I am lifted up from the earth, will draw all men to myself" (John 12:32 [RSV]; cp. John 3:14; 8:28). So, despite the absence of the Elijah saying in Luke, Luke's transfiguration narrative also becomes the occasion for Jesus to predict the passion.

Luke has nothing comparable to this phrase referring to Jesus: "to give his life as a ransom for many" (Mark 10:45; Matt 20:28). Does this mean that Luke has no concept of vicarious suffering? Probably not, because we have some postresurrection texts from Luke that explain why Jesus had to suffer. In the story of the appearance of Jesus to Cleopas and an unnamed disciple on the road to Emmaus, Jesus interprets Scripture to show that it was "necessary that the Christ suffer these things and enter into glory" (24:27, RSV). When the risen Jesus is with his disciples in Jerusalem, he says, "Thus it is written, that the Christ should suffer and on the third day rise from the dead, and that repentance and forgiveness of sins should be preached in his name to all nations" (24:46–47, RSV). The necessity of Christ's suffering has to do with the

---

8. Their mother is said to have made the embarrassing request.

## The Suffering Servant and Son of Man in the Synoptics

God's authorization of the call to repentance and offer of forgiveness. This is probably the thought-world of Isaiah 53.[9]

Probably the most dramatic citation of Isaiah 53 occurs in Acts 8:32–33. An Ethiopian eunuch is in a chariot on his way back to his home country, and Philip meets him by divine providence. The eunuch invites Philip into the chariot and asks for his help interpreting Isa 53:7–8 (in the Septuagint [Greek] translation). The eunuch wants to know who the servant is, and Philip introduces him to the gospel of Jesus. The eunuch converts and is baptized.

Did Philip grasp the concept of vicarious suffering in the passage, or was he just arguing that Jesus fulfills this "prophecy"? The verses quoted do not enunciate the vicariousness of the servant's suffering.[10] But note that the passages quoted in Luke 24 demonstrate that the author of Luke understood that forgiveness was effected by the servant's suffering.

## What Does Jesus's Suffering Have to Do with Judgment?

The question in this section title is the central one for the chapter. The answer we are looking for is the one that Christians have maintained across the centuries: the crucifixion is a judgment of all humanity and the atonement for human sin. It has, thus, a paradoxical character. What we must seek to do is to arrive at this conclusion by following the dramatic logic of the Synoptic Gospel narrative. Jesus's own preaching and action precipitate the crucifixion; we must find the line between Jesus's warning of judgment and the judgment that occurs in the crucifixion. Then we have to follow this up with reflection on the question, how can the judgment that occurred in the crucifixion be an atonement for those who participated in the event, and for others who look to it for forgiveness?

While Jesus does announce divine judgment, as we discovered in the last chapter, that announcement has nothing to do with his persecution. Jeremiah was persecuted and nearly executed for his proclamation of judgment, and his contemporary, the prophet Uriah, was executed (see Jeremiah 26). John the Baptist can be said to have been put to death for his condemnation of Herod Antipas and Herodias (so Mark 6:17–29). Not Jesus, whose primary message

---

9. So Parsons, "Isaiah 53 and Acts 8," 117.

10. The lines, according to Parsons, would appeal to the eunuch because they would make the servant's suffering similar to his own status as despised and excluded (from the temple, for example).

*Redeeming Judgment*

was the good news of the kingdom (Mark 1:14–15). Judgment was reserved for those who would not accept the good news and repent.[11]

Why Jesus was persecuted is something of a mystery. In Mark we already hear of the antipathy of the Pharisees and scribes to his teaching in chapter 2, where they take offense at Jesus's claim of authority to forgive sins (2:6–12). They grumble at Jesus's camaraderie with "tax collectors and sinners" (2:15–17). He and his disciples do not practice fasting (1:18–22); his disciples "harvest" grain on the Sabbath (2:23–27), and he himself heals on the holy day (3:1–6). A verbal battle runs between Jesus and the Pharisees and scribes, but it is hard to believe that these skirmishes resulted in Jesus's crucifixion. It would be more accurate to say that his debate with the Pharisees and their allies exemplified the rejection of the good news, and may have discouraged others from accepting it.

We get hints that Herod Antipas and his party, called Herodians, were watching Jesus (Mark 3:6) and may have sought to bring him in for questioning (Luke 13:31–33). They do not seem to have any larger role in Jesus's persecution and death.

So the causes of his trial and death are located in Jerusalem, where the high priest of the Jerusalem temple presides over a cadre of Jewish leaders, and negotiates with the Roman authorities over rule of the city and of the Jewish religious community. This was a focal point of an otherwise dispersed Judaism, which was why Jesus knew that he had to journey there to establish the kingdom.

When Jesus rides into Jerusalem on a donkey amid a demonstration staged by his followers, succeeded by a symbolic cleansing of the temple, he seems to have gone through the motions of assuming authority over the holy city and its shrine. He shows no sign of wanting to take power by force. Following his symbolic take-over, he teaches in the temple. This is consistent with his ministry in Galilee.

## Responsibility for Jesus's Judicial Murder

In *The Shadow of the Galilean*, Gerd Theissen offers a meditation on who was responsible for Jesus's death.[12] In recent years, other scholars have replaced the word *who* with the word *what*, in as much as the institutional arrangements between the temple authorities, the Jerusalem city council, and the imperial

---

11. See chapter 20 on judgment in the Synoptics
12. See Theissen, *The Shadow of the Galilean*, 165–73.

government and army can be blamed more than individuals. The Jerusalem elite consisted of the intermediaries between Rome and the masses of religious Jews. So the primary actors are institutions; nevertheless, individuals gave the institutional actions a particular nuance. Moreover, individuals have to accept blame for what happens on their watch.

We are not reconstructing history but reflecting on the role each party played in the synoptic account of Jesus's trial and execution. Events are, of course, told from the point of view of the victim. Actually, Jesus is not really a victim, for he himself is responsible for what happens. That is, he makes choices aware of the risks. He decides to go to Jerusalem; he enters ceremoniously and puts on a demonstration in the temple. He teaches in public for a period of time and does not seek to escape when he knows the authorities are after him. During the trials, he does not defend himself. He pursues a righteous, nonviolent, prophetic course of action.

According to Mark 14:1-2, the temple authorities were conspiring to arrest and kill Jesus but might well have let it drop if it hadn't been for Judas (Mark 14:10-11). According to Mark, Judas volunteers to betray Jesus for reasons unknown. Now the temple authorities have to act. They send a mob out with Judas to take Jesus into custody, and they call some sort of inquiry together in the high priest's residence. The temple authorities could have killed him without trial, but they take the legal route. They find evidence, to their satisfaction, that his claims about who he is are blasphemous. They are really not searching for evidence that would hold up in a fair trial; what they want is a pretext to dispose of him. Since so-called messiahs often urged rebellion against Rome, they accuse Jesus of this before the governor Pilate. Pilate is suspicious of the charge, and maneuvers to set Jesus free—to no avail. So Pilate signs off on his execution and has the Sanhedrin's charge written on the placard.

So the temple authorities and political elite have this upstart eliminated. It is their job to suppress all discontent among the masses and to nip in the bud any unrest during the holy days. Their hostility toward Jesus is probably compounded by his assault on their sacred institution. They are successful in avoiding a confrontation with the crowds during midday; the early morning crowd joins the authorities in condemning him. His backing by the crowds was one of the reasons Jesus is seen as a danger to the authorities, but one cannot count on the crowd to stand up for justice.

The Roman governor, Pilate, has jurisdiction over the case. He urges Jesus to defend himself, but the accused is passive. Pilate does attempt to avoid convicting a person who seems to be innocent of any serious design on the body politic. He continues to exhibit mercy later, when he allows Jesus to be buried in a tomb before nightfall. His soldiers, however, exhibit contempt for the Jewish victim.

Jesus's disciples are guilty too. Judas betrays him, but then is ensnared by his conscience. Unfortunately, he is incapable of seeking reconciliation with Jesus and his followers. A guilty conscience, unrelieved by divine forgiveness, is a killer. The other disciples abandon Jesus. Peter, of course, denies knowing him before he "goes underground." After the resurrection, Jesus restores Peter to communion and pastoral leadership (John 21). The Synoptics do not depict the uneasy conscience the disciples must have felt.

We have already touched on Jesus's responsibility. However, he is on trial not only before the Sanhedrin and Pilate but also before God and gospel readers. We want to know whether he died the death appropriate to the faithful. Mark tells an amazing story. Jesus prays in the garden of Gethsemane to have "the cup removed from me" (14:36). Though he has been predicting this moment for some time, now he pleads with God to change his destiny. From now on, Jesus will be acting against what he desires and what he expects from his God. When the trial goes its course, and God doesn't intervene, Jesus utters a cry of betrayal on the cross. Jesus has no protection from the sense of defeat and the futility of human life. God seems indifferent. This is Mark's great insight: Jesus must be inwardly vulnerable to suffering; he does not die like a martyr or a philosopher—both of whom have conquered death.

The prayer in the garden and the cry from the cross put God on trial. He must vindicate himself and his messiah.

## The Crucifixion as a Trial or Testing

Jesus's crucifixion is an indictment of the Jerusalem authorities and their Roman counterparts. The trial(s) they preside over are a miscarriage of justice. This can be said even if one doubts Jesus's Messianic claims. At least as the synoptic narratives present it, Jesus was an innocent man (as the soldier says in Luke 23:46). The Sanhedrin and the Roman prefect are responsible. It may well be that the authorities regard Jesus as a threat to the peace because of his popularity among the crowds; perhaps they deliberately execute an innocent man to eliminate the danger (cp. John 11:47–53). This would be a case of "might makes right"—in particular, the legitimate ruling power of society doing what is necessary to maintain its hold over the populace.

The theological issue is whether this exposure of the unjust action of Jewish and Roman authorities constitutes a judgment of God. By *judgment* I mean a demonstration of the evil working of the institutions and the humans who are responsible. By *divine judgment* I mean the demonstration that these persons and institutions are destined for damnation—the judgment Jesus warned of for not repenting and accepting the good news of the kingdom. Their rejection of Jesus is the rejection of the good news of the kingdom, and the rejection of the good news of the kingdom would result in damnation on the Day of Judgment.

Of course, this theological judgment makes no sense if Jesus died and that was the end of the story. The resurrection of Jesus is essential to the Christian claim. The resurrection vindicates Jesus, the Son, and his message of the dawning of the kingdom of God. If Jesus was raised, the rejection of Jesus was the rejection of the kingdom, and those who reject the kingdom face damnation. The crucifixion seals their ultimate destiny.

Almost everyone else in the gospel narratives is guilty of a lesser sin. While the authorities do the deed, the crowds withdraw their support, and Jesus's disciples betray or abandon him. On the whole, it is a moral disaster. Only Jesus's women disciples and a man named Joseph prove faithful and merciful. They were rewarded with essential roles in the resurrection.

If one believes that Jesus was raised from the dead, as all our gospels narrate, then the guilt for Jesus's death is universalized. The actors in the drama become representatives of the entire human race. Why does the resurrection have that effect? If Jesus was raised from the dead, he was God incarnate. So when Jesus was crucified, the Son of God, God incarnate in this human, was crucified. The incarnation is once for all. The act by humans to kill him is once for all. The actual participants in the event participate as representatives of the whole human race. All humans indirectly share in their guilt.

Paul seems to have it right when he says in Rom 3:23–25a, "Since all have sinned and fall short of the glory of God, they are justified by his grace as a gift, through the redemption which is in Christ Jesus, who God put forward as an expiation [Greek: *hilastērion*] by his blood, to be received by faith" (RSV). The crucifixion of Jesus is an exposure of the theological fact that "all have sinned and fall short of the glory of God." The authorities, the crowds, and Jesus's followers all were exposed as people who had rejected the kingdom of God by their contribution to this miscarriage of justice. Those who participated in one way or another represent the whole of humanity in the crucifixion of the Son.[13] In this story we should recognize that we ourselves are implicated.[14]

Jesus's resurrection reveals at the same time the atoning significance of Jesus's death. The divine gift by which we are justified is the "expiation by his blood," which is to say, Christ's suffering on the cross exposes the depth and pervasiveness of human sin and seals our condemnation, and also reverses that verdict, so to speak, offering commutation for perpetrators. This is truly a case of judgment becoming redemptive.

The Synoptic Gospels have Jesus interpret his persecution as a "ransom" (Greek: *lutron*, Mark 10:45) and a sacrifice for sin (Matt 28:27–28). Let's examine the term *ransom*, or "price of release." This is not a term describing sacrifice, but a metaphor adapted from slavery. Some would take the term literally, that is to say mythologically. The payment is to the devil, who has claims on those who have come under his hypnotic power. To regain them, God "pays" the devil. That payment is Jesus's suffering at the hands of evil humans.

One does not have to adopt this myth, however, because the word *ransom* would be better read as a metaphor. But of what is it a metaphor? We might compare sin to addiction. One becomes enslaved to drugs—or pleasures (gluttony, greed, and lust). One needs supernatural empowerment to break free from sin. Christ's death could break the grip of sin on one's will.

The crucifixion synthesizes the message of judgment and redemption. The perpetrators must see the consequences of their actions in the death of this innocent person; if they can do so, they can receive the event as an offer of forgiveness and transformation. Penitential piety is now driven by the atoning significance of their murderous deed. Judas could see only his guilt in his

---

13. It is not that the acts of the participants incur guilt for others, but that they reveal the fact that each and everyone one of us is guilty of acts worthy of condemnation and participates in corrupt institutions which perpetuate injustice.

14. What I mean is this: believers all through church history have accepted guilt for Jesus's crucifixion. Here is a verse of a great Good Friday hymn:
>Who was the guilty? Who brought this upon Thee?
>Alas, my treason, Jesus, hath undone Thee.
>'Twas I, Lord Jesus, I it was denied Thee,
>I crucified Thee. ["Ah, holy Jesus, How hast Thou offended?" by Johann Herrman (1585–1647); translated by Robert Bridges)]

Since the singer lived many years later than Jesus, it must be literally other people who he or she has harmed. To be sure, a believer experiences Jesus to be a part of every relationship, but the actual victims of our betrayal, denial and assault are contemporaries. One is reminded of the parable that teaches, "as you did it to one of the least of these, you did it to me" (Matt 25:39).

betrayal of Jesus; he is condemned to death by his conscience. Peter and the other disciples are so awestruck and overjoyed by the resurrection that their abandonment of their Lord is forgotten. However, according to John 21, Peter does have to reenact his denial in order to be restored to leadership (21:15–19).

Now we turn to the metaphor of sacrifice. Isa 53:10–12 ascribes sacrificial significance to the suffering and death of the Servant of the Lord. The idea seems to be that guilt that alienates God from humans has been removed by the human who suffers: God accepts his suffering as a substitute for the punishment of the guilty.

The orthodox doctrine of atonement worked out by Anselm invested the cross with the power to restore the order of justice and holiness. The debt owed divine justice was paid; the holiness of God, which has been tarnished by sin, is restored. Liberal Christians have been very critical, indeed hostile, to this atonement theory. Its strength is its insistence that sin alienates humans from God and injures the order of society and the universe. Justice and holiness must be reestablished in the act of reconciliation.

## The Redemptive Effect of the Cross

The gospel accounts encourage readers to take up the words of the mysterious "we" in the fourth Servant Song:

> But he was wounded for *our* transgressions,
> he was bruised for *our* iniquities;
> upon him was the chastisement that made *us* whole,
> and with his stripes *we* are healed.
> All *we* like sheep have gone astray;
> *we* have turned every one to his own way;
> and the Lord has laid on him
> the iniquity of *us* all. (Isa 53:5–6, RSV; italics added)

Those who recognize the vicarious suffering of the servant receive its benefits.

The gospels, however, do not leave us with forgiveness and a license to continue in the same vein. After the first passion prediction (Mark 8:31–33), Jesus invites followers "to deny themselves and take up their crosses"—to "lose their life for my sake and the gospel's" (8:34–35). After the second prediction (9:30–32), he commands his followers to be humble and care for "children" (9:33–37). After the third (10:32–34), he commands the leaders among his followers to be servants (10:42–45). In all of these, Jesus's suffering is interpreted to entail service and sacrifice on the part of those who would benefit from his sacrifice. This means, negatively, the renunciation of self-serving power seeking.

In summary, the crucifixion is the judgment of the world, which has been turned into a redemptive event by God.

## The Son of Man

Jesus uses the expression "Son of Man" very frequently for himself and what lies ahead in the upcoming days.[15] The words themselves are a Semiticism with a meaning of "human" but have a virtual titular character in certain statements. Ezekiel is regularly addressed as a "son of man" by the Lord.[16] Daniel 7 describes the scene of the Last Judgment as having a divine figure who looks like a human, "like a son of man." This figure sits in judgment beside the Ancient of Days (vv. 13–14). The gospels describe a similar scenario: the Son of Man[17] is accompanied by angels, but without the Ancient of Days (God). The scenario was probably a staple of Jewish tradition, as evidenced by the apocryphal writing, *Similitudes of Enoch*.[18]

Jesus uses "Son of Man" in other types of statements as well. Of greatest importance for our study is its appearance in the passion predictions:

- "And he began to teach them that the Son of Man must suffer many things" (Mark 8:31; cp. Luke 9:22)
- "The Son of Man will be delivered into the hands of men" (Mark 9:31; cp. Matt 17:22; Luke 9:44)
- "The Son of Man will be delivered to the chief priests and scribes . . . (Mark 10:33; also Matt 10:18; Luke 18:31)

While Mark 9:12 is not strictly speaking a passion prediction, it has very similar wording: "the Son of man, that he should suffer many things." Though one could replace "Son of man" in each of these sentences with "I,"[19] the titular formulation has a more formal, solemn sound; we are probably dealing with a theological formula.

---

15. See Collins, "Son of Man," 341–48.
16. Ezek 2:1, 3:1, 4:1, etc.
17. Now without the preposition *like*.
18. Charles, *The Apocrypha and Pseudepigrapha in English*, 2:163–281.
19. Matt 16:21 has "he" in an indirect quote.

We should also mention a few other utterances with a similar formality and solemnity, e.g., "the Son of man has nowhere to lay his head" (Matt 8:20; Luke 9:58). Jesus's deprived living conditions seem to be of a piece with his suffering.

## Weakness and Power

Why, we might ask, must the Son of man live so humbly? Why must the Son of man suffer? Several types of answer can be given. One has to do with dramatic logic. The text can be read as saying that Jesus deliberately provoked the authorities into killing him. But it doesn't have to be read this way, and Jesus's prayer in Gethsemane (Mark 14:32–42; cp. also Matt 26:36–45; Luke 22:39–46) encourages a more nuanced reading. Jesus pursues his calling, and this arouses opposition and ultimately a plot to eliminate him, a threat to the peace of the city. We can say that something like Jesus's execution was inevitable, given who he was, given who supported him, and given the power structure of colonial Judaism and Jerusalem. However, in theory Jesus could have withdrawn from Jerusalem; Pilate could have insisted on freeing him; or some other eventuality could have happened. In retrospect it seems that a tragic ending "had to happen," but the course of human events is contingent.

Was there a theological necessity? Many readers assume that Jesus knew that he came to earth to die an atoning death. The Gospel of John portrays his life that way, but the Synoptic Gospels are not so cut and dried. I think that we should hold that God could have accomplished his purposes in some other way. However, there were constraints that made the outcome inevitable.

What constraints do I have in mind? That God could not take a sinful, devious, or overpowering path to the judgment and redemption of the human race. Let me quote Reinhold Niebuhr: "It is impossible to symbolize the divine goodness in history in any other way than by complete powerlessness, or rather by a consistent refusal to use power in the rivalries of history.... [God can express] disinterested love only by a refusal to participate in the rivalries. Any participation in them means the assertion of one ego interest against another."[20] Any use of power in the rivalries of the struggle for power will compromise perfect goodness; what will be left is a relative goodness.

Here is a supporting argument. If goodness is a dimension of power, as Kyle Pasewark persuasively argues in *A Theology of Power*,[21] then the power of

---

20. Reinhold Niebuhr, *The Nature and Destiny of Man*, 2:72.
21. Pasewark, *A Theology of Power*, 325–36.

## Redeeming Judgment

God cannot be one power in the power struggles of history. All power is from God—both power serving the good and power perverted into evil. God does exercise ultimate control over the power communicated to creatures, and this becomes judgment: the diminishment of self-serving power or even the elimination of those who exercise power for evil. However, the rough-and-tumble world of power politics cannot embody the perfect goodness of God. Every righteous cause is corrupted; every achievement of justice is limited.

Hence, our formulation of Niebuhr's thesis is: ultimate power cannot be identified with any historical power; it would become one power among others, and that would be a form of polytheism. Although God is engaged in the rough and unstable world of power politics, knowledge of true goodness awaits a revelation in a person who exercises divine authority but renounces the will to power and adopts a pacifistic stance toward the use of coercive power against him. The renunciation of power is best symbolized, Niebuhr goes on to say, by the cross.[22]

As we said in the previous section, Jesus's execution is a judgment on the power struggle that plagues human community. It becomes an atoning event by God's acceptance of Jesus's suffering and death as vicarious in import. The raising of Jesus from the dead is the act of acceptance, a victory over the powers of sin and death. Jesus is given the power of life. He does not possess it himself, it is a gift from the Father. His resurrection overrules the judgment of the Jewish and Roman authorities, and restores the defeated disciples. It facilitates a new reading of the events of Jesus's life and a new reading of Hebrew Scriptures. It identifies the messenger of the Kingdom and the coming Son of Man.

### The Exalted Son of Man

All three Synoptic Gospel accounts of Jesus's interrogation by the Sanhedrin include Jesus's statement that those who are questioning him will see "the Son of man seated at the right hand of Power," and Mark and Matthew continue, "and coming on the clouds of heaven." Prior to this statement, Mark has Jesus answer the high priest's question about being the Christ with, "I am," whereas Matthew has him give the noncommittal, "You have said so." Luke 22:70 repeats Matthew, but Luke prefaces the Son of Man saying with "If I tell you, you will not believe; and if I ask you, you will not answer" (22:67–68). At the end of each gospel's exchange, the high priest says that Jesus has condemned

---

22. Reinhold Niebuhr, *The Nature and Destiny*, 73.

himself. Was the claim to be the Christ or the Son of man enough to bring the guilt of blasphemy on a person? If so, we could say that Jesus's forthright "I am" in Mark is what brings the wrath of the law down upon him. However, in Matthew, the offense would have to be the Son of Man saying, while in Luke the crime is muddled.

In any case, what was so offensive about the Son of Man saying from Jesus? Indeed, what was its relevance to the high priest's question? Jesus's saying does not indicate what the Son of Man is going to do. Perhaps one could construe the saying to mean, "You are going to see me seated on the right hand of God." This would be a claim by Jesus to be the eschatological figure expected by a healthy portion of his contemporaries (though not the priests). It seems likely that this construal would be an implicit threat to Jesus's interrogators. If they falsely condemn him, they will soon be held accountable.

The members of the Sanhedrin would hardly have taken Jesus's claims seriously. If they had, they would not have condemned him. But if they thought he was deluded, why did they condemn him as a criminal? Their reasoning is strange. Perhaps he had offended them, and they want to expose him as a fraud.

Mark has Jesus make several other statements about the coming Son of man. In 8:38 (RSV), Jesus says "whoever is ashamed of me and of my words in this adulterous and sinful generation, of him will the Son of man also be ashamed when he comes in the glory of Father with the holy angels." Luke 9:26 is similar, whereas Matthew 10:33 has the verb "deny," and replaces the title "Son of man" with the first-person pronoun. This saying is a warning of judgment to precisely those who are relying on Jesus's protection in the Last Judgment, that he or the Son of man (or that Jesus as the Son of man) will disown those who are not genuine devotees. Jesus plays the role of patron to his own. It is the same image of the Last Judgment that we find in Matt 7:21–23.[23]

Mark 13:26–27 describes the second coming as the resurrection of the elect: "[humans] will see the Son of Man coming in clouds with great power and glory. And then he will send out the angels, and gather his elect from the four winds, and from the ends of the earth to the ends of the heavens." Matt 24:30–31 are much the same. The scenario is not of a *judgment*; those belonging to the Son of Man are already known—"elect"—and have only to be raised from the dead. Nothing is said about non-Christians. 1 Thess 4:13–18 offers a similar scenario.

---

23. See Betz, *Essays on the Sermon on the Mount*. Cp. Luke 13:26–27.

*Redeeming Judgment*

Mark has no scenario of a Last Judgment (i.e., a trial) presided over by Christ.[24] He avoids, you might say, the challenge of reconciling justice and mercy. Jesus shows loyalty to his own and acts as judge only of those who falsely seek his protection. Of course, if the Son of Man saying before the Sanhedrin implicitly threatened judgment, we would have to expand Mark's idea of the role of the Son of Man.

Mark does have a few other passages about last things: James and John ask Jesus to sit on his right and left in the kingdom (Mark 10:35–40). This doesn't seem to have anything specifically to do with Last Judgment but with honor among the "saved."[25] It does employ an image associated with judgment—the cup of wrath—to describe what Jesus will go through and what his disciples must go through to sit beside him. Perhaps in what Jesus and the two brothers are going to suffer, they will bear the judgment of others.

Matthew is the gospel that highlights Jesus's role as judge of all humans in a judicial event. Matt 16:27b is characteristic: "and then he will repay every man for what he has done" (see Mark 8:38). A number of parables spell this out: the parables of the Wheat and Tares (13:24–30; 36–43), of the Net (13:47–50), of the Talents (25:14–30), of the Wedding Garments (22:11–14), and of the Sheep and the Goats (25:31–46). The introduction to the parable of the Sheep and Goats draws out the scene: "When the Son of man comes in his glory, and all the angels with him, then he will sit on his glorious throne. Before him will be gathered all the nations, and he will separate them from one another as a shepherd separates sheep from the goats" (vv. 31–32, RSV).[26]

Matthew's scenario of the Last Judgment has prevailed in the history of the church. Practically every medieval cathedral had a Last Judgment scene at the west end. All other scenarios we have noted can be incorporated into this truly final judgment of all humanity. All are raised from the dead and the divine decisions are declared. Never do we hear of a trial. At most the innocent and guilty can ask about why they are saved or damned (Matt 25:37–39, 44). That would also be an appropriate time for believers to appeal to Jesus to recognize that he is their patron (Matt 7:22).

---

24. The saying about being ashamed of Jesus may imply judgment by God, but there is no last judgment scene.

25. Jesus's argument in favor of the resurrection of the dead in Mark 12:18–27 does not deal with those condemned to hell. I don't know how he would have argued in that case.

26. Interestingly, this parable appeals to a common human norm rather than a revealed one. This doesn't fully solve the problem of a common judgment for all humans. Matthew 7:21–23 assumes a unique Christian responsibility.

The very fact that the judge is one of the human race who was tempted and mishandled should make him more humane.[27] The message of mercy comes and goes in the Synoptic Gospels. There are some harsh depictions of the Last Judgment. The harshness is probably driven by rhetorical considerations: an emphasis on leniency would encourage laxness. Perhaps the prophecy of judgment provides a supplement: How those who are condemned respond to the verdict actually determines their fate. God does not desire the death of sinners, but that they repent and be redeemed.

---

27. Actually, many oppressed are driven by resentment and want to "even the score." There is where Martin Luther King Jr. called for a "higher morality," a "restorative justice" in Desmond Tutu's sense.

# 22

# Judgment and Redemption in the Fourth Gospel
(John)

WE WILL BEGIN THE exposition of the Fourth Gospel with the subject of judgment. Next comes the redemptive role of Jesus. Our exposition of John will end with a discussion of the piety that goes with John's christocentric theology.

## Judgment in the Fourth Gospel

The Gospel of John tends to melt down future eschatology into an event already taking place—often called realized eschatology. Moreover, the kingdom of God—the comprehensive message of Jesus according to the Synoptics—is largely replaced by Christ in John. John's Jesus proclaims himself and calls for faith in himself. Believing will impart eternal life to the believer from henceforth. Now we have to ask what the gospel has to say about divine judgment. How can the final judgment take place in time? How consistent is the gospel with the Synoptics?

We find statements about judgment in John 3, 5, 7, 8, 9, 12, and 16. Chapters 7 and 8 depict Jesus's defense of his own claim to the Father's authority. Neither really deals with the Final Judgment of the Jews, or of all humans, or of supernatural powers. Chapter 16 concerns the action of the Paraclete—John's name for the Spirit—of convicting "the world" of sin, of righteousness and of judgment. According to C. K. Barrett, the idea runs as follows: "The Spirit, operating upon the conscience of men [and women] through the witness of the Church . . . will convince them of their sin . . . This the Spirit can do, because the sin of the world is concentrated in its rejection of Jesus."[1] In 16:11, John applies the term *judgment* to the defeat of Satan, "the ruler of this world." Nothing is said about how Satan is defeated, though one might regard the communication of the truth and righteousness as a defeat of the "father of lies" (8:44).

Several of the judgment passages deserve closer examination. Let's begin with John 5. In vv. 28–29, we read a straightforward description of what most gospel readers of the era expected at the Final Judgment: "For the hour is coming when all who are in tombs will hear his voice and come out—those who have done good, to the resurrection of life, and those who have done evil, to the resurrection of condemnation."[2] It is likely that the author expects the reader to surmise that this account of final judgment is authoritative. Any revision of the teaching to articulate a realized eschatology should be taken to be in harmony with this future expectation.

How does this depiction of Final Judgment relate to the passage in which it is embedded? Verse 28 itself ("Do not marvel at this") refers to the preceding verses. Verse 25 announces that the hour "now is" when "the dead will hear the voice of the Son of God, and those who hear will live." This verse uses the language of resurrection and Last Judgment, but should be taken metaphorically of persons who receive the Christian message.[3] The Father has shared the life-giving power of the Creator with the Son and appointed him judge as well. The Son, thus, has the power to give persons eternal life according to their character. According to v. 30, Jesus's judgment is guaranteed to be just "because I seek not my own will but the will of him who sent me." If we put these observations together, those who hear the voice of Jesus and respond in faith have been chosen by Christ to enjoy eternal life.

John 5:22–24 provide a slightly different perspective. The passage begins by stating that the Father has handed over his authority as judge to the Son. The reason is that he desires that the Son be honored.[4] Verse 24 describes the Son's act of judgment: "the one who hears my word and believes him who sent me, has eternal life; he does not come into judgment, but has passed from death to life." In other words, believers have already been judged, have already entered the order of salvation. The present decision for Christ has been fused

---

1. Barrett, *The Gospel according to St. John*, 106–7.
2. Judgment is equivalent to condemnation here and in several other places.
3. So Barrett, *The Gospel according to St. John*.
4. The text does not say why he should be honored, but the intimacy and mutuality of Father and Son makes it understandable.

with the Final Judgment. One might put it thus: the believer participates now in what is coming. One can see the similarities of this mystical appropriation of final judgment with the proclamation that the kingdom is at hand, or has come upon you, or is in your midst, despite the shift in language and framework from the Synoptic Gospels to the Gospel of John.

John 3:16–21 are a famous statement of the divine purpose for sending the Son into the world: "For God so loved the world that he gave his only Son, that whoever believes in him should not perish but have eternal life" (v. 16). Verse 17 expands upon this declaration by denying its contrary: "For God sent the Son into the world, not to condemn the world." This is the affirmation by which the liberal church lives. There is, however, no real escape from judgment: v. 18 affirms that those who believe will not be condemned; the one who does not believe has condemned himself. The world was under the power of Satan and going to hell, and God intervened to reclaim it. But those who reject his offer are doomed to continue as they were. They were in the dark, he sent light, but some choose to remain in the dark so no one will see what they are doing.

Mark 1:15 is analogous. To get something like John's phrasing, one only has to replace "kingdom of God" with "Christ," and "repent" with "believe" and you have a Johannine affirmation. Mark's Christ terms this "good news"—it is what ages have hoped for; if someone does not want to enter the kingdom—or enter into eternal life by believing in Jesus—a person has made one's own bed, so to speak.

John 3:16–21 are an interpretation of the gospel narrative in the voice of the narrator. That gives it added veracity. John 12:47–48 are similar; Jesus speaks, but no audience is specified. It is like an aside in a Shakespearean drama. Verse 47 is quite similar to 3:17: "If anyone hears my sayings and does not keep them, I do not judge him; for I did not come to judge the world but to save the world" (RSV). Even those who have come to know Jesus's teachings are not responsible for obeying them. Jesus's words are to save, not condemn. However, the next verse seems to reverse this assertion: "Whoever rejects me and does not receive my sayings has a judge; the word that I have spoken will be his judge on the last day." How is that? The truth had been made known to you, and you ignored it. Now you can claim no leniency or extenuating circumstances. In the light of what the gospel has said, the person's condemnation is being stuck with the life he chose.

Finally, a few verses earlier in the chapter (vv. 31–32) we read another judgment saying: "Now is the judgment of the world, now shall the ruler of this world be cast out; and I, when I am lifted up from the earth, will draw all men [and women] to myself." The first clause declares that Satan—the ruler of this world—will be removed from power. This is a judgment of supernatural powers; it differs from the judgment of humans. There is no reason Jesus would not condemn and destroy Satan, whereas he hopes in human reclamation.

The second clause, which alludes to the crucifixion (see v. 33), may be connected to the overthrow of Satan. Satan has been the ruler of this world, but now it will be Christ's sphere of authority. Whether this predicts the conversion of all humans or just that all will serve Christ either deliberately or against their will is not said. Of course, "all" could be an exaggeration, and the saying mean, "many."

John's interpretation of Jesus's teaching and life diverge from the Synoptics, but on the question of final judgment we can discern a convergence in structure and tenor.

## The Lamb and the Shepherd

The Gospel of John has a high Christology. Jesus is the Word of God incarnated as the Son of God. The author draws out how the actions and suffering of Jesus embody the being and action of God. Questions like the following must be answered: How can the Son of God *lose* his life? What is the purpose of the Son "laying down" his life (10:11)? Who reaps the benefits of this action? What sort of piety corresponds to the suffering of God?

The exploration of these subjects can be focused on specific Johannine texts. The first will be the declaration by John the Baptist that Jesus is the "lamb" of God (1:29, 36). The stories of chapter 2 can augment what we gain in chapter 1. In response to his mother's suggestions that he provide wine for the marriage feast at Cana, Jesus tells her that his "hour has not yet come" (2:4). Obviously there is a plan and something on the order of a schedule. In Jerusalem, Jesus condemns the commercialism of the temple and associates its destruction with his own crucifixion and resurrection. The most explicit statement of an atonement theology comes in an allegorized parable of a shepherd and his flock. In it Jesus speaks of a true shepherd sacrificing himself to protect his flock. This pericope puts emphasis on the initiative of the shepherd. This is enacted in the trial before Pilate: all the actors play their roles under Jesus's direction. The Jews who call for Jesus's crucifixion are guilty of denying God's primacy in their lives as well as murdering God's Son. Jesus has interpreted his own death and resurrection in the saying, "when I am lifted up, I will draw all men [and women] to me." Just how far does the atoning power of the cross reach? The final saying to be examined here is also about the temple. When the temple is destroyed, worshippers will worship in spirit and in truth. This is Jesus's teaching to the Samaritan woman whom he meets at Jacob's well.

## The Lamb of God

John the Baptist is the herald announcing the appearance of the Son of God. He is mentioned in the prologue to the Gospel (1:6–8) and comes on stage, so to speak, before Jesus (1:19–28). When he first spies Jesus, he announces, "Behold, the Lamb of God, who takes away the sin of the world" (1:29). This entry could not be more dramatic. It is also denser and more in need of exposition than it might appear.

"Lamb of God" refers to an animal offered in sacrifice. Thus, John's declaration already announces the most important event in Jesus's life, viz., his death on the cross. To call Jesus a sacrifice is to speak in highly symbolic language. The divine law does not allow human sacrifice. One can only say that Jesus's death, brought about by a judicial decision, has the effect of a sacrifice. Again, though, this is highly metaphorical. Jesus is crucified on the day that Passover lambs were sacrificed (John 18:28; 19:14, 31, 42). The Passover lamb was not a sacrifice that removed sin or cancelled guilt. The sin and guilt offerings belong to a different category. If Jesus's death bears away human sin, the metaphor of sacrifice is to one of these two. Yet the sin and guilt offerings did not really absolve a person of guilt. A person had to repair the misdeed and pay a penalty, and then perform the sacrifice to remove the "stain," the uncleanness of the violation of a commandment. If one had been apprehended and convicted of a crime rather than confessed it voluntarily, no purification was permitted. In other words, forgiveness was restricted and limited within Mosaic law. The rituals may have been more important for offenses of a noncriminal nature.[5]

While the exact application of the statement, "takes away the sin of the world," is left vague, it undoubtedly covers all offenses and crimes, and would appear to wipe them off one's record, so to speak. What actually takes place and how the message is to be appropriated is open to Christian development. Valuable precedents are found in Psalms like 51 and the prophets and exile and restoration.

In the Gospel of John, the Baptist's baptism is not explained. Nowhere is it said that it cleanses one of sin or seals one's repentance of sin. Mark says this first thing: "preaching a baptism of repentance for the forgiveness of sins"

---

5. Social slights and harsh words, rumors, etc.

(1:4). Luke repeats the phrase in 3:3; Matthew reports the ritual in 3:6 in these words: "they were baptized by him in the river Jordan, confessing their sins" (RSV). The synoptic tradition simply assumes that God is willing to forgive those who genuinely repent and reform. John, however, withholds such an offer until Jesus is sacrificed; then humans can be forgiven through him.

There is one other ambiguity the Baptist's statement: it says that Jesus removes "the sin of the world." This sounds like universal atonement, but we are going to find that the benefits of Jesus's death are available only to believers—to Jesus's own. John 3:36 summarizes the gospel's teaching: "the one who believes in the Son has eternal life; the one who does not obey the Son shall not see life, but the wrath of God rests upon him."

The message would, thus, be along the same lines as John's baptism in the synoptic tradition. While God's offer of forgiveness is to all Jews, forgiveness will not take place until a person repents and seals the pledge to reform by being baptized. Note that the Gospel of John does not use the word *repentance* with the same scope as we find in the Baptist and Jesus of the Synoptics. Rather, "believing" takes on the global scope. The Fourth Gospel connects believing closely with "eternal life." If we regard the sinful life as a form of death, and as leading to eternal death, eternal life means restoration of a form of obedient life, a spirit-filled life.

## *The Temple*

The Fourth Gospel locates the cleansing of the temple at the beginning of the narrative (2:13–23). The textual location has the effect of characterizing Jesus's ministry as a whole. Jesus has come to condemn the temple and to replace it with his body. The specific charge he brings against the temple is its commercialism: "you shall not make my Father's house a house of trade" (2:16, RSV). This would seem to be a rather secondary accusation, but it is enough the initiate an important exchange with temple officials.

The officials challenge Jesus to demonstrate his authority to act prophetically: "What sign have you to show us for doing this?" (v. 18). They understood him to be pronouncing the temple's destruction. Only a true prophet can do that legitimately; Jesus must prove his legitimacy by some miraculous demonstration of power.

Jesus's reply is surprising: "Destroy this temple, and in three days I will raise it up" (v. 19). Jesus addresses their central concern—the destruction of the temple. He does not, however, say that he is going to do it, or that God is. He challenges his audience to do the destroying. They ultimately pursue policies that lead to its destruction, but that is beyond their horizon. The authorities are too taken back by Jesus's seemingly ridiculous claim to be able to rebuild the temple in three days to charge him with threatening the temple. The exchange ends with their dismissal of his claim.

The narrator then tells us that Jesus was not talking about the temple: he was challenging them to kill him, and he would rise from the dead. They did ultimately take him up on his challenge, so his statement proves to be prophetic. "When therefore he was raised from the dead, his disciples remembered that he said this; and they believed the Scripture and the word which Jesus had spoken" (2:22). Thus, Jesus does provide a sign for his disciples, if not for the temple authorities.

There is an unusual appendix to the story. Jesus continues to recruit believers in Jerusalem, but he avoids any further contact with the authorities. Why? "Because he knew all men and needed no one to bear witness of man; for he himself knew what was in a man" (v. 25). This could well mean that Jesus had no need to see how the worst came out of people when their authority and self-importance was challenged. Perhaps the saying in 2:4 would fit here: "My hour has not yet come." Jesus is operating, as it were, with a schedule. It is not time for him to die; he must show the signs and provide their interpretation first.

## The Shepherd, the Flock, the Sheepfold

The Fourth Gospel has no strict parables, but it does develop scenes in a parable-like manner. John 10:1–30 presents a scene involving a shepherd, sheep flock, and sheepfold (a place for sheep to stay overnight). At first the narrator seems to be hunting for the message in the image. The shepherd enters by the gate and summons his own flock by voice; the thief enters surreptitiously and has no capacity to summon a flock. Jesus then identifies himself as the door, and all who seek admission to the fold must go through him. Then he becomes the good shepherd who cares for the sheep, in contrast to the thief.

Verse 11 turns the train of thought in a new direction. Jesus is the good shepherd, who lays down his life for the sheep. The hireling has no ownership of the sheep and will abandon them when he sees a wolf. "He flees because he is a hireling and cares nothing for the sheep" (v. 13). Jesus, on the other hand, knows his own, and his own know him. They belong to each other. Atonement is a benevolent act on the behalf, for the safety of, those who "belong" to Jesus.

Put differently, Jesus gives up his life for his friends (15:13). His death has no benefit for those outside the circle—say the wolf or the thief or even the hireling, or other flocks belonging to other shepherds.

If one can press the image, the good shepherd doesn't actually give his life deliberately; rather, he accepts the danger to himself of the predators after his sheep. He will, if attacked, fight to kill the attacker. Either the wolf dies or the sheep—and the shepherd if he stands his ground—could be killed. One would have to say that the Fourth Gospel has "distorted" the act of the shepherd: he does not lose his life defending his sheep; he "lays it down" and then takes it up—returns to life (10:18).

How does John's treatment of atonement here fit with doctrinal development of the atonement in the history of the church? It certainly does not match Anselm's conception of satisfaction or its penal-suffering variant. It is not a payment of God's mercy to satisfy the demands of justice and holiness; this produces the legal fiction of a guilty person being acquitted because Christ has suffered what the guilty should suffer. Nor is it a classical view of atonement in which Jesus is the redemptive price paid the devil for the release of sinners.[6] Indeed, there is no transaction in John between the good shepherd and those who would raid the flock.

The good shepherd protects and cares for his flock. This is comparable to the role of patron in the Synoptic Gospels. When he defends his flock against predators or thieves, the shepherd acts as protector. But a person would be a more effective protector if he stayed alive. Why is it necessary for the shepherd to lay down his life? Perhaps the good shepherd is acting like a soldier who throws his body on a grenade to save his fellows. This is a case where offering one's life is the only way to protect others effectively.

Beginning in John 10:16, the topic moves to the flock. Jesus says that he has other sheep, located elsewhere. They are to be combined with "this fold," making one flock under one shepherd. Here we get a glimpse of the history of the church, and the Gentile mission that the Johannine Jesus is concerned to keep united. Later Jesus insists that he has the power to protect his own: "My sheep hear my voice. I know them, and they follow me; and I give them eternal life, and they shall never perish. No one shall snatch them out of my hand. What my Father has given me is greater than all else, and no one is able to snatch tit out of the Father's hand. The Father and I are one" (10:27–30). This underscores the particular theology of atonement at work here: God guarantees that Jesus will be able to protect his own from all enemies.

6. Or bait in a trap!

*Redeeming Judgment*

A predestinarian motif runs through these chapters. Jesus has other sheep; "they will heed my voice" (v. 16). He tells those who are pressing him to declare his identity openly (v. 24) that he has said quite enough, but they do not believe—they want an impossible certainty. Why don't they believe? "Because you do not belong to my sheep" (v. 26). In other words, some of his audience is so keyed to the Father and open to revelation that they recognize him immediately, while others are in bondage to the world of sense and sin. People make free decisions, but they are predisposed to believe or not believe by who knows what conditioning.

John 10:17–18 underscores another claim important to John's Christology: "I lay down my life." Although the parable of the Good Shepherd would realistically say that the good shepherd is willing to fight for his flock, even till death, Jesus emphasizes the "laying down." In this application of the image, the shepherd protects the flock by dying. Jesus deliberately gives up his life for the flock. Note that 10:18 begins with the denial that others take his life. "I have the power to lay it down, and I have the power to take it again." This is a very striking claim, especially given the story of the passion. If Jesus is God, however, no one can take his life; if he is to suffer and die to redeem his own, it must be at his initiative and under his guidance. We will discover presently that that is how the trials are portrayed.

## The Trial

Readers should realize that in the Fourth Gospel there is only one trial: the trial before Pontius Pilate; the trial before the Sanhedrin has been incorporated in the trial before Pilate. In this account, Jesus and Pilate have two relatively lengthy exchanges in private: John 18:33–38 and 19:8–11. In the first, Pilate asks Jesus whether he is "King of the Jews." Jesus answers, "My kingdom is not of this world" (18:36). He explains this by comparing his kingship to instruction from a teacher who "bears witness to the truth," and those who know the truth obey (are ruled by) him. This is not otherworldly but inward. One is reminded of the sheep who know Jesus's voice. Pilate seems to dismiss this with a cynical, "What is truth?" (8:38). He recognizes only the coercive power of the state.

A public exchange follows in which Pilate tries to persuade the temple officials to execute Jesus themselves because he, Pilate, finds no crime in him. They say that Jesus has claimed to be "Son of God" (19:7) This precipitates the second private interrogation. Pilate wants to know whether Jesus really does

## Judgment and Redemption in the Fourth Gospel

claim to be "from heaven," but Jesus refuses to answer. That irritates Pilate into asserting that he holds the power of life or death over Jesus. Jesus replies that his—Pilate's—power has been given "from above" (19:11). At a literal level, Pilate has been empowered by those above him in the imperial hierarchy. He must please his superiors, or he will lose his position and perhaps his life. Of course, this political hierarchy is not the primary referent of "from above": it is God who has given Pilate power over the Son of God. No humans can exercise that power on their own.

This exchange ends with the mysterious, "therefore he who delivered me to you has the greater sin" (19:11, RSV). Within the context, the one who has delivered Jesus over to Pilate is God. Of course, one doesn't speak of God incurring guilt by sinning. We have to reach back to 18:28–32, which holds the "Jews" responsible for bringing Jesus to trial. Why does Jesus say "he" then? One might think that "he" refers to the high priest, though little has been said about the high priest's role in these events. So we are left uncertain as to who is guilty.

Now we return to the public trial. Again Pilate seeks to release Jesus, but the "Jews" warn him that he will incur the wrath of his superiors if he releases a royal pretender. This forces Pilate to continue the process. He introduces Jesus as the "your King" (19:14), which elicits an angry cry to crucify him (19:15). The "Jews" are offended by the thought that Rome should accord the status of King of the Jews to a figure they reject and despise. When Pilate taunts them, "Shall I crucify your king?" they say, "We have no king but Caesar" (19:15). Their testimony, in our author's judgment, convicts the Jews of repudiating God as their true king. Thus, they have not only sinned against Jesus, but they have broken the commandment to love God with all their being and not to honor any other being, deity or human, as God. This could be said to be their last judgment.

Thus, Jesus has "forced" both the representative of the Roman government and representatives of Judaism to perform their roles. They were destined to perform these roles. Given the character of the parties and institutional imperatives, their roles follow by a dramatic logic from who they are. There is a certain necessity, or better, inevitability, to their actions. They are, nevertheless, very much accountable for what they have done. Jesus does not coerce anyone; he simply prompts Pilate a few times.

The question of the guilt of the Jews is a sensitive subject; the Fourth Gospel raises this question to a far greater degree than the other gospels.[7] The

---

7. Only 1 Thess 2:14–16 matches its provocation.

author slips in asides through his narrative indicting the Jews, e.g.: "Some of the Pharisees near him heard this and said to him, 'Surely we are not blind, are we?'

"Jesus said to them, 'If you were blind, you would have no sin. But now that you say, "We see," your sin remains'" (John 9:40–41). It is the Jewish claim to be in the know that makes them responsible. If they knew that they were in the dark, they could be enlightened; since they are sure that they are already in the light, they will be judged mercilessly for their wrongdoing.

The Fourth Gospel does blame "the Jews" for rejecting and condemning the Son of God. This would be an accusation whose truth could only be affirmed by Christians. In other words, one would have to believe in Christ to recognize that his execution is deicide. The Gospel of John seeks to hold the Jewish people responsible to their own law. One doesn't have to believe in Jesus Christ to recognize that their confession that Caesar alone is king (19:15) is a capital offense.

As for the judicial murder of Jesus, if the religious authorities do manufacture evidence and stir up passion to get him convicted and executed, they commit a crime recognized by the human race in general. They violate, as it were, a natural law. Even if they are motivated by the desire to keep peace and preserve the country from Roman reprisals (so John 11:45–53), they have performed a criminal act and are guilty along with the Roman authorities.

## Being Lifted Up

At the end of Jesus's triumphal entry into Jerusalem, some Pharisees admit that they cannot halt the momentum of the Jesus movement (12:19). As if on cue, some Greeks approach Jesus through Philip. Jesus takes this as a sign: "The hour has come for the Son of Man to be glorified" (v. 23). The glorifying event will be Jesus's death by crucifixion (vv. 24–25). Once he has considered and rejected the idea of pleading for the canceling of his suffering (v. 27), Jesus prays to God to glorify his (God's) name, and Jesus receives an affirmative answer from God. This prompts Jesus to announce that now the world will be judged: "Now is the judgment of this world, now shall the ruler of this world be cast out" (12:31). This will, by implication, take place when Jesus is lifted up from the earth: "And I, when I am lifted up from the earth, will draw all men to myself" (v. 32). The narrator comments that this is a prediction of his manner of death. The audience points out a contradiction: "The crowd answered him, 'We have heard from the law that the Christ remains for ever. How can you say that the Son of Man must be lifted up?'" (v. 34). Jesus replies that one had better "walk by the light" while it is still around, or one will be condemned to walk in the dark. Perhaps v. 36 offers the prospect of continuing to have a lighted way once Jesus departs.

Although the reference to "being lifted up" is to the crucifixion in this passage, John means to refer to the resurrection and exaltation as well.[8] The world will be judged as sinful and destined for death, and the demonic ruler of this world will be overthrown. This foreshadows the conception of atonement known as the classical—the one Gustaf Aulen tabbed *Christus Victor*.[9] Our passage does not explain how the ruler of this world is replaced. There is nothing about a mousetrap. It may be simply that the attractive power of the exalted Christ will draw the human community away from their allegiance to Satan.

We come across that universal claim again: "all men" will be drawn to Jesus. This seems extravagant, and contradictory to the passages that speak of a division of humans over Jesus. Perhaps the "all men" means Gentiles as well as Jews. That was a decisive expansion of missionary activity in the apostolic church. So one could read "all men" as all nationalities and classes, rather than each and every individual human.

Nevertheless, one could take these universalistic statements in John and elsewhere as a basis for hope in the salvation of all humans. The church must live with the paradox that it is to proclaim a life-and-death message to all peoples, yet to hope that God will complete the universal redemption begun in time.

## Worshipping in Spirit and in Truth

To wrap up our exposition of the Fourth Gospel, we can take up the question of the piety that corresponds to the salvation offered in Christ. We have been attending to penitential piety since its emergence in postexilic Israel. The Johannine piety of inwardness and enthusiasm is a version of it. The fullest presentation of the gospel's piety is found in John 4.

The story is simple. Jesus remains behind at Jacob's well while his disciples go into a town known as Sychar. While they are away, a woman visits the well to draw water, and Jesus asks for a drink. She is shocked that a Jew would ask a Samaritan woman for a drink, and Jesus uses the occasion to announce that he is the source of "living water" (v. 10). That is, he is the "spring of water welling up to eternal life" (v. 14)—a fountain of youth, so to speak. In the ensuing exchange, it comes out that the woman has passed from "marriage" to "mar-

8. Barrett, *The Gospel according to St. John*, 356.
9. See Aulen, *Christus Victor*.

riage" throughout her life. She now realizes that she is dealing with a prophet, so she takes the opportunity to hear his opinion of the local religious tradition versus the temple-centered religion of Judaism. The Samaritans were a part of the same religion as were Jews but were considered illegitimate by the latter.

Jesus sides with Jerusalem, but then says that it is about to be replaced by a placeless religion: "The hour is coming, and now is, when the true worshipers will worship the Father in spirit and truth" (v. 23). This form of worship corresponds to the nature of God: "God is spirit, and those who worship him must worship in spirit and truth" (v. 27). Nothing further is said about this form of worship; the woman brings up the subject of the messiah, and Jesus identifies himself.

While there are a number of indications that this new era leaves behind the temple, it can only be surmised from passages like John 2:21 that Jesus's "body" is to replace it. Of course, this is a metaphor, because a human body cannot literally be a space in which people can perform a liturgy. Wherever people are gathered in Jesus's name is holy space and the transaction of worship.

How can we identify this inward piety with the penitential piety we found in the Old Testament? The Fourth Gospel says very little about repenting of sin. And there is little evidence in John of the sorrow or contrition that characterizes repentance. Thus, one has to admit that the spiritual mood of John is not penitential but more on the order of ecstatic contemplation. Nevertheless, we should not overlook the fact that the Johannine tradition gives the church the rationale for the piety of penitence: "If we walk in light, as he is in the light, we have fellowship with one another, and the blood of Jesus his Son cleanses us from all sin. If we say we have no sin, we deceive ourselves, and the truth is not in us. If we confess our sins, he is faithful and just, and will forgive our sins and cleanse us from all unrighteousness" (1 John 1:7–9, RSV). This passage captures perfectly the mood Martin Luther articulated when he said: "Justified, yet a sinner, always penitent."[10]

## Conclusions

The Fourth Gospel tells the story of Jesus, Word of God and Son of God, from the perspective of a Christology "from above." Jesus is God in the flesh, actually in the fully human person. The narrative must answer somewhat different questions from the Synoptics. In particular, John has to explain how the Son of God can suffer and die, and why. According to this gospel, the crucifixion

---

10. Clemen, *Luthers Werke in Auswahl*, 5:241.

of Jesus is the central part of the divine plan. Jesus is following a schedule: During the time when his "hour has not yet come," he reveals divine truth and recruits a community of witnesses, who are his friends; they will carry on the community when he is gone.

When his hour comes, the Son initiates and directs his trial and execution. Thus, he acts within the power of God. Humans are predisposed to play their roles, so they are fully accountable for their actions. By calling Caesar their king the Jewish authorities violate their own commandment requiring honor of God above all earthly powers, and by assenting to the crucifixion of Jesus they violate as well a common human law against murder. The Romans are also guilty of the latter.

The Fourth Gospel provides three different images or analogies to explain what the cross accomplishes. John the Baptist introduces Jesus as a sacrificial lamb who allows for sinners to be forgiven. Jesus compares himself to a shepherd who dies protecting his flock from predators. In this image, Jesus dies only for his own, for those who have joined his flock. Their election is a synthesis of freedom and destiny. Finally, Jesus is exalted—on the cross and in the resurrection—and thereby banishes Satan, the ruler of this fallen world.

There is a tension in John between limited atonement and universalism. As does a shepherd's defense of his flock benefits the sheep, so the death of Jesus benefits only his own; those who reject him continue to be under the wrath of God. On the other hand, John the Baptist introduces Jesus as the lamb who takes away all human sin, and the exaltation formula has Jesus draw "all men" to himself. The church clearly has the commission to invite all people, from all nations and religions, to believe in Jesus and gain eternal life. However, the universalistic statements leave open two possibilities—eternal perdition of some, or that what the church begins in time will be completed by God in eternity.

Those who join Jesus's flock will no longer worship God in the Jewish temple, let alone other temples. Jesus's body replaces all holy places. The piety will be inward, the mood ecstatic contemplation, humble because one's status is a gift of grace. Though the piety of penitence is not mentioned in the Fourth Gospel, it is sublimely expressed in 1 John 1.

# 23

# The Lion of Judah and Lamb of God
(Revelation)

THE CHRISTIAN KERYGMA (PROCLAMATION) may center on the historical life of Jesus Christ, but the earthly life of the messiah is only one phase in the life of the Lord, the Son of God. Before the incarnation, the Word was active in creation and was the means of communication with God's people. After Jesus's resurrection, he ascended to the right hand of God, where he is active in the life of the church and leads history toward his return to usher in the kingdom.

The book of Revelation recounts very little from the life of the historical Jesus; his crucifixion and resurrection are presupposed, but the narrative covers what he is doing between first and second coming, and what he will do at the end. You might say that this narrative complements the gospels. It covers the period that Acts covers, but from a much different perspective.

The perspective of Revelation can be called by the book's Greek name: Apocalypse. The teaching that most stands out in apocalyptic literature is the coming divine intervention to put an end to evil in the creation, and to establish an eternal saving order, the kingdom of God. This basic message frequently describes great convulsions or troubles in the time leading up to Armageddon or the Last Judgment. These are the signs that the synoptic apocalypses (Matthew 24–25; Mark 13; Luke 21) call to readers' attention. The Apocalypse of John has incorporated these troubles in its scenario. It has more, though: The events of the end are framed in a narrative that can be classified as ancient fantasy. The figures are drawn from ancient myth, though they are so synthesized and rationalized that readers are invited to allegorize them. This renders the book rather daunting to readers expecting simple, straightforward communication, and attractive to readers who relish solving puzzles and exploring mysteries.

I am going to follow David Barr's guidance into this work.[1] He divides the work into three parts: the letter(s) (chapters 1–3), the worship scroll (chapters 4–11), and the war scroll (chapters 12–22). Other interpreters break the book up differently, so we should not take our outlining too rigidly. The book has a rather repetitive plot, often telling the same events from different angles; we have to construct the story from the narrative. On the other hand, the narrator does set out the sequence for his rhetorical purposes, and we should be attentive.

The issues that we can foresee from the outset: How is the judgment of God related to the redemption in Christ? What role does Jesus play in the events of judgment? How do the acts of judgment ascribed to Christ cohere with his character as Suffering Servant? How can the Suffering Servant overcome the powers of evil? How are the supernatural powers that challenge God for sovereignty related to actual individual humans? What role does the church play in the redemption of humanity?

## The Letter Scroll (Revelation 1–3)

The first three verses of chapter 1 function as a title for the work. It is an apocalypse, or revelation, from Jesus Christ, though an angel, to John. This introduction ends with a beatitude directed to the churches that will absorb the teaching. The book ends (22:6–21) with a similar beatitude (v. 7) and a set of oaths as to the reliability and imminence of the second coming (vv. 8–9, 12–13, 16–17).

Revelation 1:4–8 depict the writing as a letter directed to seven churches in Asia Minor. There is a blessing and a thanksgiving, concluding with a divine self-asseveration (v. 8). This makes everything in the book one letter; the messages to the churches are not separate letters, and the visions are not outside the letter.

John begins the body or content of this letter with an account of the experience that initiated his visions of the end. He was living on an island in the Aegean, where he had been exiled for witnessing to Christ. The day was the Lord's day, and he was "in the Spirit" (1:10). A natural reading of this is that he was in a state of ecstasy. An unidentified voice interrupts his meditation with a command to write letters to seven churches. He looked around to discover

---

1. Barr, *Tales of the End*.

the source of the command, and first saw seven lampstands, then a human figure of very striking bearing—with a gold girdle, hoary head, flaming eyes, and polished bronze feet. His voice is "like the sound of many waters" (v. 15). He holds seven stars in his right hand and a sword protrudes from his mouth, and his face shines like the sun.

This Christ figure is not named as such, though he introduces himself as the "first and the last," an attribute of God (see v. 8), and as the historical Jesus: "I died, and behold I am alive for evermore, and I have the keys of Death and Hades" (v. 18). After alluding to the gospel story, he commands John, "Now write what you see, what is and what is to take place hereafter" (v. 19). Note that the original command is altered somewhat. John will in fact write seven messages first, and then report his visions.

The messages are within the letter that was opened properly in 1:4–7. Now John writes a message to the "angel" of each of the seven churches; we have already been informed that the seven stars in the hand of the Son of Man are the angels of these churches (1:20), which are symbolized by the seven lampstands. The angels, evidently, are only messengers, for each message is addressed to the members of the church. The message consists of commendations and criticisms of the behavior of each church. These are not private messages to each church, but messages for all recipients of the book to read. We can read each message as a part of one communication to seven churches, and the seven churches may be representative of Christian churches everywhere.

The message directed to a particular church is specific enough for one to construct an image of the congregation. The first to be addressed is Ephesus. They are commended for their bearing suffering with patience, and are criticized for losing the love they once had (2:4). This is a church that has tightened its grip, so to speak, and has become grim. Several other churches have had to survive persecution as well—Smyrna, Pergamum, and Philadelphia. This may not, however, have been recent; we are not in the era when the Roman Empire was engaged in a systematic, long-term effort to suppress Christianity. The Christians were, rather, the object of discrimination, but persecution was periodic and local.

We hear more about conflicts within the churches. Ephesus seems to have had a faction named the Nicolatians, whose "works" were scandalous (2:8). They are mentioned again in the message to Pergamum (2:15). That congregation also harbors a faction that holds a position on eating meat sacrificed to idols that is said to be "the teaching of Balaam" (2:14). The church in Thyatira has a member dubbed "Jezebel," who also supports eating meat sacrificed to idols, and some immoralities (2:20–23). Otherwise this congregation is commended: "Your faith and love and service and patient endurance" (v. 19). The congregation in Smyrna seems to be the object of slander by "Jews who are not really Jews"; they belong to a "synagogue of Satan" (2:9). That church is about to suffer persecution. The church in Philadelphia is also under pressure from a "synagogue of Satan" (3:9). That church is also persecuted, but they can survive if they continue to hold fast to the faith.

The churches at Sardis and Laodicea are afflicted by the deadly sin of sloth. Sardis is said to be "dead" (3:1) while Laodicea is "neither cold nor hot" (3:15). These are afflictions that plague churches in every era and clime. Indeed, the church evoked in John's letter is quite recognizable in the churches around us.

David Barr believes that the author of Revelation is most concerned by the accommodations the church is making, or is tempted to make, with the polytheistic and hedonistic culture of the society. That may well be, but we need not isolate the work by pegging it down to its era and the debates within the church. The Apocalypse does seem to condemn those who would eat meat sacrificed to idols. We know from 1 Corinthians 8 and 10 that this was an issue in the first-century Hellenistic church. Paul accepts the practice but warns the sophisticated in his congregation not to offend those who would mistake them for idolaters (1 Cor 8:1–13; 10:6–30). Indeed, he warns them against falling back into idolatrous ways. John seems to put all the emphasis on the dangers of accommodation.

As one reads through the messages to the churches in Revelation, the apocalyptic framework is in the background. A refrain runs through the messages: "Whoever conquers, I will grant to sit with me on my throne" (3:21; cp. 2:7, 11, 26; 3:5, 12). This is a promise whose fulfillment is the subject of the visions in chapters 4–22. Besides the promise are urgings to repent (2:5; 16; 3:3, 19) and encouragements to remain faithful (2:10; 3:11). These have the Final Judgment in the background, but not much here could be called hellfire preaching. The visions reported in the worship and war scrolls bear the weight of the characterization of John as an apocalypse.

What makes this work prophecy? The narrator does report a revelation. Though the type of revelation is not characteristic of Old Testament prophecy, the author claims authority like that of a prophet. Does he need prophetic authority for his letters to the seven churches? If anything requires prophetic authority, it would be the visions and their interpretation. There is something radically new and specifically Christian that comes to expression in the "fantastic" drama. To that we turn now.

## The Worship Scroll (Rev 4:1—11:11)

The first vision has John pass into a higher metaphysical sphere. The narrator finds himself in sacred space. It is the throne room of the Almighty, with twenty-four other "thrones" or chairs, each occupied by an elder; there are also four "living creatures" stationed around the throne (4:4-6). The creations have animal features (features of a lion, an ox, and an eagle), multiple eyes, and wings. They sing praises to God, and the "elders" on the thrones genuflect and sing along with the creatures. One can trace many details to Old Testament texts. The fragments of hymns are standard glorifications of the Creator.

The narrator notices a scroll in the hand of the Almighty, and then an angel asks, "Who is worthy to open the scroll and break its seals?" This scroll is comparable the scrolls of Scripture in a synagogue service, only this scroll is "sealed" like a legal document, with seven seals (made of clay or wax). Like a legal document too, this scroll can only be opened by an authorized person. No explanation is given as to why the document needs to be opened now. The issue is to find the right person. No one is found, until an elder tells John that there is one, the Lion of Judah, who "has conquered." This is the first introduction of the Davidic messiah.

No sooner is the one identified who is worthy to open the seals than he appears among them—as a lamb, a slain lamb—with seven horns and seven eyes.[2] How the slain Lamb can still be walking around is a part of its mystery. The line between being alive and being dead is rather blurry in this heavenly world. Christian martyrs, for example, cry out from under the altar (6:9-11).

So it is the slain Lamb, the sacrificial victim, who has conquered. How he has conquered is explained in a hymn fragment:

> You are worthy to take the scroll
>     and open its seals,
> for you were slaughtered and by your blood
>     you ransomed for God
> saints from every tribe and language
>     and people and nation;
> you have made them to be a kingdom
>     and priests serving our God,
> and they will reign on earth. (Rev 5:9-10)

---

[2]. Having many eyes, horns, and ears seems to belong to supernatural figures in this iconography. It reminds one of Hindu religious art.

This means that whatever power there is in the seals and scroll, it has been attained by gaining a holy following, by the Lamb's sacrifice of himself. The sequence he sets in motion should bring his saving purposes to a conclusion.

We are surprised by the impact of opening the seals. Usually it is the content of an opened scroll that is weighty, but in this narrative the opening of each seal unleashes some force on the earth. Though the Lion of Judah, who became a sacrificial Lamb, has participated in the life of humans on earth, he now is removed. Neither he nor God Almighty can act directly in the finite world; they must recruit agents and intermediaries. The first four seals turn loose four horses and riders on the earth—a conqueror, a "sword" (battle), famine and inflated prices, and death. This is the sort of sequence that an imperial figure typically unleashes on human society.[3]

How could the Lamb, who conquers through vicarious suffering, take recourse to imperial violence? This is an imperial power that serves the divine purpose like Assyria, Nebuchadnezzar of Babylon, and Cyrus of Persia had. Various prophets identified these rulers as agents of the Lord's wrath or mercy. But, one might ask, how can the *Lamb* manifest his power in such contradictory forms? Well, remember, the Lamb is the Lion of Judah. The long-awaited messiah was a figure who would defeat and expel Israel's enemies and establish justice and peace by exercising superior power against all who would oppose his order. The imperial power released by the seal might be driven by such an ideal. Note, however, that enlightened despotism becomes itself a source of oppression, injustice, and death despite its good intentions. So how can the Lamb adopt such contradictory means?

However one seeks to reconcile what may strike one as contradictory, the Lamb initiates and channels to his saving purpose the will to dominate characteristic of a ruler. This is the rationale of the first four seals. The result is havoc, but the narrative will now proceed to the next two seals. The fifth seal is quite unusual: the prayers of the martyrs, crying for vengeance, are answered by a promise of (delayed) judgment. The sixth seal brings the convulsions in the cosmos that accompany the Final Judgment. This is the "wrath of the Lamb" poured out on those who have rejected his protection (Rev 6:6). That protection is given the servants of God from Israel and the nations. These are marked with a cross so that they will be distinguished in the midst of judgment. This salvation may not mean protection in the body so much as the power to endure suffering and martyrdom.

---

3. Barr, *Tales of the End*, 81–88.

*Redeeming Judgment*

Notice how those who have been marked have had their robes "washed" in "the blood of the Lamb" (Rev 7:14). This is atonement language. The people have been cleansed of their sin, like a robe that has been washed. The whiteness of their robes signifies their purification from the stain of sin. What is so surprising is that among the purified, in addition to the 144,000 from Israel (a symbolic number) there is an innumerable host from the nations. This far exceeds the number of explicit Christians at the time, leaving us to wonder where they all came from.

After the seventh and last seal is broken (Rev 8:1–5)[4] comes a "story within the story," of seven trumpet blasts associated with natural catastrophes. The fifth trumpet blast reveals a "bottomless pit" (9:1–2) from which some gigantic locusts escape into the world (9:7–11). They have poisonous tails like scorpions, and they assault only humans. The sixth trumpet brings forth four angels commissioned to lead a rampage of horses. The seventh trumpet blast comes at the end of the scroll (11:15) and heralds the kingdom.

The narrative focus returns to John himself at the beginning of chapter 10. An angel appears with a little scroll, the reading of which summoned seven "thunders" (10:3). The angel swears that there will be no more delay of the fulfillment of the prophecies of old. The narrator takes the little scroll by command of a heavenly voice, and eats it at the command of the angel. The chapter ends with the duty of prophesying—passing on the message of the scroll. Next the narrator is handed a ruler and told to measure the inner areas of the temple. He is not allowed to complete the measuring, however: his action is interrupted by the introduction of two "prophets" who carry out their task, are assaulted by the "beast" and killed (11:1–7). They are not given a proper burial, but subsequently they are taken up into heaven (11:4–13). This interruption, of unidentified origin, does not seem to play any further role in the book.

The scroll comes to a close with the seventh trumpet blast, followed by a choir of heavenly voices announcing, "The kingdom of the world has become the kingdom of our Lord and of his Christ, and he shall reign for ever and ever" (11:15). Suddenly we find ourselves back in the heavenly sanctuary: the twenty-four elders are genuflecting and praising the Almighty. They celebrate the end of human rebellion, injustice, and impiety:

> The nations raged,
>> but your wrath has come
>> and the time for judging the dead,

---

4. There is silence for half an hour, then the beginning of the trumpet blasts. One might well think of Paul's last trumpet (1 Cor 15:51–55).

> for rewarding thy servants—
>> the prophets and saints
> and all who fear your name,
>> both small and great,
> and for destroying those who destroy the earth. (vv. 17–19)

This is the "completion" of the service that began in the heavenly throne room in Revelation 4. This is a classic summary of a last judgment with two outcomes.

How shall we summarize our findings from our reading of the worship scroll? The book of Revelation identifies the power capable of bringing fallen history to an end with the vicarious sacrifice of the Davidic messiah. These are not two potentially competing principles.[5] Justice and judgment belong to the redemptive action of God in Christ. The seals releasing violence and death into the world belong to the Lamb whose blood has cleansed a great people. Those will be protected during the "troubles," the convulsions that lead to final judgment.

Our narrative does not explain how so many have been "washed" in "the blood of the Lamb." At the time of the writing, the church did not have innumerable members. Is it possible that people who do not even know the story of the Lamb, or who reject it as a saving word, are included in this number? Does the author expect the church to survive and expand to include such a multitude? Is the church representative of a host of humans who are not confessing Christians?

Our narrative also does not explain why there are a host of humans not wearing robes washed in the blood of the Lamb. So far the Apocalypse has simply taken for granted that many humans, indeed all, are infected by sin and a few of these—or many—are being restored to health. But now the book will address the question of the source of sin and evil, and how humans end up in bondage. This subject is depicted as a war of sorts—that is the title David Barr gives the scroll we read next.

## The War Scroll (12:1—22:5)

This scroll begins abruptly with the introduction of the figures that are going to do battle. Four demonic figures will do battle with Christ and those associated with him. The dragon, whom we meet first (12:3), is the devil or

---

5. Say, Davidic messiah and sacrificial lamb.

Satan. He conjures two "beasts," one from the sea and the other from the land (chapter 13). Later we hear of the whore of Babylon (chapters 17–18). The two beasts and the whore are allegorical figures for the imperial power of John's day, Rome, but they are quite capable of being applied to other empires.

These figures can be compared to the "principalities and powers" that Paul and his school speak of. Romans 8:38–39 presents a long list of potential barriers to communion with God: "For I am sure that neither death, nor life, nor angels, nor principalities, nor things present, nor things to come, nor powers, nor height, nor depth, nor anything else in all creation . . ." Ephesians 6:12 describes the struggle Christians are engaged in thus: "For we are not contending against flesh and blood, but against the principalities, against the powers, against the world rulers of this present darkness, against the spiritual hosts of wickedness in the heavenly places."[6]

Many readers will be tempted to dismiss this sort of thinking as hopelessly antiquated, grossly mythological. This would be a great mistake. William Stringfellow devoted much of his theological intelligence to showing the illuminating power of the concept of principalities and powers.[7] We can understand what is meant if we think about how institutions and societies are driven by the will to live and to dominate. The values they purport to stand for will be restricted or abandoned when survival is at stake. This involves collective behavior; individuals are swept up in a collective mindset and may not even notice how the actions of the collective contradict their own moral convictions.

The contribution of the Apocalypse is to provide images for the principalities and powers. The author draws upon ancient mythical traditions to visualize what in the Pauline corpus is abstract and vague. Of course, readers need to be sophisticated enough to restrict the beasts and the whore to the imaginary world of the Apocalypse. They will become a source of illusion if they are taken too literally.

The story begins in Revelation 12 with a "cosmic" woman who is about to bear a wonder child. A dragon shows up ready to eat the child immediately after its birth. Fortunately, God intervenes to take the child into heaven upon its birth, while the mother escapes to a wilderness refuge. The dragon has come to the earth because it had been expelled from heaven. When the dragon's

---

6. Actually the Apocalypse would deny the last clause: Satan and his forces have been banished from heaven.

7. Rom 8:38; Eph 6:12. See Stringfellow, *An Ethic for Christians and Other Aliens*.

attempt is thwarted to devour the child or its mother, the dragon turns to making war on those who keep God's commandments and confess Jesus.[8]

A gruesome beast arises from the sea to join the dragon. The beast is particularly blasphemous, but nevertheless it is given authority over all peoples, and everyone but the elect worships it. Another beast arises from the land to augment the power of the first beast. The task of the second beast is to be the public relations agent for the first. Those who live in the society are marked on the hand and forehead with the number of the beast; "no one [could] buy or sell unless he had the mark" (13:17).

The narrator suddenly catches sight of the Lamb (on the top of Mount Zion) leading his loyal forces. Now a set of angels fly out announcing lessons for readers: "Fear God and give him glory," "Fallen is Babylon the great," and "If anyone worships the beast and its image, . . . he also shall drink the wine of God's wrath" (14:7, 8, 9, RSV). The section ends with a summary of the lesson: "Here is a call for the endurance of the saints" (v. 12). A voice from heaven adds consolation to those who are forced to endure martyrdom: "Blessed are the dead who die in the Lord" (v. 13).

The focus of the Apocalypse then shifts back to Christ, who is no longer a Lamb leading his forces but a Son of Man upon a cloud with a sickle in his hand. A reaping follows—a reaping of grain. Next comes a reaping of the vine. The grapes are pressed, and the earth runs blood (14:14–20). The reaping would seem to be the Last Judgment, in line with Jesus's parables involving harvesting. However, the reaping and pressing of the grapes could picture the punishment of the wicked, or could have something to do with communion. The narrative is broken off without any decipherment.

Just as in the narrative about the worship scroll, where the breaking of seven seals and blowing of seven trumpets unleashed violent power on earth, so in this narrative seven "bowls of wrath" are poured out on earth (15:7). What follows is a sequence of divine judgments: the first bowl causes "foul and evil sores [to come] upon the men and women who bore the mark of the beast and worshipped its image" (16:2). The third bowl is accompanied by angelic praise of God for judgment:

> You are just, O Holy One, who are and were,
>     for you have judged these things;

---

8. This shows how impossible it is to correlate the story told here with the sequence of the gospel story. You might think that Jesus is the child withdrawn to heaven, but that would eliminate the story of his life.

> because they shed the blood of saints and prophets,
>> you have given them blood to drink.
> It is what they deserve! (16:5–7)

The martyrs under the altar concur.

The fourth bowl says of those who suffer from it, "they cursed the name of God who had power over these plagues, and they did not repent and give him the glory" (16:9). The sixth plague ends at Armageddon, while the last plague brings ruin to Babylon. God makes sure, according to Rev 16:19 (RSV), that Babylon "drains the cup of the fury of his wrath." There are still humans remaining at the end of the sequence to "curse God" for the hailstones from heaven (16:21).

The Lamb has not directed this series of judgments. It is the work of God, executed by angels. The justifications of the blows are in terms of justice and vengeance for persecuting the saints and prophets. The actions do not achieve anything beyond judgment (e.g., they don't bring about repentance). After the last bowl is emptied, a voice speaks from the heavenly temple: "It is done!" (16:17). This scenario is deliberately different from the announcement of the kingdom (cp. 11:15).

The next two chapters celebrate the fall of Babylon. The city is depicted as a woman—a whore because of her history of impiety, greed and decadence, sexual incontinence, and love of persecution. The woman is seated on the back of a beast with seven heads and ten horns. The heads symbolize the hills of the city and its rulers. The ten horns are future kings who will make war on the Lamb. Before things are resolved, those who belong to the beast will turn against the woman.

Revelation 18 contains a dirge over the fallen city, and a lamentation by those who were enriched by the city. Early in the dirge we hear the following:

> For all nations have drunk of the wine
>> of the wrath of her fornication,
> and the kings of the earth have committed fornication with her,
>> and the merchants of the earth have grown rich with the power of
>>> her luxury. (18:3–4)

The metaphors may blur the exact indictment, but we can gather an impression: the city is extravagant, decadent and violent. It is ripe for a fall. But there is no sympathy or sorrow shown the woman in this dirge. She deserves everything she suffers.

Dirges were used periodically in the ancient Near East and the Old Testament as clothing for taunt songs directed at cities that the speaker was glad to see destroyed.[9] In the prophets, the of the taunt-song/dirge is spoken to a city or country that has not been destroyed (cp. Isaiah 47). This use of prophetic dirges or taunt songs fits the book of Revelation: the audience lives in the civilization that the dirge describes as fallen. The author uses the dirge/taunt-song as an exhortation to the audience to avoid becoming integrated into the dominant culture:

> Come out of her, my people,
>> so you do not take part in her sins,
>> so you do not share in her plagues;
> for her sins are heaped high as heaven,
>> and God has remembered her iniquities. (18:4–5)

Why, the author asks, would any believer become so dependent on the civilization that is about to fall?

After hearing of the mourning of the rulers, merchants, and shippers, an angel seals the fate of the city by casting a great "millstone," representing the city, into the sea:

> With such violence Babylon the great city
>> will be thrown down,
>> and will be found no more;
> and the sound of harpists and minstrels . . .
>> shall be heard in you no more;
> and an artisan of any trade . . .
> and the sound of the millstone . . .
> and the light of the lamp . . .
> and the voice of the bridegroom and the bride . . .
> for your merchants were the magnates of the earth
>> and all nations were deceived by your sorcery. (18:21–23)

The cultural and commercial life of the city is, according to this prophet, an infectious disease that cannot be cured, only eradicated. The crime that marked her as worthy of death was the killing of saints and prophets:

---

9. There are classes of people who do weep for the city—rulers, merchants and shippers. These classes benefited from the commerce of the city, and lost their means of livelihood when the city fell.

> And in [you] was found the blood of prophets and of saints,
> and of all who have been slaughtered on earth. (18:24)

Praise breaks out in heaven for the salvation wrought by God:

> For his judgments are true and just;
> he has judged the great whore
> who corrupted the earth with her fornication,
> and he has avenged on her
> the blood of his servants. (19:2)

Then the praises affirm the power and glory of God, and begin to look forward to the "marriage of the Lamb" (19:7). The Lamb now appears as a man upon a white horse (v. 11); he has a double-edged sword in his mouth, and a robe dipped in blood. His name is the Word of God.

Then the narrator "saw the beast and the kings of the earth with their armies gathered to make war against the one who sits upon his horse and his army" (v. 19). Before battle is even engaged, however, the beast and the kings of the earth are captured, and the "false prophet" as well, and they are thrown into the "lake of fire" (vv. 19–21). With these "principalities and powers" destroyed, their followers are slain by the Word of God. The scene ends with a banquet on human flesh by the vultures and eagles.

Why is this second battle necessary? Because the destruction of the city, as significant as it is, does not vanquish all evil, this second battle is another phase in the complete vanquishing of evil. What is so striking is that those who oppose the man on the white horse are defeated without a violent confrontation of forces. The passive construction, "And the beast was captured" (v. 20), should be read as a divine passive: God captures and destroys. Perhaps the instrument was the Word of God, who in any case disposes of the followers of the beast.

David Barr notes that battles between order and chaos, Creator and created matter, and so forth are the subject of numerous ancient myths. Our hero on a white horse seems to be of the same order, "but closer examination reveals some anomalies."[10] He has a symbolic robe (dipped in blood); his name is allegorical (Word of God), and no military engagement takes place. The instrument of power is the spoken word of Jesus. "Just when we think that good might prevail over evil by one use of force . . . , the story reverses its images and we see evil defeated by weakness."[11] "It is the word of God that slays, not

---

10. Barr, *Tales of the End*, 137.
11. Ibid.

## The Lion of Judah and Lamb of God

the coercive power of government."[12] "Rather John is showing how the death of Jesus has the power to destroy evil."[13]

One would think that our story has come to an end; but no, the dragon has not been disposed of—only those figures that he had empowered. Indeed, it seems to be very difficult to banish him altogether. Rather than killed, the dragon is locked up in the "bottomless pit." Why he must be released after a thousand years is a mystery, since this release is simply to permit one more futile gesture before he is permanently disposed of (20:1–3).

The thousand-year reign of martyrs is an odd example of retribution. Those who had suffered under the regime of Satan now have their turn to exercise power. This little detail of the convoluted conclusion has had a very productive history of application. It has encouraged radical and utopian church movements—which go under the name premillennialist—in many eras. Whether the text can bear such weight depends upon how literally one reads Revelation.

The Last Judgment proper is a rather anticlimactic event. The scene is described in 20:11–15. God Almighty is enthroned, filling the cosmos. "And I saw the dead, great and small, standing before the throne, and books were opened . . . And the dead were judged by what was written in the books, by what they had done" (v. 12). This rather conventional scenario does not have any role for Christ and does not have any role for judicial deliberation. There is no cognizance given to the "redeemability" of the persons whose "record" is not sterling.

Upon reflection, we see that the imagination of the book of Revelation is not in its teaching about individuals but in its depiction of collective redemption. The new Jerusalem is introduced in chapters 21–22, and it is in this description that we plumb new theological depths. The saving event is called the marriage of the Lamb, but to our surprise the bride is the city, not believers or the church. The city of Babylon was the demonic form of human civilization; Jerusalem is the proper, divine form of the same.[14] The heavenly city is not the simple negation of the earthly city but the redemption of human cities: "By its lights shall nations walk; and the kings of the earth shall bring their glory into it, and its gates shall never be shut by day—and there shall be no night there; they shall bring into it the glory and the honor of the nations" (21:24–26).

---

12. Ibid.
13. Ibid., 138.
14. See Ellul, *The Meaning of the City*, 183–209.

## Concluding Theological Reflection

Let's begin this reflection on what has happened in the visionary narrative with a theological observation by our guide:

> If God triumphs over evil only because God has more power than evil, then power—not love or goodness or truth—is the ultimate value of the universe... But in John's story... [it] is the lamb who replaces the lion (5:5–6); visions of the lamb bracket that of the heavenly warrior (14:1; 19:11; 21:9, 22); and even the warrior conquers by what comes from the mouth not his arm (19:21)... At every juncture in this story where good triumphs over evil, a close examination will show that the victory is finally attributed to the death of Jesus (perhaps most obvious at 12:11).[15]

We will have to place some qualifications on this statement, but let's first state our agreement with its basic contention: God's victory over evil is a case of powerlessness or defeat—being put to death by the powers ruling the society—overturning those very powers. God's ultimate power is manifested in history by nonparticipation in the power struggles that encompass human society. Or, one might say, God participates in history by accepting the part of the victims in this power struggle. These theological propositions are true to the theology of the book of Revelation, and also to most of the other writings of the New Testament.

How does God's victory through defeat effect redemption? The ultimate problem of evil is the sinful human heart. We see this again and again in our biblical text—from the Lord's observation "that every imagination of the thoughts of [the human] heart [is] only evil continually" (Gen 6:5; 8:21) to Jeremiah's and Ezekiel's realization that the people of God must have their heart transformed in order to be redeemed (Jer 31:31–34; Ezek 36:26–27, 31). The piety appropriate to this understanding is the penitential piety we discover in Isaiah 63–66 and in Psalms 51 and 130. The Servant Song in Isaiah 52–53 speaks of an objective correlative, one in whose suffering and death others can recognize their guilt and hope for redemption.

Where we have to disagree with Barr is with his simple contrast of power and goodness (plus love and truth). The Lamb does not replace the Lion; the Lion is manifested as a Lamb. God does not abandon his role as mighty Judge when he effects redemption of sinners through the sacrifice of the Lamb.

In the message of the Babylonian Isaiah, Cyrus is God's "messiah," his agent of salvation for God's people, and the one who also exposes the impo-

---

15. Barr, *Tales of the End*, 146.

tence of the gods. At the same time, God identifies with his nonviolent servant. Both have their roles in the divine economy of salvation.

We can back up our contention with the argument of Kyle Pasewark's *A Theology of Power*. He defines *power* as the "communication of efficacy." In everyday terms, power empowers those over whom it is exercised. Power is also the foundation of goodness and truth, according to Pasewark. What is good and just and holy manifests power intrinsic to it. The split between power and goodness and truth occurs because humans have sought to monopolize power rather than to share it. The redemption we hope for is the healing of this split.

Now let us return to the book of Revelation. The narrative is actually filled with violence and conflict. It would not be an apocalypse if it weren't.[16] One has to wonder whether the genre was attractive because of this feature. The modern genre of futuristic fantasy often tells of wars and destruction; *Star Wars* comes to mind.

Theological ideas are embedded in Revelation's stories of "wars and rumors of war." When the Lion/Lamb removes the seals of the scroll, scourges sweep through the world. We can deduce from this that the action leading toward the establishment of the kingdom must destroy the present order. These scourges are not, strictly speaking, acts of judgment. They seem to be the sort of random destruction and violence that the masses of people simply undergo, with either natural or historical causes. What we are getting in the removal of the seals is an intensification of events that happen time and again.[17]

In the first scroll, the Worship Scroll, Christians are mentioned only in the "cracks," so to speak. They are allied with the power ruling the world from heaven, but they only endure, pray, and praise within the temporal order. The martyrs, for example, pray for the coming of the kingdom (Rev 6:9–11). (Christians also pray this in the Lord's Prayer.) At the end of the scroll, heavenly voices declare the establishment of the kingdom (Rev 11:15). This is to be echoed by the reading or listening audience.

Immediately, however, we are plunged back into fallen history. The War Scroll returns us to the present age, reviewing events from another perspective. In this scroll, we hear of forces abroad in human society. We meet the devil and some demonic manifestations. In the Pauline school, these are called principalities and powers. In other words, supernatural evil forces seem to be in control of the governments, armies, businesses, and religions of the nations.

---

16. Actually, some apocalypses do not have violence and conflict, but most do, including those found in the Synoptic Gospels (Matthew 24; Mark 13; Luke 21)

17. One is reminded of disasters such as occurred in Haiti in 2010.

## Redeeming Judgment

They are making war against—well, at one point it is a mother and child, both of whom are spirited away, leaving only their followers, the Christians for whom the book is written.

The demonic powers must be judged, they must be defeated and disposed of. This happens with the pouring out of the seven "bowls of wrath." At the end of the series, God is praised for having accomplished the judgment (Rev 16:17). Following this praise, the fall of Babylon is celebrated. It is clear in all of these events that the powers of this world and the humans with the "mark of the beast" deserve what happens to them. In that sense, these are acts of judgment against the principalities and powers. It calls forth heavenly praise of God's justice (Rev 19:2).

Now the Christ figure appears, riding a horse; his weapon is a sword coming from his mouth, and his robe has been dipped in blood. It would appear that the hidden ruler of the new age has now appeared to assume power. His ascension, however, is interrupted by the temporary resurrection of the powers of evil. They make ready to attack the king of Glory, but they are rounded up[18] without resistance and thrown into a "lake of fire." From now on, the forces arrayed against God and his Christ have had their power removed; their challenges are futile gestures.

The accession of Christ, which is also the marriage feast of Christ and the new Jerusalem, is delayed once more. The dragon, Satan, who has survived the death of his demonic manifestations, is put into a prison; he will be released in a thousand years and then destroyed forever. During the thousand years, Christ will reign with Christian martyrs. Nothing is said about what they do—only that they will not die again. They already have a pass through the Last Judgment.

When Satan is released from prison, he stirs up the hostility of Gog and Magog against the Lamb. Gog and Magog assault the holy city, but fire from heaven consumes them, and they now are thrown into the lake of fire with their armies, who had already been disposed of. Only after the last vestiges of the principalities and powers have been destroyed can the dead be raised and judged.

Why do we have such a complex scenario of the end? Why not the simplicity of Paul's description of the end in 1 Cor 15:51–52? "Lo! I tell you a mystery. We shall not all sleep, but we shall all be changed, in a moment, in the twinkling of an eye, at the last trumpet." Well, it seems that most apoca-

---

18. By God if this is a case of a the divine passive.

lypticists feel the need for a period of transition from one era, one world, to a qualitatively different one.[19]

What we should note about the Revelation scenario is that neither Christ nor his saints actually participate in battle. The battle is won by the truth of the word of God. God backs this up with violent acts such as sending fire from heaven. It seems that those who will reign in the new age are kept unsullied by the power struggle of the dying age.

The Last Judgment itself is simply the opening of the books. The ultimate destiny of every human has been decided and must only be announced. This is a trial without deliberation. Only those who are to be saved have their names inscribed in the book, called the Book of Life. Nothing is said about their beliefs—only about their deeds (20:12, 13). There is no indication that Christ is the Judge, and none that he advocates for his own. Only the "saints" who have reigned with him seem to benefit from his patronage (Rev 20:4–6).

On the other hand, we hear in 21:5–8 that God promises his saving powers and paternity specifically to "those who have conquered." These may well be the Christians who have endured through times of persecution, whether they are martyrs or not.

Who is condemned to hell? Well, Rev 21:8 consigns those who are cowardly, faithless, polluted; who commit murder or fornication; who practice sorcery and idolatry; and all liars to the lake of fire.

What happens to the "middle group"—those who are morally upstanding but have not joined the saints? Their fate is left to readers' imaginations.

The book of Revelation was written for believing Christians. It is not a philosophical writing that seeks to answer the questions of the inquisitive. Rather, it is designed to light a fire among the spiritually dormant and to give courage to those threatened with persecution. The primary task of the church, they are told, is to pray and praise, and to endure until the second coming. This is a rather sectarian frame of mind. Christians have no role to play in the present age other than to pray and praise, and to endure. Participation in the present age would stain one, so to speak, and would threaten one's fitness for the world to come.

These people of God will participate in the "messianic banquet" in their worship service. The Eucharist makes the future saving event present proleptically to those who yearn for it. And they will continue to pray, "thy kingdom come, thy will be done on earth as it is in heaven."

---

19. We may also have an effort to draw in as many Old Testament images of the end or of great cataclysm as possible.

# 24

# The Wrath of God and Justification by Faith
(Romans 1–11)

WE CAN WRAP UP our examination of divine judgment in the New Testament with an exposition of Paul's comprehensive argument covering God's judgment and redemption of the human race. That statement describes Romans 1–11.

I originally had it in mind to follow the interpretation of Christ's vicarious suffering through a number of New Testament epistles.[1] Since I find the Romans texts to be most rewarding, I have decided to concentrate on them. Moreover, Romans has the advantage of highlighting judgment, our focus, so we are limiting ourselves to this one comprehensive text.

We can simply follow the order of the chapters as they stand. Our guide is Leander Keck.[2] I have broken the text up into arguments. The letter to the Romans is highly rhetorical in the sense of seeking to state, expound, and justify the main theses of Paul's theology about the human condition and Christ's remedy.

## The Introduction to Romans 1:18—8:39

Romans 1:16–17 states the thesis of the first eight chapters and summarizes the message of the whole letter. "For I am not ashamed of the gospel; it is the

---

1. My guide was to be Hofius, "The Fourth Servant Song," 163–88. The four primary texts identified by Hofius are 1 Pet 2:21–25, 3:18; Heb 9:28; 1 Cor 15:3b–5; and Rom 3:17ff.; 4:25; 5:6, 8, 17, 18–21.
2. Keck, *Romans*.

power of God for salvation to everyone who has faith, to the Jew first and also to the Greek. For in it the righteousness of God is revealed through faith for faith; as it is written, 'The one who is righteous will live by faith.'"

We should pay closer attention than usual to the nuances. "I am not ashamed" is a strong affirmation, on the order of, "I am confident" (in the gospel). The gospel is characterized as *powerful*. This is a message that is rhetorically effective: it has the power to save anyone who accepts it. To accept it, one must simply believe in it—trust it and rely on it. What gives the good news power is that God's righteousness is revealed in it. *Righteousness* has a broad range of meaning: the word not only describes God's character; it also involves power. That is, God rectifies or straightens out what is wrong. Let me quote our guide to Romans, Leander Keck: "Taken together, vv. 16–17 announce that the gospel is God's power to save because it is the means by which God saves, disclosing God's true character rectitude/righteousness."[3]

The message of the gospel becomes true and powerful for a sinful human being only if it is received in faith; a wait-and-see attitude will leave a person untouched and in bondage to sin. If it is received in faith, it will nourish faith. This is rather circular: faith is strengthened by believing the message of righteousness.

The thesis of Romans demonstrates just how important the theological principle that Paul formulated to accommodate the Christian kerygma for Gentiles (see Galatians 1–2) was to the apostle. Gentiles can become righteous before God without obeying the Mosaic law, for God's righteousness is available to all on the basis of faith. God's righteousness, in other words, is a gift of forgiveness and reconciliation, which sets believers on the path to sanctification and salvation. Paul had other significant theological insights, but this was the essential "breakthrough."

Leander Keck offers the following characterization of Paul's aims in the body of the letter to the Romans: "Paul's theological task is to explain how the salvation wrought by God through the gospel addresses those dimensions of the human predicament that are common to Jews and Gentiles, and why, accordingly, the same solution (the faith response to the gospel) is adequate to both."[4]

---

3. Ibid., 52.
4. Ibid., 54–55.

## The Wrath of God against Impiety and Injustice

Romans 1:18 is very jarring after vv. 16–17. We switch abruptly from salvation received by faith to judgment for sin. Paul is setting forth an argument, not preaching a sermon. He begins in 1:18 to describe the condition to which the gospel is the cure. In the rest of chapter 1 and chapters 2 and 3, he supports the conclusion that all humans "have sinned and fall short of the glory of God" (3:23). The argument does not follow the rather predictable route of exposing how rampant sin and evil are in the world, but of demonstrating that Gentiles as well as Jews know what is right and are accountable for their actions.

Romans 1:19–23 describes the impiety of the human race. The description actually applies only to Gentiles, for the Jews have the benefit of divine revelation—above all, the revealed law. The Jews, thus, have been liberated from the condition that humans on their own cannot escape. Paul is going to adopt the cosmological argument for the existence of God, but he does not think that humans are capable of escaping idolatry by rational argument.

Romans 1:19–20 inaugurates the argument by affirming what is known in theology as general revelation. "Ever since the creation of the world [God's] eternal power and deity has been clearly perceived in the things that have been made" (v. 20, RSV). This leads to the verdict, so to speak: "they are without excuse." The idolatrous instinct perverted the knowledge of God: "for although they knew God they did not honor him ... but became futile in their thinking and their senseless hearts were darkened" (v. 21). The result is the "suppression" of the truth and the deification of creatures (v. 21).

Scholars frequently note that Paul's argument resembles that of Wisdom of Solomon 13–15.[5] Nevertheless, there is a subtle but essential difference between the two arguments: "For Paul ... idolatry was not traceable to error but to disobedience."[6] Paul is thinking through the implications of the first and second commandments. Apostasy and idolatry are violations of commandments, not intellectual mistakes. Even though the Gentiles were not beneficiaries of these commandments, what God has manifested to them in creation should be enough to know that God is one and transcends creaturely reality.

What is the punishment imposed upon humans by God for its idolatry? In vv. 24, 26, and 28 we find a formula for judgment: God gave them up [handed them over] to x. The first two instances of this idea belong to the sphere of

---

5. Ibid., 60–61; also Barr, *Biblical Faith and Natural Theology*. Pseudo-Aristotle, *On the Cosmos* has a somewhat similar line of reasoning.

6. Keck, *Romans*, 61–62.

lust: "in the lusts of their hearts to impurity . . . dishonoring their bodies" (v. 24); and "dishonorable passions" (v. 26). After the first sentencing, the explanation is offered: "because they exchanged the truth about God for a lie and worshipped and served the creature rather than the Creator" (v. 25); this is a succinct definition of idolatry. After v. 26, Paul offers an example of dishonorable passions: homosexual acts by women and men. Keck observes that Paul "does not reject same-sex intercourse because of its social consequences . . . but because he regards it as a vivid demonstration of what exchanging the truth of God for a lie (v. 25) leads to."[7] Paul assumes that his audience agrees that such practices are unnatural and degrading. Evidently he had little or no problem with Christians engaging in homosexual acts, because he never isolates them for moral exhortation.

The third punishment for idolatry (v. 28) is a "base mind" and "improper conduct." Verses 29–31 list "all manner of wickedness," from the immoral motive of envy to the crime of murder, from incorrigible behavior to the violation of the commandments. All these actions are known to be condemned by God, but humans both do them themselves and honor others who do them. Clearly the human mind says one thing, but the human will and desire are out of rational control.

It is noteworthy that God's judgment for idolatry is not an intervention to destroy, say (like the flood of the earth in Genesis) but broken relationships among humans. The latter are known to be wrong, but humans have lost the proper center of life, so chaos reigns. As Keck puts it, "the consequences of idolatry run their destructive course. Paul regards this process as an act of God because God is not a bystander who merely permits the immoral consequences to develop. God's otherness and Godhood are not suspended by the results of human disobedience but are expressed in them—negatively."[8]

Paul sees the impiety and immorality that has resulted from idolatry to "lead to death" (6:16). Sin is its own punishment, but that punishment reaches beyond anything the sinner bargained for.

Chapter 2 begins with an address to a reader who is gloating over the sinfulness of most humans. This person passes judgment on others but does not examine him- or herself. The self-righteous person cannot presume the mercy of God: God's mercy is to inspire repentance, not to inflate pride in one's righteousness. All humans face the day of reckoning, when God "will repay according to each one's deeds: to those who by patience in doing good seek

7. Ibid., 69.
8. Ibid., 65–66.

for glory and honor and immortality, he will give eternal life; while for those who are self-seeking and who obey not the truth, but wickedness, there will be wrath and fury" (vv. 7–8).

Paul's depiction of the Day of Judgment ignores his doctrine of justification by faith. It has not been introduced yet. We are going to hear in chapter 3 that no human can meet the standard, which seems to make the possibility of justification by works an empty one. Here in chapter 2, however, Paul wants to insist that a person cannot be righteous by what one hears, but by what one does. Moreover, Jews do not have some advantage over Gentiles in achieving righteousness before God.

How can Gentiles be held accountable on the Day of Judgment? They have no law. For Paul (and most Jews of his time), the revealed Mosaic law is the only genuine law. Gentile law is a human construction, which in effect means that Gentiles are "without the law" (2:12). Nevertheless, Paul has already said that Gentiles "know God's decree" that a set of factious and dishonorable actions are wrong (1:32). In 2:14–15, Paul notes that Gentiles "do by nature what the law requires" and can be said to be "a law to themselves." In the next verse, he says that "what the law requires is written on their hearts." On the Day of Judgment, Gentiles will know what fate they deserve.

In Rom 2:17, we leave aside Gentile accountability for people who call themselves Jews. Paul puts it this way so he can say at the end that a true Jew is one who is inwardly circumcised. The person described in vv. 17–24, is a Jew who is proud of knowledge of God's law and quick to display it. The problem is that this person could be a hypocrite. Indeed, it is hypocrites that give Judaism a bad reputation (v. 24). Being circumcised and knowing the law only benefit a person who appropriates an identity inwardly; otherwise a Jew is worse off than a Gentile who lives a moral life without benefit of the law.

It sounds as though Paul has leveled the distinction between Jew and Gentile in his effort to show that God shows no partiality (Rom 2:11). Romans 3:1–8 seeks to rectify this misconception. Being a member of the Jewish people makes one an heir of the "oracles of God" (v. 2). However, the people may prove false to God and incur his judgment. Jews cannot complain that their wickedness is serving the just purposes of God, and therefore should not be punished; they can be held accountable even if God brings good out of evil.

In Rom 3:9, Paul seems to reverse field. While revelation is an advantage to Jews, the result is no better than if they had never received it. "All humans, both Jews and Gentiles, are under the power of sin" (3:9). Paul then quotes a series of passages from the book of Psalms and Isaiah that he regards as

## The Wrath of God and Justification by Faith

confirming the sinfulness of all his people. The law does not, in Paul's opinion, cure humans of the propensity to sin. What it does, according to Rom 3:20, is communicate knowledge of sin. (In classical Protestant theology, this is called the second use of the law.) The law condemns Gentiles because it exposes what humans know from general revelation: what humans know is enough to be held accountable, but not enough to know God. The Jews know God in revelation, but that makes them all the more accountable for their actions. In conclusion, Paul says, "no human being will be justified in [God's] sight by works of the law" (v. 20, RSV).

### Righteousness Manifested Apart from Law

Paul now states his alternative: "since all have sinned and fall short of the glory of God, they are justified by his grace as a gift, through the redemption which is in Christ Jesus" (3:23-24). One has to qualify this thesis: *if anyone* is to be saved, one must be justified by God. Paul has been arguing that Gentiles are accountable to God, and that neither Jews nor Gentiles have or can earn an acquittal on the Day of Judgment. If there is to be acquittal of anyone, it must be God's free decision. Now Paul must explain why God would choose to decide to acquit human beings, and how God's favor can be justified.

Why would God justify sinners "by his grace as a gift" (3:24) when it is discovered that no one can be righteous by one's own power? Obviously, Paul would not regard justification by faith as a makeshift policy. God has been planning it all along: he was showing forbearance toward sinners since the time of Noah.[9] That is to say, he was not enforcing the law to the full extent, but "passing over former sins" (v. 25). How could this be justified? Because God has had it in mind all along to redeem his creatures, that is, to reclaim them as his own. Thus, Paul says that this offer of forgiveness and sanctification "was to prove at the present time that he himself is righteous and that he justifies anyone who has faith in Jesus" (v. 26).

Why has faith in Christ become the condition for receiving the gift? If I understand Paul rightly, faith *is* the gift. Faith in Christ transforms the believer into the redeemed sinner. Judgment changes from punishment and despair to a redemptive action. Hence, the believer "dies with Christ" in order to be made alive by Christ's Spirit (Rom 6:7-11). In other words, the judgment imposed on the sinner becomes through faith a purgation, refinement, reformation.

---

9. God declares this to be his policy in Gen 8:20-22.

In the middle of the paragraph on the free offer of righteousness, we find a theological definition of what has happened on the cross: "Christ Jesus, whom God put forward as an expiation by his blood, to be received by faith" (3:24–25).[10] This is sacrificial language. What does it mean? The word *expiate* means "to pay a penalty" or "to make amends for sin." When *blood* is added, it must be a sacrifice that is required to neutralize the effect of sin on the holy things and perhaps on the holy order of society. In the book of Leviticus, the sin and guilt offerings use blood to cleanse what is holy of contamination caused by sin. If the altar and sanctuary were not cleansed, God would abandon the temple and the people.

Obviously the Levitical sacrifices can only be a metaphor for the crucifixion of Jesus. Here God does the offering, and a human (indeed, a human who incarnates God) is slaughtered. Human sacrifice is forbidden and condemned in the Bible. It is actually a flawed judicial action that "slaughters" this victim. Nor is Jesus's blood literally a cleansing agent.

This use of sacrifice as a metaphor for the suffering and death of an obedient, righteous human goes back to before the New Testament to Isaiah 53. In the process of being transferred from sacrifice to a tragic human death, expiation sheds the conception of blood as a cleansing agent and of atonement as repair of the sacred order. Now expiation is for the sinner him- or herself as well as for the collective bodies to which he or she belongs. Now the sinner does not offer the sacrifice but has it offered for him or her to be activated by faith. This act of faith leads the sinner to participate in some sense in the redemptive action of God. Thereby one becomes a citizen of the kingdom of God.

The one thing that Paul wants to take away from us is our boasting. Romans 3:27–31 sounds like an afterthought, but exclusion of boasting is a recurring theme in Paul's letters. One has to wonder what he has on his mind. It may be an odd way of describing pride in one's righteousness. Penitential piety requires humility, and so does Paul. If righteousness is not a human accomplishment, but a gift of God, one cannot take credit for attaining it.

One reason Paul condemns boasting is that within his social circle, it would be those who adhere to the law that would have something to boast about. Thus, Gentiles would be excluded in principle—unless they were circumcised and yoked to the law.[11] Paul is adamant about God's accessibility to

---

10. According to the RSV; the NRSV reads, "whom God put forward as a sacrifice of atonement by his blood, effective through faith."

11. The Jewish literature of the time assumes that Gentiles are not eligible for admission

Gentiles. Faith in Christ can be shared by Jews and Gentiles, as the law could not.

One could object that Paul has simply replaced the division between the elect people of God and Gentiles with believers in Christ and nonbelievers. That would be just, but it isn't what concerns Paul. He wanted to ensure that the church be inclusive. He accepted the Jewish claim to be chosen by God (see Romans 11) but simply wanted to open the door to Gentiles.

How Paul thought that he was "upholding the law" (3:31) is hard to say. So far Paul has reduced the role of Law to the "negative" function of identifying and exposing sin.

## A Canonical Interpretation of Paul's Argument

Let's pause here and look back over this sweeping argument that began in Rom 1:16–17. Paul's argument on behalf of the gospel, which he describes as empowering justification and salvation to both Jew and Gentile, reaches a climax in 3:21–31. The heart of this argument concerns the "wrath of God" (1:18). Paul's reasoning follows two tracks, one for Gentiles and the other for Jews.

Paul assumes that it is common knowledge that Gentiles are polytheists and idolaters. Thus, they are found to be lost in religious falsehood. The question is, are they culpable for their religious ignorance? Paul argues, yes, they are. The true God can be known; all sorts of evidence points to the existence of this deity. Hence, Gentiles are "without excuse," as he puts it (1:20); they have forsaken the true God for idols. Paul's appeal to evidence and reason probably echoes the popular philosophers of his day. Many of these thought that one could reason to existence of the one God who transcends all finite qualifications. These same philosophers ridiculed the worship of statues and other symbolic representations of deities.[12] If pagan philosophers know the one true God, it proves that the pagan masses are culpable; they should have known better.

God's punishment of Gentiles for apostasy and idolatry was "abandonment" to immorality and injustice. Paul believes that false religion leads to a breakdown of the moral order among humans. The argument reminds me of Hos 4:1–3. One way to look at this argument is that the punishment for sin is more sin.

---

into the kingdom because they lacked the law: Reiser, *Jesus and Judgment*, 116.

12. Consult Grant, *Gods and the One God*.

*Redeeming Judgment*

Can Gentiles be held accountable for violations of God's will if God himself abandoned them to these depredations? I suspect that Paul is assuming a synergism in which humans will freely act for their own purposes, yet their decisions conform to the plan of God. From a human point of view, Gentiles "show that what the law requires is written on their hearts" (2:15). The law to which Paul refers is the revealed law of the Old Testament; only Jews have access this law in written form, but Gentiles are not without law—it is written in their conscience. In Jewish circles, this could be referred to as the covenant God made with Noah.

So the Gentiles face a Final Judgment, which Paul refers to several times in Romans 2. "By your hard and impenitent heart you are storing up wrath for yourself on this day of wrath when God's righteous judgment will be revealed" (2:7). "For [God] will render to every one according to his works" (2:8).

Jews also face judgment. Since they have the divine law as well as revelations ("oracles") helping them to shoulder the burden of the law, they should be at an advantage (see Rom 3:1–8). However, the Hebrew Bible records Israel's constant violation of God's law (Rom 3:10–18).[13]

Paul does not speak of the historical judgments recorded in Hebrew Scripture; the only one that concerns him is the future, Final Judgment. However, since he sees both Gentiles and Jews of all times and places to be under the sign of the divine wrath, nothing prevents us from associating the judgments occurring in history with the divine wrath hovering over all humans.

Now in Rom 3:19–20 Paul seems to drop a new contention into his argument: Law exposes our sin: "through the law comes knowledge of sin." It does not seem to provide the path to salvation. Why? Paul does not explain his view of this here. Romans 7, however, seems to give an answer: the law arouses sin, it prompts the heart to desire what is prohibited and doesn't give the power to overcome this rebellious inclination.

If we correlate Rom 2:3, 5–10 and 3:19–20, we would have to say that neither Gentile nor Jew will be able to receive God's approval on the Day of Judgment.[14] Of course, some may think that they are righteous, but Paul seems

---

13. One might regard these as unfair accusations against all Jews since they originally condemned eighth- and seventh-century Israelites. That is, however, a justified way of reading the prophetic books; at least I argued for it when I was expounding the Old Testament classical prophet.

14. In his original description in chapter 2, he did regard it as possible for someone to be approved of God in the final judgment: see vv 7, 10, 15–16. That possibility is now an "impossible possibility."

to think that God has decided that question: "For no human being will be justified in [God's] sight by works of law" (3:20).

Paul has not been arguing that all is lost, however, because God has offered an alternative to justification by works, *viz.*, justification by faith in Christ, in whom the righteousness of God has been made available. "Since all have sinned and fall short of the glory of God, they are justified by his grace as a gift, through the redemption which is in Christ Jesus" (3:23-24). How can faith in Christ be a substitute for a righteous life? Has God decided that he must lower the standards in order to find someone to save?

That is, of course, a naive and unacceptable answer. So how does God go about redeeming his sinful creatures? They must be transformed, converted, and set on a path leading to faithfulness, holiness, and righteousness. Within these chapters in Romans, chapters 6 and 8 come closest to providing an explanation. Those who believe undergo a dying, participating in the death of Christ, which is also a death to sin. This is more than a metaphor for Paul. It is a quasi-metaphysical change. Nevertheless, Paul must be sober and realistic: sin continues to plague believers.[15]

Paul, here in chapter 3, asserts that the death of Jesus on the cross has the effect of justifying sinners. His death changes the situation of all sinners, all humans, whether they believe or not; faith is necessary for individuals to appropriate this justification.

How does Jesus's death have this effect? Paul uses the language of sacrifice for sin ("expiation by his blood," v. 15, RSV). He has precedence in Isaiah 53 for the employment of such a technical cultic term metaphorically. What idea is he trying to convey? Does it match any of the classical theories of atonement? In particular, one might think of Anselm's theory, known as satisfaction. The demands of justice must be met before one can offer forgiveness. That seems to fit Paul's statement that Jesus's death justifies God's foregoing strict justice through history—"because in his divine forbearance he had passed over former sins."[16] If God were strictly just, there would be no human race.[17]

---

15. Philippians treats this problem.

16. Cousar, *A Theology of the Cross*, 82-87, insists that the metaphorical character of Paul's explanations and the variation among explanations rules out identifying his views with any of the classical theories. I would put the emphasis the other way: all the theories explain some aspect or another of the meaning of Jesus' suffering and death; use each as far as it will go, and then note its inadequacies.

17. I am also reminded of God's decision at the end of the flood never again to destroy everything corrupted by sin, but to exercise forbearance in order that the human drama can continue at all.

*Redeeming Judgment*

Still we need to ask, why does Jesus have to die to perform expiation? What was inadequate about the temple rite of expiation? Why couldn't God offer forgiveness without any expiation? Why was such a drastic action required? Paul seems to address aspects of these questions in Rom 3:26: God is righteous (= not unjust) in justifying sinners who believe in Jesus. God has satisfied the requirements of justice by condemning sin but has transformed punishment into a redemptive process. That is hardly mentioned here, but Romans 6 explains how the believer "dies to sin" and is given new life in Christ.

Perhaps we can help Paul, so to speak. We might suggest the idea that Jesus's death is the "objective correlative," to borrow an expression from the poet T. S. Eliot,[18] to the penitential piety we discovered in Isaiah and the Psalms. Penitential piety accepted the judgment that all humans are sinners and should approach God in humility and compunction. Paul's argument in Romans 1–3 arrives at the same point. The difference is, Psalms like 51 and 130 do not have an objective correlate to the expectation of divine forgiveness for those who acknowledge their sin.[19] Christ's death on the cross is that correlate, fulfilling a role intimated in the Fourth Servant Song.

Having an objective correlate to the penitential attitude changes the mood: Paul no longer sounds like a compunctious sinner, and he does not instill such a mood in his congregations. Rather, he calls the Christian to rejoice in God's grace. Moreover, the Christian has been restored to dignity before God, though Paul warns his readers against boasting in their own status. Paul would seem to provide a synthesis of the classical and penitential piety.

## A Typological Justification of Christian Claims

Romans 4–5 support Paul's theological proposal that humans can only be justified by faith in Christ. First, in chapter 4, he supports his contention that God justifies not by works of law but by faith. Chapter 5 seeks to explain how Jesus's death both justifies and saves sinners.

Romans 4 is rather self-contained: it has to do with Abraham, his manner of justification, and his true heirs. Very little is said in it about sin and redemption. It is surprising to find justification proposed as a cure for the universal sinfulness of humans, and then to have it discussed without reference to sin. We might be tempted to leap over chapter 4 to chapter 5, which returns to

---

18. See Eliot, "*Hamlet*," 48.
19. Perhaps Psalm 51 now has that objective correlative in v. 19.

justification of sinners. However, it is chapter 4 that provides Paul's precedent for the elevation of faith above compliance with the law.

We will stay with the order of the argument. There are ties between chapter 4 and chapter 3, and a subtle set of references to sin and redemption in chapter 4. Romans 4:2 specifically picks up the term "boast": "For if Abraham was justified by works, he has something to boast about, but not before God" (v. 2). Paul then quotes Gen 15:6, which states that Abraham's belief was reckoned to him as righteousness. This verse is very important for Paul because it anchors his interpretation in the biblical text. Now he draws a psalm in as a textual witness: "Blessed are those whose iniquities are forgiven and whose sins are covered . . . the person against whom the Lord will not reckon his sin" (Ps 32:1–2). Note how the issue of sin and forgiveness has been fused with Abraham's justification by faith.

Paul then raises the issue of whether justification by faith only pertains to the circumcised. Paul offers two arguments in support of his contention that justification is inclusive: (a) Abraham was declared justified before he was circumcised, and (b) Abraham is promised that his descendants will inherit "the world."[20] The latter must be Gentiles as well as Jews, for the narrower reading would annul faith and promise. Abraham has been promised that he would be the father of "many nations." He clung to this promise despite the fact that he and Sarah grew too old to conceive and rear children. This is not only a story of God's miraculous fulfillment of this promise, but a promise to others as well: Righteousness "will be reckoned to us who believe in him who raised from the dead Jesus our Lord, who was put to death for our trespasses and raised for our justification" (vv. 24–25). Thus, the promise to Abraham has been integrated into the Christian kerygma. Indeed, we end with a statement of the atonement wrought by Jesus.

Romans 5:1–11 can be treated as one unit. It starts out, "since we are justified by faith . . ." The unit must be an exploration of the consequences or results of justification. While the unit may return to this starting point, it wants to go on. The first thing mentioned is "peace with God" (5:1)—at the very least, a certain security and confidence in one's relationship with God. The paragraph now reaches out toward the eschatological future: "hope of sharing the glory of God" (v. 2). This thought inspires Paul to work out a sequence of actions that arrive at hope: rejoicing in suffering, learning endurance, developing character, producing hope. Our hope is already partially fulfilled by having love

---

20. Paul has stretched the Genesis text somewhat: the word he translates "world" can mean "land," and the Genesis text promises possession of the land of Canaan; see Gen 12:7.

"poured into" our hearts by the Holy Spirit. Justification enriches a person's life by transforming experiences and relationships.

Romans 5:6–8 return to the justification of sinners. To underscore the magnitude of Christ's atonement, Paul compares it to humans offering their lives for others. It is uncommon but not unknown for a person to give his life to save a friend or family member, but it would be very rare indeed for a person to sacrifice his or her life for a stranger or enemy or ne'er-do-well. Yet, Christ's death is like the latter.

Of course, one can ask how Christ's tragic death saved anyone: that is what a doctrine of atonement is supposed to answer. All Paul says here is "we are now justified by his blood" (v. 9). This leads to a series of "much more" statements, describing the benefits of atonement: on the *Day of Judgment*, we will be saved (vv. 9, 10). Justification is the state we now exist in, but there is a decision to be made at the eschatological judgment. Since God has reestablished our status before him, we need not be anxious about what the decision will be.

Romans 5 concludes with a contrast of the effects of "Adam's disobedience" to those of "Christ's obedience." Since this material is about effects, it ties in with 5:1–11 tolerably well. However, it doesn't extend the argument of Rom 1:18—5:11. It is a rhetorical unit with the purpose of inscribing Paul's teaching about sin, judgment, and death, to which Christ is the remedy, on the memory. It does this by employing a schematic image: one man plunges the human race into sin, which is given a death sentence, and a second man reverses the effects of the first man's actions. Of course, this symmetrical scheme is highly abstract and cryptic, but it does provide the audience with "hangers" for the concepts introduced in previous chapters.

Paul ascribes the basic ills plaguing all humans to "Adam," the first human: "sin came into the world through one man and death through sin, and so death spread to all men because all men sinned" (5:12, RSV). There are several matters here to reflect on. Paul may not mean that the first man caused sin; rather, he "brought it into" the world. Not that it was someplace else. Perhaps it was like the tobacco plant discovered to have pleasing properties when dried and chewed or smoked. Once the plant was discovered, its use spread to others. Of course, sin is more fundamental than an addictive habit, but the latter may be a useful analogy.

How was death brought in through sin? This sounds like a particular reading of Genesis 3. After the couple has been convicted of violating God's prohibition, God forces them out of Eden so they have no access to the tree of life. Although humans were not immortal before the fall, this story implies that they had access to a tree whose fruit would sustain life forever. Banishment from Eden was also, in a way of speaking, a death sentence. I think that many contemporary readers would reinterpret this along the following lines: humans became conscious of death, and began to fear it, as a result of the fall into accountability and self-consciousness.

Why does Paul ignore Eve? Obviously, it would upset his one man–another man symmetry. Adam has become an abstraction, an everyman with no historical or social location, not even a gender. He is an abstract representation of humanity as it exists in itself, apart from family, community, and the like. This representation is not born into sin because he is not born into the collective connections all subsequent humans have. Other humans sin but do not start innocent. Paul does not have Augustine's idea of biological transmission, but he does assume that all other humans enter the world with a proclivity to sin.[21]

Twice in Romans 5 Paul refers to law—probably Mosaic—as an intruder like sin and death: "sin was indeed in the world before law was given, but sin is not counted where there is no law" (v. 13). In v. 20, he says "law came in, to increase the trespass." It almost sounds like humans were not accountable until Israel was given the law. However, Gentiles would, according to that reckoning, never be accountable. Yet Paul had explained in Romans 2 that Gentiles are indeed accountable, that there is a law written on their hearts. Moreover, in Genesis 4 Cain is held to account for fratricide, and Noachic law is instituted as a common human law a bit later.

In any case, Christ is the remedy for the ills unleashed on the human race by Adam. The "begracement" (*charisma*) is different from the originating sin: "For the judgment following one trespass brought condemnation, but the 'begracement' following many trespasses brings a 'verdict of acquittal'" (v. 16).[22] What act of Christ brought humans acquittal? In 5:18–19, Christ's act is designated one of "righteousness" and then in the parallel sentence, "obedience." Christ is the reverse in every way of Adam. Just as Adam brought sin into the

---

21. According to Keck, *Romans*, 149, "it is important to note some other things that Paul does not say. Not a word is said about the origin of sin, nor about either the serpent or Satan, nor about any other detail in the Genesis story. What matters to him is *that* sin and death are intruders."

22. Ibid., 152–53.

world by disobeying the divine prohibition, Christ communicated righteousness to "many" or all[23] by "obeying" God unto death.

Just as Adam is an abstraction, so is Christ in this symmetrical schema. Virtually nothing is said of the historical Jesus in this passage. Nothing is said either about the action of God in Israel's history that led up to Christ's atonement. Christ is something of cipher here. His actions have an effect on the human condition without reference to the faith of the recipient of his saving grace. The chapter has attained its memorability by simplification, and should not be pressed. Theologians should watch over the church's proclamation to make sure this oversimplification is not promulgated mindlessly.

## Atonement and Christology

Chapters 3 and 5 articulate a doctrine of atonement, or at least offer some metaphors to explain the meaning of Jesus's suffering and execution. The Old Testament precedent for such a teaching is Isaiah 53. Now it is time to consider a thesis by the New Testament theologian, O. Hofius. The thesis of Hofius's essay, "The Fourth Servant Song in the New Testament Letters,"[24] is that the teaching of Isaiah 53 is theologically unacceptable, but it is reinterpreted in the New Testament epistles in a theologically legitimate, profound way. Let's begin with his exegesis of Isaiah 53, and then show how Paul reinterprets the Song in the framework of an incarnational Christology.

On Hofius's reading, the servant of Isaiah 53 suffers in place of the speakers (we, us), sinners who deserve to suffer. This is the idea of substitutionary atonement: a victim suffers the punishment due wrongdoers. Hofius terms this vicarious suffering "exclusive place-taking." When the substitution takes place, the guilty party no longer undergoes what he deserves; the substitute does instead. The idea is stated quite explicitly in the "we" sections, Isa 53:4–6; and reiterated by YHWH in 53:11–12. "To bear sin" is to suffer the penal consequences for said sin. The sinner should suffer these consequences (cp. Lev 5:17; 7:18; 17:16, and the like), but YHWH transfers the punishment from the guilty to the innocent person. Why? In order to save the guilty without letting sin go unpunished. This creates a "legal fiction": the guilty is treated as though innocent. The system of justice is saved by this fiction, allowing for reconciliation with God and the restoration of *shalom*.

---

23. Ibid., 173–75.
24. Hofius, "The Fourth Servant Song," 163–88.

Hofius finds this idea outrageous. It contradicts the affirmation that the wicked will suffer their just consequences, e.g. in Exod 32:30–34; Ezek 18:20. The fault is, Hofius believes, conceiving of guilt like a debt.[25] One person can pay another's debt, but sin should be understood as deeper and unexchangeable. In other words, Isaiah 53 awaits a deeper understanding of sin, one that comes to expression in Psalm 51. In Hofius's words, "sin reaches rather into the *center of the* person."[26] While sin is not a part of our nature, it "completely dominates and conditions humanity . . . [and] requires a 'cleansing' from sin through the miracle of a complete new creation."[27] The redemption must remedy our propensity to sin—change us back into the creatures we were intended to be.

The New Testament, according to Hofius, replaces "exclusive place-taking" with what he calls "inclusive place-taking."[28] This latter is not substitution, but encompasses sinners as persons and affects their very being. There are four elements in this form of place-taking:

(1) Jesus Christ is God interceding for sinners: God steps over to our side while remaining qualitatively different.

(2) Jesus's place-taking is the purpose for coming over to our side; that is, his vicarious death for sinners is the meaning and goal of his coming into the world.

(3) The relation of Son and Father differs from the Lord and his servant in Isaiah 53 (and other three songs).

(4) Instead of penal suffering, Christ's death is "sanctifying atonement" (H. Gese); that is, Christ becomes one with the sinner (so 2 Cor 5:21, Gal 3:13).[29]

The fundamental point, according to Hofius, is that only God the Creator is able to free sinners from their sin. Isaiah 53, on the other hand, accords saving power to the servant's suffering—though God actually transfers the servant's meritorious suffering to others.

---

25. Note the book titled *Sin*, by Gary Anderson.

26. Anderson, *Sin*, 171.

27. See ibid.

28. See Bailey, "Concepts of *Stellvertretung* in the Interpretation of Isaiah 53," 223–50; and Bailey, "The Suffering Servant," 251–59.

29. Hofius, "The Fourth Servant Song," 173–75.

Hofius has projected onto Isaiah 53 a concept of substitution that is regarded in many circles as the orthodox doctrine. In theological history, this idea of the transfer of punishment from sinner to Christ has been associated with Anselm of Canterbury.[30] Hofius, following Immanuel Kant, finds this kind of atonement doctrine logically false and morally offensive. Guilt cannot be transferred from one person to another as if it were a monetary debt.

There are other ways to construe Isaiah 53, but our task here is understand Paul's idea of Christ's atonement. Perhaps Hofius is right that the New Testament "corrects" the substitutionary idea of atonement. The incarnation is the key: In Christ, God shares our death (for sin) with us and empowers us to live a new, redeemed life by his resurrection. Hofius calls this "inclusive place-taking"—an event that is shared; the sinner still must pass through judgment (death) to destroy the power of sin and be given a supernatural power to continue to live despite dying.[31]

Human analogies to Christ's suffering (e.g., Rom 5:7)[32] do not have the constitutive character of the crucifixion of the Son of God. When a righteous person dies a vicarious death, it has a limited scope of effects.[33] Jesus's death has an expiatory effect for past sins and justifies God's mercy toward sinners, but it also becomes a redeeming power in the life of believers, as we will discover in Romans 6. I am arguing that we can identify the redeeming effect of judgment, I have argued throughout this work, with Paul's "dying with Christ."

Another dimension of the uniqueness of Christ's suffering comes from Hebrews and 1 Peter, e.g., "Christ suffered once for all to make atonement for sins, the righteous for the unrighteous, in order to bring you to God—he was put to death in the flesh, but made alive in the spirit" (1 Pet 3:18).[34] "For Christ did not enter a sanctuary made by humans hands, a mere copy of the true one, but he entered into heaven itself, now to appear in the presence of God on our behalf. Nor was it to offer himself again and again, as the high priest enters the Holy Place year after year with blood that is not his own; for then he would

---

30. Though in fact the church universal has never come to a definitive teaching on the meaning of the cross.

31. Hofius, "The Fourth Servant Song," 163–88.

32. Rom 5:7 compares Jesus's death on the cross to the vicarious death of others: "Why, one will hardly die for a righteous man—though perhaps for a good man one will dare even to die."

33. Moreover, there is no continuing existence for the victim, as there seems to be in the Servant Song (viz., 52:13–15, 53:10–12). King and Gandhi live on only as a memory and inspiration.

34. In Hofius, "The Fourth Servant Song," 187.

have had to suffer again and again since the foundation of the world. But as it is, he has appeared once for all at the end of the age to remove sin by the sacrifice of himself" (Heb 9:24–26).

Only an event in which God is both subject and object, the One who destines and the One who is destined, can give an event a once-for-all character.

## Justification and Sanctification

Romans chapters 6–8 explain how faith in the righteousness of God communicated by Christ accomplishes what the law, weakened by the flesh, cannot do. Chapter 6 sets forth two analogies to show that it would be contradictory for a believer in Christ to fall back into sin. Law has no role in the sanctification of the Christian, who is no longer obligated to it. The law expresses God's will, but it actually arouses sinful desires rather than dampening them. The "law of the Spirit of life in Christ Jesus" frees a person from the inclination toward sin (8:2).

Paul adopts a diatribe style in chapter 6. An objection is formulated in question form, then answered. Objections are cited in Rom 6:1 and 6:15. The first says it all: "Are we to continue to sin that grace may abound?" If a person holds that law is necessary to keeping sin in check, and that violation of the law should be severely sanctioned, removing law sounds like an invitation to chaos and depravity. Since Paul has indeed taken obedience to law off the table, so to speak, he must show his interrogator that faith does the job. He answers the question with a question: "How can we who have died to sin still live in it?" Note how Paul has shifted to the first person: he now is speaking as a believer who has been baptized and transformed, and is led by God. But why does he say we have "died to sin"? He says that the ritual of baptism represents our death, or dying with Christ. This is obviously metaphorical. Yet Paul does expect us to undergo such a change in identity that our continued life has Christ acting through us.

Although Paul describes the believer as having died to sin, he knows that temptation has not disappeared. Hence the need to exhort his addresses: "Do not yield your members to sin as instruments of wickedness, but yield yourselves to God as people who have been brought from death to life" (6:13, RSV).

Romans 6:15–23 repeats 6:1–14 under another metaphor: slavery or servanthood. According to Paul, the liberal ideal of a free, rational decision maker is an abstraction. In fact, humans are slaves to sin, and sin leads to death. The best example of slavery to sin is an addiction. Something has to intervene to break the addiction, and one must submit to a discipline. "Thanks be to God that you who were once slaves of sin have become obedient from the heart to the standard of teaching to which you were committed, and having been set free from sin, have become slaves of righteousness" (vv. 17–18). Being delivered from enslavement, the addressees "become slaves [or, better, servants] of God, [and] your return is sanctification and its end, eternal life" (v. 22).[35] Just as sin drags one toward death, sanctification prepares one for eternal life.

Paul's argument returns to this contention in Rom 8:1–8. Romans 8:3–4 (RSV) reiterates the thesis of chapter 6: "For God has done what the law, weakened by the flesh, could not do: sending his own Son in the likeness of sinful flesh and for sin, he condemned sin in the flesh, in order that the just requirement of the law might be fulfilled in us." Paul has now introduced the divine law as the standard that we should meet; chapter 7 brings it into the equation. We will survey that chapter presently. Here we should note Paul's polarity of flesh and spirit/Spirit. He defines these terms further in vv. 5–8. For Paul, "flesh" harbors the rebellious impulse in humans. One might think of the sexual desires arising in the flesh, but Paul has a broader spectrum of desire. Indeed, we might define "flesh" as the source of desire, and as a source of sin when it is bent on satisfying these desires. In this section, "spirit" is the Spirit of God or of Christ. If I read correctly, the power of Spirit is, above all, the power of resurrection. Since sin is the power of death, the Spirit rescues the person from sin as well as death.

## Romans 7

The chapter begins with an explanation of why divine law plays no role in sanctification. Evidently Paul wants to set out his concept of sanctification without the confusion of the debate over law. He does, though, link law and sin closely in Rom 6:15. Romans 7:1–6 draws a rather far-fetched allegory, but the point is clear and striking. With Christ's death, divine law has no further claim on Christ or on those who have died with Christ. "Now we are discharged from the Law, dead to that which held us captive, so that we can serve not under the old written code, but in the new life of the Spirit" (7:6). For Paul, who had to fight a conservative movement in the church to circumcise Gentile men in Galatia and perhaps elsewhere (see Phil 3:2–3), there is no "third use of the law."

---

35. There is an echo of "yoke of the law" in the slave image.

Having disposed of the claim of the law on Christians, Paul now answers the objection that he has equated law with sin. That surmise is actually not too far fetched. The law does represent God's will: it is good. But its role in ambiguous: it teaches us the actions that are approved and disapproved by God, but it also arouses the desire to do what is forbidden. Of course, we usually suppress the desire to do what is forbidden, but we sometimes succumb and must regularly battle sinful desire. The flesh has subtle ways of gaining satisfaction.

Paul's example was well chosen: "You shall not covet" (v. 7). This is the only one of the Ten Commandments that prohibits an attitude or inclination. One has much less control of desire than of our actions. The more we try to suppress desire, the more it wells up in us.

Paul is also well instructed when he chooses to write in the first-person singular. He avoids a self-righteous tone by doing so. The audience is expected to plug themselves into Paul's description.

The incapacity of law to overcome sinful desire is why it fails as an instrument of salvation. The commandment can restrain, but it cannot redeem. According to Paul, redemption can only happen by dying to sin, with Christ, and living in the divine Spirit, which communicates the power of the risen Christ.

## The Role of Law

It is worth reflecting on the role of law in the saving action of God. For Paul, law means the Torah revealed through Moses, preserved in the written Scripture and the oral tradition of interpretation.[36] Common human law, the law written on the heart, is not a substitute for revealed law—or if it is a substitute, it is a deficient one. Whatever is true of this common human law, it is filtered through sin. Gentiles do not even know the meaning of idolatry, and that is the root of their perversion of the laws, which they recognize as God's decrees (Rom 1:32).

Mosaic law is not manmade, it is divine in origin, therefore "holy and just and good" (7:12). Any perversion or misapplication of the law is due to the sinfulness of the interpreters. In other words, Paul probably accords Mosaic law greater justice and goodness than modern interpreters would. The shortcoming of the law resides elsewhere.

In the history of the church, many branches have not followed Paul in restricting the role of law to identifying and exposing sin. The Reformed tradi-

---

36. I interpret Paul as a Pharisee as regards the law.

tion spoke of the "third use of the law," the use of the law to guide the like of the redeemed community. Actually, church teachers have learned all too well that the believing community is *not* the redeemed community. Rather, at best it is a community on the road toward redemption. It needs the discipline of the law. If the community has been transformed by the Spirit, we should be preserved from misusing law, whether by arousing desire or by falling into legalism and literalism and the like.

Moreover, the divine law is a depository of theological and spiritual and ethical revelation. The Gentiles need the Old Testament to keep them from returning to their idolatry and polytheism. Likewise in whatever era, the church cannot rely on the inspirations of the Spirit apart from the revealed commandments; these inspirations are often the spirit of the age. The task of interpretation and reflection on application must guide the church.

Yet we are not to favor ritual circumcision and yoking ourselves to the law. With Augustine, we can recognize and reform the Gentile legal systems.[37] The divine law should never be imposed on civil societies or on the church; no, it should be used heuristically in the reform of the laws of our society and the moral and religious teaching of the church.

## Summary of Exposition of Romans 6–8.

Let's begin at what I take to be the goal of Paul's argument in Romans 6–8. The goal is stated succinctly in 8:3–4 (RSV): "For God has done what the law, weakened by the flesh, could not do: by sending his own Son in the likeness of sinful flesh, he condemned sin in the flesh, so that the just requirement of the law might be fulfilled in us, who walk not according to the flesh but according to the Spirit."

This statement needs to be unpacked at bit. The law should be fulfilled; it makes just demands on us. We, however, are unable to fulfill its demands as long as we rely on "the flesh"—ourselves and the world we are a part of. Christ has been sent to exercise judgment on all of us, inasmuch as we are sinners. Judgment has another side, that of liberation. By sending the Spirit, Christ facilitates our fulfillment of the law.

It is actually unusual to hear of Christ passing judgment in Paul. The cross is interpreted in sacrificial terms, and that hardly elicits the idea of condemning sin in the flesh. What does this mean, and how is it effected? Perhaps Paul means that the believer participates in Christ's death, which is simultane-

---

37. Augustine, *City of God*, 19.17.

ously death to sin. We still need a model of atonement that gives Jesus victory over sin and death.

Romans 7:7–25 sets forth the idea that the law cannot redeem us because we are enslaved to sin. Sin, according to those verses, arouses the desire to do what the law forbids. Coveting is Paul's example of what the law forbids but what we are aroused to do. We can all agree, Paul would argue, that coveting what belongs to others is wrong, and we may well end up acting on our desire. "I delight in the law of God in my inmost self, but I see in my members another law at war with the law of my mind, making me a captive to sin which dwells in my members" (7:22–23, RSV).

This line of reasoning hardly accounts for all sin; what it does is show how the law—yes, divine law—fails to master the sinful inclinations of the will. If there is to be redemption, it must come from elsewhere. The self must die to sin; the driving force of our wills must be replaced. This line of reasoning echoes Jeremiah's in the New Covenant passage of chapter 31:31–34 and Ezekiel in 36:26.

How does Paul articulate the reformation of the human will? Chapter 6 does so. The chapter begins with an implied allegation that replacing works of law with faith in Christ will simply unleash the human will to whatever impulses come one's way. Paul, of course, denies this allegation and interprets his counterclaim with a discussion of what happens in baptism. The rite has, for him, metaphysical import: the believer is "buried . . . with [Christ] by baptism into death, so that, just as Christ was raised from the dead by the glory of the Father, so we too might walk in newness of life" (6:4, RSV).

The death we share with Christ overcomes our bondage to sin: "our old self was crucified with him so that the body of sin might be destroyed, and we might no longer be enslaved to sin" (6:6). "So you also must consider yourselves dead to sin and alive to God in Christ Jesus" (6:11).

Such language may seem exorbitant; it is the sort of thing religious people say in liturgy and contradict in their daily living. Well, Paul knows that he must urge his audience to practice what they purpose to believe (6:12–14).[38]

After the analogy of "dying and rising with Christ" (baptism), the second analogy he offers to explain sanctification is slavery (6:15–23). In this passage, death is classified as the punishment for sin. It is not considered a means for redeeming the sinner.

---

38. The rest of chapter 8 moves beyond sin and judgment to the life in the Spirit in the hope of the return of Christ and unconditional salvation.

## Jews and Gentiles in the Plan of God

Romans 9–11 are driven by the question, why have the Jews rejected their messiah? Paul allows this question to surface in a highly personal expression of feeling. "I have great sorrow and unceasing anguish in my heart" that "my brothers [and sisters], my kinsmen by race," have not believed that Jesus is the long-awaited messiah (9:2). After all, the messiah had to come from this people, who are God's elect, and the beneficiary of revelation throughout their history, and it would be incomprehensible for the Jewish people to reject their savior. Yet, that is the Christian claim. One could well take Jesus's rejection by his people as evidence that Jesus is not their messiah.

Paul formulates the challenge in a way that allows for a successful Christian answer: "It is not as though the word of God has failed" (9:6). Jesus has fulfilled the divine promises of the Old Testament for his Jewish followers. A look at biblical history shows that often God chooses some person or group and rejects another. Those who have accepted Jesus are a "remnant," the faithful among the stiff-necked people. Paul proposes this line of thinking in Rom 11:1–6.

In Rom 9:6–24, Paul seeks to show that God's power is manifested in the election of some and rejection and "hardening" of others (v. 18). Paul is operating with a predestinarian scheme: the power to believe is a gift of God, and the resistance to God's revelation is an act of God hardening the human heart. Paul realizes that this divine determinism makes human accountability problematic. He seeks to silence the objection by questioning the standing of the questioner: "who are you, a human, to answer back to God?" (9:20). After all, the pot can't object to the potter's decision to make it to serve a menial task.

This argument, though influential in Christian theology, does not really get Paul very far. He wants to argue that the positive reception of many Gentiles proves the truth of the Christian kerygma despite its poor reception by Jews. God must have understood this all along. Paul finds evidence of the divine plan to include Gentiles in the prophecies of Hosea (9:27–29). We can now see that paradoxically: "the Gentiles who did not pursue righteousness have attained it, that is, righteousness through faith; but that Israel who pursued the righteousness based on law did not succeed in fulfilling that law" (vv. 30–31, RSV). Evidently, Paul is equating rejecting Jesus as Christ as failure to fulfill the law. The Old Testament prophets particularly Isaiah, testifies to the lack of faith among the people of God (Rom 9:33).

Paul has a unique explanation for the resistance of Jews to Jesus's claim to be messiah: they are so bent on pleasing God by their obedience to God that they have no need or desire for the free gift of righteousness. Here is Paul's formulation: "being ignorant of the righteousness that comes from God, and seeking to establish their own, they do not submit to the righteousness of God" (10:3, RSV). This is known by the revelation in Christ: "For Christ is the end of the law, that everyone who has faith may be justified" (v. 4, RSV).

Of course, in the first decades of Christianity, many Jews simply had not heard of Jesus's teaching, crucifixion, and resurrection. Thus, it was imperative that the church send out preachers. Nevertheless, Paul seems to have realized that the vast majority of the Jewish people would not convert. He quotes several Old Testament passages to the effect that they have "heard" but refused to listen. Why he thinks passages condemning previous generations are still applicable is hard to say; perhaps he first realized that Jews were predisposed to reject the messianic claims of Jesus, and then discovered the passages to interpret it.

At the beginning of chapter 11, Paul returns to where he started, but now the issue is whether the Jewish rejection of Jesus as Christ is irreversible. Paul could have simply stopped in 11:5 (RSV): "So too at the present time there is a remnant, chosen by grace." A remnant—Jews who have accepted Jesus as their messiah—is all that is necessary to validate the Christian kerygma.

However, Paul is not satisfied with the abandonment of a majority of the Jews. While Israel has failed "to obtain what it sought," it had not "stumbled so as to fall" (vv. 7, 11, RSV). The Jews have not, that is, lost God's favor—have not been "unchosen," so to speak. God aroused resistance to the Christian gospel among the Jews in order to redirect the church's missionary outreach to the Gentiles. In other words, Jewish rejection of God's gracious gift allows Gentiles to receive it. The invited guests made excuses so that the poor and needy, whoever was on the streets and roads, could share in it (cp. Luke 14:15–24). Unlike Jesus's parable just referenced, however, the invited guests will, according to Paul, become jealous and finally take God up on his gift.

Paul comes up with the analogy of an olive tree to illuminate God's plan (11:16–21). The tree is the people of God, with the ancestors of Israel as the root and trunk. The Gentiles are being grafted into this tree. In order for them to be grafted in, branches have to be broken off, and these broken branches happen to be the Jews that have rejected Jesus's messiahship. The "wild olive" branches—the Gentiles—should not boast, but bear fruit lest they be broken off. The limbs that were broken off can be grafted back at the right time.

The horticultural practices described by Paul may deviate from actual practice, but analogies are not meant to be exact. The image affirms the continuity of God's plan throughout history. It is still the same tree that is being nurtured; the grafting simply includes new strains of olive on the one true. The unsatisfactory behavior of the native limbs has occasioned this.

Now Paul returns to the hardening of the Jews. God is behind this hardening because it has meant a lively, successful mission to Gentiles. Israel will continue to be hardened "until the full number of the Gentiles comes in" (11:25). Paul is still operating with his predestinarian scheme. In any case, the Jews will not be left "outside" forever, they are God's chosen people, and that is unconditional. They have been "consigned . . . to disobedience" (v. 32) now so that mercy will be offered the Gentiles, but then the Jews will be converted. "For God has consigned all humans to disobedience, that he may have mercy on all" (v. 32). This resolution of the division of the human community evokes a shout of praise for the "depth of the riches and wisdom and knowledge of God" (v. 33, RSV).

We can in conclusion say that Paul's interpretation of the Christian kerygma holds out the prospect of universal salvation. This is not salvation of each and every human but of collective bodies of humans. Jews will not be saved while Gentiles remain outside, and Gentile Christians will not be saved while non-Christian Jews are left out. Paul's is not a modern liberal doctrine that regards all religions as equal and all humans as good, but he does work out an inclusive, Christ-centered eschatological resolution.

## Reflections on Romans 9–11

Paul returns in these last three chapters of the letter's body to Jew and Gentile. I say "returns" because his argument in Rom 1:18—3:31 sought to prove that Gentiles and Jews will be in the same situation before God the Judge at the Final Judgment. Neither Jew nor Gentile can avoid a judgment of guilty unless they appeal to faith in Jesus Christ.

Only now do we realize that Paul's discussion of Gentile and Jew is insufficient; it had only to do with individual members of collectivities. Paul feels the need to confront the collective division of humanity into Jew and Gentile itself. This division has been created by God—by the election of the people of Israel as God's unique possession. Now we need to understand how God can be the same for Gentiles.

Paul is actually forced to deal with this question because the vast majority of his people have rejected Jesus as the Messiah promised them. This fact produces a contradiction. The Jews are God's elect: the recipients of the revelation of the one true God, the people who have been promised a Messiah (see Rom 9:1–5). If Jesus is not accepted as Messiah by the people to whom he was promised, it raises the question whether he is the Messiah in truth. If he is, have God's saving purposes been thwarted by the hardness of the Jewish heart?

Paul won't even discuss Jesus's messianic qualifications, so the issue must be the power of God: "It is not as though the word of God had failed" (9:6). He must now explain how God's purpose is succeeding when most Jews are not accepting their Messiah. His solution is to take recourse to remnant theology: God chooses a few to be his true people and rejects the rest. Paul is justifying the unstated proposition that only the Jews who have accepted Christ now represent the true Israel.

Paul's defense of this position requires him to adopt a harsh version of predestination. God not only intervenes to convert some to Christ, but he intervenes to harden the hearts of others so that they cannot accept his offer of grace. Nothing happens in heaven or on earth without God's deliberate ordination of it.

God's predestination, in Paul's scheme, does not take place above our heads, so to speak. Rather, it is our predispositions and decisions that destine us. In 10:2–3, Paul attributes the Jews' rejection of Jesus to their desire to establish their righteousness on their own. "For, being ignorant of the righteousness that comes from God, and seeking to establish their own, they have not submitted to God's righteousness" (10:3, RSV).

Of course, if it is simple ignorance, that can be corrected by education. Paul does discuss the need for bearers of the word (10:14–17). However, he immediately admits that a mission to Jews will continue to prove largely futile. The Jews already know all that they need to know in order to be held responsible for their decision (10:18–21). One suspects that Paul has had his proclamation rejected and disputed by a sufficient number of his brethren to know how such a mission will fare.

So Paul is back to remnant theology (11:1–6). But he is dissatisfied; it results in the abandonment of a vast majority of Jews to perdition. He is sure that God would not give up on them. Indeed, he goes so far as to say in 11:29 (RSV), "the gifts and the call of God are irrevocable."

If Paul looks back over the biblical story, he will discover that Israel repeatedly stumbles, but gets up, or rather is helped up by God. That story must have been in Paul's mind, because he decides that the same thing is happening in the present: "Have they stumbled so as to fall? By no means!" (11:11, RSV). Actually, the image might work better if Paul had said that the Jews fell but had not hurt themselves so badly that they could not get up.

Well, in any case, Paul sees their stumbling as serving God's purpose: Christian missionaries have directed their efforts to Gentiles, who are receptive to their message. The Jewish rejection of Jesus is due to God's hardening, as Paul says in chapter 9, but it is a *temporary* hardening.

It is God's purpose to bring in the Gentiles in great numbers, and that should arouse jealousy among the Jews and they will convert. His reasoning climaxes in this paradoxical statement: "Just as you [Gentile Christians] were once disobedient to God but now have received mercy because of their disobedience, so they have now been disobedient in order that by the mercy shown to you, they too may receive mercy. For God has imprisoned all in disobedience so that he may be merciful to all" (11:30–32). We have here a grand reconciliation of collectivities, the collectivities that really count for Jews: Jew and Gentiles. One is reminded of the passages in Isaiah, *viz.*, 19:18–25 and 45:20–25, which speak of the incorporation of the Gentiles qua Gentiles into the people of God. For Paul, the culmination of history must entail reconciliation at a collective as well as an individual level.

An essential element in this reconciliation is the "grafting" of Gentiles into the people of God (11:17). The people of God are the descendants of the patriarchs. Until Christ, these were "natural" descendants of Abraham (v. 21), but now there are adopted descendants as well; that is, those who share the faith of Abraham. To put it another way, the people of God is an olive tree that has had new shoots grafted in.

# 25

# Final Judgment and Redemption

WILLIAM SHAKESPEARE HAD A penchant for making allusions to the Last Judgment at the end of his tragedies. When King Lear, for example, bears the dead body of his daughter Cordelia on stage and cries out,

> Howl, howl, howl! O, you are men of stones
> Had I your tongues and eyes, I'd use them so
> That heaven's vault would crack. She's gone forever,

Kent says, "Is this the promised end?" and Edgar seconds him, "Or image of that horror?" (5.3). Later in the same scene Albany promises that his rule will rectify the wrongs of the previous regime: "All friends shall taste the wages of their virtue, and all foes the cup of their deservings."

I find this to be a subtle theological framing of the denouements of history. The conclusion of a great tragedy has such weight and portent that the Final Judgment comes near. On the one hand, the Final Judgment is the measure, so to speak, of each judgment within history. On the other hand, the need for a Final Judgment arises from the incompleteness and distortions of the judgments of history.

We are bringing our study of redeeming judgment to a close. Our objective here is to explore the *doctrine* of divine judgment. We will attempt to abstract a conceptual scheme from the passages we have studied. These passages were embedded in historical particulars. The objective of theological reflection is to free the conceptual content from its temporal determinations.

First, we will review the textual studies for salient features of divine judgment. This is the first step in the abstraction process. Then we will examine the treatment of judgment in a major voice in twentieth-century Protestant theology: Jürgen Moltmann. We find his most systematic treatment of judgment in a chapter on the Last Judgment. The Last Judgment is a proper home for the abstractions we have been discovering in biblical passages as long as we remember that the Last Judgment is an extension of the divine judgments in history.

## Review

We have been putting together the exegetical findings for constructing the doctrine of divine judgment. It has been relatively easy to identify the depictions of transactions that can be classified as divine judgment. Humans act against the good of their communities and the will of God, and God declares his verdict for their behavior; punishment follows. These transactions are not between the perpetrator or perpetrators and God alone, but normally involve other humans.

Judicial process has the primary purpose of restoring right order after a breach. The punishment is usually retribution of some sort. It may also be to stop a wrongdoer from continuing to harm others. It may also be to discourage repetition by others. Deuteronomy has several formulae that articulate the purposes of judicial actions: "So you shall purge the evil from the midst of you" (Deut 13:5, etc.). The guilty person shall be removed in order to restore health to the body politic. Moreover, eliminating the evildoer removes the black mark from the nation's record, so to speak. "And all Israel shall hear, and fear, and never again do any such wickedness as this among you" (Deut 13:11). Deterrence was a desire of ancient as well as modern societies.

What is true of the judicial system is also true of God's own judgment. The commandments of the Book of the Covenant (21:2—23:33) not to wrong sojourners, widows and orphans are backed up by the following warning: "If you do afflict them, and they cry out to me, I will surely hear their cry, and my wrath will burn, and I will kill you with the sword, and your wives shall become widows and your children fatherless" (Exod 22:23–24, RSV). The poetic justice entailed in this sentence re-enforces its logic.

Divine judgment is also meant to straighten out the violator of God's law. The wrongdoer should recognize the evil of the deed, feel sorry for doing it, repent of such behavior, and allow God to lead into right paths. Judgment of a community or nation may also purge it of its evildoers and shatter the patterns of oppression and injustice. God never judges solely to recompense the wickedness of the nation, but rather he judges in order to steer it away from its perverse ways: "Have I any pleasure in the death of the wicked, says the Lord God, and not rather that [they] should turn from (their) way and live?" (Ezek 18:23).

*Judgment Prompting God's Adjustment*

We were able to trace a theme of divine judgment through the Old Testament and into the New. Every judgment, it seems, prompted an adjustment on God's part so as to avoid a repetition. After the great flood, for example, God renounces any further annihilation of the human race. From now on, he will put up with the evil that pervades human society and plagues the human heart; humans are to police themselves with a judicial system, and God will intervene when the human judicial system and government break down.

Israel is different from the other nations. It has been chosen to be a mediator of divine blessing to other nations. It is given a special law, as a part of a covenant, which requires individual and collective obedience. "I have chosen [Abraham] that he may charge his children and his household after him to keep the way of the Lord by doing righteousness and justice" (Gen 18:19, RSV). "If you will obey my voice and keep my covenant, you shall be my own special possession among all peoples" (Exod 19:5, RSV).

With its special calling, Israel becomes vulnerable to a level of scrutiny above all other nations. On the one hand, she owes obligations to YHWH that no other people owe their deity or deities: the relationship is to be exclusive, so recognition or worship of other gods is strictly forbidden as is the worship of images (of any other deity or creature). Moreover, violations of morality and equal justice are added to criminal law. Both individuals and the people as a whole are held accountable to Mosaic law.

No sooner have the people been given the Ten Commandments and the Book of the Covenant than they break the first and second commandments egregiously with the construction of the golden calf. This action calls for divine judgment, but not annihilation: Moses intercedes for his people and procures a less severe penalty. The covenant is reestablished with new provisions for avoiding national judgment. Nevertheless, the people do arouse the Lord's wrath again, during the trek through the wilderness, resulting in a delay of the conquest of Canaan and settlement for a generation. During the conquest several events could have resulted in divine judgment of the people but were resolved short of that. Wars of conquest could have been envisaged as divine judgment on the previous inhabitants but were not. Israel itself experiences various crises during the period chronicled in the book of Judges, which could have become divine judgment; but these events are reduced to the status of corrective measures.

The establishment of the monarchy changes the equation. From now on, divine judgment will be focused on the behavior of kings. The three kings of the united monarchy (Saul, David, and Solomon) are subjected to prophetic judgment, as are most of the kings of the northern kingdom, Israel, in the divided monarchy that follows Solomon's reign. In these events the people both suffer as subjects whose rulers had aroused the divine wrath, and benefit from the removal of an unjust or apostate ruler.

By the middle of the eighth century BCE, judgment can no longer be limited to rulers. With Amos, Hosea, Micah, and Isaiah we have collective judgments of Israel and Judah. The prophets are commissioned to announce God's decision against their addressees. Each prophet's task was to discover the reasons for God's decisions; the reasons are formulated as accusations. Since the trial has already taken place in the mind of God, the prophet's rhetorical task is to persuade the people of their guilt deserving a harsh punishment. All the prophetic books announce salvation as well, usually as a prospect for the time after judgment.

Since the southern kingdom of Judah survived the incursions of Assyria, which had wiped out the northern kingdom of Israel, the prophets Jeremiah and Ezekiel have the task of reviving the message of judgment at the outset of the Neo-Babylonian empire's rise. They essentially repeat the accusations of the eighth-century prophets, but now must penetrate the indifference or denial of their compatriots. The preaching of these two prophets provides the basis for the people's survival with their identity in tact.

The people beaten down by Assyria and Babylon and taken into exile have plenty to say to YHWH. We have a string of communal laments that accuse YHWH of betrayal and indifference. The laments are the human side of the divine-human dialogue. Various prophets compose laments as well, and formulate God's negative or positive answer. Ultimately, all the prophetic books have oracles promising restoration and new life, some such a qualitatively different life that we can call them "eschatological" promises.

Final Judgment and Redemption

## Judgment Intended for Transformation

The argument of the second part is that divine judgment is intended to transform those who undergo it. That is to say, judgment is not restricted to retribution but seeks to reform those who suffer from it. It can become mere retribution if those who are subjected to it refuse to acknowledge their guilt, lacking all remorse and sympathy. Repentance is required for transformation.

Those who do take God's judgment to heart are malleable. When we speak of redemption, we mean the state of compunction that renders one malleable by the Spirit of God. This malleability has been called "sanctification" in the theological tradition. The end toward which this action moves is described by Jeremiah in 31:33: "I will put my law within them, and I will write it upon their hearts; and I will be their God and they shall be my people" (RSV).

We followed this action through a sequence of stages in the book of Isaiah. Isaiah of Jerusalem is commissioned by YHWH to deliver a message of judgment. The Lord does not tell Isaiah what the people is guilty of, only that they would reject the truth of what he says. Nothing is said of redemption. Isaiah discovers and seeks to convince his contemporaries of what they are guilty of and would suffer for. There is little hope of escaping punishment. However, Isaiah sees judgment purifying and converting his sinful countrymen. In other words, judgment will redeem the people and make them capable of receiving salvation. The book of Isaiah, chapters 1–39, have been designed to communicate Isaiah's message of redemptive judgment to all future readers.

The prophet who speaks in chapters 40–55, a figure we have named the Babylonian Isaiah, is commissioned to announce the end of Babylonian exile and the beginning of a new era of salvation. This message is the sequel to Isaiah 1–39. The divine judgment proclaimed by Isaiah of Jerusalem has run its course; now his message of redemption and salvation are being fulfilled. The exiles are not allowed to forget that they are in exile as a result of YHWH's judgment; only if they take this to heart can they accept the new message and put their hope in God's saving action.

The scope of this prophet's message is extraordinary. The exiles will participate in a new exodus, which will convey them back to Zion, where they will rebuild the city and the temple, and enjoy eternal salvation. Never again will the people of YHWH be subjected to judgment. The nations will see the salvation of Israel and abandon their idols for the true God and will join his people.

We must also speak of the mystery figure, the servant of the Lord, woven into the message of these chapters. He plays a role analogous to the messiah of

First Isaiah, but actually coalesces with the prophet himself. The servant ends up suffering vicariously for others.

The agent of YHWH, Cyrus of Persia, takes sovereignty over the Near East and grants exiled Judeans the right to return to Palestine; among them are the disciples of the Babylonian Isaiah. The prophet or prophets who write Isaiah 56–66 are among the disciples. Their contribution to the book of Isaiah originates in the first twenty or so years following their return from Babylonian exile.

Third Isaiah emerges from the testing of the traditions of First and Second Isaiah, producing a working synthesis. The prophet of Third Isaiah, according to chapter 61, shares the calling of the master (Babylonian Isaiah); namely, to proclaim the time of salvation. A particular audience within the community—the poor, the oppressed, the slaves—is singled out for consolation. The prophet confronts the persistence of sin within the people of God. Since the master, Isaiah of Babylon, had promised that the people of God would never again be subject to judgment (chapter 54), the disciples interpreted the delay of salvation as their punishment. In the final chapters of the book of Isaiah, the society of Jerusalem is divided between the establishment and the servants of YHWH. The former face rejection, a final judgment, whereas the latter, the servants, will be adopted as the true people of God and rewarded with a new earth.

There are at least two emanations from the book of Isaiah. First, the distinctive piety of the servants begins to make its way into the broader postexilic literature. The piety involves the appropriation of the message of the prophets of judgment. It elevates contrition and humility, and profound reverence toward the Holy. In our study this spirituality has been called penitential piety. A practitioner of this piety does not rely on ritual action to establish or repair a relationship with God, but seeks to please God by his or her inwardness.

This new piety clashes with the spirit of the classical laments, which were not shy about claiming the supplicant's righteousness and even, on occasion, blamed God for betrayal or indifference. The book of Job dramatizes the clash between these two different pieties, and leaves readers with an ambiguous resolution.

Another emanation from the book of Isaiah is the doctrine of a last, final judgment at the end of history. This judgment is not immanent in the movements of history but imposes a resolution from outside. In this way, the partial and temporary judgments that occur in history are corrected and completed at the end. This Final Judgment can be something hoped for or something

## Final Judgment and Redemption

feared. The dominant mood in the Psalms is hopefulness, though there is an undercurrent of fear that none can meet God's expectations.

The Last Judgment can be called the horizon of history. The judgment promised in the last two chapters of Isaiah transcends the judgment announced by Isaiah of Jerusalem and terminated by the Babylonian Isaiah. Everything mentioned in the preceding sixty-four chapters of Isaiah belongs within the final, future horizon,[1] though many of these chapters contain an "eschatological surplus" that awaits the end for fulfillment.

Now we take up the New Testament. Many Christian readers either deny the presence of judgment in the New Testament altogether, or try to reduce it to a residue from the Old. One can even find an occasional statement in the New Testament encouraging such a distortion: "For the law was given through Moses; grace and truth came through Jesus Christ" (John 1:17).

Our first chapter devoted to the New Testament sets out to expose this distortion. The Synoptic Gospels actually preface Jesus's message with judgment preached by John the Baptist (Mark 1:6). Jesus affirms John's calling and attaches his own message to John's. Eschatological judgment is affirmed by the gospels, not repudiated. The "horizon" is now brought into the present; the end, the Day of Judgment as well as the establishment of the kingdom, is "at hand," invading the present, dawning on those who receive the message (Mark 1:14–15). One may also hear the sound of thunder (cp. John 12:27–32).

Judgment is centered on response to the message of the kingdom. The refusal to repent, to turn away from the fallen world to the new order being created by God, means abandonment to the fate of the dying world. The condemnation and crucifixion of Jesus seals the judgment of God on this world.

Yet Jesus's death is redemptive as well. It is said to have the force of a sacrifice of atonement. Various metaphors explain this impact; they have the force of God himself "bearing" the judgment for sin, either in place of or along with the guilty. This has redemptive efficacy not only for those who accept the offer of grace but also for the collectivities of which they are a part.

There remains the continuing power of sin over all humans, including believers. The cross must not only communicate forgiveness but also liberate from the power of sin. Only if the audience members take up their crosses and follow Jesus can they embark on the road toward sanctification. Following Jesus entails obedience to the "laws" of the kingdom. Thereby Jesus's proclamation converges and coalesces with the Synoptic Gospels' proclamation of Jesus as suffering Messiah.

1. Actually, Isaiah 24–27 is an early apocalypse, called the Isaiah Apocalypse.

## Redeeming Judgment

The Fourth Gospel differs substantially in its formulations, but is analogous in structure to the Synoptics. The premise of the narrative is that Jesus is the incarnate Word, the Son of God. Every narrated action involves a clash between humans and God the Son, and complexities arise from the paradox of the Eternal, Unconditional living among humans as a human. Divine judgment occurs when those who meet him reject his claim to be God, Redeemer, and Lord. He judges them by being who he is; those who reject him judge themselves.

The Son of God has been "sent" to human society to suffer crucifixion. John the Baptist identifies Jesus as Lamb of God because he will die a sacrificial death. Jesus describes himself as the Shepherd who protects his sheep. Jesus predicts that his death and resurrection will draw all humans to him. We are left with a tension between limited atonement and universal salvation.

The Apocalypse of John follows the story of Jesus beyond his earthly life. There is a "transcendent countdown" to the end, and Jesus—the Lion of Judah who is the Lamb of God—is initiating each stage. The sequence of events leading toward the end is told on two different "scrolls"—the same sequence from different perspectives. We see or hear of a series of catastrophic events caused by the removing of the seals on one scroll. These events are judgment-like but not punishment. The other scroll tells of the assault of demonic forces, which are defeated and ultimately destroyed by God. The Lamb of God does not participate in these wars but is presented in purity to assume rule in the world to come. The demonic powers are defeated by the divine word.

Perhaps the Apocalypse of John requires a rather carefully nuanced doctrine of the Trinity. The Father is the figure who confronts and ultimately undoes the demonic forces that challenge his rule. Christ seems to remain above this conflict, which means that he can assume power in the heavenly Jerusalem without a record of violence. As the Lamb of God sacrificed for sin, he embodies the purity of the world to come. Even the Father seems somewhat removed from war, for the demonic seems simply to crumble when condemned by the Father. Divine power is simply overwhelming vis-à-vis contesting powers, though the these powers are capable of flourishing for a time. The demonic seems to generate conflict between nations, classes, and the like.[2]

Romans 1–11 has the most comprehensive treatment of judgment and redemption in the New Testament. Judgment ("wrath") hangs over the whole human enterprise. Gentiles and Jews have different degrees of responsibility,

---

2. There are many inexplicable features to the Apocalypse, some of which may be of no theological consequence.

but both are in the same situation: they face divine judgment, and none can escape condemnation. The gracious God has offered a means to please him—by accepting the righteousness offered by God in Christ's death. God desires to redeem sinners, not to condemn them. However, sinners must acknowledge their condition and "die" with Christ—die to sin and the world—to enter on the road toward sanctification.

Reconciliation is also taking place at a collective level. The Jews, the chosen people, have rejected Jesus's messianic claims, so God has sent the apostles to the Gentiles, who are being grafted into the people of God. At some future time, the Jews will accept Christ's justification and the division between Jews and Gentiles will be transcended.

## Doctrine

The title of this section is meant to recall the second part of the traditional Protestant sermon. Following exegesis of a biblical passage, a preacher would seek to identify the teaching of the passage. In this section we will be seeking to spell out the doctrinal implications of what we found about divine judgment.

### Toward a Concept of Redeeming Judgment

We still need to abstract a concept from its embeddedness in narrative. To do so, we can enter the discipline of systematic theology where ideas are woven together into conceptual schemes. What we propose to do is to examine a respected and influential theological layout for its treatment of judgment and redemption. We can assess how it squares with our findings, and propose amendments that would bring the theologian's doctrine into better alignment with Scripture.[3]

We need to choose a worthwhile dialogue partner. This theologian obviously must be pledged to rendering Scripture faithfully. He should also accept critical biblical scholarship and be abreast of the best modern science and contemporary philosophy. I would hope to find a dialogue partner who is a churchman committed to the church's flourishing.

I have selected the theology of Jürgen Moltmann, a Protestant theologian who spent most of his career teaching at the University of Tübingen. He meets all the specified criteria well. He was a leading voice in the theology of

3. Somewhere in James Barr's writings he proposes that one of the tasks of biblical theology is evaluate systematic theologians' treatment of Scripture. This works best with theologians who really care whether they represent scriptural teaching.

hope, a successor to the neo-orthodoxy of Karl Barth and his contemporaries.[4] His theology opened the door for Latin American liberation theology, but Moltmann remained committed to working out his original thesis.

Three books of his I will cite: *Theology of Hope* (from the 1960s), *The Crucified God* (from the 1970s), and *The Coming of God* (from the 1990s). These span much of Multmann's productive career and represent a serious, mature theology.

Recovering the future orientation of the gospel was Moltmann's original rallying cry and long-term commitment. It suited the political and cultural radicalism of the youth of the '60s and early '70s, which made Moltmann a popular figure until liberation theology inherited the energy of radicalism. Moltmann identified the "eschatological" hopes of the Old and New Testaments and sought to represent them conceptually in his theology. He drew heavily on the neo-Marxist philosopher Ernst Bloch for a future-oriented worldview.

Strangely, judgment is rarely mentioned in Moltmann's early works. Of course, anyone who highlights apocalyptic must recognize the fact that the present world is out of joint and must be overturned to make a better one. However, judgment is largely sublimated into the status quo, which must be undone for the new to appear.

We do find a chapter on the Last Judgment in Moltmann's later work, *The Coming of God*. The title of the chapter is, "The Restoration of all Things," which foreshadows what he is arguing toward. Nevertheless, he explores the subject of last judgment explicitly and forthrightly. We will allow this chapter to order our train of thought; the other two books of Moltmann's will be consulted when they supplement our primary text.

## The Issue of the Outcome of the Last Judgment

The title of the first section of the chapter just mentioned is, "'The Last Judgment' and its Ambivalent Outcome."[5] By that title Moltmann means that the Last Judgment is usually thought to result in the acquittal of some and the eternal damnation of others. This is the picture one sees in medieval and Renaissance depictions of the Last Judgment, and it is reflected in the liturgy of the requiem mass. Most theologians through church history, including Protestant Reformers, depicted the Last Judgment as entailing the eternal

---

4. Moltmann cites Barth more often than anyone else of his teachers' generation.
5. Moltmann, *The Coming of God*, 235–37.

damnation of many. This result, however, is ambiguous because sound arguments can be made for universal salvation.

A few theologians have taught that all humans will ultimately be saved. Origen is probably the most famous. Among Protestants, some pietists took a universalist position, as did the Blumhardts, who founded the Bruderhof. The Blumhardts passed this stance on to a number of theologians, including Karl Barth. We should also mention the Universalist Church, which has merged with the Unitarians.

Moltmann surveys the biblical text for support of the orthodox position, which speaks of a "double outcome," as well as for the universalist position. Matt 7:13–14; 12:32; 25:31–46; Mark 9:45, 48; Luke 16:23; John 3:16, and 36 all support a double outcome. Matthew 7:13–14 distinguishes between the way that leads to life and the one that leads to death. Matthew 12:32 speaks of the unforgivable sin. Matthew 25:31–46 is the parable of the Last Judgment, which speaks of the actions that result in acceptance into the kingdom—the absence of which leads to rejection. Mark 9:45, 48 threaten everlasting fire. The parable of Dives and Lazarus (Luke 16:19–31) assumes that people go to heaven or hell in compensation for what they enjoy or suffer during their lifetimes. The Fourth Gospel has its own way of speaking of heaven and hell: "The one who believes in the Son has eternal life; one who does not believe in the Son shall not see life, but the wrath of God rests upon him" (3:36). Paul speaks openly of the double outcome of judgment in Rom 2:5–10, and refers to being lost in 1 Cor 1:18; 2 Cor 2:15; Phil 3:19; and elsewhere.[6]

Another set of passages, primarily from Paul and his disciples, speak of universal salvation. Eph 1:10 says that God will "unite all things in Christ," and Col 1:20 promises that Christ will "reconcile to himself all things." Philippians 2:10–11 says that "every knee shall bow" to Christ, and "every tongue confess" his lordship. First Corinthians 15:25–28 affirm that Christ will gain rule of all things and then hand creation over to the Father. This great chapter on resurrection makes no mention at all of a Last Judgment with a double outcome. In Rom 5:18, Adam is said to make all humans inherit death, while Christ makes all alive. In Rom 11:32, Paul says, "God has consigned all humans to disobedience, that he may have mercy on all."[7]

---

6. Ibid., 241.
7. Ibid., 240–41.

## Redeeming Judgment

### Some Matters for Debate

Moltmann has lined up these passages on the two sides of the issue in order to establish a standoff. Since the Bible does not come down unequivocally on either side on the question of the double outcome, the issue will have to be resolved by theological reasoning.

Moltmann is surely right in his contention that the New Testament has universalistic as well as dualistic passages. However, it is clear that Moltmann does not intend to engage the New Testament in any depth. He has not taken up the larger question of judgment in the gospels or epistles. Indeed, one gets the impression from Moltmann that there is no common concept of judgment, no doctrine shared by all theological voices in the New Testament.

Even more distortive is Moltmann's silence about judgment in the Old Testament. It seems to me that a systematic theology that means to speak to the whole church has an obligation to synthesize the whole canon. This assumes, of course, that the whole canon is equally authoritative. Surely the Old Testament needs to be consulted on the subject of judgment, since the New Testament is based upon and continues Old Testament teaching on the subject. Moreover, it is impossible to interpret Jesus's role in the action of God without reference to messianic prophecies and the portrayal of the servant of YHWH.

Moltmann does discuss Old Testament law and prophecy in *Theology of Hope*.[8] He follows an established tradition of subordinating law to covenant. Covenant is a promise, and law is the guidance given by God for living within the covenant. The law and commandments "are explications of the one commandment, to love God and cleave to him (Deut 6:5)."[9] This in turn is the reverse side of the covenant promise: Israel is commanded what it is offered. Nonfulfillment entails its own punishment and also the withholding of accompanying blessings. Legalism develops when Israel begins to ascribe flourishing to obedience, and decline to disobedience. Otherwise Israel would have to blame God for failure to deliver what he promised.[10]

Let me offer some alternatives to Moltmann's reading. Covenant is indeed promissory, but both parties must commit themselves.[11] Each party agrees to the provisions. It looks forward not to a particular outcome but to an

---

8. Moltmann, *Theology of Hope*

9. Ibid., 121.

10. Ibid., 121–23. Moltmann throws around the word *legalism* rather promiscuously, and probably should be censured for it. I will leave that task to someone else.

11. Moltmann wants to assimilate the covenant to his future-oriented type of promise with its eschatological horizon.

ongoing relationship. In the covenant between YHWH and Israel, Israel agrees to acknowledge YHWH's authority to command, and itself pledges to obey. YHWH is made sovereign, Israel his subjects.[12] The divine law is the exercise of YHWH's sovereignty.

Israel's law is unique. It is directly commanded, so every Israelite is obligated to YHWH and accountable for violation. Every violation is a sin against YHWH as well as a wrong done to self, neighbor, or God. The first commandment, and the prohibition of images, are unique to Mosaic law.[13] The first commandment is indeed summarized by, "love God with all your being," but its revolutionary impact was in its negative formulation. Compliance with it produced monotheism.

The first (and second) commandments have a significant effect on law dealing with human society. Moshe Greenberg has shown how Mosaic law introduces a radical distinction between the value of persons and the value of property.[14] The same commandments had a revolutionary effect on marriage law, if one takes Jesus's interpretation of the tradition as commentary (see Mark 10:2–12). The prophets expand duty to neighbors under the aegis of this law. The cult itself is "internalized" by the Deuteronomic reform: obedience to law replaced rite as the means of pleasing God. The bottom line is, Mosaic law cannot be reduced to an abstraction or a cipher for the common rules that govern human behavior in all societies; it is unique and belongs to revelation as much as divine promise does.

Moltmann cannot avoid discussing the prophets, for they introduce eschatology into the stream of Old Testament tradition. However, he insists on subordinating their message to promise.[15] This is how he treats judgment within the prophetic message: "The threat that the history of the attacking peoples will bring Yahweh's judgment upon Israel marks a decisive universalizing of the divine action. The experience of being crushed between the great world powers is understood as a judgment of Yahweh. Yet even as early as Amos this threat of judgment is universal."[16]

---

12. I have elsewhere compared the covenant to a constitution; see Patrick, *Old Testament Law*, 223–33.

13. And Israel's heirs, Judaism, Christianity, and Islam.

14. Greenberg, "Some Postulates of Biblical Criminal Law," 5–28; developed in Finkelstein, *The Ox That Gored*.

15. Moltmann, *Theology of Hope*, 127.

16. Ibid., 128.

*Redeeming Judgment*

Moltmann finds the most important thing to say about judgment is not its correspondence to Israel's sin but its inclusion of nations.[17] "The moving horizon of the assurances for the future given by the God of promise, once it is extended to embrace 'all peoples,' then reaches the utmost bounds of human reality as such, and becomes universal and so also eschatological."[18] When it really comes down to it, judgment seems only to be a stepping stone to something better: "The prophets' message of judgment... points once more to a different future, to a day of Yahweh, which will arise out of the night of judgment... It can therefore be conceived as a judgment that paves the way to something finally new, as annihilation for the sake of greater perfection."[19] From now on, the theologian needs only think about the new, the eschatological. At the end of the day, Moltmann even pits salvation against judgment: "If this were to be expressed in theological terms, we should have to say: it shows itself in the overcoming of God by God—of the judging, annihilating God by the saving, life-giving God, of the wrath of God by his goodness."[20]

Evidently Moltmann cannot take the prophets at their word: according to Amos 7–8 and Isaiah 6, the prophet was commissioned by God to announce judgment. I do not hear a commission to warn the people that they will be judged if they do not change their ways, or a promise of a rosy future; no, the people are guilty, the divine decision is being announced in the prophet's message, and from now on all events lead toward retribution. Hosea and Jeremiah are given the authority to declare judgment *and* promise salvation, e.g., "to build and to plant" (Jer 1:10). Still, judgment is the first order of the day.

The promises that our prophets felt commissioned to deliver were not God's goodness overcoming his wrath. After all, God's anger was an expression of his concern for the welfare of his people.[21] Rather, God's judgment serves his redemptive purposes, as we have argued earlier in this volume.

Let me add, Moltmann's passion for the origins of eschatology is a source of confusion. Eschatology should be regarded as the outgrowth of historical experience and quest for understanding. The judgments of history bring about a "rough and ready" justice, peace, healing; but there is always the need of a final settlement that completes and corrects the judgments of history. Eschatology

17. I suspect that Moltmann does not accept Israel's eternal election.
18. Moltmann, *Theology of Hope*, 129.
19. Ibid., 129.
20. Ibid., 131.
21. Heschel, *The Prophets*, 279–98; Moltmann, *The Crucified God*, 271–72, actually cites Heschel approvingly on this subject.

*Final Judgment and Redemption*

also looks beyond a healed finitude to eternal life with the vision of God. It is indeed the "last horizon," nicely symbolized in the last two chapters of Isaiah.

Let me say something more about promise, commandment, and judgment. Moltmann seems to have held that God's revelation belongs entirely to the category of promise. This is mistaken. If we take promise to be a primary category of performative discourse, as I would, we have to acknowledge that the God of the Old Testament also speaks commandments and judgments, and backs up his promises, commands, and judgments with appeals to memory, feeling, and the like.[22] Jews have traditionally highlighted God's commanding while Protestant Christians focus on his promising; it would be better to acknowledge the "many and various ways God spoke of old to our ancestors by the prophets" (Heb 1:1).

## *The Theological Debate over the Outcome of Final Judgment*

Let's return to Moltmann's argument in *The Coming of God*. Once he has shown that the Scriptures actually support both a single and a double outcome, he sets out the arguments for each side.

Moltmann locates one single foundational principle in support of a double outcome. This is, God has decided to save humans by faith, and faith requires free decision.[23] Grace, it is said, cannot be forced on people. If humans are free to decide their ultimate fate, God must win them by persuasion.

The investment of the decision regarding salvation solely in the will of the individual human reduces God to the status of a salesman, so to speak.[24] Theologians have often corrected this anthropocentric soteriology by a doctrine of prevenient grace. Indeed, many believers themselves testify that God intervened to turn them around and set them on the path to Glory.[25] This may be too successful in giving God credit: it could take away human decision. One can, with a careful, sophisticated metaphysic, harmonize human freedom and divine intervention, but one must be careful not to take away (viz., human freedom) what one has given.

The doctrine of prevenient grace is often thought to require a doctrine of predestination: God has decided who he is going to convert and save. If God

---

22. See Patrick, *The Rhetoric of Revelation*.
23. Moltmann, *The Coming of God*, 244–46. By the way, freedom of decision would also be necessary for salvation by works, or by a combination of faith and works.
24. Isa 55:1–2 actually portrays YHWH as a vendor.
25. Moltmann, *The Coming of God*, 245–47.

decides to save some, he must have rejected the rest. Paul goes so far as to say that God "hardens their hearts" (Romans 9, 11). Suddenly God's grace sounds rather cruel and unjust. If God restricts admission to his kingdom to the righteous—however they have attained their righteousness—all should have equal access. And if the capacity to receive the gift is itself God's gift, why hasn't God granted all the gratitude due the Creator and Savior?

John Calvin explains God's parsimony thus: God needs "vessels of wrath" to show the severity of his justice. This ascribes a rather sadistic side to God: he creates some creatures solely to destroy them.

If one wants to hold out for the possibility that God will in fact persuade all his creatures, one must hypothesize a continuation of the moral struggle beyond temporal life. Why? Because it is evident that many people do not die in grace. If they are to be redeemed, it must be after their death.

Moltmann holds that the decisive argument against a double outcome and for universal salvation is that God's grace is more powerful than sin (Rom 5:20). Love overpowers wrath; indeed, "God judges the sin of the world so as to save the world."[26] Psalm 30:5 sums up the univeralist stance: "His anger is but for a moment, and his favor is for a lifetime."

Martin Luther was able to escape theological ruminations about predestination by concentrating on Christ's suffering. He had been counseled by Johannes von Staupitz, a fellow Augustinian, that "if he wished to wrestle with predestination he should begin with the wounds of Christ, after which the dispute about predestination would cease of itself."[27] Christ's descent into hell was his experience of the wrath of God on all sin. "Christ suffered this hell on the cross in order to reconcile this world, damned as it is, with God."[28] "Death has been swallowed up in victory" (1 Cor 15:54).

We still need a theological conceptualization of what transpired on the cross. Moltmann sets forth Karl Barth's argument.[29] God has determined himself to be Creator, Reconciler, and Redeemer from the outset. He has decided to be incarnate even before sin entered the world. Once sin entered the world, the incarnate Son is called upon to suffer on the cross to take upon himself the rejection of sinful men and women. Christ is rejected on the cross, and the rejection is overcome by the resurrection. Now all humans have been elected

---

26. Ibid., 243. This agrees with the position I took in criticism of Moltmann earlier; either I have misread him, or he is inconsistent.

27. Ibid., 251.

28. Ibid., 252.

29. Ibid., 248–49.

and reconciled, freed of their sinful record and their propensity to sin. This happens whether they know it or not. Faith is the subjective appropriation of reconciliation, which sets one on the road to redemption and sanctification.

This seems to be a universalistic revision of Anselm's conception of atonement. Christ suffers death in place of sinners, satisfying the requirements of justice while offering mercy. Barth's atonement occurs over our heads, so to speak; it is objective.

Barth's exposition of atonement, like Anselm's, is vulnerable. Immanuel Kant objected cogently to equating guilt with debt; guilt is a personal blotch that only the guilty can satisfy.[30] My own objection is that in this view Christ's atonement becomes a legal fiction—the sin of one person is imputed to another person; the righteousness of one person is imputed to the other in an exchange.

Hofius offers a remedy for this flawed conception of atonement: he interprets the suffering of Christ not to be "in place of" the punishment of sinners, but "along with" sinners.[31] One's punishment would thereby be transformed from condemnation to purgation. Moltmann adopts a position along those lines when he writes, "*Christ's descent into hell* means: you have suffered the experience of hell for us, so as to be beside us in our experiences of hell."[32]

## Christ's Suffering and the Doctrine of the Trinity

A theological doctrine lies behind the atonement: the doctrine of the incarnation. We have assumed up till now that what Christ does and undergoes can be predicated of God. This can only be so if God is incarnate in this fully human person.

But we cannot simply ascribe Christ's suffering to God, given the long history of the rejection of patripassionism. It is Christ who is tried and crucified; the Father remains in heaven, so to speak. Indeed, Jesus cries out that he has been abandoned by God. Yet 2 Corinthians can say, "God was in Christ reconciling the world unto himself" (5:19). The only way to reconcile these affirmations is to work out the doctrine of the Trinity.

Moltmann probes the theology of Christ's suffering very profoundly in *The Crucified God*. It is his thesis that the doctrine of the Trinity comes into being in the effort to interpret the suffering of the Son. He begins with the

---

30. See Hofius, "The Fourth Servant Song," 163–88.
31. Ibid.
32. Moltmann, *The Coming of God*, 252 (italics original).

narratives in the gospels of Christ's death. For him, the singular "last word" on the cross was the cry of dereliction: "My God, my God, why have you forsaken me?" (Mark 15:34).[33] This utterance, which was drawn from Psalm 22, is shocking on the lips of the figure whom Mark names "Son of God," and who has foretold his suffering and death numerous times. How can God feel or be abandoned by God?

It is common to ascribe the cry to Christ's humanity alone, and then to give a psychological explanation. What happened to the unity of the person of Christ? Obviously the cry was uttered by the one person who was dying on the cross. What we must say, therefore, is that the Son experiences abandonment by God, his Father, Abba. He suffers "God-forsakenness" on the cross. "This is the very meaning of hell, and thus his experience, as expressed in the cry of dereliction, was a descent into hell."[34]

Anti-patripassionists could possibly tolerate this affirmation, but they would have to deny that the Father is moved by the cry of the Son, or by anything that happens to him. God the Father is unchangeable, immutable, impassive. To this stance Moltmann objects. He borrows rabbi Abraham Heschel's concept of the *pathos* of God. Jews (and Christians) accepted a philosophical ideal, including a philosophical theology, from the Greeks and Romans, which regarded absence of emotion, of passion, to be the ideal of true manhood; deity would therefore have to be removed from feeling. According to Heschel and Moltmann, acceptance of this reasoning by Jews and Christians was a disastrous accommodation to an alien spirituality.[35]

The upshot of Moltmann's argument is that the Father does not suffer *like* the Son but does suffer—certainly grief at the loss of his Son, perhaps even something like remorse for having "delivered him up" to be crucified (e.g., Acts 2:23). Some have compared what God did in the crucifixion to child abuse, though in fact it would be better compared to what parents do when they hand over responsibility to their children. The Father does not protect Jesus from the assaults of his violent world, and the results are Jesus's struggles, his disappointments, his trial and humiliation at the hands of the authorities, and finally his execution. The rough-and-ready justice of the fallen world puts the Son the death, and the Father is the ultimate sovereign of this very world.

---

33. Ultimately, he would have to adopt a canonical reading that takes into account all of the last words, but I would indeed give the cry of dereliction a special place.

34. For this whole paragraph, see Moltmann, *The Crucified God*, 235–48.

35. See ibid., 267–73; for Heschel, see *The Prophets*, 221–334.

# Final Judgment and Redemption

This set of events calls for a Trinitarian theology—a theology that envisages two centers of experience and will, interacting with each other and through the creatures of the world. It is a Trinitarian rather than a binitarian Godhead because the love of the Father for the Son and Son for the Father is an active immanent force in humans: the Spirit.

The resurrection of Jesus Christ is the revelation of the deity of the Son. It is the divine answer to the cry from the cross. The cry is not, however, drowned out by the joy of the resurrection. It is like a scar; it is also a reminder that many others die betrayed by humans and abandoned by God. Not until the end of time will the resurrection be the answer to the injustice and God-forsakenness suffered by the righteous.

Although it is not my task to justify the doctrine of the Trinity, I find Moltmann's line of thought utterly persuasive. We need to be able to speak of the suffering of God in the suffering of the Son and of the Father. I would add that the Father has suffered—experienced *pathos*—in Israel's history and hiddenly in the histories of other peoples.

It is also theologically proper to take into account that God is the ultimate source of all power, and exercises the final disposition of all power, and, between beginning and end, limits the evil uses of power.[36]

We can see the *dual* expression of God's power in various biblical texts: Isaiah 40–55 has two human figures manifesting the power of God: Cyrus the military conqueror, and the servant, who would not even break a bent reed. This duality appears again in the Apocalypse of John.[37]

## Last Judgment and Redemption

I would like to focus our discussion of this critical conundrum by quoting Moltmann's formulation of what will happen at the end:

> Judgment is the side of the eternal kingdom that is turned toward history. In that Judgment all sins, every wickedness and every act of violence, the whole injustice of this murderous and suffering world, will be condemned and annihilated, because God's verdict effects what it pronounces. In the divine Judgment of sinners, the wicked and the violent, the murderers and the children of Satan, the Devil and fallen angels will be liberated and saved from their deadly perdition through transformation into their true created being, because God remains

---

36. This is what I take to be the import of Pasewark's *Theology of Power*.

37. This is my amendment of Moltmann, who speaks only of the inner history of the Father and the Son: Moltmann, *The Crucified God*, 145–53, 240–49.

true to himself, and does not give up what he has once created and affirmed, or allow it to be lost.[38]

I find the statement very appealing and will support it the best I can. I do think that Moltmann has jettisoned important dimensions of judgment and redemption, which leaves him silent about how to get from here to there.

Moltmann has an aversion to retaliatory justice and specifically excludes it from the Last Judgment: "The person who in the history of Christ has experienced the righteousness of God which creates justice for those who suffer injustice and which justifies the godless knows what the justice in which at the Last Judgment will restore this ruined world and put everything to rights again: it is not retaliatory justice, Ulpian's *suam cuique*, to each his due—the justice that gives everyone their 'just deserts'"[39] Moltmann also excludes "expiatory penal code(s)" from Christ's court.[40]

I would hold that retaliatory justice is the foundation of criminal law. This is how wrongdoing is evaluated. There is no reason to distinguish divine justice from human justice on this point. Human justice aspires, in fact, to enforce the will of God. Yes, the poetic expression of retaliatory justice, "an eye for an eye and a tooth for a tooth . . . a life for a life," may sound harsh, but it depends upon how it is administered. No one needs to maim people to require that a wrongdoer suffer proportionately to the suffering caused.

Readers may object, Jesus put an end to the exacting of an "eye for an eye" (Matt 5:38–42). I regard the requirements of the Sermon on the Mount as supererogatory; we cannot expect such a renunciation of a person's rights from most members of society. But, you say, Jesus's justice will follow this higher norm. That is a legitimate point, but I would remind readers that Paul assured his readers of Romans that God would retaliate: "Beloved, never avenge yourselves but leave it to the wrath of God; for it is written, 'Vengeance is mine, I will repay, says the Lord'" (Rom 12:19).

I am restricting myself to defending retaliatory judgment because Moltmann and I probably agree on prevention and restitution as aims of justice, divine as well as human. What I am arguing is, we cannot dispense with "the left hand of God," to use Luther's expression. The prophets announce it without embarrassment. God works through Cyrus as well as the Servant.

38. Ibid., 255.
39. Ibid., 250.
40. Ibid.

This issue is directly relevant to the transition from history to the kingdom of God. One cannot break the power of sin and evil simply by fiat. God's intervention is a judicial event in which evil is condemned. Moltmann himself says as much. It seems to me that that is of a piece with the judgments of history. The perpetrators cannot escape responsibility for their actions. Whatever else happens in the Final Judgment, humans must come to acknowledge what they have wrought.

The proper state of the godly mind, according to Psalms 51 and 130, and Isaiah 56–66, is compunction and humility. "This is the one to whom I will look, the humble and contrite in spirit, who trembles at my word" (Isa 66:2). Only a person who has such a state of mind can be reformed by the Spirit. A society that cannot recognize its injustice and inhumanity will resist the prophet's condemnation. A nation that is willing to sacrifice everything to survive will lose whatever was worth preserving. Judgment is an inevitable, if not necessary, stage on the road to redemption.

All through these two volumes I have insisted that God intends to redeem humans, and that judgment is not an end in itself. I have reserved the word *redemption* for the transformation of the human heart and mind so that they belong completely and unconditionally to God.

## Universal Salvation

It sounds like I have chosen a double outcome, since the Last Judgment applies retaliatory justice along with restorative justice.[41] Actually, I shall not join either camp. I hope that all can be redeemed and saved, but I cannot rule out the serious possibility that some of us will be lost.

The reason I cannot come down on either side is simply that neither biblical passages nor theological arguments are decisive. Some biblical passages fall on each side of the question, though candor requires that we acknowledge a preponderance on the side of the double outcome. As a pastor it would be embarrassing, at the least, to have to face a layperson, to look someone in the eye, and say that the Bible really does not say that the wicked or unbelievers are destined for judgment. The bigger task is to persuade church people that there are universalistic passages in the Scriptures.

As for theological arguments, we have to admit that the current theological climate probably favors a message of universal salvation, though the preponderance of the finest theological minds of church history defended a

---

41. "Restorative justice" is Desmond Tutu's term: see Tutu, *No Future without Forgiveness*.

double outcome. Moltmann has stated the arguments in favor of universal salvation well; he does, unfortunately, ignore the theme of judgment running through Scripture, and only occasionally does he admit that judgment serves the redemptive purposes of God.

One can raise all sorts of questions about the possibility and legitimacy of a Last Judgment. Would all humans be measured according to the same norms? Wouldn't judgment require that the defendants know the law they are accountable to? Perhaps, however, the norms that a body of people recognized were not good.[42] Also lurking here is the problem of collective and individual responsibility and accountability.

I do not propose to address the problems I just raised. There is probably a defensible answer to each one, though it would make any picture of Last Judgment more complex than any depiction of the event could be.

I propose to consider another question: redemption is not simply a matter of forgiveness. Most theories of atonement, particularly those that use the metaphor of sacrifice, only explain how God can legitimately forgive sin without abandoning the standards of right and holiness and justice. It is equally important to explain, however, how Jesus's death on the cross moves us, changes our wills from the propensity to sin toward trust and steadfast love. Or, to paraphrase Augustine, how we can be broken of the inclination to "love self even to the contempt of God" in order that we may "love God even to the contempt of self."

We have tentatively adopted the idea that the cross is meant to shock us into recognizing the impact of our sinful actions. It provides an "objective correlative" to the inward sorrow for our actions. This is what I take Janowski to have proposed.[43]

Surely this rhetorical understanding of the suffering of Christ is not adequate. Christ died *for* us. But we backed away from substitutionary atonement because guilt cannot be transferred from one person to another. Instead, we favored Hofius's idea that Christ suffers *with* us rather than *instead of* us. He transforms our suffering from punishment unto death into remorse unto repentance and restoration.

Our transformation is not one-sidedly passive, despite Luther's emphasis. The Synoptics report that Jesus commanded his followers to take up their crosses and follow him (Mark 8:34). Paul speaks of dying with Christ in order

---

42. Like the institution of slavery in the ancient world.

43. Janowski, "Er trug unsere Sünde," 1–24, now in English ("He Bore Our Sins"). I am actually relying on Bailey, "Concepts of *Stellvertretung*," 223–50.

to be given life by Christ's Spirit. We probably could lay out a "third use of the law" on the basis of the call to discipleship/to die with Christ.

If we were to adopt a universalistic hope, we have to ask when this transformation would take place. Does it take place completely in history? Then how do we account for those who have never taken a step on the road to the kingdom? Do we follow Origen in projecting a period of punishment, repentance, and restoration after death? This sounds like purgatory, though it would not entail the option of eternal damnation. Purgatory might solve our problem but would create others. It is theologically unsatisfying to have to project a metaphysical realm beyond time to complete the course of time. Moreover, some humans would have to be forced to enter the path to redemption.

Moltmann and Barth counsel us to put our trust in God's capacity to save. As long as we do this, we can rest assured of our own salvation. The minute one begins to examine one's own heart, the outcome becomes much more iffy. If we are ruthlessly honest with ourselves, we will know we are infinitely far from redemption. The father of the epileptic speaks for us: "I believe; help my unbelief" (Mark 9:24).

## Postscript

It was a rather odd turn that centered this concluding chapter on the Last Judgment, for our exegetical studies were not focused on the eschatological dimension of the theme. It was Moltmann's location of his systematic discussion of divine judgment in a book about the last things that dictated ours.

There is a certain advantage to focusing on the Last Judgment when one considers the doctrine of divine judgment. We are not just speaking of the last in a series; indeed, that may be a misunderstanding. The Last Judgment is the definitive judgment that determines the measure of all things. So the Last Judgment is an "ideal type," so to speak. It is a judgment free from the accommodations, limits, and distortions of every historical judgment.

Though God transcends time and circumstance, he must accommodate himself to what is going on in time when he intervenes. He operates through human agents. These agents have amassed their power to perform their assignment by overwhelming or outmaneuvering others in the struggle for power. They have been corrupted in one way or another by the struggle. God's action is compromised by his sin-prone human agents. Every judgment in history, therefore, leaves a residue of injustice and injury.

The judgments of history are also incomplete. A judgment successfully resolve a particular conflict, put an end to a particular wrong, or repay a shameful act, but evil continues, humans continue to injure each other and dishonor the Holy One. The Final Judgment promises "no more."

The Final Judgment, however, is not different in objective from other judgments; indeed, it is the correction and completion of the judgments of history. The judgments of history seek to give to each their due, to rectify injustice, to reestablish equality, to honor the good and true. They also seek to reclaim and reform those subjected to judgment. The Final Judgment, I have argued (sometimes against Moltmann), seeks to do the same.

Judgments test the convicted, allowing us to participate in our own punishment. There is, thus, room for repentance and reform. The Lord does not desire the death of the sinner, but that the sinner repent. This is the redemptive potential of judgment.

Let me bring the book to a close with a passage from Romans: "Since all have sinned and fall short of the glory of God, they are justified by his grace as a gift, through the redemption which is in Christ Jesus, whom God put forward as an expiation by his blood, to be received by faith. This was to show God's righteousness, because in his divine forbearance he had passed over former sins; it was to prove at the present time that he himself is righteous and that he justifies [those] who [have] faith in Jesus" (3:23–26, RSV).

# Bibliography

Albright, W. F., translator. "The Moabite Stone." In *Ancient Near Eastern Texts Related to the Old Testament*, edited by James B. Pritchard, 320–21. 3rd ed. Princeton: Princeton University Press, 1969.
Alt, Albrecht. "The Origins of Israelite Law." In *Essays on Old Testament History and Religion*, 81–132. Translated by R. A. Wilson. Oxford: Blackwell, 1966.
Anderson, Gary A. "Does the Promise Still Hold?" *The Christian Century*, January 13, 2009, 22–24.
———. *The Genesis of Perfection: Adam and Eve in Jewish and Christian Imagination*. Louisville: Westminster John Knox, 2003.
———. *Sin: A History* New Haven: Yale University Press, 2009.
Ateek, Naim Stifan. *Justice and Only Justice: A Palestinian Theology of Liberation*. Maryknoll, NY: Orbis, 1989.
Augustine, Saint. *The City of God*. Translated by Marcus Dods et al. The Modern Library of the World's Best Books. Modern Library Giants 74. New York: Modern Library, 1950.
Aulen, Gustaf. *Christus Victor: An Historical Study of the Three Main Types of the Idea of Atonement*. Translated by A. G. Herbert. 1951. Reprinted, Eugene, OR: Wipf & Stock, 2003.
Aune, David. *Prophecy in Early Christianity and the Ancient Mediterranean*. 1983. Reprinted, Eugene, OR: Wipf & Stock, 2003.
Bailey, Daniel P. "Concepts of *Stellvertretung* in the Interpretation of Isaiah 53." In *Jesus and the Suffering Servant*, edited by William H. Bellinger, Jr., and William R. Farmer, 223–50. 1998. Reprinted, Eugene, OR: Wipf & Stock, 2009.
———. "The Suffering Servant: Recent Tübingen Scholarship on Isaiah 53." In *Jesus and the Suffering Servant*, edited by William H. Bellinger Jr. and William R. Farmer, 251–59. 1998. Reprinted, Eugene, OR: Wipf & Stock, 2009.
Barr, David. *Tales of the End: A Narrative Commentary on the Book of Revelation*. The Storyteller Bible. Santa Rosa, CA: Polebridge, 1998.
Barr, James. *Biblical Faith and Natural Theology*. The Gifford Lectures for 1991. Oxford: Clarendon, 1993.
———. *The Garden of Eden and the Hope of Immortality*. Minneapolis: Fortress, 1993.
Barrett, C. K. *The Gospel according to St. John: An Introduction with Commentary and Notes on the Greek Text*. London: SPCK, 1960.
Barton, John. *Understanding Old Testament Ethics: Approaches and Explorations*. Louisville: Westminster John Knox, 2003.
Betz, Hans Dieter. *Essays on the Sermon on the Mount*. Philadelphia: Fortress, 1985.

*Bibliography*

Biddle, Mark E. *Missing the Mark: Sin and Its Consequences in Biblical Theology.* Nashville: Abingdon, 2005.
Bellinger, William H., Jr., and William R. Farmer, editors. *Jesus and the Suffering Servant: Isaiah 53 and Christian Origins.* 1998. Reprinted, Eugene, OR: Wipf & Stock, 2009.
Boda, Mark A. et al., editors. *Seeking the Favor of God.* Vol. 1, *The Origins of Penitential Prayer in Second Temple Judaism.* Early Judaism and Its Literature 21. Atlanta: Society of Biblical Literature, 2006.
Brueggemann, Walter. "The Costly Loss of Lament." In *The Psalms and the Life of Faith*, edited by Patrick D. Miller, 98–111. Minneapolis: Fortress, 1995.
———. *Theology of the Old Testament: Testimony, Dispute, Advocacy.* Minneapolis: Fortress, 1997.
Brueggemann, Walter, Martin Jeschke, and Donald Wagner. "Responses to Gary Anderson." *The Christian Century*, January 13, 2009, 25–29.
Charles, R. H., editor. *The Apocrypha and Pseudepigrapha in English.* Vol. 2, *The Pseudepigrapha.* Oxford: Clarendon, 1913.
Childs, Brevard S. *Biblical Theology of the Old and New Testaments: Theological Reflection on the Christian Bible.* Minneapolis: Fortress, 1992.
———. *Introduction to the Old Testament as Scripture.* Philadelphia: Fortress, 1979.
———, *The Struggle to Understand Isaiah as Christian Scripture.* Grand Rapids: Eerdmans, 2004.
Clements, R. E. *Jeremiah.* Interpretation. Atlanta: John Knox, 1988.
Coats, George W. *Rebellion in the Wilderness: The Murmuring Motif in the Wilderness Traditions of the Old Testament.* Nashville, Abingdon, 1968.
Collins, Adela Y. "Son of Man." In *NIDB*, 5:341–48. 2009.
Conzelmann, Hans. *The Theology of St. Luke.* Translated by Geoffrey Buswell. 1960. Reprinted, Philadelphia: Fortress, 1982.
Cousar, Charles B. *A Theology of the Cross: The Death of Jesus in the Pauline Letters.* OBT. Minneapolis: Fortress, 1990.
Dalton, William J. *Aspects of New Testament Eschatology.* Lectures in Biblical Studies 4. Nedlands, Perth: University of Western Australia Press, 1968.
Daube, David. *Studies in Biblical Law.* New York: Ktav, 1969.
Davies, Eryl W. *Prophecy and Ethics: Isaiah and the Ethical Traditions of Israel.* JSOTSup 16 Sheffield: JSOT Press, 1981.
Daye, Russell. *Political Forgiveness: Lessons from South Africa.* Maryknoll, NY: Orbis, 2004.
Driver, S. R. *A Critical and Exegetical Commentary on the Book of Job.* International Critical Commentary 14. 2 vols. New York: Scribner, 1921.
Dworkin, Ronald. *A Matter of Principle.* Cambridge: Harvard University Press, 1985.
———. *Taking Rights Seriously.* Cambridge: Harvard University Press, 1977.
Eissfeldt, Otto. *The Old Testament: An Introduction.* Translated by Peter R. Ackroyd. New York: Harper & Row, 1965.
Eliot, T. S. "Hamlet." In *Selected Prose of T. S. Eliot*, edited by Frank Kermode, 45–49. New York: Harcourt Brace Jovanovich, 1975.
Ellul, Jacques. *The Meaning of the City.* Translated by Dennis Pardee. Grand Rapids: Eerdmans, 1970.
Evans, Craig A. *To See and Not Perceive: Isaiah 6:9-10 in Early Jewish and Christian Interpretation.* JSOTSup 64. Sheffield Academic, 1989.
Feuerbach, Ludwig. *The Essence of Christianity.* Translated by George Eliot. Great Books in Philosophy. Buffalo: Prometheus, 1989.

Finkelstein, J. J. *The Ox That Gored*. Philadelphia: American Philosophical Society, 1981.
Fitzmyer, Joseph A. *Luke*. Anchor Bible 28-28A. Garden City, NY: Doubleday, 1981-1985.
Fowler, James W. *To See the Kingdom: The Theological Vision of H. Richard Niebuhr*. 1974. Reprinted, Eugene, OR: Wipf & Stock, 2001.
Frankfort, Henri. *Kingship and the Gods: A Study of Ancient Near Eastern Religion as the Integration of Society & Nature*. Phoenix edition. Chicago: University of Chicago Press, 1978.
Frei, Hans. *The Identity of Jesus Christ: The Hermeneutical Bases of Dogmatic Theology*. Philadelphia: Fortress, 1975.
Frymer-Kensky, Tikva. *In the Wake of the Goddesses: Women, Culture, and the Biblical Transformation of Pagan Myth*. New York: Fawcett Columbine, 1992.
Goldhagen, Daniel. *Hitler's Willing Executioners: Ordinary Germans and the Holocaust*. New York: Knopf, 1996.
Gottwald, Norman K. *All the Kingdoms of the Earth: Israelite Prophecy and International Relations in the Ancient Near East*. New York: Harper & Row, 1964.
Grant, Deena, "Wrath." In *NIDB*, 5:933-34. 2009.
Grant, Robert M. *Gods and the One God*. Library of Early Christianity. Philadelphia: Westminster,1986.
Greenberg, Moshe. "Some Postulates of Biblical Criminal Law." In *Yehezkel Kaufmann Jubilee Volume*, edited by Manahem Haran, 5-28. Jerusalem: Detus Goldberg, 1960.
Hanson, Paul D. *The Dawn of Apocalyptic: The Historical and Sociological Roots of Jewish Apocalyptic Eschatology*. Rev. ed. Philadelphia: Fortress, 1979.
Heidel, Alexander. *The Gilgamesh Epic and Old Testament Parallels*. 2nd ed. Chicago: University of Chicago Press, 1949.
Heschel, Abraham Joshua. *The Prophets*. 2 vols. New York: Harper & Row, 1962.
Hofius, Otfried. "The Fourth Servant Song in the New Testament Letters." In *The Suffering Servant: Isaiah 53 in Jewish and Christian Sources*, edited by Bernd Janowski and Peter Stuhlmacher, 163-88. Translated by Daniel P. Bailey. Grand Rapids: Eerdmans, 2004.
Hollenbach, Paul. "John the Baptist." In *ABD* 3:887-88.
Janowski, Bernd. "*Er trug* unsere Sunden: Jes 53 und die Dramatik der Stellvertretung." *Zietschrift für Theologie und Kirche* 90 (1993) 1-24.
———. "He Bore Our Sins: Isaiah 53 and the Drama of Taking Another's Place." In *The Suffering Servant: Isaiah 53 and Jewish and Christian Sources*, edited by Bernd Janowski and Peter Stuhlmacher, 48-74. Translated by Daniel P. Bailey. Grand Rapids: Eerdmans, 2004.
Janowski, Bernd, and Peter Stuhlmacher, editors. *The Suffering Servant: Isaiah 53 in Jewish and Christian Sources*. Translated by Daniel P. Bailey. Grand Rapids: Eerdmans, 2004.
Johnson, Luke Timothy. *Luke*. Sacra Pagina 3. Collegeville, MN: Liturgical, 1991.
Kaminsky, Joel S. *Yet I Loved Jacob: Reclaiming the Biblical Concept of Election*. Nashville: Abingdon, 2007.
Keck, Leander E. *Romans*. Abingdon New Testament Commentaries. Nashville: Abingdon, 2005.
Kegley, Charles W., and Robert W. Bretall, editors. *Reinhold Niebuhr: His Religious, Social, and Political Thought*. The Library of Living Theology 2. New York: Macmillan, 1961.
Kierkegaard, Søren. *The Concept of Anxiety: A Simple Psychologically Orienting Deliberation on the Dogmatic Issue of Hereditary Sin*. Kierkegaard's Writings 8. Translated by Reidar Thomte with Albert Anderson. Princeton: Princeton University Press, 1980.

# Bibliography

———. *Fear and Trembling; Repetition*. Translated by Howard and Edna Hong. Kierkegaard's Writings 6. Princeton: Princeton University Press, 1983.
Knierim, Rolf. "*ḥṭ'*." In *TLOT*, 1:406–11.
———. "*'awel*." In *TLOT*, 2:849–51.
———. "*'awon*" In *TLOT*, 2:862–66.
———. "*pesha'*." In *TLOT*, 2:1033–37.
Koch, Klaus. "Gibt es ein Vergeltunsdogma im Alten Testament?" In *Spuren des hebräischen Denkens. Beiträge zur altestamentlichen Theologie*, edited by Bernd Janowski and Martin Krause, 65–103. Gesammelte Aufsätze 1. Neukirchen-Vluyn: Neukirchener, 1991.
———. "Is There a Doctrine of Retribution in the Old Testament?" In *Theodicy in the Old Testament*, edited by James L. Crenshaw, 57–87. Issues in Religion and Theology 4. Philadelphia: Fortress, 1983.
Labuschagne, C. J. *The Incomparability of Yahweh in the Old Testament*. Pretoria Oriental Series 5. Leiden: Brill, 1966.
Leeuwen, C. van. "*rš'*." In *TLOT*, 3:1261–65.
Levinson, Bernard M. *Deuteronomy and the Hermeneutics of Legal Innovation*. New York: Oxford University Press, 1997.
Liedke, Gerhard. "*dîn*." In *TLOT*, 1:335–36.
———. "*rîb*." In *TLOT*, 3:1232–37.
———. "*špṭ*." In *TLOT*, 3:1392–98.
Lind, Millard. "Monotheism, Power, and Justice: A Study in Isaiah 40–55." In *Monotheism, Power, and Justice: Collected Old Testament Essays*, 153–70. Elkhart, IN: Institute of Mennonite Studies, 1990.
Lohr, Joel N. *Chosen and Unchosen: Conceptions of Election in the Pentateuch and Jewish-Christian Interpretation*, Siphrut 2. Winona Lake, IN: Eisenbrauns, 2009.
Luther, Martin. *Luthers Werke in Auswahl*. Edited by Otto Clemen. 8 vols. Berlin: de Gruyter, 1950–1959.
Melugen, Roy F. "On Reading Isaiah 53 as Christian Scripture." In *Jesus and the Suffering Servant: Isaiah 53 and Christian Origins*, edited by William H. Bellinger, Jr., and William Farmer, 55–69. 1998. Reprinted, Eugene, OR: Wipf & Stock, 2009.
Mendenhall, George. "Covenant." In *The Interpreter's Dictionary of the Bible*, edited by George Buttrick et al., 1:714–23. Nashville: Abingdon, 1962.
Miller, J. Maxwell, and John H. Hayes. *A History of Ancient Israel and Judah*. Philadelphia: Westminster, 1986. 2nd ed., 2006.
Miller, Patrick D. *Sin and Judgment in the Prophets: A Stylistic and Theological Analysis*. Society of Biblical Literature Monograph Series 27. Chico, CA: Scholars, 1982.
———. *They Cried to the Lord: The Form and Theology of Biblical Prayer*. Minneapolis: Fortress, 2000.
Moberly, R. W. L. *The Old Testament of the Old Testament: Patriarchal Narrative and Mosaic Yahwism*. OBT. Minneapolis: Fortress, 1992.
———. *Prophecy and Discernment*. Cambridge Studies in Christian Doctrine 14. Cambridge: Cambridge University Press, 2006.
Moltmann, Jürgen. *The Coming of God: Christian Eschatology*. Translated by Margaret Kohl. Minneapolis: Fortress, 1996.
———. *The Crucified God: The Cross of Christ as the Foundation and Criticism of Christian Theology*. Translated by R. A. Wilson and John Bowden. Philadelphia: Fortress, 1974.
———. *Theology of Hope: On the Ground and the Implications of a Christian Eschatology*. Translated by James W. Leitch. Harper & Row, 1967.

# Bibliography

Morrow, William S. "Consolation, Rejection, and Repentance in Job 42:6." *JBL* 105 (1986) 211–25.

———. *Protest against God: The Eclipse of a Biblical Tradition*. Hebrew Bible Monographs 4. Sheffield: Sheffield Phoenix, 2006.

Mowinckel, Sigmund. *He That Cometh: The Messiah Concept in the Old Testament and Later Judaism*. Translated by G. W. Anderson. 1959. Reprinted, with a new Foreword by John J. Collins. Grand Rapids: Eerdmans, 2005.

Muilenburg, James. "The Book of Isaiah, Ch. 40–66." In *The Interpreters Bible*, edited by George Arthur Buttrick, 5:381–773. New York: Abingdon, 1956.

Niebuhr, H. Richard. *The Kingdom of God in America*. New York: Harper & Row, 1959.

Niebuhr, Reinhold. *Christian Realism and Political Problems*. New York: Scribner, 1953.

———. *Faith and History: A Comparison of Christian and Modern Views of History*. New York: Scribner, 1949.

———. *The Nature and Destiny of Man*. 2 vols. New York: Scribner, 1943.

———. *The Irony of American History*. New York: Scribner, 1952.

Parsons, Mikeal C. "Isaiah 53 and Acts 8: A Reply to Professor Morna Hooker." In *Jesus and the Suffering Servant: Isaiah 53 and Christian Origins*, edited by William H. Bellinger Jr. and William R. Farmer, 104–20. 1998. Reprinted, Eugene, OR: Wipf & Stock, 2009.

Pasewark, Kyle A. *A Theology of Power: Being beyond Domination*. Philadelphia: Fortress, 1993.

Patrick, Dale. *Arguing with God: The Angry Prayers of Job*. St. Louis: Bethany, 1977.

———. "Avenge." In *NIDB*, 1:356. 2006.

———. "Avenger of Blood." In *NIDB*, 1:357. 2006.

———."Bloodguilt." In *NIDB*, 1:481–82. 2006.

———. "Crimes and Punishment, OT and NT." In *NIDB* 1:790–802. 2006.

———. *Arguing with God: The Angry Prayers of Job*. St. Louis: Bethany, 1977.

———. "Election, Old Testament." In *ABD*, 2:434–41.

———. "The First Commandment in the Structure of the Pentateuch." *Vetus Testamentum* 45 (1995) 107–18.

———. "Job's Address of God." *Zeitschrift für die alttestamentliche Wissenschaft* 91 (1979) 268–82.

———. "Law in the Old Testament." In *NIDB*, 3:602–14. 2008.

———. "Lex talionis." In *NIDB*, 3:651. 2008.

———. *Old Testament Law*. 1985. Reprinted, Eugene, OR: Wipf & Stock, 2011.

———. "Ordinance." In *The New Interpreter's Bible* 4:339. Nashville: Abingdon, 1994.

———. "Redeem, Redeemer." In *NIDB*, 4:753–54. 2009.

———. *The Rendering of God in the Old Testament*. OBT. Philadelphia: Fortress, 1982.

———. "The Rhetoric of Collective Responsibility in Deuteronomic Law." In *Pomegranates and Golden Bells: Studies in Biblical, Jewish, and Near Eastern Ritual, Law and Literature in Honor of Jacob Milgrom*, edited by David P. Wright et al., 421–36. Winona Lake, IN: Eisenbrauns, 1995.

———. *The Rhetoric of Revelation in the Hebrew Bible*. OBT. Minneapolis: Fortress, 1999.

———. "Short Note: The Translation of Job XLII, 6." *Vetus Testamentum* 26 (1976) 369–71.

Patrick, Dale, and Allen Scult. "Finding the Best Job." In *Rhetoric and Biblical Interpretation*, 81–102. JSOTSup 82. Sheffield, UK: Almond, 1990.

Patrick, Dale, and Kenneth Diable. "Persuading the One and Only God to Intervene." In *My Words Are Lovely: Studies in the Rhetoric of the Psalms*, edited by Robert Foster and

## Bibliography

David Howard. Library of Hebrew Bible/Old Testament Studies 467. New York: T. & T. Clark, 2008.

Paul, Shalom M. *Amos*. Hermeneia. Minneapolis: Fortress, 1991.

———. *Studies in the Book of the Covenant in the Light of Cuneiform and Biblical Law*. Vetus Testamentum Supplements 18. 1970. Reprinted, Eugene, OR: Wipf & Stock, 2005.

Preiser, W. "Vergeltung und Sühne im altisraelitischen Strafrecht." In *Festschrift für Eberhard Schmidt zum 70. Geburstag*, edited by Paul Bockelmann and Wilhelm Gallas, 7–38. Göttingen: Vandenhoeck & Ruprecht, 1961.

Rad, Gerhard von. *Old Testament Theology*. Translated by D. M. G. Stalker. 2 vols. 1962–1965. Reprinted, with a new Foreword by Walter Brueggemann. Louisville: Westminster John Knox, 2001.

———. "The Theological Problem of the Old Testament Doctrine of Creation." In *The Problem of the Hexateuch and Other Essays*, 131–43. Translated by E. W. Truman Dicken. Edinburgh Oliver & Boyd, 1966.

Reiser, Marius. *Jesus and Judgment: The Eschatological Proclamation in Its Jewish Context*. Translated by Linda M. Maloney. Minneapolis: Fortress, 1997.

Rendtorff, Rolf. *Canon and Theology: Overtures to an Old Testament Theology*. Translated by Margaret Kohl. OBT. Minneapolis: Fortress, 1993.

———. *The Canonical Hebrew Bible: A Theology of the Old Testament*. Translated by David Orton. Tools for Biblical Study 7. Leiden: Deo, 2005.

Ricoeur, Paul. *Essays on Biblical Interpretation*. Edited by Lewis S. Mudge. Philadelphia: Fortress, 1980.

Sanders, E. P. *Jesus and Judaism*. Philadelphia: Fortress, 1985.

Sauer, G. "nqm." In *TLOT*, 2:767–69.

Schlatter, Adolf von. *Johannes der Täufer*. Edited by Wilhelm Michaelis. Basel: Reinhardt, 1956.

Schottroff, W. "pqd." In *TLOT*, 2:1018–31.

Seitz, Christopher R. *Figured Out: Typology and Providence in Christian Scripture*. Louisville: Westminster John Knox, 2001.

———. *Word without End: The Old Testament as Abiding Theological Witness*. Grand Rapids: Eerdmans, 1998.

———. *Zion's Final Destiny: The Development of the Book of Isaiah*. Minneapolis: Fortress, 1991.

Stamm, J. J. "g'l." In *TLOT*, 1:288–96.

———. "pdh." In *TLOT*, 2:964–76.

Sternberg, Meir. *The Poetics of Biblical Narrative: Ideological Literature and the Drama of Reading*. Indiana Literary Biblical Series. Bloomington: Indiana University Press, 1985.

Stringfellow William. *An Ethic for Christians and Other Aliens in a Strange Land*. 1973. Reprinted, Eugene, OR: Wipf & Stock, 2004.

Suggs, M. Jack. *Wisdom, Christology, and Law in Matthew's Gospel*. Cambridge: Harvard University Press, 1970.

Taylor, Joan E. *The Immerser: John the Baptist within Second Temple Judaism*. Studying the Historical Jesus. Grand Rapids: Eerdmans, 1997.

Theissen, Gerd. *The Shadow of the Galilean: The Quest of the Historical Jesus in Narrative Form*. Translated by John Bowden. Philadelphia: Fortress, 1987.

Trible, Phyllis. *Rhetorical Criticism: Context, Method, and the Book of Jonah*. Guides to Biblical Scholarship. Minneapolis: Fortress, 1994.

Tutu, Desmond Mpilo. *No Future without Forgiveness*. New York: Doubleday, 1999.

*Bibliography*

Via, Dan O. *Divine Justice, Divine Judgment: Rethinking the Judgment of Nations.* Facets. Minneapolis: Fortress, 2007.
Ward, James M. *Hosea: A Theological Commentary.* New York: Harper & Row, 1966.
Watts, Rikki E. "Jesus' Death, Isaiah 53, and Mark 10:45: A Crux Revisited." In *Jesus and the Suffering Servant: Isaiah 53 and Christian Origins*, edited by William H. Bellinger Jr. and William R. Farmer, 125–51. 1998. Reprinted, Eugene, OR: Wipf & Stock, 2009.
Weinfeld, Moshe. *Deuteronomy and the Deuteronomic School.* 1972. Reprinted, Winona Lake, IN: Eisenbrauns, 1992.
Westermann, Claus. *Basic Forms of Prophetic Speech.* Translated by Hugh Clayton White. Philadelphia: Westminster, 1967.
———. *Isaiah 40–66: A Commentary.* Translated by David M. G. Stalker. Old Testament Library. Philadelphia: Westminster, 1969.
———. *Praise and Lament in the Psalms.* Translated by Keith R. Crim and Richard N. Soulen. Atlanta: John Knox, 1981.
———. *The Praise of God in the Psalms.* Translated by Keith R. Crim. Atlanta: John Knox, 1965.
———. "Sprache und Struktur der Prophetie Deuterojesajas." In *Forschung am alten Testament: Gesammelte Studien zum Alten Testament*, 1:92–170. Theologische Bücherei 24. Munich: Kaiser, 1964.
———. *The Structure of the Book of Job: A Form-Critical Analysis.* Translated by Charles A. Meunchow. Philadelphia: Fortress, 1981.
———."Struktur und Geschichte der Klage im Alten Testament." In *Forschung am alten Testament*, 260–305. Theologische Bücherei 24. Munich: Kaiser, 1964–1974.
Williamson, H. G. M. *The Book Called Isaiah: Deutero-Isaiah's Role in Composition and Redaction.* Oxford: Clarendon, 1994.
Wills, Garry. *Lincoln at Gettysburg: The Words That Remade America.* New York: Simon & Schuster, 1992.
Wright, G. Earnest. "Deuteronomy." In *The Interpreter's Bible*, edited by George Buttrick et al., 2:311–537. New York: Abingdon-Cokesbury, 1953.
Yadin, Yigael. *The Art of Warfare in Biblical Lands.* 2 vols. New York: McGraw-Hill, 1963.
Zimmerli, Walther. *Ezekiel.* 2 vols. Translated by Ronald E. Clements. Hermeneia. Philadelphia: Fortress, 1979–1983.

# Scripture Index

## OLD TESTAMENT

### Genesis

| | |
|---|---|
| 1–11 | 11, 18, 36 |
| 2–3 | 31 |
| 2:7 | 26 |
| 2:16–17 | 21 |
| 2:18 | 34 |
| 2:19–20 | 34 |
| 2:20 | 34 |
| 2:24 | 24 |
| 3 | 5, 18, 19, 22, 25, 26–27, 28, 31, 34, 39, 252, 574 |
| 3–4 | 27 |
| 3–11 | 37 |
| 3:3 | 23 |
| 3:6 | 23 |
| 3:10 | 24 |
| 3:11 | 24 |
| 3:14–15 | 25 |
| 3:19 | 25–26 |
| 3:20–21 | 26 |
| 3:22 | 21n3, 26, 35 |
| 3:22–24 | 26 |
| 4 | 5, 18, 19 |
| 4:7 | 28 |
| 4:9 | 29 |
| 4:10 | 443 |
| 6 | 18, 19, 30 |
| 6:1–3 | 18 |
| 6:1–4 | 31 |
| 6:4 | 31 |
| 6:5 | 9, 30, 31, 39, 290, 420, 558 |
| 6:5–12 | 18, 31, 38 |
| 6:5—9:17 | 31 |
| 6:9 | 31 |
| 6:11 | 30 |
| 8 | 58 |
| 8:20 | 32 |
| 8:20–22 | 567n9 |
| 8:20—9:17 | 18 |
| 8:21 | 9, 31, 32, 291, 295, 420, 558 |
| 9:1–10 | 58 |
| 9:1–17 | 291 |
| 9:4–6 | 58 |
| 9:4–7 | 61 |
| 9:5 | 32 |
| 9:5–6 | 33 |
| 9:6 | 29 |
| 9:21–22 | 420 |
| 9:24 | 32 |
| 11:1–9 | 19, 291 |
| 11:4 | 35 |
| 11:6 | 35 |
| 12 | 41 |
| 12–50 | 11 |
| 12:1–3 | 44 |
| 12:3 | 249n38 |
| 12:7 | 44, 573n20 |
| 12:11–12 | 42 |
| 12:17 | 43, 45 |

## Index

### Genesis (continued)

| | |
|---|---|
| 12:18–20 | 42 |
| 12:19 | 42 |
| 14 | 42 |
| 15:6 | 573 |
| 15:14 | 46 |
| 15:18–21 | 40 |
| 16:5 | 99 |
| 18 | 5 |
| 18:16–22 | 4 |
| 18:16–33 | 37, 40 |
| 18:18 | 46 |
| 18:19 | 46, 591 |
| 18:20 | 45 |
| 18:21 | 4 |
| 18:25 | 4, 81, 134 |
| 19 | 275 |
| 19:15 | 6 |
| 20:6 | 43 |
| 20:11–12 | 42n1 |
| 20:25–34 | 44 |
| 21:10–14 | 51 |
| 22:11–19 | 45 |
| 22:16–18 | 45 |
| 26:2–5 | 45 |
| 26:26–33 | 44 |
| 27:5–45 | 42 |
| 28:13–15 | 45 |
| 29:15–30 | 42 |
| 31:19 | 43 |
| 31:33–35 | 43, 44 |
| 31:43–54 | 44 |
| 31:53 | 4 |
| 32:2–4 | 44 |
| 32:28 | 103 |
| 34 | 42 |
| 34:30 | 42 |
| 35:3 | 40 |
| 35:22 | 43 |
| 44:1–17 | 43 |
| 45:4–13 | 40 |
| 45:4–15 | 43 |
| 49:3–4 | 43 |
| 49:5–7 | 42 |
| 50:15–21 | 43 |
| 50:20 | 51, 381 |

### Exodus

| | |
|---|---|
| 1 | 47, 54 |
| 1:7 | 47 |
| 1:9 | 47 |
| 1:11 | 47 |
| 3:1–6 | 47 |
| 3:7–8 | 47 |
| 3:8 | 126 |
| 3:9–10 | 47 |
| 3:10 | 47 |
| 3:13 | 47 |
| 3:18 | 47 |
| 3:19–20 | 47 |
| 3:19–22 | 47 |
| 3:21–22 | 50 |
| 4:17–31 | 48 |
| 4:21 | 49 |
| 5:1 | 48 |
| 5:1–9 | 48 |
| 5:2 | 48 |
| 5:3 | 48, 49 |
| 5:4 | 48 |
| 5:15–21 | 48 |
| 5:22–6:1 | 48 |
| 6:9–13 | 48 |
| 7:1–13 | 48 |
| 7:14ff. | 48 |
| 7:22 | 48 |
| 8:7 | 48 |
| 8:18 | 48 |
| 9:11 | 48 |
| 9:12 | 49 |
| 9:14–16 | 49 |
| 10:1 | 49 |
| 10:7–11 | 49 |
| 11:4–8 | 49 |
| 12:12 | 48 |
| 12:31–32 | 50 |
| 12:33–36 | 50 |
| 12:38 | 54 |

## Scripture Index

| | | | |
|---|---|---|---|
| 13:13 | 7 | 20:23 | 56, 58, 59, 60 |
| 14:1 | 47 | 20:24 | 114 |
| 14:5 | 50 | 20:24–26 | 60 |
| 14:10 | 47 | 21:1—22:17 [18–20] | 60 |
| 14:10–14 | 47, 103 | 21:2–6 | 7 |
| 14:17 | 49 | 21:16 | 43, 117 |
| 14:28 | 5 | 21:22 | 56n6 |
| 15:1 | 50 | 22:7–13 | 61 |
| 15:1–3 | 51 | 22:9 | 61 |
| 15:2 | 50 | 22:16–17 | 61 |
| 15:3 | 122n2 | 22:18–19 | 60 |
| 15:6 | 50 | 22:20 | 60, 151n16 |
| 15:7 | 5 | 22:21–24 | 61 |
| 15:9 | 50 | 22:21–27 | 61, 67 |
| 15:11 | 50 | 22:23–24 | 590 |
| 15:13 | 50 | 22:25–27 | 61 |
| 15:19 | 5 | 22:28 | 60 |
| 15:23–25 | 103 | 22:29–30 | 60 |
| 15:24 | 54 | 22:31 | 60 |
| 16:2–3 | 54, 103 | 23:1–3 | 62 |
| 16:3 | 99 | 23:4–5 | 61 |
| 17:2–3 | 54 | 23:6–8 | 62 |
| 17:2–4 | 103 | 23:7 | 67 |
| 17:8–16 | 51 | 23:9 | 61, 62 |
| 18:14–23 | 54 | 23:11 | 61 |
| 19–24 | 55, 57 | 23:12 | 61 |
| 19:3 | 116 | 23:13 | 60 |
| 19:3b | 55 | 23:19 | 56 |
| 19:4 | 55 | 23:20–33 | 56n4, 126 |
| 19:5 | 55, 591 | 23:23–33 | 44, 109 |
| 19:5–6 | 57 | 24 | 57 |
| 19:6a | 56 | 24:3 | 57 |
| 19:6b | 55 | 24:3–8 | 56, 64 |
| 19:7–8 | 56 | 24:7 | 56, 57 |
| 19:16–20 [21–25] | 56 | 24:8 | 57 |
| 20 | 63n14 | 24:9–11 | 64 |
| 20:1–17 | 56 | 24:9–12 | 56 |
| 20:3–11 | 58 | 24:10–11 | 57 |
| 20:4 | 59 | 24:12–14 | 65 |
| 20:5 | 7 | 24:38 | 116 |
| 20:10–11 | 61 | 25–31 | 65 |
| 20:12–17 | 58 | 31:18 | 65 |
| 20:16 | 62 | 32:1–4 | 62 |
| 20:18–20 | 56, 56n3 | 32:4 | 62 |

623

## Index

### Exodus (continued)

| | |
|---|---|
| 32:5 | 62 |
| 32:7–8 | 63 |
| 32:7–10 | 105 |
| 32:9–10 | 63 |
| 32:11 | 63 |
| 32:11–13 | 105 |
| 32:11–14 | 398 |
| 32:20 | 63 |
| 32:27 | 64 |
| 32:28–29 | 64 |
| 32:29 | 64 |
| 32:30–34 | 64, 577 |
| 32:31 | 6 |
| 32:33–35 | 63 |
| 32:34 | 7 |
| 33:1–6 | 64, 65 |
| 33:12–16 | 64, 65 |
| 33:17–23 | 65, 151 |
| 33:17–28 | 64 |
| 33:19 | 208 |
| 34 | 64 |
| 34:1–28 | 64 |
| 34:6 | 208 |
| 34:6–7 | 65 |
| 34:6–9 | 64 |
| 34:7 | 7, 59 |
| 34:9 | 65 |
| 34:10 | 64, 65 |
| 34:11–16 | 126 |
| 34:12–16 | 44 |
| 34:15–16 | 109 |
| 34:20 | 7 |
| 35–40 | 65 |
| 40:34 | 65 |

### Leviticus

| | |
|---|---|
| 1–7 | 65 |
| 5:17 | 576 |
| 7:18 | 576 |
| 8–9 | 65 |
| 11–15 | 66 |
| 16 | 66, 67 |
| 16:14 | 67 |
| 16:16–19 | 68 |
| 16:18–19 | 68 |
| 16:20–22 | 68 |
| 17 | 66 |
| 17–26 | 66 |
| 17:7 | 66 |
| 17:16 | 576 |
| 18 | 71, 125 |
| 18–20 | 66 |
| 18:1–5 | 68 |
| 18:24–25 | 124 |
| 18:24–28 | 68 |
| 18:29 | 68 |
| 19 | 71 |
| 19:2 | 66 |
| 19:4 | 59, 66 |
| 19:11 | 66 |
| 19:12–16 | 66 |
| 19:17–18 | 66 |
| 19:34 | 67 |
| 20:22–26 | 44, 68 |
| 21–22 | 66 |
| 23–25 | 66 |
| 23:26–32 | 67 |
| 23:39–43 | 69n18 |
| 24:10–16 | 66 |
| 25 | 7, 67 |
| 25:25–31 | 7 |
| 25:35–54 | 7 |
| 26 | 68, 71 |
| 26:1 | 59, 66 |
| 26:3–13 | 68 |
| 26:14–46 | 68 |
| 26:27–32 | 68 |
| 26:33–39 | 68 |
| 26:39–40 | 6 |
| 26:40–45 | 68 |
| 26:46 | 66 |
| 27 | 67 |
| 27:15 | 7 |
| 27:19 | 7 |
| 27:31 | 7 |

## Scripture Index

### Numbers

| | |
|---|---|
| 5:1–4 | 67 |
| 5:1–31 | 63n16 |
| 5:5–10 | 67 |
| 5:5–31 | 102 |
| 5:11–31 | 61n12, 67 |
| 6:1–21 | 67, 102 |
| 11:3 | 104 |
| 11:34 | 104 |
| 12 | 107 |
| 13–14 | 103 |
| 13:28 | 104 |
| 13:31 | 104 |
| 13:32–33 | 104 |
| 14:1–3 | 104 |
| 14:4 | 104 |
| 14:8–9 | 105, 127 |
| 14:11–12 | 105 |
| 14:13–16 | 105 |
| 14:17–19 | 105 |
| 14:20–23 | 105 |
| 14:22 | 104 |
| 14:24–25 | 105 |
| 14:28–35 | 105 |
| 14:36–37 | 105 |
| 14:39–45 | 105 |
| 15 | 105 |
| 15:1–10 | 106 |
| 15:2 | 105–6 |
| 15:17 | 106 |
| 15:17–21 | 106 |
| 16 | 106, 107 |
| 16:1–40 | 66 |
| 16:3 | 106 |
| 16:8–10 | 106 |
| 16:13–14 | 106 |
| 16:22 | 107 |
| 16:23 | 107 |
| 16:26 | 6 |
| 16:27 | 107 |
| 16:29 | 106 |
| 16:30–33 | 106 |
| 16:32 | 107 |
| 16:35 | 107 |
| 16:41 | 107 |
| 16:46–49 | 107 |
| 17:1–9 | 107 |
| 17:10 | 107 |
| 17:13 | 107 |
| 18:1–7 | 107 |
| 18:8–32 | 107 |
| 18:15–16 | 7 |
| 18:16 | 7 |
| 20:2–13 | 108 |
| 20:10 | 108 |
| 20:12 | 108 |
| 20:13 | 104 |
| 22:12 | 108 |
| 22:18–20 | 108 |
| 22:35 | 108 |
| 22:38 | 108 |
| 25:4 | 109 |
| 25:5 | 109 |
| 25:6–8 | 109 |
| 27:1–11 | 67, 102 |
| 27:3 | 6, 72 |
| 32:13 | 6 |
| 35 | 67 |
| 36:1–12 | 102 |

### Deuteronomy

| | |
|---|---|
| 4 | 112 |
| 4:25 | 6 |
| 5:3 | 113 |
| 5:7 | 58 |
| 5:8 | 59 |
| 5:22–27 | 56n3 |
| 6:4–5 | 112–13 |
| 6:5 | 600 |
| 7–11 | 112, 116 |
| 7:1–16 | 44, 126 |
| 7:2–4 | 126 |
| 7:3–4 | 109 |
| 7:6 | 112 |
| 7:7 | 112 |
| 8 | 180n34 |

## Index

*Deuteronomy (continued)*

| | |
|---|---|
| 8:2–3 | 111–12 |
| 8:5 | 112, 116 |
| 8:19–20 | 116 |
| 9:4 | 112 |
| 9:4–5 | 124, 125 |
| 9:5 | 124 |
| 9:6 | 112 |
| 9:18–19 | 398 |
| 9:25 | 398 |
| 10:12–13 | 113 |
| 10:14–15 | 112 |
| 11:26–28 | 113 |
| 12 | 12, 114 |
| 12–26 | 118 |
| 12:2–4 | 114 |
| 12:5–7 | 114 |
| 12:8–9 | 114 |
| 12:11 | 114 |
| 12:12 | 113 |
| 12:13–15 | 114n5 |
| 12:15 | 115 |
| 12:17–18 | 114 |
| 12:18–19 | 113 |
| 12:20–21 | 115 |
| 12:29–31 | 44, 114, 117 |
| 12:30 | 125 |
| 12:31 | 125 |
| 13 | 59, 114, 118, 151n16 |
| 13:1–2 | 117 |
| 13:1–5 | 114 |
| 13:5 | 114, 128, 590 |
| 13:6 | 117 |
| 13:6–11 | 114 |
| 13:11 | 117, 590 |
| 13:12 | 117 |
| 13:12–18 | 114 |
| 13:17 | 114 |
| 14–16 | 115 |
| 14:1–2 | 117 |
| 14:23 | 115 |
| 14:26–27 | 113 |
| 14:28–29 | 113 |
| 15:1–11 | 171n22 |
| 15:12–18 | 7, 113 |
| 16 | 115 |
| 16:11 | 113 |
| 16:14 | 113 |
| 16:18–20 | 115, 117–18 |
| 16:19–20 | 118 |
| 16:21–22 | 181n36 |
| 17:2 | 6, 117 |
| 17:2–3 | 59 |
| 17:2–7 | 114 |
| 17:2–13 | 115 |
| 17:4–7 | 114 |
| 17:7 | 114, 195 |
| 17:8–13 | 115, 118 |
| 17:14–20 | 115 |
| 18:1–5 | 115 |
| 18:1–8 | 115 |
| 18:6–8 | 115 |
| 18:9 | 125 |
| 18:9–11 | 114, 117 |
| 18:9–14 | 115 |
| 18:9–22 | 115 |
| 18:12 | 125 |
| 18:15–17 | 115 |
| 18:15–22 | 245 |
| 18:18–19 | 115 |
| 18:20–21 | 115 |
| 18:22 | 115 |
| 19:1–13 | 114, 117, 118 |
| 19:10 | 114, 117n9 |
| 19:13 | 195 |
| 19:15 | 114 |
| 19:15–19 | 114 |
| 19:15–21 | 114, 118 |
| 20:1–9 | 118 |
| 20:10–18 | 118 |
| 20:19–20 | 118 |
| 21:1–9 | 118 |
| 21:2—23:33 | 590 |
| 21:8 | 117n9 |
| 21:18–21 | 114, 117 |
| 21:21 | 114 |
| 21:22–23 | 118 |
| 22:6–7 | 113 |

| | |
|---|---|
| 22:12–20 | 119 |
| 22:13–29 | 61 |
| 22:20 | 59 |
| 22:22 | 114, 117 |
| 22:23 | 117 |
| 22:24 | 114 |
| 22:28 | 117 |
| 23:10–15 | 118 |
| 23:13 | 59 |
| 23:15–16 | 113 |
| 23:18–19 | 117 |
| 24:1 | 117 |
| 24:1–4 | 221 |
| 24:7 | 114, 117 |
| 24:16 | 6, 113, 116 |
| 24:18 | 7 |
| 24:19–22 | 113 |
| 25:1–3 | 113–14, 118 |
| 25:17–19 | 118 |
| 26 | 116 |
| 26:4 | 113 |
| 26:12–15 | 113 |
| 26:16–19 | 116 |
| 26:18 | 116 |
| 27:9–10 | 116 |
| 27:15 | 59 |
| 28 | 116, 118 |
| 29–31 | 118 |
| 29:14–15 | 113 |
| 30 | 118 |
| 30:1–2 | 118 |
| 30:1–10 | 118, 120, 158 |
| 30:2–3 | 158 |
| 30:3–5 | 119 |
| 30:6 | 119 |
| 30:7b | 119 |
| 30:15–27 | 119 |
| 30:36–38 | 119 |
| 32 | 157–58 |
| 32:1–38 | 120 |
| 32:17–18 | 158 |
| 32:21 | 158 |
| 32:34–43 | 158 |
| 34:14 | 59 |

## Joshua

| | |
|---|---|
| 5:9 | 122 |
| 6:1–21 | 122 |
| 7 | 122 |
| 7:2–15 | 127 |
| 7:16–21 | 127 |
| 7:22–26 | 127 |
| 8 | 122 |
| 10 | 122, 123 |
| 10:29–43 | 123 |
| 12 | 123 |
| 23 | 131 |
| 23:13 | 131 |
| 24 | 131 |
| 24:2–15 | 131 |
| 24:19–20 | 131 |
| 24:19–27 | 155 |
| 24:21–28 | 131 |

## Judges

| | |
|---|---|
| 1 | 123, 129 |
| 1:1–3 | 129 |
| 1:4–8 | 129 |
| 1:19 | 129 |
| 1:22–26 | 123n3, 129 |
| 2:1–3 | 130 |
| 2:3 | 123 |
| 2:4–5 | 130 |
| 2:11 | 6 |
| 2:11–12 | 130 |
| 2:11–23 | 129–30 |
| 2:14–15 | 130 |
| 2:16 | 130 |
| 2:18–19 | 130 |
| 2:21 | 123 |
| 3 | 124 |
| 3–16 | 129 |
| 3:4 | 124 |
| 3:7–9 | 129n15 |
| 3:11 | 129n15 |
| 3:12 | 129n15 |
| 3:12–30 | 129 |

## Index

**Judges (continued)**

| | |
|---|---|
| 3:15 | 129n15 |
| 3:30 | 129n15 |
| 4–5 | 129 |
| 4:1–3 | 129n15 |
| 5:31b | 129n15 |
| 6–8 | 129 |
| 6:1–2 | 129n15 |
| 6:7–8 | 129n15 |
| 6:7–10 | 130, 131 |
| 6:25–26 | 132 |
| 6:27 | 132 |
| 8:22–23 | 132 |
| 8:24–27 | 129n14 |
| 8:24–28 | 59 |
| 8:27 | 132n18 |
| 8:33–35 | 129n15 |
| 9 | 124, 133 |
| 10:1–5 | 124 |
| 10:6 | 6 |
| 10:6–16 | 129n15 |
| 10:10–16 | 130 |
| 11–12 | 129 |
| 11:27 | 4, 81 |
| 12:7 | 129n15 |
| 12:8–15 | 124 |
| 13:1 | 129n15 |
| 16:31 | 129n15 |
| 17–18 | 124, 133 |
| 17:3–5 | 59 |
| 17:6 | 133, 139 |
| 18:30–31 | 59 |
| 19–21 | 124, 133 |
| 19:16–30 | 46 |
| 21:3 | 133 |
| 21:25 | 133 |

**1 Samuel**

| | |
|---|---|
| 1 | 138 |
| 1–2 | 72 |
| 2 | 131, 140n6 |
| 2:11 | 141 |
| 2:12–17 | 141 |
| 2:15–17 | 141 |
| 2:18–21 | 141 |
| 2:22 | 141 |
| 2:22–25 | 141 |
| 2:23–25 | 141 |
| 2:26 | 141 |
| 2:27 | 141 |
| 2:27–28 | 141 |
| 2:27–36 | 141 |
| 2:29 | 141 |
| 2:30 | 141 |
| 2:31–32 | 141 |
| 2:33 | 141 |
| 2:34 | 141 |
| 2:35–36 | 141 |
| 3 | 131, 141 |
| 3:11–12 | 141 |
| 4–6 | 59 |
| 7:6 | 6 |
| 8 | 115, 132, 133, 183 |
| 8–12 | 137, 155 |
| 8–15 | 139 |
| 8:4–5 | 133 |
| 8:7 | 133 |
| 8:11–18 | 139 |
| 8:20 | 139 |
| 9:1—10:16 | 139 |
| 9:16 | 140 |
| 10:1 | 140 |
| 10:8 | 142 |
| 11 | 140 |
| 11:12–15 | 140 |
| 11:15 | 183n40 |
| 12 | 132, 140, 183 |
| 12:6–11 | 133 |
| 12:9 | 144 |
| 12:12–15 | 133 |
| 12:16–18 | 140 |
| 12:19–24 | 140 |
| 12:19–25 | 133 |
| 12:22 | 140 |
| 13:8–10a | 142 |
| 13:8–15 | 142 |

| | | | |
|---|---|---|---|
| 13:10–11 | 183 | 12:13 | 145 |
| 13:13a | 142 | 13–20 | 145 |
| 13:13b–14 | 142 | 17:14 | 7 |
| 14:45 | 7 | 21:1–7 | 128n8 |
| 15:1–2 | 142 | 24:10 | 6 |
| 15:1–35 | 142 | | |
| 15:19 | 6 | | |

## 1 Kings

| | | | |
|---|---|---|---|
| 15:22–23 | 142, 229 | 2 | 138 |
| 15:24 | 6 | 2:26–27 | 141 |
| 15:24–31 | 142 | 11 | 145 |
| 16:1–13 | 143 | 11:1–8 | 145 |
| 24 | 143 | 11:6 | 6 |
| 24:8–21 | 143 | 11:9 | 146 |
| 26 | 143 | 11:9–10 | 146 |
| 26:13–25 | 143 | 11:10–13 | 146 |
| 28:8–19 | 142 | 11:14–25 | 146 |
| | | 11:26–28 | 146 |
| | | 11:31 | 146 |

## 2 Samuel

| | | | |
|---|---|---|---|
| | | 11:33 | 146 |
| 1:19–26 | 266 | 11:35 | 146 |
| 3:6–11 | 145n12 | 11:40 | 146 |
| 3:33–34 | 266 | 12 | 13, 146 |
| 4:9 | 7 | 12:4 | 146 |
| 4:11 | 6 | 12:25–30 | 59 |
| 5:1–5 | 147n14 | 13 | 147 |
| 5:3 | 55 | 14:1–5 | 147 |
| 7:1–2 | 143 | 14:9 | 147 |
| 7:3 | 143 | 14:12–13 | 100 |
| 7:4–7 | 143 | 14:22 | 6 |
| 7:8–17 | 143 | 16:31–33 | 150 |
| 11 | 143 | 17 | 150 |
| 11:1–2 | 143 | 17–18 | 178n30 |
| 11:3–4 | 143 | 17–19 | 138, 147, 149–52 |
| 11:5 | 143 | 17:1 | 149 |
| 11:6–8 | 143 | 18:3b–4 | 150 |
| 11:9–13 | 143 | 18:13 | 150 |
| 11:27–12:1 | 144 | 18:21 | 150 |
| 12 | 64, 143 | 18:31–32 | 151 |
| 12–20 | 72–73 | 18:41–46 | 151 |
| 12:1–7 | 144 | 19 | 151 |
| 12:7 | 144 | 19:10 | 151 |
| 12:7–8 | 162 | 19:15–18 | 131, 151 |
| 12:8 | 145 | 19:19–21 | 151–52 |
| 12:10 | 145, 162 | | |

## Index

### 1 Kings (continued)

| | |
|---|---|
| 20:35–43 | 141n9 |
| 21 | 138, 147, 148 |
| 21:1–2 | 147 |
| 21:17–19 | 147 |
| 21:19 | 162 |
| 21:20–26 | 148 |
| 21:23 | 148 |
| 21:25–26 | 149 |
| 21:27 | 149 |
| 21:29 | 149 |
| 22 | 152, 152n17 |
| 22:8 | 153 |
| 22:10 | 153 |
| 22:16 | 153 |

### 2 Kings

| | |
|---|---|
| 1 | 138 |
| 1–2 | 147 |
| 1–10 | 137 |
| 1:1 | 128n11 |
| 1:2–4 | 149 |
| 1:2a | 149 |
| 1:3–4 | 149 |
| 1:5–16 | 149 |
| 2 | 475n19 |
| 8:7–15 | 152 |
| 8:28–29 | 152 |
| 9–10 | 138, 148, 149 |
| 9:1 | 137n1 |
| 9:1–10 | 152 |
| 9:1–11 | 141n9 |
| 9:25–26 | 148 |
| 9:33–36 | 148 |
| 9:36–37 | 148 |
| 10:18–27 | 152 |
| 13:1–2 | 156 |
| 13:4 | 137n1 |
| 17 | 131n17, 156–57 |
| 17:1–6 | 156 |
| 17:6 | 157 |
| 17:7–8 | 156 |
| 17:7–23 | 146n13 |
| 17:19 | 157 |
| 17:19–20 | 157 |
| 17:24–25 | 157 |
| 17:26 | 157 |
| 17:27–28 | 157 |
| 17:29–34 | 157 |
| 18:13—20:19 | 354 |
| 21:2–6 | 221 |
| 21:16 | 221 |
| 22:3—23:25 | 218n9 |
| 23 | 12 |
| 23:1 | 119 |
| 23:3 | 119 |
| 23:4–14 | 119, 221 |
| 23:8a | 119 |
| 23:15–21 | 119 |
| 23:29–30 | 217 |
| 24:1–7 | 250 |

### 2 Chronicles

| | |
|---|---|
| 20:15 | 271 |
| 20:15–17 | 271 |
| 33:10–13 | 216n7 |

### Ezra

| | |
|---|---|
| 7 | 69n18 |
| 7:6–7 | 69 |

### Nehemiah

| | |
|---|---|
| 1:6 | 479 |
| 8 | 459–60 |

### Job

| | |
|---|---|
| 1–2 | 435 |
| 3 | 236n24, 435, 436–37 |
| 3:1—42:6 | 435 |
| 4–5 | 435 |
| 4:7 | 435, 437 |

## Scripture Index

| | | | |
|---|---|---|---|
| 4:8 | 435 | 14:13 | 440 |
| 4:12–16 | 445 | 14:13–17 | 435 |
| 4:17 | 437 | 14:14b | 442 |
| 4:17–19 | 445 | 14:21–22 | 441–42 |
| 5:6–7 | 437 | 15:14–16 | 445 |
| 5:8–27 | 435 | 16–17 | 443 |
| 6–7 | 436 | 16:18–19 | 442–43 |
| 6:2–3 | 438 | 16:18–21 | 435 |
| 6:4 | 438 | 17:13 | 443 |
| 6:8–10 | 442 | 17:15–16 | 443 |
| 6:8–13 | 438 | 19:23–27 | 435 |
| 6:14–30 | 438 | 19:23–27a | 443–44 |
| 6:15–20 | 235n23 | 21 | 436, 444 |
| 7:7a | 438 | 21:1–34 | 435 |
| 7:8a | 438 | 21:7–8 | 81 |
| 7:11 | 438 | 21:13–16a | 81 |
| 7:12 | 438 | 21:28–32 | 287n25 |
| 7:17–18 | 438 | 22 | 436, 444 |
| 8 | 436 | 23:3–17 | 435 |
| 9–10 | 436 | 24 | 436, 444n15 |
| 9:2 | 439, 439n12, 450 | 24–27 | 436n9 |
| 9:14–15a | 439 | 24:1–12 | 435 |
| 9:14–20 | 450 | 24:22–25 | 435 |
| 9:16 | 439 | 25 | 445n17 |
| 9:19 | 439 | 25:2–3 | 439 |
| 9:20a | 439 | 25:4–6 | 439, 445 |
| 9:21 | 439 | 26:2–4 | 439n12 |
| 9:32–35 | 436n11 | 26:2–14 | 445n17 |
| 9:33 | 439, 443 | 26:5–14 | 439 |
| 10:2 | 264n12, 439 | 27 | 435 |
| 10:3–7 | 439 | 27:6 | 440 |
| 10:8–13 | 440 | 28 | 436 |
| 10:14–17 | 440 | 29 | 444 |
| 10:18 | 437 | 29–31 | 441, 444 |
| 10:21–22 | 441 | 30 | 444 |
| 11 | 436 | 31 | 444, 450–51 |
| 12 | 440 | 31:13–15 | 77 |
| 12–14 | 436 | 31:35–37 | 444 |
| 12:13–14a | 442 | 38–41 | 398 |
| 13:13–16 | 440 | 38:2 | 447 |
| 13:13–27 | 435 | 38:3 | 447, 451 |
| 13:15–16 | 447 | 40:2 | 448, 451 |
| 13:23 | 440 | 40:7 | 447 |
| 14:7–12 | 442 | 40:7–8 | 451 |

## Index

### Job (continued)

| | |
|---|---|
| 40:8 | 447, 448 |
| 40:9–14 | 448 |
| 41:1–9 | 449 |
| 41:1–11 | 447, 449 |
| 41:10–11 | 447 |
| 41:11 | 449 |
| 41:12–21 | 439 |
| 42:1–6 | 398, 452 |
| 42:2 | 449 |
| 42:5 | 449 |
| 42:5–6 | 449 |
| 42:6 | 446, 450 |
| 42:7 | 451 |
| 42:7–8 | 398 |
| 42:7–9 | 450 |
| 42:7–17 | 435 |
| 42:7–28 | 398 |

### Psalms

| | |
|---|---|
| 1 | 457 |
| 1:5 | 457 |
| 2:5 | 5 |
| 6 | 92 |
| 6:5 | 92 |
| 6:7 | 92 |
| 6:8 | 92 |
| 7 | 83, 456 |
| 7:3–5 | 83, 88, 456 |
| 7:6 | 83 |
| 7:7–8 | 83 |
| 7:9 | 456 |
| 7:9–11 | 83 |
| 7:10 | 456 |
| 7:11 | 456 |
| 7:12–14 | 83 |
| 7:15–16 | 83 |
| 7:17 | 83 |
| 9 | 456 |
| 9:5 | 4, 81 |
| 9:7–8 | 456 |
| 9:8 | 456 |
| 10 | 456 |
| 13 | 89–92, 97 |
| 13:1 | 89 |
| 13:1–2 | 89 |
| 13:3–4 | 90 |
| 13:5–6 | 90 |
| 13:5b–6 | 428 |
| 14:1 | 87 |
| 17 | 83, 84, 457 |
| 17:1 | 457 |
| 17:1–2 | 84 |
| 17:2 | 457 |
| 17:3–5 | 84, 88, 457 |
| 17:6–9 | 84 |
| 17:13–14 | 84 |
| 22 | 92–94, 97, 606 |
| 22:1–2 | 93 |
| 22:3–5 | 93 |
| 22:6–8 | 93 |
| 22:11 | 93 |
| 22:12–13 | 93 |
| 22:16–18 | 93 |
| 22:19 | 90, 93 |
| 22:19–21a | 93 |
| 22:19a | 93 |
| 22:21 | 93 |
| 22:21b | 93 |
| 26 | 83, 84 |
| 26:1–2 | 84 |
| 30:5 | 604 |
| 30:9 | 442 |
| 31 | 85–86 |
| 31:11–13 | 85–86 |
| 31:19 | 86 |
| 32:1–2 | 573 |
| 35 | 83, 84–85 |
| 35:1 | 84 |
| 35:4 | 84 |
| 35:6 | 84 |
| 35:9–10 | 85 |
| 35:11 | 85 |
| 35:18 | 85 |
| 35:19 | 85 |
| 35:22–23a | 85 |

## Scripture Index

| | | | |
|---|---|---|---|
| 35:26a | 85 | 50:1–2 | 431 |
| 35:27 | 85 | 50:1–6 | 458 |
| 37 | 457 | 50:5 | 431 |
| 37:28 | 458 | 50:6 | 4, 81, 458 |
| 39 | 94–95, 97 | 50:7 | 459 |
| 39:1–3 | 94 | 50:7–23 | 431 |
| 39:4 | 94 | 50:8–9 | 431 |
| 39:7–8a | 94 | 50:8–15 | 459 |
| 39:9–11a | 94–95 | 50:10–13 | 431 |
| 39:12b–13 | 95 | 50:14–15 | 431 |
| 42 | 87 | 50:16 | 431–32 |
| 42–43 | 87–89 | 50:16–22 | 431–32, 459 |
| 42:1–2a | 87 | 50:22 | 432 |
| 42:3 | 87 | 50:23 | 432 |
| 42:4 | 87 | 51 | 88n11, 308, 426–30, 429, 430, 432, 433, 458, 472, 486, 534, 558, 572, 577, 609 |
| 42:5a | 87 | | |
| 42:5b | 87 | | |
| 42:9 | 87 | | |
| 42:10 | 87 | 51:1–2 | 426 |
| 42:11 | 87 | 51:3–4 | 427 |
| 43 | 83, 87 | 51:4 | 427, 458 |
| 43:1 | 87 | 51:5 | 427 |
| 43:2 | 87 | 51:6 | 428 |
| 43:5 | 87 | 51:6–7 | 427 |
| 44 | 127, 256, 257, 259, 260, 262, 413n6, 458n3 | 51:7 | 472 |
| | | 51:8 | 428 |
| | | 51:8–9 | 427–28 |
| 44:2 | 127 | 51:9 | 428 |
| 44:2–3 | 257 | 51:10 | 428 |
| 44:4–8 | 257 | 51:10–12 | 428, 433 |
| 44:9 | 257 | 51:11 | 428 |
| 44:10–14 | 258 | 51:13 | 433 |
| 44:17–18 | 259 | 51:13–14 | 428 |
| 44:17–22 | 264 | 51:14a | 429 |
| 44:20–21 | 260 | 51:14b | 429 |
| 44:22 | 260 | 51:15 | 429 |
| 46 | 461, 464 | 51:16–17 | 429, 431, 458 |
| 46:9–10 | 464 | 51:17 | 426, 429, 433 |
| 47 | 461, 463, 464 | 51:18–19 | 429–30 |
| 47:2 | 463 | 55 | 83, 86 |
| 47:6 | 463 | 55:6–8 | 86 |
| 47:7 | 463 | 55:9–11 | 86 |
| 47:8 | 463 | 55:12–13 | 86 |
| 50 | 431–32, 458–59 | 55:15 | 86 |

## Index

**Psalms (continued)**

| | |
|---|---|
| 55:18–19 | 86 |
| 55:20–21 | 86 |
| 55:23 | 86 |
| 60 | 257n1 |
| 69:18 | 7 |
| 72:14 | 7 |
| 74 | 256, 257, 260, 262, 413n6, 458n3 |
| 74:1 | 259 |
| 74:4–8 | 259 |
| 74:9 | 259 |
| 74:10 | 259 |
| 74:11 | 259 |
| 74:12–14a | 259 |
| 74:18 | 260 |
| 74:18–23 | 259 |
| 74:18b | 260 |
| 74:21 | 260 |
| 74:22b–23 | 260 |
| 77 | 87, 95–96, 97 |
| 77:1 | 95 |
| 77:3 | 95 |
| 77:4 | 95 |
| 77:7–8 | 87 |
| 77:7–9 | 95 |
| 77:8 | 87 |
| 77:9 | 87 |
| 77:10 | 87, 96 |
| 77:11 | 96 |
| 77:14–15 | 96 |
| 77:16–20 | 96 |
| 78 | 109–10 |
| 78:17–18 | 109 |
| 78:21 | 109–10 |
| 78:22 | 110 |
| 78:40–41 | 110 |
| 78:56–66 | 110 |
| 79 | 256, 257, 260, 413n6, 460 |
| 79:6 | 260, 460 |
| 79:10b | 460 |
| 80 | 256, 257, 260, 413n6 |
| 80:1–3 | 258 |
| 80:8–9 | 258 |
| 80:12–13 | 258 |
| 80:14–15a | 258 |
| 80:18 | 260 |
| 82 | 460 |
| 82:1 | 460 |
| 82:2 | 460 |
| 82:3–4 | 460 |
| 82:5 | 460 |
| 82:6–7 | 460 |
| 82:8 | 4, 460 |
| 83 | 257n1 |
| 85 | 257n1, 413n6 |
| 88 | 96–97 |
| 88:3 | 96 |
| 88:5 | 96 |
| 88:6–8 | 96–97 |
| 88:9 | 97 |
| 88:13 | 97 |
| 88:15a | 97 |
| 89 | 256, 257, 260–62, 413n6 |
| 89:1–4 | 261 |
| 89:5–13 | 261 |
| 89:14–18 | 261 |
| 89:19–37 | 143, 261 |
| 89:29–37 | 261 |
| 89:38–39 | 261 |
| 89:38–51 | 261 |
| 89:46 | 261 |
| 89:49–50a | 262 |
| 89:52 | 262n6 |
| 93 | 461, 463 |
| 93–99 | 463 |
| 93:1 | 463 |
| 94 | 463 |
| 94:4–7 | 463 |
| 94:8–11 | 463 |
| 94:16–19 | 463 |
| 94:16–23 | 463 |
| 94:22–23 | 463 |
| 95 | 461, 462, 463 |
| 95:1–7a | 462 |
| 95:4–5 | 462 |

## Scripture Index

| | |
|---|---|
| 95:8 | 463 |
| 96 | 461, 462, 464n8 |
| 96:1 | 462 |
| 96:2–5 | 462 |
| 96:3 | 462 |
| 96:7 | 462 |
| 96:9 | 462 |
| 96:11–12 | 462 |
| 96:13 | 4, 462 |
| 97 | 461, 462, 464n8 |
| 97:8 | 462 |
| 97:8–9 | 462 |
| 97:9 | 462 |
| 97:10–11 | 462 |
| 98 | 461, 462, 464n8 |
| 98:1 | 462 |
| 98:2 | 462 |
| 98:4 | 462 |
| 98:7–8 | 462 |
| 98:9 | 4, 442, 462 |
| 99 | 461, 463 |
| 99:4 | 463 |
| 103 | 261n5, 262n6 |
| 103:9 | 264n12 |
| 104 | 261n5, 262n6 |
| 105 | 459–60 |
| 105:2 | 459 |
| 105:5 | 459 |
| 105:7 | 459 |
| 105:8–11 | 459 |
| 105:45 | 459 |
| 106 | 110, 242n31, 326, 459–60 |
| 106:12 | 459 |
| 106:13–14 | 110 |
| 106:13–15 | 459 |
| 106:16 | 110 |
| 106:19 | 110 |
| 106:20 | 110 |
| 106:28 | 110 |
| 106:34–46 | 110 |
| 106:40–46 | 459 |
| 106:43a | 459 |
| 106:44–46 | 459 |
| 106:47 | 459 |
| 108 | 261n5, 262n6 |
| 130 | 8, 86n9, 88n11, 308, 432–33, 434, 459, 558, 572, 609 |
| 130:2 | 432 |
| 130:3–4 | 458 |
| 130:7–8 | 8, 433 |
| 132:1–12 | 143 |
| 132:17–18 | 143 |
| 139 | 5 |
| 143 | 83, 86–87, 88n10 |
| 143:3 | 86 |
| 143:4 | 86 |
| 143:7 | 86 |
| 143:9 | 86 |
| 143:12 | 86 |

### Proverbs

| | |
|---|---|
| 1:7 | 74 |
| 9:10 | 74 |
| 10:3 | 75 |
| 10:12 | 78 |
| 10:19 | 79 |
| 10:26 | 78 |
| 10:27–30 | 79 |
| 11 | 79 |
| 11:1 | 76 |
| 11:2 | 78 |
| 11:20 | 74 |
| 11:24 | 79 |
| 11:25 | 79 |
| 12 | 79 |
| 12:2 | 74 |
| 12:6 | 6 |
| 12:22 | 79 |
| 12:24 | 77 |
| 13 | 79 |
| 13:3 | 79 |
| 13:10 | 79 |
| 13:23 | 77 |
| 14 | 79 |
| 14:5 | 76 |

## Index

*Proverbs (continued)*

| | |
|---|---|
| 14:31 | 77 |
| 15:1 | 79 |
| 15:18 | 78 |
| 15:19 | 77 |
| 15:29 | 75 |
| 15:32 | 79 |
| 15:33 | 74 |
| 16:1 | 74 |
| 16:2 | 74 |
| 16:5 | 78 |
| 16:9 | 74 |
| 16:11 | 76 |
| 16:18 | 78 |
| 16:32 | 78 |
| 17:4 | 79 |
| 17:8 | 79 |
| 18:12 | 78 |
| 19:6 | 79 |
| 19:17 | 77 |
| 19:21 | 74–75 |
| 20:10 | 76 |
| 20:21 | 76 |
| 20:24 | 75 |
| 21:2 | 74 |
| 21:13 | 77 |
| 21:31 | 75 |
| 22:22–23 | 76 |
| 22:24–25a | 78 |
| 22:28 | 77 |
| 23:10–11 | 77 |
| 23:29–35 | 79 |
| 24:23–26 | 76 |
| 24:30–34 | 77–78 |
| 24:34b–25a | 76 |
| 25:18 | 76 |
| 26:21 | 78 |
| 28:7 | 74 |
| 29:18 | 74 |
| 30:6 | 75 |

*Isaiah*

| | |
|---|---|
| 1 | 321, 421–22 |
| 1–5 | 334 |
| 1–11 | 174, 320, 324, 343 |
| 1–12 | 332–43 |
| 1–39 | 317, 320–25, 358, 360–61, 362, 365, 371, 399, 400, 422, 423, 593 |
| 1:1 | 317 |
| 1:2–3 | 210, 334 |
| 1:4 | 320, 321, 392 |
| 1:4–9 | 194 |
| 1:7–8 | 198 |
| 1:8 | 334, 350n11 |
| 1:10 | 334, 392 |
| 1:11 | 323, 429 |
| 1:11–15 | 176 |
| 1:11–17 | 334 |
| 1:15–17 | 335 |
| 1:16–17 | 176 |
| 1:18 | 323 |
| 1:18–19 | 163 |
| 1:18–20 | 333, 335, 356, 357, 465 |
| 1:20 | 163 |
| 1:21 | 165, 335 |
| 1:21–23 | 358 |
| 1:21–28 | 210–11, 336, 349, 359 |
| 1:23 | 335 |
| 1:24 | 165, 335 |
| 1:24–26 | 358 |
| 1:25 | 165, 335 |
| 1:25–28 | 342 |
| 1:26 | 165, 336 |
| 1:27 | 358 |
| 1:27–28 | 336 |
| 1:28 | 358 |
| 1:29–31 | 336 |
| 2 | 187, 321 |
| 2–12 | 323 |
| 2:1 | 336 |

| | | | |
|---|---|---|---|
| 2:1–4 | 204n3, 211, 247, 323, 359, 464 | 7–8 | 198, 247, 339, 360 |
| 2:1–5 | 191 | 7–9 | 354 |
| 2:2 | 359 | 7:1–9 | 337 |
| 2:2–4 | 336, 346, 359 | 7:1–14 | 359 |
| 2:3 | 359 | 7:1–17 | 359 |
| 2:4 | 359 | 7:1—9:7 | 337–43 |
| 2:5 | 323 | 7:6 | 337 |
| 2:6 | 187 | 7:7–9 | 337 |
| 2:8 | 187 | 7:7b–9 | 189–90 |
| 2:11–12 | 187 | 7:9 | 357 |
| 2:18 | 187 | 7:9b | 194 |
| 2:20 | 187 | 7:10–12 | 190 |
| 2:22 | 187 | 7:16 | 21n3 |
| 3:1–5 | 198, 200 | 7:17 | 190 |
| 3:12 | 200 | 8:5–8 | 190, 337 |
| 3:13 | 264n12 | 8:8 | 337 |
| 4:2–5 | 342 | 8:10 | 337 |
| 5 | 174, 259, 334, 421 | 8:13–14 | 357 |
| 5:1–7 | 210, 220n12 | 8:16 | 323 |
| 5:7 | 175, 259, 357 | 8:19–20 | 188 |
| 5:8 | 175 | 8:21 | 358 |
| 5:8–24 | 175 | 8:22 | 323, 338 |
| 5:13–17 | 198 | 8:23—9:7 | 359 |
| 5:14–17 | 175 | 9:1 | 323, 338 |
| 5:18 | 321 | 9:1–7 | 359 |
| 5:18–19 | 191 | 9:2 | 323, 338 |
| 5:25–30 | 323 | 9:2–7 | 337, 339, 341 |
| 5:26 | 323 | 9:3 | 338 |
| 5:26–30 | 198 | 9:4–5 | 338 |
| 5:30 | 323 | 9:6 | 337 |
| 6 | 167, 322, 332, 356, 411, 602 | 9:6a | 338 |
| 6:1 | 322 | 9:7 | 338–39, 359 |
| 6:3 | 320 | 9:7a | 360 |
| 6:5 | 323 | 9:8–10 | 339 |
| 6:7 | 321 | 9:8–21 | 360 |
| 6:9–10 | 224n15, 294, 322, 333 | 9:8a | 206 |
| 6:10 | 352, 411 | 9:9 | 206 |
| 6:11–12 | 323 | 9:11–12 | 198 |
| 6:11–13 | 160, 333 | 9:14–15 | 198 |
| 6:12b | 175 | 9:20–21 | 198 |
| 6:13 | 479 | 9b–10 | 343–44 |
| | | 10 | 198, 339, 422 |
| | | 10:1–2 | 175 |
| | | 10:1–4 | 334 |

## Index

*Isaiah (continued)*

| | |
|---|---|
| 10:5 | 165, 211, 339 |
| 10:5–6 | 191, 193, 334, 339–40 |
| 10:5–19 | 36, 193, 247, 360 |
| 10:6 | 203 |
| 10:7 | 194, 340, 355n13 |
| 10:7–11 | 203 |
| 10:7–14 | 203, 247 |
| 10:13 | 194 |
| 10:15 | 203, 247, 340 |
| 10:16 | 198, 340 |
| 10:16–19 | 191, 203 |
| 10:18 | 198 |
| 10:19 | 198, 340 |
| 10:20 | 340 |
| 10:21–23 | 340 |
| 10:24–25 | 341 |
| 10:27b–32 | 198 |
| 11 | 339, 342 |
| 11:1 | 341 |
| 11:1–5 | 341 |
| 11:1–9 | 359 |
| 11:1–10 | 359 |
| 11:2 | 341 |
| 11:3b–4 | 360 |
| 11:3b–4a | 341 |
| 11:4 | 360 |
| 11:4b | 360 |
| 11:5 | 341 |
| 11:6–9 | 359, 417 |
| 11:9 | 342 |
| 11:10 | 323, 342 |
| 11:11–16 | 323, 342 |
| 11:12 | 323 |
| 11:13–14 | 338 |
| 12 | 321, 322, 323 |
| 12:1 | 320 |
| 12:4 | 343 |
| 12:5 | 343 |
| 13 | 344 |
| 13–14 | 248, 323, 454 |
| 13–23 | 174, 247n36, 344, 454 |
| 13–27 | 323, 324, 343–47 |
| 13–35 | 321 |
| 13:1 | 343 |
| 13:2 | 323 |
| 13:3 | 479 |
| 13:17 | 344 |
| 13:19 | 344 |
| 14 | 254, 344, 345, 422 |
| 14:1–2 | 345 |
| 14:5–6 | 344 |
| 14:12 | 254 |
| 14:12–21 | 344 |
| 14:13 | 344 |
| 14:14 | 344 |
| 14:16b–17 | 344–45 |
| 14:21 | 6 |
| 14:24 | 345 |
| 14:24–25 | 355 |
| 14:24–26 | 203–4 |
| 14:24–27 | 191, 211, 247, 345, 355 |
| 14:25 | 345 |
| 14:26 | 346 |
| 14:27 | 346 |
| 14:28 | 347n10 |
| 14:28–32 | 247 |
| 15 | 347 |
| 15:1 | 343 |
| 17 | 346 |
| 17:1 | 343 |
| 17:1–6 | 190n45 |
| 17:1–9 | 247, 347n10 |
| 18 | 247 |
| 18:1–6 | 192 |
| 18:13 | 323 |
| 19:1 | 192, 343 |
| 19:1–15 | 247 |
| 19:3 | 192 |
| 19:5–10 | 192 |
| 19:11–15 | 192, 247 |
| 19:16–17 | 347 |
| 19:16–25 | 347, 359 |
| 19:18 | 347 |
| 19:18–25 | 588 |

| | | | |
|---|---|---|---|
| 19:19–20 | 347 | 28–39 | 324 |
| 19:19–22 | 359 | 28:1–4 | 200, 347n10 |
| 19:21–22 | 347 | 28:4 | 323 |
| 19:23 | 347 | 28:5–6 | 347 |
| 19:23–25 | 359 | 28:7 | 188, 348 |
| 19:25 | 347 | 28:7–8 | 348 |
| 20 | 343, 346, 354 | 28:8 | 188 |
| 20:1–6 | 247 | 28:9–11 | 200 |
| 20:2–6 | 191 | 28:9–22 | 348 |
| 21 | 248 | 28:11 | 348 |
| 21:1 | 343 | 28:12 | 212, 348, 357 |
| 21:1–10 | 343 | 28:13 | 200 |
| 21:11 | 343 | 28:14 | 348 |
| 22:1 | 343 | 28:15 | 193, 348 |
| 22:1–8 | 194 | 28:16 | 212, 348, 357 |
| 22:8b–11 | 193 | 28:16–17 | 176–77 |
| 22:11 | 357 | 28:17a | 348, 357 |
| 22:12–14 | 194 | 28:22 | 165, 348 |
| 22:14 | 321 | 28:23–29 | 191, 348 |
| 22:15–25 | 140n6, 343 | 28:26 | 348 |
| 23 | 248 | 28:29 | 348 |
| 23:1 | 343 | 29 | 348–50 |
| 24 | 344, 347 | 29:1 | 348 |
| 24–27 | 248, 320, 323, 325, 327, 343, 453, 454, 455, 595n1 | 29:1–8 | 200, 211, 348, 349, 358 |
| | | 29:3 | 348 |
| 24:1–13 | 343 | 29:4 | 349 |
| 24:14–16a | 343 | 29:6 | 349 |
| 24:16b–23 | 343 | 29:7 | 349 |
| 25–27 | 344 | 29:7–8 | 355 |
| 25:1–5 | 343 | 29:8 | 349 |
| 25:6 | 343 | 29:9–16 | 349 |
| 25:7–8 | 343 | 29:13 | 189 |
| 25:9–12 | 343 | 29:14 | 200 |
| 26:1–6 | 343 | 29:15 | 349 |
| 26:7—27:1 | 343 | 29:15–16 | 189, 323 |
| 26:9b | 454 | 29:16 | 350 |
| 26:19 | 344 | 29:17–19 | 358 |
| 27:1 | 344 | 29:17–21 | 350 |
| 27:8 | 264n12 | 29:20–21 | 358 |
| 27:9 | 321 | 30 | 347, 352 |
| 28 | 347–48 | 30–31 | 247 |
| 28–32 | 174, 334, 346, 347–53 | 30–32 | 350–53 |
| | | 30:1–2 | 192 |

*Index*

Isaiah (continued)

| | |
|---|---|
| 30:1–5 | 192 |
| 30:1–7 | 354 |
| 30:5a | 350 |
| 30:6–7 | 192 |
| 30:7 | 192, 323, 350 |
| 30:8 | 323 |
| 30:9–11 | 188, 350 |
| 30:10 | 351 |
| 30:13 | 6, 321 |
| 30:15 | 350, 357 |
| 30:15–17 | 190, 200, 354, 355 |
| 30:17 | 323 |
| 30:17b | 350 |
| 30:19–22 | 351 |
| 30:19–24 | 358 |
| 30:19–33 | 351 |
| 30:20–21 | 351 |
| 30:23–26 | 351 |
| 30:27–28 | 351 |
| 30:29–33 | 351 |
| 31 | 347, 352 |
| 31:1 | 351 |
| 31:1–3 | 192, 200, 350, 354 |
| 31:3 | 192, 351 |
| 31:4 | 351 |
| 31:4–9 | 351 |
| 31:5 | 351 |
| 31:8–9 | 355 |
| 31:8a | 351, 355 |
| 31:9 | 323 |
| 32:1–2a | 352 |
| 32:1–8 | 358 |
| 32:3–4 | 352 |
| 32:5 | 352 |
| 32:6–8 | 352 |
| 32:9 | 352 |
| 32:9–14 | 352, 358 |
| 32:9–20 | 358 |
| 32:10 | 352 |
| 32:11 | 352 |
| 32:12 | 352 |
| 32:13a | 352 |
| 32:17 | 358 |
| 32:18 | 352 |
| 33 | 321, 324, 353, 354 |
| 33–35 | 353–54 |
| 33:2–4 | 353 |
| 33:5–6 | 353 |
| 33:7–9 | 353 |
| 33:10 | 323, 353 |
| 33:11–12 | 353 |
| 33:13 | 353 |
| 33:14–16 | 353 |
| 33:17 | 353 |
| 33:17–22 | 358 |
| 33:18–19 | 353 |
| 33:18–20 | 358 |
| 33:20–21 | 353 |
| 33:22 | 81, 353, 358 |
| 33:23 | 323 |
| 33:24 | 321 |
| 34 | 353 |
| 34–35 | 320, 323 |
| 34:1–4 | 353–54 |
| 34:5 | 354 |
| 35 | 321, 354 |
| 35:1–4 | 354 |
| 35:2 | 320 |
| 35:5–6a | 354 |
| 35:6b–7 | 354 |
| 35:8 | 354 |
| 35:9 | 354 |
| 35:9–10 | 7 |
| 35:10 | 354 |
| 35:10b | 354 |
| 36–37 | 174n24, 193, 271n16, 346, 351, 354 |
| 36–39 | 320, 323, 354–56 |
| 37 | 352 |
| 37:22–29 | 193, 247 |
| 37:23 | 355 |
| 37:24 | 355 |
| 37:26 | 355 |
| 37:29 | 355 |
| 37:36–37 | 355 |
| 39 | 356 |
| 39:6–7 | 356 |

| | | | |
|---|---|---|---|
| 40 | 356, 369, 388, 389, 402 | 41:15 | 369 |
| | | 41:17–20 | 369 |
| 40–45 | 368 | 41:18–19 | 369–70 |
| 40–48 | 364–88 | 41:20 | 323, 370 |
| 40–55 | 7, 13, 14, 249, 317, 317–20, 322–25, 354, 360, 362, 363, 399, 400, 403, 421, 422, 423, 593, 607 | 41:21 | 323, 370 |
| | | 41:21–29 | 370 |
| | | 41:22b | 370 |
| | | 41:23 | 370 |
| | | 41:24 | 370, 371 |
| 40–66 | 354, 362 | 41:25–27 | 387 |
| 40:1 | 323 | 41:26 | 371 |
| 40:1–5 | 364 | 41:26–27 | 422 |
| 40:2 | 320, 321 | 41:27 | 371 |
| 40:3 | 472n6 | 41:28–29 | 371 |
| 40:3–5 | 364, 370 | 42 | 308 |
| 40:5 | 320 | 42:1 | 371, 392, 516 |
| 40:6 | 364 | 42:1–4 | 371, 388, 394, 422, 516 |
| 40:6–8 | 323 | | |
| 40:8 | 364 | 42:1–9 | 394 |
| 40:9–11 | 364–65 | 42:2–3 | 371 |
| 40:10–11 | 365 | 42:3 | 392 |
| 40:12 | 365 | 42:3c–4 | 372 |
| 40:12–26 | 366 | 42:4 | 323, 372, 392 |
| 40:12–31 | 363, 365–68 | 42:5 | 372 |
| 40:18–20 | 366 | 42:5–9 | 393 |
| 40:21 | 323 | 42:6 | 372, 393, 394 |
| 40:25 | 323 | 42:6–9 | 372 |
| 40:25–26 | 366 | 42:7 | 372, 393 |
| 40:27 | 366 | 42:8–9 | 372 |
| 40:28b–29 | 366 | 42:9 | 378 |
| 40:31 | 366 | 42:10–12 | 363, 373 |
| 41 | 204, 364, 379, 380, 460 | 42:10b–11 | 378 |
| | | 42:12–13 | 378 |
| 41–43 | 387 | 42:13 | 373 |
| 41–48 | 318 | 42:13–16 | 373 |
| 41:1 | 368 | 42:13—44:5 | 373 |
| 41:1—42:12 | 368–73 | 42:13—44:8 | 373 |
| 41:2–3 | 380 | 42:13—44:23 | 373–79 |
| 41:4 | 368, 370 | 42:14 | 373 |
| 41:5–7 | 371 | 42:14–16 | 373 |
| 41:8–10 | 368–69 | 42:15 | 374 |
| 41:11–13 | 369 | 42:16 | 322, 323, 374 |
| 41:13 | 369 | 42:17 | 373n11 |
| 41:14–16 | 369 | 42:18–19 | 322, 376 |

## Index

*Isaiah (continued)*

| | |
|---|---|
| 42:18–20 | 378 |
| 42:18–25 | 373, 375, 376 |
| 42:20–21 | 376 |
| 42:21 | 323 |
| 42:21–25 | 322 |
| 42:22 | 376 |
| 42:24 | 323 |
| 42:24–25a | 376 |
| 43:1 | 7–8, 377, 378 |
| 43:1–7 | 373, 377 |
| 43:8 | 322, 378 |
| 43:8–13 | 373, 378 |
| 43:14 | 8, 374 |
| 43:14–21 | 373, 374 |
| 43:15 | 323 |
| 43:16 | 374 |
| 43:16–17 | 374 |
| 43:18 | 417 |
| 43:19a | 374–75 |
| 43:19b–20 | 375 |
| 43:21 | 375 |
| 43:22–23 | 377 |
| 43:22–28 | 373, 375, 376 |
| 43:24 | 377 |
| 43:24–25 | 321 |
| 43:25 | 377 |
| 43:26 | 377 |
| 43:27–28 | 377 |
| 44 | 204 |
| 44:1–2 | 378 |
| 44:1–5 | 373, 377 |
| 44:2 | 377 |
| 44:6 | 323 |
| 44:6–8 | 373 |
| 44:7b | 323 |
| 44:9–20 | 373, 379 |
| 44:14 | 8 |
| 44:21–22 | 373 |
| 44:22–23 | 8, 373 |
| 44:23 | 373 |
| 44:24 | 379 |
| 44:24–28 | 379 |
| 44:24–45:25 | 379–83 |
| 44:25 | 379 |
| 44:28 | 380 |
| 45 | 204, 367, 373, 378, 404 |
| 45:1 | 318, 380 |
| 45:1–6 | 367, 379 |
| 45:1b–3 | 380 |
| 45:3 | 367 |
| 45:4 | 367, 380 |
| 45:4a | 380 |
| 45:5 | 367 |
| 45:6 | 380 |
| 45:7 | 323, 367, 380 |
| 45:8 | 381 |
| 45:9 | 323, 367 |
| 45:9–10 | 381 |
| 45:10 | 367 |
| 45:11 | 367 |
| 45:13 | 367, 381 |
| 45:14 | 381 |
| 45:14–17 | 381 |
| 45:16 | 382 |
| 45:18 | 323, 382 |
| 45:18–19 | 367 |
| 45:19 | 382 |
| 45:20–25 | 588 |
| 45:20b–21a | 382 |
| 45:21b | 382 |
| 45:22 | 382, 404 |
| 45:23 | 383 |
| 45:24b | 383 |
| 45:25 | 383 |
| 45:3b | 380 |
| 46–47 | 383–86 |
| 46:1–2 | 383–84 |
| 46:3–4 | 384 |
| 46:5 | 384 |
| 46:12 | 384 |
| 47 | 383, 384, 555 |
| 47:1 | 385 |
| 47:3–4 | 384 |
| 47:6 | 385 |
| 47:7 | 385 |
| 47:8a | 385 |

| | | | |
|---|---|---|---|
| 47:8b | 385 | 49:22 | 323 |
| 47:9 | 385 | 50 | 308, 372, 388 |
| 47:10 | 385 | 50:1 | 321 |
| 47:12–13 | 385 | 50:2 | 8 |
| 47:15 | 385 | 50:4 | 394 |
| 48 | 318, 386–88, 389 | 50:4–9 | 422–23 |
| 48:1–2 | 386 | 50:4–9 (10–11) | 388 |
| 48:3–5 | 387 | 50:4–10 | 393, 394 |
| 48:4–5 | 387 | 50:6 | 394 |
| 48:6 | 387 | 50:10 | 323 |
| 48:6–8 | 387 | 51:3 | 320 |
| 48:7 | 387 | 51:4 | 323 |
| 48:8 | 387 | 51:7 | 323 |
| 48:9–11 | 386 | 51:9–10 | 323 |
| 48:10 | 8, 386 | 51:10 | 8 |
| 48:11 | 387 | 51:12 | 320 |
| 48:12 | 323 | 51:17–23 | 515 |
| 48:14–16 | 388 | 52–53 | 388, 558 |
| 48:14b | 388 | 52:7 | 323 |
| 48:15 | 388 | 52:9 | 8, 320 |
| 48:16a | 388 | 52:13 | 322, 397 |
| 48:16b | 388 | 52:13–15 | 397, 578n33 |
| 48:17–19 | 387 | 52:13—53:12 | 308, 388, 395, 423, |
| 48:18–19a | 387 | | 512 |
| 48:20 | 318 | 52:15 | 323, 397 |
| 48:20–21 | 386 | 53 | 399n29, 415, 512–15, |
| 48:22 | 386n17 | | 517, 568, 571, 576– |
| 49 | 308, 372, 388 | | 78 |
| 49–53 | 388, 392, 400 | 53:1–6 | 395–96, 397 |
| 49–55 | 321, 363, 388–92 | 53:2 | 397 |
| 49:1 | 393 | 53:3 | 397 |
| 49:1–4 | 422 | 53:4–6 | 395–96, 576 |
| 49:1–6 | 394 | 53:4b | 397 |
| 49:1–6 (7–11) | 388 | 53:5–6 | 523 |
| 49:1–8 | 393 | 53:7–8 | 517 |
| 49:3 | 393 | 53:10–12 | 523, 578n33 |
| 49:4 | 394 | 53:11 | 6 |
| 49:5 | 397 | 53:11–12 | 396, 397, 576 |
| 49:6 | 323, 393, 394 | 54 | 391–92, 594 |
| 49:8 | 394 | 54:1–2 | 391 |
| 49:9 | 394 | 54:1–3 | 323 |
| 49:9b–11 | 394 | 54:3 | 391 |
| 49:13 | 320 | 54:4 | 391 |
| 49:14–21 | 323 | 54:5 | 391 |

# Index

*Isaiah (continued)*

| | |
|---|---|
| 54:7 | 391 |
| 54:8 | 391 |
| 54:9 | 391 |
| 54:10 | 391 |
| 55 | 388, 389–90, 391 |
| 55–56 | 453 |
| 55:1–2 | 603n24 |
| 55:1b–2a | 389 |
| 55:3 | 380 |
| 55:3a | 389 |
| 55:3b | 389 |
| 55:4–5 | 390 |
| 55:6 | 390 |
| 55:7 | 390 |
| 55:8–9 | 390 |
| 55:10 | 389 |
| 55:10–12 | 364 |
| 55:11 | 389 |
| 55:12 | 389 |
| 55:12–13 | 389 |
| 55:13a | 389 |
| 55:13b | 389 |
| 56 | 404 |
| 56–66 | 14, 317, 318, 320, 324, 325, 326, 362, 363, 401, 402, 421, 423, 424, 594, 609 |
| 56:1 | 322, 403, 404, 423 |
| 56:3 | 404 |
| 56:4–5 | 404 |
| 56:6 | 417n9 |
| 56:6–7 | 404 |
| 56:7 | 404 |
| 56:9 | 404 |
| 56:9–12 | 404 |
| 57 | 404 |
| 57–59 | 408 |
| 57:1–2 | 404 |
| 57:3 | 404 |
| 57:5 | 404 |
| 57:6b | 404 |
| 57:7 | 405 |
| 57:9 | 405 |
| 57:11–13 | 405 |
| 57:14 | 405 |
| 57:15 | 322, 405, 421 |
| 57:15b | 416, 426 |
| 57:16 | 264n12 |
| 57:16–18 | 406 |
| 58 | 406 |
| 58:1 | 406, 423 |
| 58:2 | 406 |
| 58:3a | 406 |
| 58:3b | 406 |
| 58:4–5 | 406 |
| 58:6–7 | 406 |
| 58:9b–10 | 407 |
| 58:13–14 | 407 |
| 59 | 321, 404, 407 |
| 59:1–2 | 407 |
| 59:2 | 321 |
| 59:3 | 321 |
| 59:9–15a | 407, 410 |
| 59:12 | 321 |
| 59:17–18a | 407 |
| 59:20 | 8, 321, 407 |
| 60–62 | 403, 408, 409, 419 |
| 60:1 | 320 |
| 60:1–3 | 408 |
| 60:5–7 | 408 |
| 60:7c | 408 |
| 60:9 | 322 |
| 60:10b | 408 |
| 60:11–13 | 408 |
| 60:13b | 408 |
| 60:14 | 322 |
| 60:14–16 | 408 |
| 60:16 | 8 |
| 60:16b | 408 |
| 60:17–19 | 408 |
| 60:19c | 408 |
| 60:20–22 | 408 |
| 60:22 | 408 |
| 61 | 408, 594 |
| 61:1–2 | 403, 423 |
| 61:1–4 | 402, 415 |
| 61:5–6 | 408 |

## Scripture Index

| Reference | Page(s) |
|---|---|
| 61:8 | 409 |
| 61:10 | 409 |
| 62 | 409 |
| 62:1 | 409 |
| 62:3 | 409 |
| 62:4–5 | 409 |
| 62:6–9 | 409 |
| 62:10 | 323 |
| 62:10–11 | 409 |
| 62:12 | 409 |
| 63–64 | 421, 433 |
| 63–66 | 558 |
| 63:1–6 | 409 |
| 63:7 | 410 |
| 63:7—64:12 | 326, 409, 460n5 |
| 63:9 | 410 |
| 63:10 | 410 |
| 63:10–12 | 410 |
| 63:14 | 410 |
| 63:15 | 410 |
| 63:16 | 8, 411 |
| 63:17 | 411 |
| 63:17b | 411 |
| 63:18–19 | 411 |
| 64 | 411 |
| 64:1–2 | 411 |
| 64:2b | 411–12 |
| 64:4 | 412 |
| 64:5 | 321 |
| 64:5a | 412 |
| 64:5b | 412 |
| 64:6 | 412, 458 |
| 64:6–7 | 321 |
| 64:6b | 412 |
| 64:7 | 412 |
| 64:8 | 413 |
| 64:9 | 321, 412 |
| 65 | 409, 413 |
| 65–66 | 327, 404, 418–19, 453, 454, 455, 595 |
| 65:1 | 413 |
| 65:1–16 | 417 |
| 65:2–7 | 421 |
| 65:5 | 411 |
| 65:5a | 413 |
| 65:5b | 413 |
| 65:8–9 | 413–14 |
| 65:11–12 | 414, 417 |
| 65:13–14 | 414 |
| 65:13–16 | 414, 417 |
| 65:15 | 414 |
| 65:16 | 413, 414 |
| 65:17 | 423, 455 |
| 65:17–25 | 417 |
| 65:17a | 417 |
| 65:17b | 417 |
| 65:18–19 | 417 |
| 65:21–22 | 417 |
| 65:23 | 417 |
| 65:24 | 417 |
| 65:25 | 417 |
| 66 | 416, 417 |
| 66:1–2 | 416, 421 |
| 66:1–4 | 326 |
| 66:1–5 | 416 |
| 66:2 | 421, 426, 609 |
| 66:2b | 426 |
| 66:3 | 416 |
| 66:5 | 416 |
| 66:6 | 418n10 |
| 66:7 | 417 |
| 66:7–9 | 417 |
| 66:7–14 | 417 |
| 66:10 | 417 |
| 66:11 | 417 |
| 66:12 | 417 |
| 66:13 | 320, 417 |
| 66:14 | 417 |
| 66:15–16 | 418 |
| 66:18 | 320 |
| 66:18–21 | 418 |
| 66:19–14 | 417 |
| 66:21 | 418 |
| 66:22 | 418, 423, 455 |
| 66:22–23 | 418 |
| 66:24 | 418n10 |

# Index

## Jeremiah

| Reference | Pages |
|---|---|
| 1:2 | 217 |
| 1:2–10 | 217 |
| 1:5 | 393 |
| 1:10 | 160, 217, 248, 286–87, 602 |
| 1:11–19 | 217 |
| 2–3 | 221 |
| 2–6 | 214, 227 |
| 2:1–3 | 242 |
| 2:1–13 | 219, 241, 264 |
| 2:2 | 111 |
| 2:2–3 | 219 |
| 2:5 | 219, 220 |
| 2:9 | 264 |
| 2:10–11 | 220 |
| 2:11 | 220 |
| 2:14–18 | 222 |
| 2:20 | 220 |
| 2:21 | 220 |
| 2:23–24 | 264 |
| 2:23–24a | 220–21 |
| 2:25 | 222, 264 |
| 2:34 | 222 |
| 3 | 221 |
| 3:6 | 218 |
| 3:6–14 | 242 |
| 3:6—4:2 | 218 |
| 3:10 | 218 |
| 3:12–13 | 218 |
| 3:14 | 218 |
| 3:25 | 218 |
| 4 | 222 |
| 4:1 | 218 |
| 4:2 | 218 |
| 4:18 | 225 |
| 4:19 | 225 |
| 4:23–28 | 225 |
| 4:27–28 | 225 |
| 5 | 222 |
| 5:1 | 223 |
| 5:1–5 | 223 |
| 5:2 | 223 |
| 5:3 | 223 |
| 5:4 | 223 |
| 5:5a | 223 |
| 5:5b | 223 |
| 5:7 | 224 |
| 5:10 | 223 |
| 5:12b | 223 |
| 5:13 | 223 |
| 5:14 | 223 |
| 5:15–17 | 223 |
| 5:20 | 224 |
| 5:21–22a | 224 |
| 5:26 | 6 |
| 5:26–28 | 224 |
| 5:29 | 224 |
| 5:30–31 | 224 |
| 6 | 222 |
| 6:27 | 224 |
| 6:28 | 224 |
| 7 | 214, 228, 229 |
| 7–20 | 214 |
| 7:1–15 | 227 |
| 7:3 | 227 |
| 7:4 | 227 |
| 7:5–7 | 227 |
| 7:8 | 227–28 |
| 7:10 | 228 |
| 7:11 | 228 |
| 7:15 | 228 |
| 7:16–19 | 229 |
| 7:16–20 | 228, 243 |
| 7:22 | 429 |
| 7:31 | 230 |
| 8–20 | 231 |
| 8:18—9:1 | 232 |
| 8:20 | 232 |
| 8:21 | 233 |
| 8:22 | 233 |
| 9:1 | 233 |
| 9:2–6 | 233n22 |
| 9:2–9 | 233n22 |
| 9:7–9 | 233n22 |
| 9:10 | 233 |
| 9:18 | 233 |

## Scripture Index

| | | | |
|---|---|---|---|
| 9:20–21 | 233 | 15:5–9 | 232, 495 |
| 10:2–5 | 75 | 15:6 | 232 |
| 10:2–10 | 75 | 15:7a | 232 |
| 10:7 | 75 | 15:7b | 232 |
| 10:8–9 | 75 | 15:10–21 | 235 |
| 11 | 234 | 15:15–18 | 235 |
| 11:1–14 | 218 | 15:16–17 | 235 |
| 11:13 | 218 | 15:18 | 235 |
| 11:14 | 229 | 15:19–21 | 99n14, 235 |
| 11:18–20 | 234 | 16:1–9 | 231 |
| 11:18—12:6 | 234 | 17:14 | 235 |
| 11:21–23 | 234 | 17:14–18 | 235 |
| 11:22–23 | 99n14 | 17:15 | 235 |
| 12:1–4 | 234 | 17:17 | 235 |
| 12:5 | 234 | 17:18 | 235 |
| 12:7 | 233 | 17:19–27 | 230 |
| 12:7–13 | 233–34 | 18:1–11 | 230 |
| 12:10 | 234 | 18:6 | 230 |
| 12:12 | 234 | 18:7 | 230 |
| 12:13 | 234 | 18:7–8 | 230 |
| 12:56 | 99n14 | 18:10 | 230 |
| 13:1–11 | 230 | 18:11 | 231 |
| 13:15–26 | 231 | 18:12 | 231 |
| 13:16–17 | 231 | 18:19–23 | 235 |
| 13:18 | 232 | 18:20 | 235 |
| 13:19 | 232 | 18:21–22 | 235 |
| 13:21 | 232 | 19:1–13 | 230 |
| 13:22 | 232 | 19:1—20:6 | 230 |
| 13:24 | 232 | 20 | 234, 236 |
| 13:26 | 232 | 20:1–6 | 140n6 |
| 14 | 229, 279–80, 413n6, 478n28 | 20:7 | 236 |
| | | 20:8 | 236 |
| 14:1–10 | 229 | 20:8–9 | 236 |
| 14:7–9 | 279–80 | 20:9 | 236 |
| 14:10 | 280 | 20:10 | 236 |
| 14:11–12 | 229 | 20:14–18 | 236 |
| 14:13 | 229 | 21–23 | 214 |
| 14:17–22 | 229 | 22:10 | 226 |
| 14:19 | 280 | 22:13 | 227 |
| 14:20 | 280 | 22:13–17 | 217 |
| 14:21 | 280 | 22:13–19 | 227 |
| 14:22 | 280 | 22:15–16 | 219 |
| 15:1–3 | 280 | 22:17 | 227 |
| 15:1–4 | 229 | 22:18–19 | 227 |

# Index

*Jeremiah (continued)*

| | | | |
|---|---|---|---|
| 22:30 | 226–27 | 31:7 | 282 |
| 23:9–40 | 238 | 31:9c | 283 |
| 23:13–14 | 238 | 31:10–14 | 283 |
| 23:13–14a | 238 | 31:15 | 283 |
| 23:17 | 239 | 31:16–17 | 283 |
| 24 | 237 | 31:18–19 | 283 |
| 24:3–10 | 237 | 31:20 | 283 |
| 25:15–31 | 515 | 31:29–30 | 244n33 |
| 26 | 517 | 31:31 | 284 |
| 26:1 | 227 | 31:31–34 | 558, 583 |
| 26:1–24 | 227 | 31:33 | 593 |
| 26:20–23 | 228 | 31:33–34 | 284 |
| 27:5 | 248 | 31:34 | 284 |
| 27:5–7 | 237 | 32 | 279 |
| 27:8–9 | 237 | 32:6–12 | 7 |
| 27–28 | 237, 279 | 33 | 279n22 |
| 27–29 | 204 | 36:29–31 | 227 |
| 28 | 238 | 37 | 239 |
| 28:2–4 | 238 | 37–39 | 239 |
| 28:6 | 238 | 38 | 239 |
| 28:6–9 | 287 | 38:2–4 | 239 |
| 28:8–9 | 238 | 38:7 | 239 |
| 29 | 237, 279, 284–85 | 38:15–16 | 239 |
| 29:1 | 284 | 38:17–18 | 239 |
| 29:5–6 | 248, 285 | 38:19 | 239 |
| 29:7 | 248, 285 | 41:26–27 | 278 |
| 29:10 | 248 | 44:7–8 | 278 |
| 29:10–11 | 237 | 45:21 | 278 |
| 29:15–23 | 240 | 45:4–5 | 236 |
| 29:16–19 | 285 | 47 | 250 |
| 29:24–32 | 240 | 48 | 250 |
| 30–31 | 279, 280–84, 285n24 | 49:1–6 | 250 |
| 30:5–7 | 280–81 | 49:23–27 | 250 |
| 30:10 | 281 | 49:7–22 | 250 |
| 30:12–13 | 281 | 50:1—51:58 | 248 |
| 30:14 | 281 | 50:2 | 248 |
| 30:15 | 282 | 50:3–5 | 249 |
| 30:17 | 282 | 50:8 | 249 |
| 30:18–22 | 282 | 50:13a | 249 |
| 30:22 | 282 | 50:15b | 249 |
| 31 | 282, 284 | 50:33–34 | 249 |
| 31:2–3 | 282 | 51:5 | 249 |
| 31:4a | 282 | 51:6 | 6, 249 |
| | | 51:34–35 | 249 |

## Scripture Index

| | |
|---|---|
| 51:36–37 | 249 |
| 51:61–64 | 248 |

## Lamentations

| | |
|---|---|
| 1 | 266–68, 270, 271 |
| 1–4 | 266 |
| 1:1–2 | 267 |
| 1:3 | 267 |
| 1:4 | 267 |
| 1:5 | 267 |
| 1:5b–c | 267 |
| 1:6 | 267 |
| 1:7 | 267 |
| 1:8 | 267, 270 |
| 1:9 | 267 |
| 1:9b–c | 267 |
| 1:9c | 268 |
| 1:10 | 267 |
| 1:11a | 267 |
| 1:11c | 268 |
| 1:12a | 267 |
| 1:14 | 267 |
| 1:16 | 267 |
| 1:17 | 267 |
| 1:18 | 268 |
| 1:19 | 267 |
| 1:20 | 268 |
| 1:21 | 267 |
| 1:22 | 268 |
| 2 | 268–69, 270 |
| 2–3 | 270 |
| 2–4 | 270 |
| 2:1–8 | 268 |
| 2:14 | 268–69 |
| 2:17 | 269 |
| 2:19–22 | 268 |
| 3 | 269, 270 |
| 3:21 | 269 |
| 3:32–39 | 269 |
| 3:39 | 269 |
| 3:40–41 | 269 |
| 3:40–47 | 269 |
| 3:42 | 269 |
| 3:48 | 269 |
| 3:58 | 7 |
| 4 | 270 |
| 4:1–16 | 270 |
| 4:11 | 270 |
| 4:16 | 270 |
| 4:17–22 | 270 |
| 4:21–22 | 270 |
| 5 | 265–66, 270, 413n6 |
| 5:2 | 265 |
| 5:2–18 | 265 |
| 5:7 | 265 |
| 5:8 | 265 |
| 5:11 | 265 |
| 5:16b | 265 |
| 5:19 | 266 |
| 5:20 | 266 |
| 5:21 | 266 |
| 5:22 | 266 |

## Ezekiel

| | |
|---|---|
| 1:1–3 | 240n27 |
| 2:1 | 524n16 |
| 3:1 | 524n16 |
| 4:1 | 524n16 |
| 4:1–8 | 244 |
| 4:9–15 | 245 |
| 5 | 245 |
| 5:1–4 | 245 |
| 6 | 245 |
| 6:4–7 | 245 |
| 6:7 | 241 |
| 6:10 | 241 |
| 6:14 | 241 |
| 7:4 | 241 |
| 7:9 | 241 |
| 7:19 | 479 |
| 8–11 | 243 |
| 8:3 | 243 |
| 8:7–13 | 243 |
| 8:11 | 241 |
| 8:14–15 | 243 |
| 8:16–18 | 243 |

## Index

Ezekiel (continued)

| | | | |
|---|---|---|---|
| 11:25 | 241 | 25 | 250 |
| 12 | 245 | 25–32 | 241, 250 |
| 12:3 | 245 | 26:2 | 250n40 |
| 12:18 | 245 | 27 | 250, 251 |
| 12:19–20 | 245 | 27:12–25 | 250 |
| 13:5 | 240 | 27:26–36 | 250 |
| 13:9 | 240 | 28 | 251 |
| 13:10 | 240 | 28:1–10 | 36, 252 |
| 13:11 | 240 | 28:2 | 251 |
| 14:1–8 | 241 | 28:6–8 | 251 |
| 14:2–6 | 243–44 | 28:11–19 | 251, 252 |
| 14:12–23 | 244 | 28:12 | 251 |
| 16 | 241 | 28:12–14 | 251 |
| 16:8 | 241 | 28:15 | 251 |
| 16:23–34 | 242 | 28:16 | 251 |
| 16:35 | 242 | 28:16b | 252 |
| 16:36–43 | 242 | 28:17b | 252 |
| 17 | 240 | 28:18 | 252 |
| 17:1–4 | 241 | 29–30 | 252 |
| 17:16 | 240 | 29–32 | 250 |
| 17:22–24 | 240n28 | 29:17–21 | 250n39 |
| 18 | 6 | 30:14–16 | 479 |
| 18:1–32 | 244 | 31–32 | 252 |
| 18:2 | 244 | 31:2 | 253 |
| 18:5 | 6 | 31:10 | 252 |
| 18:20 | 577 | 31:12 | 252–53 |
| 18:23 | 10, 591 | 31:15 | 253 |
| 18:25–26 | 244 | 31:18 | 253 |
| 20 | 110–11, 242, 459 | 32 | 253 |
| 20:1–4 | 241 | 32:1–16 | 253, 254 |
| 20:4 | 242 | 32:2 | 253 |
| 20:5–8 | 110 | 32:4–5 | 253 |
| 20:11–26 | 110–11 | 32:13–15 | 253 |
| 20:21b–24 | 111 | 32:17–32 | 253 |
| 20:25–26 | 111 | 32:23 | 253 |
| 20:30–32 | 242 | 32:25 | 253 |
| 20:32 | 241 | 32:27 | 253 |
| 20:33–39 | 241 | 33–37 | 241 |
| 20:33–44 | 242 | 36:26 | 583 |
| 23 | 242 | 36:26–27 | 558 |
| 24:16–17a | 245 | 36:31 | 558 |
| 24:19–24 | 245 | 40–48 | 241, 363 |
| 24:25–27 | 245 | | |

## Daniel

| | |
|---|---|
| 7 | 524 |
| 7:10 | 465 |
| 7:13–14 | 524 |

## Hosea

| | |
|---|---|
| 1 | 166, 276 |
| 1–3 | 177 |
| 1:1 | 177n28 |
| 1:2 | 166, 208 |
| 1:4–5 | 179 |
| 1:7 | 272 |
| 1:10–11 | 272 |
| 1:24–25 | 200 |
| 2 | 178, 198, 272, 273, 276–78 |
| 2:2 | 166n10, 178 |
| 2:2–13 | 178, 272, 276 |
| 2:3 | 178 |
| 2:5a | 178 |
| 2:5b | 178 |
| 2:7b–8 | 178 |
| 2:9 | 178 |
| 2:10 | 178 |
| 2:10–12 | 200 |
| 2:11–13 | 178 |
| 2:12 | 276–77 |
| 2:12–13 | 198 |
| 2:13 | 277 |
| 2:13–14 | 179 |
| 2:14 | 272 |
| 2:14–15 | 198, 277 |
| 2:14–23 | 278 |
| 2:16–20 | 209 |
| 2:17–20 | 277 |
| 2:19 | 200 |
| 2:19–20 | 277 |
| 2:21 | 200 |
| 2:21–23 | 208, 277 |
| 2:21–23a | 179 |
| 2:23b | 179 |
| 3 | 166, 272, 278 |
| 3:1 | 200 |
| 3:1–3 | 208 |
| 3:5 | 272, 278 |
| 3:13–14 | 200 |
| 3:17 | 200 |
| 4 | 178, 179, 180, 273n18 |
| 4–14 | 177, 178 |
| 4:1–3 | 569 |
| 4:1b–2 | 179 |
| 4:3 | 198 |
| 4:6 | 179 |
| 4:7 | 6 |
| 4:7–8 | 179 |
| 4:10 | 199 |
| 4:12 | 179 |
| 4:13 | 179, 220n11 |
| 4:13b | 179 |
| 4:13b–14 | 199 |
| 4:18 | 180 |
| 5–8 | 178, 198, 209 |
| 5:4 | 180 |
| 5:8–15 | 177, 184–85, 274 |
| 5:8–6:6 | 274 |
| 5:9 | 185 |
| 5:10a | 185 |
| 5:11 | 185, 198 |
| 5:12 | 200, 202 |
| 5:13 | 198 |
| 5:13a–b | 185 |
| 5:13c | 185 |
| 5:14 | 200, 202 |
| 6:1–3 | 185, 274 |
| 6:4–6 | 274 |
| 6:6 | 163, 429 |
| 6:7–10 | 177, 198 |
| 6:11—7:7 | 177 |
| 6:11a | 272 |
| 6:11b—7:7 | 200 |
| 7:1 | 184 |
| 7:1–7 | 184, 198 |
| 7:3 | 184 |
| 7:5a | 184 |
| 7:7 | 184 |

## Index

### Hosea (continued)

| | |
|---|---|
| 7:8–9 | 185, 202 |
| 7:8–13 | 185 |
| 7:11 | 185 |
| 7:11–12 | 200, 201–2 |
| 7:11–12a | 201–2 |
| 7:13 | 7, 198 |
| 7:16 | 198, 276 |
| 8:1–3 | 185 |
| 8:4 | 183 |
| 8:4–6 | 181 |
| 8:4–10 | 185 |
| 8:6 | 200 |
| 8:7 | 202 |
| 8:7–10 | 200 |
| 8:8b–10 | 198 |
| 8:14 | 200 |
| 9–13 | 178, 180 |
| 9:3 | 198, 203, 276 |
| 9:6 | 276 |
| 9:10 | 109, 180 |
| 9:15 | 183, 209 |
| 10:1–2 | 181 |
| 10:5 | 200 |
| 10:9 | 183, 209 |
| 10:10 | 273n20 |
| 10:13 | 183 |
| 11 | 209, 272, 274, 276 |
| 11:1 | 180 |
| 11:1–2a | 275 |
| 11:1–7 | 209, 274–76 |
| 11:1–9 | 180 |
| 11:2 | 180 |
| 11:3 | 275 |
| 11:5 | 180, 198, 275n21 |
| 11:8 | 275 |
| 11:8–9 | 180, 286 |
| 11:9 | 209, 275, 390 |
| 11:9a | 275 |
| 11:10–11 | 209, 276 |
| 11:12—12:1 | 182n39 |
| 12:1 | 185, 202 |
| 13:1 | 181 |
| 13:1–3 | 181 |
| 13:2 | 181 |
| 13:3 | 200 |
| 13:4–6 | 208–9 |
| 13:4–8 | 180, 223 |
| 13:8 | 200 |
| 13:9–11 | 209 |
| 13:13–15 | 177 |
| 13:14 | 7 |
| 14 | 178, 182, 272–74 |
| 14:1–2a | 273 |
| 14:1–3 | 209 |
| 14:1–8 | 215 |
| 14:2 | 183 |
| 14:2b | 273 |
| 14:2b–3 | 182, 273 |
| 14:3 | 182, 273, 447n20 |
| 14:4 | 209 |
| 14:5–6 | 274 |
| 14:5–7 | 209 |
| 14:8 | 274 |

### Joel

| | |
|---|---|
| 2:3 | 479 |
| 3:3 | 479 |

### Amos

| | |
|---|---|
| 1–2 | 5, 168 |
| 1:3 | 6 |
| 1:3–5 | 246 |
| 1:3—2:5 | 197 |
| 1:6 | 6 |
| 1:6–8 | 246 |
| 1:9 | 6 |
| 1:9–10 | 246 |
| 1:11 | 6, 168 |
| 1:11–12 | 246 |
| 1:13 | 6, 168 |
| 1:13–15 | 246 |
| 2 | 162 |
| 2:1 | 6, 168 |
| 2:1–3 | 246 |

| | | | |
|---|---|---|---|
| 2:4 | 6 | 6:1–3 | 172–73 |
| 2:4–5 | 246 | 6:4–6 | 171 |
| 2:6 | 6 | 6:4–7 | 171, 175 |
| 2:6–8 | 168 | 6:7 | 199 |
| 2:6a | 162 | 6:9–10 | 197 |
| 2:6b | 162 | 7 | 247n35 |
| 2:6b–7a | 169 | 7–8 | 602 |
| 2:7a | 162 | 7–9 | 166 |
| 2:7b | 162, 169 | 7:1–6 | 166 |
| 2:8a | 169 | 7:4 | 264n12 |
| 2:8b | 169 | 7:7–9 | 166 |
| 2:9–10 | 205 | 7:8 | 229 |
| 2:9–11 | 168, 169 | 7:8c | 179n31 |
| 2:11 | 205 | 7:10–17 | 140n6 |
| 2:12–16 | 168 | 8 | 247n35 |
| 2:14–16 | 197 | 8:1–3 | 166 |
| 3:1–2 | 205–6, 247 | 8:2 | 229 |
| 3:2 | 40 | 8:2c | 179n31 |
| 3:11 | 197 | 8:3 | 197 |
| 3:12 | 207 | 8:4–6 | 170 |
| 3:14–15a | 171 | 8:8 | 198 |
| 4 | 489n56 | 8:9 | 198 |
| 4:1 | 170, 197 | 8:10 | 197 |
| 4:4–5 | 172 | 8:11 | 199 |
| 4:6 | 197 | 9 | 247n35 |
| 4:6–11 | 164 | 9:1–4 | 166, 206 |
| 4:6–12 | 50, 228 | 9:4 | 166 |
| 4:7 | 197 | 9:7 | 206, 478 |
| 4:8 | 197 | 9:7–8 | 206, 247 |
| 4:9 | 197 | 9:9–10 | 173, 196, 197 |
| 4:10 | 197 | 9:10 | 206 |
| 4:11 | 197 | 9:11–15 | 215 |
| 4:12 | 50, 164, 198, 201 | | |
| 5:3 | 197 | *Obadiah* | |
| 5:4 | 163 | | |
| 5:4–6 | 172 | 8 | 479 |
| 5:7 | 170 | | |
| 5:10 | 170 | *Jonah* | |
| 5:11 | 199 | | |
| 5:12 | 170 | 3:9 | 207 |
| 5:15 | 207 | | |
| 5:18–20 | 199 | | |
| 5:21–24 | 172 | | |
| 5:22 | 429 | | |

## *Scripture Index*

*Index*

## Micah

| | |
|---|---|
| 1 | 186 |
| 1:1–7 | 207 |
| 1:2–4 | 368n8 |
| 1:7 | 186 |
| 1:10–16 | 201 |
| 2:1–2 | 173 |
| 3:5 | 152n19, 174 |
| 3:8 | 167 |
| 3:9–11 | 173 |
| 3:12 | 228 |
| 4 | 207 |
| 4–5 | 246 |
| 4:1–5 | 204n3 |
| 4:10 | 7 |
| 5 | 207 |
| 5:5–6 | 201n3 |
| 5:7–15 | 201n3 |
| 5:7–9 | 201n3 |
| 6:1–2 | 368n8 |
| 6:1–5 | 207 |
| 6:2 | 207 |
| 6:3 | 207 |
| 6:5 | 207 |
| 6:6–8 | 174 |
| 6:10–11 | 6 |
| 7 | 207 |

## Habakkuk

| | |
|---|---|
| 3 | 410 |

## Zephaniah

| | |
|---|---|
| 1:17 | 6 |
| 1:18 | 479 |
| 2:2 | 479 |
| 2:3 | 479 |

## Zechariah

| | |
|---|---|
| 1:4 | 163 |

## Malachi

| | |
|---|---|
| 3 | 484 |
| 3:1a | 484, 484n47 |
| 4:1 | 479 |
| 4:5 | 475 |
| 4:5–6 | 475, 476 |

∾

# NEW TESTAMENT

## Matthew

| | |
|---|---|
| 3:2 | 490n57 |
| 3:6 | 535 |
| 3:7–12 | 477, 487 |
| 3:7b | 478 |
| 3:9 | 478 |
| 3:10 | 479, 487 |
| 3:11 | 480 |
| 3:11–12 | 479 |
| 3:12 | 480, 487, 492 |
| 3:13–14 | 482n37 |
| 3:14 | 474n17 |
| 3:17 | 516 |
| 4:17 | 490n57 |
| 5 | 425, 502 |
| 5–6 | 500 |
| 5–7 | 500 |
| 5:13–20 | 500 |
| 5:17 | 501 |
| 5:17–20 | 507n89 |
| 5:20 | 501, 503 |
| 5:21–26 | 500 |
| 5:25–26 | 497 |
| 5:27–32 | 500 |
| 5:31–32 | 501 |
| 5:33–37 | 500 |
| 5:38–42 | 500, 608 |
| 5:43–48 | 500 |
| 5:48 | 502 |
| 6 | 500 |

## Scripture Index

| | | | |
|---|---|---|---|
| 6:1–4 | 500 | 11:21–24 | 494 |
| 6:1–18 | 501 | 12:6 | 509n92 |
| 6:2 | 503 | 12:18–21 | 516 |
| 6:3–12 | 500 | 12:28 | 498n71 |
| 6:5 | 503 | 12:32 | 599 |
| 6:5–8 | 500 | 12:41–42 | 493, 504 |
| 6:7 | 500 | 13:16–17 | 509 |
| 6:16–18 | 500 | 13:24–30 | 528 |
| 6:19–21 | 500, 502 | 13:36–43 | 528 |
| 6:22–23 | 500 | 13:47–50 | 528 |
| 6:24 | 500 | 16:13–23 | 515 |
| 6:25 | 500, 502 | 16:18 | 515 |
| 6:25–34 | 500 | 16:21 | 524n19 |
| 6:36 | 502 | 16:27b | 528 |
| 7 | 502 | 17:9–17 | 516 |
| 7:1–2 | 496 | 17:10–12 | 476n21 |
| 7:13–14 | 599 | 17:13 | 476 |
| 7:21–23 | 502, 527, 528n26 | 17:22 | 524 |
| 7:22 | 528 | 18 | 502 |
| 7:23 | 502–3 | 18:23–35 | 497 |
| 7:24–27 | 498n71, 502 | 19:1–12 | 501 |
| 8:11–12 | 494, 504 | 19:21 | 502n77 |
| 8:20 | 525 | 20:28 | 516 |
| 10:13–15 | 504 | 21:41 | 493 |
| 10:18 | 524 | 21:43 | 493 |
| 10:32–33 | 498n71 | 22:1–14 | 493 |
| 10:33 | 527 | 22:11–14 | 528 |
| 11:2–6 | 481 | 22:34–40 | 502 |
| 11:3 | 481 | 23:1–5 | 496 |
| 11:5 | 482 | 23:1–31 | 492 |
| 11:5–15 | 481 | 23:6–13 | 496 |
| 11:6 | 483 | 23:16–22 | 496 |
| 11:7–9 | 473n9 | 23:25–28 | 496 |
| 11:7–15 | 484 | 23:29–31 | 496 |
| 11:7b–9 | 484 | 23:37–39 | 495 |
| 11:10 | 484, 484n47 | 24 | 559n16 |
| 11:11 | 484 | 24–25 | 544 |
| 11:11–13 | 485–86 | 24:30–31 | 527 |
| 11:11–13a | 484 | 24:37–39 | 498n71 |
| 11:12 | 485 | 25:14–30 | 528 |
| 11:12–13 | 481, 485 | 25:31–32 | 528 |
| 11:13a | 485 | 25:31–46 | 465, 504, 528, 599 |
| 11:13b | 484 | 25:37–39 | 528 |
| 11:16–19 | 473n9, 481, 483 | 25:39 | 522n14 |

655

# Index

## Matthew (continued)

| | |
|---|---|
| 25:44 | 528 |
| 26:36–45 | 525 |
| 28:27–28 | 522 |

## Mark

| | |
|---|---|
| 1:2–3 | 472 |
| 1:2–11 | 472 |
| 1:3 | 473 |
| 1:4 | 472, 474, 534–35 |
| 1:5 | 472, 474 |
| 1:6 | 595 |
| 1:7 | 473, 480 |
| 1:7–8 | 486 |
| 1:11 | 510, 516 |
| 1:14 | 14 |
| 1:14–15 | 518, 595 |
| 1:15 | 400, 490, 532 |
| 1:18–22 | 518 |
| 2 | 518 |
| 2:6–12 | 518 |
| 2:15–17 | 518 |
| 2:18–22 | 473 |
| 2:23–27 | 518 |
| 3:1–6 | 518 |
| 3:6 | 518 |
| 3:28–29 | 490–91 |
| 3:29 | 491 |
| 4:24 | 491 |
| 4:24–25 | 491 |
| 4:25 | 491 |
| 4:26–29 | 491 |
| 4:35–41 | 510 |
| 6:11 | 492 |
| 6:17–29 | 517 |
| 6:18 | 474 |
| 6:45–52 | 510 |
| 8:9–10 | 510 |
| 8:29–30 | 510 |
| 8:31 | 514, 524 |
| 8:31–33 | 511, 523 |
| 8:32 | 515 |
| 8:32—9:1 | 514 |
| 8:34 | 610 |
| 8:34–35 | 523 |
| 8:38 | 491, 527, 528 |
| 9:2–8 | 510 |
| 9:8 | 510 |
| 9:9–13 | 516 |
| 9:11 | 475 |
| 9:11–13 | 475 |
| 9:12 | 476, 524 |
| 9:12a–13 | 476 |
| 9:12b | 476, 476n21 |
| 9:24 | 611 |
| 9:30–32 | 511, 514, 523 |
| 9:31 | 524 |
| 9:33–34 | 511 |
| 9:33–37 | 514, 523 |
| 9:35 | 511 |
| 9:43–48 | 491 |
| 9:45 | 599 |
| 9:48 | 599 |
| 10:1–12 | 501 |
| 10:2–12 | 503, 601 |
| 10:4 | 501 |
| 10:5 | 501 |
| 10:8–9 | 501 |
| 10:17–22 | 491 |
| 10:17–31 | 502 |
| 10:18 | 501 |
| 10:21 | 502n77 |
| 10:25 | 491 |
| 10:31 | 491 |
| 10:32–34 | 511, 514, 523 |
| 10:33 | 524 |
| 10:35–37 | 511 |
| 10:35–40 | 528 |
| 10:35–45 | 514 |
| 10:42–45 | 523 |
| 10:43–45 | 511 |
| 10:45 | 514, 516, 522 |
| 11:11–26 | 490 |
| 11:15–18 | 492 |
| 11:18 | 492 |
| 11:25 | 502 |

## Scripture Index

| | |
|---|---|
| 11:27–33 | 475 |
| 11:28 | 475 |
| 12:1–12 | 492–93 |
| 12:18–27 | 528n25 |
| 12:27 | 442n14 |
| 12:28–34 | 502 |
| 12:38–40 | 492, 496 |
| 13 | 544, 559n16 |
| 13:1–2 | 492 |
| 13:1–4 | 492 |
| 13:1–37 | 487n50, 492 |
| 13:5–8 | 492 |
| 13:9–13 | 492 |
| 13:14–23 | 492 |
| 13:24–27 | 492 |
| 13:26–27 | 527 |
| 14:1–2 | 519 |
| 14:10–11 | 519 |
| 14:32–42 | 525 |
| 14:36 | 520 |
| 14:61 | 492 |
| 14:62 | 510 |
| 14:62–64 | 492 |
| 15:34 | 606 |

### Luke

| | |
|---|---|
| 1:40–45 | 482n37 |
| 1:68 | 8 |
| 2:38 | 8 |
| 3:3 | 535 |
| 3:7 | 477 |
| 3:7–9 (10–14) | 487 |
| 3:7–17 | 477 |
| 3:7b | 478 |
| 3:9 | 487 |
| 3:10–14 | 481 |
| 3:10–15 | 477, 480 |
| 3:15–17 | 487 |
| 3:16–17 | 480 |
| 3:17 | 487, 492 |
| 4:18–19 | 402 |
| 6:37 | 496 |
| 6:37–38 | 496 |
| 6:47–49 | 498n71 |
| 7 | 485 |
| 7:18–23 | 481 |
| 7:19 | 481 |
| 7:23 | 483 |
| 7:24–26 | 473n9 |
| 7:24–30 | 481 |
| 7:27 | 484, 484n47 |
| 7:28 | 485 |
| 7:29–30 | 485 |
| 7:31–34 | 473n9 |
| 7:31–35 | 481, 483 |
| 9:18–22 | 516 |
| 9:22 | 524 |
| 9:26 | 527 |
| 9:31 | 516 |
| 9:44 | 524 |
| 9:58 | 525 |
| 10:13–15 | 494, 504 |
| 10:23–24 | 509 |
| 10:25–28 | 502 |
| 11:4 | 502 |
| 11:20 | 498n71 |
| 11:31–32 | 493, 504 |
| 11:39–51 | 496 |
| 11:46 | 496 |
| 11:52 | 496 |
| 12:8–9 | 498n71 |
| 12:33–34 | 502 |
| 12:57–59 | 497 |
| 13:1–5 | 495 |
| 13:3 | 495 |
| 13:26–27 | 527n23 |
| 13:28–29 | 494, 504 |
| 13:31–33 | 518 |
| 13:34–35 | 495 |
| 14:15–24 | 496, 585 |
| 16:1–8 | 497 |
| 16:8a | 497 |
| 16:9–13 | 497 |
| 16:16 | 481, 485 |
| 16:17 | 507n89 |
| 16:19–31 | 498n71, 599 |
| 16:23 | 599 |

# Index

## Luke (continued)

| | |
|---|---|
| 17:26–27 | 498n71 |
| 18:6–9 | 479n31 |
| 18:9–14 | 425, 501 |
| 18:19 | 501 |
| 18:22 | 502n77 |
| 18:31 | 524 |
| 20:45–47 | 496 |
| 20:46 | 496 |
| 20:47 | 496 |
| 21 | 544, 559n16 |
| 22:24–27 | 516 |
| 22:39–46 | 525 |
| 22:67–68 | 526 |
| 22:70 | 526 |
| 23:46 | 520 |
| 24 | 517 |
| 24:21 | 8 |
| 24:26 | 515 |
| 24:27 | 515, 516 |
| 24:46–47 | 516 |

## John

| | |
|---|---|
| 1:6–8 | 534 |
| 1:17 | 595 |
| 1:19–28 | 534 |
| 1:29 | 329, 533, 534 |
| 1:30–31 | 480 |
| 1:35–37 | 482 |
| 1:36 | 329, 533 |
| 2 | 533 |
| 2:4 | 516, 533, 536 |
| 2:13–23 | 535 |
| 2:16 | 535 |
| 2:18 | 535 |
| 2:19 | 535 |
| 2:21 | 542 |
| 2:22 | 536 |
| 2:25 | 536 |
| 3 | 530 |
| 3:14 | 516 |
| 3:16 | 532, 599 |
| 3:16–21 | 532 |
| 3:17 | 532 |
| 3:18 | 532 |
| 3:25–30 | 482 |
| 3:36 | 535, 599 |
| 4 | 541 |
| 4:10 | 541 |
| 4:14 | 541 |
| 4:23 | 542 |
| 4:27 | 542 |
| 5 | 530, 531 |
| 5:5–6 | 558 |
| 5:22–24 | 531 |
| 5:24 | 531 |
| 5:25 | 531 |
| 5:28 | 531 |
| 5:28–29 | 531 |
| 5:30 | 531 |
| 7 | 530 |
| 8 | 530 |
| 8:28 | 516 |
| 8:33–39 | 479n32 |
| 8:38 | 538 |
| 8:44 | 23, 531 |
| 9 | 530 |
| 9:40–41 | 540 |
| 10:1–30 | 536 |
| 10:11 | 533, 536 |
| 10:13 | 536 |
| 10:16 | 537, 538 |
| 10:17–18 | 538 |
| 10:18 | 537 |
| 10:24 | 538 |
| 10:26 | 538 |
| 10:27–30 | 537 |
| 11:45–53 | 540 |
| 11:47–53 | 520 |
| 12 | 530 |
| 12:11 | 558 |
| 12:19 | 540 |
| 12:23 | 540 |
| 12:24–25 | 540 |
| 12:27 | 540 |
| 12:27–32 | 595 |

## Scripture Index

| | |
|---|---|
| 12:31 | 540 |
| 12:31–32 | 532 |
| 12:32 | 516, 540 |
| 12:33 | 533 |
| 12:34 | 540 |
| 12:36 | 541 |
| 12:47 | 532 |
| 12:47–48 | 532 |
| 14:1 | 558 |
| 15:13 | 537 |
| 16 | 530 |
| 16:11 | 531 |
| 18:28 | 534 |
| 18:28–32 | 539 |
| 18:33–38 | 538 |
| 18:36 | 538 |
| 19:7 | 538 |
| 19:8–11 | 538 |
| 19:11 | 539, 558 |
| 19:14 | 534, 539 |
| 19:15 | 539, 540 |
| 19:21 | 558 |
| 19:31 | 534 |
| 19:42 | 534 |
| 21 | 520, 523 |
| 21:9 | 558 |
| 21:15–19 | 523 |
| 21:22 | 558 |

### Acts

| | |
|---|---|
| 2:3–4 | 480 |
| 2:23 | 606 |
| 8:32–33 | 517 |

### Romans

| | |
|---|---|
| 1 | 564 |
| 1–3 | 572 |
| 1–11 | 15, 317, 562, 596 |
| 1:16–17 | 562–63, 564, 569 |
| 1:18 | 564, 569 |
| 1:18—3:20 | 8 |
| 1:18—3:31 | 586 |
| 1:18—5:11 | 574 |
| 1:19–20 | 564 |
| 1:19–23 | 564 |
| 1:20 | 564, 569 |
| 1:21 | 564 |
| 1:24 | 564, 565 |
| 1:25 | 565 |
| 1:26 | 564, 565 |
| 1:28 | 564, 565 |
| 1:29–31 | 565 |
| 1:32 | 566, 581 |
| 2 | 564, 565, 566, 570, 570n14, 575 |
| 2:3 | 570 |
| 2:5–10 | 570, 599 |
| 2:7 | 570n14 |
| 2:7–8 | 566 |
| 2:8 | 570 |
| 2:10 | 570n14 |
| 2:11 | 566 |
| 2:12 | 566 |
| 2:14–15 | 33, 566 |
| 2:15 | 570 |
| 2:15–16 | 570n14 |
| 2:17 | 566 |
| 2:17–24 | 566 |
| 2:24 | 566 |
| 3 | 564, 571, 573 |
| 3:1–8 | 566, 570 |
| 3:2 | 566 |
| 3:9 | 566 |
| 3:10–18 | 570 |
| 3:15 | 571 |
| 3:17ff. | 562n1 |
| 3:19–20 | 570 |
| 3:20 | 567, 571 |
| 3:21–31 | 569 |
| 3:23 | 564 |
| 3:23–24 | 567, 571 |
| 3:23–25a | 8, 521 |
| 3:23–26 | 612 |
| 3:24 | 567 |
| 3:24–25 | 568, 573 |

# Index

Romans (continued)

| | | | |
|---|---|---|---|
| 3:25 | 567 | 7 | 570, 580–81 |
| 3:26 | 567, 572 | 7:1–6 | 580 |
| 3:27–31 | 568 | 7:6 | 580 |
| 3:31 | 569 | 7:7 | 581 |
| 4 | 572–73 | 7:7–25 | 583 |
| 4–5 | 572–73 | 7:12 | 581 |
| 4:2 | 573 | 7:22–23 | 583 |
| 4:16–25 | 479n32 | 8 | 571, 583n38 |
| 4:24–25 | 298 | 8:1–8 | 580 |
| 4:25 | 562n1 | 8:2 | 579 |
| 5 | 572, 574 | 8:3–4 | 580, 582 |
| 5:1 | 573 | 8:5–8 | 580 |
| 5:1–11 | 573, 574 | 8:38 | 552n7 |
| 5:2 | 573 | 8:38–39 | 552 |
| 5:6 | 562n1 | 9 | 588, 604 |
| 5:6–8 | 574 | 9–11 | 584, 586–88 |
| 5:7 | 578, 578n32 | 9:1–5 | 587 |
| 5:8 | 562n1 | 9:2 | 584 |
| 5:9 | 574 | 9:6 | 584, 587 |
| 5:12 | 574 | 9:6–24 | 584 |
| 5:13 | 575 | 9:18 | 584 |
| 5:16 | 575 | 9:20 | 584 |
| 5:17 | 562n1 | 9:27–29 | 584 |
| 5:18 | 599 | 9:30–31 | 584 |
| 5:18–19 | 575 | 9:33 | 584 |
| 5:18–21 | 562n1 | 10:2–3 | 587 |
| 5:20 | 575, 604 | 10:3 | 585, 587 |
| 6 | 571, 572, 579, 580, 583 | 10:4 | 585 |
| | | 10:14–17 | 503, 587 |
| | | 10:14–21 | 503 |
| 6–8 | 579, 582–83 | 10:18–20 | 503 |
| 6:1 | 579 | 10:18–21 | 587 |
| 6:1–14 | 579 | 11 | 569, 585, 604 |
| 6:4 | 583 | 11:1–6 | 584, 587 |
| 6:6 | 583 | 11:5 | 585 |
| 6:7–11 | 567 | 11:7 | 585 |
| 6:11 | 583 | 11:11 | 585, 588 |
| 6:12–14 | 583 | 11:11–36 | 505 |
| 6:13 | 579 | 11:16–21 | 585 |
| 6:15 | 579, 580 | 11:17 | 588 |
| 6:15–23 | 579, 583 | 11:21 | 588 |
| 6:16 | 565 | 11:25 | 586 |
| 6:17–18 | 580 | 11:28–36 | 10 |
| 6:22 | 580 | 11:29 | 587 |

| | |
|---|---:|
| 11:30–32 | 588 |
| 11:32 | 586, 599 |
| 11:33 | 586 |
| 12:19 | 608 |
| 15:8–29 | 505n83 |

## 1 Corinthians

| | |
|---|---:|
| 1:18 | 599 |
| 8 | 547 |
| 8:1–13 | 547 |
| 10 | 547 |
| 10:6–30 | 547 |
| 15:3b–5 | 562n1 |
| 15:25 | 513 |
| 15:25–28 | 599 |
| 15:27–28 | 296 |
| 15:51–52 | 560 |
| 15:51–55 | 550n4 |
| 15:54 | 604 |

## 2 Corinthians

| | |
|---|---:|
| 2:15 | 599 |
| 5:19 | 605 |
| 5:21 | 577 |

## Galatians

| | |
|---|---:|
| 1–2 | 563 |
| 3:13 | 577 |
| 3:29 | 479n32 |

## Ephesians

| | |
|---|---:|
| 1:10 | 599 |
| 6:12 | 552, 552n7 |

## Philippians

| | |
|---|---:|
| 2:10–11 | 599 |
| 3:2–3 | 580 |
| 3:19 | 599 |

## Colossians

| | |
|---|---:|
| 1:20 | 599 |

## 1 Thessalonians

| | |
|---|---:|
| 2:14–16 | 539n7 |
| 4:13–18 | 527 |

## Hebrews

| | |
|---|---:|
| 1:1 | 603 |
| 9:24–26 | 579 |
| 9:28 | 562n1 |

## 1 Peter

| | |
|---|---:|
| 2:21–25 | 562n1 |
| 3:18 | 562n1, 578 |

## 1 John

| | |
|---|---:|
| 1 | 543 |
| 1:7–9 | 542 |

## Revelation

| | |
|---|---:|
| 1–3 | 545–47 |
| 1:4–7 | 546 |
| 1:4–8 | 545 |
| 1:8 | 545, 546 |
| 1:10 | 545 |
| 1:15 | 546 |
| 1:18 | 546 |
| 1:19 | 546 |
| 1:20 | 546 |
| 2:4 | 546 |
| 2:5 | 547 |
| 2:7 | 547 |
| 2:8 | 546 |
| 2:9 | 547 |
| 2:10 | 547 |
| 2:11 | 547 |

## Index

*Revelation (continued)*

| | |
|---|---|
| 2:14 | 546 |
| 2:15 | 546 |
| 2:19 | 547 |
| 2:20–23 | 546–47 |
| 2:26 | 547 |
| 3:1 | 547 |
| 3:3 | 547 |
| 3:5 | 547 |
| 3:9 | 547 |
| 3:11 | 547 |
| 3:12 | 547 |
| 3:15 | 547 |
| 3:19 | 547 |
| 3:21 | 547 |
| 4–11 | 545 |
| 4–22 | 547 |
| 4:1—11:11 | 548–51 |
| 4:4–6 | 548 |
| 5:6 | 330 |
| 5:9–10 | 548 |
| 6:6 | 549 |
| 6:9–11 | 548, 559 |
| 7:14 | 550 |
| 8:1–5 | 550 |
| 9:1–2 | 550 |
| 9:7–11 | 550 |
| 10 | 550 |
| 10:3 | 550 |
| 11:1–7 | 550 |
| 11:4–13 | 550 |
| 11:15 | 550, 554, 559 |
| 11:17–19 | 550–51 |
| 12 | 552 |
| 12–22 | 545 |
| 12:1–22:5 | 551–57 |
| 12:3 | 551–52 |
| 13 | 552 |
| 13:17 | 553 |
| 14:7 | 553 |
| 14:8 | 553 |
| 14:9 | 553 |
| 14:12 | 553 |
| 14:13 | 553 |
| 14:14–20 | 553 |
| 15:7 | 553 |
| 16 | 547 |
| 16:2 | 553 |
| 16:5–7 | 553–54 |
| 16:9 | 554 |
| 16:17 | 554, 560 |
| 16:19 | 554 |
| 16:21 | 554 |
| 17–18 | 552 |
| 18 | 554 |
| 18:3–4 | 554 |
| 18:4–5 | 555 |
| 18:21–23 | 555 |
| 18:24 | 556 |
| 19:2 | 556, 560 |
| 19:7 | 556 |
| 19:11 | 556 |
| 19:19 | 556 |
| 19:19–21 | 556 |
| 19:20 | 556 |
| 20:1–3 | 557 |
| 20:4–6 | 561 |
| 20:11–15 | 557 |
| 20:12 | 557, 561 |
| 20:13 | 561 |
| 21–22 | 557 |
| 21:5–8 | 561 |
| 21:8 | 561 |
| 21:24 | 10 |
| 21:24–26 | 557 |
| 22:6–21 | 545 |
| 22:7 | 545 |
| 22:8–9 | 545 |
| 22:12–13 | 545 |
| 22:16–17 | 545 |

# APOCRYPHA

*Wisdom of Solomon*

13–15    564

# GREEK AND LATIN WORKS

Augustine
*City of God*

19.17    582n37
20.14    418n12

www.ingramcontent.com/pod-product-compliance
Lightning Source LLC
Chambersburg PA
CBHW021220300426
44111CB00007B/367